Copyright 2016 Nancy Alvarez

Printed in the United States of America

ISBN: 978-0-578-18152-3

All rights reserved.

Other books by the author:

Fiction:

Ladycat (as Nancy Greenwald)

The Girls and Me (as Nancy Alvarez)

Non-fiction:

Little Nancy, the Journey Home (a memoir and workbook) (as Nancy Alvarez)

ACKNOWLEDGEMENTS

Book design by Kristina Romero

For August & Ezekiel

MISHPOCHEH: BOOK ONE
("Family")

By Nancy Alvarez

THE TEACHER: ONE

She burrowed under her quilt, but resisted the impulse to pull the cover all the way over her head so she could hide. There was no one to hide from: Ernie, her husband of thirty years, had died three months earlier. It hadn't been a sudden death. The prostate cancer that finally killed him had given them two and a half years between prognosis and the end. Both believed he had beaten it after the first year. No, their marriage hadn't been a bed of roses. He hadn't been Robert Cummings and she hadn't come near the perfection of Jane Wyatt, smiling at the door every time anyone came home. But they had loved each other dearly. Jen wasn't sure whether she missed his voice the most, or his touch. She had loved the joking tone he frequently used with her when she plunged into the darkness of her concerns, personal or worldwide, with an intensity that had always made people uncomfortable. Ernie had enjoyed her fervor from the very first. This particular morning Jen ached with longing for the feel of his hand on her hip, the warmth of his palm, the weight of his finger pads, and the softness. Not the sex, although even at her advanced age of almost sixty, she also missed the feel of him inside her. Their big bed felt huge without him. She still inched over to his side during the night while she slept, her body searching for his unconsciously, without the awareness that would remind her belly, her back, her butt, that he was buried at sea.

Ernie would have enjoyed the burial. He loved a good joke, and always seemed to find hilarious new ones to tell her, their children, and their friends and neighbors. Jen, their grown son Jacob, and Toni, the baby of the family, had taken his remains in the box she had been given by the mortuary and rented a skiff at the local marina, despite the cold and the sideways stares of the local fisherman. One of them, his face wizened by years spent in the elements, wearing one of those red and black checked jackets, offered to skipper the little boat when he saw Jake struggling with the motor pull. Ernie had raked their lawn in the same kind of jacket for years. Before either of the children could respond, she had assented, feeling reassured by the notion that Ernie's jacket would be aboard the boat that would take him to his final, and chosen, resting place. The fisherman had steered the little craft out of the marina and around the break wall, the chop buffeting them from side to side as soon as they passed the shelter of its rocks. Because the boat was bouncing around, she had found herself unable to open the box holding her husband's ashes. The fisherman grabbed it before her son even realized there was a problem, opened it with ease, and turned it upside down, dumping Ernie unceremoniously into the deep. She and the children were so shocked none of them said a word. Then Toni grabbed the bouquet they had brought along to sprinkle into the sea with the ashes, thrusting flowers into their hands. Frantically, they hurled roses, lilies, nasturtiums and angel's breath at Ernie as he disappeared into the broiling seawater. The fisherman merely grunted when the last rose hit the water, turned the boat around, and deposited them upon the dock as unceremoniously as he had rid himself of Ernie.

It wasn't until they were safely locked inside her Volvo, seatbelts fastened, that she started to laugh. At first Jacob looked at his mother sternly, but when his sister's chortle joined Jen's, he just gawked at them both, bewildered by their hilarity. His mother managed to blurt "This is what your father would be doing" in-between bursts of laughter, and the light dawned. His laugh, so like his father's, joined theirs until his mother realized tears were streaming down her cheeks. She never knew whether it was because of the unstoppable laughter, or because of grief. She didn't sink into that dark hole until the children had gone back to their normal lives, her son to his unhappy marriage in Cambridge, and her daughter to her last year of law school at Stanford.

Now she struggled to get herself out of bed every day. During the week the realization that her absence would disappoint her students forced Jen to pull aside the comforting covers, and swing her legs over the edge of the bed. She knew today would be no exception, but had allowed herself two more minutes. It was still surprising to her that even after three months she often felt unwilling to leave the bed she and Ernie had shared for almost twenty-five years of marriage, replacing their original box springs and mattress a few years after Toni had been born. It was probably time to again replace both, but somehow the task seemed daunting to Jen. It would be like throwing away one more piece of Ernie. For most of her adult life Jen had bounded out from beneath the sheets, excited to see what the new day would bring, but always startling her more sedate husband. Unlike her father, Ernie had thoroughly enjoyed her enthusiasms, never berating her for one of them. He always said that each new path she explored broadened his own world. Even if he didn't try the same path, her energy spurred him to try out a new one of his own. Perhaps there wasn't any point to her enthusiasms now that she didn't have anyone to influence. This was not a comforting thought: that she only felt excited about life when she had someone to share it with. 'How shallow,' Jen thought, 'and dependent', a word she hadn't ever employed about her own psyche.

She worried she was returning to the fear and despair that had haunted her as a child, when each new day was something to be dreaded, not enjoyed. Fortunately, once she had left her parents' home at eighteen to attend college, that early morning anxiety had disappeared. Jen loathed its return, but felt helpless within its grasp. Perhaps, she thought to herself, she was being punished for her lack of compassion for her father's debilitating fear, half believing this might be so. She hadn't told either of the children about her escalating dread, because they each had their own worries. They could hardly take care of her; besides, it wasn't their job. At least her sense of responsibility hadn't abandoned her, she told her reflection in the bathroom mirror.

By the time she was downstairs boiling water for her morning oatmeal, most of the heaviness had been left behind in their marital bed. She had always been good as an adult at forging ahead with what she had planned for the day whether she had a cold, an upset child, or an irritated husband. Even when she and Ernie fought, which was rare: their battles were more frequently underground, creating craters of silence between them until somehow they were filled in or merely boarded over; she hadn't usually had a problem getting on with her day.

She supposed she should be grateful, at least, for her continued ability to plan out her weekly schedule. Today she was giving a surprise quiz on the first half of "Crime and Punishment" to her first period advanced English class, had planned a discussion on the paper her second period students had handed in at the end of the preceding week, would enter the grades from the quiz in her record book third period, and so forth. If she didn't think ahead to the weekend, and how the hours within those two days loomed, she would be fine. One of her teacher friends had even commented a few days before that she was bouncing back amazingly well; she, herself, had been in the dumps for years after her husband passed away. Of course, her colleague continued, she had had children in high school to contend with, so perhaps that had been the reason for her angst. If the woman had been a close friend, Jen's apparent recovery wouldn't have fooled her. That reminded Jen to write a note to herself to call her friend Margaret, and leave it next to the phone so she wouldn't forget that evening. Margaret was an old friend who was living in Maine. They had gone to high school together. Even over the phone, Margaret would not be fooled. Jen cried when they talked, which Margaret didn't seem to mind, and then she felt better for a few days. What she didn't understand was why she had such a hard time crying if no one was at the other end, so to speak. She could lie in bed feeling lousy for hours, but tears rarely fell.

Halfway to the high school she realized she had forgotten to make an appointment at Circle & Square, the repair shop she and Ernie had been using for years. Her 3000-mile oil change was due, and the steering wheel was pulling to the left. Ernie had always taken care of the cars. Another job that was now hers. Jacob had sold his father's car to a friend in Cambridge, after they had all decided that her Volvo, though older, was still in better shape than his Subaru. It might seem odd to a stranger that although he accepted responsibility for their cars over the many years of their marriage, Ernie's own vehicle had been a disaster. The one thing she didn't miss was his mess. Her husband had left papers, books, sweaters, and even shoes behind him whenever he moved from room to room in their spacious colonial house. Sneakers she hadn't seen him wear in years were discovered beneath the towel he kept on the floor behind the driver's seat of the Subaru for emergencies. Jen hadn't kept a towel in her car, despite his fairly frequent urging, because her car was always neat. Jen reached for the pen she kept clipped to her visor, and jotted down "Circle" so she wouldn't again forget to call when she got home. Then she pulled into the high school parking lot, and found herself waving to several of her students.

The day had finally begun.

Talking to a couple of the kids in the hallway on the way to her first class lifted her spirits, as did the fact that the kids quieted themselves as she wrote a quote from an expert on Dostoevsky on the chalkboard, asking that they defend or dispute it. Sitting at her desk while they bent to the task, she couldn't concentrate on her plan for second period. Instead Jen found herself staring into space with a blankness of mind that was discomfiting. Even when her favorite student, a young woman who had applied to Brown early decision, placed her neatly written answer on the desk with her familiar smile, Jen was unmoved. A year from now this child would have forgotten her, caught up in the excitement of her new school and the life of a college freshman. What difference did it make that she and her student related well now? As the words 'what's the point" crossed her mind, she had to fight to hold back her tears. The girl glanced at her, but moved back to her desk when Jen smiled.

Why couldn't she get a grip?
Jen had never been prone to tears; when she needed to cry, she had done so in the privacy of her bedroom or on the phone with a very close friend. This new Jen was insupportable. Grading her papers in the teacher's lounge during her free period, she chose a table in the corner because she didn't trust her voice to sound normal if she was forced to converse with someone. Her throat actually ached with the effort of keeping the tears tamped. She remembered her friend Phyllis telling her with great excitement how helpful the twelve-step phrase 'One day at a time' had been for her when her oldest boy was drinking. Sighing, she supposed it could have other uses: a romantic disappointment, stomach distress, even the death of a spouse. At the end of third period, Anita, who worked in the office, stuck her head into the teacher's lounge to tell Jen that she had a visitor, ushering a young woman who looked vaguely familiar into the room.

Walking towards her with a smile reminiscent of her first period favorite, the woman held out her hand as she said, "Mrs. Roth. You have no idea how often I have thought of you!" Indeed she did not. The pert brunette blithely continued, "I sat in the second row, second seat, and wrote down every word you uttered. Believe it or not, I still have that notebook." And then it came to her: Hillary Roth. Ten years ago, twelve? She had been a good student. Another favorite. "Hillary," she grasped the outstretched hand. "It has been a very long time."

"My name is Hillary Hansen now," she said, as if that was explanation enough, and it was.

Jen hadn't realized that one of her favorite new fiction writers had been one of her favorite students. She rarely looked at author photos, and hadn't connected the dots.

"Your first book was marvelous. When I read it I had no idea you had been my student. How amazing!" she blurted. Blurting was no more typical of her than crying, but Hillary didn't seem to notice.

"Could I take you out for a cappuccino at the end of the day? There's so much I'd like to talk to you about. God, I don't usually end my sentences with a preposition," Hillary said. And then she laughed.

As the bell sounded and Jen picked up her books, slipping the corrected papers into their proper folder, she realized her former student had become very comfortable with herself. "I'd enjoy that," she found herself replying, startled that it was true. Now that she remembered her she realized she had been very fond of Hillary. Talking with her about her writing would be enjoyable; perhaps she'd divulge what she was working on now. They agreed to meet at "The Dive", a coffee shop in the center of town that had recently undergone a transformation to bring it into the 21st Century.

Later, in the teacher's cafeteria, one of her friends sat down with a bottle of purified water for Jen and one for herself and opened her brown lunch bag. Ruth made the best sandwiches Jen had ever eaten, thick with meat, sprouts, tomatoes, mayonnaise and hot spicy mustard, all of which came packed inside the town's best, fresh multi-grain bakery bread. When she offered Jen half, there was no way she could decline despite the fact that she was on one of her frequent diets and had packed a large, vegie-filled salad for herself that morning. After she had picked up a plastic bowl from the counter and deposited half of her salad into it for Ruth, she bit into the welcoming sandwich, turkey this time, slathered with cranberry sauce. They talked easily about their respective days. Ruth was as surprised as Jen that the writer whose first novel they had both enjoyed had been a student at the high school. She had taught the now-famous novelist geometry. Laughingly, the sandwich maker said that the math problems she had forced upon the girl hadn't left much of a mark. Jen marveled at her ability to laugh about this: when Jen had to admit that she hadn't made much of a difference in a student's life, she usually felt bereft. She presumed the truth lay somewhere in-between, and that Ruth wasn't as jolly about her lack of impact within as she appeared to be without. They parted at the bell, each hurrying off to their fifth period classes with a wave.

Both fifth and sixth period passed without incident. One student spoke about 'Tess of the D'Urberville's' with stunning clarity, a boy who rarely opened his mouth. He was obviously as pleased with Jen's response as she was by his eloquence. There were the usual groans at the homework assignment, and in sixth period, the announcement of an imminent test, but by the time the kids cleared their desks and headed off to their after school activities with the usual chatter, pushing, shoving and chaos that accompanies teenagers, Jen's classroom was left blessedly quiet. She stayed behind to put some questions on the board for the next day's 2nd period class, which would give her another five minutes in bed the following morning, packed the day's quiz papers that she hadn't had time to grade into her leather briefcase, a gift from Ernie weeks before his death, and walked to her car with surprising purpose.

For some reason the idea of talking to a former student who had achieved success was brightening her outlook. She noticed the changing leaves, probably for the first time that fall, marveling as she drove at the bright reds and oranges, much as she had the previous fall with Ernie. Instead of becoming sad at his absence, she felt relief that she was again noticing the season that had always been her favorite. How did one enjoy what was, she wondered, when what wasn't, was so pervasive? She knew she wouldn't have the opportunity to meet a famous former student every day and decided to try to enjoy the occasion. Assuming their coffee date was the cause for her newfound sparkle, she knew that would be important because she had no idea if she'd be able to hold on to it later that evening. For the past three months mourning her loss had taken up most of her time outside of school, as well as worrying about Jacob and his crumbling marriage. Nothing had seemed worth the energy of a smile, a stunning admission she realized. Her husband might have passed away prematurely, but that didn't mean she had to live a gray existence. She vowed to work at finding a pathway out of her grief.

Hillary was seated at one of the tables next to the windows that overlooked the street, but was so engrossed in what she was reading, she failed to notice Jen pull neatly into a narrow parking spot almost directly in front of her. Her former teacher sat and watched her: the pose tickled memory and was familiar. She would have to ask Hillary if she had worn her hair longer in high school, so that it had fallen across her cheeks as she bent over her notebooks. Jen ordered a cappuccino as she entered the shop, and picked out a muffin as well, cranberry, a treat she rarely allowed herself. If she was going to hell, she might as well go all the way, she thought as she carried the plate to Hillary's table. When she slid into the booth Hillary looked up, startled, but her smile was immediate as she realized who was interrupting her. "It's amazing, but even after all these years that look of concentration is so familiar," Jen commented. The young woman shrugged, bemused. "No matter how much I try to break the habit, when I'm reading I'm in another universe. Writing is even worse." The two smiled comfortably across the table at one another, the awareness that this was a trait they shared, immediate.

Much to Jen's surprise Hillary remembered she had two children, even though her son had graduated before Hillary entered high school, and her daughter had been a senior when Hillary was a freshman. Kids from one grade back then hadn't socialized with kids from another; even now there was a pretty big divide. After giving Hillary a short update on the lives of her children, she suggested her former student call her 'Jen', since Mrs. Roth no longer seemed fitting. Although their conversation was a bit stilted the first few minutes, once they were launched, the exchange became fluid and quite enjoyable for them both. Hillary had gotten her masters from Berkeley, and as it turned out, often spent weekends in Palo Alto with friends. It was the only activity that freed her from the intensity of graduate school. She was surprised Jen hadn't visited Toni since Ernie's death, and urged her to do so in the earnest manner of the young. "Hopping on a plane, strolling around the campus and seeing her new apartment – all of that would probably make you feel a lot better," she said. Despite herself, Jen felt her eyes fill, an unheard of occurrence with a near stranger, and a former student to boot. She kept talking, as if the words would belie what was happening. Hillary didn't interrupt, but let her ramble. Jen recalled that she had always been sensitive, even as a teenager.

When her motor slowed down and Jen paused, Hillary simply said, "I'm sorry for your loss."

"Oh God," Jen muttered, reaching for the Kleenex in her purse. "I am so sorry."

"Don't be silly. I cry at the oddest times over next to nothing. God, I can't imagine losing someone I've lived with for so many years." After hesitating for a few seconds, she reached across the table and took the older woman's hand in hers, just as the counter boy delivered her cappuccino.

For some reason this simple gesture freed the words that had been locked inside her head, her chest, and her body since Ernie's death, and Jen began to talk, as she hadn't even with her closest and oldest friends. She admitted that California felt continents away, and that perhaps she should visit. But she was so depressed she had been unable to even consider the long trip. She didn't want to burden her daughter. Of course she knew this was probably ridiculous, but her daughter was in her last year of law school, consumed by an unbelievable workload. Her son was headed for a divorce, and though caring, was struggling himself to hold his life together. He couldn't possibly have any energy left over for his mother's grief. And besides, she found herself acknowledging, her descent into this pit was so embarrassing. She was not a person who cried easily. She was not a person who asked for help. It had taken years for her to accept comfort from Ernie, she explained, and now when she needed him the most: at that, she began to laugh, although tears were still wetting her cheeks.
"This is ridiculous," she said when she was able to catch her breath. Then she sighed. "Or maybe not."

"I don't have anyplace I have to go," Hillary said. "I'm a pretty good listener."

And she was. There was so much Jen had never told anyone these last months. About the dinners she ate in front of the television. The television, for God's sake! She never watched the news; it was too depressing and biased. And the silly entertainment programs that came on immediately after the stupid, sensational news reports? Please. She was also hooked on some of the sitcoms. It didn't matter which ones were on; if she couldn't get herself to read, she watched the boob tube. She felt less ashamed about her addiction to Grey's Anatomy and Chicago Fire. At least someone with a modicum of intelligence wrote them. 'Law and Order' was an embarrassment, but she watched every iteration, and amused herself by having imaginary conversations with Ernie about them. She couldn't possibly have told her daughter, who was determined to become a public defender, about all the versions of 'Law and Order' she watched. Toni wanted to save people, not incarcerate them. Actually, her mother's views were remarkably similar, but she still looked forward to Special Victim's Unit and Criminal Intent. How would she ever find time to read 'The New Yorker' if they added a fourth spin off? she asked Hillary with a laugh.

It was such a relief to be telling someone how she had been living. It shouldn't have mattered that Hillary loved the nighttime medical soaps and secretly watched the 'Law and Order' shows, too, but it did. She sometimes spent the entire Sunday in her robe too, and loved reading The Times in bed. Jen and Ernie had always read the Sunday paper in the den, sitting side by side on their two plush leather lounge chairs, each with its own ottoman. She couldn't bear to sit in hers now – and most assuredly not his – so she had retreated to their bed, buying new sheets and two new comforter covers, stealthily throwing out the ones she had shared with her husband. She didn't want them in the house, and she didn't think she should offer them to her children. Goodwill hadn't come to mind until the week after they had been picked up by the garbage truck.

"Is there anything you can read that holds your interest?" Hillary asked her when she paused for breath.

So Jen told her the rest. The only relief she had been able to find was in tracking down books relating to her parents and grandparents: tomes on the Polish Ukraine, Vienna at the turn of the Century, New York City and the Bronx in the early 1900's. These books more then held her interest. She finished one and immediately ordered the next. The 700-page book she had found on Eastern European shtetl life had been utterly consuming. When she had neared the end, she felt as she did after she had put down 'Pillars of the Earth', or 'A Suitable Boy'. She wanted more pages to magically appear and slow down her own inexorable march to the end of the book. As she described what she was learning about her own beliefs through the history of the lives of her grandparents, Hillary became as animated as she. The path her ancestors had taken to New Jersey had long been a fascination for her as well, but she hadn't found the time, with all the research she had done for her first novel, or the one she was now working on, to pursue her genealogy.

They rose in unison, and Hillary followed Jen home. There she copied the list of books Jen had been reading and purchasing so she could order them, like old friends, and revisit pieces of her grandparents' lives that were particularly memorable. Vienna was similar to Berlin, where Hillary's great grandparents had come from twenty years before Hitler's youth had marched in its streets. Her grandfather's parents had been Eastern European Jews, like Jen's grandparents. Though one generation further removed, her longing to reconnect with her roots was even greater than Jen's. She believed that was because her family's assimilation ran deeper.

They hugged when they said good-bye well after seven. Jen realized she should have invited her former student to an impromptu dinner, but her car was gone by the time she ran back outside. She dumped a can of Campbell's into a pot, sliced some cheddar, onion and tomato for a grilled cheese sandwich, and sat down at the kitchen table with a smile on her lips to wait for the bread to crisp in the frying pan. Tomorrow she would go to the library for the next book on her own list without any shame. Although the purpose of reading about what life was like all those years ago wasn't clear to her, she did know it had to be profound in some way. However, at this particular juncture what was most important was that it held her interest.

She fell asleep that night grateful Hillary had come to see her. She was inordinately pleased at the influence she had had on the young novelist's life, and felt content for the first time in over a year. Of course, she never expected to see her again.

CHAPTER ONE

Addie could barely sit through the family breakfast, let alone eat the eggs Marlena, the parlor maid, slid onto her plate. That afternoon she was to sing three songs in the parlor for a group of her parents' friends, many of whom served on the Board of the Vienna Opera or Symphony. Although her parents attended both institutions regularly, and her mother was clearly proud of her talent – after all, she had sent out printed invitations, and spent days in the kitchen making little yeast cakes, apfel kuchen, and stollen for her daughter's concert – she thought of the afternoon as a pleasurable event for her friends, not a precursor of things to come. Even at seven, this was not Addie's view. Becoming a hausfrau was not her goal; singing was, although in the late 1800's in Vienna, that admission would have shocked every woman in her mother's circle of friends.

"Adelaide!" Her mother's stern voice interrupted her reverie. "You are skin and bones, and have already had a nasty influenza this year. You must eat your breakfast, or I will cancel the Salon."

Terrified, Addie filled her fork with an overflowing lump of scrambled eggs and began to chew. She also chose a roll from the basket in the center of the table, and as she did so, glanced at her father whose eyes were twinkling at her from his end of the long, shiny, mahogany dining room table. The concert would go on: she was certain. The uncomfortable fluttering in her chest remained, but much to the little soprano's surprise, the bite of egg the cook had scrambled with cream cheese and onions tasted good. By the time she had finished every morsel on her plate, her mother was beaming at her.

"You are a good girl, Adelaide. Your frock and petticoats have been laid out on your bed, as have Sophia's, but you shouldn't get into them for several hours. We will have a light lunch at noon, and neither of you would want to spill anything on them." Her mother paused, noticing the look of panic transforming her daughter's face. The crease of concern furrowing her childish brow distorted Adelaide's features, giving her an almost comical appearance.

Her father's laugh filled the dining room. "Lisl, I think today it is enough that our little singer has finished her entire breakfast. You wouldn't want her to be worrying about her stomach when she's reaching for that high note in the Schubert lieder, would you?" Addie glanced from one parent to the other until her father stood, walked to the opposite end of the long table where his wife was sitting, placed his hands on her shoulders and kissed the chignon that always graced the crown of her head. Sighing, her mother looked up at him as he rubbed her shoulders. The smile she bestowed on her younger daughter was strained, but it was a smile. "All right, little one. You don't have to eat lunch with us. Sophia will come upstairs when we are finished, and then you can put on your dresses."

Her father beamed at Addie across the table, his wink hidden from her mother who was still seated in front of him. Adelaide adored her father, frequently wishing his bank didn't keep him so busy. When he strolled with her in the Volksgarten on a Sunday, or came home early enough from the bank to turn the pages of the sheet music for Sophia, the older sister who accompanied her when she practiced at home – those were the moments that would stay with her forever. She could close her eyes and remember their dining room and that particular breakfast well into her eighties. Her father was the only man she had ever loved with all her heart, because she knew he understood her.

With his hands resting lightly on his wife's shoulders, he asked his youngest child in a gentle voice, "So, my precious Addie. Would you like to practice this morning, or would practicing strain that marvelous voice of yours?"

"I would like to practice the Mozart, Papa" she immediately replied, continuing, "Sometimes I miss the e-flat. If I were sharp this afternoon, it would be…I can't even imagine."

Sophia grabbed her hand, pulling Addie to her feet. "Then come with me," she ordered. "I will accompany you, even though I am not as good as Herr Lieberman. Still, you'll get to practice."

Addie was grateful for her sister's offer, even though her sister didn't seem to have much concern for the mistakes she made when she played the piano. She was also relieved that Mr. Lieberman, who accompanied many singers in the concert halls of Vienna, had heeded her father's entreaties to accompany her that afternoon, although he had never worked with a child before. The two men belonged to the same club, and had known each other for years. Lieberman had said yes because of the long-standing friendship. Practicing with him several afternoons a week during the preceding month had been revelatory for Adelaide. His touch on the keyboard was delicate but precise, making her task a joy because for the first time she could just close her eyes and let the notes flow out of her. What was even more significant and thrilling was that he had told her the very first day she had gone to his house to sing for him that she had a gift, a gift that should be nurtured. But he hadn't stopped there. He had told her parents over tea that very afternoon that he knew a teacher who would be terribly excited to work with a talent like hers. The teacher he was proposing even lived in Vienna 9, like them.

Many Jews lived in this neighborhood, of course, but even at her age Adelaide knew the teacher could have lived far away in another part of the city like her Oma and Opa did. If she could walk to his apartment by herself, her mother couldn't complain about the danger, or the need for the maid to accompany her. After all, she went to the grocer by herself to pick up little things for her mother, like the freshly ground nutmeg she had run down to get just the day before. Her parents had told Mr. Lieberman they would consider the idea after the afternoon concert. The very thought was too exciting to dwell on: her mother would never let her take voice lessons. Addie could even imagine her mother's plaintive tone coming from the room she shared with her father, asking what the child would ever be able to do with her trained voice. Sing, Addie thought as she made her way to the parlor. Sing. Ever since she could remember, she had either taught herself tunes note by note at their piano in the parlor, or sung with a group at school. Sometimes the teacher wouldn't even let her join in, because her voice intimidated the other girls. She didn't mean to be loud, but she so loved to sing.

The little girl practiced with extra concentration and effort that morning. If she could perform all three numbers without a flaw that might convince her mother she deserved the lessons. Sophia, sensing how important the afternoon was to her little sister, played for almost two hours, even after their parents came into the parlor to suggest it might be better for Adelaide to get a bit of rest before the concert.

"If I was performing in front of all those people this afternoon, I'd want to practice just to have something to do. Otherwise I'd get more and more nervous, and I'd just…I'd just want to crawl under my featherbed and die," Sophia explained to them, her hands resting lightly on the piano keys.

"Let us just go over each song one more time, Mama, and then we'll stop," Addie implored. She looked so little as she stood beside the new Bluthner piano, and so very dedicated, the two adults left the room without another word. Neither child knew their parents remained standing outside in the hallway, arm in arm, listening to their little girl sing all three pieces. Victor brushed the tears from his wife's eyes, and they tiptoed away as the last notes from the final tune faded away behind the parlor door. "I want her to have a normal life, Victor," Lisl whispered as they made their way down the hall to the kitchen to check on the tapioca and chocolate puddings their kitchen maid was cooking on the stove. None of their guests would lack nourishment after the concert. This would be their reward for coming to hear Addie sing, or so Lisl believed. It never dawned on her that the reward might be the child's voice.

Sophia came racing upstairs after the family's simple luncheon, and burst into Adelaide's room. Both of their dresses had been hung from the younger girl's wardrobe so they could change together. Although they were three years apart in age, and in temperament as opposite as two siblings could be, the girls were close. Each appreciated the qualities the other possessed, especially the ones she, herself, lacked. Sophia would have liked to have the commitment and dedication about her painting that her younger sibling had about singing. Addie's only focus seemed to be music. Perhaps Sophia didn't believe she was as talented. Or perhaps she enjoyed going to the Prater with her girlfriends too much, and being part of the popular group at the girls' gymnasium to put in the hours required to nurture her own gifts. For her part, Addie would have liked to be less fearful about her mother's powerful opinions, and have the gumption to stand up to her the way Sophia did. She certainly wished she felt less fear about what life might hold in store for her, especially if she had to give up her singing. She really couldn't imagine such a thing. As for friends, Addie enjoyed the Prater as well, but if given the choice between practicing with Herr Lieberman or going to the amusement park with all the girls, that would have been no choice at all.

When Addie lifted the white dress off of the hanger, with its miles of lace from bodice to hem, and raised her arms so the maid could slip it over her head, she could feel the calm slide down her entire frame along with the linen and lace. It was as if the butterflies plaguing her all day had flown from her belly right into the lace itself, she thought, smiling at the image in the mirror. She loved the way she looked in the frilly frock, even though she knew the raven-haired Sophia, at ten, was much prettier than she. Addie felt pretty when she sang and that would have to do. She had worked as hard as anyone could have for this concert, her first, to make her whole family proud. She believed this all the way down to her toes, which she squeezed into the white leather heeled boots her mother had ordered for this special occasion. Sophia and she beamed at each other in their new dresses, Sophia's boasting the barest suggestion of peach to offset the extreme white of her sister's costume. Sophia was very proud of her little sister and almost as excited as Adelaide, listening to the ebb and flow of the voices floating up the back stairs as the guests arrived. Much to her surprise the older child realized she was actually more nervous than the performer herself seemed to be.

The sisters descended together to greet the guests before they were all seated for the performance as they had been taught was proper. Addie, who found this custom excruciating because of her shyness, reminded herself of the grander purpose – singing well enough to warrant private singing lessons with this new teacher – and smiled at first one couple and then another, moving among the adults who filled her parents spacious parlor. Mr. Lieberman was already there, and winked at Addie as she glanced his way. She couldn't help but smile, which her father noticed, marveling at the poise exhibited by his slender seven year old. Her older brother Sidney, who was already apprenticing at a prestigious law firm in Vienna 1, wrapped her in his arms and lifted her off the floor. "Sing your heart out, little Addie. If you break some glasses, I'll replace them," which made her laugh. He was even busier all week than her father, because he had to 'prove himself' which she didn't quite understand. Wasn't his graduation from the legal academy proof enough? He had graduated second in his class, which seemed pretty impressive to both his little sisters. Neither one was overly fond of the gymnasium even though they had been told again and again by everyone how fortunate they were to be going to school at all. Their mother and aunt had been tutored at home, but had been forced to stop their education at twelve, because even ten years earlier anything else would have been unseemly for a girl.

When Addie stepped up to her place beside the piano stool, the voices in the parlor quickly quieted and then Mr. Lieberman began to play. As she looked out over the familiar faces, Addie felt an amazing sense of peace, just as she had when she had donned her dress and it had floated into place a short while before. The first note she sang came out in perfect pitch, as did each one thereafter. Some of the audience began to clap in-between the first and second number, but her father shushed them so she could go on without having to lose momentum. As usual she was grateful for his sensitivity. She had never told her father she would prefer singing all three together; he just knew. From time to time Mr. Lieberman would glance up at her with a little turn of his lips so the smile would not be obvious to the audience, and then his eyes would return to the pages of music resting on the piano before him. His encouragement helped her hit the e-flat in the Mozart piece perfectly, and she could not contain her own smile. When she finished with a tremolo, the family friends sitting before her were at first stunned. Then the room erupted in applause, her brother Sidney leading the bravos of course. The rest of the event passed in a blur for Addie, though she knew she was hugged by almost everyone, and suddenly felt ravenous. She ate apfle kuchen as well as two little yeast cakes along with a healthy serving of her mother's tapioca pudding, which she had always relished. Her father tried to sneak her a bit of coffee, but her mother's stern look prevented that indiscretion. She had to make do with tea, which was good enough.

Several of the adults stayed on into the late afternoon, when her father suggested she and Sophia go upstairs. Both girls ran up the back stairs, hiding on the top step in order to be able to hear what the adults were talking about below. When they heard one of the women say that Addie's voice was amazing – "Can you imagine what it might be with professional training?" Sophia grabbed her sister's hand and squeezed. Neither girl could tell who had spoken, even though they conferred about it in whispers so as not to be heard. Mr. Lieberman was loud and clear when he agreed, urging private lessons on the Welts. When several other adult voices joined in agreement the sisters stared at one another, huge grins plastered across each of their young faces. Without knowing why, Addie began to giggle, which was contagious of course. Clinging to each other, hands hugging their mouths, the girls tiptoed up the remaining stair to their rooms, lest the grown-ups below hear them. After the sisters had managed to hang each of their dresses back on the hangers, Sophia jumped into Addie's bed, snuggling beneath her comforter. Neither had been able to hook the hangers over the wardrobe door until Addie thought to go for a chair in their parents' bedroom. She longingly looked at her sister, whose nose peeked out from beneath the fluffy down comforter, but knew she had to return the chair before she could join her.

In the hallway she heard the raised voices of her parents downstairs. After dragging the chair to its proper place in her parents' bedroom, she raced back to her own and pulled Sophia out of bed and back to the stairwell so they could hear the argument. Instinctively Addie knew it was about her, and it was. Her mother, with her voice raised to a level neither child had ever heard before, was furious that so many of the adults were urging the Welts to give Adelaide private singing lessons. But she was angrier at her husband for agreeing. What kind of life did he think his daughter would have as she grew into a woman if she pursued singing in a serious way? Was he even considering how a female artist would live in the Vienna they both knew? Even in her sheltered environment Lisl had heard stories after she married, and the thought of her little girl being subjected to 'the whims of men' was unendurable to her. Confused, Addie looked at her older sister; but Sophia had no idea what the words meant either. She whispered 'it sounds exciting', but Adelaide wasn't so sure. She did love the order of her mother's home: a day for baking; one for cleaning the rugs; one for polishing the mahogany dining room set until it sparkled, even on a cloudy day. The regularity of it made her feel safe. Was her mother suggesting that if she were actually good enough to become a singer with the symphony she would be forced to lead a life different from the one that gave her so much comfort? If so, how would it be different? Knowing her father disagreed gave her racing mind some relief, but nevertheless, it was a subdued Addie who climbed back up to her bedroom. She was still awake when her parents came upstairs, and was therefore aware that neither tiptoed in to give the sisters, who were being allowed to share Addie's bed that night, a goodnight kiss. She had never known her parents to be so angry, and most certainly didn't like being the cause of it.

The very next week Sidney was coming to dinner with Robert, who had been his best friend since the days the two had attended the gymnasium; Robert was also apprenticing at a law firm, though not the same one as Sidney because he was a gentile, and worked at the gentile firm run by one of his uncles. The two firms were only several blocks apart in the center of the City, and the two young men often met for lunch to discuss a thorny legal problem. Sophia had a crush on Robert, and followed him around from parlor to kitchen whenever he came to visit. The young men were well aware of the little girl's infatuation, and were both indulgent about her obviously flirtatious behavior. That afternoon their mother was lunching with her knitting group, but had assured her son she would return in ample time to supervise the cook over the preparation of the leg of lamb, which she herself had seasoned with garlic cloves, flour and pepper. The young men were early, which was purposeful though not obvious to either sister. After the cook set out a plate of cakes left over from the weekend Salon for them all, and boiled water for coffee and tea, Robert asked Sophia if she would play one of the pieces her sister had sung the previous Sunday, so that he might hear it. Since she would have eagerly climbed to the top of their apartment building and gone out on the steep roof had he asked, Sophia agreed without any prodding.

Addie felt a bit shy. Somehow singing for one person, someone she had known her whole life, seemed more difficult than performing before a roomful of adults, even though they were almost all friends of her parents. What if he thought she was dreadful, or, more likely, just didn't understand what the fuss was about? She possessed a large voice for someone so small, but perhaps that was all it was: big. She stood at her usual place by the piano stool, afraid to say she wasn't prepared, but also afraid to begin. When she didn't enter at the appropriate place, Sophia stopped playing to see what was wrong. Addie merely shrugged because she had no idea how to explain, and Sophia began again. The little chanteuse knew her voice wasn't as clear as it had been on Sunday, but she didn't hit any false notes either, which was a plus given how shockingly nervous she was. When the last note escaped her lips, Addie realized her knees were trembling, and abruptly sat down next to her sister on the piano stool.

"You have a beautiful voice, little Addie. The power of it is a bit surprising in someone so tiny," Robert smiled at her, taking her hand in his much larger one. Mortified, Addie started to cry. "Sweetie, what on earth is the matter?" he asked, squatting beside the stool so he could put his arm around her shaking shoulders.

"I want to be normal," was all she could manage before she was overtaken by another squall of tears.

Sidney picked his sister up and set her on his knee as he sat back down on the tufted parlor chair. "Why do you think your beautiful, beautiful voice will keep you from having a normal life?" he asked, totally bemused.

"We heard Mama and Papa arguing about it, and that's what Mama said," piped up 10-year-old Sophia.

Robert pivoted to face Addie, once again taking her hand in his. "Your Mama's from a different generation, precious. She doesn't understand how much is changing in Vienna. Why, we've been told that they will be opening the University to women within the next five years."

His words amused Sydney no end. "You better watch your step in that firm of yours, Robert. A woman might best you, especially if she's anything like Lydia," he teased.

"Who is Lydia?" asked Addie, her curiosity getting the better of her tears.
Both men burst out laughing, which infuriated the sisters. "Who is she?" demanded Sophia, emboldened by her younger sibling who was usually more reticent

"A friend of my cousin's," Robert replied, and blushed when Sidney added, "A very pretty friend with a very sharp tongue."

That didn't satisfy little Addie, who wanted to know what 'a sharp tongue' was. When her brother explained that Lydia spoke her mind without any fear, Addie seemed satisfied by the explanation. Inside, she hoped she would be as courageous as Lydia when she grew up. When Sophia blurted out the very same thought, "That's how I'm going to be!" the two men laughed again. Sidney reached out and pulled her into his chest, spreading his legs so she could stand comfortably between his knees. "Just not in front of Mama, little one, if you want to have any freedom at all once you've graduated from your finishing school," he suggested.

That night at dinner, the little girls sat mutely as their mother talked with Robert about all the people she knew who were converting. She wanted to know if Sidney would be acceptable to the legal firm where he worked if her son converted as well. Robert thought he would, adding that it might be a good idea, if his friend thought going to Temple was something he could give up without undo distress. Sidney explained that he wasn't worried about that; he was more concerned about having to attend church services with the partners and their wives. Getting on his knees and praying at St. Stephens was a little beyond his ability, at least for now. Robert was amused because he found Sunday mornings a trial as well, a fact that seemed to appall Addie's mother. Later Sydney sat quietly in the parlor while his mother lectured him about how important converting might be for his advancement in Vienna's legal community, glancing at his father every now and then for affirmation. The old man remained stoic, his countenance betraying nothing of his thoughts. Robert didn't intrude, but sat beside his friend, equally mute.

Before Adelaide could think of the proper question to ask so the adults would explain what they were talking about, Robert began to describe what he had experienced that afternoon hearing her sing. Her mother's face, which had looked strained throughout the conversation with Sydney about 'converting', became even more stressed, her rather full lips drawing together in a tight little line. The words the young man used to describe Addie's voice brought a flush to both her cheeks and ears, which the seven-year old imagined would feel hot to the touch. Focusing on the plate in front of her, Addie was even afraid to steal a glance at her father. There had been too much talk altogether about her voice and she was beginning to wish it would stop, except if it did, she might not be allowed to go to Herr Goff's house to learn how to sing like a professional. This was the name she had heard Mr.

21

Lieberman suggest when she and Sophia had been eavesdropping the day before. Even at her young age Addie knew what the word 'professional' meant. She had attended small concerts with her parents, and had heard both men and women sing Lieder, a very popular practice at the Musikverein as well. How could anyone believe she could sing in such a place, to such a large audience? She was relieved when he and her brother moved on to a discussion of the changing times, including the news that women would soon be attending University, which forced her mother's lips to compress even further. Sidney assured everyone at the table that within the next ten years women in their class would be working outside the home, doing jobs other than tutoring in wealthier homes and taking care of children. Robert added with enthusiasm that this was a just development, to which Victor also assented.

"My sweet, you don't have to be concerned," he told his wife. "By the time Addie and Sophia are grown, they and all their friends will have been trained for meaningful work," noticing the disapproval in her eye and adding immediately, "This does not mean they won't also learn how to manage a household, bake, knit and keep a watchful eye over their children."

"They will do all this in addition to working for ten hours a day in a bank like yours?" she asked, sounding incredulous.

"With the added income women might provide, Mama, there will be funds for extra household help," Sidney reminded her.

Her response: "Household help do not raise children. You may not realize it, but that takes more time and energy than you can imagine."

"I wouldn't want Rosa to teach me how to make yeast cake. I like taking lessons from Mama," Addie piped up, which almost brought Sidney to tears. When the laughter subsided, Lisl agreed with a sigh to let her youngest daughter take singing lessons. "How can I refuse, when she compliments my baking?"

"As well as your teaching!" Victor added, beaming at his child.

Although she had no idea what had just happened, or why, she did understand that she was going to be allowed to walk to Herr Goff's house at the end of her school day two afternoons a week for singing lessons. She could not stop smiling.

* * *

Simon raced out of his father's small tailoring establishment in Vienna 1 with a suit over each arm, anxious to make the deliveries as quickly as possible so he could have enough time to study the book his friend Otto had found about the new world. Hyman Liebman watched his handsome young son leave the shop, concern etched upon his face. Seated at his sewing table, surrounded on three sides by bolts of fabric to suit every season stacked from floor to ceiling, Liebman sighed loudly. He was well aware that his son did not want to become a tailor, even if it meant inheriting his father's thriving business. The boy preferred sports, exploring the city with his friend Otto – including sections of the City boys their age should not have been visiting – and keeping track of new-fangled inventions. For the boy these discoveries signaled an exciting future, he often told his father, who would have preferred Simon attend more frequently to his studies of the Talmud as he, himself, had done. Instead, the preceding evening the boy had not been able to contain his excitement as he talked about a vehicle he knew was in the making, a vehicle that would run without the help of a team of horses. "Like a bicycle with seats for four, but one you don't have to peddle," he had told his parents before desert was served. After the table had been cleared so the boy could tackle his latest assignment, the section of the Talmud he was meant to be studying lay open before him, utterly ignored. Again Hyman found himself sighing. Simon was his only male child, and though his wife was pregnant – thanks be to God – it was for his elder son that he had worked this hard, building his business and his reputation until he had become the tailor for all the wealthy Jews in Vienna. And just the week before, a member of the aristocracy, a gentile, had ordered two suits and not even remarked upon the price, which was well above anything Liebman had ever charged a Jew, even Mr. Lowenberg.

As for the Talmud and its study, Simon's father had to acknowledge that he knew he hadn't a prayer. He had given up sending Simon to the shul to study after his regular school day, but had ordered his son to study with him at night in their parlor. Because Simon was obedient, and loved his papa, the boy tried hard to please him. But it was obvious the learned tome bored him. He almost always fidgeted in his seat, his eyes wandering about the room looking at anything but the book on the table before them. He often had to be brought back to the page in front of him by his father, who would ask the boy to read a paragraph or two aloud. At the gymnasium the only subject at which Simon excelled was figures. Reading literature, even in German, was obviously a chore for him, as was the history of his own people. To be a doctor or lawyer, or even to work at a bank, he would have to complete a rudimentary education and finish towards the top of his class at the gymnasium. There was no way for the father to hold on to the illusion that this could happen. Hyman worried about what would become of his son, where he would find his place. All he could pray for, and pray he did, was that the handsome lad would not become a dandy, a growing plague with the younger generation in Vienna as far as he was concerned.

As soon as Simon had dropped off the two suits, and eaten the goodies the doting maids offered him at each of the sumptuous apartments, he raced to the Volksgarten to meet his friend Otto. Today Otto had brought a book about America with him, a new book that neither boy had seen before. Without the knowledge of either of their parents, the two friends dreamed about immigrating to the land of opportunity. There, the boys were certain they would be able to choose professions they enjoyed, and not be held back because they were Jewish, or because they had not been to University. Neither had any intention of continuing with their education. They often argued about who hated school more. Otto usually won because his friend at least liked the math classes, a subject he himself detested. His friend actually excelled at figures, something that amazed both boys. If Simon didn't move on to University when he graduated from the gymnasium and couldn't find work immediately in Vienna, he had grudgingly agreed to apprentice for an insurance company that belonged to a client of his father, or at the bank where his father held his business account. There he would slog through his work life without much chance of real advancement. He could become head clerk if he worked very hard, but being head clerk didn't interest him. Simon believed that in America his skill with numbers would enable him to advance to a position of authority in either profession without a University diploma, despite the fact that he had found nothing in writing to support this belief. In the city of his birth he accepted that the lack of a university diploma, as well as the fact that he was a Jew, would be a definite hindrance.

Neither of the boys had ever seen pictures of San Francisco, a growing city on the west coast of America. Otto loved the hills, which seemed very much like the outskirts of Stuttgart, where he and his family often vacationed during both the summer and winter holidays. Simon complained that the foreign city looked small. The hilly paradise didn't beckon him the way the bustling avenues of New York did. Simon had enough confidence in himself, as well as his friend, that this was where he believed they should go: in New York they would succeed.
Together the two boys poured over their new book for at least an hour, until daylight began to fade, and both realized they must hurry home or be scolded by their mothers, who still worried about them. At ten, they each felt this was demeaning and denoted a lack of respect, though neither said so aloud. Despite their dissatisfaction with the opportunities available to boys without intellectual acumen in the city of their birth, both boys loved their parents and were loathe to disappoint them. Nevertheless, they knew how to take care of themselves and couldn't understand why their fathers did not know this as well. If trouble loomed, both boys knew how to fight, and each was sure they could win in a dual of fisticuffs. The two left the park together, shaking hands at the entrance before each hurried off to his respective house in order to arrive before the streetlamps were lit.

When Simon burst through the front door into the hallway of his family's apartment in Vienna 9, his worried mother was standing there waiting for him. She brushed lint from the sleeve of his jacket, and then gently pushed a lock of hair back from his forehead without offering a word of reproach for the worry his late arrival had caused her. His mother's adoration had become more difficult for him to endure as he grew older, but there were benefits as well. He enjoyed being given the choice piece of beef, after his papa, and being asked his opinion on world events, something his younger sisters would never be asked even though they had both been tutored for years. Fortunately one of them had inherited the same good looks, although the strong nose and full lips weren't quite as attractive on her face as on her brother's. Nevertheless she, too, was treated with deference, because it was assumed she would have her pick of suitors. At dinner that night Simon found himself wishing his father would focus his attention on her dowry, rather than worrying about what business he would pursue when he was ready to 'enter the adult realm' as his mother frequently said.

After dinner he played a game of cards with his mother and aunt. When his father came into the parlor to ask if he had brought home any schoolwork, he looked down in shame – of course he had, but obviously hadn't tackled any of it yet, though it wasn't long before his bedtime. Fortunately it was not a night set aside for studying the Talmud with his father, but he was expected to finish his schoolwork before indulging in more trivial pursuits, or so his father said. Both women came to his defense, saying the game wasn't nearly as good without three, and he had only played at their insistence. As he rose from the table to go upstairs to his studies, his aunt pressed a piece of his favorite candy into his palm, sustenance for the hard and disagreeable task ahead of him. The boy actually winked at her as he left the parlor, already pleased by the effect he had on women, even those too old to hold his interest. An hour later his father entered his room, glancing at the books spread out across his son's desk, his mouth pinched in concern. It was obvious the boy had not yet finished.

"It's late, my son. Perhaps you should finish in the morning, if you want me to wake you a bit early," he suggested.

Simon didn't even look up from the paper in front of him. He dunked the pen nib in the ink and wrote with great concentration as he explained to his father that this was his last paragraph. "Please, Papa don't wake me early," he implored without raising his head. "Let me sleep as late as possible."

"Your Mama will want you to eat a hot breakfast," Hyman reminded his son, the very idea that he might ever leave the house without either hot cereal or eggs filling his body amusing them both. For that moment they became men together, amused by the behavior of the fair sex, united in their desire to withstand it. Hyman exited only after the two had agreed that he should awaken the boy at 6:30, so that he could steal an extra fifteen minutes of sleep but satisfy his mother's need to feed him properly.

By the time Simon was fourteen he was already beginning to shave, much to his mother's secret pleasure and his father's dismay, and he was chafing at the bit. The dream he and Otto had hatched two years before, to immigrate to America, was no longer merely a dream. Simon intended to persuade his father to let him leave the gymnasium early. His intention: to apprentice to Mr. Waxman, his father's client in the insurance business. Despite Simon's obvious laxity with his studies, he had long heard his father talk about what a good-and-growing business insurance was, and he had paid attention. It was obviously a skill he could transport across the ocean, and though working behind a desk held no appeal to the energetic youth, possessing such a skill made the idea palatable. Although he had no intention of sharing his plans about emigration with his father, he had chosen this field because of his father's belief in the soundness of that business, and because he believed his math skills would serve him well there. It hadn't escaped his understanding that the insurance his father had purchased for the entire family several years earlier had given him peace of mind. He believed he would be able to approach other burghers in the city with ease because he genuinely believed they would benefit from the product he would be offering. He was therefore bound to do well.

There were now three children in the family besides Simon, including a baby boy a year and a half old, with pink cheeks and a cheerful disposition, the apple of everyone's eye. Much to his surprise, Simon never felt a moment of jealousy for the robust, laughing child. The boy's arrival meant there was a son to take over their father's business: Simon could leave Vienna without guilt or worry, which had come as a great relief. He loved the little boy, and often volunteered to take Ralph to the park, racing around the huge meadow with him, sometimes tackling him – lightly so he didn't get so much as a scuffed knee – but hard enough to make him laugh out loud. As selfish as he could be about his own needs, Simon had always been a good brother to each of his siblings. He enjoyed children, and looked forward to the time when he would have some of his own. Of course he knew that day was far beyond the horizon. There were too many lovely ladies to pursue and no reason at all to settle down before he had amply tasted of the fruit spread before him.

One morning in the early fall after he had turned fifteen, Simon asked his father if he could come to the shop at the close of the workday, and speak to him before they returned home for the evening meal. For once the notion of a heart to heart with his happy-go-lucky son did not seem to trouble the trim tailor. He knew how much his son had always disliked school, and had actually been thinking through some notions he had come up with for the young man's future. At 5'8" tall and still growing, Simon had already outdistanced his father. With his voice deepening on a daily basis and an afternoon shadow darkening his cheeks, talking with his son had started to feel like talking with another man. Hyman raced through the work he had prepared for the day, looking forward to the afternoon meeting. He felt proud of the person his son was becoming.

When the bell tinkled as he opened the door to his father's shop, Simon was a bit surprised to see that he was not hunched over the sewing machine or standing beside the cutting table. Hyman had already cleaned off both areas in preparation for their conversation, depositing the scraps in a box underneath the cutting table, and rethreading the machine to be ready for the first job of the following day: a suit for Mr. Horowitz, who demanded everything be just so.

"Hello Papa." Simon said, immediately blurting before he could stop himself, "I've never seen you stop work this early." With some surprise the young man realized he was more anxious about this encounter than his father. His expectation that they might chat about the local rugby team before getting down to business was dashed, which brought him up short. He wasn't yet ready to divulge his plans, and was at a loss about how to begin.

"I, too, want to talk with you, my son. Sit, sit," Hyman said, motioning to the upholstered chair he had placed across from his work area. Sensing his son's discomfort, he added, "Would you like to begin, or would you prefer that I do?"

Simon believed he would have more control over the conversation if he set the tone as well as the subject to be discussed, by beginning himself. He therefore cleared his throat and said without any hesitation in his voice, "Papa, I do not want to go on to the University. I am not a good student, and I have never enjoyed going to school." Inside he was quivering, but the young man was already adept at hiding his feelings.

Smiling, his father leaned forward and patted his knee. "Do you think this comes as a surprise to me?"

"A disappointment," his son replied.

Leaning forward, Hyman again patted his son's knee. "I made peace with myself about your proclivities several years ago, Simon. But I do want to ask: do you have any idea what you would like to do?"

Because he felt the acceptance in his father's words, Simon plunged ahead. "Yes, father, I do. I hope you do not think it out of place, but I have talked to Herr Waxman, who would be very happy to have me apprentice in his office."

Hyman was both impressed and shocked. He had known and worked with Harold Waxman for almost twenty years, but his friend and insurance agent hadn't breathed a word to him about the conversation he had had with the boy. It was difficult not to see this as a betrayal, but Hyman also understood that the other man had probably been the one to urge Simon to have this conversation with him.

When his father didn't respond immediately, Simon had to force himself to breathe let alone continue. "I don't intend any disrespect, father, by not offering to work with you here. But I don't think I would be happy as a tailor. So it seemed important to me to show you I have initiative, as well as a plan, and that I am capable of moving forward on both."

It was a tremendous relief when his father reached out to clasp his hand. "I am very proud of you, my son. You will just have to give me a moment to digest all of this new information."

"Of course, father. I just hope I have not caused you too much disappointment," the boy managed to say, looking down at their entwined fingers. The two sat this way for several moments before Hyman stood, releasing his son's hand. "So. You will move on. All I ask is that you wait until your sixteenth year, when you have graduated from the gymnasium. I think that would be a good idea if you truly want to advance in your chosen career. Now. Let's go home and share this news with your mother."

Simon stared up at him. "But father, I thought you had something you wanted to talk with me about."

"Your future. I wanted to discuss your future with you because I was worried. Your dislike of school has been apparent to both your mother and me for some time," he explained.

"And you can accept my choice?" Simon asked his father. He couldn't believe the turn the conversation was taking, or how easy it had been.

"You are a good boy, Simon, even though you will never pursue a scholarly life. Today you have shown you possess both courage and initiative, which pleases me a great deal." He pulled his son to his feet, and threw his arms around him, patting him on the back. Since physical affection was not often exhibited in the Liebman home, Simon was as startled by his father's actions as he had been by his words. He was relieved his father had nothing more to say to him, because Simon had no idea how to handle what had already transpired between them. Simon just prayed he would not embarrass either one of them by allowing a tear to escape. On the way home, they talked about a local sports team and its hope to take the title in Vienna, thereby moving on to Berlin for a match with the first place team there. Vienna had not advanced so far in many years. This proved much easier terrain for both father and son.

Within a week of the young man's graduation from the Gymnasium, he had begun his new job at the insurance office of Herr Waxman. To his surprise, he actually enjoyed the work. Computing various financial solutions for the problems faced by Herr Waxman's clients, and then discussing the ramifications of these choices with them was a simple task for him, and one the older man loathed. Waxman didn't want to discuss anything; he just wanted to choose a direction for them himself, and then expect them to take his advise, but the business had changed, and not in a way the older man found comfortable. For this reason Simon quickly became indispensable to the office. His voluble nature, good looks, and the open charm he couldn't help but exhibit when he met with clients pleased his new boss immeasurably. The boy was a natural. Before he turned seventeen he had sold his first policy without any assistance from Herr Waxman or any of the other salesmen.

The best news for Simon was the grace with which his father accepted his choice, excitedly asking him to describe each meeting he had with prospective clients. Hyman would then enquire if he had felt prepared, and finally ask with bated breath, "So, what happened my son?" It was he who opened the special bottle of schnapps after dinner that first day, and he who poured the boy both his first and second glass, beaming down at him each time he raised the bottle.

Simon had some guilt about his ultimate plan, but of course his planned emigration with Otto was still over a year away, so he was able to squelch it easily. He didn't miss his buddies from the Gymnasium at all, nor did he envy the studies most were pursuing at the University. He was in the real male world, and was already experiencing success. The wife of the man who bought this first policy had a sister who was alone, and needed advise. Simon fared especially well with women, and had done so since he was a boy and stolen his first kiss from Any Tannenbaum behind a bush in their neighborhood park. Amy was beloved by all the boys, but it was Simon she chose to kiss. Simon knew he would have a second policy within the week, and was correct. Life was enfolding before his very eyes, and there was no aspect of it that did not fill him with joy.

Then, of course, there were the coffee houses of Vienna. It was clear that his popularity there would lead him to some sweet woman's bedroom, and Simon was more than ready. His only concern was that he often had an erection while seated at the coffee house tables conversing and joking with the women he met there, and usually had to remain behind when everyone else got up to leave. Otto, who seemed to have more self-control, perhaps because the women did not actually drape themselves all over him, couldn't help but tease his friend about the problem, which he quickly understood. Simon did convince him, however, not to share his knowledge with any of the other men who regularly trolled the coffee houses with them. He told no one about the agony he endured on sheet-changing day at home, not even Otto. The maid obviously said nothing to his mother about what she found in his linens each week when she washed them either, though she did look at him with some amusement when she passed him in the hallway. Once, when he felt himself begin to blush, she actually chuckled as she raced by, her arms filled with his bedding, but neither said a word.

All in all, the young man had no complaints. Life was better than he ever thought it could be, even one short year before.

* * *

Noah Unger was born to Zanvil and Leah in the small shtetl of Monasterzyska in the Polish Ukraine in 1863. His mother, a very energetic woman who ran her household with an iron hand and warm heart, owned and operated the best small apothecary shop in the little village. She was revered by many of the villagers who lived there because she cared about her clientele, often prescribing medicines to the poorer residents when they couldn't afford a visit to one of the two community doctors. Often her remedies eased a patient's suffering, and sometimes, even did away with the originating complaint. Her husband, Zanvil, was a scholar who spent many of his hours at the beth medrash, studying. The remainder of his time was spent teaching Torah to the boys in the village, whose parents could afford his small fee for the higher education of their sons. Noah was reading most of the aleph beth by the time he was two. The little boy loved to sit with his father at night, often on his lap, pouring over the text of the Talmud with him, or some other Hebrew tome. He sometimes read the letters aloud for his father, and sometimes Zanvil read aloud to him, especially if the little boy was sleepy from the exertions of his day. Helping others was greatly valued in the Unger household. Noah often helped his older brother, Harry, deliver bread to families in need, which his busy mother somehow found time to bake in her spare time.

Noah was a rambunctious boy. He loved playing with the other little boys in the town square, only two short blocks from the shack his parents called home. After he finished his chores, which included milking the cow, weeding his mother's garden with Harry because there were no girls in the family to complete this task, sweeping out the main room of the hut and the kitchen, and throwing away the kitchen slop which his mother collected in a pail by the back door, he ran outside to find another little boy to play with, even if dusk was already falling. The first time she added this final task to all of Noah's other chores, she watched the little tyke struggle to carry the pail from the back door to the compost in the corner of the yard, setting it down twice to rest, and quite obviously close to tears though unable to admit defeat. She covered her smiling mouth with her hand. This was a son who would accomplish much; this was clear to her even though he was only two years old.

Unfortunately, the morning he was told he was old enough to attend the village heder with his older brother Harry, Noah ran out into the street in front of their little house, sat down and began to howl with fury. He already worked very hard, he said, and read with his papa at night. Why did he have to give up the games he so loved to play in the afternoon with his little pals in the center of the town square? He didn't hurt anyone with them and it could be said, even helped Hymie, the crippled boy who was allowed to play with the others only because he, Noah, insisted upon it. Harry sat down next to his brother and put his arm around the toddler's shoulders. He assured Noah that he would come to love the heder. The melamed was a kind man, though not as gentle as their father; still, the world of men which would open up for Noah as he began to learn would come to mean even more to him than his childish games, his reticent older brother assured him. Finally the usually quiet Harry took his brother's hand in his own, and the two little boys stood, Noah waiting while Harry brushed off his pants, and then his own, so they wouldn't track the dirt from the road back into their parents cottage. He stood equally still while his father wrapped him in the family prayer shawl, took him in his arms, and carried him to the square, past the market street where some of the shops were already bustling with activity, and down the block to a cabin very similar to their own, where a man with a red beard stood outside, awaiting his arrival. Leah, who watched her husband leave with her two sons, knew she would miss Noah's daily visits to her shop, but she and Zanvil were both well aware how bright their younger son was. He could become a rabbi if he worked very hard, and this would make them proud, as well as give them stature in Monastyryzka.

When his father handed Noah over to the rebbe, he was determined not to cry. Of course it helped that Harry walked in beside him, along with two of the older boys with whom he had been playing in the square in the afternoon. This was their first day at the heder as well. Perhaps, like Noah, they hadn't known until this morning that their time of being a playful child was at an end, so they hadn't told him they would no longer be able to play. The room he found himself in was very similar to the main room in his own home, where his father ran a heder for six to eight year old boys every day. Because his father was a teacher, Noah had always been able to count on someone at home if he scraped a knee, or wanted to eat a few dried fruits or an extra apple in the middle of the afternoon. Now, like the boys in his father's care, he would spend ten hours each day with this red-bearded man who seemed quite stern to the little boy, especially when he pronounced the ritual prayer Pura, the angel of forgetfulness, that was embroidered on a tablet above his head. When the reb handed him his aleph beth he managed to mutter that he already knew most of his letters. This brought a smile to the teacher's lips. "Is your aleph beth covered in honey?" he asked the new little student, smiling down at him. After the melamid read from the little plaque of Hebrew letters, he handed it to Noah, as well as the kilorit, or tiny cake, which Noah was allowed to eat along with the two other new boys, who had tablets and cakes of their own. "That's why it's sticky," Noah exclaimed, surprised, but also pleased by his own understanding. Each student received a hard-boiled egg as well, upon which was written a saying from a religious Jewish text. Noah was delighted that his saying was one his father often read to him at night, after Zanvil's students had left for their own homes.

Although Noah didn't hate school the first day, he didn't like it either. Sitting on the hard bench for hours to read the pages prepared for him by the teacher felt agonizing to the little boy, whose body all but crackled with energy. Although he already knew the aleph beth, he loved the honey-covered aleph beth tablet, and the taste of the little kilorit. His heart thumped with excitement when he discovered he would be allowed to keep the tablet once he had licked off the honey coating. The two other new boys spent the morning learning their letters on their tablet, both stealing glances at the page Noah was already reading from the Siddur, lying open before him on the big table. They were not surprised or jealous even though he was merely three and they were both four; after all, his father was a melamid also, and one well-thought of throughout the village. Besides, they liked Noah: although younger, he had been their playmate for two years, and always had ideas for new games they could play. When all three newcomers were finally given a break, the boys immediately raced outside and began to play one of their favorites, even though they knew they would only be allowed to stay outside for a few minutes. In this game the boys chased each other from one rock to another, rocks Noah had quickly placed at strategic places around the small yard as soon as he had raced outside. The boys had to follow a pattern: whoever finished first won. None of the boys took time to bite into the bread their mother's had stuffed into their pockets, and none of them, even Noah, had had the courage to sneak a bite inside the classroom. By the time the bahelfer, an older boy who assisted the teacher with the youngest students, brought them their lunches, all three were ravenous, and could barely mumble the few words of prayer that would enable them to eat.

By the third week Noah was excited by the words he was reading on his own, and the fact that he could connect them in a string so that they became phrases, and sometimes even full sentences. He did not have to be persuaded to sit longer on the hard benches by Harry or the bigger boys. His own intelligence did the job. As his facility with the Hebrew letters increased, the phrases became little paragraphs, and the paragraphs stories. Noah was entranced by the world that was opening before him, just as Harry had assured him he would be. When the other boys, even some of the older fellows, were asked to read aloud, many stumbled over the unfamiliar sounds, but Noah rarely did. If it was possible to love one part of his studies more than the others, Noah loved the sound of the words as they rolled off his teacher's tongue. He would practice in his bed at night, whispering to himself so that he would sound like the teacher the next day when it was his turn to stand up and recite a phrase or a sentence or a paragraph. His only frustration was that he was unable to intone the syllables in the way the older boys did, but he was sure he would improve with practice, and eventually, find his own facility acceptable. He accepted that it would take years for him to reach the heights of the older men in the temple, but was also grateful he was expected to study for hours and hours each day so that he might equal them. It was only in the evening, when he began to long for the milk and yeast cakes he knew his mother had prepared for him, that he had trouble concentrating. He and Harry always hurried home after saying good-bye to the other students, stomachs growling. Noah would never forget the scent of his mother's baking that wafted all the way outside to their little lane when Harry pulled open their front door each and every night. "My little scholars" she smiled at them as she placed the daily treats on the table in front of their seats, watching them inhale the little goodies with obvious pleasure before she shoed them upstairs to their bedroom, and to sleep.

By the time Noah joined Harry at his father's heder, he had become the leader of the students in his school, many moving on to study with him there. When some of the boys groaned at the number of pages they had to read each day in the Torah, Noah made interesting stories out of them for his compatriots, much to the amusement of his father. Rather than being distressed by his son's fertile imagination, he was pleased by the wit he displayed with these little tales, as well as how apt each one was to the pages being perused. Now, like Harry, Noah was considered "bohrim", a young man. If he could not play like a child, he did not want to be one any longer, so the new appellation didn't bother him. Because of his love of learning, he found it difficult to understand the fear that seemed to consume his older brother, Harry, who was always worrying he wasn't smart enough. Though the older boy had never loved the actual learning as much as Noah, he couldn't accept that his skill level was lower than his younger brother's. Fortunately on Sunday afternoons the brothers were allowed some hours to again be boys. When Harry refused to play two Sundays in a row, Noah determined to find out what the problem was.

That very evening the mystery was solved. Sneaking back down the stairs to hear the conversation being conducted between Harry, his mother and his father, Noah was careful not to awaken his little sisters. The two girls now shared the upstairs loft bedroom with their brothers in an area partitioned from theirs by a cloth curtain. Leah had somehow managed to make the divider look decorative, rather than a mere divider between the boys and girls. He heard his father's voice first.

"My son, I do not want you to stop your studies. Your mother and I will make do," he heard his father say.

"I am the oldest of four," his older brother's voice was firm, though muted. "You know as well as I do that it is time I help you in supporting our family."

It seemed to Noah that his heart had moved into his upper chest, and lodged there like a lump of hard clay. He could not imagine the heder without his brother; but even more, he could not imagine not being able to continue learning himself. The youngster strained to hear the rest of the conversation.

"No, son, I want you to be a man of education," Leah told Harry. "Your father and I have talked about this for weeks now. If I open the shop a bit earlier, and close a little later, we will have enough. "

"Two of the balebatim have spoken to me about their sons. When they come into the heder, their fathers will pay the full amount. Do not worry about the family, my son. The family will be fine," his father added.

When Harry came up to bed, he knew instinctively that Noah had been listening. He was not surprised when the younger boy climbed into his bed. "What are you going to do?" Noah asked him. For a short while Harry didn't answer him, and the two brothers lay side by side beneath Noah's comforter.

"If I was a scholar, like you, Noah, this would be much harder for me. But I know I am not. I don't excel at my studies, and they don't thrill me they way they do you. What I see in your eyes when you are pouring over the Talmud, is not something I have ever felt," Harry whispered. Neither boy wanted to awaken the younger girls. Nor did they want to be heard by their parents, who had not yet gone to bed below.

"But what kind of work will you do?" Noah asked his brother.

"Tomorrow I will go to talk to Mr. Bronstein. I know he has had to work very long hours since both of his sons died last spring from influenza. He has no family to help him, no nephews even. I think I would be a good cattleman, and perhaps someday could even become a partner in his business," Harry replied without any hesitation.

"What do you know about cattle?" the younger boy asked, startled by this idea.

"What ever country boy knows, and if there is anything else I need to learn, I will learn it," replied his brother with quiet assurance. For once he didn't seem afraid of what lay before him.

The two boys snuggled beneath the cover until Noah felt himself begin to drift into sleep. He almost didn't hear Harry whisper, "Don't worry, Noah. I will become a good salesman, and I will earn enough so that you can stay in heder."

* * *

Yetta Bloom was born in the smaller, neighboring village of Krynicja four years after Noah Unger entered his father's heder. From the beginning she was a feisty, opinionated child, the apple of her father's eye. Because he was the community scholar, he studied at the beth medrash from dawn till early evening every day except Saturday, when the entire village worshiped. Fortunately Yetta's mother Rosa had a head for business, and had taken over her own mother's shop shortly before her third child was born. The little family was kept comfortable by her work, although no one would have called them wealthy. They had a decent life. Yetta began to help her mother in the fabric shop when she was three, following in the footsteps of her older sister, Mara. By the time she was five she had taken her sister's place at their single sewing machine; she had made her first jacket for a distinguished member of the balebatim by the end of the year. Even her mother Rosa was surprised by the quality of the little girl's workmanship.

When Yetta suggested she start a tailoring business from her mother's fabric store at age eight, everyone but her father was appalled. Yetta, distraught by his negative reception to her novel idea, ran from the shop and couldn't be found for hours. It was her father, the scholar, who tracked her down. He hiked down to the river towards Monastyrzyska, and traversed the quickly flowing water by log, walking quickly towards a tree-lined bluff where he and his daughter had often picnicked. Here they shared weighty conversations about the state of mankind, and womankind, as well as the reason for the dislike the peasants exhibited towards the Jews of their shtetl and those of Monastyrzyska, the largest Jewish town in the area. Yetta had always been wise beyond her years. She had an obvious head for mathematics, and was already helping her mother with the accounts for the shop, even though still a child. Nevertheless branching out at her young age seemed a little over-reaching, even to her attentive and supportive papa. The only council her father had offered on those outings he and she had shared regarding the limits placed on women in their community, had been that she forego the notion of a formal education. He promised that he would teach her the aleph beth if she did not tell her mother. To this she had readily agreed. When he found her lying on the huge rock slab on the edge of the embankment still sobbing hours after running away, the wise man merely stroked the child's back until she was calm. Gently he suggested she postpone her business venture until she was twelve. Yetta's eyes slammed shut again: after all, four years was half her current life span. However, when her father assured her he would continue discussing the idea with her mother, as well as her older sister, so that when she was twelve the entire family would be prepared, she agreed.

On the walk home, she agreed to renew her efforts in the kitchen as well. Her kugle pudding had, thus far, been inedible, and her challah so dry her mother threw out her first, second and third attempts, despite the fact that the entire family was looking forward to eating the loaves with their midday meal. True to her word, Yetta dropped her business suggestion, although she continued to improve her sewing skills on the shop's single sewing machine. She also became a passable cook. Not a good one like her mother or her older sister, but at least her attempts no longer landed on the garbage heap in the backyard. Yetta also frequently volunteered to watch her younger sister and brother when they were infants, freeing her mother to work in the shop longer hours. Truthfully, she enjoyed playing with them in the garden, weeding and watching the two toddlers, sometimes crawling on all fours with them through the rows of carrots, beets and lettuce, when there were no adults around to report her unladylike behavior. As a result, her little brother howled with despair when he was dressed in his best clothes to attend the heder at the age of three, and only stopped when Yetta picked him up in her arms and carried him down their muddy street and across the main square to the synagogue where classes were held. He agreed to go inside when she promised she would play with him for an hour each night when he returned home before he had to go to bed. She promised she would talk to their Papa, assuring the little boy he would be on their side.

The day she turned twelve, after cleaning up the breakfast dishes as well as preparing a morning snack for her three sisters, who were now all working at the shop, Yetta marched with purpose along the narrow side street which housed the most popular shops in the village, including her mother's fabric store.

"I am twelve today, Mama, and I plan to start my tailoring business," she declared.

Amused, her mother asked who her customers would be, not terribly surprised when Yetta had an answer at hand. Rosa told her ambitious daughter she could clear a space for her, and then they would see. Yetta spent the morning moving the fabric piled in front of their one window, where she planned to display the man's jacket she had been working on all month during her lunch break. Within days she had gained a commission to complete a suit to be worn by an honored belabatim for an important town occasion. She was thrilled, knowing other commissions would follow, but she kept that belief to herself. If her mother allowed her the freedom to sew during working hours when the shop wasn't crowded with shoppers, she would use her lunch hour to inform all of the other shop owners of her new business, as well as the few women in the small village whose husbands were so wealthy they didn't have to work at all. By the time she approached them, they already knew about her tailoring skill; the wife of the man who had ordered the first suit because of the jacket he had seen hanging in the window of her mother's shop, had already showed their friends the fashionable suit Yetta had made for him. When Yetta received her second order that afternoon, Mara offered to run the family home, taking over all the chores Yetta had handled, as well as her own. After dinner Yetta's mother agreed to let Yetta begin her business in earnest. Since her father had kept his word, Rosa was expecting her daughter's request, and had already agreed to accede to it.

Within half a year, Yetta was so busy she had to hire two seamstresses to help her keep up with all the orders. A year after she opened her new business, the Bloom family was able to move to a larger, more comfortable cottage closer to the shop and temple. For the first time since their first child was born, her parents had a room of their own, and the children all slept upstairs in the loft. Although Mara was tired from all the chores she had to complete each day: in the garden, the kitchen, the living area and in the shop itself, she, too, was delighted by the success of her sister. With the family's new-found wealth, her mother was less adamant that Mara consider the community doctor as her potential mate, allowing her to take afternoon strolls with the man's son, a well-respected rabbinical student at the Yeshiva in Buchach, whom she had loved for three years. Yetta's father was both amused and proud of his younger daughter's assessment of her sister's situation; she declared that although the doctor was a wealthier man, Mara would have had a much more difficult life with him, since he still had three young children at home. Those children would have become her sister's responsibility. Even though a rabbi did not earn a large income, the son would become one of the most respected members of the community, and certainly in time a member himself, of the balebatim. Initially when Mara married the young rabbi she took care of both homes, but this wasn't a burden since her own cottage was small. Even if she became pregnant immediately Yetta's younger sister would be able to take over more and more of the household chores for the family, aided by the youngest girl, who at 5 was already an enormous help to the older girls. The family joke was that the baby of the family also was a better baker than her sister, the tailor, despite the years Yetta had spent improving her culinary skills.

More and more of the balebatim began to frequent the shop to use Yetta's services, and while in the shop, also noticed the quality of Rosa's fabrics. They began to order dresses for their wives there as well. Thus Rosa's business improved along with her daughter's; within the following year, the family added another room to the back of their home, which their father used for his classes, and the two older girls as a bedroom at night. By the time Yetta was 15, she was making suits for the most important members of their little community. When she told Mara she felt guilty that her older sister had the burden of caring for two households, Mara was shocked.

"Without you, Chaim and I would never have been able to move, or to afford the clothes for our child, or the one on the way. You are the most generous person I know, Yetta, and the hardest worker," Mara assured her sister on their way to temple one Saturday morning. Though Yetta was appeased, her discomfort about the burden she had left for her older sister remained hidden in her heart. More important, and even more secret, Yetta believed that no man would ever want to join his life with hers, because in the important ways, she was not a woman. All she did in her home was eat and sleep.

* * *

When she was in her last year at the Gymnasium and it was time to consider applying to the University, an honor newly available to some of the upper class girls in Vienna, Addie's singing teacher, Herr Goff, asked to speak to her parents. Lisl, who still only allowed the singing lessons on sufferance, at first stubbornly refused to go to the teacher's house, but at Victor's urging, finally agreed to go there with him. Despite herself she was excited by what Herr Goff had to say. He believed Adelaide could sing at the opera; at the very least, she could sing in an a cappella group of some renown; if she was allowed to give one concert with them at the symphony hall, people would flock to hear her solo at the next one. Such was the depth of their daughter's talent. He urged Victor and Lisl to consider sending Adelaide to the music academy when it was time for her to move on to university, because her gifts could only be fully explored in such an environment. Though painfully shy, it was clear the girl loved to sing. When the piano began to play and she opened her mouth to begin, the shyness that hung like a shroud around her slim body slid away. That soaring voice, Goff told them, needed nurturing.

It was Lisl who urged her husband to consider the proposal that evening as they prepared for bed, shifting roles for the first time in their long marriage. Of course Lisl still wanted her daughter to have a married life, and to experience the joy of motherhood, but she feared that neither would happen if Addie had to squelch her musical ability. She had seen her daughter practice at home, seen the look of transport Goff had described on her face. How, she asked Victor, could they deny her that joy? Distressed, Victor listened to his wife, wishing in his soul that he had not allowed the music lessons to begin. Her talent was enchanting in a child. But he also knew pursuing a life in singing could become a detriment to her enjoying a fulfilled life as a woman in bourgeois Vienna. Much to his surprise his wife was now suggesting that to put a halt to the singing might erode Addie's chances for a normal, happy life as well. Neither had any idea what to do, though both suspected they would follow Herr Goff's advise. The singing lessons, which had seemed harmless, had taken them and their daughter beyond the point of return. As they prepared for bed each of the adults found themselves thinking about their first-born daughter, Sophia, who was also unhappy with the possibilities afforded her by the turn-of-the-century world of Jewish Vienna. She lacked Adelaide's talent, which might have enabled her to pursue an alternative path, although neither parent knew if this would have been a good thing or not. Perhaps, Victor thought as he drifted into sleep, it was time to put his energies into finding a husband for Sophia, ensuring the safety of at least one of his daughters.

Had either of the adults been aware of the depth of their older daughter's malaise, they would have been extremely distressed. In the afternoons after school, Sophia had been sneaking off to the Stierboche Café on her way home, or the Griensteidl, at first merely listening to the conversations between the free-thinking artists who frequented the cafes, but then, slowly making friends and joining in the conversations herself. Here, the young people were interested in her opinions, which they most certainly were not at the gymnasium. Here, she learned enough to actually develop her thinking skills. One day when she picked up her younger sister, which she had been ordered to do after each and every singing lesson, Sophia confessed that she had not come from home, but from the Stierboche. Addie was shocked by her sister's revelation, as well as startled that their mother had not asked Sophia what she did each afternoon after leaving school. Sophia suggested Addie go with her the following Wednesday afternoon, when she did not have a lesson with Herr Goff. Their mother would be out until four that day, meeting with her weekly knitting club. Frightened by the very idea, Addie immediately declined. That she was pursuing an art form was one thing; to frolic with 'artist' types quite another.

Nevertheless, Sophia continued to frequent the coffee shops on her own, although the sisters did not discuss the issue again. One day a pale, intense young painter joined the table where she sat, deep in discussion with a struggling writer and two portrait painters. When one of the other women mentioned Sophia's desire to paint, as well as her concern that she had no talent, the young man was appalled: if she didn't attempt it, how would she ever know? Before she could even reply, everyone at the table joined in, urging her to get her hand wet, so to speak. Sophia hesitantly agreed. Without a second's hesitation the young man offered to take her under his wing, to tutor her at his small attic studio. Sophia had no idea if she was feeling terror or excitement. How would she ever tell her parents what she intended to do? Of course she could never tell them. She sat mute at the table while her mind raced over the pit falls and possibilities as the others watched her expectantly. Finally she explained that she would have to hide these lessons from her parents, and had to consider how she would pay for them. Obviously interested in the young woman, the painter couldn't keep the grin from his face: he would tutor her at first for free; if she had talent and wanted to continue, then they would see. Sophia, who was so excited by the notion that she, like her little sister, could take lessons and become something more than a mere hausfrau, immediately agreed. She failed to notice the conspiratorial look that passed between the painter and the writer, or the smile exchanged by the two women who early on had befriended her at the Griensteidl. All she knew was that her life was beginning, and she was becoming a participant in its development.

* * *

Although Simon Liebman was one of the young men Sophia had noticed during the months she had been going to the coffee houses, he was too young to hold her interest. Good looking yes, and clearly confident in the attraction he held for the opposite sex, the young man was a bit too taken with himself to elicit any real interest on her part. In addition, despite her own naiveté, it was clear to Sophia why he was there. The way he looked at her and the other women made her very uncomfortable. Fortunately it was easy to ignore him because there were so many young men and women drinking coffee and chatting every afternoon.

Indeed, Simon did frequent the coffee houses because, at 15, he found it difficult to think about anything other than women. In a constant, and embarrassing state of tumescence, he knew he must solve this problem before his parents became aware of his predicament. Within weeks of his first attendance at one of the café's frequented by artists of every gender and inclination, Simon realized he had been noticed by Hilda, an actress of some repute in the local theatre scene. Almost ten years older than he, Hilda was immediately aware of the young man's problem, which she found amusing. He was certainly not the first young man she had initiated into the world of love, and wouldn't be the last, but he was easily the most enthusiastic. As soon as she sat down in the empty seat across from him, Simon jumped up to order a cup of coffee for her with the funds he secreted from his weekly school allowance. This momentous event occurred the year before he left the gymnasium to work for Herr Waxman. By evening's end, he had agreed to meet her at her flat the next day at four. When he seemed disappointed at the delay, Hilda had actually laughed aloud.

"You have waited this long, my anxious young man. Another day shouldn't be a problem," she said when she was able to catch her breath. She told him she had a performance that evening; he would have to practice patience.

"I've been practicing that this whole year," he replied without pause. "I'm sure I won't sleep, or be able to study for my science test either."

"On the contrary. If you won't be able to sleep, you will have the entire night to study. You may surprise your teacher and yourself," she laughed.

"Most of all, my teacher," he grinned at her, agreeing that might be a good way to spend the hours instead of tossing and turning and messing up his bedclothes.

Much to his surprise, his concentration was extraordinary and he studied late into the night, and the next day finished the test before anyone else in his class. The young man was amused that the very idea of losing his virginity had improved his study skills. Ten minutes early to his assignation, he waited up the block so as not to appear too anxious. He even managed to knock on her door five minutes later than the appointed time, awarded for his patience by the fiery actress grabbing his jacket and pulling him into the flat. At first he was dismayed to discover that one of her three room mates was at home, but when the young woman patted him on the back, kissed his cheek, and wished him well in this, his first encounter, he was too amazed to be embarrassed or disgruntled.

His only embarrassment during the big event was when the actress led him into the bathroom, undressed him, and washed his private parts with a clean washcloth. It was also tremendously exciting. Initially he had to resist the impulse to push her hands away from the buttons on his pants, but his curiosity about what she had in mind overpowered his discomfort. By the time he was totally disrobed he was, of course, standing at full attention, despite his efforts to control himself. When he saw the way she was looking at him, everything but his desire to see and wash her as well vanished.

"My my my," she smiled up at him from her perch resting on her knees beside the sink. "I don't think you have to worry about size. You do know that, don't you?"

And although he had never seen another erect penis, he believed his own dimensions were satisfactory. Before he could stop himself Simon blurted, "I'm not too big, am I?"

As she slid the washcloth down and around his appendage with relish, she assured him that he needn't worry about that either.

Lifting her chin so that she was again looking up at him he murmured, "I want to do that to you too," which made her laugh aloud. Without another word, she stood, placed his fingers on the buttons of her blouse, and unzipped her skirt, stepping out of it inches from where Simon stood. By the time she, too, was naked, Simon was afraid he would lose his seed without even touching her. Determined to comport himself with dignity, he began to wash her body, starting with her neck, delighted when she murmured, "What a surprise...."
Although he had never even seen a naked woman before, he gently parted her legs so that he could wash the place he had been dreaming about for years. He squatted on his haunches and looked up as he worked, utterly thrilled. Not only did Hilda him allow this liberty, she

closed her eyes and began to moan, which of course excited Simon beyond belief.

"We'd better go to my room right now," she whispered, blindly reaching behind herself for the two robes that were hanging on a hook beside the door. Handing him the plainer of the two, she took his hand and led him down the hall to her room. Thankfully, the roommate had disappeared.

As soon as her bedroom door closed behind them, Simon reached for the sash of her robe, undoing his own at the same time with one easy tug. Again Hilda laughed. Without thinking about the propriety of his move, he bent his head and began to kiss and then lick the nipples of her breasts. "Are you sure you've never done this before," she asked with a sharp intake of breath. All he could manage was a shake of his head. His mouth was occupied as were his hands, roaming down the length of her back until they had lightly cupped her buttocks. He inched her backwards to the bed, which they both fell onto with some relief.
"Is there anything you want me to teach you," she asked him languidly, as she too, stroked his back.

"What do I do…there?" he asked, wishing he knew what to call that part of a woman's anatomy. Without a word, she joined her hand with his, showing his fingers how best to please her. When it became obvious he needed little tutelage, she lay back with a moan, opening her legs to him eagerly. As she began to shiver from head to toe, the muscles in her stomach actually undulating beneath his other hand, Simon pulled back in fear that he was hurting her. But Hilda pressed his hand back between her lips, rolling her head from side to side with abandon as his fingers again began to move.

When he asked, "What happened?" she replied, "Let me show you." And she did.

The affair continued for months, with Simon arriving home for dinner at a later and later hour, until his mother spoke to his father, and his father decided to follow the young man when he left his school to see what he was up to. Hyman stood on the corner across the street from the coffee house where Simon had initially met Hilda, horrified but not totally surprised that this was where his son had been going. Nonetheless, when he saw him exit the place some moments later with the obviously older Hilda clinging to his arm, his feelings were not nearly as sanguine. No one who frequented the coffee house was shocked by the passion the two exhibited for one another despite their obvious age difference; their affair actually tickled some of the more romantically inclined. Hyman Liebman was appalled. On that fateful day neither the boy nor the woman noticed the older man walking a mere half block behind them; neither realized that he caught the outer door to the apartment building as they headed up the stairs to Hilda's second floor apartment. By the time Hyman found the courage to knock on the door, neither had a stitch of clothes on, although Hilda had hurriedly slipped into her rose-colored robe before stumbling to her front door. At first she had no idea who the older gentlemen standing before her was, until Simon called out from the bedroom with a giggle, "Who is it, Hilde…come back!" and the old man's face lost any trace of color. Without a word, she ushered him inside, pointing to the sitting room, then disappeared down the hallway to fetch his son.

It was a chastened and hastily dressed Simon who stepped into the room where his father was sitting, hat in hand. All he could think to say was "I'm sorry, Papa. We were very discreet."
Hyman didn't bother to argue with his son's lack of veracity. "I won't tell your mother, my boy, but you know that you cannot see this woman again," he said as he stood, setting his hat back atop his head. As he pushed the boy in front of him towards the front door, his tone, if not his words, showed the extent of his distress. "My God, Simon, she is as old as your Aunt Greta!"

Much to the shock of both man and boy, Hilda was already standing at the entryway. "Mr. Liebman, I really do love your son. I certainly haven't meant to upset you, or anyone in your family."

"No one but me will know of this, Miss…" he sighed. "I would tell you to be ashamed but I doubt there's any purpose to that."

"Papa, please!" Simon implored as Hilda smiled a sad little smile, shaking her head 'no'. Instead she took Simon's hand, pressing it to her breast. "I will never forget you, Simon Liebman, and wish you only the best in life."

With that, she released him, opened the door for father and son, and closed it quietly behind them upon their exit from her apartment. As they walked slowly down the stairs, Simon could hear her begin to cry, a sound that haunted him for years, even after he had enjoyed the company of many women. Perhaps it was because she was his first, or because in some way she touched him as much as he had her. In any event, after his father took him to a clinic to be tested for syphilis, a humiliating experience for them both, neither father nor son ever spoke of the matter again, and Simon began to come home from school earlier. It was months before he again began to frequent the coffee houses, avoiding the one where he knew Hilda might be.

He never saw her again, until years later when he returned to Vienna from America with his wife and daughters, and then, only from a distance.

* * *

By the time he was seventeen, Noah was the most revered scholar at the Gemara Heder, the stepping-stone for admittance into the Yeshiva at Buchach. Noah's longing to further his education, and perhaps become a rabbi, was not a surprise to anyone in the family. Of course Zanvil would have loved his son to continue his education, and could not keep the pride from his voice when he discussed his younger son with the other men at the synagogue. He was also pleased with Harry's progress in the cattle business, although the reticent young workingman didn't hold quite the place in his heart that Noah did. Harry had prospered in Mr. Bronstein's employ; everyone expected him to take over the business completely within five years. The old man was saving his money so that he could move to Ternopol, where his wife's sister had moved years before with her husband. Despite his success in their little village, Bronstein's wife, who had never quite recovered from the loss of both of her sons, longed to live closer to family. Towards that end one daughter already had been sent ahead, and wrote glowing letters about life in the city. She had been introduced to a wealthy young merchant who seemed enchanted with her, according to his sister-in-law. He was convinced the move would be a boon for his younger daughter as well and was doubly relieved that he had had the foresight to hire a young man who was adept at speaking with his customers.

Unlike his boss, Harry married a young woman from the village who was both religious and concerned with community life, a young woman much admired by both Leah and Zanvil. She became pregnant sooner than either the young couple who were struggling to set up their own household, or their parents, would have wished. Because she worked for the Bikkur Holim, Molly understood that her pregnancy could be fraught with peril if she continued to work their garden by herself and do all her own cleaning, as well as help her mother with her younger siblings and the work of that household. Much to the shock of the entire family, Leah, too, became pregnant within a month of her daughter-in-law, much more at risk because of her age. She, too, needed to scale back. Even with the help of her two daughters at home and in the shop, Leah was clearly exhausted at the end of every day. It was unthinkable that Zanvil, as a town scholar of great renown, should give up his studies. Neither could he abandon his students, for both moral and financial reasons. Now more than ever the family would need the income, since it would again be expanding.

Although no one said a word, Noah knew it was his turn to make the ultimate sacrifice for his family. No matter how learned he might become, and how much he could eventually earn as a rabbi, there were no funds to send him to Yeshiva. Besides, the family needed what he would earn in order to pay a poor young woman from the village to come and help out in both his brother's household and his mother's. Nevertheless, it was with a heavy heart that he walked to his brother and sister-in-law's small cottage one night to talk to his brother about his idea: that he join him in the cattle business. At first, of course, Harry would hear nothing of it. But as Molly poured each of the men a glass of hot tea, they all knew that the change Noah was suggesting was inevitable. By the time Noah wended his way home, his heart burdened with a grief that would never completely disappear as long as he lived in Monasterzyska, he and his older brother had agreed that by spring, when he had finished his last weeks at the Gemara heder, Noah would learn the cattle business from Harry. All that remained was for Harry to talk to Mr. Bronstein, who would certainly agree. Another hand would mean the business could expand, which in turn would mean more profit for Bronstein. His move into the city could happen all the more easily and better yet, more quickly.

Noah was not surprised to find his father awaiting his return, or his mother taking a kugle pudding from the oven for him. No one wanted to talk about what must occur, but talk they did. Noah understood that he had to convince his parents this was a move he was making by choice: he was not a city boy, and might not do well at the Yeshiva if he were lonely for his parents, his sister, and his brother. Much as he loved his studies – Noah was wise enough to know he could not deny this because then his decision would be suspect and opposed by his father – he longed to become a man by supporting his family, as Harry had. He also wanted to marry some day, but if he went to the Yeshiva, that event would be years and years away, because he could never afford to care for a wife while he studied to become a rabbi. Of course he also acknowledged he would not be able to help the family during that time either. "The family needs my help now," he told them in summation. His parents did not demur. They, too, had realized the necessity of this step.

Within months Noah's affable nature enabled both Harry and him to expand the business so that they were soon selling Kosher beef to surrounding villages. Harry began to look towards Warsaw as an additional market for them. If they could sell in the City, they would be able to make a good settlement with Mr. Bronstein, a settlement that would allow him to move without financial worries, and them to earn enough for Harry and his wife to buy a new cottage for their rapidly expanding family. They could also look to a future where Noah might marry, and buy a house of his own within six or seven years.

Noah did his grieving privately, when he was taking cattle to market. It was during that time that Noah began his life-long habit of keeping his deepest suffering to himself, but doing what he had to do for his family without complaint.

CHAPTER TWO

On Tuesday Adelaide informed Sophia that she would meet her at the Café Griensteidl on Wednesday afternoon because Herr Goff had told her he had to shorten her Wednesday lesson to keep a doctor's appointment. Neither sister mentioned the change to their mother, so neither was expected home before five, which would give them almost an hour at the bohemian coffee bar. Addie followed her feet to the café so she wouldn't have to think about where she was going. She loved Sophia, and was also worried about her, so she kept walking. Unlike her sister, Addie knew she would never be comfortable with bohemians. At first she was startled by the cacophony of sound that greeted her when she slipped inside the inner door, but then felt relief: her silence would be less noticeable in this crowd because everyone was engaged in his or her own conversation. No one would care what she had to say or, indeed, if she had anything to say at all. She spied Sophia, as engaged as everyone else in the room, seated with a group of ragamuffins at a corner table towards the back of the large, cheerful room.

As she was introduced to each of the men and women seated at the table, she was sure her mouth fell open when Sophia reached the young man seated directly across from her and said his name: Arnold Schoenberg. She couldn't keep herself from staring at him, so of course he smiled broadly at her, making her cheeks flush with shame. That she was behaving with such a complete lack of sophistication felt utterly humiliating. The young man had been making quite a name for himself in the symphonic circles of Vienna, his atonal music causing a stir, though not always a favorable one. His reputation as a rake preceded him; even innocent Addie had heard about his exploits, though certainly not in detail. She found herself praying no one at the table had noticed her stares or his response as she made an attempt to sink into her seat and become invisible.

"You have a perfectly stunning voice, Miss Welt," he said, just as her ears were beginning to cool.

"Excuse me," she managed, again in utter emotional disarray.

"I often go to student recitals to find voices for my lieder. I was most impressed at your recital for Herr Goff," he explained to her with a broad but gentle smile.

"Oh. I never notice the audience. If I did I might not be able to sing a single note," she mumbled, forcing him to lean even closer to her. Addie, utterly bewildered by the closeness of his face to hers, felt herself flushing yet again.

"Perhaps I will drop a new piece off with your teacher, and we can see how you do with it," Schoenberg suggested.

Sophia finally noticed the exchange taking place between her little sister and the well-known ladies' man. She was horrified. How could she have made such a mistake, subjecting little Addie to such a man? Without missing a beat, she pulled Addie to her feet.

"Sorry everyone. I didn't realize how late it was getting. Your conversation, has been, as usual, just too scintillating to ignore. But we have to get home to Papa and Mama, or they will discover where I have been spending my afternoons," she finished with a laugh.

Adelaide longed to grab her sister in a huge bear hug in front of everyone in the crowded coffee house, but of course knew this was out of the question. Before she could escape completely, Schoenberg grasped her hand and gave it a little squeeze. As the sisters turned to find their coats, hats and other paraphernalia, he called after the student singer, "I will get those pages to Herr Goff, and come by when he thinks you're ready to sing the piece all the way through for me."

No one else at the small table seemed to notice what a short time Sophia's sister had spent in their midst. Conversation resumed its fever pitch before the sisters had even reached the exit. Sophia was appalled by what she had apparently set in motion. But shy Adelaide was thrilled despite her intense fear of the man.

He believed she could sing!

Over the next few weeks, Sophia did nothing to encourage her sister to return to the café, although she met her painter there every afternoon before she had to retrieve Adelaide from Herr Goff's apartment so they could walk home together. Sophia did this for their mother, although she had assured their Mama that it was perfectly safe for Addie to walk the four blocks by herself. Sophia could not imagine what her mother would think if she knew that the composer, Schoenberg, had dropped off the sheet music for a new piece he had composed at Herr Goff' apartment the day after meeting Adelaide at the café. Not only was Herr Goff supporting Adelaide in her attempt to learn the piece, he intended to invite Schoenberg to his house so that he might hear her perform it. Sophia thought this a poor idea but couldn't think of anything to do about it. After all, she was female and clearly inferior to any man, let alone the renowned Herr Goff.

What a dilemma! She and Harold, the painter, agreed that if she told her father what had happened, he would know where she had been going, and then they would no longer be able to see one another. After the first year of her 'painting lessons' it had become apparent to them both that Sophia's talent was minimal, but by then their interest in one another no longer held even the pretext of a teacher/student bond. In reality, the two were a mere five years apart, a five-year gap that would have horrified both of Sophia's parents, though not nearly as much as his life style. Harold had been disowned by his bourgeois parents two years earlier and had been living hand to mouth until he and his artwork would be discovered. Sophia knew her parents would be less appalled by his age if Harold was a banker, but he was what he was: her parents could not find out about him. Although her concern vis-a-vis Adelaide and the urges of men was precisely the concern her parents would have had about her and Harold, the older girl didn't see any similarity in the two situations.

At the end of the week when Addie was rhapsodizing on the way home about Schoenberg's visit: he had indeed come to hear her sing his melody, and had nothing but praise for the grace of her voice; Sophia decided she had to put her self-interest aside. She had been able to keep Harold at bay when they embraced, and even kissed, and had been tutored in this maneuver by some of the older women at the café. Sexual freedom, though something they themselves believed to be important in the development of a complete woman, was certainly unhealthy for a girl not yet old enough to attend University. Their advise had held Sophia in good stead; her refusal to even consider his more amorous advances had propelled them both into a discussion about how best to approach her parents about their possible marriage. Sophia had no such faith in Schoenberg's intentions. He was already married, and famous for his peccadillos.

One evening after dinner, rather than racing upstairs to complete her homework from the lyceum as quickly as possible, Sophia remained behind, helping the maid remove the dishes and serving platters from the dining room. Because her parents assumed she had gone upstairs as she did every evening, they began their drawing room conversation within her purview. Much to the relief of the free-spirited young girl, it seemed her mother was already petitioning for her marriage, but the young man she had in mind was not Harold. It was Martin Goldblum, a rather taciturn and stout young man Sophia had known since she was a child. Even when their parents used to meet on Sunday afternoons in the Volksgarten for a stroll along the winding pathways there, she had found the boy odious. He enjoyed pulling her hair when their parents were involved in deep discussions, and even pinched her cheeks and pulled her ears when he knew he could get away with it. Of course as a young man he no longer engaged in these activities, although merely thinking about what might spark his interest now, sent a chill down Sophia's spine. She stood transfixed between the dining and drawing rooms, holding a platter in her hands, unable to move, not even when the maid, Linka, tapped her on the shoulder to propel her towards the kitchen. Sighing, the servant took the dish from the girl, who remained standing where she was.

Although Victor did not really approve of his wife's choice of a suitor for Sophia, he had concerns about his elder daughter that he could not reveal to his wife. Sophia had always been more affectionate with him than his little Addie; but in the past few months she had curtailed the usual hugs and kisses with which she had always greeted him upon his arrival home from the bank. She could barely look him in the eye, which was disturbing, to say the least. As he left the bank early on Wednesday, Victor assured himself it was because of this concern that he was standing across the street from his daughters' lyceum at the end of the school day. He watched as Addie and Sophia met just inside the school fence, chatting for a few seconds before Addie raced off, obviously heading in the direction of Herr Goff's apartment for her singing lesson. He watched Sophia cross the street with two other girls with relief, but then the three embraced and his daughter took off on her own. His heart heavy with trepidation, Victor followed Sophia, realizing a block away where she was headed. The awning of the Café was easy to make out, and as soon as he saw it, he knew. When Victor saw Sophia run into the arms of a bearded young man who somehow managed to look mangy even in a proper frock coat with cravat and pocket hanky, he could not believe his own eyes. Unable to watch for another moment as the young man lifted his daughter off her feet, Victor turned away, blindly heading back the way he had come.

At the bank he ordered his secretary not to interrupt him, after assuring his assistant he knew he could handle anything that should arise until the close of the workday. Rather than completing the report Victor had informed the young man he needed to finish that afternoon – a fabrication of course – Victor sat with his head in his hands as he tried to calm himself in the peace and quiet of his own office, and to figure out what to do about Sophia. He tented his hands in front of him but could find no reasonable solution even after several moments of contemplation. A quick marriage to the plump, and slightly cruel Martin was out of the question of course. He feared with some certainty that forcing such a marriage would push his daughter to leave home at best, or worse, move in with the bohemian young man, a thought too horrible to consider. What if the two youngsters found a rabbi who would marry them without their parents' knowledge? He closed his eyes to try to bring into focus the face of another boy within their social circle. Simon Liebman popped into view, but Victor soon dismissed the boy as too young, and not artistic enough to interest Sophia. When he remembered Samuel Siegel, at 18 already a master chess player and violin virtuoso who was preparing for a career in law, content to pursue his artistic interests in his spare time, the father sighed with relief. This young man would appreciate the longings of his eldest daughter, but be a comfort and support for her throughout her life, unlike the wastrel she obviously believed she loved. Finally Victor was able to relax. This was a solution that would appeal to both his wife and daughter, he believed, and one that would free his daughter from the clutches of the disheveled bohemian, whomever he might be.

That evening when Victor explained his objections to the planned betrothal of Martin to Sophia, Lisl did not immediately agree but neither did she deny his concerns, which gave him the strength to continue. The idea of opening a conversation with the Siegel's about their son Samuel startled Lisl, but she found it interesting as well. She, too, could see the wisdom of offering her daughter a suitor with an artistic temperament, but a young man who obviously also understood his responsibilities to society. Before suggesting this possibility to Sophia, the parents agreed to propose an outing to the parents, where they would broach the topic amidst the splendor of the Vienna Opera. If the boy was not already betrothed, and the parents were amenable, then they would approach their daughter. Fortunately the outing took place early the following week, and the four adults found themselves in complete accord. They agreed to discuss the matter with their respective youngsters immediately, each couple returning home with a lighter heart. Not only did their children seem a good match, both couples also knew that they would greatly enjoy being in-laws. They would spend more time with one another than they had in the past, but this possibility was not at all distasteful to anyone. Each of the women discussed this reality with their husbands as they prepared for bed, and all were of like mind.

Unfortunately the very next day before either of her parents could approach her with this plan, Sophia decided to display a bravery she had thus far been unable to summon in her young life, disrobing for the man she considered the love of her life so that she might pose in the nude for him. Unfortunately she continued to think of Harold in this light until her dying day. When Rima, one of the older women who was advising Sophia about how best to love Harold without giving into his baser needs, dropped by the studio she was startled, and greatly distressed, by what she discovered. Without telling the humiliated young Sophia what she intended, the older woman, a mere twenty-two but decades older than the innocent she had been trying to protect, Rima covered the young girl with her own wrap, ordered her to dress, and hustled her out of the studio without even bothering to say a word to Harold. The look on her face was enough. Heart sinking, the young man knew this day would be a turning point in his young life, and that his desire to paint his beloved as nature intended her to be seen had perhaps been the worst idea he had ever entertained in his young life. As she was pushed from his studio, Sophia looked back at him with tears in her eyes, but could think of nothing to say besides his name – 'Harold" – which was clearly not enough.

The very next day during her lunch break Rima found herself standing outside the bank managed by Sophia's father. Pacing back and forth with great uncertainty, the choice was made for her: Victor exited the bank on his way to a luncheon meeting, politely pausing to ask the young woman if she needed help. Steeling herself, Rima introduced herself as a friend of his daughter, Sophia, and asked if she might have a word with him. Without any hesitation, but an obvious look of concern, the older man led her to a café a few blocks from the bank. He explained that he only had a short time as he was meeting a colleague in twenty minutes. It was only because the teashop was around the corner that he could talk to her at all. Motioning her to a table towards the back of the room where they would have privacy, he ordered them each a pot of tea, and carried them to the table. They sat across from one another, both filled with trepidation. Mr. Welt cleared his throat, but did not know what to say to the young woman, who appeared to be only a few years older than his daughter.

"Mr. Welt. This is very difficult for me. I am not sure how to tell you...." She began, and then plunged ahead. "Your daughter, Sophie, has begun a friendship with a painter named Harold. At first he just gave her a few lessons because she wanted to become an artist. But it has developed into more than that." The young woman paused again. Victor pictured the bearded bohemian whose arms had enfolded his daughter a few weeks before. "Does this young man have a beard, which he doesn't keep trimmed as he should," he found himself asking, despite his desire not to learn what he suspected was true. He was not surprised when she nodded her assent.

"He is not a bad sort, Mr. Welt. And he is a fine painter, already selling his work at several smaller galleries here in Vienna. But Sophia, Sophia is very naïve," she explained.

"Isn't this trait to be encouraged in a young woman?" he asked, startled by the dismay he could hear in her tone. Most of the women he knew could be called naïve, but they ran households, gave their time to charities, and planned cultural events for their friends.

"If she is going to spend time with the artists who congregate at the Café Griensteidl in the afternoons, no, this is not a desirable thing to be. There is no easy way to say this, but I stopped by Harold's studio the other day, and Sophia was modeling for him." The man across from her gasped, and visibly paled, but she continued. "Of course I took her away, but … I might not be there the next time she decides to explore…a world she finds unfamiliar."

The two sat and stared at one another, neither touching the coffee cups on the table before them. "I am very grateful you have come to me," Victor assured the young woman. "It cannot have been easy for you to do. I presume you met my daughter at the café?"

"Yes. Several of us have taken her under our wing and tried to teach her a bit about the world. About men. I really thought she understood, but now I think I, myself, may have been naïve as well."

"You have been a wonderful friend to Sophia and I can only tell you again that I am grateful." Victor's outward demeanor may have been calm, but his insides were broiling.

"What will you do? She is truly a lovely young woman, and just wants…more to life than becoming an arts matron. Do you understand what I mean?" Rima asked with a concern for his daughter that even Victor could see in her eyes.

"Yes, my dear, I do. Why she is this way, I cannot say for sure. But I do understand. I also believe I know how to handle this situation, and I do thank you." He took her hands and squeezed them, quickly pulling back as propriety dictated.

With that the two left the café, the father with grave disquiet and the young woman with relief. Rima felt it would have been wrong to allow Sophia to destroy the possibility of living the kind of life she had been brought up to expect, even if some of those expectations seemed constraining. She had not had that advantage or choice, coming from a very different neighborhood in Vienna. She hoped she had not betrayed her young friend, but had protected her, instead, from ruining her life.

* * *

Simon had been promoted to the post of assistant manager at the insurance company. After he had been there for only six months, Mr. Waxman took him aside to tell him how pleased he was at Simon's ability to pick up the more complicated details of the business: he was clearly a clever young man, and one who was not afraid of hard work. He set Simon some new and difficult tasks to accomplish, watching with pleasure as the young man completed them in record time. His promotion, as well as the pay raise that accompanied it, excited even Simon. He didn't object to the celebration dinner his mother lavished on him, appreciating the brisket she served with his favorite whole potatoes crusted the way he liked, and the rich strudel she had asked the cook to prepare for desert although it was only midweek. Simon didn't let himself think about the extra money he would now be able to save for his emigration to the new world until he was alone in his bedroom. He understood how distressed his parents would be about this plan, but he also knew that he could not stay in Vienna. The society in which he had grown up was too constraining for his social ambitions, the people within it gossiping spitefully about good-looking young men like him who had a penchant for seducing members of the opposite sex. From what he had read about New York City, neither would be a problem for him in that freethinking society. The young man was grateful that his mother had presented the family with another child since he had begun to work at Waxman's. At least he was no longer the only son, and the only hope his parents had for the continuation of the Liebman line. His boss was correct in saying he was not afraid of hard work. He wasn't, especially if it would enable him to make the kind of life for himself that he and Otto had been dreaming about for years.

The next day the two young men met in the Volksgarten for lunch, which they had been doing several times a week since they had begun their respective apprenticeships. Simon's father had hopes that if he did well in his administrative job at the insurance company he would become willing to attend law school, expanding his potential for a good life with the family he someday would surely have. If he worked hard, it was even possible Waxman would urge him to return to school, assuring him a job of significance at the company once he completed the necessary course work. Otto's parents were no more aware of the plans being hatched by the two friends then were Simon's. Otto had brought the itinerary of various ocean liners traveling from Rotterdam to New York with him that very day, which the boys poured over. It was a minor set back that the fare on all of them was more than either boy had anticipated, but one they were both sure they could handle. With his quick mind, Simon suggested they write to the city of New York for a newspaper. He was certain they could find the name of one at Vienna's large, central library. Once it arrived they could each scour the paper for jobs, applying by post if necessary. If they were both assured of a position before they approached their respective parents, he reasoned, both families might view the journey be as less perilous. Otto agreed to go to the library on his lunch break the next day and to order the paper immediately, paying with the savings account the boys had opened together for such expenditures. Simon's assignment: to open a postal box where the newspaper could be delivered. Both eagerly awaited its arrival. The day it arrived Simon slipped his key into the slot in the postal box, saw the newspaper resting in the back, and feared he might faint. His heart was beating so fast he was certain the man standing beside him opening his own box could hear it. Simon stopped by Otto's law firm on his way back to his own office to suggest he and Otto go out for a cup of coffee after work at a café they often frequented. When Otto said he had errands to run for his mother, Simon replied, "You may want to look at the mail I received this morning before you rush off to the market for your mother." Neither of the young men had any idea how he would manage to get through the rest of their workday.

They poured over the job advertisements in the New York Tribune; initially, both were quite disappointed. The only advertised job at an insurance firm was for a lowly assistant broker, a job description Simon had surpassed two years before. No law firms advertised at all, but there was a position for a salesman at a clothing firm that didn't seem too bad; at least it didn't make Otto's blood run cold. Like Simon he had always been a personable boy, his pleasant disposition paving his way through the gymnasium despite his less than stellar grades there. His charm had helped him climb the ladder at the Vienna law firm where he had been employed since graduation as well. Nonetheless, over the past year Otto had become bored with the work there, even as he advanced within the management hierarchy. Despite his mother's dreams, he had no interest in continuing to work in the legal profession. Perhaps the dearth of jobs in his chosen field could be fortuitous: in the New World he would find a new career, one that better suited his personality.

Again filled with good cheer, Simon's longtime compatriot proved his worth: we will both advance quickly, he told Simon, just as we have here.

"In America it will be more difficult. I will have to learn the language before I will be promoted to the position I hold here," Simon reminded Otto with a worried expression on his face.

Undeterred, Otto clapped him on the back. "Ach, within a month you will be teaching me. My only worry is that I will have no one to explore this new place with me, because you will be always studying." Simon could not help being cheered by his friend's laughter as they quickly walked to the postal exchange to return the newspaper to their private box. Each had copied the name and address of the firm they needed to contact, and neither wanted to be late for dinner. They had long ago discovered that avoiding explanations was the expeditious approach in all arenas, especially the home front. In addition to the two job opportunities they believed most promising, there were several lowly positions available in disparate fields, which the two agreed to divide between them. Any job seemed better to the boys than none for the aforementioned reason: it would ease the distress their plan would engender in their respective families. Each had four letters to write, and planned to do so that very night. As Simon made his way home, he felt relieved he had conceived this plan with Otto all those years ago instead of one of the other boys he had known since childhood. Otto always saw the brighter side of any situation, and had usually been proven correct in his pronouncements. Simon told himself that he must trust that his friend was again more prescient than he, and that life in the new world would be all that he had dreamt it could be. Never did it enter the mind of either young man that they would not be able to emigrate.

The response to Otto's job inquiry at the clothing establishment took longer to makes its way across the sea than Simon's. He had received a letter telling him that there would be a job for him at the insurance firm if he could leave within the month, although the pay would be less than that advertised in the newspaper until he proved himself proficient in the English language. Nevertheless this was fortunate, since neither he nor Otto received any replies from their other inquiries. A Mr. Wilkens applauded Simon's use of English in his inquiry letter, which pleased Simon no end: he had spent hours at the central library with the two dictionaries and an English grammar book in order to transpose both his letters and those of his friend, Otto, who had found the task daunting, Otto promised Simon he would buckle down with his study of English as soon as he arrived on the shores of the new land. Simon had already begun to study the language at night, hiding both the grammar book and dictionary beneath his mattress, in the center so the maid wouldn't find them when she made his bed each day. He worked late into the night, every night, which didn't sap his energy because he had much to spare, given his excitement about the giant leap forward his life was about to take. Both young men awaited a response to Otto's inquiry with some nervousness, although Otto assured his friend he should emigrate whether a job came through for him or not, a possibility Simon would not consider. It wasn't that he was fearful about going by himself, but that he had always pictured making this move side by side, which is what he intended to do. It was part of the picture in his mind's eye, and he had long believed in that picture.

When Simon spied Otto waiting outside for him at closing time on a Wednesday afternoon, he knew immediately why his friend was there. With an hour of work remaining, Simon could barely concentrate on the tasks before him. Nevertheless he persevered, managing to clear his desk with ten minutes to spare. Grabbing his overcoat and hat, he raced out the door without his usual words of cheer for the office girls, who often stayed even later than he did. As he approached Otto, who had been pacing at the corner since his arrival at Waxman's office, Simon could not tell whether the news was good or bad. As it happened, Otto didn't know either because he had not been able to muster the courage to open the letter alone. It was Simon who sliced the flap with a letter opener he had taken from his carrying case as the crowd of workers hurrying home eddied around them. With a shout, he grabbed Otto in a huge bear hug.

"We're on our way to America! We're on our way to America!" he shouted over and over again.

"Aren't they concerned about my lack of English?" Otto asked him, voice trembling, before he even inquired about the job awaiting him.

"Of course they are. But they say if you are willing to enroll in a course of English, and have the funds to pay for the four week session, they will agree to hire you at its conclusion." Simon was clearly elated.

"What firm is this," Otto asked Simon, who had forgotten he was the only one who had read the letter.

Grinning, he said, "You're going to get to charm hundreds of people, although I don't know if this place makes men's clothing or women's."

Otto's grin was immediate, but faded as quickly as it had appeared.

"I am not good at school," he reminded his friend. "What if I cannot learn this new language?"

"We will learn together. I have enough saved to take this class as well. Perhaps we can take it in the evenings, and both find temporary work during that first month."

"Ach, doing what?" Otto groaned

Simon was nonplussed by his friend's attitude, because it was Otto who had always buoyed his spirits. He had never heard a negative note from him before, and they were already 18 years old. He realized with a start that it was his turn.

"Who cares?" he shouted. "We will be in America!" With that he grabbed his friend's arm and pushed him towards a café on the corner. "We are both strong. We can unload boats if we have to. Come on. It is time to celebrate!"

* * *

Within the last month Yetta had been able to hire two more seamstresses in her little business. She had been sewing for the balebatim for almost two years, but she and the two women who had been working for her since the beginning were no longer enough. There was little room for anything or anyone else in the storage area of the fabric shop, but her father had built a shed along the back wall to house the supplies for both businesses, so they had endured. Although she was almost sixteen, no suitors had come to the Bloom door because Yetta was always at her sewing machine with no time to spare for frivolous social events. At the temple when Saturday service was over, she rushed home to help Sarah with the family dinner, rarely staying to chat with the girls and boys in their tiny stet. Despite this grueling work schedule, Yetta felt guilty that she didn't have the time to help her older sister with more of the household chores. Mara, with a small two-year old clutching at her ankles and already big with a new child on the way, did the cleaning in her own small cottage, as well as helping Yetta's younger sister with the housework at her parents' home. Together, they weeded the family garden, harvested and canned the family produce, and seeded the garden each spring. Mara never complained: she was proud to have a husband who was becoming a community scholar, a man who was sure to become the rabbi at their own temple when their revered childhood rabbi retired, which his wife had been begging him to do for several years. He was old and frail so that event was likely to occur within the year.

For her part, Mara worried about Yetta. Aside from the work she did to support the family, her younger sister had no life. As they worked together at the crowded counter next to the sink in their mother's tiny kitchen before the evening meal, Mara was determined to talk to her about the solstice fair planned for the following weekend in Monasterzyska. There would be young men at the fair plying their wares, as well as looking over the local girls from both communities. It was time for Yetta to consider life outside her little factory. Though not beautiful, Yetta's smile could light up a room all by itself. Besides, the fact that she already had a thriving business at her young age would appeal to many parents, if not their sons. There were more ways to skin a cat, Mara thought as she slid the roast into the oven. Much to her surprise, when she brought up the fair, Yetta did not immediately suggest she keep her thoughts to herself.

"If I can finish the suit I have promised Mr. Goldblum by the Sabbath, perhaps I will walk to Monasterzyska with a few of the frocks the girls are working on," she mused as she was lifting the dinnerware from the well-used mahogany cabinet in the dining room. The small room was so cluttered by the old hutch with its matching large mahogany table and chairs that Yetta had to edge her way around the chairs to the corner of the room before unburdening herself of the heavy storage case.

"You can't be thinking of expanding your business again?" Mara exclaimed from the kitchen. "You can't possibly sit at that machine any longer. There aren't enough hours in the day!"

Smiling, Yetta agreed, though secretly she knew she wouldn't object to gaining a few extra customers in the larger town. Where she would put more seamstresses to complete their orders was another matter. Besides, she knew why Mara wanted her to go to Monasterzyska the following weekend, and had no objections though she didn't have much hope either. "Do you think I can walk there in my old shoes?" she teased, not at all surprised when Mara immediately took her own newer ones from the ledge by the back kitchen door. The sisters had worn the same shoe size for several years, and often switched shoes so they would last longer.

When Yetta asked her sister in a whisper, "Do you really think someone there might notice me?" Mara turned back to the sink so her sister would not see her eyes fill.

"With my shoes and the dress you made for yourself a few months ago, how could every man at the fair not turn to stare?" she managed. For the first time she found herself wondering if Yetta worked so hard because that was what she feared. Seeing her sister's uncertain expression almost broke her heart. Mara moved awkwardly from the tiny kitchen to the dining room and hugged Yetta as much as her growing stomach would allow, assuring her sister she would help her prepare, and would even walk with her part of the way, if their mother would agree to watch her toddler.

With her back to Mara, Yetta spoke quietly as she folded the napkins for the family dinner. "I do have dreams of loving someone someday. A man with energy. A thrifty man. A man who will also love me..." her voice trailing off at the obvious improbability of such a thing.

"But of course you do," Mara agreed, although she hadn't known her sister harbored these longings.

After a short silence, Yetta continued, but so quietly her sister had to strain to hear her words. "I am out of practice in the art of talking to men. Or really, I suppose, I've never known how. I had an easy time when I was little and played with the boys in the square, but then I was always in charge!"

At this admission, both sisters laughed.

"I don't suppose being in charge is appreciated by a grown man." Yetta moved next to her sister at the dining room table, surprising Mara with a tiny smile twitching at the corners of her mouth. She was not renown for her rollicking sense of humor.

Mara's arm snaked around her shoulders again. "My little one, I have faith in your ability to be in charge, even if this man of yours doesn't know you are." She and Mara again hugged one another quickly as they heard the rest of their rowdy family coming home from the synagogue.

The following weekend after the Sabbath meal Yetta, two of her seamstresses, and Mara walked the six miles to Monasterzyska. Yetta actually felt pretty in her new dress and her sister's shoes, with her hair tucked beneath a new kippah. Mara and the two seamstresses had helped her dress, all of them excited at the prospect of Yetta attracting a man from the nearby town. Although it, too, was small, compared to their tiny village it seemed a major metropolis, and one all the women loved to visit. The solstice fair was famous throughout the region, famous enough for Leah to have offered to watch little Mikha'el for the entire afternoon so Mara could shop for some cups for her cottage. She, too, hoped that her younger daughter might attract the attention of a young man, though she admitted this hope to no one, not even her husband.

Throngs of people filled the main square as they entered the town, hawkers hawking, women pushing to get to the front of the most popular lines, youngsters playing underfoot: chaos prevailed. At first Yetta tried to protect herself with her arms as she was jostled from side to side, but then she became so enthralled by all the wares she saw at the makeshift stands within the square that she ceased to notice the crush. Within minutes her sister had stopped in front of some very pretty ceramic ware, her eyes glowing when she spotted the elegant little blue and white cups that would nicely match the white dishes with painted blue rims she had already managed to squirrel away as her fleishig set. Ida, the prettier of the two seamstresses, was happily flirting with two of the 'city' boys, despite having promised herself she would do no such thing. It was Yetta who needed to be noticed, and Yetta was her boss.

The crowd pushed Yetta and the other little seamstress along until they found themselves in front of the matjes shop. They bought a small container of creamed herring, which they ate with their fingers. Ida pushed her way through the throng, joining them with a giggle as she waved in the general direction of the ceramic stand. Yetta was not sure whether she was pointing the way for Mara, who had been looking around for her little sister with some concern, or the gaggle of boys milling about nearby. The four women agreed that having a cup of coffee in the local tavern would not be too great an extravagance, and slowly wended their way along the periphery of the square until they reached the small shop. It was already filled with young people, pushing closer to the counter to order their items, and then waiting, cups in hand, for a place to sit. As they entered the cafe Yetta noticed a group of young men who seemed about ready to leave the shop, which she pointed out to the others. Ida shouted into her ear that she would order Yetta's coffee: why didn't she take the table.

Noah Unger was at first thrilled to see the young woman he had noticed earlier at the herring stand heading towards his table. Then he realized he felt tongue tied, having no idea what to say to this strange, and interesting-looking creature.

"I don't mean to hurry you," she shouted to Noah, Martin and two of their friends, pointing to the three women she had left in line and adding, "But it looked to my friends and I as if you might be ready to go back into the mayhem out there." The only reason Yetta was able to speak to these strange young men at all was that she was thinking about the table, not the men staring up at her. She wondered who the young man with the bushy moustache and heavy eyebrows might be, or how she could find this out, but he looked away with utter disinterest and didn't say anything in response. It was another boy, with full black peyos and blossoming beard who answered her. "Yes, we are done here and would happily give you our seats." He rose, holding out his chair for her to sit in, which she did with a shy smile and a mumbled 'thank you'.

It wasn't until years later that she learned that her husband-to-be could not stop talking about her all the way back to his cattle stall. Noah found her very voice delightful, and couldn't help but notice the smart lines of the lavender dress she wore, and the quality of the fabric. He and his brother Martin agreed that she must be a woman of wealth to be able to dress in such a way, but a woman of wealth from a smaller village would not necessarily be beyond Noah's grasp now that their cattle business was expanding. For days Noah could not stop seeing her large, soulful eyes before him, even when he was talking to a customer, or negotiating the price of a cow.

Before the four girls headed back to their own village, Ida managed to learn a little bit about Noah. A cattleman, he was also a well-known scholar in Monasterzyska, although he had been forced to give up his formal studies to help support his younger siblings and his parents. It was well and good, Yetta told her friends on the walk home, to have learned his name and what he did for a living, but what practical help was any of that information? There was no way she could ever go to his business stall let alone his family home to find him. Behaving in such a brazen manner was both beyond her abilities, as well as behavior all the young women considered improper. "Perhaps he noticed you, too," Mara suggested in her gentle way, taking her sister's arm in hers and adding, "And perhaps he will come to our door." All four women laughed aloud at this notion, although Yetta felt a sadness inside because she knew that would never happen.

Several days after the Solstice Fair, Noah boarded the train to Warsaw with twenty of their finest cattle to deliver to a longtime buyer from the old days, when Mr. Bronstein had owned the company. The young man was also determined to approach some of the butchers in the meat market, to see if he and Martin could expand their business. The trip was a profitable one. Much to his surprise, Noah got along well with the butchers he met because he had done his homework about cuts, loss and trim. He returned to Monasterzyska in very good humor, but what he found there was utterly devastating. Zanvil, who had not been feeling himself for over a month, had been diagnosed with cancer. Once Leah had realized what was wrong, it was clear to her and the others that the cancer was advancing at a rapid pace. Although she managed to be cheerful so that Zanvil would not realize the gravity of his condition, she was actually inconsolable. When one of the boys was sitting with his father, who no longer had the energy to teach, she would take long walks in the fields surrounding the town, howling her grief aloud, sure that no one could hear her. When Noah, who understood his mother better than any of the others, followed her one afternoon, at first she was furious to be discovered in such a state, but then gratefully fell into his arms and cried without respite for more than an hour. By the time they returned home, the mask of calm once again covered her face. She was holding her husband's hand when he died, and would not release it until it became cold.

After his funeral, Leah became obsessed with the single status of her favorite son. In secret she visited the better of the town's matchmakers, and began to arrange dinners at the cottage for him with prospective brides and their parents on days when he wasn't away selling cattle. Neither Noah nor Martin could bear to dissuade their mother from putting together these evenings because both feared that she would slip into a void if she didn't have something significant to do to hold her attention. Finally Noah, who still dreamt about the young woman with the huge eyes from Krynicja, told his mother about his infatuation. Rather than upset her, this newfound information galvanized Leah into even more frenzied activity. She spent hours with Martin's wife and together they concocted a plan. Martin and Noah would drive some cattle over to Krynicja to find new customers, and make discreet inquiries so they might ferret out the young woman's name.

So on a windy Monday morning the two brothers jumped up onto the bench seat of their wagon at dawn, with several cattle tied loosely behind, and made the short trek to the tiny neighboring village. Even though they managed to sell two of the cows, none of the butchers of Krynicja were wealthy enough to order on a regular monthly or bi-monthly basis. Since expanding the business was not the real reason for the day's journey, neither brother was disappointed. On the contrary, each was pleased by the sale of the two Kosher beef cows. However, by the end of the morning Noah was despondent: no one they met had any idea who the young woman from the fair might be. The lavender dress was unfamiliar, and large eyes… well… many of the young women of Krynicja had large eyes. As they sat in a small coffee shop off the town square fortifying themselves for the journey home, Noah suddenly jumped up from the table, almost upsetting both his coffee and Martin's. A totally startled Martin watched his brother race from the shop into the street, even more shocked to see him all but accost a pretty young woman walking past the coffee shop. The excited look on Noah's face as he returned to their table wiped away any need for an explanation.

"Her name is Yetta. Yetta Bloom! She has a thriving business here. Ida is one of her seamstresses, and was in Monasterzyska with her at the Solstice Fair." Noah beamed at his brother, a look Martin rarely saw on his serious younger brother's face.

"Did you get her address Noah," he inquired, even more surprised to discover that his younger brother had possessed the presence of mind to do just that. Although Noah preferred waiting until their next visit to Krynicja to try to find her shop, Martin paid no attention to his objections. He knew his brother was terrified about actually meeting, and speaking to the young woman he had been dreaming about for more than six weeks. They had to hurry, because the address Ida handed him was for both the pharmacy and sewing studio, and dusk was already falling outside. They tethered the cattle to the wagon, and hurried off to the business district on foot.

* * *

When Simon wrote to tell the insurance company he would have to save a hundred more krone before he could make the voyage to America, the boss replied that there should be another opening in six months, and wished him well. All Simon needed to do was inform the man by post when he was arriving, come to the office on lower Broadway, and then he would see what he could do. The owner of the clothing company Otto had contacted was even more sanguine. They always needed young, energetic salesmen. Finding him a position, once he learned English, would not be a problem. A young man who had the gumption to apply for a job in New York from across the ocean in Austria was just the kind of go-getter they were seeking for their growing company. After trying to figure out the meaning of the phrase 'go-getter', both boys agreed to work longer hours in order to accrue the necessary funds as quickly as possible. Neither could have been more thrilled by these prospects for a new life.

Seeing how hard his son was working, Hyman Liebman suggested the young man open a savings account. Moving some of the money from the account he and Otto had shared for almost two years, Simon opened the account at Victor Welt's bank, impressing his father's old friend with his thrift. It wasn't often that a young man, new to the work force, saved some of his earnings rather than spending them in the café's or on the women who would happily exchange favors for a good meal. When the young man accepted a second job at the bank itself, tallying funds at the end of the day in one of the bank ledgers, his father began to wonder what plan was being hatched in his son's head. Afraid to ask, he complimented the young man about his dedication, winking as he suggested that his son must have met a young woman with whom he wanted to set up house. This, Simon of course denied, which his father found even more disturbing. The old man suggested that such a move would not be untoward. After all, he was almost 19 years old. Neither father nor son knew how to continue the conversation, though each left the room in a state of consternation. Hyman was worried about what was inspiring his son to work so hard, and Simon that his father would discover his intentions before he was ready to reveal them.

* * *

Relieved, and thrilled that her voice was flowing from her in clear ringing tones, Addie actually had the courage to glance at Arnold Schoenberg, who was sitting on the couch in her teacher's study watching her with total intensity. After the last note hung suspended and then slowly faded away, no one said a word. Addie stood by the piano, head lowered, eyes riveted to the buttons on her new boots. She had been so sure of hitting every note on the page, so sure of the purity of the tone, she could not understand why both men were silent.

Trying desperately to hold back her tears, she clenched her graceful little fingers in each palm, attempting to take simple small breaths.

"Adelaide," Schoenberg's voice broke the silence. "No one has sung that piece with perfect pitch and just the right amount of vibrato before. I cannot believe you are only seventeen years old. Lisa Schumann, who is already a woman of twenty-five, cannot compare."

Addie was afraid to look up at the great composer. She had no idea what to say.

"This is a good thing. Look at me," he urged as he took her chin in his hand and raised her eyes to his. Because she had been staring at her own feet, she had not even heard him stand and walk over to the piano. "Don't look so frightened, my sweet. You have an amazing talent. You must never deny it again."

"Yes, sir," was all she could think of to say, which made Herr Goff laugh aloud. Schoenberg merely smiled, the gentle gaze of his limpid brown eyes filling her with wonder. He turned to her teacher asking, "So Herman, what do you think? Is Adelaide ready to sing in a small concert hall?"

Adelaide could barely believe her ears. Her first thought was that this new development might ease her parents' worry about Sophia, who daily raged around the house, furious about the new suitor they had found for her. She didn't seem to like him anymore than she had the horrid fat Martin, which Adelaide did not fully understand. The new young man seemed kind, and he was also pleasant to look at. Sophia no longer gossiped with her at night when they lay side by side beneath the fluffy fat quilt they had shared since early childhood. Busy with her music, and trying not to fall behind with her studies, Addie hadn't had the time to wonder about her older sister's reticence, which was why it was surprising that thoughts of Sophia popped into her mind at this particular moment. She realized she was holding her breath, unsure which possibility frightened her more: Herr Goff saying she was not yet ready, or the daunting thought of singing in public, in front of hundreds of strangers. Or could it have something to do with the way the famous composer was looking at her?

"What I think," she heard her teacher's say, "is that Adelaide has been ready for more than a year. She just didn't know it." Her head turned of it's own accord as she stared at her teacher in disbelief, her demeanor again sparking laughter in both of the men.

Gently, Schoenberg brushed her cheek asking, "So my precious. What do you think of that! Are you ready to go into the Glasener Saal in the Weinber Musikverein in three months and sing, just as you do here, letting that vibrato soar out into the gallery mesmerizing everyone there with the sound of my music?"

By this point her throat felt so congested she could not force a single word past her lips. She felt terrified: singing in a concert hall, in front of hundreds of people?

"Do not look so frightened, liebchen. That hall only holds about four hundred souls. That won't be so daunting, no?" he teased her gently. His hand upon her cheek seemed to burn.

All of it was just too much for her to assimilate. The only thing she could offer the two men was a nod, which seemed to satisfy them both. When Schoenberg explained that he would walk her home, since he wanted to broach the subject of the proposed concert to her parents before booking the hall, she didn't feel she could deny him. She just wished she understood the heat that seemed to be enveloping her breasts, and the flush on her cheeks that wouldn't be denied. No matter how much she wished it away, the pinkish hue rose from her high lace collar to tint both of her cheeks. She wanted to crawl beneath the teacher's carpet and jump in the air with the thrill of it all at the same time.

Adelaide and Schoenberg arrived at the apartment building where she had lived her entire life only steps before her father, who met them on the sidewalk in front of the entryway. Smiling with pleasure at seeing his Addie, Victor took his daughter by the arm and turned to the famous man beside her. "So Herr Schoenberg, tell me. Is Addie destined for stardom?" Partly in jest and partly with anxiety, Victor climbed the front stairs with them, waiting for the composer's response.

"That, sir, I believe will be up to your daughter. Her talent knows no bounds," Schoenberg replied.

It was obvious that his words were not ones Victor had expected. Inviting the man inside for an aperitif, he called out to his wife – "Lisl, Lisl, see who I have brought home with me!" In part he called out to hide his own discomfort; in part, he sought the solace of his wife's company during this clearly momentous meeting. As Schoenberg explained to Adelaide's parents what he had in mind for their youngest child, she watched her mother's hand reach out to grasp hold of her father's. She wanted desperately to perform this young man's composition, but she also felt a need to please her parents. When her father told Schoenberg that there was no way he could deny either him, or his child, such an opportunity if he and Herr Goff truly believed she was ready, Adelaide thought she would never take breath again. She heard her father tell Schoenberg that their little Adelaide, despite her worldly talent, was an innocent. His only concern about allowing this event to take place was how such a child would handle that sort of exposure.

"In the art world, sir, I am sure this concert will assure Adelaide's future. But what I believe you are asking is if such a life will preclude the world of family and a life as a wife and a mother for your daughter." As soon as the older man nodded in agreement, Schoenberg continued. "The world is a different place from the one you knew when you were a young man. Within a few years women will be admitted to the University. Women perform great classical works alongside men. Such women are often revered, and are not expected to live a bohemian life. Frankly, I can't imagine that for Addie…" he paused, at a loss about what else to say to reassure Adelaide's father what he envisioned for the man's talented daughter. Victor was thinking about Schoenberg's profligate reputation with women. Those fears he could never air with either his respectable wife, or his youngest daughter. Nevertheless, he found himself assuring the young man that he would carefully consider what had been said, but also explained that he would have to discuss the matter with his wife before giving the composer a definitive answer. Of course he also knew the actual decision would be his own to make, which did nothing to ease his mind.

That evening Lisl went to her daughters' bedroom, as she did every night, to brush Addie's hair before tucking her into bed for the night. However this night she had a more important motive for entering her daughters' bedroom. Lisl had chosen to climb the stairs well before Sophia had finished her homework so that she would be able to talk to Adelaide alone, with no ears prying, especially her older daughter's.

"Dear little one, you must be so thrilled by what Herr Schoenberg is asking of you," she began as she pulled the brush through her daughter's thick auburn hair.

Addie, who was actually quite confused by the turmoil she experienced whenever the young composer came to the apartment of Herr Goff to hear her sing, had no idea what to say to her mother. "Yes, mama," was all she could think to reply. What she wondered was if she was going to become one of 'those women' because of her feelings around Schoenberg.

"I am excited for you as well, but I am also concerned for you," her mother continued.

Misunderstanding, Addie blurted, "I know I can do this, Mama. I no longer strain to reach the higher tones because I have learned a great deal from Herr Goff."

Smiling to hide her own discomfort, Lisl pulled the brush back and forth through the thick hair with even more vigor. "It is not your singing I am concerned about, little one." Sighing, she continued. "What do you know of men, Adelaide?" she asked.

"I…I don't know what you mean," Adelaide stammered.

"That is what concerns me," her mother sighed yet again. "Men have needs," she began, clearing her throat because she wasn't sure how to proceed. "They have urges, and sometimes they cannot control them, especially young men." Lisl felt totally inadequate for the task at hand.

"Does Sidney experience these things?" the startled Addie asked her mother, the concern she felt for her older, and adored brother, apparent.

"I have never discussed the matter with him. That is something I have left for your father to do. I don't imagine he is as…ferocious as many men, but I imagine he does experience urges, nonetheless," she replied with hesitation.

Mother and daughter both became mute, Addie experiencing an odd sort of unrest because of the unusual tenor of their conversation, and the mother unsure how to proceed now that she had begun the unthinkable. Perhaps, Lisl finally decided, the less detail shared the better. "Has Herr Schoenberg ever placed his arm around you, my dear?" she asked.

"No mama," Addie replied, her shocked tone belying the dreams she often had where he was doing just that.

"Good. If he does, you must tell Papa or me, and I can tell Papa, so that he might talk to Herr Schoenberg."
"Yes Mama," Addie agreed, although she had no idea what her Papa would talk to Herr Schoenberg about. She was able to intuit that an arm around the shoulder might be the beginning of some other, dangerous behavior, which was a rather terrifying thought. Nevertheless, the idea also made her heart flutter, and this feeling shamed her. Adelaide was grateful her mother was sitting behind her, having just completed their nightly ritual, so that she could not easily see the flush spreading from her neck to her cheeks.

When Sophia finally came up to bed, Adelaide had not yet fallen asleep. "Mama had a talk with me tonight," she blurted, startling her older sister who had thought she was already asleep.

"About what?" she asked with curiosity.

"Men. She made them sound …dangerous. But surely she doesn't see Papa that way…," Adelaide mused aloud, clearly confused by what had transpired moments before with their mother.

"Ah," said her sister, understanding immediately. "She was talking about men's needs."

"Yes! But what are they?" Adelaide asked her, curious as well as fearful.

"It has to do with how babies are made," Sophia explained.

"You mean if a man puts his arm around you, you could have a baby?" Adelaide asked, incredulous.

"I don't know, but I don't think so. My friend, Harold, has held me close to his chest, and nothing like that has happened to me," Sophia said. When Adelaide asked her who Harold was, Sophia regretted her lack of discretion.

"You mustn't tell Mama or Papa, Addie, but I have continued to see my painting instructor. I am still chaste, you must believe that," Sophia explained with great earnestness.

"I don't know what it means to be chaste," her younger sister admitted with some hesitation.

"We haven't ever kissed," Sophia replied. The sisters lay in Addie's bed, arms touching, each decidedly pleased they could trust one another enough to have such a discussion. Sophia entwined her fingers with those of her younger sister. "You mustn't say a word, but I have even modeled for Harold. And I think I love him."

"Sophia!" the younger girl gasped.

"I know they would never approve of him as my suitor. He has no money, and is quite bohemian," Sophia explained, sadly.

Adelaide's thoughts had nothing to do with their parents' approval. "Did you wear clothes?" she asked.

When Sophia didn't answer immediately, Adelaide knew the answer. "Oh my. I think I would die if anyone saw me without my clothes. But a man! I can't imagine."

At that, Sophia began to giggle. "I thought my heart would burst from my chest, even though he only looked at me as a professional would."

"How do you know that?" her sister asked in absolute amazement.

"Well, he didn't say anything, and when he had finished his sketch, he told me I could get dressed."

"Why do you think you love him?" Adelaide then asked her.

"When I see him, my heart always skips a beat and I think about him all of the time. I can't wait for my next lesson. I have never felt this way before, and certainly not about Martin!"

At this, both girls began to laugh, instinctively smothering the sound with their quilt so their parents wouldn't know they were still awake.

"Or even Samuel, though he's a lot better," Sophia whispered with a giggle.

"You will be careful, won't you?" Adelaide admonished.

"You are one to talk! One of the most famous skirt-chasers in Vienna comes to hear you sing on a regular basis, and you are worried about me!" Sophia exclaimed.

To cover her embarrassment and the awareness that she, too, felt fluttery when she knew Herr Schoenberg would be coming to Herr Goff's studio to hear her sing, Adelaide blurted, "That's silly. I am just a voice to him."

What she didn't say, even to Sophia, was that every inch of her wished that this were not so. She feared she thought about the young composer much more often than was proper for a young woman, but this she would ever admit to anyone either.

Within weeks of this conversation with her sister, Adelaide returned home from a session at Herr Goff's studio with the great composer, lost in her own world of music and titillation. They parted at her front door, Schoenberg continuing on to his own apartment. The past year Lisl had relented, allowing her youngest child to make the walk by herself every day, at least when it was still light outside. As Addie was hanging up her wrap in the hallway, she was startled to hear the angry voice of her father overpowering Sophia's quieter tones. Before she could even stand on her toes to reach the hook on the coat rack, Sophia wrenched open the parlor door, pushing past her troubled sister and racing up the stairs to their bedroom. Not only was the older girl obviously angry, she was sobbing uncontrollably and didn't even seem to notice Adelaide, standing in the hallway with her coat still in her hand.

Adelaide had no idea where to go. If she went upstairs, she knew she would be intruding upon her sister. On the other hand, Sophia might need her help in wading through whatever disaster was afoot. What if her father stormed out of the parlor? Would he want to talk to her about the problem, whatever it was? Might he be equally angry with her for some unfathomable reason? As she stood there frozen in indecision, her mother opened the door and walked into the hall, looking utterly devastated.

"Adelaide. How long have you been standing here?" she asked.

"Only for a little while. I arrived a few seconds before Sophia ran upstairs. I…I didn't know what to do." Voices were rarely raised in the Welt household, which was one of the reasons Adelaide was immobilized by her father's rage.

"Come to the kitchen with me, Adelaide. Please," Lisl urged.

She followed her mother down the hallway bordering the staircase that ascended to the upper floors of their home without demur. Her mother put the kettle on to boil, setting a tray of little yeast cakes on the kitchen table, a spot usually reserved for the kitchen maid and rarely used by the family. Adelaide stood awkwardly by one of the kitchen chairs, not even thinking of pulling it out to sit on. She didn't want to be in the kitchen with her distraught mother at all, let alone to stay in it.

"Your sister has refused an engagement to Samuel Siegel, and your father is not used to having his wishes denied," her mother explained, as if she were discussing a normal, everyday event.

"I thought it was Martin who….who…you preferred," Adelaide sputtered, utterly confused. She agreed with her sister about the horrors of a proposed match with him. But Samuel Siegel was another matter. He loved to attend both the theater and the symphony, a big plus for any man as far as Adelaide was concerned. Her parents, who had introduced their daughters to both venues at an early age, would have felt the same as she. Adelaide understood her father's fury, and her mother's confusion. She was sure neither of them knew about the painter.

"Apparently your sister believes she is in love with a painter she has met at the Griensteidl. That's a café…" she continued.

Adelaide interrupted. "I know what it is," but her mother was too distressed to ask her how she knew about the café, a known spot for artists to congregate.

"A place she shouldn't have been visiting in the first place," Lisl declared with distaste. The biggest surprise to Addie was that Sophia had admitted her infatuation to her parents. Again Adelaide hadn't a clue what to say. Lisl poured a cup of tea from the pot, which had been steeping on the kitchen counter, and placed it in front of her. "You don't seem surprised, little one. How long have you known of this…love interest."

"Not long," she mumbled, her clear voice low and barely audible.

"You should have told me, liebchen," her mother gently chided.

"I…thought…I don't know what I thought. A painter seemed a better choice for Sophia than Martin, Mama." Addie had begun to shake, knowing her mother would not approve of her thoughts on the matter, let alone want to hear them.

Her mother sat down heavily on one of the wooden chairs, and glanced up at her daughter. "You don't truly believe that, Addie. You can't." When Addie failed to reply, Lisl sighed heavily.

"What will happen now?" Adelaide asked her mother.

"Your father is going to this young man's studio tonight. And your sister will marry Samuel Siegel. Your father and I believe Sophia will not find that choice so unendurable in time."

Adelaide heard her mother's words with a sinking feeling in her stomach. What if they chose someone for her whom she could not bear? Or didn't believe she could come to love? Would she have Sophia's courage and refuse?

* * *

One day, after a particularly long and grueling afternoon at the sewing machine in her small shop, Yetta was surprised to see two young men standing across from her parents' cottage when she turned the corner onto their lane. At first she couldn't place either one of them, and then her heart started to beat so quickly she pressed her hand against it, as if that would stop the pounding. One of the men was the young man from the cafe in Monasterzyska, the young man Ida said might call on her. What in the world could he be doing standing with another young man across from her very bungalow? To make matters worse, at that very moment her mother opened the front door and came down the two steps to the street, carrying a challah she had made for their next-door neighbor who was recuperating from a bronchial ailment. Although Yetta would have preferred to turn and run back up the block, she continued to walk towards her house, her mother, and the two young men. Seeing the young man in question cross the street as she drew closer did nothing to quiet the beating in her chest. Nodding to Yetta he spoke the first words she ever heard Noah Unger utter.

"Mrs. Bloom. I would like to ask your daughter to take a walk with me this Saturday after the Shabbos meal. My name is Noah Unger and I am from Monasterzyska," he managed, flushing mightily.

Noah realized immediately he should have introduced himself first, and then made his request. But having gotten any words out at all seemed a major miracle to him.

It did not escape Mrs. Bloom's attention that both the young man and her daughter were blushing mightily. Wishing to ease their discomfort, she invited the two young men inside for a cup of tea and a piece of stollen, nudging her daughter up the steps in front of them. Yetta was so shocked by the young man's appearance at her home she could barely make her legs move. Her mother rarely invited anyone inside, other than family or very close neighbors. Yetta could not remember a stranger ever being asked to tea as if it were an everyday occurrence.

The first few excruciating moments inside the small cottage parlor passed with exchanged pleasantries about the countryside, the difference between their two villages, as well as people they discovered they knew in common: but as the young men sat down at the dining room table for their piece of coffee cake, a stifling silence fell. Finally Marty, Noah's older brother, addressed Yetta, saying he had heard she was a fine young seamstress with a thriving business. At her young age, this was quite an accomplishment, he added. To keep another silence from descending upon the small room, Yetta found herself describing the commencement of her venture, as well as the addition of the new seamstresses the year before due to her increasing business with the town balebatim. Humiliated by her own awkward words, Yetta then clamped her mouth closed. She hoped the brothers wouldn't think her brazen, or self-aggrandizing, not realizing this was an accomplishment both young men would appreciate. Noah talked about the business his brother had all but inherited, flushing again when Marty credited his younger brother with its rapid growth, including the expansion into Warsaw. He, himself, was much too fearful to have ventured there, Marty continued; he was grateful to have his more venturesome brother as a partner. Mrs. Bloom cut the cake, her heart expanding with extraordinary relief. Her accomplished young daughter would not live the life of a spinster, of that she was now certain. This young man was adventuresome as well, and would not be threatened by her achievements.

That Sunday the young couple wended their way through the woods towards the cemetery. Perusing the gravestones to learn about Yetta's family history was a natural ritual for both of the young people. What came as a surprise to them both were the words Noah spoke as they stood beside the stones commemorating the young woman's ancestors.

"I have come to ask you if you would consider becoming my wife," he said, unable to tear his eyes from her face, too anxious to see and hear her response.

Even more surprising, Yetta replied without any hesitation. "I believe I would be willing to marry you." The two stood only feet apart, grinning at one another like fools. Then Yetta murmured, "But I think we should spend some time together before we announce this decision."

Unable to stop smiling, Noah's response was immediate as well. "In that case, may I invite you to Shabbos dinner next Friday evening. I will come to get you in the wagon before dusk, but we will have to walk back."

"I enjoy walking after the Shabbos meal. I have heard walking aids digestion," Yetta replied. By now, she, too, was smiling again.

When Mrs. Bloom saw her daughter's face, she knew what had transpired, especially since Yetta declined to say a word about her conversation with Noah Unger. Lonely as her daughter had been, Mrs. Bloom was pleased, as well as proud that she had not agreed to an immediate wedding. Yet again she was impressed by her daughter's wisdom, which seemed an innate characteristic, not one she had been taught. Once Noah departed, the older woman hugged her daughter, a rare gesture for the reserved woman, who reminded Yetta that she had a distant cousin who lived in Monasterzyska: she would ask the woman about Noah and the Unger family, to make sure this shidduch would be a wise one. But it was clear to her from the expression on Yetta's face that her opinionated daughter would make that decision herself, no matter what the cousin discovered. She thanked God that her daughter was religious, which had always tempered her obstinate nature. Belief would help her withstand whatever difficulties this marriage might present.

The wedding was held at the smaller schulhoyf in Krynicja, the bride's village, as dictated by local custom. At the outskirts of Monasterzyska, Noah's extended family said their good-bye's to him, also according to custom, although they would be following him to Yetta's village several hours later. Accommodations for the groom's entire family had been arranged weeks before. Fortunately the community cottage reserved for poor families, guests, and travelers was vacant, so the immediate family was to be housed there. Leah Bloom and her daughters had scoured the place from top to bottom on Thursday afternoon so that it would be ready for the grand occasion. When Noah reached the bridge to Krynicja, he could see the men of Yetta's family waiting to welcome him on the other side. They walked him to his temporary home, where he was joined by the men from both families.

At the Bloom cottage, a badkhan, or jester, entertained Yetta and her female guests. In word and dance, he lamented the loss of the bride's carefree childhood, and sang his grief at the burdens she was to take on as a wife. Since Yetta had been running her own business from the time she was twelve, this tradition was not terribly suitable to the young bride. Nevertheless, all of the women, including Yetta, participated because this was part of the wedding ritual in the shtetl.

For his part, the groom was signing the ketubah, or marriage certificate, promising to leave money for his prospective wife, should he predecease, or God forbid, divorce her. Because of his scholarly nature, Noah himself delivered the expected discourse to the assembled men, his chosen subject the sanctity of marriage, in which he fervently believed. Noah was certain he was marrying the person for whom he was intended, and this he meant to make clear, in religious terms, to his male relatives and guests. Despite the fact that his speech was powerful and erudite, he was interrupted time after time, as dictated by custom, with jokes, singing, and general group hilarity. This he accepted with extreme good humor. At the conclusion of his speech, ashes were placed on his forehead, a symbol of the destruction of the Temple in Jerusalem, and he and the others, preceded by the Klezmer band, proceeded to walk slowly to the house of his intended.

At the Bloom home, Yetta was so thrilled by the magnificent wedding dress that had been made for her by two of her best seamstresses, she was able to shed the anxiety she had been feeling. Once she raised her arms to let Ida and Mara drop the gown down her arms, she knew the most momentous day of her life was truly beginning. When she sat down in the chair that rested high atop the upside-down trough of dough that had been prepared earlier by the women for the pre-wedding ceremony of abundance that would take place in front of the entire wedding party, Yetta felt like a queen. Her eyes shimmered with tears as her father moved in front of her in their front room, placing his hands atop her head to bless her with the words, "May God make thee as Sarah, Rachel, and Leah who built the house of Israel." She could not take her eyes from Noah, who then lowered the veil over her face, inviting everyone from both families to take part in the final blessing. "Our sister, be thou the mother of thousands of ten thousands, and let thy seed possess the gate of those that hate them."

As the Havdalah candles were lit, the Klezmer band split into two, one preceding the group of men as they walked to the town square and across it to the shul, the other leading the women there. Candles shined in every window along the route, the procession joined by everyone in the small shtetl as they moved towards the schulhoyf to attend the wedding ceremony. By the time the men entered the building, and Noah stood beneath the huppah awaiting his bride, the line of celebrants spread from the shul all the way across the small town square. Candles sparkled in the hands of every person to light the way for the bride, the musicians and the rest of her family. The Monasterzyska tailor had done such a good job altering Marty's wedding suit for Noah, that Yetta did not even think about how the suit might have been improved when she came to stand beside him. Her husband crushed the glass with one step, which sent both families, as well as the villagers who could actually see the glass break, into gales of laughter.

As Noah, Yetta, and the rest of the wedding guests made their way back to the Bloom's cottage for the first of the weekend's wedding meals, the bride and groom were showered by wheat kernels thrown by all of the villagers along the route. Because it was fall they didn't have to contend with being pelted by snowballs, which Noah laughingly reminded Yetta as he picked wheat kernels from the hair peaking out of her head covering. As soon as they entered the main room of the Bloom home, Mrs. Bloom offered them the huge braided challah she had baked during the night as well as salt to bless their union. Both families crowded into that room as well as the small, open kitchen. Yetta and Noah were given enough food to satisfy them until the Sabbath meal, which would take place after the service at the shul, and then led to the master bedroom, which had been cleared so that they could break their fast in privacy. The rest of the guests were fed honey cake before the men and then the women, hurried off to shul for the evening service.

Although there was much teasing when Noah and Yetta emerged from the bedroom, they had had no time to do more than kiss one another, after consuming enough food to not insult the women who had prepared it. Having discovered that she loved kissing Noah even more than she had imagined she would, Yetta had no trouble raising a blush to her cheeks, which of course caused even more laughter. For the first time in his life, Noah could not concentrate on the rabbi's sermon, nor Yetta hear the soaring voice of the hazzan, a sound she had relished since early childhood. Each was focused on the festivities to come, the Sabbath meal, and the time when they would be allowed to excuse themselves, and retire to the bedroom in the bungalow that had been prepared for them. There they would be allowed to sleep until morning when the festivities would continue, although truth be told, neither was thinking about using the time for sleep.

The Sabbath food, though simple, was ample, tasty village fare. Laid out on the Bloom dining table as well as the sideboard were gefilte fish for whetting the palate, small sweet-and-sour meatballs in a delicious sauce passed down from generations of Bloom women, sliced veal in a different, but equally scrumptious sauce, jellied calves feet, a particular favorite of both Noah and Marty, carrots with prunes, potatoes with prunes, and sauerkraut with red berries and pickles. Mara would not let Yetta get up from the table until she had eaten, though she, herself, had difficulty consuming everything set in front of her. "You will need sustenance for the night to come," she explained to her sister. Both women blushed, but they also smiled at one another in conspiratorial anticipation. Mara was the only person to whom Yetta had dared whisper, "Why didn't you tell me kissing was so…so…splendid?" As for Noah, he was surprised by his own hunger, consuming easily as much as his brother Marty, who was famous for his healthy appetite.

When the time finally came for Noah and Yetta to change their clothes and walk to Mara's home, which had been vacated for this first night of their union, the catcalls and hilarity did not shock the young woman. Unlike Adelaide, she had been raised in the country, and knew full well what was in store. After the kissing she had experienced only a few hours earlier, she was eager to depart, which she managed to hide by lowering her eyes and focusing on her new shoes. As she and her husband walked hand and hand to her sister's cottage, Yetta found her heart beating rapidly again, as it had when she had first seen this young man in his village on the day of the Solstice Fair. But this time it pounded with anticipation, not fear. Finally she would be allowed to feel the body of her groom pressed against hers.

Noah need not have feared his wedding night. His slender young bride, who would have been called skinny in the big city, was ashamed of neither her body nor that of her young husband. It was she who unfastened the buttons on his shirt, and she who stepped out of her undergarments without hesitation. The beauty of the woman standing before him stunned Noah, who could not believe his good fortune. He took her hand in his and led her to their marriage bed. Their lovemaking that first night was both passionate and gentle, Yetta touching and exploring her husband with a relish equal to his. After she fell asleep in his arms, he lay awake until dawn, watching his new wife with both wonder and awe.

CHAPTER THREE

When Simon and Otto crested the hill and could see the boat nestled in the harbor of Hamburg, they both leapt from the cart that had carried them from the railway station. Simon raced down the hill towards freedom followed by Otto, the heavy bags banging against their shins feeling weightless in both of their arms. They clambered up the gangway side- by-side, idiot grins plastered across both of their faces. Simon handed his ticket to the purser, who directed him to a cabin below deck. Again Otto followed. Their miniscule cabin, with no porthole, seemed like a castle to them both. Finally, they were beholden to no one but themselves. Neither had to eat with the family, or on a timetable, although they quickly discovered that meals on board were a group experience, albeit a rowdy one: all of the immigrants below decks talked at once, too excited about starting new lives to follow any sort of decorum in their discourse with one another. Simon was disappointed at being barred from first class, where he had hoped to make a business contact or two for himself, ever hopeful that he would not have to begin his new life on the low end of the totem pole at the New York insurance firm. Otto was more sanguine about it: his friend's family was more cultured than his own; he wouldn't have easily melded into an upper class environment in any event. Neither boy suffered from seasickness, and both came to love the raucous group meals.

Within days Simon was walking the small promenade on the deck used by the immigrants with a young woman from Salzburg. He and his parents had often summered there, so the two had a quick rapport and easy frame of reference for conversation. Instead of being deterred by Otto's jealousy, Simon decided to utilize the crossing to tutor his friend in the art of approaching a woman. First, he and Otto perused the noisy dining room at breakfast for a likely candidate for the young man's attentions. By lunchtime of the second day, Simon forced his friend to make his choice. They knew from the accent of a little redhead that she hailed from Vienna, which made her the top candidate. By late that very afternoon Simon pushed Otto onto the small promenade with these suggested words of introduction, "Didn't I see you at the Opera on Shaumstrasse? Carmen, wasn't it?" It made no difference if she attended Opera or not, Simon had assured Otto. If she said no he could play a guessing game about where they might have run into run another. Actually, Simon suggested, it would be better if she said no. Then Otto could discover all he needed to know about her habits, preferences, family and the like, learning about the places she frequented at home in Vienna. If she had seen Carmen, he could talk about the Opera, which both boys had seen with their parents a month prior to their departure, a bon voyage gift from the Liebman's. Either way, Otto would have begun his conquest.

The first meeting went even better than planned: the young woman had not seen Carmen, because by the time she and her friends went to the Opera House for tickets, all of the performances had been sold out. But she was from Leopoldstrasse as was Otto, so there were many places they both loved and enjoyed talking about. They agreed to take their meals together, which didn't bother Simon in the least, because it freed him to do the same with the young woman he was courting. Unlike Otto, he had high hopes that he would lure the pretty young thing to his cabin one day when his roommate was otherwise occupied. Otto was merely relieved to finally be having a 'relationship' with a young woman who seemed to enjoy his company. He had never been to bed with a bourgeois girl, and had some discomfort about attempting such a bold act on board the boat. What if she were a virgin? Simon merely laughed: then she would remember him for her entire life. What could be wrong with that?

One day, when Otto was occupied walking the small deck with his Vienna sweetie, Simon made his move to the upper deck. He had spent days watching the porters and maintenance staff to ascertain when the stairway would be unattended. Simon still believed he could make a contact or two up in 'the heavens' that would ease his entry into life in the new world. When he emerged from the stairway he was amazed by the depth and breadth of the large deck. Well-dressed men and women sauntered along both an inner and outer walkway, each infinitely wider than the one Simon's compatriots were allowed to traverse below. In addition, each promenade was wide enough to accommodate rows and rows of lounge chairs. The entire area was crowded with people, all of them dressed in the finest attire of the day. Even the children wore outfits made of the best materials, clearly hand tailored to fit their active little bodies. Idly, Simon wondered if any of them had been clothed by his father, and was grateful he had worn one of the two new suits Hyman had made for his journey to the new world.

He joined a group of men walking around the circumference of the ship with an ease born of youthful disregard for propriety, closing the gap between himself and the last two men. So caught up was he in the swell of humanity around him – a world closed to him and well above his station in Vienna – Simon barely heard the conversation of the group strolling before him. When an older gentleman from the middle of the pack slowed his gate, falling into step beside him, Simon didn't notice his presence at first, not until the older gentleman cleared his throat. Startled, Simon glanced at him directly, quickly averting his gaze as he had been taught to do. He had no idea what to say. Like Otto when he would see a pretty young woman in the Volksgarten, Simon was tongue-tied in front of such a cultured and wealthy gentleman, an unusual occurrence for the usually affable young man.

"I haven't seen you before, young man. Where have you been hiding these past few weeks?" the gentleman asked, the open, kind look in his eyes indicating that he had no suspicion of the truth. The frankness in his gaze had a profound effect on Simon.

"Actually, sir, I have been below you for the entire journey," Simon was startled to hear himself reply with equal candor. He held his breath, fearing whistles would blow to call for ship security personnel and he would be thrown in an isolated cubicle for the remainder of the voyage.

Instead the white-haired man inquired with genuine interest, "Is it very different up here?"

Again Simon told him the truth: about the windowless sleeping quarters; the watery soup and breakfast gruel, which they all laughed about, but ate for lack of anything better; the narrow, short outdoor promenade; the group bathrooms with open showers, and lastly, the excitement of the passengers squeezed into the quarters below-deck, all of whom were journeying to a new life in a world they hoped would offer them both wealth and less judgment than the one they were leaving behind. Before long Simon realized the other men had quickened their pace and long since disappeared around the curve of the ship's deck, or perhaps he and the man beside him had slowed theirs. No matter. He was alone with his newfound friend. The dapper gent asked many questions about life below-deck, and seemed genuinely interested in Simon's responses. When he finally asked why Simon had risked censure by climbing the stairs to first class, the young man thought for some moments before replying.

"I determined to make this journey when I was just a boy," he began. "Although my parents belong to the middle class, and have always believed in the value of both learning and culture, the careers available to me were not any I longed to pursue. I am a quick learner, and am also gifted with a mind for numbers, but I do not enjoy schooling. In Vienna, where I was born, I could not improve my lot in life without going on to the university, and pursuing a career in law or in medicine. I don't think I am suited to either."

When he finally paused, it seemed natural for the older man to ask him what sort of position he envisioned for himself in this new world, and in what field of endeavor. Simon talked about Waxman's insurance office, and the ease with which he had advanced there. He quickly explained that he didn't mean to brag, but he thought it important to assess one's own gifts and liabilities if one were to succeed in life. Chuckling at this revelation, the gentleman beside him agreed wholeheartedly.

"And what do you think your strengths are, young man?" he asked with total sincerity.

"I am very personable. Because I enjoy talking about a wide range of subjects, and listen well, I quickly ascertain the needs of another. I believe I could work in sales, especially if I possessed a real belief in the product, and that I would quickly improve the business potential of whatever company hired me," he replied slowly, quite obviously thinking about the question before putting his thoughts into words.

It came as a surprise that the gentleman had heard of the small Jewish firm where Simon had worked these past three years. He also seemed impressed by the speed of Simon's rise from lowly clerk to assistant office manager, and asked the young man if he was pleased with the advance.

"Yes and no," Simon answered with total honesty. "I think I did the job well, and that is why I was promoted, but taking care of the details of office life is not my greatest strength." The other man wanted to know why Herr Waxman had kept him behind a desk. Simon explained that his boss needed him to take over for a man who had left his employ, and the young man had felt honor-bound to accede to the request. Although he knew he would eventually be promoted to the manager of Waxman's entire enterprise, he also knew this was not a position that would give him real pleasure.

"Have you already inquired about a position in a New York firm, young man, or are you arriving without such a possibility?" the man asked. Simon told him about the newspaper search he and his friend, Otto, had undertaken, and that each of them had a job awaiting them. Although neither job was what they dreamed of attaining over time in this new country, each job would afford them the opportunity to begin their respective journeys without fear of having to sleep in the streets. For now, that would have to be enough.

For a while the two walked side by side in companionable silence. Simon no longer feared the man would turn him over to the authorities. He also understood that risking such a thing had been worthwhile: sharing his thoughts, his dreams, his beliefs with this stranger had helped him to clarify them for himself. The young man actually felt serene about his decision to take this giant leap into the unknown, a comfort he hadn't experienced since telling his parents about it. The older man reached into his pocket, removing a simple white card. This he handed to Simon.

"I think you are a very brave young man, and one who will go far because you have already taken an honest appraisal of your strengths and weaknesses. My name is Robert Dowling and this is my card. If your new job is a big disappointment, give me a call. There might be something I could do for you." He held out his hand and Simon took it. The two men smiled at one another, Simon with utter disbelief and joy. Then the older man took his leave. Simon watched until he, too, disappeared around the curve of the ship deck, and he then turned to walk back to the stairway that would take him to the deck below. He had to hold himself in check so that he wouldn't throw his hat in the air, leap as high as he could, and shout his joy for all the world to hear. Had he written a fictional account of what he hoped to find by sneaking up to the highest deck on the ship, it wouldn't have been better than what in reality he had found there.

* * *

Despite the fact that young Simon had recently travelled to New York City in the new world to begin a new life, the Welts decided to invite the Liebman's over for dinner. Now that they had settled upon Samuel Siegel as the appropriate mate for Sophia, Lisl turned her attention to Adelaide. Because Arnold Schoenberg was now attending her daughter's singing lessons with Herr Goff at least once a week, the woman felt compelled to act. The day Adelaide raced home to tell her parents that the renowned composer had become involved in the 'training of her instrument', this news was much less thrilling for the mother than her daughter. Although she knew he was married to Alma Mahler, the sister of another famous composer, Schoenberg's interest in her daughter was still disturbing. Even Victor agreed that with 'artistic' types, the normal rules of society didn't seem to count. Who knew where Schoenberg's interest might lead, married or not. In addition, the mother sensed that the composer's attentions were exciting to her child in a way that had nothing to do with music. She told herself that if Adelaide was engaged, he wouldn't dare. And if her daughter's betrothed happened to live across the ocean where Adelaide would have to live as well, that might be even better, her mother told herself as she prepared for the dinner. Much as she would hate losing her younger daughter, knowing she was safely married and beginning to raise a family as far away from the famous rake as possible would be an enormous relief. Both husband and wife agreed that until they knew whether the Liebman's would also be interested in such a union, they wouldn't discuss it with their daughter. As for her singing, as far as Lisl was concerned, whatever she was able to manage once she completed her responsibilities as wife and mother – well, what harm could there be in that?

Devious when life seemed to call for such devises, Lisl planned the dinner party on an evening when both Addie and Sophia would be attending a play at the Hofburgtheater with Samuel and his parents.

The girls were so eager to be gone, that neither thought to ask who was coming to the house for dinner, although both knew guests were expected. That afternoon after her lesson, Adelaide had actually helped her mother make Viennese apfle kuchen, rolling the dough while her mother peeled and cut the apples. As they were donning their evening wraps, the sisters teased their mother about making sure she left a piece of the kuchen for each of them and didn't let their guests gobble it all up before they returned. "And one for Samuel," the mother agreed, which caused additional hilarity because it meant that Samuel was not only allowed to come into the house with them, but into the kitchen as well, even if the old folks had gone to bed.

"What if I leave you alone with him?" Addie giggled as they tramped down the front steps to the waiting carriage.

"Don't you dare!" Sophia shrieked. "We are nowhere near ready for that!"

Once they were inside the cab, Addie quietly asked her sister, "Do you miss Harold, Soph?" She was not overly surprised when her sister's eyes filled with tears, and reached over to take her hand. They rode the rest of the way to the theater this way, which was a comfort to them both.

The dinner with Addie's prospective in-laws went well. The two couples discovered that they shared a number of friends, despite that fact that their immediate social circle was different. Their interests merged as well – in theater, the current show at the museum, opera, and the beautification of the Volksgarten – so the conversation never flagged. They had been seated at the dinner table, halfway through the main course, before a momentary silence fell.

Clearing his throat, Victor began, "We are very glad you were able to come to our home for dinner. I don't know what you know of our younger daughter, Adelaide…."

"Oh my. Naomi Ganz, one of my closest friends, heard your daughter sing last month at the Musikverein. I cannot wait to hear her myself. Naomi told me her voice just soared, soared to the rafters!" Simon's mother gushed her words, her blush signifying the authenticity of her enthusiasm.

Of course Lisl and Victor were pleased by her reaction. "She has been taking singing lessons from Herr Goff since she was 7," Victor explained.

"I had to be convinced to allow it. My daughter is not an artiste. She is merely a person with a tremendous talent," added Lisl. "Fortunately she has the same aspirations as other girls her age."

As the main course was cleared from the table the Liebman's waited expectantly for their hosts to continue. When the maid left the room, Harold admitted, "Raising children these days can be terribly trying. We were very concerned about our son, especially when he told us he planned to emigrate to New York City."

"I can certainly understand that," Victor commiserated. "How did you make peace with his move…and your loss?"

"Simon has always been a spirited young man. His aspirations go beyond what he would have been able to achieve here in Vienna without more schooling. He convinced us that this would not be the case in the new world," Hyman replied.

Ever the good host, Victor poured desert wine for his two guests. "Actually, we asked you here to talk about our two children," he explained as he hovered behind them.

Unable to keep the words from escaping her lips Mrs. Liebman blurted, "But what would your daughter do about her music if she were to move across the ocean?"

"First of all, our hope would be that she would begin her family life as soon as Adonai intends her to. Until then, I'm sure there are music clubs or organizations that would welcome Adelaide," replied Mrs. Welt.

Simon's parents glanced at one another as the desert was served. The only words spoken until the maid again left the room were pleasantries about the meal, and the new lamp Lisl had purchased for the low hutch that dominated the wall to the left of the mahogany dining table. Simon's father cleared his throat.

"You must understand that our son has just reached the New World. We have only received one letter from him," he explained, his wife interrupting, "A very enthusiastic letter!"

"Of course," Victor agreed. "Adelaide is not yet 18. We understand that your son will want to have solid employment, as well as some savings before he could commit to sending for a wife."

"Nevertheless this is a very interesting idea, and one we should discuss further as Simon's position in his new firm becomes more assured," Hyman added with a warm smile. He had imbibed a significant amount of wine during the meal, and had thoroughly enjoyed the conversation as well. He knew he would enjoy having this couple as his in-laws.

"We are very excited about the possibilities for our son in his new city. It seems Simon met a gentleman aboard the ship who is trying to help him attain a position at a more prestigious firm then the one where he is presently employed," his wife agreed with evident excitement.

"We are very pleased at your good fortune," Victor beamed.

Hyman smiled broadly as well. "We would be quite pleased at the joining of our two families."

After they saw their guests out to their waiting carriage, Lisl and Victor climbed the stairs to their bedroom with lighter hearts. As she began to brush her hair, Lisl turned to smile at her husband. "This was a very good decision. Perhaps we will be able to announce an engagement by summer. If Schoenberg does divorce by then, Addie will be safe." "You are not displeased that the young man's father is merely a tailor?" her husband rested his hands upon her shoulders.

"A bohemian would be much worse. Addie will have few music contacts in New York City. She will become pregnant, God willing, and begin her life as a normal young woman. With an interest in music."

* * *

The first year of the marriage between Yetta and Noah was one of growth: newfound intimacy as well as trust for another human being that neither had experienced elsewhere; of Harry and Noah's cattle business; and of Yetta's business as well because of orders from the balebatim of Monasterzyska. When Yetta told Noah she was pregnant in the midst of all this expansion, he was beside himself with excitement. Delighted by the joyous expression on her husband's face, Yetta admitted, "I was afraid you would not be pleased. Both of our businesses are expanding; this is not the best time to have a child to care for...." Before she could finish this thought, her young husband reached out for her, pulling her close to his chest, "How could you imagine I would not want this, Yetta-la? It is the best news you could have given me." Snuggling close to him, Yetta shook her head in agreement. They had often talked about wanting to start a family: she just hadn't expected they would begin so quickly.

When Harry told Noah that a small, but comfortable house with an unfinished loft upstairs had become available across from the home his small family had lived in for three years in Monasterzyska, Noah broached the suggested move to his young wife with some trepidation. He knew they could not move to the larger town unless they could find a spot for her business there. But she would also not be able to walk back to her own village for work very much longer because of her growing belly. He waited to tell her about the cottage, unsure if was even the right choice. Then one day his mother raced over to the cattle yard to tell him she had found a large grocery store quite near her own apothecary shop whose business had fallen off precipitously. Because of her financial woes the woman who ran the grocery was open to the suggestion that they partition the large space, making room for Yetta's little factory in the rear and cutting down the woman's costs at the same time. Noah waited anxiously overnight for the woman to discuss the matter with her sons, trying to hide his anxiety from Yetta. Although it would take some months to prepare the shop for the two businesses, the sons approved. Noah wanted to move his wife to the larger town, especially now that she was pregnant, but was afraid she would not be willing to leave her mother. One evening, when husband and wife were standing by their kitchen sink, Yetta washing the dinnerware, and Noah drying each piece before putting it in its proper place on the shelves above the sink, he took a deep breath, and told her what he had discovered. Since Noah had already come to trust the business acumen of his young wife, she was quite surprised that he had taken it upon himself to investigate all of the aspects of such a big move by himself, and not displeased. It was the first time in her young life she felt cared for in every aspect of her life. Clearly, this young man whom she had married only months before would do whatever was necessary, not only to assure their financial security but their home life as well. She planted a happy kiss on his lips, assuring him she had many reasons to be pleased about his discoveries.

In the first place, the new workspace sounded larger than the one she was already using, which would enable her to hire one more seamstress. Given the new orders she had already accepted, the space and the new seamstress she could hire would relieve the workload, which was already becoming a burden to Yetta and the women she employed. Secondly, the tiny apartment they have been sharing two houses away from her parents, behind the larger home of a neighbor Yetta had known since childhood, hardly had room for the newlyweds let alone space for a bassinette, and later, a bed. She wanted to know when he could take her to Monasterzyska so that she could see both their new home, and the proposed workspace. They agreed to take the wagon there together on Friday, after the midday meal. They would attend shul with his family and later eat the shabbos meal with them. Since Harry had already added a room to his house upstairs in preparation for their third child, they would be able to sleep there rather than walking back to Krynicja that evening. If Yetta liked the bungalow and approved of the space behind the grocery, they would go directly to the home of Yetta's mother to discuss the move with her when they returned home on Saturday evening.

The new shop was considerably larger than the one in Krynicja, but the grocery owner seemed loud and overbearing to Yetta. Or perhaps the woman was a disappointment because she wasn't Yetta's mother, whose tiny fabric shop Yetta now shared. Nevertheless, it was a good space, with plenty of room for an expanding business. The house was absolutely perfect, much larger than what Yetta had imagined. Downstairs there was a kitchen, living/dining room, and wonder of wonders, a small room that had already been added behind the kitchen by one of the former owners. The present owners used it as their bedroom. Upstairs was a large open room with plenty of room for the couple's four children, all of whom were boys.

Anticipating Yetta's concern, Noah whispered, "We can turn this into two rooms of a decent size," which made her smile. "You think we're going to have more than one child, and that they might not all be boys?" she whispered back. They stood in the little attic, which seemed huge to them, grinning at one another like fools. Both knew they were standing in their new home.

The Sabbath meal was absolutely glorious. Not only was Leah a fine cook, helped as usual by her youngest child, Anna, but Harry's wife, Sarah, also contributed, and her challah was renowned, even in a village as large as Monasterzyska. Of course it wasn't just the food that made it such a celebratory affair. Noah's entire family was thrilled to have their scholar son moving back to their own village. They had given him up to Yetta's family with grace, especially since they had all become quite fond of her during the months between their engagement and marriage. Nevertheless they couldn't deny their excitement at having the young couple a few blocks away rather than six miles down the road. Although Yetta had also come to love Noah's parents, she knew she would miss her mother desperately. She felt relieved that the new work space wouldn't be ready for several months, even though this meant she would be walking the six miles from the bungalow to her village every day to get to work. The journey was one she didn't fear; it would be good to be outdoors. By the time the first snow fell, the shop, too, would be ready, and both she and her mother would be used to the idea of her leaving the village of her birth.

Because of the new customers Noah had recruited from far away Warsaw, neither he nor Harry actually had the time to help with the refurbishing of Yetta's new shop. She could not move her sewing machines, or hire a second seamstress for almost five months. No matter how often Noah begged his wife to let her younger sister, or Ida handle the major portion of the sewing so that she didn't have to walk to Krynicja every day with her growing belly, Yetta belittled his concern. She was a strong peasant woman, and enjoyed her time in the woods, she told him time and again. The child within clearly did as well, since he kicked with abandon as soon as they were on their way. This she explained one night with a laugh when she opened their front door, bending Noah's head to her belly so he could feel the movement within. He could not deny that both she and the baby seemed fine. As a compromise, she agreed to let Ida run the new shop for the last few months of her pregnancy as well as the first weeks after the delivery until she regained her strength. The last day in her mother's shop was a very sad one for both mother and daughter. At the noon meal, they shared a large repast at Yetta's childhood home, actually closing the shop for over an hour, a singular event in the life of the Bloom family. By the time Yetta said her goodbyes, and hugged both Ida and her mother at least three times, she was bone weary. Of course she didn't tell either of them because she knew neither would sleep through the night, worrying instead about her long trek back to Noah in Monasterzyska.

She had crossed the bridge at the edge of Krynicja, and was just beginning the most difficult part of her journey, a climb up the long, winding, unpaved hill towards the little shtetl, when she noticed a wagon, much like the one Noah and Harry used for their business travels, coming towards her. For a fleeting moment, she wished the wagon were headed in the opposite direction, so she might beg a ride for a few miles, anything to ease her journey, but then she raised her chin, and walked with new purpose towards home. "This is silly,' she chided herself. 'I am a strong young woman. Five more miles is nothing for someone like me.' Lost in her own thoughts, she barely glanced at the occupants of the wagon as she strode past it, and then stopped in her tracks. It was her husband, Noah, and his brother, Harry who occupied the bench seat above her.

"Would you care for a ride, young woman?" she heard her husband ask her in his kind, deep baritone.

"I don't know, Noah. She walks with such purpose, she might be insulted by the offer of a ride," teased her brother-in-law.

She turned to stare at them, placing her hands on her hips, which caused much laughter on the part of the Unger men, since her stance forced her belly forward, almost making her lose her balance. "Stop that this instant," she demanded. "And help me up there before I land on my rump in the dirt," she added with a broad grin. This young woman, who had never felt appreciated or protected, was pleased beyond her wildest imaginings by the thoughtful behavior of her young husband and his brother. It was even more touching because she realized being thoughtful was part of Noah's character, and always would be.

Once they were home and fed, and Yetta had enjoyed a half hour with the women in the bathhouse, she curled up on their small parlor couch, resting her feet on Noah's lap. He began to massage her left foot immediately, smiling when an inadvertent sigh escaped her lips. After several minutes, she said to him, "There is something I want to suggest to you, my dear."

"And what might that be," he asked, working by now on her right foot.

"I know that you sorely miss your study of the Torah. Now that I will only be working during the day close to our new home, I think you should begin a study group. You could meet several nights a week if you don't have to wait up for me."

"I wouldn't want to leave you here alone either," was his immediate response.

"I wouldn't be alone, Noah. Sarah is right across the street. If I needed her, all I would have to do is open the front door and call out to her. Besides, I have sewing to do for the baby to come, and that would be easier without interruptions." Her tone was gentle. She knew he was worried that she could go into early labor. "I can see the longing in your face, Noah. Why deny yourself?"

And so it was that a study group began, made up of six other businessmen besides Noah and Harry. All of them had been forced to go to work to help their families, and none could afford to attend the Yeshiva in Buchach. Men in the village who studied, did so all day long at the shul, supported by their working wives. Because these young men were either supporting large families already, or were building a new business, none could afford the luxury of constant study. It was a radical idea for them all that working might not preclude the study of their precious Torah. All of them, to a man, were grateful to Noah's little wife for suggesting this intellectual venture. As for the wives, they sometimes met at the same time as their husbands to gossip as they sewed, or cooked, or mended bedding, which they all found quite enjoyable. In this way, Yetta began to make friends, not only enriching Noah's life by her suggestion, but her own as well.

When she went into labor, Yetta was taking a walk to the cemetery, where she loved to meander among the gravestones of her new family, thinking about her place with them and this new life she was living, a life she had never even dared dream about. Because she had grown up around animals, and helped with the birth of her niece and nephew, she did not panic, assuming her first labor would not be over in an hour and that she had ample time to walk slowly back to the village and alert the midwife. By the time she reached her cottage in Monasterzyska, her pains were coming two minutes apart; she had to stop to hold on to several trees along the way and catch her breath. The midwife and a neighbor who happened to be returning from the town market, ran to her side to support her, one under each arm, as they made their way down the pathway to her small bungalow. The neighbor raced across the street for Sarah and then over to the cattle pen to find Noah, who fortunately was working in the shack he and Harry used as an office there, doing the month's billing. Noah hastily dropped his pen onto the ledger book and raced to his cottage, which he needn't have done. Yetta's labor was long and arduous. Every scream from their bedroom seemed to ricochet from the walls of the small house, echoing from every corner before the walls again fell silent, only to begin again moments later. Sarah urged Noah, who was in torment, to go outside to stand with his brother and his friends from the study group who had all gathered outside to offer support. The men persuaded him to spend a half hour in the bath house, after the midwife assured them that the little one would not be appearing for some hours yet. The next-door neighbor's son promised to run to the bathhouse should the midwife be wrong in her estimation. In truth, comely little Clara did not actually see the light of day for another two and a half hours, so the men needn't have hurried either.

Despite Noah's protestations, Yetta was on her feet preparing breakfast for him two days after Clara's birth. She shushed him when he ordered her back to bed, reminding him that he married a woman who did not long for a life of leisure: she enjoyed being productive and was quite ready to get up and greet the day. She promised him that should she tire, she would lie down; he did not have to come home to check up on her. Little Clara did not fare as well. She was sickly when she was born, and did not easily take to her mother's milk. No matter how many herbal concoctions the young mother drank to make her milk more palatable, and no matter how many concoctions she tried to feed directly to the little girl, the baby's lack of weight gain was a worry. Noah, Sarah and Harry discussed the situation one afternoon, after persuading the exhausted Yetta to nap with the baby. All three were certain the child would not survive. What they were trying to figure out was whether to talk about this belief with Yetta. Noah argued for silence. His young wife would have to deal with it soon enough, which, as it happened, was correct. Clara died days before the three-month anniversary of her birth.

Yetta took to her bed and refused to get up. When Noah sat down next to her, she turned her back to him, closing her eyes and facing the wall. After a week, Harry suggested Noah take the wagon to Krynicja to speak to Yetta's mother about the state of her daughter's health. Perhaps she would have some ideas about how to deal with her daughter's despair. Although his own mother was totally supportive of her daughter-in-law because she, too, had lost a child, like many of the women in the village, this didn't seem to be having much effect. She knew not to talk to the young woman about her loss, but to focus on less volatile subjects instead. Leah spoke about village life, about the repairs at the women's bathhouse, and about Yetta's growing business, as well as sharing stories about Noah's childhood, stories the young woman had never heard. By the time Noah arrived back in Monasterzyska with his mother-in-law, Rosa, his wife was lying in bed facing Leah who had finally fallen silent. When Yetta saw her own mother enter the room, the tears she had been holding inside since Clara's death cascaded down her cheeks. Rosa immediately took Yetta in her arms, while Noah's mother stroked her back and her hair, whispering another story about Noah's childhood. That night, Yetta came out to dinner fully dressed, pale but present. When her mother suggested Noah and Harry get started on partitioning the shop in

Monasterzyska so that Yetta could get back to work, everyone at the table realized the wisdom in the suggestion. Their cattle business would survive the time it would take for them to ready the shop.

Having her own business again did wonders for Yetta's morale, and within a month she was the same vibrant, active human being Noah had met less than a year before. Although both were enormously busy – he with his business and she with hers – they each set aside an hour each evening to spend with one another, and tried occasionally to spend it outside their tiny bedroom so they could discuss current events, and more importantly, their dreams. The only sadness in their lives, which they religiously did not discuss, was the fact that nine months after Clara's death, Yetta was still not pregnant. Much as they enjoyed the life they were making together, they knew it would not be complete for either of them without a child to nurture and raise. Both Ida and Sarah, who had become Yetta's closest friends, could see Yetta's sadness as well as Noah's, though not a word had been spoken about its cause. One day at lunch the two suggested the three women take sandwiches to the meadow and share a picnic. Once they had eaten Yetta acknowledged that she was terribly disappointed to have not yet conceived. She had not talked about her sadness with Noah, because she didn't see the point. What could either of them do about it? When Sarah tried to lighten the mood by suggesting they repair to their bedroom earlier in the evening, Yetta, blushing, laughed in response. "I don't think that's the problem! My renewed ardor came as a big surprise to us both, but Noah has adjusted." This sent all three women into gales of laughter as they packed up their basket and headed back to the shop. On the way there Sarah suggested Yetta see the town herbalist who might be able to help.

The following week, Yetta did just that, leaving work early, which came as a surprise to her new seamstresses. Neither of them could complain about their hours, because Yetta worked more tirelessly than anyone, and never, in their memory, had left earlier than they. The herbalist spoke to Yetta for almost an hour, asking hundreds of questions about her life: with Noah, with work, with the community. Some of the questions were intimate, and some seemed to bear no relation to the problem at hand. Nevertheless, Yetta accepted the little package the herbalist handed her with more hope about her situation than she had felt in months, and was rigorous about following the woman's instructions.

When she realized she had skipped a period three months later, Yetta was elated. She said nothing, fearing a jinx. Of course Noah realized as well, because of their very active sexual life, but he said nothing either. When four more weeks passed, and still nothing, Yetta visited the town doctor who confirmed what she had been afraid to believe. Yetta was again pregnant. Although the mood in the Unger household was one of celebration, Noah's concern was sharp and immediate; he needed to share it with someone, and it certainly couldn't be Yetta.

One morning on the way to Buchach with several head of cattle shortly after the doctor's confirmation, Noah, more quiet than usual, haltingly began to talk with Harry. During the last pregnancy Yetta was insulted that he wanted a woman to come in to clean the cottage and help her with the more difficult household tasks. Nor had she taken kindly to the suggestion that she sit at the sewing machine for less hours than was her habit. For over a year Noah had worried that his wife's active schedule and heavy workload had contributed to or been responsible for the frail constitution of their first child. He wanted to urge, even demand, that Yetta slow down and accept assistance, but had no idea how to bring up the subject for fear of upsetting her. Harry agreed it was essential that he raise these issues with Yetta. They discussed how he might do this all the way to market, even looking at the possibility of Sarah talking to her sister-in-law instead, but in the end, Noah decided that it was his responsibility. After all, Yetta was his wife, and the baby growing inside her his as well.

That evening after dinner when they were in their small kitchen, Yetta washing up the dishes and pots and Noah drying, which had become their custom over the past year, Noah cleared his throat. But before he could utter even one word, Yetta teased, "It must be serious," splashing him with some water from the bowel she always filled with hot, soapy dish water.

Noah knew he could not beat around the bush with his wife. "I think you need to get some household help, Yetta. I am worried about how hard you work even now, and now you are only two months pregnant.

I worry…" he continued, but Yetta again interrupted before he could continue.

"I agree. I couldn't bear to lose another one," she whispered, leaning up to kiss him. "When do you think we should begin?"

Noah was so delighted he could barely think let alone reply. "Right now!" he all but shouted after catching his breath.

"I know I am not the best of cooks," Yetta admitted. "What I would like, I think, is to have someone do most of the cooking. For now, I think I can do the light cleaning…"

"I can do the stooping, and the lifting," Noah chimed in. "In a few months, you can do less, or even right now, whenever you feel enervated."

The two held hands as they moved towards the dining room table, where they both had bills waiting. Noah decided to leave the question of his wife's work schedule for another day. That she agreed to have help come into their home was victory enough.

The birth of Jules was no easier than Clara's had been, but the baby was robust, crying with gusto when the midwife spanked breath into him. By the time he was toddling around their small home, Yetta was again pregnant, and this time, she had needed no assistance from the village herbalist. Neche, or Nellie as she would later be called, was born a year later, which troubled Noah because he still worried about his wife's health, both mental and physical. He helped with the heavy cleaning when he could, and worried silently. Because of the hours Yetta spent at her sewing shop, the children were expected to help around the house as well, Jules in the small garden, and Neche at her mother's side in the kitchen. By the time she was four, Nellie was doing most of the baking, which she did with more ease than her mother, even at that tender age. The quiet little girl was relieved to have two more sisters arrive, again within a year of one another, both for the help they would afford her, but also for the company. Her brother, Jules, was in the town's heder, and she was lonely. By the time Rivho was three and Matel, two, both little girls were going to the shop with their mother, the older toddler helping with the folding of fabric and the younger often undoing what her older sister had just done. Because she was tiny, and utterly charming, no one could be angry at Matel for very long, no matter how much chaos she wreaked at the shop or at home. Rivho was an even better baker than her older sister, so the growing family ate quite well. Of course they always had the best cuts of beef, and with the earnings from both parents, could buy the freshest produce, quality flours, and even some delicacies from the local bakeries. Yetta told Noah she had no idea why her daughters were so proficient in the kitchen: neither girl inherited their abilities from her, that was certain.

Jules quickly became the star pupil at the heder. Like his father, he had a natural gift for his studies, but unlike Noah, he was also endowed with a generous streak of boisterousness. If the boys at the heder were in trouble, the teacher didn't have to look far to find their ringleader. He adored the boy who reminded him of his own son at that age, and because of his adoration, was particularly strict with Jules. When he spoke to Noah about him, to the old man's surprise Noah took the side of his son: there must be joy in life; he didn't want this marvelous spirit stifled just yet. He cautioned the man to give the boy room.

The Unger household brimmed with life. Neither Yetta nor Noah could believe their good fortune: in their life together, with their respective businesses, and with their offspring. Though Neche was singularly serious, and had been so since she could talk, Rivho was a whirling dervish, filling the house with both tumult and laughter. She tortured her younger sister by urging her to participate in every game she invented, and was even occasionally able to rouse Neche to laughter, especially when she pulled her to the ground and tickled her with an utter lack of mercy. Although Jules enjoyed the role of wise older brother, he could not resist the temptation to join in the games Rivho invented. Sometimes he even embellished them with mischief of his own. The house was often a noisy place when Noah came home from his cattle selling trips but he stopped Yetta when she attempted to quiet the children for him. He loved the life that filled his home, and couldn't imagine living in a house that was more subdued. Despite his wife's lack of culinary skill, Noah knew that his cup runneth over.

* * *

Simon and Otto found a rooming house in lower Manhattan by asking other young men they met in a bar near the boat dock for advise, and immediately plunged into the life of their new city. Unable to sleep on Sunday night because of the bustle going on in the streets below their tiny room, Simon and Otto headed out without caution, giving little thought to the hour, or any possible danger. They were city boys, after all, and used to pickpockets and the like. Neither thought about where they would have been in Vienna at 2 AM: at home in bed, with their front doors safely locked against possible intrusion. They never experienced danger on the streets of their native city because they were rarely out alone after midnight. When the two Austrians saw four huge Italian men moving up the street towards them, neither gave it much thought, which was, as it turned out, a big mistake. Within seconds they were surrounded. What little money they were carrying was forked over to the toughs without any resistance. Nevertheless, because they were carrying so little, they were roughed up before the four louts raced around the corner. Even Simon couldn't manage his usual jocular response to the tragedy. His nose was bleeding, and he thought a rib might be broken as well. The two immigrants limped back to their rooming house, each keeping to himself the thought that perhaps this journey to a new world and a new life had been a mistake after all.

The next day at work, the first for each of them in their new jobs, neither hesitated to inquire about better living arrangements. Simon was given the name of two inexpensive hotels downtown in a bohemian area near Union Square, while Otto's boss suggested a different rooming house, in the Bronx. He explained that there was a brand new underground train line to the area, and prices had yet to rise in reflection of the easy commute to downtown Manhattan. Both of the young men still preferred the bohemian area. Not only was it closer to work, but Simon hoped they would meet women there, women like the ones who had frequented the cafes he loved in Vienna. Even at the age of eighteen, Simon had a healthy sexual appetite. His job was boring, which made his fantasy life even mover vivid. Until he learned the new language well enough to have a route of his own, he had been asked to arrange the schedule for the four young salesmen already plying the trade. When he felt confident about his ability at the job and with his new language, he would contact his friend from the upper deck. Until then, he knew he had much to learn. Otto was happier in his job at the dress factory. His boss, Barney Solomon, was a jolly man who remembered his first years in the City, and was impressed by the bravery of this young man, foreign born, who had come all the way from Europe to make a better life for himself. Making the journey from upstate New York all those years ago had seemed a huge move to the older man. Otto worked hard, quickly learning how to cut the fabric he stacked on huge racks in the cavernous loft room in the center of the west side garment district. Unlike Simon, he had often watched his friend's father lay fabric beneath his patterns and cut the fine wool into the shapes he would then sew into the suits known all over Vienna for their quality and style. The young man therefore picked up that part of the garment trade with ease, during his lunch hour, and knew he had impressed Mr. Solomon.

After work Otto followed the more gregarious Simon from tavern to tavern, although he was often exhausted and would actually have preferred to return to the hotel room they were sharing so they could save enough funds to put down the security on an apartment of their own with a kitchen and sitting room. He hated the fact that his friend seemed depressed. Never in all the years he had known Simon had he seen him in such a mood. Without his friend's constant assurances that they would both prosper, Otto would never have moved away from his family across the ocean to this new, rough-and-tumble country. Neither boy knew how to deal with this turn of events: Otto, the one who believed he had made the right move and would advance in this new business; Simon, slow to learn English, stuck in a lowly job in a business he had always thought of as temporary, and certainly not his life path. Fortunately for them both, the handsome young man still managed to attract women. During their first month in New York he cut a wide swath through downtown Manhattan, never staying with one woman more than a few nights, and never overnight. The women he met were clearly not close to the caliber of the artists' models he had known in Vienna. None were middle class. Some were even used to charging for their services, though none suggested such a thing to the handsome young foreigner. One morning Otto, who sometimes pleasured himself with the women they met as well, noticed a blemish on the tip of his penis. He was so terrified that he raced from the bathroom at the end of the hallway all the way to their room with his penis still in hand. When Simon saw his friend hurtle into their room with his fly unbuttoned, his sense that something serious was afoot kept him from bursting into laughter at the sight of his friend waving his member in the air and yelling something utterly incoherent.

After work that afternoon both boys visited a clinic on the lower east side that specialized in immigrant health issues. Simon had been so distraught with fear he hadn't even known how he would get through a full day's work, let alone ask his boss where he could go to be tested for venereal disease. When the doctor suggested they both young men be examined after questioning Otto about his evening activities, Simon complied without demur. He knew that the women he had been bedding had probably had as many nocturnal partners as any of the men he had known in Vienna. When the doctor gave them both a clean bill of health, he also told the boys that they were extremely lucky. After showing them pictures of what could happen to them should a blemish appear that was not benign, neither boy had the heart to go to any of the taverns peppering the streets of lower Manhattan. That night Simon actually composed a letter for each of them to their respective parents, telling them about their jobs, their move to the inexpensive hotel until they could afford an apartment, and finally, their need to find an appropriate wife with whom they could share this new life. He hadn't expected to seek such advice, but the pictures he had seen at the clinic had totally terrified him. He knew he needed sex, but he didn't want to die because of it. Omitting a discussion of his own place of employment, which he had grown to despise, since the truth would make such a request seem irresponsible, he rhapsodized about the garment business for Otto's parents. Indeed, Otto's hope was that he would someday run a factory like Mr. Solomon's, having no intention of remaining a cutter the rest of his life. If Simon had had any influence on his friend in this grim time, it was to hold on to dreams of glory, and pursue whatever steps he must to attain them.

* * *

As Addie placed the pins in her sister's hair for the proposed meal with her fiancé's family, she wondered what she herself would do if she were to find herself in Sophia's situation. Pretending sleep, she had nonetheless heard the quiet crying beside her each night, as well as the angry sounds coming from behind the parlor door when her father had laid down the law about this proposed marriage. Wanting to assure her older sister's privacy, and unsure what words of comfort to offer, Adelaide remained mute, even in the seclusion of their shared bedroom. Neither had she spoken to Sophia about the flutter she felt in her chest when Schoenberg, the famous composer, attended her singing lessons, occasionally resting his hand on her shoulder as he explained how he wished her to sing a particular phrase. In her heart she felt shame for those sensations, because she knew that Schoenberg had recently married the sister of Gustav Mahler. Not only was it wrong for her to have these stirrings, she worried there was something poisonous about her very nature that she should feel this way about someone who was not single. The anger and distress her father was feeling now about Sophia would be tripled if he knew what was in the thoughts of his younger daughter, of this Adelaide was quite certain. Grateful to be considered too young to worry about her own future as a married woman, she ached for Sophia who merely had the misfortune to love an artist who also apparently loved her. His only crime was that he was not yet successful, which made him a poor match for her sister in the eyes of both of their parents.

When Addie was finished pinning up Sophia's hair, she sat down in the chair herself so that Sophia could dress hers as well. Usually the girls took care of their own toilette, but in this special instance, when the entire family was invited to dine with their prospective in-laws, Addie suggested they help one another in an attempt to ease Sophia's anxiety. It was all she could think of to do.

"I actually like Samuel, Addie," Sophia explained as she plaited her younger sister's hair. "I have tried to love him, but the man I dream about at night is still Harold."

"You don't still see him, do you?" Addie asked, the fear apparent in the tremor of her voice.

"No. I am obeying Papa." She sighed. "But I cannot imagine my life continuing without him for ever and ever...."

Robert, who left his law firm earlier than his schedule usually allowed so he could drive to the dinner with his family, was waiting downstairs in the parlor when the girls descended in all their finery. Samuel's parents also lived in Vienna 9. Nevertheless the Welt family took a hansom there, because that was the cultured thing to do. Besides, Victor explained to his womenfolk, it would be difficult for them to walk the six blocks in their delicate evening shoes. When the cab arrived at the Siegel's front door, both Samuel and his father stood outside the cab to help the women alight. Addie noticed how solicitous Samuel was of her sister and even had the fleeting thought that he was a nice-looking young man. It was a shame he was a banker and not a successful artist, she thought to herself as she placed her hand in his so he could help her step down to the sidewalk. If he were only a little more bohemian, Sophia would have to make less of an adjustment in her heart to marry him.

The dining room was larger than that of the Welt's, but Addie knew her mother preferred her own oblong mahogany table to the Siegel's heavy rectangle, both for its style and the ease of conversation afforded by its shape. She, herself, thought the sideboard in this large room magnificent, especially the inlay work on the drawers and doors, which had been carved in a lighter and contrasting wood to accentuate the design. Dinner was a genial affair, with conversation never flagging, not even between courses when the maid and butler were clearing the plates, tureens and dinnerware. Samuel was clearly intelligent, though he lacked somewhat in the humor department. Although Sophia might be pining for her painter, her prospective husband was clearly smitten with his bride-to-be. Not only did he include her in every conversation, he could not take his eyes from her face the entire meal. When he led her back to the waiting hansom, Addie and Robert noticed that his hand, holding her elbow to guide her down the steps, was shaking. "Soon this will be you, my little singing sister. Does the prospect make your heart beat faster?" Robert whispered in her ear, ever the tease even though she was nearly grown. "Shhh," she whispered back, unable to hold back the flush inching from neck to cheeks. He helped her into the cab, smiling broadly, which she ignored. "If anything, it is you who should be concerned. Mama will set her eye on you again, if you don't find yourself a mate on your own," she managed, startling both her brother and sister by her spirited remark.

Once they were home, Sophia burst into tears. "I cannot do this," she wailed to her father. "I cannot!" she repeated to everyone standing in the foyer, their coats still in their hands. Then she fled up the stairs.

Addie watched as her mother turned to her father with concern.

"She will do as I demand," her father declared, turning to Adelaide before she could follow Sophia up the stairs to their bedroom. "And you, my little one. You will not give me any difficulty, will you?"

"No, papa," Addie of course replied, although she was sure of no such thing. What if he wanted her to marry soon, and her proposed husband did not approve of her singing? What in the world would she do?

Indeed, alone in their boudoir, Lisl persuaded Victor that it was time for them to tell Addie they had met with the Liebman's and that both families thought this proposed match a good idea, once Simon settled into his new job and managed to find himself a real apartment. "We certainly don't expect you to live in a hotel in this big city in your new country," Victor explained to his daughter with forced joviality the next morning at breakfast."

Stony-faced, Sophia said, "I have seen Simon Liebman at the Stierbock many times, and every time he was escorting a different model. His reputation is that of a rake. Is this alright with you, father, if it means that Adelaide will be married and safe?" Sophia asked with some asperity.

"Young men often sow their oats before they settle down. His former boss in Vienna has assured me of his dedication to the insurance business, and his skill as a salesman. These are qualities I expect in a young man who will marry one of my daughters, liebchen."

"And not kindness, or a gentle manner?" Sophia somberly asked.

"Sophia. I know you don't believe me, but I truly have your best interests at heart. I cannot envision a life in a garret for you, or one where you have to worry where you will find the money to purchase food for your children."

"If you would only talk to Harold, father…." She begged nonetheless.

"I have talked to Harold. He can offer me no assurance of a better life, Sophia, and he is man enough to admit that," her father replied, the set of his lips precluding the response aching to escape Sophia's lips.

Adelaide listened to the conversation between her sister and father in a state of total dismay. Try as she might, she could not even remember Simon Liebman. Although his work habits were important to her father, and perhaps, over time might even be to her, his attitude about her music was the only thing that really counted in her mind. Of course she had no faith that admiration of her musical ability was even in the purview of either of her parents. Holding her hands in her lap so that their trembling would not betray her, she asked, "When do you think he might return so that we could meet one another?"

For the first time in her life, her father appeared to hesitate, until he finally managing to stutter, "All of the details will be worked out in Vienna, little one. And when they have, we will book you a birth on the SS Bremer for your journey to the new land."

Addie was no nonplussed she could not even respond. "Papa! You can't expect Addie to marry someone she doesn't even remember," gasped Sophia, appalled as well, although she was quickly silenced by the glare leveled at her by their father. Lisl, of course, said nothing, and the breakfast passed in an awkward silence. This time Addie knew that being adored would offer her no shelter. She knew their father could become relentless when pushed. That evening he again began the dinner time discussion with words of praise for Samuel: for his intellectual prowess; his stellar reputation at his new law firm; his obvious respect and love for his parents; his wit; and on and on. Finally even his wife had had enough.

"Victor, you sound like you have become feeble-minded," she suggested quietly, which even made Sophia smile.

Victor was undeterred. He turned to his oldest daughter. "Could you come up with such a list for your painter?" All three women turned to stare at him, none of them able to speak. "Of course you can't, " he answered his own question.

"I like Samuel very much, father. But I don't love him. I love Harold. Doesn't that count at all?" Sophia finally managed.

"Your mother and I had barely spoken to each other when we were married. Love is something that grows, liebchen. I know that to be true and you will have to trust me in this," he explained to her in a gentler tone of voice.

"Your father is right, Sophia. Well before I became pregnant with Robert, I knew I had come to adore your father," Lisl added, taking advantage of this softening in her husband's tone. She reached for her daughter's hand across the table.

"And the hole that is left in my heart where Harold used to be, what will happen to that?" Sophia asked no one in particular.

Her father answered immediately. "It will fill, first with love for Samuel, and then with love for your children. In a year, it will be completely healed."

By the end of the week, he had arranged a second meeting with Simon Liebman's parents. When they readily agreed, suggesting the Welts come to their home for dinner this time, Victor proposed they bring their daughter Adelaide to meet them. When he told his daughter that the young man's sister played the piano and would accompany her on some Shubert tunes before they dined, Adelaide agreed to attend. If his parents appreciated music, perhaps their son would as well.

* * *

The growing Unger family was very content in the house Noah had purchased across the street from his brother six years earlier. The upstairs had been divided into two unequal rooms; one for the three girls and the smaller, with its very own window, for Jules. Fortunately the parents' bedroom was downstairs, where the activity within had barely been dimmed by the care of four children and the heavy work schedule of both parents. Their ardor for one another was still electric, and a formidable mutual respect had grown between the two as well.

Yetta never believed she would find a man who worked as conscientiously as she, but over the years of their marriage, she realized she had met her match in every respect. Although the men in her village and the ones she knew in Monasterzyska relied on their women to run both their households and the family business, leaving the world of Torah to them, Noah not only shared the responsibility of supporting their family, but trusted Yetta with decisions about his business life as well as her own. Her ability in mathematics had always been stellar, but she had known instinctively that she had to show respect for her husband's point of view. It was only after much discussion between the two that decisions affecting either business were reached, which allowed Noah to retain his sense of manhood, and not feel diminished by his wife's acumen. It was Yetta's suggestion that the brothers borrow funds to expand their business into two additional, and wealthier, Warsaw neighborhoods. As usual Yetta's vision had been prescient: the money was already returned, and Harry now had plans to expand his little house by adding a sitting room behind his small kitchen. Yetta, who coveted such a room, nevertheless determined that their additional income should be saved, lest the following year or the one after that be slow, or their family grew larger, necessitating more funds, especially if the child were a boy.

Weeks after Harry's sitting room had been completed, there was a precipitous drop in the price of beef in both the Ukraine and Poland. Whether it was caused by the turn of the century, or other, unforeseen economic conditions, no one knew. But the effect on the Unger business was devastating. Because their stock was larger than ever before, the cost of feeding the animals was greater than they could manage, even if they rented an extra field. After much discussion the men decided to take their usual load to Warsaw despite the declining market to see if they could unload the cattle for half their usual price. At least they wouldn't have to feed them throughout the winter months if they were successful. Before the train departed, Jules came running to the train station waving the weekly newspaper in his hand: there had been another price drop. The men turned their cart, and the cattle, back to their cattle yard. Even Harry, the more upbeat of the two, was dejected. On the way home Jules explained that his mother thought they should attempt to weather the next few months, because selling the cattle now would not only cut their gain, but induce a loss that neither family would be able to weather. The brothers could not discount this conclusion, but Noah could not help feeling pride in his young son's understanding of the information he was sharing. The brothers drove the cattle back to the field they had thought they would be able to lease with a heavy heart. They both knew the farmer would want the cattle moved as quickly as possible. On the way there Harry suggested that Noah take the train to Warsaw nevertheless, to speak with their clients about the current market, and to see if there was anyone who would buy the prime Kosher beef at a price they could live with. Noah grabbed his overnight bag from the wagon, and ran with it flapping against his thigh all the way back to the train station, just managing to jump aboard as it slowly pulled out of Monasterzyska.

The news he returned with two days later was even more devastating than either he, or Harry had expected. Because of economic conditions countrywide, the belief in Warsaw was that the price of beef, lamb and even pork – which of course was not an issue for the Jewish cattlemen – would remain low until the summer. Because of Yetta's business and their savings, Noah's family would not starve. Harry's circumstances were much more precarious; Yetta and Noah stayed up discussing the situation long after the children went to bed, even Jules, who stayed downstairs reading much later than usual in the hope of learning what was being decided by his parents. A sensitive boy, he knew as soon as he saw his father, whose outward demeanor was calm, that something serious was occurring.

It had become obvious, at least to Yetta, that the men would have to unload the beef at whatever price they could manage to get for it, because feeding the livestock through the summer months without the extra field, should that be necessary, would be an impossibility if the two families were to survive. Before Noah's return from Warsaw, she had hoped they could hang on, but it was clear that was now impossible. The only question was price, and how bad their loss would be. Her second suggestion was one Noah resisted, because he didn't know how he would be able to comply. Yetta was determined that they abstain from their nocturnal activities until the price of cattle returned to a normal level, because they could ill afford a house helper anymore. She had to admit to herself and then Noah, that she could not manage her business, the children, and the household without the helper if she again became pregnant. The next morning they released Maya, which they both knew would make life more difficult for Yetta. If his wife had the strength to endure, and to do so with good cheer, Noah would have to be content with holding her close at night, and nothing more.

Jules, who was hiding in the stairwell above the parlor and was not in his bed as his parents believed, was very disturbed by their conversation. The sensitive youngster agonized over the situation for days before he broached the subject with his father. Telling the melamid at the humash, or middle school, that he was not feeling well, Jules left early enough to help his father herd the cattle back into the barn for the evening. Noah was so distressed about his business woes that he didn't even think to ask his son what he was doing home from his studies at such an early hour. In truth, he was grateful for the company, although neither father nor son had the energy for the Talmudic discussion they both relished. It was only when the cows were milked and fed for the evening, that Jules brought up the subject that had been haunting him for days.

"Papa, I know what is happening with the cattle," he began, and when Noah didn't think to ask him 'how?', continued. "It is time for me to become a man, to get a job to help support our family."

Totally shocked by his son's suggestion, Noah turned to stare at him. "No Jules. These problems will pass, and they are not insurmountable in any event. Your mother and I can certainly handle them until the economy turns around."

"That is not what I see in your faces," the boy stubbornly replied.

"I will not have you give up your studies," Noah said, equally stubborn.

"Please talk it over with Mama," the boy pleaded. He knew his mother would see the sense in his suggestion.

Although Noah nodded his agreement, he repeated, "But you will not be leaving the humash."

That night before sitting down to discuss the matter with his wife, Noah tiptoed over to the stairs. He was not surprised to find his son huddled there, and it was with a gentle touch that he sent the boy upstairs. Neither uttered a word, but Noah knew Jules would not sneak back down. He had been brought up to revere honor and would obey his father. Yetta laid out all of the letters they had received from Elias, the oldest Unger brother, who had settled in a place called Elizabeth in a state named New Jersey in the United States of America. Elias had begun his life there as a butcher's assistant, but had done so well that he had bought that very shop from the original owner. Yetta and Noah knew that his brother cut kosher meat for the Jewish community in one side of the shop, but used the other to serve the gentile population non-Kosher meat. It was the way his predecessor had built his business, and Elias had seen no reason to change the set-up. He had plans to buy his own home because his new wife was certain she was pregnant again. His letters sounded so enthusiastic about the opportunities in this new land, Yetta had determined that moving there was something they not only needed to consider, but had to act upon as well. She believed her job that evening was to persuade Noah to book passage immediately to start a new business alongside his brother. That way she and the children would be able to join him all the sooner.

Her hope for her own journey was to be able to leave within the first year, but perhaps, if it took him a bit longer than it had Elias, or Elias was exaggerating, at least there would be the possibility of improvement for their growing family the year after. That very night they composed a letter to Elias, explaining their situation. They had saved enough to cover more than half the price of a ticket already, due to Yetta's long-standing thrift, but would need help with the rest. Of course Noah would reimburse his brother once he set up a business of his own in Elizabeth. Neither had any idea what that business would be, but they assured Elias that they were both very hard workers; Yetta was so certain they would succeed in their plan for a better life, she even convinced her husband. When they finally went to bed, Noah said nothing about their son's suggestion, in the hopes they would not have to accept it.

Harry could not be persuaded to join them in their new venture. He, too, had saved, but his savings would be used to keep his little family afloat until he could either return to the cattle business, or find another to take it's place. Much to the surprise of Noah and Yetta, it had been Harry and not Sarah who had the foresight to plan ahead by saving money for a dark day. Harry was old enough to remember the famine of his youth, and was determined his family would never suffer as others had in the village of his birth when he had been just a boy.

It was more than a month before Noah and Yetta received a return letter from Elias, and the news was not as promising as they had hoped. Although he could not afford to loan them the $50 they would need for the remainder of Noah's ticket to the new world, he had sent half, an enormous sum in its own right. Again the couple sat down at their dining table after the children were asleep. And again Yetta convinced her husband that with some scrimping over the next months, they would be able to raise the rest. She pushed aside his anxiety about what would happen to her and the children if they used up all of their savings in this way and something untoward occurred after his departure. Although she was anxious about the very same thing, she realized if she shared her misgivings with her husband, he would not go. Because she was convinced, utterly convinced, that go he must, Yetta held her own counsel. Otherwise the Unger family could lose their home, and have to live in the community house held in trust by the entire town for just such misfortunes. An even more disturbing possibility for her was that they might not be able to afford even this place when their year's lease there was up, and she and the children might find themselves homeless. This Yetta could neither fathom nor allow. If she had to work in her shop after the children were in bed for the next year to protect them all that was what she would do.

At the Shabbos meal on Friday evening after they came home from shul, Yetta and Noah laid out the pictures Elias had sent of Elizabeth, and told their children about their plan. When Jules realized they didn't yet have the full fare for his father's ticket, he again suggested he leave the humash, an idea that both parents opposed with vigor. Rivka and little Min broke into tears at the thought of their father's departure, and were only consoled when he assured them he would either return to them in a year, or they would travel with their mother all the way across the ocean to join him. At this, Min asked, "What is this thing…this ocean?" her curiosity warming his heart. The ensuing discussion stopped the flow of tears in both girls.

However, unbeknownst to his parents it was Jules who cried himself to sleep that night. He knew he must become a man, even at the age of six, because his father would be leaving, and it would become his job to care for the family. When little Min came crawling into his bed before dawn, whimpering because she was frightened about her papa leaving them all alone, Jules bravely offered comfort, although he, himself, felt exactly as she did. It was not only Min who never realized his true feelings; neither of the boy's parents did either. Noah and Yetta were grateful for the strength exhibited by the tough little fellow, amazed at the boy's stoicism. Unbeknownst to anyone, Jules first approached his grandmother at the apothecary shop as soon as he knew his mother would be at the home of one of the balebatim measuring the man for a new suit, to see if she knew of anyone who needed shop help and would consider hiring a little boy. The words he used with his grandmother were 'young man' because that was how he knew he must now view himself. Gently she enfolded her grandson in her arms, assuring him that he needn't worry. What the family wanted him to do was concentrate on his studies, especially since his father had been forced to go to work at an early age. The last thing Noah would want for his son was for him to have to give up his schooling as well, even in this time of crisis, his grandmother whispered as she held him close to her narrow chest. But Jules was no more deterred by Leah's words than he had been by those of his parents. The next morning he rose even earlier than usual, stoked the fire for his mother, and then trudged over to the humash to speak to his teacher. His serious tone commanded the attention of both the man and his wife.

"Since I will be the only remaining male of my family remaining in Monasterzyska, I know I must behave with responsibility," the ever-so-serious Jules explained, failing to notice the look of admiration that passed between husband and wife. "Is there any work you might have for me so that I might continue my studies as my father wishes, but not burden my mother with the cost of my education?" he asked.

Although the teacher and his wife were the age of his grandparents, Jules thought of them as second parents, often remaining behind when the other boys left, either to work for another hour with the melamid, or to help his wife with some of her weeding. While they discussed his proposal in their tiny kitchen, Jules lit the lantern so he might begin his studies, even though the actual school day would not begin for another half hour. When the old man set a cup of steaming tea before him with a piece of challah smothered in honey, the boy looked up startled, so engrossed was he in the section of the Talmud resting on the table before him.

"Esther and I have talked it over, my boy, and we think your idea is a sound one. You will continue to help Esther in the garden, as you have been doing for the past year out of the goodness of your heart, expecting no remuneration, and help her with the milking of our two cows as well," the melamid explained. The look of gratitude on the little boy's face was thanks enough for the man, although he and his wife depended on the small income they received from each boy to survive. Not wanting Jules to feel any guilt at receiving tuition for work he had always done for free, the old man explained, before Jules had the opportunity to actually say anything, "Esther's fingers can barely bend anymore. I am more than grateful for the help you will be giving her, and am happy to exchange this job for the one of continuing to teach such a fine scholar."

Jules' smile filled his entire little face, not only because of the help he would be giving his own family, but for the words of praise he had just heard from this man he so admired. Continuing his studies was actually more important to the little boy than for his father, because in his heart Jules believed he was learning for them both, and that he must continue to do so at all cost.

That evening when he explained to his parents what he had arranged, he could see the pride in his father's eyes before Noah enfolded him in his arms. Jules could tell that Yetta, too, was very pleased with his accomplishment, although she merely pressed her lips together and didn't say a word. After dinner they persuaded him to leave his studies for the night and go to his bed since he was clearly exhausted. After she had tucked him into his bed and returned to the kitchen, Yetta fell into Noah's arms and began to cry. Both husband and wife understood that in this job they had taken on as parents they were experiencing success beyond their wildest dreams. Not many had a boy as noble as theirs.

The very next day Yetta began to collect clothing for her husband's journey, sewing additional shirts for him to take to the new country long into the night after she had finished her chores and everyone else had gone to bed. Her husband sat beside her reading Torah, because he was sure he wouldn't have the time once he left the village. Yetta knew this loss was almost as great for her hard-working and kind husband as leaving all of them behind, so she never urged him to get the rest he needed in preparation for the trip ahead. Besides, each wanted the other's company for as many hours each day as possible, as if they could store up their love to keep them warm for the months, and possibly years, of their chosen separation.

CHAPTER FOUR

As she stood at the rail, clutching it in both hands because she was so afraid she would fall overboard, Adelaide peered at all of the people standing on the dock below, every now and then letting go with one hand so she could glance at the picture she was holding of the young man she would be marrying in a few days. She could tell he was good-looking from the photograph, but it revealed nothing of his character to her. 'What is he like?' was not a question she could have asked his parents, let alone 'Is he a person of integrity?' Despite Sophia's urgings, Addie didn't ask her parents to try to find out what sort of person Simon was either. Her father was clearly satisfied with what he had learned, and hadn't investigated the information brought to him by his irresponsible older daughter: that Simon Liebman had been a rake in his teens, when he frequented the coffee houses, and had often been seen with one actress or another during that time. His former boss in Vienna sang his praises and his teachers at the gymnasium remembered him quite clearly as a boy with promise. This has been enough for Victor.

What he told his daughter was that Simon was a young man with ambition and courage, and she was a lucky young woman to be able to follow him to a new country, where Jews had a better chance to advance than they did in Vienna where there was so much prejudice. Even though her brother, Robert, had converted to the Protestant faith some years before, as had most of his more ambitious friends, his rise in the law firm that had engaged him had still been slow. Simon would have no such problem, her father assured her; and he would not have to convert. When the woman standing beside her asked Adelaide if she was all right, she could merely nod, because her heart was beating so hard it seemed to leave no room for her voice. Still, the woman kept glancing at her with concern, but then her husband saw someone he recognized in the crowd below, and took her arm to lead her to the gangplank, which was just now being set in place from the deck beneath the rail to the dock below. Addie, herself, didn't move for some moments, although she turned every now and then to make sure her luggage was still stacked behind her, two trunks and several boxes of her hats, as well as boxes of gifts for Simon from his family. Suddenly she noticed a man with a moustache waving wildly at her from below. At first she wasn't sure it was her prospective husband because he had grown a moustache, and his build appeared more virile in person than in the picture she tightly gripped in her left hand. But yes, she believed, this was the man she had been sent to marry, so she raised the hand with the picture, and waved at him with some hesitation. After all, she didn't want to seem bold, if he was not who she suspected him to be.

When he shouted with glee upon seeing her raised hand, jumping into the air, throwing his hat above him, and whooping so that everyone could hear, there was no longer any doubt, either for Adelaide or anyone standing anywhere near her on the deck. An older gentleman, his hand resting on the ship's rail next to hers, asked if she would like to be escorted down the gangplank, an offer she gratefully accepted. Her protector signaled to the steward, who followed them with the trunks, ordering two well-muscled deck hands to heft the rest of Adelaide's belongings and follow them to the dock below. The older man was amused and then touched at the awkwardness with which the young couple greeted one another. Obviously this young woman was a mail-order bride, he believed, as his own wife had been so many years before. Asking the young man's name, he doffed his hat and introduced the young couple to one another, which elicited a laugh from Simon, a good omen for the young couple's future together the man thought. Simon explained to him that he and his bride-to-be had known each other as little children in Vienna, but agreed with her that they had probably never met as adults. Still, their families were acquainted, and before the week was out, they would be husband and wife. When Adelaide finally moved into his embrace, the young man couldn't help but notice how brittle her body felt, as if it might break if it touched his. He, in turn, was amused, wondering idly how long it would be before their embrace was a more happy experience. Trusting totally in his expertise with women, the young man had no doubt that it would only be a matter of time before her body was as welcoming as the women who had preceded her.

As her bags were loaded into the waiting hansom cab, Simon explained to Adelaide that he had arranged a meeting with the Rabbi for that very afternoon. He had understood this would not be the time to introduce his young bride to the underground that had opened only months after his own arrival in this major metropolis, even if she hadn't come with so much baggage. He had hired a cab to take them all the way to the Bronx after the cabman had assured him that his horses were fully capable of such a long journey. He didn't tell Adelaide that this extravagance would cost him a week's wages: he knew his new boss would give him a bonus as a wedding gift, and besides, he wanted to impress this lovely young woman whose voice, according to his mother, was the talk of cultured Vienna. On the way to Crotona Park, which was only blocks from the building Simon had been living in since he and Otto had moved to the outer borough from Manhattan, Simon pointed out places of interest in this new, and bustling city. Although Vienna was also large, even crowded, and comprised of every sort of person from working class louts to the nobility, the crowds in New York were a bit overwhelming for Adelaide, who was tired from lack of sleep, and anxious about what her new life would be like.

Because she had no one else to rely upon so far from home, the young woman shyly slipped her hand into his, which delighted Simon no end. As they passed the Metropolitan Museum of Art on Fifth Avenue, a bastion of the city's cultural life, Simon told his prospective bride he was most anxious to hear her marvelous voice. There were several music halls in Manhattan, and he had already been inquiring about a teacher for her there, since his mother had written to him that finding such a person was of great importance to his wife-to-be. Addie turned to smile at the young man sitting beside her. She had been severely reprimanded by her mother after she had made this request to Simon's mother at one of the many dinners she and her parents had shared with Simon's parents, but obviously she had been right to do so. She thanked Simon with genuine warmth, explaining that her teacher in Vienna had also gotten a name from Arnold Schoenberg, whose music she had been performing for some years. When the young man squeezed her hand with a returning smile and said, "Perhaps you will introduce New Yorkers to his music!" she could feel her eyes brimming. 'At least he is a gentleman,' she thought, as he immediately pulled a handkerchief from his pocket and gently wiped the tears away.

Addie didn't have the heart to tell him that she did not enjoy Temple, and hoped to find a religion more akin to her own spirituality in this new country, because she knew it was proper that they be married by a Rabbi. She believed it would be best to wait at least a few weeks to discuss her feelings about God with Simon, a connection that since childhood has been strongest for her when she was performing. The only person she had had the courage to share this fact with in her short life had been her sister Sophia, who was now miles and miles away and pregnant with her second child, but nevertheless unwilling to share with Addie anything about the relations between a man and a woman. Addie only knew that when she and Sophia had heard that the painter, Harold, had married the year before, her sister had become very withdrawn, but never said a thing about her feelings to anyone, even Addie. Although his paintings were beginning to sell in certain sections of Vienna, his career was by no means one that would have inspired her father to accept him as a son-in-law, even then.

The Rabbi, who had laughing eyes and a gentle voice, captured Addie's heart immediately. She was pleased by Simon's choice, and said so after they had left his office. When the Rabbi asked her some questions about religion, Addie hesitated. He grasped both her hands in his and assured her that there are many ways to honor God and to pursue the Jewish faith. He would welcome spiritual conversation with her where they could address some of these issues. Much to her surprise, Addie realized she would enjoy talking to this man, and made a promise to herself that she would do just that once she was settled. They agreed to hold their marriage ceremony the following Saturday, which was only three days away. Thankful that she had packed her wedding dress on the top layer in one of the trunks, but sad as well that none of her family would be present when she said her vows, the young woman was quiet on the journey from the temple to the apartment building on 174th Street in the East Bronx.

The apartment Simon now occupied was new for him as well, since he had moved two floors below his original residence a few days before Adelaide's arrival. The new space was larger, a two-bedroom place with both a living and dining room, as well as a small pantry behind the kitchen that could easily be converted to another bedroom, should the marriage be a fertile one. This he explained to Adelaide as he led her from room to room; she felt positively petrified. Although she has no idea how a woman became pregnant, she did know that she felt ill-equipped for motherhood. Her goal was to build a singing career, even in this new country. Watching Sophia become more and more somber in her new role as wife and then mother over the past two years had done nothing to open Adelaide's heart to what lay before her. Of course she hadn't shared any of her thoughts with her father or her mother, both of whom would have been appalled. Nor had she spoken with Sophia, who seemed to be struggling with enough burdens of her own. The building Addie would be living in with her new husband was a six-story brick structure, less elegant than the narrow, three-story one where she had been raised in Vienna. When Simon opened the front door of the building for her she was shocked to realize that the building inside housed not one, two or even three families, but easily more than ten.

By the time the driver had carried each of her trunks up the four flights to their apartment, there was nothing more to be said. The driver seemed pleased by the tip Simon offered him, and departed after leaving his card, lest they should ever require his services in the future. When the front door closed behind him and Simon returned to Adelaide in the kitchen, he could tell his new bride looked frightened and thought he understood the reason. "Addie, my dear. You won't be staying with me until we are married. I have arranged for you to board with my neighbor, Mrs. O'Reilly. She's a widow who could use the extra income, and she's the warmest human being you can imagine…."

When his words seemed to have no affect, he stopped mid sentence. Finally, he asked her, "Tell me what the matter is," quite baffled by her demeanor.

"What kind of name is O'Reilly?" Adelaide stammered. She might not be religious, but she was, nevertheless, a Jew.

Simon burst into a loud laugh. "Addie, neighborhoods in New York are mixed. There are Jews, and Irish, and Poles, and Russians, all living together. Though to tell you the truth, I think there are more Jews in this twenty-block area than in any other neighborhood in the Bronx."

"And they all get along?" she asked, totally surprised by this information, and having no idea what to make of it.

"Come and meet Fionella and tell me what you think," he suggested, and led her up the narrow stairway to the sixth floor. As they passed Simon's old apartment, he pointed it out to his fiancé. She merely nodded, disappointed by the worn doors and poor paint job in the hallway, but certainly unwilling to share her feelings with Simon. Insulting him the very first day they met one another did not seem a good idea, so she kept her mouth closed. At least their apartment had a fresh coat of paint throughout. The young woman reminded herself to ask her husband if he had painted it himself, and if so, to compliment him on his work.

Fionella O'Reilly was a spry sixty, with a huge bosom hanging almost to her waist across the breadth of her chest. Before Addie could say a word, she opened her arms although her hands were still dripping with water and she held a dish towel in one of them, enfolding the young woman in her warm embrace. She was the most motherly woman Adelaide had ever encountered, her cheeks round and pink, a halo of frizzy hair escaping from her bun and encircling her head, her mouth open in a welcoming smile as she pulled the young woman towards her. Thoughtful as well as loving, she held her hands away from Addie's back, so as not to soil her fashionable jacket with water.

"My sweet and brave Miss Welt. You must be exhausted and overwhelmed with everything you're seeing. Your bed is made, with crisp clean linen, but if you're hungry, I have some tea steeping and a coffee cake still warm from the oven," she said as she released her.

"Oh Addie. I'm so sorry. I never even thought about food," Simon blurted, a look of real concern on his face.

"Whenever I turned around there was another meal being offered on the ship," she told them. "Until you mentioned it, I didn't realize I might finally be a little hungry."

"Is the coffee cake enough, or would you like a sandwich? I have cheese and tomato and sliced beef in the ice box," Mrs. O'Reilly beamed at her, as if she had given a brilliant answer to a difficult test question in school.

"You sound just like my grandmother," Addie blurted terribly embarrassed by her outburst. She needn't have been. Both Simon and Fionella O'Reilly burst into laughter, the older woman's deep and deeply contagious. Even Adelaide could not help joining in as she was led into the woman's kitchen. The smells in the cozy room were intoxicating, and Addie gratefully sank into the chair Fionella pulled out from the table for her. Within seconds her plump, roughened hands had placed a sandwich stuffed with mouth-watering ingredients in front of her, as well as a second plate with the still-warm coffee cake.

"Go ahead, you sweet thing. Don't wait for Simon. I'll have his sandwich in front of him in a jiffy," she said as she turned back to the counter next to the sink. "He's been very nervous about this, you know," she whispered, patting him on the shoulder as she passed him, but he didn't say a word to deny or refute her remark. He was embarrassed; he didn't share his anxieties with women, at least not the ones he dated, and certainly not with one he was about to marry but barely knew. For her part, Adelaide hadn't even considered how Simon might feel about her arrival in New York; but she found she was pleased by this information. It made her prospective husband seem human, and not just a name on her father's lips, or a young man staring out at her from a piece of photography paper.

Simon was indeed hungry, and wolfed down his sandwich with delight, which was slightly unnerving to the bourgeois Viennese girl who had barely finished the first half of hers. Her discomfort must have been obvious, because Fionella O'Reilly gave her shoulder a squeeze when she placed a cup of tea next to her plate. The conversation between Simon and his former next-door neighbor was both genial and lively. By the time she had eaten her piece of coffee cake – "Smaller please. I can't eat a great deal at one sitting." – Addie had learned she should frequent the grocery two blocks away rather than one on their own block; explore the wonders of Crotona Park as well as experience the delights of the American game baseball; and appreciate the glories of the underground, or subway, as they both called it. Afterwards, she was regaled with stories about various tenants in the building whose travails sounded like a Trollope novel to her.

"Simon. I don't know what is wrong with the two of us," Mrs. O'Reilly boomed out above her shoulder. "Look at this poor child. She is falling asleep at the table." Which, much to her shame, she was.

"I am sure I will enjoy shopping at Mr. Rosen's grocery," she managed, which made both of her companions smile.

Simon put his arm around her to help her from her seat, leading her down the hallway, this time turning towards the back of the woman's apartment. Mrs. O'Reilly, only steps behind, somehow managed to wiggle her girth around the two younger people so she could turn back the covers on the bed in the small, but spotlessly clean spare bedroom. Adelaide had to turn sideways to pass the bureau in order to sit down in the room's one small chair, which looked like it belonged in her parents' dining room, and began to unlace her shoes.

"Scoot, young man. I'll come get you when she wakes up," Mrs. O'Reilly admonished Simon, adding as an afterthought, "Unless it's in the middle of the night."

"If you can tell me what time it is, I can adjust my timepiece," Adelaide suggested. "Then I wouldn't wake either of you up if I sleep for a long time. I just need to find one of my books," she said, turning her head this way and that in search of her trunks.

"I left them in the living room," said Simon. "But if you know which trunk they're in, I'd be glad to get one for you."

"You go home. I'll take care of your little bride," ordered the neighbor. And she did as promised, bringing both a book and linen nighty to Adelaide, who couldn't seem to do more than unlace her shoes. She didn't even object when the older woman unbuttoned the back of her dress, and slid it from her shoulders. The last thing she noticed before she drifted into a deep and luxurious sleep was the crucifix hanging on the wall above her head.

* * *

As the freighter steamed slowly into New York harbor, Noah Unger stared at the ever-expanding metropolis of New York City, with its many tall and imposing buildings, in dismay. Although he had spent a great deal of time in Warsaw, a large city filled with imposing buildings itself, that city's architecture bore no relation to the spectacle he saw displayed before him. He and his fellow immigrants stared at the buildings as they glided past them, some wondering aloud how they would survive in such an enormous, crowded place. Noah, too, wondered about his future and that of his family. He was, after all, a country boy from a tiny shtetl in the Polish countryside who was used to dirt roads and tiny houses. The largest buildings in Monasterzyska bordered the town square: the government building, the temple and its outbuildings, and the village administrative offices. None of those buildings was more than five stories high, though they were constructed with stone and brick, like the structures he saw in this huge city. During the journey across the wide ocean, despite some trouble with seasickness, Noah had felt a building excitement about the life he was about to create for his family, never letting himself think about the possibility of not succeeding. Suddenly he experienced the same kind of anxiety he had felt the first day he was forced to attend his father's heder. What if he didn't have the moxie to succeed in such a place? What, after all, was he prepared to do in this new country? He didn't know very much English, although he had been studying the language by himself at night for months, and hadn't even finished a secondary education in Hebrew. Because of Yetta he had continued his studies with other workingmen in the village, and even might have been able to enter the second year at the Yeshiva in Buchach, had he possessed the funds to do such a thing, which had never been considered of course.

When the freighter docked at Ellis Island Noah was pushed off the boat in a jumble of immigrants, all shoving and pushing, or being pushed and shoved down the gangplank to the dock below, where they were immediately herded into a huge, cavernous building with endlessly long lines. Immigration workers paced the floor, barking out orders to the flood of people entering the already packed room. Of course Noah couldn't understand a word they were saying, and stood rooted in his tracks with no idea how to proceed. It could have been the way he had been pronouncing the foreign words at home, or the fact that the Americans were speaking so quickly. No one around him seemed to understand the commands any better than he did. He stood on his toes to better see what lay ahead, immediately noticing the large letters which hung in front of the lines that had already formed before the current tide of immigrants had entered the room. Discussing the situation with the two men closest to him in the crush of people near the entryway, they all agreed the letters must represent the first letter of their country of origin, or the initial of their last names. Opting for the latter, which seemed a more reasonable supposition to all three, they pushed and shoved and weaved their way through the room until they were standing side by side. One man's name was Ullman and the other Tisch, so one stood behind Noah and the other in the line next to theirs, though further back in the huge room.

The process was endless. Exhausted, the men finally sat down on their suitcases, each one taking stored food from within before sitting down, and sharing the little they had left from the long voyage with one another. In this way, they managed a meal of sorts, learned a bit of history about each other, and passed the time. Birthed on the opposite side of the freighter from Ullman, Noah had seen him a few times but never spoken to him. He was surprised to learn that Tisch had even been on the same ship, and even more startled to hear that the man came from Buchach. As it turned out both of his new friends had dreamed of attending the Yeshiva there, but Tisch's situation had been worse that his own. He had managed to complete almost two years at the Yeshiva, and then, because of illness in his family, been forced to take over his father's business. No one was to blame in his case either, Noah thought to himself as Tisch unburdened his soul to his two compatriots. At least Noah had been working since early childhood, and hadn't experienced the loss of his studies after several years of study at the revered school of higher learning.

Noah watched as Ullman tried to deal with the inspectors after he sat down at the imposing table spanning the width of the room in front of the endless lines of immigrants. In reality, the desk was a simple table scarred from years of use, but for the thousands upon thousands of newcomers waiting to be welcomed into their new home, every guard, every inspector, every potential judge seemed larger than life. Since Ullman, like almost all the rest of them, spoke very little English, finding a spelling for his name that even resembled its European derivative seemed a daunting task. Finally Noah, who believed he understood the difficulty the inspector was having, pulled at Ullman's sleeve, and mimicked writing each letter down on a piece of paper. When neither Ullman nor the official seemed to understand what he was suggesting, Noah reached for the piece of paper and did it himself. Because of Noah's intercession the Ullman family spelled its name the same way its forbears had for generations with two 'ell's' and one 'm'. Close to tears by then, Ullman clung to Noah in thanks, while everyone behind them stood in line, numb and exhausted, waiting their turn. Finally, the woman behind Noah suggested in Hebrew that the two either step aside or let Noah take his turn so the line could move on. Noah pointed to a spot nearby, where the distraught Ullman could wait for him, and was processed in much the same way his friend had been. 'Unger' he arrived in this new country, and Unger he remained. When his passport was finally stamped, Noah felt the sense of elation he had boarded the liner that would take him to a new life. He had done it: he had been admitted to the land of promise. He vowed to make a life for himself and his family as he crossed the room to Ullman who was waiting atop his one battered suitcase. Noah was strong, and knew he would survive.

He and Ullman, who hadn't thought to look for Tisch – he had either finished his procedure before they and disappeared or was too far back to be seen – were herded with many others towards what appeared to be a gaping hole in the wall near their point of entry, where two huge open doors were letting both light and the early afternoon chill into the cavernous room. As he stumbled outside, Noah was startled to see another boat tied up at the dock, much smaller than the freighter, but with two decks nonetheless. The lowest level was already loaded with carts and horses that had come from God-only-knew where, the upper with hordes of immigrants. Clutching each other by the arms to gain purchase in the rush of bodies barreling up the gangplank, he and Ullman stumbled aboard, finding places near the back of the boat at the railing of the crowded lower deck. Both were surprised when the ferry disembarked from Ellis Island to find themselves not in the back of the vessel as they had assumed, but in the front, with a marvelous view of the New Jersey shore as they approached it. Of course Elias had explained the entire procedure to Noah by letter, but he had completely forgotten about the ferry ride to Hoboken, where Elias had sworn he would be waiting with horse and buggy to carry him to his temporary home in Elizabethport.

Neither Ullman nor Noah could remember whether Tisch was going to New York City, or like them, to a town in New Jersey where one or two relatives had already settled. As Noah turned to see Ellis Island disappear behind the body of the sturdy ferry, he heard a voice yelling above the cacophony of voices speaking in so many languages it almost made him dizzy, "Unger! Unger! Over here!" First the words came in Hebrew, then Polish, and finally a familiar Ukrainian dialect, but by then Noah had spotted Tisch leaning over the deck above them, shrieking at the top of his lungs to be heard. He and Noah motioned at the same time, in agreement that Tisch should come down rather than the two below making their way to the top deck. In moments, much faster than Noah would have thought possible given the crush of human beings in every imaginable place on the small ferry, Tisch appeared by his side and the three men embraced, as if they were long lost friends or relatives. And it was thus they arrived in Hoboken, arm in arm, each man peering anxiously towards the shoreline to try to find their relatives in the huge crowd awaiting the ferry. Noah again despaired: how would he ever find his brother in this mess; and would Elias wait until every last person had gone? It had been over five years; would they even recognize each other?

At just that moment he heard another scream in the sudden miraculous lull of the hundreds of voices on the ferry as almost all of the passengers stopped talking so they could also search for a familiar face.

"Little scholar! "Notchke!" And then even louder, "Unger! Over here. On the wagon near the tall maple tree!" And there, grinning broadly from ear to ear, was his older brother, sitting on the bench seat of a very old wagon, wearing a suit cut in a manner Noah was quite sure his wife had never seen, looking prosperous, or just chubby: who could tell? Noah would have known him anywhere. Whatever the cause, his brother was certainly doing a lot better than Noah had been over the last year. Never had Noah been as conscious of his bony wrists, and his pants, hugging his waist only because of the leather belt Yetta had forced him to buy before he set out on his journey. He, Ullman and Tisch exchanged addresses, promising not to lose touch with one another, in this, their greatest adventure. Indeed, until they were old men Noah and Ullman met once a month in Newark, a central location for them both, and both kept in touch with Tisch who lived too far south to join them very often, until his death from tuberculosis when he was only in his forties.

All three joined the horde of bodies pouring off the ferry after the departure of the animals, carts, wagons, and carriages, all three anxious because, of course, in the melee they had lost sight of their relatives. Fortunately Elias, who had borrowed both the horse and the old wagon precisely because of its high front seat, was well above the crowd milling along the quay in a logjam, hundreds of bodies turning this way and that in utter confusion. He again spotted his brother, with the unhealthy pallor of a long-distance traveler, and began to sing the tune Noah used to sing to him when they were little boys, and Elias was having trouble falling asleep, and their mother, exhausted from her long workday, had given up comforting him. "Singing" was a euphemism for the sounds brought forth by Elias, but the surrounding hordes forgave him because they quickly realized he was bellowing the notes as loudly as possible, so he could be heard by a relative on the ferry.

When Ullman turned to Noah to ask, "What is that dreadful noise?" Noah grinned at the shorter man. "It is my brother. Ruining the tune I used to sing to him when we couldn't sleep at night." The other man laughed long and loud, finally managing, "I can't imagine falling asleep to that!" and was off again, great barks that made heads turn and others join in without even knowing what either man was laughing about. When Noah, who couldn't see any further than the people pressed closest to him, felt a hand grasp his shoulder from above, he reached up with both hands, hefting his suitcase first, so his brother could grasp it. Then, helped by both Ullman and Tisch, who both realized what was happening without being able to see Elias either, Noah again stretched his arms above his head so that his brother could pull, and the two below, push, until he found himself scrambling into the wagon. The last sight he had of his friends was of the two men, hanging on to each other as they were pushed and shoved by the crowd between two huge oak trees, and then disappeared beyond them. Both had seen family from the ferry deck above as well, so Noah knew they would be reunited with family eventually, once people like him who had found their relatives quickly, left the vicinity, clearing the way for other reunions.

Several blocks from the ferry terminal, Elias pulled over so that the two brothers, who hadn't seen one another in almost five years, could clasp each other in a grateful embrace. Elias was not surprised that his younger brother had only brought one suitcase, albeit a large one, but he was surprised by the canvas bag he had been carrying over his shoulder, and was now unloading: several shirts Yetta has made for her brother-in-law, too small for him now, as well as a new jacket she had finished only hours before Noah had left Monasterzyska. Elias couldn't have worn any of the clothes, which had been sewn for a younger, more slender young man, not the heavier solid citizen he had become.

"With a little altering," Elias suggested, "All of these things can be fixed so they make you look as if you haven't just fallen off the boat from Eastern Europe." Noah was so nonplussed he could think of no response. He had thought his brother was the one 'out of fashion', but clearly in this new land it was actually the reverse. "We can't fatten you up right away," his brother chuckled, "or your pants will be out of style as well." Indeed, compared to the lose trousers his brother wore, Noah's seemed unsuitably form fitting. "Perhaps it is a good thing we have all been hungry this past year," he grinned. "Otherwise I would have arrived with pants that hugged my hips even more." Both brothers smiled contentedly at one another, totally comfortable with this familiar brand of shtetl humor.

First Elias wanted to know about his mother and how she was faring. He didn't trust the letters he received; after all, given the difficulty of life in the Polish Ukraine, she couldn't be as full of health as she had been when he had left the shtetl behind in the hopes of finding a better life. Assuring his brother that their mother was actually in amazing health, still working a full day in the apothecary and often helping Yetta with the cleaning in their home as well, since they now had four small children and couldn't afford outside help. Knowing what his brother's next request would be, Noah removed a linen-wrapped packet from his canvas bag, unfolding the napkin so that he could show his brother pictures of his wife, and of each of their children. Elias couldn't believe how much Jules looked like him as a little boy. The brothers agreed his posture was an exact replica. Elias thought the girls a delight, the mischief in Beck's eyes apparent, even in a photograph.

"It's amazing how little Monasterzyska has changed. Even the clothes look the same!" Elias exclaimed.

"Yetta would shoot you for that," Noah laughed. "She is very proud of the suits and dresses she makes in her little factory, and has kept up with fashions in Warsaw through newspaper articles and postcards I bring back from my business trips there."

"How funny! They just look Eastern European to me." Until that moment Noah's brother had not realized how far he had come in so few years.

Both men fell silent as they wended their way towards Elizabethport, the underprivileged neighborhood of the thriving New Jersey town of Elizabeth, where many Jewish immigrants had settled in the past fifteen years. Both men were thinking about how much their lives had changed since they had been boys in the Ukraine together. Elias not only had become a butcher, he had owned his own business for two years already, and it was thriving. Though not a rich man by any means, he was doing amazingly well for a man who had only immigrated five and a half years earlier. In those few years he had also met and married a young woman from the Austrian countryside and started a family, and though living in a rented apartment, was setting aside savings so that he would be able to purchase a home of his own within the next couple of years. Noah, who had left the heder to join Harry's business as a teen and become instrumental in its growth, had been forced to watch the business shrivel, long after Elias had left the Ukraine. Here he was, in a wagon borrowed by a brother he hadn't seen in years, headed for an unknown town in a land thousands of miles across an ocean from the land of his birth, and thousands more by wagon from the only home he had ever known. Exhausted and hungry, his head spinning from this momentous moment, Noah suddenly became aware that he was dizzy: trees in the distance were waving with considerable force although there wasn't even a breeze, and the road ahead was tilting at an odd angle. Holding on to the side of the wagon with his right hand, he prayed he would not embarrass them both by falling out of the wagon altogether.

"What a nudnik I am," his brother's voice broke into the muddle inside his brain. Elias reached into a bag at his feet, pulling out first a loaf of homemade challah, then a block of cheddar cheese, and finally a jug filled with pure, clean water. "Here. Marta would be furious if she discovered I had forgotten to offer you this snack as soon as I saw you. She still talks about how faint she felt when she disembarked from that very same ferry four years ago. Eat, eat, don't be shy," urged Elias as

Noah reached for the challah. He broke a piece for himself and one for Elias, and cut two chunks of the rich-looking cheese with the pocket knife he always carried; the two munched contentedly as the horse brought them closer to their destination. Noah's head began to clear and he said aloud, "It will be fine. I will make a life here for us all." Elias patted him on the back, as the two nodded in agreement.

* * *

The wedding of Simon and Adelaide was a quiet affair, with only Otto, the young woman he had been seeing, Mrs. O'Reilly and several other neighbors from the building in attendance. Although her family had never been particularly religious, Adelaide was surprised at the relief she felt when she entered the temple and spied the traditional huppah in the front of the room. When Simon broke the glass beneath it, Otto whooped almost as loudly as Simon had at dockside only a few days before when he had first spied his bride. Even the Rabbi smiled. Surprised but undaunted on this, his wedding day, Simon said nothing when Addie turned her cheek to him for the traditional kiss, avoiding his lips even though they were now married. In that moment the young and innocent young woman felt a depth of fear she had never known before: if she could get pregnant from touching her lips to his, then she would have to avoid doing so, at least until she had a singing teacher, and, perhaps, had attained a position in a New York choral group as well. She couldn't become pregnant before launching her singing career in this new world, of that she was certain. Otto's woman, the only one who noticed the exchange or lack of one, thought she should speak to the young bride. She suspected what the problem might be, but was not sure. As the evening unfolded, it turned out there was never an opportunity.

Simon had rented a large room in the back of a local kosher restaurant where the small wedding party retired for their wedding feast. The owner of the restaurant had suggested hiring a small band of local boys who would not be too expensive, and they were surprisingly good. Simon was a fine dancer. He led his new bride around the dance floor with ease, quickly switching from a contemporary slow dance to an old-country hora with no difficulty whatsoever. Addie found herself humming with the tunes despite herself, thoroughly enjoying this young man's touch, the music and the festivities. When the small ensemble broke out in a well known Jewish song, Addie's voice soared above the others as she taught Mrs. O'Reilly the words until hers was the only one to be heard in the entire room. Every one of the band members turned towards the young bride. Her young husband was stunned, despite what he had heard about her talent. This magnificent sound was beyond anything he had imagined. Impulsively he grabbed Addie's hand and urged her on to the small raised platform upon which the three band members were standing, asking her to sing for them all, right now. Flustered, she had no idea what to sing, stuttering in confusion that she knew little English, and certainly didn't know songs popular in this new country. The violinist asked if she would prefer something classical, perhaps some Schubert, and startling the young bride, suggested a favorite concerto of her, which he began playing immediately. At the urging of one of the other band members she turned to face the audience, beginning to sing before she realized what she was even doing, the familiar music drawing her in. Within seconds, the celebration room filled with other restaurant patrons, drawn by the lovely singing coming from within it. Mrs. O'Reilly joined the musicians, sitting down at the piano and playing several pieces by Mozart from memory, a total surprise to Addie, who had assumed the woman came from peasant stock and certainly wouldn't know the Viennese composer. She sang while her host played for almost an hour, the room packed by then with everyone in the restaurant, including the waiters, the chef and the owner. When the bass player suggested he teach her some local tunes, the cheers of the crowd urged her on, and the young woman, following his lead, picked up the simple tunes in moments, thrilling the already enraptured crowd.

Simon, stunned, watched in awe as the young woman he had just married mesmerized the entire restaurant, customers and staff, taking over the evening in front of his very eyes. He found himself watching this tiny woman, entranced by her voice, her presence, and her curves. She was much prettier than her pictures had indicated, and became truly beautiful when she was performing. His heart began to beat with a sudden fierceness as he realized he couldn't wait to take little Addie home to their apartment. Because of his own passion, he barely thought about the kiss that had been avoided earlier in the day. Tonight they would truly join, something he was sure they would both relish once he relieved her of her modesty. He had become adept at this job after his initial New York scare, because he only wooed middle class American girls, girls who were less likely to carry disease. Simon had rarely thought about the consequences of his actions, assuming the American beauties were allowed more leeway in the realm of physical expression than their European counterparts, although not enough to make them dangerous. He would have been horrified to learn that at least one of the girls he had enjoyed had become pregnant after several encounters with him. A marriage for her had been quickly arranged, and she was now living in Brooklyn with a one-year old in a loveless marriage, still dreaming about the young handsome immigrant who had taken her virginity. Had she known he was finally marrying, she would have cried.

After Adelaide was finally allowed to leave the stage, promising to return to the restaurant with the little band, and be paid for a performance the restaurant would advertise in the local paper, Otto ordered Schnapps for the entire party. Of course the restaurant owner refused to let them pay for it, and also cut Simon's bill in half because of the money he had made bringing drinks to the crowd listening to his young bride. For some reason this enhanced his anticipation of the celebration awaiting him at home. Despite the fact that he longed to grab his new wife and escape back to 174th Street, he managed to maintain his gracious and charming manner for the rest of the evening.

When the door finally closed behind them and Simon crushed Addie to his chest, he was mildly surprised by how stiff she became. For her part, Adelaide had no idea what to do. She was terrified. Neither her mother nor her sister had told her any details of what she might expect on her wedding night, or thereafter. In her naiveté she had assumed that Sophia had merely been fortunate to not become pregnant with Harold, whose kisses had transported her to a place Addie, herself, had no interest in visiting. When Simon turned her face to his, so that he might kiss the lips he had been watching with longing for hours, Adelaide burst into tears and pushed herself back with both hands upon his chest.

"I can't become pregnant, Simon. My singing is so important to me, and I don't even have a teacher here yet," she blurted, fear leaching from her pores.

Simon, not an insensitive lout, gently stroked her hand, and then her cheek. "Addie. Sweet Addie. How do you think you will become pregnant?"

Blushing furiously, she looked at her own feet as she replied, "By kissing you...."

Simon's laughter filled the room. Gently, very gently, he again took his young wife in his arms, whispering into her hair. "I assure you, kissing won't make you pregnant. Even what we will do in the privacy of our own bedroom now, won't make you pregnant. I will pull out, and you, my sweet wife, will find a singing teacher and a doctor next week."

With that he led her into their bedroom, which she herself had decorated during the past few days with furnishings much like those they both had grown up with in Vienna, and began to unbutton her lovely linen frock with its lace-trimmed bodice and shirred skirt. Adelaide found herself thinking that when she, Sophia and her mother had ordered it from the dressmaker after months of deliberation, this night was not what she had imagined. Although she did believe him, Addie could not stop her body from trembling as he removed the bodice, gently releasing her arms from the sleeves with a little tug, and dropping it behind her back. At first she was unclear why he took her hand in his, but then she realized it was so that she could step out of the skirt, which she managed, just barely, since her legs were now trembling along with her body. Still holding on to her hand, he scooped up her dress and laid it across the back of the chair on her side of the big bed in the center of the room. Then he pulled back the comforter and sat so that she was on his lap. Addie was afraid to move, afraid not to move, and terrified that her chest would burst. Her heart had never beaten with such vehemence.

And then she found herself lying on top of Simon, at least with the upper half of her body, though her legs were skewed to the right, half atop his, and half hanging over the edge of the bed. When he finally kissed her mouth it was not an unpleasant sensation, though his moustache tickled her top lip. She was just beginning to relax, because this was not as bad as she had imagined it would be, when his tongue pushed aside her lips, and engaged with her own. Adelaide was horrified. She had no idea how to keep the saliva in her own mouth from dripping down her chin, and didn't want his filling her mouth because she was afraid of gagging. When he gently adjusted her mouth with his free hand so that her lips were closer together, she froze into position, her tongue heavy and immobile, while his darted in and out of her mouth.

"Liebchen, relax," he smiled up at her. "I promise I won't hurt you. Kissing is playful, like this." His tongue again began its dance inside her mouth. She did manage to move her own tongue so that it brushed his a few times, but inside, in her heart, she felt herself closing herself off from him. What he was asking of her seemed revolting. How her mother endured such 'play' was beyond her comprehension. Then Simon shifted beneath her, and she found herself lying on her back, their tongues still moving around her mouth. But now his hand was brushing down the length of her leg, and pulling her slip aside so that he could actually explore each limb. Adelaide held herself in place, barely able to breathe.

"Liebchen, relax," he chided her yet again. "Don't you want me to prepare you?"

The new bride, who had only been in New York for a week, with no family or friend to offer her counsel, stared up at the man who now owned her, mute. How could she tell him she had no idea what he meant?

She let him roll down first one stocking and then the other, wondering when this ordeal would be over, and then gasped, as his hand clasped her most private place, his fingers pulling aside her panties, and actually touching her there. She, herself, when washing, moved the cloth over and around that 'place' as quickly as possible, and now this man, this man was touching her with his fingers, no cloth protecting her, no way to escape. She held her breath. Finally he removed his hand, and raised up on both arms, looking down on her with sad, hurt eyes.

"Addie, if you don't relax I won't be able to keep you from pain. Please," he begged.

The breath she took was ragged, her fear palpable to them both. She whispered, "What…is it …you want me to …do?"

This stopped Simon completely. With most of the women he had known, by this point in a seduction even the 'good' girls were sighing with enjoyment, despite their fear about what might be about to happen. He took one of her little hands in his, and uncurled her fingers, one by one. "You can begin by unclenching your hands. And letting your legs fall apart, just a bit."

When a tear escaped her right eye and dribbled down onto the sheet, he wiped it away, leaving little kisses in its wake. "If you allow me to…release you, I think you might even come to enjoy…love making," he suggested with some hesitation. Since he had never faced a woman so resistant, Simon was at a loss. All he knew how to do was to persevere.

Closing her eyes, Adelaide gulped air several times, much as she would have done before warming up her voice, knowing there was truth in his words despite her terror. When she was tight, the notes didn't soar. If she was tight here, perhaps she was preventing another kind of soaring. But as soon as she felt one of his hands lifting her hips, and the other pulling her panties down and off her legs, she knew that here she would be defeated. She loathed the feeling of his fingers probing her most private place, and cried out in alarm when he tried to poke his middle finger deep inside her, her body arcing up on the bed, totally rigid.

By this point neither husband nor wife was looking at the other. Addie's eyes were squeezed shut, as if to block out what was happening to her, and Simon was by now gritting his teeth, determined to gain admittance. He knew that if he stopped this trial would only be postponed until the next day or the day after that. Perhaps after the initial shock the next time would be easier, the young groom told himself as he unbuttoned his underwear, and placed his erect penis at the entry to his new wife's portal. When he tried to move inside her, the dryness there, something he had also never experienced, destroyed any remaining pleasure he might have derived from the experience. It took everything the young man possessed to retain his erection, as the woman beneath him began to moan with discomfort, and toss her body from side to side.

Oddly, this movement allowed him entry. And then the woman beneath him began to scream.

"Help! Help! Help!" she screamed at the top of her lungs. Within eight or nine thrusts, he was spent. Instead of collapsing on top of his new wife and covering her with kisses, as he had imagined in the restaurant, he rolled off of her, and lay by her side, staring at the ceiling above the bed. At that very moment there was a loud banging at the door to the apartment. Simon grabbed his pants, struggling into them as he raced to the door. "Coming," he called out, opening the door to a very frightened-looking Mrs. O'Reilly.

"Is everything alright, Simon? Adelaide was calling out for help, and I didn't know…." she paused, noticing for the first time that all Simon was wearing was his pants, and then she understood.

"Addie," the young man called out. "Tell Fiona that everything is alright, please."

Although she could barely hear the new bride, Mrs. O'Reilly heard the muffled 'I'm fine' with relief. She could not wait for Simon to close the door so she could flee back to her own apartment.

This time Simon did not wipe the tears from his bride's face when he returned to their bed, although he did lift her legs one more time so that he could cover her with their comforter. Simon had no idea if the chill in the room was real, or was just within his own heart.

As for Adelaide, she did not think she could endure a life filled with such encounters. Returning to Vienna was impossible: what reason could she give? After all, from the beginning of time women clearly had suffered through this bestial act. Why should she be any different? Quietly crying herself to sleep, the young immigrant could only hope that she would mend, and that time would ease the horror of her wedding night.

* * *

The apartment where his brother Elias lived was above the butcher shop. Although it was larger than Noah and Yetta's cottage in

Monasterzyska, it felt much more crowded. Every room was filled with heavy European furniture, the wood dark and varnished, the fabrics covering each piece heavy, in dark tones of maroon and deep blue. In the dining room, where all of the adults were sitting after consuming a marvelous meal of brisket, roasted potatoes, green salad, home-made rolls, and hamentashen for desert, Noah pushed back from the round, shiny mahogany table to unbutton his pants, relaxing for the first time in over a month. His sister-in-law Marlene, a homely woman with a large nose and watery eyes, was the warmest, most welcoming person Noah had ever known. Older by several years than his stout brother, the two clearly adored each other. Often interrupting one another's sentences to complete a thought, which neither husband nor wife seemed to notice, Noah could no longer conceal his astonishment by the forth interruption. Marlene stopped in mid-sentence after cutting her husband off in mid-thought to laugh at the expression on his face.

"We understood each other from the very first date, Noah. I don't mind when he finishes my sentences because it's what I was going to say anyway, and he feels the same way," she chuckled, patting her husband's arm with obvious affection.

"When did I interrupt you, Mar-lee?" Elias asked with genuine surprise, proving the point. He turned to his brother. "I don't even know I do it anymore. Isn't that something? And what do you think of my English?"

"It's better than mine," Noah replied, causing Marlene, Elias, Marlene's brother Robert, and Marlene's parents, Elihu and Bess, to burst into raucous laughter. Noah joined in with equal mirth. When he was able to regain control, he asked in Hebrew, "How long do you think it will take me to be able to understand, and make myself understood?"

Elihu explained that the local "Y" offered an English class for foreigners that met three times a week in the evenings after dinner when most working men were home. He had actually met Elias at the class, and one thing led to another, and now he had two grandchildren. Marlene, whose accent was thicker than her husband's, added that she signed up for the very next class at the urging of Elias, who by then was her husband, although very few women managed to find the time to attend. She was grateful her husband wanted her to become fluent in this new country. One of the rewards was being much more comfortable talking to her young son's teachers than any of her friends. "What she isn't telling you is that she is the interpreter for the entire neighborhood of women. Everyone relies on her to explain their children's behavior to the teachers, and to learn what is expected of them in these American schools. Here boys and girls all attend school until they are eighteen. It is a very different place," Elias explained. "But that doesn't answer your question. It took me a few months before I was comfortable. Until then I did whatever odd jobs I could find where I didn't have to speak much, or be taught what to do. Once I thought I didn't sound like a complete dummkopf, that is when I had the courage to talk to Mr. Vincent."

"The butcher who hired him over four years ago!" Elihu and his wife all but shouted in unison, the pride for their son-in-law apparent to all.

"He sold Elias his shop several months ago. Did that letter reach you before you left Monasterzyska?" Marlene asked him.

"No. I'm amazed to have a brother, even an older brother, who is already a big macher in this new country." The two men grinned at each other across the table.

The next morning Noah was up by 5, a half hour before either Elias or Marlene began to stir. Even the children were quiet when he slipped into the kitchen, lit the stove, and put the kettle on to boil for the coffee the adults would drink to begin their day. He quietly searched the pantry, finding oatmeal, raisins, and a loaf of bread wrapped in a linen cloth, and began to make breakfast for Elias, Marlene and their two children. During each of Yetta's four pregnancies, Noah would make breakfast for the family so that his wife, often ill the first few months, could get a few more minutes of much-needed sleep. It was a task he actually enjoyed, rummaging around by himself in the kitchen while the rest of the world slept, his mind released to wander along an otherwise forgotten intellectual landscape by the simple tasks. When Marlene joined him, wrapped in her robe, distressed that he felt the need to feed her family on this, his first full day in America, he assured her he had frequently prepared breakfast at home, and that doing so was something he enjoyed. By the time the rest of the family straggled in, the two were singing folk songs together as they set the table.

The first person Noah approached in his search for work was the shoemaker, at his brother's suggestion, although he had never repaired a shoe. The man had come to America from a town on the other side of Buchach over twenty years earlier, and had a soft spot for fellow immigrants, especially those from the Polish Ukraine. Their conversation was a pleasant one, full of news from 'home', as this wizened old man still called it. Yes, the man could use an apprentice he said, very good news indeed. Noah began to feel excited. Perhaps this wouldn't be as difficult as he had feared. It took longer for the shoemaker to admit to this pleasant and brave young man that he could not afford to pay him to learn, but suggested he try the grocer at the corner store. Perhaps the grocer could use a man to unpack boxes; for that Noah's lack of English would not be such a problem. Unfortunately the Irish grocer, who finally understood what Noah wanted, needed no more workers. By the time he climbed the stairs to his brother's apartment at midday, Noah was berating himself for feeling discouraged. Either the local shopkeepers had workers aplenty, or they lacked the funds to pay for additional, and needed help. Noah couldn't work for free, even in the hope that eventually he would be paid.

At lunch he talked to his brother about the Singer sewing factory he had been hearing about all morning. The factory employed many residents of Elizabethport; Noah knew a great deal about sewing because he had been watching Yetta for years. He knew he couldn't expect a supervisory position at first, despite his experience in his wife's business, but he assured Elias he was certain he could operate a sewing machine. At his sister-in-law's urging he stopped by the three story red brick factory that afternoon to enquire about a job as he broadened the circle of streets he walked in his search for work. Having practiced the words he would have to say to the factory manager at lunch, he did not have a terribly difficult time making himself understood to the man's secretary. He was not bothered by the frown of concentration on the woman's face as she strained to understand him because he was so concentrated himself. When he left the building with an appointment for the following morning at 11, he was positively elated. If only Marlene had owned a machine, he would have practiced what he had only watched before, never dreaming that he, himself, would one day apply for the job of 'seamstress'. That night Elias told him he was fortunate to have gotten an interview with the big man himself, rather than being shuffled down the line to a lower level floor manager, who might not have been willing to even think about hiring a worker with such a poor command of English, and a man at that. After dinner, Elias walked his brother to the local school, where he enrolled in his first English class. Staying up even later than he had the night before to read the first chapter of the book he had been given so he would be prepared for his initial class the following evening, he easily memorized the words therein. Noah didn't tiptoe to the sink to brush his teeth, or lie down on the couch to sleep until well after 1 AM.

Nevertheless, he was again in the kitchen before Marlene, waking early with anxiety about the interview. Brother and sister-in-law worked in companionable silence as they prepared the morning meal. Leaving her to clean up the dishes, Noah assured Elias he didn't have to close the shop for the few minutes it took him to walk his children to school. Noah now knew the way, and could easily walk them there himself as he again began to canvas the area for jobs. Because he received virtually the same response – no money – at every shop he entered, by 11 Noah was more determined than ever to impress the factory manager with his knowledge of sewing machines. With the words he had learned only the night before, Noah explained his situation to the busy man. The fellow, in his ill-fitting suit with its wide lapels and tie, was friendly enough despite his stiff manner, and followed Noah onto the floor, seemingly willing to allow the young man to show him that he could, indeed, stitch a straight line. Confident in his ability to imitate his wife, Noah didn't remove the jacket the little seamstress, who had risen from her machine at the manager's bidding, had been working on. He easily stitched the back of the jacket to the left side, and than pinned the sleeve in place as well. Even the young woman was surprised at the ease with which he accomplished these tasks, smiling at him in surprise, and then lowering her flushing face in embarrassment at such forward behavior.

Heart pounding, Noah followed the factory manager, whose name was Brennan, back to his office and stood behind the chair across from the man's desk. At first he did not understand what Brennan was offering.

And then it began to dawn on him that the manager was saying that he had lost a floor manager the month before, and had been unable to find someone to replace him because no one he had interviewed was knowledgeable enough about the sewing business. Obviously, language would be a problem, but he thought Noah might be able to demonstrate what he expected of a new girl, and even help a seasoned woman with a difficult task until he gained mastery over English. In this way he might surmount the problem of language for a short while. Noah pulled his registration slip for night school out of his jacket pocket, and laid it on the man's desk in explanation, since he certainly didn't yet have the necessary words to explain that he had already enrolled in a class the night before. The factory manager was obviously pleased by Noah's display of resourcefulness – after all, few immigrants would enroll in such a class their very first day in a new country. The young man left the factory with the direction to report for work the next morning at 5 to begin his orientation. Brennan suggested he buy an English dictionary, or if possible, an English/Polish one, so that he could look up words he didn't yet know to ease his job the first months as a floor supervisor.

On his way home Noah stopped at his brother's butcher shop to tell him the news: the two hugged each other long and hard, neither giving a thought to the blood covering the front of Elias' apron. That night he brought home a special cut of beef so they could celebrate, a cut he usually reserved for his more prosperous clients. Marlene made a fruit tart for desert, and opened a bottle of sweet red wine they had been saving for a special occasion. All three agreed this night qualified even though it was not a religious holiday. Noah again stayed in the dining room studying words after he finished a letter to Yetta telling her the good news. He included little tidbits for each of his children, information about this new country he knew would interest them, and finally doused the lantern at midnight. The next morning Marlene had his breakfast prepared by 4:30, though he had assured her this wasn't necessary. Nonetheless, he was grateful, and said so, the tea and challah warming his belly all the way to the doors of the factory.

The day was long and difficult. Noah had no trouble showing the women how to do particular tasks on the sewing machine, but he often did not know what they were asking of him. After several frustrating attempts by an older woman to make him understand her complaint, and more frustration on his part when he clearly could not figure out what she was wanted, he suddenly had a solution. Holding up his finger to tell her to stay where she was, he raced up the stairs two at a time and into the office where Brennan's secretary sat, returning with a small handful of lined paper. First he drew a stick figure sitting at a table and then pushed the pad towards the seamstress. She looked up at him in puzzlement, finally breaking into a raucous laugh as she showed the women on either side of her his awful little drawing. Slowly she, too, put figures on the page, and in this way, they reached understanding with one another. Within moments her problem had been solved. Unfortunately the entire episode took more than a half hour, a long time to deal with one minor problem in one small department at the large factory. By lunchtime Noah's shirt was drenched in sweat, and he barely had the appetite to eat the roast beef and tomato sandwich Marlene had prepared for him. He had just managed to stuff it down when the whistle sounded for the seamstresses to return to the floor. Within moments, he was engulfed in yet another problem that he didn't manage to solve for twenty minutes.

That night, although he was clearly exhausted, he refused to listen to Elias who urged him to skip his second evening class and rest. In a few weeks he would be used to life at the factory and less tired, Elias argued. Noah didn't agree. He believed that if he didn't attend each and every class, he would never learn enough words to keep this new job, which he was determined to do. When the two-hour class was over, Noah stumbled home, again staying up to memorize the lesson for the following class. In the morning he didn't scold Marlene for rising early enough to prepare his breakfast and make him a sandwich for lunch. He was as grateful for the few minutes of extra sleep as he was for the food, and he told her so.

The days and nights fell into a grinding and seemingly endless routine, one made bearable by the knowledge that the harder he worked, the sooner his family would be able to join him in this new country. In a way it was fortunate Noah didn't have a moment in his work day to sit and take a breather; if he had, he might have fallen asleep, an action that would certainly have reached the attention of Mr. Brennan. Noah had vowed to himself that his behavior would be so exemplary he would avoid the scrutiny of both Brennan and the man who was his immediate superior. Despite the fact that each day he arrived at work with at least thirty new words beneath his belt, the women he supervised still had difficulty understanding what he said to them because of his thick, Eastern European accent. Most of them were already second generation Americans, whose accents were as foreign to him as his was to them. The pad of paper and pencils he brought with him daily was a help, since pictures were a universal language, but if the task at hand was complicated, there was no way on earth that Noah's drawing skills were adequate to the task. If there had been a business manual for the factory that might have helped, but that type of text had not yet been invented. The first woman he helped with his stick figures often stopped to talk to him at lunch, teaching him words for some of the parts of the machines used in the Singer plant. Remembering her own struggles, she had empathy for the young man who was obviously striving so hard to make a go of it. Very few of the other seamstresses were as empathetic.

When the teacher of the English class realized that Noah was by now two chapters ahead of his fellow students, he pulled Noah aside to request he help some of his slower contemporaries. Noah was too shy to say he didn't have the time: how could he deny others the help many people in this new land had already been giving him. In days already filled to the brim, the young man met two other immigrants before class to explain the sections of the assigned chapter they didn't understand. In a way his task was easier than the teacher's because he and the two men he met with had at least one language in common. This task helped him too, since explaining the grammar issues gave him a greater understanding of the rules as well. This he explained to Elias and Marlene one evening after dinner, because both of them were worried about his lack of sleep and his obvious exhaustion. The one joy in his otherwise grueling existence was Friday nights, when the entire family attended shul, and he was able to take his own talus and yarmulke, sit with the men in the main area of the temple, and pray with them. This precious time took him back to Monasterzyska, and all the Friday night services he had attended with his father and brothers. The words the men read aloud in this new country were identical to the ones he had spoken his entire life in Poland.

On the last Friday of his second month at the Singer Sewing Machine Factory, Noah was called down to Mr. Brennan's office in the middle of the morning when the supervisors were usually allowed a short, five-minute coffee break. Of course Noah brought his coffee in a thick canister from home, and was actually sipping from it when the messenger arrived from above with the summons. Several of the women working at their machines turned to watch him go, including his one friend whose expression was quite sad, which he found discomfiting. Noah realized he was as anxious approaching the factory manager's office as he had been on the day of his initial interview there. Noah sensed immediately that whatever news the man had to impart, it was not of a positive nature.

"Mr. Unger. This is difficult for me to tell you, because everyone on the floor is in agreement about how hard you have been working, and how conscientious you are," Brennan paused, watching Noah's face to make sure he understood him thus far.

Noah nodded, but didn't say anything, because not only didn't he have the words in English, but wouldn't have known how to defend himself against what he believed was coming next even in Yiddish.

"The women have come to me in a group," he continued. "They have a very hard time understanding what you are telling them to do." Again, he paused.

At this point it seemed a good idea for Noah to say something. "I learn new words at every class. I go to school…" he hesitated, unsure of the English word for 'night'.

"Night school," Brennan prompted. He obviously hated this conversation, and the necessity of having it. "I know that, Mr. Unger. But the progress, though amazingly quick, I admit, is just not quick enough. Production is down in your department."

Noah's quick mind moved rapidly through his options as the other man spoke. Memorizing more words each night would not do. Suggesting he take an additional class during the day and return to the factory in a month was a decent idea, but what would he do for money during the interval? He could not live on the charity of others, even his own brother. Studying privately with his night school teacher was out of the question: there was no way he would be able to pay for the lessons without this job. Even with the job, there was barely enough. The only thing left was the suggestion that he work alongside the women, rather than as their superior.

"Sir. I could…sew," he suggested, but Brennan shook his head. They only used tailors for the detail work, and those men came to the factory after years of training either in small shops here in the states or in their native lands. Having a wife who was a seamstress with her own business was too far removed from the actual labor for Brennan to risk hiring Noah in such a capacity. He had no choice but to let him go, and wish him 'God speed'. The notion that Noah could do 'women's work' and was totally willing to work as a 'seamstress' and not a tailor had not entered the man's mind. Noah did not have the English to fully explain his reasoning. There was no way for either man to continue the conversation.

Although Brennan did not request it of him, Noah was adamant that he would finish out the day. Not only was he being paid to do so, Brennan had offered to give him pay for half a week more, to 'tide him over' until he found another job. At lunch his usual companion was too embarrassed to sit with him, so the half hour passed in total silence. Knowing he had solved multiple problems for the women did nothing to assuage the anxiety that threatened to overwhelm him as he worked that afternoon. It was only the necessity of finishing the day's quota that compelled him to work through it, keeping the darkness at bay until he was walking home.

As soon as he opened the front door of his brother's small apartment and stepped inside, Marlene knew what had happened. Without a word she took her brother-in-law in her arms and held him there, much as she would have held one of her children. When she released him, Noah sat down at the kitchen table with his English book, and proceeded to memorize the words from yet another chapter. The one thing he understood was that if he was to succeed in this new place, he would have to become proficient in this strange language as quickly as possible. He could not let sadness gain prominence if he were to remain a provider for his family so many thousands of miles away. He could not allow the possibility that he might not achieve what he had set out to do in America invade his soul. Noah knew he had to persevere.

After reading a nighttime story to the children of Elias and Marlene in Hebrew, which he had been doing whenever he could since his arrival in Elizabethport, Noah returned to the living room with a heavy heart. Finding no one there, but hearing voices in the kitchen, he slowly walked towards the room, but could not get himself to sit and join in the intense conversation. Instead, he upended one of the kitchen chairs, which seemed to be on its last legs both literally and figuratively, pulled it apart, and then rummaged in the kitchen drawers until he found a hammer, nails, glue and other paraphernalia necessary for its repair. While his brother and sister-in-law talked about their day, occasionally glancing his way, Noah fixed the first chair, setting it upright and sitting on it to make sure it was sturdy. He then upended the other unoccupied chair and repeated the process. By the time he was finished, both Marlene and Elias were watching him work.

"Elias has two left thumbs. I've been after him to fix those things for months," his sister-in-law exclaimed.

"I collected all of our furniture in Monasterzyska from the waste lot, took it home and repaired it. Our hutch was badly scratched, with one missing leg. I never did get that one to match the other three completely, but after I refinished the piece, you could barely tell," Noah replied, chuckling, "I found it relaxing, after a long day 'handling' with cattle buyers."

"Why on earth did you look for a job at Singer?" Elias blurted, looking at his younger brother with utter astonishment.

"What do you mean? To make money," Noah replied, obviously puzzled by the question. Then he realized where Elias was headed. "I don't even have enough money to buy glue, or nails, or anything else I'd need to repair furniture as a business, Elias." He stood and pulled a bottle of milk from the ice box, pouring himself a glass and cutting a piece of cake for himself as well. He stood at the counter next to the sink to eat, his very posture indicating his defeat.

"That much I can front you," declared his brother with some excitement. "If you comb the alleyways, you'll find more junk than you can imagine. There's plenty of room in the yard behind my shop for you."

"What if it rains?" Marlene asked her husband. "The furniture would be ruined."

It was Noah who responded. "I could build a little lean-to to protect the pieces from the weather. I would just need...a few pieces...."

"We have some lumber under the shop," Elias jumped up, his growing enthusiasm contagious. "You can use that!"

"Do you really think people would buy what I fix?" Noah asked them both, afraid to feel hope, let alone excitement, at the thought of beginning such a venture.

"Are you kidding? In case you haven't had time to notice, everyone here is struggling to have a better life for themselves and their families. People can't go downtown and buy new, fancy furniture!" Elias declared, actually sounding indignant.

"But that doesn't mean they don't know good workmanship when they see it," Marlene added with a broad grin.

"If you can really refinish the stuff you pick up and not just nail it back together, I think you'll sell most of it before the glue dries," Elias added with absolute assurance.

"Don't sit on those chairs before morning. You want to give the glue time to harden," Noah said around a mouthful of Marlene's delicious cake. All three were silent, each thinking about what they were proposing while Noah finished his snack. "If you really think I could make a business out of this" – his arms swept over the two upturned chairs – "then I'll spend tomorrow seeing what I can collect."

"I can borrow David's wagon at least one day a week, so you can drive around the neighborhood showing your wares. I'd bet my life you'll have enough for your own wagon in a few months."

Finally, a smile creased Noah's cheeks. "My shop on wheels," he said.

* * *

Simon didn't tell a soul about the sexual difficulties he was experiencing in his marriage to Adelaide or how unsatisfied he felt. But the hope he had held onto the first few months, that she would come around and eventually welcome his touch, had long since evaporated. Were it not for his overly sexual nature this might not have been a problem, given his young wife's talent in the kitchen as well as the pride she took in keeping a clean and sparkling home. Several of the fellows at his insurance company had taken to teasing him about the sandwiches he brought to the job, thick with slabs of juicy brisket, tender chicken, and upon occasion, tasty morsels of thinly sliced leg of lamb. Her apple cake, streusel, sponge cake and stollen were so mouth-watering, that one day he brought her apple cake into the office to share and when he returned home that evening told his wife of the response with pride. Afterwards when she baked for their home she always packed a second cake for him to take into Manhattan with him. Her generosity made him even more uncomfortable about his unhappiness; although he frequently felt guilty about it, that didn't ease his discontent.

Left to her own devises, Adelaide managed to find a singing teacher who had been recommended by Herr Goff, although the woman no longer lived at the address she had brought with her from Vienna. Addie's resourcefulness was enhanced by the boredom she felt cooking and cleaning. Overcoming her usual shyness, Adelaide knocked on Mrs. O'Reilly's door one day, and over tea, asked the native New Yorker about the New York Underground. Writing down the names and numbers of the trains she would be taking, she clutched her purse to her chest, descended the steps to what felt like the bowels of the earth, and traveled into Manhattan. After conquering her fear of enclosed spaces, it seemed like nothing to the young woman to canvas the appropriate building door to door until she located a neighbor who not only remembered the music teacher, but had kept her forwarding address in her little red address book. The next day Addie again decamped for the burrow where her husband worked, easily locating the teacher, who, as it turned out, had recently received a letter from Herr Goff asking how her work with his former star pupil was going.

The letter had been forwarded by the local post office from the address Adelaide had brought with her from Europe.

"I am so glad you have found me," the woman exclaimed after closing the door behind Addie, and smiling warmly at the young woman. "I had already begun a letter to Alan to ask him if he had an address here for you, and now I won't have to finish it!"

Ruth Geiger was a tall, bony woman of indeterminate years. Younger looking than Alan Goff, but with the authority of someone comfortable with her own expertise, Ruth, as she asked to be called, moved immediately to the piano. "Let's see about this voice of yours," she suggested, running her fingers over the keys, and selecting a Mozart tune with a glance at Adelaide, who nodded in agreement as she removed her coat and laid it over the back of the sofa. The Mozart piece was one of her favorites, a tune she had learned when she was only 13 years old, in the early years of Herr Goff's tutelage. After the first few notes escaped her lips, the older woman glanced at her with eyes that were positively shining with pleasure. When she played the last bar of music, fading the final notes with a grace rarely heard outside a concert hall, she sat on the piano stool smiling.

"Well. I would be honored to teach you, Adelaide, although I think I have as much to learn from you as you may have from me." They agreed to meet three times weekly, just as she had with Herr Goff, before Addie returned to the Bronx. When she told Simon that she had found the teacher, he was in the midst of consuming the corned beef and cabbage she had set before him and barely reacted. His lack of response was actually a relief to his young wife, who had been concerned that he would not want her to travel into Manhattan to study, even though he had assured her over and over he was not opposed to her studying.

Simon was also relieved. If his young wife became engrossed in her studies, she would be less likely to object to his evening meetings. Although he could not find satisfaction at home, several of the women he met at the offices of his ever-expanding client list were more than willing to meet his needs. Good-looking and personable, the young man had no trouble finding women who were not only willing to do his bidding, but who seemed to enjoy his efforts as well. Usually they were older fading beauties, who had given up on the idea of marriage, but like Simon, had not abandoned their libidos. Simon, alone, could have disproved the accepted theory of the day, that women did not find sex as necessary as men. Thus husband and wife found peace with one another during their first year together. Each was content with the home life they were creating, largely because of the life they were each pursuing outside of it.

The first time she felt overwhelmed by nausea was on the subway ride back to the Bronx after her Wednesday lesson. Since she had never gotten used to descending into the bowels of the earth, as she thought of it, Adelaide believed that the sick feeling in her stomach was due to her fear of being belowground. By the time she had snapped the green beans for dinner, peeled and chunked the potatoes for the pritschen kartoffel Simon loved, and gotten the roast into the oven, she had all but forgotten about it. When she awakened the following morning unsure she would even make it into their bathroom in the hallway, she was totally nonplussed. Perhaps it was her innocence, or perhaps her need not to know, but it never dawned on her that she might be with child. She continued to cook and clean and practice and sing, but nevertheless, found herself on her knees in front of the toilet several times a day during the initial week of her first pregnancy. Finally, unable to deny any longer that something was wrong, she again knocked on Mrs. O'Reilly's door, this time asking for the name of a doctor. Unwilling to even entertain the possibility of pregnancy, she certainly was not going to voice the thought aloud, instead telling her concerned neighbor that she thought she might have a mild case of the flu.

She was actually so concerned that she didn't give a thought to seeing a doctor named Hennessy, and was greatly relieved he could see her that very afternoon. Surprised that she was asked to disrobe after explaining her symptoms to him, she nevertheless complied behind the screen in the corner of the sterile, white room. Utterly humiliated by the order to place her feet in the stirrups at the foot of the examining table, and feeling utterly violated by the scapula and the doctor's probing fingers, she didn't even care what he might find: she just wanted the exam to be over. Adelaide dressed quickly and then sat down on the doctor's stool until she gained the courage to open the door, walk down the hall, and enter the man's private office, despite her overwhelming need to never see the man again. After all, he had looked at her most private parts with an intimacy she had never even allowed her husband. This she found unendurable.

It was only because she knew she had to catch the bus to the subway and get home early enough to make dinner for her husband, that she did get up, and did open the door, and did find her way to doctor's office. There she sat in the chair opposite his desk, refusing to look up from her own hands, the one sign of protest she allowed herself.

"Mrs. Liebman, I have wonderful news," his voice boomed across the heavy wooden desk at her. "You are pregnant. Now there is no need for any anxiety. You are young and healthy and you will be just fine."

"I am sick every morning," she said, unable to make her voice rise above a whisper.

"I can assure you that will pass," he chuckled. "I will want to see you in two weeks…"

"Whatever for?" she blurted, shocking both herself and Hennessy.

"To take your blood pressure and make sure things are moving along," he replied, adding with both tact and a gentleness she found unexpected, "I won't have to do another internal exam for several months."

Mortified, she felt a tear run down her cheek into her high collar.

"Believe me, you're not alone in feeling embarrassment, Mrs. Liebman. I've been doing this a long time, and I try to make my patients feel at ease. I promise you will get used to me, and I to you, which will make it easier to bear."

'Never' she thought on the ride home. But she was determined to endure the entire, gruesome experience nevertheless, as had her mother and sister before her. She did wish, and not for the first time since arriving in this new country, that she could talk to Sophia. She had never felt as alone.

When she told Simon what she had learned at dinner, after he finished his desert, he jumped up with absolute glee, spinning her around their tiny kitchen in utter delight. "Simon, stop. You will make me sick!" she ordered in a quavering voice. The two stood facing one another beside their kitchen sink, Simon's arms still loosely encircling her waist.

"I suppose I won't be able to do this much longer," he grinned at her. "Ah Addie. This may be just the thing for us, my sweet. A child will make us closer, you'll see."

He actually lay awake for some time after she fell asleep, noticing that her slumber was both heavy and deep. Watching his young wife breathe in and out in the shadowy room, her breath barely ruffling the shirring of her night gown, he felt an unbelievable tenderness towards this stranger he had married, and more hopeful about the union than he had in months. Perhaps the pregnancy and the birth of their first child would make Adelaide more comfortable with the obligations of a wife, and more able to open herself to the joy that could come with them. He believed that the experience of pregnancy, and the medical exams necessitated by it, would help ease his new wife's modesty, which would be a start at least.

A child. They were going to have a child. He realized he hoped the baby would be a girl. The young man fell asleep with a smile on his face, more at peace than he had been since their wedding night. He would love to be a father to a pretty little girl.

CHAPTER FIVE

Yetta was too busy to be lonely. Every day she arose before dawn and stoked the fire to warm the kitchen area so she could prepare a hot breakfast for all four children. In an effort to create additional funds for their current needs, as well as for the growing but small pile of coins she was adding monthly to the cotton bag in the closet beneath her darned and re-darned underwear, Yetta had been able to hire two additional seamstresses since her husband's departure. This meant she could take in more work, of course, but it also meant she had to arrive earlier at the shop and leave later, after the day's work has been completed. Fortunately Nellie was big enough to cut fabric, another task the little girl had gladly taken on. Within the month her oldest daughter would be cutting the patterns for all of the seamstresses in the shop, which would be an enormous savings because it would release two of the women to return to their machines full time. Beck was more of a problem. The little hellion was just learning to toddle about the room, but seemed to have insufficient common sense about what to touch and what to leave alone. Teaching Nell the various skills she would need had taken longer than it should because when Beck was awake, the older child had to mind the younger. Matel was still a baby, so caring for her was not difficult. She dozed in her little basket near her mother's sewing machine, or looked around the room with great interest. Yetta dreaded the day when she, too, would be up and about, because she didn't think Beck would be as reliable a sitter as her older sister. Aware that worrying about an event that wouldn't take place for several months yet was a waste of precious time and energy, Yetta was usually able to push this concern from her mind. Sometimes when she finally lay down in the bed she had shared with Noah since their wedding night, she was less successful at keeping such thoughts at bay. But she was also so exhausted that she usually fell asleep despite them.

One day, when Nell was intent on a particular piece of fabric, she failed to notice that her younger sister had awakened, and was sitting up on the blanket her mother had set up in the corner of the room behind the row of seven sewing machines. Before Nell could catch her, Beck was on her feet, toddling precariously between the machines, happily reaching a wooden box that contained spools of brightly colored thread. Within seconds she had sat down on her rear so that she could reach inside to get a grip on the wondrous things for a closer look. By the time Nell had looked up, spools of thread were unraveling all over the floor, sliding this way and that, beneath the machines, under the seamstresses feet, and rolling towards the apothecary store in the front.

"Nellie!" Yetta turned on her stool to scold her oldest daughter. "I told you watching Beck was more important than that piece of fabric. Can't you do what I ask?"

The only sound in the place was that of the machines continuing to hum. None of the women dared to look at the child or to say a word in her defense. As fair as a boss could be, Yetta also had a temper that could wither the strongest weed. Before she could add another word to the damaging ones she had already uttered, Nell had scooped up the little trouble-maker under one arm, and with the other was grabbing at the rolling spools. Despite fearing for their jobs, two of the younger women grabbed the ones they could reach to help the child. Nell said nothing to her mother, mumbling her thanks to the helpful seamstresses whose movements had been so quick, she wasn't sure they had actually handed anything to her. All of the spools were back in the box in five minutes and everyone was back at work. Little Nellie sat down on the floor with Beck in her lap, one arm resting across her chest so she could massage the other. The child was thankful she neither dropped her sister, nor let any tears sneak down her cheeks, because then she would have had to add humiliation to an already damning experience. Yetta, with concerns of her own, never noticed her daughter's sad countenance, so she never felt the need to offer an apology for her harsh words. Of course the offence was never repeated. Even at four Nell would do anything to avoid her mother's ire.

However, that night, despite her best efforts, Nell could not hold back her tears. She covered her head with her pillow, hiding beneath the quilt she shared with her two sisters. The fear that they might awaken was less a problem than the thought that her mother might hear her and be disappointed. Downstairs Yetta was writing a letter to Noah by lamplight when she thought she heard a strange sound coming from the room above her head. Tip-toeing upstairs so she wouldn't awaken the sleeping children, she nevertheless wanted to discover the source of the sound. Tilting her head as if that would bring the low keening closer, she stopped in surprise when she realized it was coming from the girls' room. She stood in the doorway until her eyes were used to the dark and she could make out the shaking little form hidden by both comforter and pillow. Yetta crossed to the bed, knowing immediately that she had been a harsh taskmaster. The ache in her heart at the distress she had caused this marvelously responsible little maidshen felt huge. Gently she enfolded her daughter in her arms.

"I'm sorry, Mama. I tried to be quiet," Nellie managed between gulps.

Stroking her head and her back, at first Yetta merely crooned, "Shhh. Shhh," until the shaking sobs subsided. "Oh my little Nellie. It is your mama who needs to say I'm sorry. Don't you know how much I depend on you, my little mainstay. If I didn't know you were going to the shop with me every day, I don't know how I would manage."

This newfound information came as a total surprise to the little girl. "What do you mean?" she couldn't help but ask.

"My sweet little one. How could I sew, or show the other women what I want if I had to watch Beck and Matel. I couldn't have this business if it wasn't for you," she explained, continuing to rub the child's back and covering the top of her head in little kisses. Nell was as shocked by the warmth in her mother's actions as she was by her words. Since her father had left for far away, Nell had been afraid to ask for affection from her mother. She had seemed too distracted, too tired, too busy for such a silly request. Nell longed to be strong like her big brother, and as big a help.

Yetta quietly continued, "I have not been a good mama…" only to be interrupted by Nell's "Oh no," but she hushed the child immediately. "No, little Nellie, it is true. I love you so very much, but I haven't taken the time to tell you in so long, or to hold you. Until tonight, I didn't even realize how much I missed our quiet time together."

With a deep sigh, Nell crawled deeper into her mother's embrace, and the two sat that way until she fell asleep. Before Yetta slid into her own bed, she finished her letter, anxious to share what had just transpired with Nell, but knowing she could not because her gentle, thoughtful husband would just worry about the burden he had left behind for her. That night, for the first time she could remember, Yetta quietly cried herself to sleep.

But in the morning, she was herself again, quickly taking care of one chore after another. She was also different, or more herself. She had risen earlier than 4:30 AM, the time she usually rose to begin her day, and by five she had the children's favorite home-baked sweetbread in the oven. Hot cereal was cooking on the stove. Each one of the children, including Jules, entered the kitchen looking expectant. Nell and she glanced at one another, Nell immediately moving to the stove to help her mother pass out the bowels of hot cereal. When Yetta set the hot bread in front of them, Nell insisted that today she sit with them instead of standing by the counter to quickly gulp down her breakfast, and Yetta complied. She let Jules race to the town well to pump enough water for the day before he left for the hahem, and Nell do the dishes by standing on a chair in front of the sink. She dressed the younger girls herself, a real treat for them. Rarely had they received this kind of attention from their mother, who was always a dervish in the mornings, at least since their father's departure. Jules called up the stairs to say good-bye to her and then was out the front door so he would reach his school on time, but not before he heard his mother's voice, thanking him for all his help. As he raced around the block, Jules wondered what had happened to his mother, but then he was at the school, and too busy to think about it. Before Yetta and the girls left for the shop, she buttoned Nell into her warm winter coat, bending down to kiss the top of her head. Together they left the house, Beck's hand in her sister's and Yetta carrying Matel in her arms.

Jules was still late to the hahem, where every morning he helped the melamed's wife with all of her chores, a task he had taken on months before. In this way, the little boy was able to continue his studies, his schooling now free. The only thing that gnawed at his heart was that he was not actually contributing to the needs of his own household, or to the savings fund he was sure his mother had created to help his father pay their fares to the new country. Although he had spoken to his mother about this, she had been adamant in her refusal to let him leave school altogether in order to help the family meet its financial obligations. The second time he raised the issue, she took a letter from an envelope and let him read the instructions Noah had sent from across the ocean months before. By no means was she to remove his son from school: whatever either of them needed to do so that the boy could continue his studies, they would do. Their exceptional son would have the life that Noah's family had been unable to afford for him. When Jules went to bed that night he was still not easy in his mind, but he understood he had to obey his parents. And truthfully, he was grateful to them both for allowing him to pursue his studies, which he relished.

Despite his heavy workload at the hahem and at home, Jules was still an amazing student. He excelled in his studies of Torah, and was usually pages ahead of the other boys. Nevertheless, he had many friends because he was also a personable boy, and like his father before him, filled with a love of play and make-believe. Since most of the boys had many chores to fulfill at home, his life was only a bit harder than theirs, so no one felt a need to ostracize him. The melamid encouraged his young student's gifts without discouraging the other boys, so that Jules would not be seen as 'other' by his peers. Occasionally Jules felt guilty that his closest sister, Nell, had to work so hard without the stimulation of books to help her endure. Even though she was only 4, Jules knew she was very bright, often sitting beside him in the evening learning the aleph bet, and even reading a few paragraphs aloud to her older brother at his urging. As long as all of her chores had been completed, their mother didn't complain. Independent herself, she was proud of her daughter, seeing nothing wrong with a girl learning to read, despite community norms to the contrary. What took place in their own home was their business as far as Yetta was concerned. Noah, from thousands of miles away, seemed to agree, encouraging Jules to teach Nell whatever he could.

One night, Lev Ostrow, the melamed, knocked on their front door, somewhat nonplussed to see his star pupil sitting beside his younger sister with an open study book, clearly teaching her as he had been taught. But the man brushed aside his concern, having come on more important business. After all, this family was planning to immigrate to America, and he had heard it was the norm there for a girl to receive an education, even if it wasn't a religious one. Perhaps after he and Mrs. Unger had talked, he could ask her what she had heard about education in the new land. After moving the children to the parlor couch where they could continue their studies, the adults sat down at the kitchen table over a glass of tea. The teacher spoke softly. He did not want to give his imaginative student a swelled head.

"Mrs. Unger, I have come to talk to you about your son, Jules," he began. Yetta merely nodded, since she assumed that must be his mission. "I haven't had a student as talented in more than five years. The boy excels at every aspect of his learning, and is often a full chapter ahead of the other boys."

Yetta beamed at him, her face alight with parental pride. All she said aloud was, "He is a good boy."

"Yes, he is that as well," Ostrow agreed, immediately continuing. "I have come to urge you to let him apply to the Yeshiva, and attend as long as you remain in this country."

Suddenly Yetta felt shame rather than pride, looking down at her hands because she lacked the courage to raise her eyes to the man's face. If she had to set aside money for Jules to study at the Yeshiva in Buchach, it would be years before the family could be reunited. How her first thought could be about her own need, rather than her son's, she had no idea. "My business is a good one. But the fare for all five of us to join Noah in New Jersey is prohibitive," she said, and stopped. What else was there to say?

"Yetta, there must be a way to allow the boy to flourish while he is still here. He might be able to become a lawyer in your new country if he can't stay at Yeshiva long enough to become a rabbi here. His stature could affect the life of your whole family," he urged, the tone of his voice compounding the power of his words. When he saw the pain in the young mother's eyes, the teacher, more sensitive than most men in the village, reached across the table to take her hand in his. "I am sorry. I did not intend to add another pressure to your life."

"I know Zanvil would have wanted his grandson to continue his studies as he did his son, but we are a family without means. We have taken steps towards another kind of future now because we had no choice, Reb Ostrow. It has been a difficult decision."

"Perhaps I can speak to the Rabbi and a fund could be started," Ostrow mused aloud.

A proud woman from a very early age, Yetta experienced no conflict about what she must do, even if she did not know how. "We do not need the charity of Monasterzyska. I will find a way, even if it means working longer hours. What you have told me is too important to ignore," she agreed, rising from the table. After he had gone, and Jules and Nell had been tucked into their beds, the young woman sat down at the table to begin another letter to her husband. She knew she had to share this conversation with him, even though she knew it would increase the pressure he was already experiencing. Although she had no idea how, since the children had fallen asleep she had gained strength in her resolve to find a way to honor the intelligence of their son by writing to her husband, and was able to retire with a clear mind and open heart. She would manage.

* * *

Adelaide was standing at her kitchen counter, kneading the dough to make a challah for their Sabbath meal when her water broke. Her hands continued to roll the dough from top to bottom, but her attention was on the floor by her feet, where a puddle was rapidly forming in-between her new shoes. At first she felt humiliated that at her age she was unable to hold her water, and then realized that she hadn't _feel_ a need to urinate at all. Stumbling backwards she managed to fall into one of the kitchen chairs, stunned but unable to move as her pains began. For once she was sorry to be in the apartment alone, and wished her husband was beside her. Because she was not expected to give birth for several more weeks, neither she nor Simon had discussed what they would do when the time for her labor approached. They did not have a phone in their apartment yet, but like the other tenants in the building, used the one in the hallway two floors below their apartment. As Adelaide sat in her kitchen, contemplating going down the stairs to call him, she realized she would not be able to climb back up.

'Fionella', she thought to herself before she actually began to panic, pulling herself to her feet by gripping the side of the kitchen table. She managed two faltering steps, but was stopped by a very powerful contraction that took her breath away. Again she hung on to the table, and in this way, using first the table, then the counter, the doorway, and finally the wall in the hallway all the way to her front door, Addie made her way to her neighbor's apartment. Fortunately, Mrs. O'Reilly had not yet left to do her grocery shopping, although she was already standing at her wooden coat rack, wrapping her warm scarf around her neck when Adelaide knocked. Realizing immediately what was happening, she took the young woman's arm in her strong one, brought her into the living room and sat her down on the couch.

Humiliated, Adelaide tried her best to stay on her feet, pleading, "Please, Fionella, I don't want to stain your cushions." She struggled for only a few seconds, finally succumbing to the other woman's gentle shove.

"Pshhh. As if I care about that at a time like this," she grumbled. "Let me have your key, Adelaide, so I can collect your things. Have you packed a bag?" she turned to ask before she reaching the living room door.

Numbly, Adelaide shook her head 'no'. "We didn't think…the doctor said next month…." At which the older woman barked out a laugh. "Shows you how much you can rely on the medical profession!" And then she was gone. Addie had all she could do to breathe during her contractions, let alone spare the energy to worry how the older woman would find what was needed in her apartment. She was not the least bit surprised when Fionella appeared moments later with a small suitcase as well as her coat, scarf and purse. After the older woman managed to get the younger woman's arms into the sleeves of her coat and wrapping the scarf around her head to keep out any chill, she managed to grasp the suitcase in her free hand while holding tightly to Adelaide's arm with the other. It took them at least ten minutes to reach the street because Adelaide had to stop with each contraction, her free hand gripping the stair railing until it passed. She didn't even notice Mrs. O'Reilly leave the vestibule where she still hung on to the railing, or walk in her usual duck waddle down the front stairs to the curb to try and hail a cab. Several raced by, the horses moving at a quick trot, each with a passenger or two within, none available for the young woman in labor. Finally, in despair, the older woman hiked up her skirts, climbed back up the stairs to the front door of their apartment building, and helped the younger woman down them. They made quite an odd pair: the one woman rotund and robust, walking with the short little steps she had adapted years earlier to manage the stress to her knees caused by her weight; and the younger woman, who could barely walk at all, slender except for her belly, which protruded from her winter coat.

They made their slow way to the corner where the trolley stopped, still pausing every few feet while Adelaide waited for her contraction to pass, the older woman holding her up during their entire arduous journey. The trolley driver had spotted their strange routine, and realizing the women were making their way to his tram stop, was waiting for them, a most unusual occurrence in New York City. Fionella managed to push, lift and drag the laboring woman inside, wishing the driver's good will had extended to helping her with the task. Thankfully the trolley was not crowded because it was only 3:30 in the afternoon and rush hour had not yet begun, so Adelaide was able to sit close to the front of the bus.

"Do you stop near the hospital," Mrs. O'Reilly asked the driver, who replied, "Not usually. But I will today. Go sit next to her," he added, motioning to the passenger in that seat next to the laboring mother to move out of the way. "Even if I have to pull over at every stop between here and there, it shouldn't be more than ten minutes," the driver explained in a gentler tone, appearing to understand that he should have risen and helped the women up the stairs.

Sighing heavily, Fionella lurched the short way down the aisle, sitting down with a thump next to the panting Adelaide as he pulled away from the curb. Years later, when both her daughters asked her to tell them about this amazing trolley ride, Adelaide remembered far less than their neighbor. On the day her first daughter was born Addie was barely aware of the stopping and starting of the tram, or the stares of the passengers as they embarked or disembarked. She was too overwhelmed by the pain of each contraction, and the effort it took her not to cry out on a public vehicle, which truly would have been unendurable. When the driver called out "Bronx Hospital, next stop", a young man across the aisle jumped up to take the young mother's other arm and helped Mrs. O'Reilly get her down the trolley stairs to the sidewalk. When he realized that the woman was not ill but pregnant and in labor – a condition made obvious as soon as Adelaide was standing – the color spreading across his cheeks betrayed his mistaken belief and dawning realization. Had she not been so concerned about her young neighbor, Mrs. O'Reilly would have broken into raucous laughter at the young man's expression. But she was actually too relieved to have his help to find him amusing. Thankfully, Simon was already pacing in front of the entrance to the hospital, and raced forward to help his wife, allowing the young man to turn and sprint back to the trolley before the driver pulled away. The three never gave him another thought.

While Simon argued with the admitting nurse about his insurance coverage, Addie sat next to Mrs. O'Reilly across the way from the front desk, terrified that she would have another flood, this time in public. The young woman understood as little about childbirth as she had about what would make her pregnant, and had been too ashamed to ask her doctor. No matter how often Mrs. O'Reilly had told her in passing that nothing embarrassed her, and that Addie could say or ask anything she wanted, there was no way the young bride would have talked to a virtual stranger about such personal matters. Instead she blundered along with practically no understanding about her condition, praying only to survive it. Finally she was helped to her feet by a nurse in white, settled into a wheel chair, and wheeled down the hallway away from the only faces familiar to her in the crowded hospital lobby. She felt a moment of blind panic, but refused to succumb. Her terror was lessened by her immediate need to control her contractions, which were now barely a minute apart and unbelievably strong, all but consuming her normally small frame. When she was wheeled into a room with four beds, three of them already occupied by other young women in labor, at first she felt comforted: at least she would not be alone for this ordeal. But then one of the women let out a blood-curdling scream, which seemed to go on and on and on endlessly. Addie swiveled in the chair as best she could to look at the woman, and then turned back to the nurse who was unbuttoning her blouse, because she had no idea what to make of what she was seeing. Her eyes were frantic, but the nurse didn't seem to notice. As the blouse came off, she did stroke Addie's arm, explaining rather brusquely that all of her clothes would have to be removed so she could put on the hospital gown the other three were already wearing.

"Oh no!" Addie moaned, utterly beside herself. She did not know any of these women, and could not imagine undressing in front of them. Quick to understand modesty when she saw it, the nurse grabbed a screen that was leaning against the wall across from the beds, and unfolded it, affording the reserved young woman a modicum of privacy. With the help of the nurse, Adelaide managed to slip out of her skirt by herself, and then, utterly spent by the effort, raised her arms so the nurse could lift her slip over her head. She held her brassiere close to her chest while the nurse unsnapped it from behind, and was able to slip into the open backed gown before removing it. The last thing she remembered was the relief she experienced at having been able to retain some dignity during the undressing process, and then the pains increased, precluding any further thought at all.

Despite her best efforts, before being wheeled into the delivery room Addie did cry out, "Oh my God, please help me!" In too much agony to even feel embarrassed by this breach of etiquette, she did nevertheless hope that she had not been as loud as her nearest neighbor. Before she could utter another sound, the nurse had started to examine her, much as the doctor had been doing every humiliating month since her initial visit to his office. Then she noticed the needle, and then, mercifully, everything receded from consciousness, including the pain.

When she awakened everything was blurry at first, and confusing. Someone was bending over her bed, although she couldn't at first imagine who it was or why this person was bending down to look at her, and then Simon swam into focus. He was smiling at her in utter delight, which was also confusing at first. And then he stepped aside, and a woman dressed in white handed Addie a bundle wrapped in a pink cotton blanket. The face within it was hot pink, the features squeezed together with effort as the infant began to cry, slowly at first, and then in earnest.

"She's a hungry little thing," the nurse said, opening the dressing gown to allow Addie's breast to fall free. Without even thinking, Addie grabbed the gown and pulled it closed, a loud "Please!" escaping her lips. She barely managed to hold on to the infant with her other hand. The nurse barely reacted, instead shooing Simon from the room and closing the door behind him. Obviously Adelaide was not the first new mother to have responded this way.

"It's a little overwhelming at first, dearie. I've had three, and the first time I had no idea what to do and I was already a nurse," the women explained as she again loosened Addie's gown. Taking the infant in her arms, she maneuvered the crying baby into a better position, inside the crook of Addie's right arm. "You can hold your breast with your other hand, and move the nipple so the little thing can feel it. She can't see quite yet, but she'll know what it is, believe me!"

Hating every moment of it, Addie did as instructed. Indeed the baby knew what to do immediately, grabbing hold with her gums and pulling. The sensation was unpleasant, but certainly bearable after what she has already been through, and at least it stopped the screeching. Closing her eyes for a moment in relief, she heard the nurse tell her that she would leave her and the child alone for ten minutes, so that she could enjoy this, her first experience nursing her own baby.

As the door to the room swished closed behind her departing body, Adelaide wanted to scream aloud in frustration. She had no idea what she was supposed to be enjoying. Looking down at the infant's face, calm now, but intense with concentration, she was shocked at how ugly she found her own child. She wondered for a fleeting moment if her own mother had felt this way when she first looked down at her or her sister, Sophia, who had come before her, after all, or Robert, the firstborn. The notion that her mother had to endure this experience the very first time with a son was unfathomable. Fighting tears at her own lack of motherly instinct, Addie found herself longing to be in her own bed in Vienna, back in the bedroom she and Sophia had shared their entire lives. If she could admit this coldness to anyone, it would have been her sister. Of course she knew that would never happen: first of all, they were worlds apart; secondly, there was no way she could translate these thoughts and feelings into letter form. Adelaide realized in that first moment that she would have to be her own confident, and that she would have to hide her feelings from her husband, who, for some reason, seemed thrilled at becoming a father.

Within seconds her daughter, Holly, had been whisked away in the nurses capable arms, and Simon had returned to the room, followed by

Mrs. O'Reilly. The two of them were so loudly enthusiastic about the beauty of this strange-looking infant, and amazed by the ease with which she had learned to nurse, as well as what that implied about her obvious intelligence, Adelaide did not have to say a word. With infinite relief she closed her eyes and began to drift into sleep. "Whatever are they babbling about," she thought to herself as she sank into her pillows and thankfully lost consciousness yet again.

After a month of baring her breast every five minutes - which was how it felt to the new mother - washing diapers, lugging the baby carriage down and up the steps of their apartment building, grocery shopping, making three meals a day for Simon and herself, Adelaide began to believe she was losing her mind. She could picture the rest of her life unfolding in this manner, where she would become slave to both her child and her husband, these duties becoming all that was or ever would be of her life. So one day as soon as she had put Holly into her crib for her morning nap, Addie took some change from her purse and, leaving the door ajar so that she would be able to hear the baby, she ran down the stairs to the hall telephone. Ruth Geiger was delighted to hear from Addie as well as totally willing to begin their lessons again, even if the young mother had to bring the baby with her into Manhattan. It was with a much lighter tread that Adelaide climbed back upstairs. Knowing that she would be able to continue to have a life of her own altered her entire perspective. She bumped the stroller down the front stairs, bought fresh vegetables for dinner, and walked all the way to Crotona Park, the furthest she had ventured since Holly's birth. She sat on a bench overlooking an expanse of field, holding Holly up so that she, too, could see the man throwing a ball to his son in the middle of it. She was startled to realize she felt content.

Although Simon was distressed to learn his young wife had been taking Holly into the City so that she could resume her singing lessons, he knew, instinctively, that he could not forbid this activity. In awe of her voice and her obvious talent, he contented himself with suggesting she leave the child with Fionella instead. Addie immediately agreed: she was sure she could hand express enough milk for an entire bottle and thus have almost three hours to herself three days a week, more than ample reward for sore nipples. He could not have explained why, but Simon was disappointed that his wife so easily gave up those hours with their new child. Even knowing how important her singing was to her, he could not understand why she didn't relish every moment with Holly as he did. He thought about his little girl on his way from appointment to appointment each day, and found himself anxiously counting subway stops on his way home in the evening, because he could not wait to take Holly into his arms, hold her close to his heart, and then walk with her around the apartment pointing out the cupboard, his new easy chair, a picture of his family taken in Vienna and one of Adelaide's. Just a few days earlier Holly had actually held up her little arms to make it easier for him to pick her up. He found her very scent: baby powder, ivory soap and baby shampoo; enchanting. Much to his surprise, Simon could not imagine a time when he didn't have a child. He told himself that he must remember that he only spent time with Holly in the morning before he had to rush off to catch the subway, and when he returned home before she was put down in her basinet in the evening, a bare hour after his arrival at their apartment. Of course on the weekends he did not find her care burdensome, whether he was changing a diaper or walking with her through the park. He reasoned that perhaps if Adelaide were able to pursue her singing, she would relax with Holly and begin to take pleasure in her company as well. But this did not dispel his unease.

When she arrived at her Wednesday singing lesson, out of breath because she had run all the way to the singing teacher's apartment from the subway station, Addie was startled to discover a well-dressed and obviously cultured man sitting in the parlor. She was quickly introduced, but had no time to become anxious about singing for the conductor of the prestigious Schola Cantorum of New York City. The a cappella singing group had just completed its first tour of Europe, singing to glowing notices in England, France and Germany, which Adelaide had read about in the Sunday New York Times. Although the article had stated that another tour was being planned for the following spring, and that Austria might be added to the agenda, she had never dared dream that she, herself, would ever be auditioning to join the group.

She stepped up to the piano without hesitation, partly because there was no time to allow any, and partly because she felt reassured by Ruth, who smiled at her from her place on the piano stool. Her singing was indeed glorious, her voice soaring to the ceiling, lightly gliding over the notes with ease, and grace. As she finished the Mozart piece, Adelaide realized that she had never felt as excited by anything in her life as singing, or as complete, especially when she performed well, which she had just done. She was also startled to realize that the man's glowing response did not come as a surprise to her. It was his offer of work that was shocking.

"Your voice is an utter delight, as is your command of the room, Mrs. Liebman. There is going to be a full audition next Thursday at our rehearsal room at Carnegie Hall. I will be there, as well as the tour producer, the singing coach, and our two pianists. I would love it if you would come to sing so the others can hear you, though my recommendation that we hire you immediately will count for a great deal, " he explained, rising to shake her hand.

"Yes of course," she managed to stammer, having no idea how she would manage yet another day in Manhattan. She certainly could not ask Mrs. O'Reilly to watch her child for another whole day. The woman clearly admired her for keeping her home, managing a child, and pursuing her singing. But admiration went only so far before it became unease, and finally, disapproval. Adelaide did not want her neighbor to think her a woman with few motherly instincts, though she herself believed that to be true.

After Mr. Gordon left, she explained the situation to her teacher, who came up with a very easy solution. She should skip the Friday lesson, and use Monday and Wednesday to prepare. That way her Ms. O'Reilly would not be watching Holly for any extra time at all. Then Ruth offered to meet Addie at Carnegie Hall for support. She was sure Gordon would allow her to sit in the back of the audition studio. Smiling, she added, "I imagine my presence might make the event less of an ordeal." Adelaide agreed immediately, quite relieved not to have to attend her first audition in the city by herself, let alone an audition for such a prestigious group.

When she told Mrs. O'Reilly that her lesson had been changed from Friday to Thursday the following week, her neighbor assured the young mother that the time change would be no problem. Addie did not like dissembling, but she didn't want anyone to know about the audition. Whether she was more afraid that Simon might think her silly to audition for a group she couldn't possibly join because of her family commitments, or that his attitude could keep her from pursuing such a significant venture, she had no idea. Adelaide just knew that this momentous opportunity was something she needed to keep to herself, especially since it might bare fruit.

On the morning of the audition Adelaide awakened with a surprising sense of calm. She fed Holly with a smile upon her face, which, in turn, pleased her husband enormously. Their morning interaction was easier than usual, Simon even offering to clear away the breakfast dishes when Holly's loud cries bespoke a need for an additional feeding. Adelaide managed to nurse her daughter as well as to dress her to take her shopping at the local butcher and grocer so that dinner supplies would be there for her when she returned from the audition. She was ready to drop Holly at her neighbor's apartment by 10:30, which gave her ample time to make the noon appointment. As she descended the subway stairs she prayed she was taken at the scheduled time, so she would be home in time to have her house in order when Simon returned from his workday. That everything had fallen into place with ease increased her confidence in the day to come.

"Fionella. I never mentioned to Simon that the day of my lesson changed this week. Sometimes simple explanations become so complicated with men," she found herself saying, in absolute amazement at the untrue words flowing from her mouth.

"In thirty years of marriage I never knew what would upset my husband and what wouldn't, Addie. Trust me. There's no reason for Simon to be bothered with our arrangement," the other woman instantly agreed. Her words were both welcoming of further confidences and indicative of the empathy she felt for her young and talented neighbor.

Addie smiled all the way to the subway station. She hummed quietly to herself, sure that the click clack of the train wheels on the track would mask the scales she intended to practice all the way into Manhattan. When she spied Ruth waiting for her on the corner of 57th Street, she greeted her teacher with more warmth than she usually exhibited to others. "My throat feels totally open," she told her mentor. "I've been doing my scales."

"Good. Now let's get you a cup of tea with honey and lemon to soothe it before we go inside. We have fifteen minutes," she replied, sliding her arm into her student's, and leading her to a little coffee shop diagonally across the street from the studio.

Adelaide's confidence faltered momentarily when she and Ruth entered the large audition room. Five other young women were already waiting to audition. Addie had to control herself so she didn't bolt and give in to the words in her head that were telling her she couldn't be as good as any of the others. The first singer missed a high note and then had a difficult time completing her audition piece, which helped Addie considerably. Of course she felt some compassion for the other woman, but her failure also strengthened Addie's confidence. When she was called to perform after the second singer, she was delighted. Not only would she be spared having to wait through the two other applicants, she was sure to make it back to the Bronx in ample time. Nevertheless, her throat momentarily tightened as she stood, and she had to force her breath into submission as she walked to the front of the room and climbed the two steps up to the small platform that was serving as a stage. She handed her sheet music to the pianist, wondering for a fleeting moment why there was an accompanist at all since the group performed without one, and then heard the first notes of the Mozart lieder and began. Addie wasn't aware that the room around her had become utterly still until she had almost completed her piece. Having no idea what this might mean, she forced herself to continue without any hesitation to the end of the piece. Only when the applause began, did she realize what had happened. There had been no applause for the first two singers.

The conductor, voice couch, manager and producer thanked her for coming into Manhattan. As she walked back to her seat, the producer's assistant asked her for a phone number where she could be reached. Adelaide felt her face flush with shame as she explained that they did not have a phone in their apartment, but used the one in the hall, as did all of the other tenants in the building. He assured her that several of the singers in the group had the same limitation, wrote down the hall phone number on his yellow lined pad, and explained that he would be calling her within the next couple of days. "Yes, that will be fine" she replied, voice firm. "We all take messages for one another. We leave them on the board next to the phone." Then she continued to the back of the room, sitting down next to Ruth and listening to the remainder of the singers because she would have wanted them to do the same for her had she been last. But she heard very little, the voices passing in a blur. She realized that Ruth had taken her hand when she sat down and given it a squeeze, but had no idea if she had been the one to let go or if it had been her teacher. When they passed in front of Carnegie Hall on the way to the subway, Addie merely stared at her teacher when she joked that she was sure that someday she would be coming to this great building to hear her student sing, perhaps with someone even more famous than the Schola Cantorum. Adelaide had no remembrance of her subway ride home, or of picking up Holly, or of making dinner, although she certainly did all three. She even allowed Simon his marital due, lying awake afterwards to relive every moment of her thrilling afternoon.

* * *

Noah was very lonely in Elizabeth, despite that fact that he continued to live with his brother Elias and his small family. He loathed sleeping alone on the narrow living room couch and often found himself reaching for his wife, and then waking in confusion when his groping produced no warm body. Afterwards, he would have difficulty falling asleep. When Marlene commented that he was developing deep gray rings beneath his eyes, he shrugged, having no idea how to explain. Coming in one day from a long, fairly fruitless day foraging for junk in his borrowed wagon, he was nonplussed to see a small, narrow bed against the living room wall in place of the treasured family bookcase. Marlene led him into the bedroom she shared with his brother to see its new home next to their bureau. He hadn't the heart to tell her that his sleeping problems had nothing to do with the couch, nor did he suggest they return the bed because he knew that would be insulting. Actually, he did sleep better on the new mattress, no longer having to contend with the cracks between the couch cushions or the two big lumps in the middle cushion that always poked up between his knees and had been unavoidable no matter how he had twisted or turned. He still awakened almost every night with his arm outstretched, groping for his missing Yetta, but was able to fall back to sleep with much less difficulty.

Every evening he stayed awake long after the rest of the family had gone to bed, to re-read the letters he received from Yetta and compose one for her in return. He reread hers so often that the crinkled paper became almost unreadable after only a week had passed. His own letters took hours to compose, because he wanted to sound hopeful about their future; neither did he want to dissemble. Since he felt discouraged, this was no easy task. When he learned that Matel had been sick with the chicken pox, he wanted to race out, buy a boat ticket, and return to take his rightful place beside his wife, watching over both her and their sick child. Of course he knew he could not do this. He also knew that although he was reading the letter now, little Min was probably long over the illness unless it had taken a terrible turn. This thought he pushed from his mind, because there was no point in allowing it to dwell there. Jules had become the 'head of the household', accepting his new responsibilities with grace, Yetta told him again and again. Their son arose as early as she so that he could sweep out the hahem before the other students arrived, and help the teacher's wife cut vegetables for lunch, or any other task she required of him. Their eldest son did all these tasks without demur, helping Yetta with the dishes each night as well before sitting down at the table to pour over his studies before going to bed himself. Hearing about his diligent boy helped Noah persevere, his paternal pride immeasurable.

When he sold his first refurbished table, Elias and Marlene were almost as excited as Noah. The price was a good one, because Noah worked magic with the broken wooden furniture pieces he collected from the trash. He was very pleased that he could begin to contribute to his brother's household, save one dollar for Yetta's journey with the children, set aside two dollars for the purchase of a second-hand wagon and horse of his own, and still have a bit left over for his own necessities. After he sold his first repaired and refinished wardrobe, people from blocks away begin to drop in to see what he was working on, or to ask him to repair a piece they had been thinking of throwing away. Soon the little backyard shed was filled with furniture waiting for his attention. Because he longed to have Yetta by his side, Noah found himself working longer and longer hours, often unable to write his daily letter home until well after 11 at night. Nevertheless, he rolled out of his narrow bed by 4:30 every morning to help Marlene in the kitchen, despite her protests that he should do no such thing. It was another way he could contribute and show his gratitude for all his brother and sister-in-law were doing for him.

The morning he awakened with pains in his thighs and shins, Noah assumed it was because he had hauled two heavy pieces of furniture into the yard on his back the day before, since the wagon could get no closer to his destination than the back gate in the alley. By mid-morning he knew he was not experiencing mere muscle soreness. The aches and pains had traveled up his torso to his arms, his neck, and finally invaded his head with a deep and steady throbbing. Unwilling to give up a day's labor, he pushed himself to collect the pieces of scrap he had spotted in an alley blocks and blocks from home. He knew that if he left it, by the time he came back the next day it would be gone, either to some other collector, or to the garbage dump. He had spied a small dining table that would repair easily with a little sanding and gluing. Small pieces of furniture were sought after by the inhabitants of the many small apartments and cottages in Elizabethport. Several wooden chairs, some without any legs at all, had been thrown in a heap near the table. He could make legs to replace the ones that were missing. Together, the set would sell for a tidy sum, which he was unwilling to give up despite how much his body ached. In an apartment without a dining room such a table would allow a growing family to eat together in the kitchen, or next to a wall in the parlor without taking up so much space that there was no room left for a couch or a comfortable chair.

By the time he had all of the pieces stored away inside the shed, which he had to rearrange first in order to fit them inside it, Noah could barely crawl up the back stairs to the kitchen door. When he stumbled inside, Marlene, who was stirring a stew on the stove, screamed out in fright, bringing Elias on the run. They each supported the trembling man, one under the left arm, the other buttressing the right, and managed to half carry, half drag him into the parlor. The influenza he had contracted was debilitating but not virulent. His life was in jeopardy only the first week. At his urging, Elias wrote to Yetta twice during that time, because Noah was terrified that she would worry that he had been injured or worse if she didn't get any letters at all. Marlene ordered her husband not to tell Yetta the seriousness of the illness, only that it had been incapacitating, which he did in his first letter. By the end of the first week, he sent a second note, saying that though weak, Noah, would be writing to her in a few days himself.

The first week of the illness passed in a blur for Noah, who alternated between throwing off all his covers because he felt so warm, or reaching for them with hands trembling from the chills that had overtaken his entire body so that he could barely pull them up to his chin. He lost almost twenty pounds that week, certainly more than a slender man could afford, but was still adamant that he could walk down the back steps to the privy by himself. By the middle of the second week, he was no longer willing to have Marlene help him back up the stairs into the house, and was strong enough to write a letter to his wife. Towards the end of the second week, when his brother brought him his dinner plate, Noah asked him to sit for a minute.

"You must take three dollars from my savings, so that I am still contributing to the household," he began.

Elias reached out to touch his brother's arm with a gesture that clearly said 'don't be silly'. "Noah, I know how lonely you are. There is no way I would take money from your fund and make you and Yetta wait even longer for her to come here so that your family can be together."

"Yes, Elias. I am lonely. But I am also a grown man. I cannot live here without contributing, like some scrounger. I can see you have another child coming. You cannot afford to support me in the way you have been. I will explain to Yetta." With that, Noah lay back exhausted from the effort of saying so many words, resting the dinner plate on his chest. Marlene had come into the parlor to see why her husband had disappeared, and returned shortly with a plate heaped high with food for him. Elias propped Noah up with two of the pillows from the couch, and the two brothers quietly ate their dinners together, content because they had reached agreement.

Because Noah could not work for more than a month, his savings towards the boat fare for his family dwindled to twenty dollars. He could not afford to wait any longer to buy his own wagon, and knew he had to set aside the extra dollars he was earning in his expanding business for that purpose. Money for boat fare would have to wait even longer, a reality that caused him both pain and shame. It might be months, or even more, before he could again begin to save money for his wife and children. When he explained the necessity of this decision to Yetta by letter, she assured him that a year in the grand scheme of things was nothing. It was more important for him to expand his business so they would be able to afford a place to live when she and the children did come to join him in America. It was important that they both prepare for this future so their children would be assured a better life.

"You must take care of your health with rigor," she wrote to him. "If this means cutting back your hours for some months, that is what you must do."

Of course by the time he received this suggestion, he was again working ten hours a day so that he could not only buy the needed wagon, but begin to replenish the savings he had used to fund his recuperation. Realizing his brother was depressed by this setback, Elias bought an English primer for his brother's children; they could begin to learn the language now, in preparation for their trip to the new country, he explained at the dinner table. Because Noah's focus has been building the business, and being able to bring his family to live beside him, he had not given a thought to the issue of language in relation to either his wife or his children. It was a marvelous gift. Somehow the notion that his children would be preparing for their new life with him in America while they were still living in their Ukrainian village made them feel closer, almost within reach. He was delighted when Yetta wrote to tell him that all of them, under the tutelage of Jules, studied several pages every night except shabbos, and that even she was learning the meaning of the words. Pronunciation might be a problem, since there was no one in Monasterzyska who knew the language, but they could learn that when they arrived in Elizabeth.

By the time Noah had been living in the United States for three years, he had managed to save enough to cover fare for Yetta and two of the children. However, by that time it was also clear that he needed a larger shed. He bought lumber, and he and Elias built an addition over a long weekend. Again, he started to save. Then the wagon broke down and needed a part Noah could not repair himself. It was expensive, and set him back months. The cost of horse feed rose. And on an on, one thing after another. In his heart, he began to wonder if this move had been the right decision. The years seemed to stretch ahead endlessly, the days filled with work and shul and someone else's family. He felt guilty because he loved his brother's children and was grateful for the company of Elias and Marlene, whom he had come to love like a sister. But he longed to hold and teach and talk to his own family. The notion that his children were growing and changing without knowing him had become unendurable. He had already missed the loss of Matel's baby teeth, and she was the youngest. Yetta descriptions of the incidents in the lives of each of the children he had left behind were informative as well as inventive, but he wasn't there to experience any of it, and this had become an ongoing and deepening pain. The meager amount Yetta had managed to set aside from her business would not even cover the cost of the family's trip by train across the Continent to the boat that would carry them to America. Noah began to think that he should return to Monasterzyska, but told no one. At least if he went home, his bright little boy, who was rapidly growing towards manhood, would be able to go to the Yeshiva, and perhaps become a rabbi.

Unbeknownst to Noah, Elias and Marlene had several conversations about his situation in the privacy of their bedroom. Marlene was becoming more and more concerned that he would fall into a deep depression. They had no idea how much he had managed to save since they were hesitant to ask, but they knew by his demeanor that it was less than he would have liked.

"Tonight when he came in the back door, he looked like an old man, stooped over, his step dragging," Marlene sighed, pulling the brush through her hair as she prepared for bed.

"At least when I came here I was alone, with no family back in Poland to take care of, and no one to care for but myself in this new country. I don't know how he does it," Elias agreed.

"I don't think he will be able to go on much longer, Elias. We have to do something to help him. Something he will be able to accept."

"He has become a part of the community here. I don't think our neighbors will want to lose him either," mused Elias.

And thus began the plan. Within the next few days, unbeknownst to Noah, his problem had become a community issue, much as it might have were he still in his shtetl in the Ukraine. On Sunday morning Elias and Marlene pressured Noah to go on a picnic with them to Warnanco Park, a forty-five minute ride by wagon. Of course he had planned to work, since Saturday had long been his day of rest for religious reasons. When Marlene's face dropped in disappointment as she shrugged and walked slowly back to the kitchen, he realized he must relent. These people had done so much for him, how could he refuse to celebrate the beauty of the spring day with them? He followed his sister-in-law into the kitchen to tell her that he had changed his mind. What could he do to help her prepare? Her face immediately broke into the endearing crooked smile he had come to love, which was reward enough for his lost hours of work. After paring and cutting some apples and pears for the ride, he and Elias carried two picnic baskets heaped with food for the five of them – Noah, Elias, Marlene and the two children – who were racing up and down the back stairs in excited anticipation about the outing. The ride, itself, was quite lovely. Noah sat on the bench behind his brother and wife with the two children, pointing out sights he knew, like the sewing factory and railway station, and listening to the descriptions of those he had never seen before with the same eager interest as the children. The fruit he and Elias had cut up earlier were crisp and delicious. As the children tumbled from the wagon, Noah looked around him at the beauty of the fields leading down to a small lake in the distance. Turning around with a grin to grab one of the over-stuffed baskets, he thanked both Elias and Marlene for urging him to come. The beauty of the place reminded him how much he had missed the countryside.

While Marlene spread the blanket and emptied the baskets, he and Elias threw a big ball to the children, roaring with laughter when little Elsie, only 4, could not grasp the thing in her little arms but laughed with absolute abandon as she chased it down the hill towards the lake. The picnic was a big success. There was sliced meat, and tomato, and lettuce, corn on the cob, an American invention, three-bean salad, pickled herring, deviled eggs, fresh seeded rye bread, and for desert, a marvelous kugle pudding with raisins, which they all devoured. When they were done eating, the children were so exhausted from the excursion, the games and the meal they both drifted into sleep. With a loving smile, Marlene gently covered them with the cotton blanket she had brought along for just that purpose. Then she and the men lay down on the 'adult' quilt a short distance from the sleeping children so they wouldn't disturb their slumber.

"Noah, dear Noah," Marlene began, the gentleness in her tone surprising him; he turned his head to look at her as she continued. "You are working so hard I am worried about you again." He shrugged to indicate there was nothing for her to be concerned about.

"We know how depressed you are," Elias jumped in. "You are not a good dissembler." When his brother started to open his mouth to deny this obvious truth, Elias held up his hand. This silenced Noah, who turned away to stare out over the lake. Elias forged ahead. "We may not have a Bikkur Holim here, but we do have a caring community. People who live as much as ten blocks away from the shop came to help Marlene when Elsie was born. Our little one had developed a fever almost immediately. It was very comforting to have those women stop by so that Marlene was never alone."

"I don't know what I would have done without them, Noah."

"No one in this little community wants to lose you, my brother. Most of us have come to depend upon you, not only for your ability to restore the most useless looking piece of furniture, but for your intelligent counsel as well," Elias said, reaching out to take his brother by the arm. "Noah, I need you to listen to me."

"I am listening," Noah muttered.

"Everyone is afraid you will return to Monasterzyska because it is taking so long for you to earn the money to bring Yetta and the children here," Marlene explained.

Again the shrug. "If that is what must be, than it must."

"That is not what we believe, as a community," replied his brother. He then removed a small leather pouch from the pocket of his jacket, tossing it across the blanket to Noah.

"What is this?" he asked as he automatically reached up to grab it.

"Open it and see," Elias suggested.

When Noah saw the dollar bills, and the coins, he dropped the bag as if it contained hot coals. "What can you be thinking?" he asked, his voice rising in anger, unusual for the reserved young man.

"This comes from your neighbors, Noah. It is just the beginning," his brother gently explained.

"No. Absolutely no. This must stop!" Noah sprang to his feet, looking as though he might run all the way back to Elizabeth. With quiet fury he glanced down at his brother and wife. "I may not be a member of the balebatim, but I am also not a beggar. My family has never borrowed a penny from anyone, Elias. And you should know that!" Noah was so furious he could not even continue.

"No one is lending you a dime, Noah. All of your neighbors and clients are giving you this money in thanks for all you have given them," replied Elias, shocking Noah into silence.

"I cannot accept this," he finally managed. "And neither would Yetta. You must know that." His demeanors was deflated, all of the anger drained away. All that remained was anguish.

For several moments all three were silent, the only sound the ducks quacking occasionally in the distance. Noah sat back down on the blanket, wrapping his arms around his knees and staring again into the distance.

"You can't give back this gift, Noah. That would insult all of the people who have given to you out of heartfelt sympathy," Marlene murmured.

"Noah. When we helped people who were having hard times back in Monasterzyska, did you ever blame them for accepting what our community was able to offer them?" When Noah did not respond, Elias again asked him, "Did you?"

Sighing, Noah replied, "Of course not. But this feels different."

Kindly, Elias suggested, "It feels different because you never expected to be someone who would need help."

"Did you?" Noah's voice again rose in annoyance.

"Of course not.

"And Elias would have had as hard a time as you are," Marlene suggested to them both.

"Yes. I would," Elias agreed. "I would have been miserable. But I also know you have to accept this, because you need your wife here. It is time. Between the money in this pouch what is still being collected, what you have saved, and the money Yetta will receive when she sells your house, you won't have to wait any longer."

The very idea felt so marvelous that Noah was afraid his heart might fly out of his chest and travel all the way to Monasterzyska without him. "By the time she gets my letter explaining all this, there will be enough money," Noah marveled. "I don't know what to do."

"You must accept, Noah, so that you can have the life you have dreamed of for more than three years now," Marlene told him.

"I will think about it tonight," he replied.

One of the children stirred, and Marlene jumped up to sit next to the other blanket so the toddler would know she was there when he awakened. Her face, however, remained glued to her brother-in-law, so that she could assess his feelings from the expression on his face.

"I won't take days, Marlene. I just need to give it some thought."

* * *

When the hall phone rang downstairs and no one answered it by the third ring, Simon yelled to his wife that he was going down to answer the phone, taking the stairs two at a time and grabbing the receiver before it stopped ringing.

"Hello? Yes?" he asked, his inflection still European.

What he heard on the other end came as a total shock. Had anyone been watching him they would have thought that someone close to him was either ill, or dead. He replied in monosyllables and then slowly hung up the phone. He didn't take the stairs two at a time on his way back upstairs. It wasn't that Simon disapproved of his wife singing with the prestigious Schola Cantorum, but that he was shocked she hadn't even told him she had auditioned for the prestigious singing group. He wondered if she had taken Holly with her, or left her with Fionella. If she had left the baby behind, had Fionella also been keeping this secret, or hadn't she known where Adelaide was going either? He stood outside the door of their apartment for several minutes to collect himself. He wanted to appear excited for Adelaide, but he felt numb. Simon knew the anger at being somehow betrayed would come later; now he had to share the news he had just received with his wife.

"Addie!" he called out from their front hallway.

"What is it?" she called back. "My hands are covered with flour. Can't you come back here?"

Walking back to their kitchen, he managed a forced smile with the hope that it would appear natural to her.

"Well, that was an interesting phone call," he began.

She looked up from the dough she was kneading. The fleeting look that momentarily crossed her face seemed a guilty one to Simon, but that might have been because of what he had just learned. He was dismayed to realize that his wife was afraid of him, but instead of arousing compassion, the very idea infuriated him.

"How could you keep your audition for the Schola Cantorum from me?" he began in a normal voice. "What did you do with Holly? Was Fionella part of the conspiracy?" As the questions mounted, so did his voice, until he was yelling at her across the width of the kitchen. Holly started to cry. He reached his daughter in three long strides and lifted her from the high chair. "Stop looking at me that way, damn it! Yes, you've been accepted. I just wish I could feel pleased for you."

"Well, maybe that tells you why I didn't share the news of my audition with you," Addie glared at him, equally angry. How could he ruin this marvelous moment for her?

Clasping the child to his chest, he spoke in a quieter voice, but one obviously filled with both hurt and anger. "Don't you dare make your secrets my fault!" Holly, who had been silenced by their exchange, looked from one to the other, almost as if she was following their conversation.

Adelaide could not argue with him. He was right. She had kept a secret and it had not been a little one. She wiped her hands on her apron without any awareness that she was doing so, took a deep breath, and looked directly at her husband. Her entire body was shaking.

"It was wrong of me not to tell you, Simon. But I was so afraid they would turn me down, and then I would have to handle not only my disappointment, but my shame in front of you as well," she said, voice faltering.

Since the idea that being rejected might seem shameful to his wife had never entered Simon's mind, he was almost silenced by her response. He was finally able to manage, "I would hardly think less of you, Adelaide. I am smart enough to know that the competition to be accepted into the Schola Cantorum must be enormous."

"I wasn't sure you would want me to audition," she finally admitted, close to tears. She had only cried once in front of Simon, and that had been on their wedding night.

Because she was being honest, Simon felt forced to be honest as well. "I might have tried to stop you," he muttered.

"I can't merely be your wife and Holly's mother, Simon. I hope in time you will come to accept that," she replied, sweeping past him with an imperiousness surprising in one so young, and left him in the center of their kitchen, alone, holding their child in his arms. He was immediately sorry he had said nothing about the pride he felt to be married to someone with such a talent and now it was too late. Although he realized it might be unreasonable, he didn't totally understand why she couldn't be satisfied taking her lessons and singing for their friends. Between those little pleasures and their child, shouldn't she have been satisfied? Even at this early stage of their life together, Simon realized he did not offer his wife all that she needed. If he was willing to live with that knowledge – surely a daunting task – why couldn't she live without performing?

That night, and for many more over the months ahead, the two slept side by side and back to back, each facing the edge of the bed, careful not to touch one another when they turned over during the night. They had sex, because Addie felt she could not deny him, but it was even less loving than their usual thrashings. For the first time in his adult life, Simon experienced little desire for a woman's body, any woman. It was as if that part of his nature had retreated along with the hope that his home life would improve.

Addie actually celebrated with Fionella, who was terribly excited at her news. Over tea and scones, she asked where Simon was taking her to dinner, a question Addie deflected with mumbled words describing their busy schedules. Because she was so proud of this young woman whom she almost felt as if she had raised, it never entered Mrs. O'Reilly's mind that Simon might not be pleased with his wife's accomplishment, even though a woman pursuing a career in 1910 was most unusual. Despite the continued tension in her home, Adelaide could not hold back her excitement when she sat down on the subway train for her practice sessions in Manhattan. It had gotten easier for her to expel enough milk for the two bottles Holly would require, so the three-hour rehearsal sessions would not be a problem. She had also become adept at getting the child dressed and down the stairs by 9 AM with ample time to do the daily grocery shopping, stop in the park for the toddler to crawl around on the grass, and return home to nurse her and put her down for her nap at Fionella's before she had to leave for the city.

An uneasy truce developed between husband and wife. Adelaide made Simon his favorite dishes, making sure she included a homemade pastry in the lunch she packed for him every day as well as an extra sandwich. She never asked if he ate it all, and wouldn't have been upset to learn that he usually fed the extra bread to the pigeons in the park. When one of the other salesmen saw him trying to open his mouth wide enough to bite into his sandwich, which he had stuffed with the meat from both sandwiches, he burst into applause when he succeeded. After the two men were able to contain themselves, Simon explained that he could not eat two sandwiches, but didn't want to waste the extra meat. The other man, who was not nearly the salesman Simon was, and had no wife to make him lunch, was delighted when Simon offered to share his daily repast with him. And thus, unbeknownst to Adelaide, the huge meal she prepared was enjoyed by two men, not one.

The evening Simon returned home with a bouquet of flowers for his young wife, and a new toy for the apple of his eye, Addie removed two of her European crystal wine glasses from the dining room hutch, although she had no idea what had occasioned her husband's generosity. The red wine he selected from their small stock went well with the evening's pot roast dinner. Addie did not object when he poured her a second glass, nor when he offered to give Holly her evening bath. By the time the little girl was in bed, she had washed the dishes and put them all away. Although she had certainly not come to enjoy the sexual act, that night she vowed to try to welcome the touching that seemed to mean so much to Simon before he actually climbed on top of her. He was, after all, making an effort, and so must she. Finding a way to live in close quarters seemed as essential to the young wife as it did to her husband, since neither would have dreamed of asking the other for a divorce. It was actually a relief to them both when she came to bed wearing only a loose robe, and one that was easily opened. When she took his hand to kiss each of the fingers, Simon was shocked by his body's immediate response, as well as relieved to discover that he hadn't become less a man, which he had begun to fear. When he finally used his arms to lift himself above his wife, who wrapped her legs around his back, she didn't turn her head aside as was her habit, but actually met his lips with her own. Much to her own surprise, kissing him while he moved inside her made the usually abrasive movement almost pleasurable. For once, the two fell asleep wrapped around one another instead of back to back, and as a result both had a better night's sleep.

Several days later Simon was even able to ask his wife when her new group would be performing, adding with a grin, "Or do you only rehearse?"

Addie, at last understanding the flowers and wine from earlier in the week, turned from the stove where she was stirring the soup that had been simmering all day for their dinner. "Would you really come to hear us?" she asked him with surprise.

"Of course I would, Addie. Whatever could you be thinking?" he replied with equal surprise. He might not understand why she needed to do this thing, but he was also proud of her gifts, something he had yet to share with her. When she didn't immediately respond, he added, "There are a couple of men at work I thought I'd invite. I'm sure they and their wives would enjoy a night on the town."

And so it was that Simon, his lunch buddy, two of the other salesmen and their wives, as well as the boss and his wife entered Town Hall together for the fall concert of the Schola Cantorum, which would become a yearly New York event, and one popular with the city's elite. Fionella was also in attendance, arriving at the last minute with another neighbor from the third floor whose daughter had offered to watch the already sleeping Holly but had been kept late at work. The two women almost hadn't arrived in time for the first number, which would have upset Addie greatly, since she could see the first few rows of the orchestra where they all were to be seated.

Simon's mouth opened in complete surprise when, in the middle of the concert, his young, pretty wife stepped forward and began to sing alone, her voice soaring out into the hall with a clarity even he knew was unique. Fionella, who had known Addie had been given a solo to perform, turned to Simon with a huge smile plastered across her face, her brown eyes almost obliterated by her chubby cheeks. "Isn't she amazing?" she asked him. Simon took her hand in reply, his throat too constricted to respond.

Indeed, his heart could not help but swell in pride as he looked about him, and saw the rapt attention on face after face in the audience surrounding him: for his wife, for Adelaide Liebman. When their guests crowded into the dressing room after the concert, Adelaide smiled modestly, with flushed cheeks, at the rush of compliments. She laughed aloud when Simon lifted her off the floor and spun her around the small room, protesting that he must put her down before they broke a jar of makeup or she kicked someone. Everyone, including the concert master, walked to Rumpelmeyers for coffee and pastries after the concert, Addie linking one arm through the arm of a fellow singer with whom she often had tea before returning to her duties in the Bronx, and the other around the waist of her husband. When he stood to offer a toast to her in front of everyone, she was startled to find she was pleased rather than embarrassed and raised her glass to him as well. The entire room erupted into applause.

It was a grand evening. In many ways, it was also the beginning of their marriage. Certainly for Adelaide, the beginning of the marriage she had always wanted, and a union Simon was coming to accept.

CHAPTER SIX

Yetta began to dread the dawn, barely managing to sit up, take several shuddering but deep breaths, and finally rise so that she could stoke the fire and make breakfast for the four children. She was unbearably lonely, unable to remember life with Noah or to imagine it without him. The only person with whom she had been able to share her distress was Nell. Even at eight, the little girl seemed adult: serious, dutiful, and remarkably aware of the feelings of those she loved. She had not admitted to her mother that she could not remember what her father looked like, but she had shared that she, too, found his continued absence unbearable. Although there were many village children with fathers living in the new world, none had been gone as long as hers. Nell had no idea what to think: was her papa less able than the fathers of her playmates who were already packing, or soon expecting the requisite funds for their trip to a new life? One night, shortly before the family received the letter telling them the separation was at an end, all of the children, led by Beck, sat their mother down after dinner and urged her to write to their father to tell him to return to the Ukraine. It would be better to be a family than to wait endlessly for a move that somehow seemed too much for them to arrange. The family sat in the tiny parlor staring at one another until Yetta held out her hands, which were grasped by first Nell, and then Jules, who in turn each reached out for Rivka and Matel until all of them were hanging on with no clear notion how their father might respond. No one in the village would have believed the sight: affection was part of shtetl life, and certainly that of the Unger family, but clinging was unheard of.

That night Yetta stayed up even later than usual struggling to compose a letter to her husband that would not make him feel a failure. She realized that if it were humanly possible for him to have raised the necessary money, Noah would have done so. She concluded that conditions in the new world must not be much better than those he had left behind. Though terribly grieved to admit it, Yetta was in agreement with the children; she knew she had to urge her husband to come home. The following morning she again had a difficult time getting out of bed, and was therefore late ushering everyone out of the bungalow. Her carefully composed letter remained on the kitchen counter, forgotten in the scramble to be on time. It became a family legend over the years, this unsent letter that would have crossed Noah's more optimistic missive somewhere in the middle of the Atlantic Ocean. Unbeknownst to anyone in the family, Beck saved that letter for years, hiding it with her underwear in the suitcase she and Nell were to share on their way to a better life. Before Yetta's death many years later, she took it out of the same suitcase, which she had stowed in her attic all the years she had been married to Morris, to show to her mother. Fortunately for all of them, Noah never returned to Monasterzyska, and the rest of them were living with him in New Jersey before the year was out. Within three years to the day Yetta first set foot on American soil, she and her husband were planning to buy and renovate their own building, with a workshop downstairs and an apartment above, something they never would have been able to achieve had they remained in the Polish Ukraine.

In Monasterzyska when Yetta returned home a few evenings later, exhausted by the long day in her shop, she found her own letter under a pile of socks waiting to be darned on the kitchen table, as well as an answering one from her husband on the front stoop. When she finally sat down to read the words within it after the dinner dishes had been laid out on the table and the meager dinner soup set on top of the burner to heat, she raced from their home so that she could reach the butcher shop before it closed. There she bought an entire leg of lamb for their evening meal, even though it would mean a late dinner. That letter was worthy of celebration; none of them had had such a feast since the last religious holiday and it was time. When Jules arrived home from the heder at 8:30, the smells wafting from his mother's kitchen were enough to make him set down his schoolbooks and look at her and sisters in total puzzlement. Their father's return wasn't cause for such festivity, even though he would certainly be happy to see him again, and go for a walk in the woods by his side. Jules stood in the middle of the parlor, looking from one sister to another, as each shook her head in confusion.

"I made the lamb, don't worry. I didn't leave it to Mama," Beck explained, but those were the only words any of his sisters uttered. None knew more than he.

Then Yetta came into the small front room from the kitchen, smiling broadly. "She did let me boil the potatoes, and I have mashed them the way you like, with gobs of butter and creamy milk, fresh from the cow." She beamed at them all, motioning them to the dining room table, which she had already reset with the family's best dishes. When they had all sat down, Yetta handed one wine goblet to Beck who sat beside her, and then another, until all of them, even six-year old Min, held one. She then reached for the carafe of wine they had not finished at Pesasch, and poured each of them a small tot.

"I have something I want to read to you, my sweet children" she said as she placed the eyeglasses she now used for close work low upon her nose.

"My dearest Yetta. Before you object, understand that accepting this gift has been very difficult for me as I know it will for you, but Elias and Marlene have helped me see the wisdom in doing so."

He had written in Yiddish, of course, but the children all stared at her in puzzlement. From her other apron pocket, she removed a bank draft and continued to read Noah's letter aloud. "Although Elizabeth is not a small town like our Monasterzyska, the little neighborhood we live in operates in much the same way. The neighbors, people whose furniture I have repaired and sometimes even advised about a personal problem when they have come to me with one, raised this money so that I could be reunited with my family. At first I refused to accept it, but Marlene helped me understand that to do so would be an insult to the good will of the entire neighborhood."

"Does this mean Papa is coming home?" little Min asked, unable to restrain herself a moment longer. Some of the words in the letter were beyond her scope, despite her evening studies with Jules, who was determined that all of his sisters learn to read.

A beaming Jules stood, pulled his youngest sister to her feet, and waltzed around the room with her, pushing aside furniture as he twirled her around in the small space. His awkward movements were hilarious to watch as he dodged a chair, a cushion, a pile of books; within seconds everyone was laughing and whooping, even the usually temperate Nell, which confused little Min all the more.

Yetta continued to read in the midst of the chaos and laughter, including her own. "With the money you will collect from the sale of our house and its furnishings, you should be able to immigrate as soon as that is accomplished. Make haste. Now that I have accepted this gift, I fall asleep every night awaiting your arrival, and awaken in the morning disappointed that you are not beside me, and the children in the next room."

"What room? Where?" Min shouted so that her siblings would pay attention to her, tears of frustration beginning to slide down her cheeks.

Yetta took her youngest daughter in her arms, and to the shock of the other children, continued the dance begun by Jules. "We are going to America, little one. We are joining Papa!" she repeated over and over, almost making a song of it.

The feast that had been prepared by Beck was consumed with utter joy despite the late hour. Every plate was filled until it overflowed, and every mouthful that was not consumed was wrapped and saved for the next day's lunches. None of them had eaten such fare in a very long time. "Do you think we will eat this way every day in America," Nell mused aloud as she chewed a piece of lamb liberally dipped in mashed potato. For once her mother didn't scold her for such slovenly eating habits. "Perhaps not quite this well," she replied with a smile. "After all, it did take Papa a long while to be able to send for us, and he has only been able to do so now because of the help of his community." When she noticed the look of concern that immediately filled the faces of her three daughters, she added, "But I am sure we will eat well. Elias was a skinny young man when he left here, and look at him now." She grabbed the picture of Elias, Marlene and the children that had been sent by Noah only months before, and everyone crowded around her chair, looking down at a plump man with a mustache but no beard.

"Jews must not let their beards grow in this new country," noted Beck. "I presume our Uncle Elias, Jewish through and through when he departed, has remained so in Elizabeth." Her witty remark caused even more hilarity as the children carried plates and serving bowls into the kitchen to help their mother with the evening cleanup.

It was only when he was drying the dishes Yetta had set on the counter after the girls had been persuaded to go up to bed, that Jules realized this meant he would never attend the Yeshiva. It was with deep shame that he also realized how disappointed he felt about this loss, despite the obvious benefits of this move for his family. Startled, he knew his mother was staring at him,

"Whatever happens in America, son, your father and I will make sure you receive the education you deserve. It may not be a Jewish education, or have the depth of learning you would have attained at the Yeshiva, but you will not be left behind," Yetta assured him. To hide his tears Jules turned to carry the platter he was drying back into the parlor where it belonged, but stopped when he felt his mother's hand lightly touch his wrist. "I am disappointed for you, too, Julie. But I am a fighter, and I mean what I say." She pulled her son into her arms, and the two stood thus enfolded, saying nothing, but offering comfort to one another on this very special night.

Yetta found a buyer for the house the very next day during her lunch hour, and thus the family began their journey to their new life.

* * *

On the subway ride back to the Bronx after her Friday rehearsal, Addie practiced different ways to tell her husband that the Schola Cantorum had been invited to tour the Continent, beginning with a concert at the new Konzerthaus in Vienna. Although she realized he would want to see his family, she expected objections because of the expense if the entire family were to join her on this tour. Even more worrisome was how her husband would feel about her expanded rehearsal schedule, and the growing conflict between her life as a singer and her role as a mother. In Europe she would not only be rehearsing but giving weekly performances as well. Even she did not know how she would manage it all. By the time she climbed the subway stairs to the street, she had decided she would suggest writing to her sister, Sophia, who had two children of her own, and would certainly know the name of a Nanny. Perhaps Holly could join her cousins each day, and the entire experience would be one of adventure for her rather than loss. At any rate this was what she planned to suggest to her husband at dinner.

With the need for persuasion in mind, she stopped at the butcher shop to pick up a large New York style steak, an American staple Simon had come to relish. She would garnish the meat with his favorite potatoes, thinly sliced, slathered in butter, roasted in the oven for more than an hour, and then topped with cheese under the fire the last few minutes before the platter was brought, steaming, to the table. Climbing the stairs to the apartment, Addie found herself smiling. If she was honest, and shared this news with her husband the day she, received it, he would accept the inevitable. He must, she told herself, key in hand.

When Simon smiled at her across the dinner table, set with their best China and glassware, and said with a broad grin, "I'm one step ahead of you, baby" Addie's mouth gaped. The American slang was not a surprise – Simon picked up new words on a daily basis, probably from his customers, and loved using them – it was the smile that shocked her into silence. "To our trip abroad!" he saluted, raising his wine glass and motioning his wife to raise hers. She picked up her glass, which he clinked with his, a habit she detested because the glasses came from her mother's house in Vienna, and she was terrified of losing even one of them. As she sipped, she eyed her husband over the rim, waiting for him to explain.

"I knew it was only a matter of time before your group again toured Europe," he began.

"How did you know the Schola had performed on the Continent?" she blurted, surprised that he would be privy to information even she hadn't known until Lotte had found an old program for her after she had been accepted into the group.

"I called the business office and asked what countries the group had visited in the past, and when the next tour was planned, explaining that I had family in Vienna," he beamed at her.

"Why?" she asked him with genuine puzzlement. She, herself, had never thought about it. Singing in New York's Town Hall had been a highlight, and quite enough for Addie to take in. In truth, she hadn't wanted to know because she and Simon had achieved a peace she didn't want to threaten in any way, even with information.

Her husband relished the wine he held in his mouth and finally swallowed. "It was a natural assumption. And it gave me a business idea."

This news was in fact very interesting to Adelaide, who had come to respect her young husband's acumen in that arena. "What kind of idea, Simon?" she asked with both curiosity and enthusiasm.

Proud of what he had accomplished as well, Simon was only too happy to explain. "I told Cohen that your group would be singing in Vienna, Berlin and Prague in the fall and suggested that I query a few of the smaller firms in each city to see if they might welcome a partnership with us. That way, when a family planned to emigrate, they could order insurance before they ever set foot on a boat. The two companies could share the commission."

"What a good idea. Wherever do you get them?" she asked, utterly amazed at how clever this young man could be when it came to business opportunities.

"I really don't know, my little songbird. But it's a good idea isn't it?" He beamed at her, not really expecting an answer. "Anyway, Cohen is pleased with me, and has gotten the names of several companies there. While you rehearse I will meet, and Holly will play with Sophia's children. Ach, the world is an exciting place," he concluded. With that he arose, taking her plate in his hand, stacking it with his own, and carrying them both into the kitchen, an action in and of itself a cause for concern. "I will put up a pot of coffee, to go with your apfle kuchen. But you see…" he turned back to shower another glowing smile on his stunned wife. "You didn't have to win me over with your marvelous cooking. Not tonight."

Addie was left alone in their small dining room, astounded. Not only would the entire family be going to Europe, Simon had already thought about leaving Holly with Sophia and her girls. She hadn't had to suggest it. In amazement she realized that he had accepted that she, too, had a career. During the entire dinnertime conversation her husband had not uttered a word that would inspire guilt.

The voyage by ship to the Continent was perhaps the most romantic holiday Addie and Simon had taken with one another. The older couple in the cabin next to theirs found Holly enchanting, and even offered to babysit a few evenings so the younger couple could join other young couples on the dance floor. On the way to the ship's salon Adelaide told Simon she felt too shy to dance with him in such a public place, especially with the dances now in vogue, but was nevertheless cajoled, laughing, onto the dance floor by another couple who were seated at their table. "We'll teach you how to dance, American style, and then you can show us Vienna, sweet Addie," Naomi, the wife urged, grabbing her hand and pulling her onto the already crowded space. "You see," said Simon. "No one is even watching." Despite her natural inhibitions, Addie enjoyed the evening, and never thought to suggest she and her husband leave early to check on their child. Looking around her with some surprise, she realized that the four of them were among the final dancers on the floor. The dances had felt less risqué than she had feared they would. Delighted by the evening, Simon pulled his wife into his arms, whispering into her ear, "Thank you, my dear, for one of the best evenings of my life." Before she could take them back, the words, "Yes, Simon, for me too," bubbled up from within, which made her hide her head in embarrassment. After saying goodnight to Naomi and her husband Phillip, the transplanted Austrians slowly sauntered back to their cabin holding hands. Addie allowed his whispered words of endearment, and even welcomed them. She did not object to his lovemaking either, because she knew that their child's sleep was deep in the middle of the night. For the first time Simon's deep kisses didn't seem repellent, although they caused an embarrassing flutter deep within her tummy. For once the rest of the evening wasn't repugnant either, although she didn't experience actual pleasure. It was bearable, and that was enough. She lay awake in wonder long after he had drifted off to sleep. How her life had changed in an amazingly short time.

Little Holly charmed everyone she met in Vienna starting with all four grandparents, her aunts and uncles, and particularly Adelaide's father. The very first morning he heard her gurgling in the tiny trundle they had moved into the guest room for the child, he tiptoed into the bedroom so that he wouldn't wake his daughter and son-in-law, finger to lips. After lifting the little girl into his arms, he carried her down to the kitchen where he prepared a bowl of cereal for her, a cooking chore he had never before admitted he even understood. It was too early for the cook to have begun her household tasks, so the old gentleman gallantly put up water to boil to take care of his little granddaughter's needs. When Addie awakened with a start, noting the empty crib, Simon pulled her back down beside him with the words, "Your papa came and got her hours ago, my sweet. Stay here with me just a little longer." She again allowed his advances, though her ardor was much dampened by the thin wall separating her from her mother, which Simon found amusing.

When the young couple finally entered the family dining room, an argument was already in progress. Sophia wanted to take Holly to the dressmaker with one of her own daughters, so that a little gown could be made for her in anticipation of Addie's concert, only a week away. Finally grandpa, who had planned an excursion to the amusement park with his youngest grandchild while he had been feeding her the cereal he had made, relented, agreeing that having such a dress made for her was more important. It was with some bemusement that both father and mother watched their daughter happily leave the house without them, holding her Aunt's hand and never once looking back at them, although they were both standing in the front doorway waving. They left the house a half hour after their daughter, Addie going to her rehearsal, and Simon to his first appointment with a European insurance company, the firm where he, himself, had begun his career.

His old boss was obviously proud of the distance Simon had traveled since leaving his employ, clearly claiming credit for the young man's rapid advancement in the new world. Although he could not afford to join his young protégé's project, he suggested several larger firms and called ahead to arrange a meeting for Simon with the head of each firm. The manager at larger of the two was, indeed, excited by his proposal; by the time he met his own father for lunch near the tailor's shop, Simon had his first contract in hand for a new business he had created. Too embarrassed to decline, his father allowed the young man to buy him lunch, pride and self-doubt warring in his breast. It was obvious to Hyman that his son had entered a world he had never even dreamed of for himself, and overall he was relieved. It had been worth losing his son to the new country and a better life, he decided as he hunched over his sewing machine after Simon departed.

Unbeknownst to the old man, who would have been horrified, Simon had decided to stop by his old stomping grounds, the Cafe Griensteidl, to see if any of his old friends were sipping a cup of black and white, or arguing over some article they had read in a local newspaper. Much to his surprise the young woman who had initiated him into the world of love years before was sitting alone in a corner leafing idly through the day's news. When she saw him standing in the doorway, she jumped to her feet, almost spilling her half full cup of steaming coffee onto the floor. Within minutes it was clear to Simon what she wanted – her studio was but minutes away by foot, as she was only too happy to tell him – but he was also startled to find that he was not willing to dishonor his young wife in this way.

It was with surprising bemusement that Simon walked back to Adelaide's childhood house, declining the cabbies who stopped to ask him if he wanted to ride instead. He realized he needed the time to think about what had just transpired. Of course his first love had aged considerably, but Simon still found her demeanor attractive, and wouldn't have found a romp in the hay with her a hardship. Like his father but for different reasons, Simon realized on his long walk through the city that he had entered a different world, one of excitement to be sure, but a world of responsibility as well. In addition his young wife was finally beginning to respond to him physically. Knowing that what he might have done with Hilda would not actually have affected Adelaide made no difference. In his heart he had not been willing to take the risk. He was no longer the Simon Liebman who would have done anything with any woman who was willing ten years earlier. He had become a man.

It was with great pride that Simon donned the suit his father had only finished the day of Adelaide's concert, watching Holly skip down the stairs in the long, pale blue dress with the flounce on the back of her skirt that had also been created for this special occasion. She held the skirt in her hands so that she wouldn't step on it with her new, leather shoes that had been dyed perfectly to match the shade of the dress, despite the impracticality of that choice. His little girl looked like an angel, her eyes glowing and riveted to his as she carefully pranced down each step.

"Do I look like a lady?" she asked him.

"You look like an utterly beautiful lady," her father replied, wanting to scoop the child up in his arms, but knowing all of the other assembled adults, including his own mother, would object because it would wrinkle the lovely dress. Simon contented himself with taking her hand, and ushering everyone else down the front steps to the two hansom cabs waiting below.

Simon, who had never attended the famous concert hall with his parents as Addie had with hers, was impressed by the grandeur of the Konzerthaus. It was he who spotted Arnold Schoenberg moving towards them to congratulate the Welt's on the debut of their daughter, singing with the renowned New York group in the city of her birth. Even Adelaide's mother was pleased to see the famous composer, now that he posed no threat to her daughter's virtue. As she smiled and chatted about the concert with the composer, and Adelaide's life in New York, she was relieved that no one around them, even the closest members of the family, knew the real reason she and her husband had been so willing to marry their youngest child to a man they hadn't seen since he had been a boy, and even then, had barely known. As they moved into the hall, she walked with a regal bearing natural to the mother of such a person. Simon noticed Mrs. Welt's expression as well as that of his own mother, who was beaming with joy, utterly thrilled to be included in such an event, let alone be the mother-in-law of one of the performers. He picked his daughter up gently around her waist so that he wouldn't cause any damage to the silk gown, to help her see the hall as they entered it. Her whining stopped immediately: even such a small child was silenced by the grandeur of the hall where she knew her mother was about to sing.

The Schola Cantorum, with a reputation for excellence in the United States, had also caused a stir on the Continent, and attracted an unusually large audience. As Simon glanced around him, he noticed that the only seats not filled were those in the back of the highest balcony. Much to his own surprise his chest constricted with anxiety for his young wife. He finally understood the American slogan "my heart was in my throat" as the curtain rose and he could see Adelaide, close to center stage. The musicians, singing a capella as usual, sounded magnificent, the ten singers more than managing to fill the large hall with their clear and beautiful voices. The applause after each number was very respectable, the sophisticated audience clearly enjoying the group's selection of numbers. When Adelaide stepped forward Simon, and all of the family members surrounding him, gasped, almost in unison. She had told no one she had been given a solo number. As her voice soared from the stage to the rafters above, a hush fell on the audience. Not a program rustled; no one even adjusted an arm or a leg: the only sound was Adelaide's soprano, it's vibrato, the perfect pitch, and the wonder of such a powerful voice emanating from such a tiny woman. When the piece was over, there was utter silence as she stepped back, which made Holly look up at her father with concern. Simon, sensing the movement, stroked the top of her head, his eyes riveted on his wife. Until applause spontaneously erupted, the few seconds between the end of the number and the swell of that sound felt like an eternity. Laughing with relief, Simon held his daughter's hands so they could both clap, amazed by Adelaide's calm demeanor on the stage before him. The rest of the concert passed in a blur for him, although his mother and Addie's both seemed enraptured by every note. The phrase 'this is why she needs to sing' kept sounding in his head; it was not just for her own self-expression, but so that the world could take pleasure in the gift she had been given.

"This is an amazing young woman you have married, my son," his mother said to him as they made their way through the crowd at the end of the concert. "You must show her respect, and support everything she needs to do to pursue her singing."

"Yes, I am coming to understand that, mother," he admitted. "I haven't been all that I could have been in that regard." He took his mother's arm and squeezed, which was not what she expected. "I suppose I wanted a wife more like my Mama, but I am beginning to understand the woman I have married and what I must do to keep her."

His mother, educated at home with tutors along with the more enlightened females of her time, nonetheless had a quick mind and was able to grasp emotional issues quickly. "We knew she had studied singing, and even had worked with Arnold Schoenberg, but we had no idea the breadth of her talent," she agreed. "You have never been truly conventional yourself, Simon, or you wouldn't have longed to live your life in a new country across the ocean from your home. Perhaps, in the end, this marriage will be what you really needed all along, even if it wasn't what we expected for you either."

Of course Simon did not tell his mother that there were other areas of his marriage that were not what he had hoped for either. He had never even shared details of his American sexual life with Otto, because Simon still suffered from self-doubt about his wife's lack of ardor in their boudoir. If her talent was more than he expected, and life in their bedroom less, he still hoped he would find a balance with Adelaide in the various arenas of their married life that would be acceptable to them both.

By the time the family was able to wend its way through the crowded foyer, abuzz with comments about the little soloist, who, people had discovered, had grown up right there, in cultured Vienna. Schoenberg was already standing in the doorway of the dressing room in animated conversation with Adelaide. It was clear by the expressions on the faces of some of the other singers in the group that they had had no idea their newest member had known the infamous composer when she had lived in Vienna, and were impressed. Since he was doing most of the talking, with Adelaide, who had reverted to her habitually shy persona as soon as she had left the stage, merely nodding in agreement or saying nothing, it was she who noticed the larger, looming presence who was pushing his way past her husband to stand behind Schoenberg. If the members of the group were impressed by the self-confident composer, they were totally silenced by the presence of Enrico Caruso, whose picture Adelaide had stared at for years on the few recordings she had managed to collect.

"Mr. Caruso," she stammered. "Thank you so much for coming to see us all. We had no idea you were in attendance this evening." She feared she would faint, and certainly had little breath for more words.

While the great man told the group how lovely their voices, how marvelous the selection of material, and how poignant the last number, Simon, who knew instinctively how his young wife must be feeling, managed to move a chair closer to her body so she could lean upon it. When the great Caruso turned his attention to her, and held out his hand to grasp hers, she instinctively held back the other hand so that she could still support herself, with a grateful glance at her husband.

"Mrs. Liebman. You were a joy, a true joy this evening. I certainly hope you will consider doing some tunes with me when the group next visits Europe," he bellowed, even his speaking voice magnificent.

Adelaide was so shocked she had no idea how to respond and was therefore silent. Before her lack of etiquette could be noticed, the concertmaster, who was standing in the midst of the other singers, bowed to the great man. "Of course we will find the time for such an event, sir. It would be a great honor for one of our singers to perform with you. If I could have the name of someone on your staff, our producer will contact him so this momentous event can be arranged."

Caruso immediately reached into the pocket of his jacket, and handed an embossed card to the man. "You have done a splendid job, sir," the famous singer replied, grasping the older man's hand as well. "To take ten voices, each special in its own way, and blend them in the way you have, takes an amazing talent."

Before the other man could demur his chorus broke into applause, which brought a smile to the faces of both men and helped alleviate the tension of the moment. As soon as the famous singer has gone, Simon lifted his wife off the floor, and despite the hazard in such a small space, swung her in a full arc just as he had at Rumpelmeyers. "I am so proud of you, my little Addie, I cannot tell you in words."

No one else heard, because all of the singers were hanging on to one another, shrieking with excitement. Even the concertmaster did not try to stop them, though he had concern for their voices. Instead he allowed them their excitement, and only after a few moments began to quiet them, reminding everyone that their next concert in Berlin was a mere week away. He wouldn't want any of them to develop laryngitis.

* * *

By the time the final financial installment arrived from Noah in New Jersey, four trunks were stacked in the parlor in place of the couch. Yetta had sold it to a young married couple; the wife had been working in her little factory for several years, so she was not troubled by the worn places on the velveteen fabric Yetta had used more than eight years before. She could easily re-cover the cushions; it was the body of the couch that mattered; and the quality of the workmanship was obvious to anyone with an eye for these things. The couch had been one of the first pieces of furniture Noah had built for his wife, and her favorite, but there was no way she could take it with her to Elizabethport. He would have to make another, even finer model. Yetta sat at the dining room table, which was also promised to a local family, bent as usual over one of the sewing machines she had borrowed from her shop, putting the finishing touches on a new coat for Min, who was rapidly outgrowing her old one. Yetta couldn't bear the thought of her youngest child boarding the train with her little mittened hands sticking out below the cuffs of her otherwise perfect little coat. Even if it meant staying up till all hours to finish the new one once all her other chores had been completed, Yetta believed it would be well worth it. The older girls knew what their mother was up to, but kept their knowledge from Matel because they too, knew how excited she would be the day they left Monasterzyska for good, when Yetta took it from the wardrobe, exchanging it for the one that had become too small. The seamstress who had bought the couch was also buying the coat; though she had no children yet, she knew, eventually she would have a daughter. This particular evening Yetta was working on the coat because the girls had taken Min directly from the shop to play on the town square before they all traipsed over to Harry's for dinner.

By the time she heard her children's laughter in the street outside, the coat was put away and almost the last of the kitchen utensils had been packed into the top trunk, ready for their departure at the end of the week. When Min burst through the door ahead of her sisters, Yetta had just sat down to look at the train schedule from Warsaw to Rotterdam, where the Potsdam, the boat that would take them to Ellis Island in New York City, would be waiting. She pocketed the schedule, reached for her own coat, lying across the back of one of the dining room chairs, and hurried the children across the street. Her sister-in-law was very prompt, and would hate it if her roast were overcooked. In this way Beck seemed more her daughter than Yetta's, who probably wouldn't even notice the overdone meat; it was Harry's wife who had taught her daughters to cook, Beck taking to it with a fervor her own mother reserved for sewing. It was after dinner, when the adults and Jules were sitting around the cleared table pouring over the train schedule, that Yetta realized she would be leaving this village where she had made her home for almost 12 years. Suddenly she was unable to concentrate on the various possibilities the children were discussing about getting first to Buchach, and from there to Warsaw. It wasn't that she was leaving behind her business: two of the seamstresses had bought it, enabling her to purchase second class tickets for herself and the children on the train, a luxury that meant they wouldn't have to pack themselves in like cattle. It wasn't even that she would be traveling to join her husband, a man she hadn't laid eyes upon in almost four years. Nor was it that she would be leaving all of her friends behind in Monasterzyska; she didn't have many because she hadn't had the time it would have taken to make good friends. It was her parents whom she knew she would never see again, a realization she had not allowed into her conscious thoughts until that very moment. It almost took her breath away.

Jules, who didn't miss even a slight change of mood when it came to his mother, asked if anything was the matter. He had just come downstairs from reading a fairy tale to Min, and then whispering with the older girls about the coming train ride, the big city of Warsaw, and the boat that would take them to the New World. He didn't believe his mother when she answered in surprise, "Nothing!" But he knew enough to let her be. If she wanted to talk to him, she would. It didn't bother him that she sometimes confided in Ruchel, the young seamstress who had bought some of their furniture, because even at his young age he realized that women needed to talk to one another. Mother and son worked side by side, Jules on his studies, especially now that he would have to give them up, at least for a while, so that he could help his parents settle into their new life, and Yetta, putting the finishing touches on the coat. Their silence was companionable. Working side by side in the evenings was part of a routine that each hoped to continue in Elizabeth, after everyone else had gone to bed and Noah was sanding furniture in the shed in Elias' backyard that he had described long ago. Both the Rabbi and the Melamid had given Jules books to take with him for his continued studies, in Hebrew, of course, as well as lesson plans voluminous enough to take a year to complete. Jules was determined to read every last word, as well as send back written work to his teacher, whom he had come to love, even if he was able to attend school in America. School in the new world would be different, and certainly have little to do with Jewish history, legal matters, or beliefs.

Before he climbed the stairs to his bed in the loft above them, Yetta gave him a hug and assured him, "I am really fine, Julie. You don't have to worry."

As she let him go, he looked her right in the eye. "I won't, mother. You take care of yourself better than anyone I know. I love you." He turned and raced upstairs. Despite the warmth of their home, those final words were not ones he had often said to either parent, though he certainly felt them in the depth of his being. Yetta stood at the foot of the stairs for some time before moving into her own bedroom. She knew she was fortunate in many ways, especially in the character of her children; this awareness somehow increased the shame she felt about the depth of her grief at having to leave her parents.

The next morning Yetta asked Ruchel to mind the shop, packed a water container as well as some nuts and dried fruits in a bag that she slung across her back, and set out to hike the six miles to the tiny village of her birth. When she arrived at her parents' cottage, her mother was already taking down the wash from the line in the side yard, although it was only ten in the morning. The sun was shining brightly, warm for a day in late fall. Yetta dropped her pack, immediately moving alongside her mother to help fold her wash. When they were done her mother put the things away inside while Yetta set the teakettle on to boil, moving around the kitchen with an easy familiarity, even though it had been many years since she had lived in the home of her birth.

"Papa thought we should come the night before you leave so we can help you with any last minute packing. Not that there'll be any," she added with a wry humor. She knew her daughter well, and clearly respected her organizational skills.

"If I am able to start a business in Elizabeth, I would like to send for you both, Mama," Yetta explained to her mother without any preamble. She didn't object when her mother reached across the table to take both of her hands in her own.

"Yetta-la. Papa and I are too old for such a trip now. Imagine our aches and pains in three or four years."

Both women fell silent, grasping hands, their tea forgotten. Yetta had no idea how to express what she was feeling, but she finally managed to say, "I don't know if I can bear never seeing you again, Mama."

Her mother replied, "You didn't think you could stand one more minute of your separation from Noah, and he had only been gone a year. It's amazing what human beings can endure, my sweet child."

"But I knew that wouldn't be forever," Yetta mumbled.

"I believe that we will meet again, don't you" her mother quietly asked her.

"I'm not sure. How do we know?" By now tears were streaming down Yetta's cheeks, but her back didn't bend. She sat as straight as she always did, ready to take whatever blows might befall her.

"We don't know, we believe." The older woman got up from her stool to reach for her hands, pulling Yetta from her stool and enfolding her against her ample bosom. They had not stood this way since Yetta had been a child, not because her mother parsed out her affection, but because the little girl would not allow such a display after she had turned seven or eight. Even now, though what she longed for was exactly this embrace, Yetta remained stiff and apart.

Only when her mother whispered, "You can let yourself go, my dear. Your father won't be home for hours," did Yetta's body give in, falling in to her mother's embrace and resting there for awhile. By the time her father returned home for lunch, the two women were both bustling around the kitchen preparing it. He hadn't expected to see his daughter for a couple of days, and was delighted to find her shelling peas next to his wife at their immaculate kitchen counter. Yetta had brought new pictures of Elizabeth for them to see. After the three had eaten their soup and challah, they poured over each of the pictures together, marveling at the beauty of the local park, one of many, Noah had explained in a letter, and the size of the public school building, intended only for children ages 5 to 11. Such an imposing brick building for such a small number of children. Neither parent could believe that in America their grandchildren would all attend school until they were eighteen years old, as Noah had assured them time and time again. Such a wonder, to receive that kind of education for free, even the girls.

On the walk home Yetta picked a bouquet of fading fall flowers, as well as a few small branches with brightly colored leaves, even though she and her children would be long gone before they died in her sister-in-law's vase. She had a need to fill the parlor with these local plants so that she could breathe them in until the very last moment. What kind of trees and flowers grew in this new country was just one of the many questions she had not thought to ask her husband. She realized she was crying, because when she bent to snap off some nasturtiums, her tears splattered across her wrist and she had to wipe them away. When she neared Monasterzyska, she sat down on a rock to compose herself, and only arose when she was sure the tears had abated.

THE TEACHER: TWO

When Jen played her phone messages, she was surprised to hear Hillary Roth's voice inviting her to dinner the following weekend, and stood in the hallway staring at her phone machine as if it had something more to tell her. Jen reminded herself that the girl's name was now Hillary Hansen as she pushed the rewind button, unreasonably pleased that she had remembered. After listening to the message a second time, she was no less startled by it. "Why?" she found herself thinking. "Why would such a young, bright, successful young woman want to spend an entire evening with me?" It wasn't that she thought she had nothing to offer, but she also wasn't sure she would choose to spend one of her free evenings with someone who was younger than her son. Perhaps it was she who was lacking, she thought, as she waited for the water in the kettle to boil. She relished this after-school cup of tea, whether she allowed herself a biscuit with it or not. By seventh period she had already been picturing herself ensconced on the couch with the new James Welch novel, her cup of steaming peppermint tea on the coffee table beside her.

Why had Hillary invited her into New York for dinner?

Jen rested her portable phone on the book, carrying the tea in her free hand, and gratefully sank into the down cushions of her couch. When the damned thing started ringing, she almost dropped it. Her right hand was still holding the hot tea. The only disaster was a bit of hot tea splashed on the area rug. Sighing, she pressed talk as she made her way back to the kitchen for a rag to mop up the spill. "Yes?" she said into the receiver, regretting her tone immediately. It certainly wasn't her caller's fault that she had spilled her tea. Without waiting to find out who was on the other end, she added, "Sorry. I just spilled my tea all over the living room rug."

"Good thing it's red, Mom," her son replied. "I should have waited a few more seconds for you to settle onto the couch and set the tea down before I dialed, but being telepathic doesn't seem to be one of my strengths," he added with his usual wit.

"Like hell! You know me well. I was just sitting down with my book.

"OK."

Instead of an immediate, and humorous rejoinder, her son was silent at the other end of the line.

"Are you all right, Jacob?" she asked, trying not to sound too concerned. Her son was in the early stages of a divorce. He was not having an easy time. It wasn't he who had wanted to separate, let alone divorce.

"Actually, I'm a little worried about you," he said, which gave Jen pause.

"You're worried about me?"

"Yes, mother, I am. When was the last time you went out?"

"Last night. To my book group. So there," she replied, by now back in the living room attending to the wet blotch on the Persian rug.

"Wise guy," he said. "You don't get away with that. You'd never give up your book group."

"I had dinner with my son. It was a very pleasant affair because he wasn't grilling me on my social life," she retorted.

"No," he chuckled. "She was grilling me on mine. Kind of."

Back she went into the kitchen, where she dumped the rag into the sink. She longed for her place on the couch and no interruptions. Rinsing the rag could wait. "Is anything new?" she asked him as she sat back down, hoping not. Carole couldn't be asking for more money from him – they hadn't had any children. Though that issue had been one of the thorns in their turbulent relationship, now it seemed fortunate to Jen that none of the in-vitro sessions had been successful.

"Carole's moving back in," he said, deadpan. When Jen didn't say anything, he added, "Joke, Mom. That was a joke. Nothing's new."

"Jesus, Jacob." Then, to change the subject, she said, "I just got the strangest phone message. From a former student."

"How so?" he asked.

"Remember the young woman who came to see me a few weeks ago?"

"The writer?"
"Yes. Hillary Hansen. I wonder if she married whomever she married because of the way his name would sound with hers...."

"I *am* worried about you, Mom. Is this the kind of thing you used to talk about with Dad?" he asked.

"Probably. So now I do it with myself, or with you if you happen to call. Anyway, she invited me to dinner." When Jacob didn't respond immediately, she added, "In New York."

"What's strange about that? Or is there something else you're not saying?"

Jen sighed. "Don't get on my case. I just don't know why she'd want to have dinner with me."

"Because she likes you. Because she really is grateful for all she learned from you. Because she thinks you're interesting." He paused. "This is a multiple choice, although if I had my pick, I'd probably say a little of all three. Jesus, Mom."

"I know all that, Jacob. I do. I'm just a little bit surprised, I guess. Come to think of it, I'm probably kind of pleased, now that I've had the rest of my hot tea to fortify myself," she added.

Once he was sure she was going to call back and accept Jacob was willing to talk about his own life. No, he wasn't yet dating, although there was a new young lawyer at his firm that he thought was awfully bright. He laughed at his mother's question about what she looked like, which was a reversal of the usual question a mother might typically ask her divorcing son. He acknowledged that she was attractive, petite but curvy, with huge brown eyes a fellow could get lost in. "Jeez," he concluded. "I had no idea I'd noticed that much about her...."

"Don't feel guilty, Jacob. It just means you're still among the living, and that's OK. Noticing her attributes won't keep you from going through your grieving process," Jen assured her son.

"I don't feel as low as I did a couple of months ago," Jacob sighed. "But I was starting to worry that maybe I was pushing the feelings aside, or that I was moving into denial."

"Honey, it's been over a year. Be grateful for whatever relief you get," she suggested."

He and Jen talked for a few more minutes, about the psychology of loss, how each of them spent evenings and weekends, which still loomed long and empty for them both. When Jacob told his mother that he wouldn't be able to meet her for brunch on Saturday and heard the disappointment in her voice, he totally understood. He explained that the partners were meeting for breakfast to go over developments in their new cases. Of course she told him not to worry, she would fill in with one of her friends. But Jacob realized this was a perfect opening for him to return to the subject of Hillary Hansen. By the time they finally hung up, she had again agreed to accept the young woman's invitation, and seemed to mean it.

Jen knew, that like her son, she needed to push herself out of the house, and back into the flow of life.

The following Saturday as she filled her tank at the local Exxon station, she was not so sure. What in the world would she find to talk about with this talented and successful young woman? She supposed Hillary might be interested in some of her current students, and what material she was having them read, especially new authors. Anna Quindlen had been an interesting choice, and caused quite a gender division in the discussions within her honors English class, despite the fact that the boys were among the best and the brightest in the school. This brought her thoughts back to her son: she found his depth of self-awareness unusual in someone so young, especially someone of the male gender. Of course Jacob had spent much more time with her than his father, who had always been working on a brief, even over the weekend. It was no accident that Jacob had become an attorney. As a little boy he had noticed her every mood, especially the dark ones, which he tried to ameliorate whenever he could. Once she was on the interstate Jen found herself wondering whether her constant attention, which had continued once he was grown, might have felt smothering to Carole, his estranged wife. Or were there other issues Jacob had chosen to keep to himself? As much as they talked, and as often, she was surprised to realize how little she knew about the reasons for his separation and impending divorce. Jen was so engrossed in her thoughts that she almost missed the turnoff to the Henry Hudson Parkway, which would have taken her miles and miles out of the way.

"Pay attention," she admonished herself out loud. "You're not old enough to be this spacey." Then she recalled driving out to Long Island when she had been working on her masters, and realized this particular failing had nothing to do with age, at least in her case. That route had become so familiar she would often find herself beyond Great Neck without any memory of passing Levittown at all. Then and now such a lapse of consciousness struck her as dangerous. Turning onto 86th Street she resolved anew to increase her effort to stay in the present, at least when she was driving. 'How often have I made such a resolution?' she asked herself with a frown, knowing the answer. Perhaps this could be a conversation she and Hillary would have over dinner: the distraction of daydreaming on the road. What a joke!, as Jacob would say.

When Hillary opened the door to her modest west side apartment, surprising given the degree of her renown, Jen was startled to hear voices within. She had assumed she and Hillary would be dining alone, and hadn't bothered to ask. As she handed her hostess the bottle of Chardonnay she had bought for their dinner that afternoon and kept chilled in a small cooler on her front seat, Jen felt an unfamiliar flutter in her stomach, similar to what she had experienced as a young woman going to a dance or out on a first date. Before she had a chance to be flummoxed by her own jitters, she was ushered into Hillary's surprisingly spacious living room and introduced to the three other people already seated around the coffee table. As she waited at the hutch for Hillary to pour her a glass of wine, she glanced around the room with approval.

One wall was lined with bookcases, most of the books standing in neat rows like hers, though Hillary's shelves had more books than space. A number of them were lying flat, as if they were waiting to be put in place within the rows of upright novels. Jen noticed that most of the books were fiction, though there was one row of shelves filled with sociology, psychology, history and the like, probably books collected during Hillary's college career. An overstuffed chair and ottoman rested comfortably at an angle in the corner to the left of the bookcase, a very attractive lamp curving down over the chair. Both the chair and ottoman were upholstered in a sage green fabric that looked luxurious, and much used, as did the couch Jen was sitting on, accented with brightly colored pillows in red, navy and dark green. A young man who was sitting in a rocker perpendicular to the couch, leaned forward to ask her name, and then offered her a platter of crudités. He told Jen that he had gone to graduate school with Hillary at Sarah Lawrence, and that she had often spoken about her amazing high school English teacher. He was delighted, he explained, to finally meet her.

"How embarrassing," Jen blurted. "I fear I'll never live up to such a recommendation."

Another young man who was sitting next to Jen on the couch laughed. "Don't worry about it. When she introduces me she says I'm the only boyfriend on the planet worth having, and I'm her brother!"

At that, everyone started to laugh, the ice broken. By the time the seven of them repaired to the dining room for the magnificent feast Hillary had prepared – coq au vin with potatoes, baby onions, peas, and chives in a wine sauce spiced with tastes that 'tease the pallet', as one of the guests suggested with a grin – everyone was so engrossed in conversation that the room vibrated with the din. As she bit into a piece of the chicken, Jen realized she hadn't had such a good time in months. Because Henry had been sick for so long, she actually could not remember the last time she had felt so engaged by the conversation of her fellows. She decided to call Jacob the next day to thank him for urging her to come.

Over a desert Hillary had bought at a local bakery, one of her women friends mentioned a recently published historical novel. Apparently there had been several articles about it, one in an historical journal of some renown, and there was considerable doubt about the authenticity of some of the supposed facts of the novel. The author had been interviewed on NPR about the research he had done before even beginning to outline, but admitted that there might be some errors. He never thought to check the background details with a scholar who was expert in the period, and was quite embarrassed by the furor incurred by his mistakes.

"It was obvious to me it wasn't purposeful, but he was clearly sloppy about some of the details. He was probably a novice at culling information from history books," Hillary suggested.

Her brother teased her, "Ah, you just don't want a fellow novelist raked over the coals for any reason."

"I'd never try an historical novel, if I was a writer. I'd be much too worried about making mistakes," one of the other women said, ignoring Brian completely.

Jen chuckled. "You two must have known each other for ages."

"Oh yes," the woman agreed. "We used to change Brian's diapers."

"So you say, but I don't believe you. I was out of diapers by the time Hillary was three and a half." Brian smiled with total good will, not the least bit disturbed by this exaggeration. Jen wished he had been her student as well. His ready wit and easy manner would have been a pleasure in a high school classroom. Although he might have been a gawky, awkward teenager with pimples, braces and a whole lot of attitude to cover up his actual, and embarrassing nature.

"I've done quite a bit or research about my family of origin," Jen was startled to hear herself admit. Not even her son knew this, although Henry had encouraged her in this pursuit. When he was so ill, pouring over family photo's and records was one of the only things that made her feel sane. That was something she hadn't admitted to Hillary the last time they met, although she had told her about some of the books she had read.

"Maybe you should write a novel," Hillary suggested, obviously delighted by the idea.

"I don't think so. I teach better than I write, and gave up the idea of writing my own novel before I was out of college. I've always loved teaching. Anyway, I started investigating my family history when my husband was going through our old albums because I became curious," she explained.

"Where did your family come from," Brian asked her.

"One side came from a small shtetl in the Polish Ukraine, and the other from cultured, bourgeois Vienna," she replied.

Excited by this, Hillary jumped in. "Have you read, "There Once Was A World" yet? It was Jen who told me about it," she told Brian.

"No. I don't remember. What's it about?"

"It's a book about shtetl life in eastern Russia, pretty close to Poland and the Ukraine. It goes into detail about every facet of life there. Dad's reading it too, because I got him interested in his grandparents. Did you know they came from Russia when they were teenagers?" Hillary asked her brother. She bounded up from her chair at the head of the dining table, returning moments later with an extremely thick, hard cover book. "Here. You're welcome to borrow it," she said. "I found it so interesting I bought my own copy."

Brian reached for the book with real curiosity. "I can't believe Dad's reading a book about shtetl life," he mused. Turning to Hillary he added, "Our family has never been religious."
"You may have to write that novel for people like us, so those stories don't just fade away," Hillary's woman friend teased Jen.

Laughing, Hillary turned to her as well. 'You'll certainly have enough information!"

Rather than feeling overwhelmed by such a proposal, as she would have in the past, Jen was intrigued. She joined the laughter. "I'm really

222

not a writer, but I certainly know one. And Janet's right: someone should do it so all those stories aren't lost."

"Ah, perhaps a collaboration," Brian suggested.

The room burst into chatter, as the friends began to talk about family, background, and research, eventually returning to the unfortunate novelist whose problems had spearheaded the original conversation. As some of the group members made motions to rise and wend their way home, Jen glanced at Hillary who was looking at her as well. The younger woman mouthed, "We should have lunch." Jen found herself nodding in agreement, anticipating the conversation she would have with Jacob about it. She decided she would leave out the part about historical novels; there would be plenty to tell him about without that tidbit. The last thing she wanted was pressure from her son to become a writer. As if that would fill the void left by Henry's death!

Nevertheless all the way home she told herself it had been an amazing evening.

The next weekend she started to reread the shtetl book she had suggested to Hillary weeks before, and had trouble putting it down. By sixth period on Monday she was itching to get back home so she could brew a cup of tea, sit down in her favorite reading chair, actually, one very similar to Hillary's, and return to the strange, old fashioned world of her grandparents. Her parents had each died within the last ten years, but her father's brother, Nathan, who at 93 was still practicing law, if only for the residents of the retirement community in northern Jersey he and his wife had moved into almost fifteen years earlier, was alert and active. He was delighted by the notion of talking to her about the past, and readily invited her to come to their apartment at the Hyatt the following Saturday for lunch. Eating in a dining room with the other tenants, who were all over 80, would be an experience in and of itself, and she, of course, agreed. When she told Jacob about it he was disappointed she was going on Saturday, because he had season tickets for the symphony in New York, and wouldn't be able to go with her. But he suggested she take along a tape recorder so she could collect their family information for posterity, and any future grandchildren that might come along.

Jen took this as a helpful sign about his emotional wellbeing. If he could imagine having children, he must be feeling less wounded by the divorce. She, too, was feeling less dreary than she had even a week before, and realized it was because of the reading and research. As long as she didn't think about having to create a novel out of it all, she could barely contain the excitement she felt at what she was discovering. She chuckled about what her son would think if she told him about Hillary's silly suggestion, realizing she was actually happy to be going to see Lil and Nathan by herself, although she didn't understand why.

Her aunt and uncle were frailer than she remembered. As she walked slowly with them from their apartment down to the community-dining hall, a wash of guilt swept over her for not visiting them more often. When Henry had done the driving, they had come down to visit at least once a month. Now, although it was just a little over an hour's drive, Jen hadn't been down to see them in months.

Nevertheless, even in their apartment conversation had been animated. All of them read The Nation, and had a heated argument about the Israel/Palestine situation. Though none of them were particularly religious – could this have been something instinctive she and Hillary had sensed about one another? – the older couple defended the need for more Israeli villages, emotional about Jews being chased from their homes everyplace else. Of course they had concern about displaced Palestinians, but not enough to feel they had an equal right to the land in dispute. They were still arguing about the West Bank as they entered the dining hall and moved towards the table Nate had reserved for them all, which took at least ten minutes, partly because her Aunt Lil was now using a walker, but also because the two were clearly community favorites. They had to stop at almost every table to accept and offer greetings, ask about health matters, and exchange information about children, grandchildren, and sometimes, great grandchildren. At each table they introduced their niece, Jen, an amazing high school English teacher.

When they returned to their apartment her Uncle was happy to have their conversation taped as long as she operated the 'damned machine', but her aunt was silenced by the little player at first, only speaking when she was coaxed, repeatedly, by both her husband and her niece.

Some of the information about the family's move from the Polish shtetl to New Jersey was familiar to Jen, because her mother had often talked about it when she was growing up, even though it was her husband's family that had come from there.

"Dad hardly ever talked about any of this," Jen told the other two, "But my Mom did. Where do you think she learned so much about your family?" she asked.

It was her aunt who replied, "Because she and I used to visit Noah, when he stopped working," suddenly unafraid of the little microphone. Noah had been her father-in-law. "Like his son, he loved talking about his past. I think your mother actually looked forward to those conversations more than I did, even though it was awfully difficult to keep Stephen and Susan occupied while he talked."

Because she had been in that living room often as a child herself, Jen could picture the entire scene: the old man sitting back in the wooden chair with the overstuffed seat covered in a maroon velveteen fabric his wife had found years before, when they had first moved to Elizabethport. Both of them refused to recover the chair, or to give it away and purchase a new one because it was the first piece they had collaborated on in their new country, once Yetta had been able to immigrate with the four older children. Jen had never known about these conversations, because they had occurred before her birth. Her grandfather had been lost in thought when she had been taken to his home.

"What else did you talk about?" Jen asked Lil.

"Elizabeth. Noah's first shop. It was just a shack in the back of his brother Elias' butcher store. It was Yetta who talked him into buying the building and remodeling the upstairs into two apartments, one for themselves and one they rented to another family."

Nathan, who wasn't a terrific listener, knew all about this story and couldn't keep himself from interrupting. "If it hadn't been for that shop, and my mother, I wouldn't have gone to law school, and your father wouldn't have been able to go to medical school," he told her.

"But he didn't go to medical school," Jen reminded him. Perhaps he wasn't quite as sharp as she had thought.

Clearly he found her comment irritating. "Of course he didn't. He had to go to the Sanitarium, for his TB. But the money was there, between what he earned in high school and what my parents saved for us both."

By the time Jen left their apartment hours later, after they had all taken a painfully slow walk around the grounds, she had taped more memories about various cousins and their children. Nate and Lil kept in touch with everyone, and most of the cousins and their children kept tabs on them as well, given their age. Jen had learned so much about the family she had never known before, she resolved to begin a file with cards for each individual, especially her grandparents and all the aunts and uncles.

She truly didn't think she was a good enough writer to attempt a novel, but she certainly had collected some interesting stories for Hillary.

CHAPTER SEVEN

When they arrived at the train station in Buchach, anyone observing the huge entourage from Monasterzyska might have thought they were watching a funeral procession. Not only had Noah and Yetta's immediate families walked beside the wagon transporting the children and their goods on the six mile trip, all of Yetta's seamstresses had closed up the shop so they could say their good-bye's as well. Both of Jules' teachers and their wives had come, trailed by the boys from both heders. Many friends and neighbors had found themselves joining the trail of people heading out of the village because Yetta and her children were beloved: everyone knew they would never see them again. Because she didn't want to upset the children, Yetta held back from saying good-bye to her parents until they had to board the huge train that had pulled into the station only moments before, already a half hour late according to the schedule tacked to the wall beside the waiting room door. Her father, unable to wait another moment, reached out and enfolded his daughter in his massive arms, and that was her undoing. Despite the flood of tears, Yetta kept saying, "It's all right. It's all right," over and over, especially to Min, who looked terrified. Until Jules called out to her from the steps leading into the car, she clung to her mother with a desperation that shocked even Yetta. She resisted when her son rushed down the steps, pulling at her until she finally released her arms and he could propel her up onto the steps of the slowly moving train. By then all of the children were screaming and Min was crying, even though Nell was holding her tightly in her arms. As soon as she was aboard, Yetta raced to the window beside the bench seats her children had chosen, tugged at the window sash until she and Jules managed to pull it upwards, and lunged out of the open space with the top half of her body so she could see her parents until the entire station platform had disappeared from view.

When she could no longer even see the speck the station building had become on the horizon, she pulled herself inside, shoved the window back down to protect them all from both the cold and the black smoke billowing beside the train, and sat down on the narrow bench next to her youngest child. Only then did she realize how packed the car was – with people, with boxes, with trunks, with bundles wrapped round and round with rope and tied together, and with animals on their way to market. Jules was now standing, squeezed between two other young men in-between the two rows of benches lining both sides of the car. He was already engaged in an animated discussion with one of the boys, who was pointing out the window at the trees whizzing by and describing something to her son.

Beck handed her a handkerchief, saying, "It is all right Mama. You'll start a new business in this place, Elizabeth, and we'll send for Oma and Opa." Her eyes were as red as her mother's, the handkerchief she always carried balled in her hand lying open on her lap.

"We're going so fast," little Min shrieked. Her fascination with the passing countryside had quelled her tears. "Look, Mama. It's another village like Monasterzyska. Hurry!" She tugged at her mother's sleeve to get her to turn her head.

"My oh my. Your father described this to me many times, but I never imagined…" Yetta murmured, eyes wide and mouth dropping open as she stared at the countryside slipping away. All she could actually see were the disappearing forms of her parents, but her children didn't discover this for many years.

"Did he say anything about Warsaw?" asked the ever-practical Nell.

Yetta took the young girl's hand in her own. "He said we wouldn't believe how tall the buildings were. He even reminded me about that in his last letter," she replied, smiling at each of the children in turn. All the girls were clearly relieved their mother had stopped crying, since it was something they had rarely seen before.

When the train reached the outskirts of the capitol of Poland, with its three and four-story brick buildings, Beck urged Jules to open the window again so she could lean out to see the city in all its grandeur as they approached it. This he did, over his mother's objections, assuring her he would hold on to both Nell and Beck so they wouldn't fall out of the moving train. Yetta picked up Min, who was desolate to be missing this momentous event, and she and Jules leaned over the girls, so that they, too, could watch the approach of Warsaw.

"All of the buildings look like the city hall in Monasterzyska," Beck exclaimed in amazement. "Papa told me that it took over six months to construct. How did they ever do this?" she asked no one in particular.

All of them were equally amazed by the size of the train station. Once they had moved all of their belongings to their departure gate, beyond which they could see an even longer train than the one they had just taken, they took turns, two at a time, exploring the huge terminal. Min raced back to her mother clutching a sucker on a stick, and clung to her skirt with a "please mama, please can I eat it now!" Yetta had planned to make them all sandwiches once they were settled on the new train, but realized that was several hours away, so she relented. For some reason her daughter's slurping made the silly thing seem appealing; Yetta found herself asking Beck, who was about to leave with her brother to explore more of the station, to bring back a red or purple one for her. Both children grinned broadly. Neither had ever seen their mother indulge herself with sticky candies. Before they boarded the new train, Yetta took the girls to the bathroom, which was actually inside the station, a huge room with many stalls and running water, so the customers could wash their hands. They all found the entire experience of the station and its various amenities amazing. There were certainly some advantages to city life, Yetta realized.

On the train she stacked the sandwiches with meat and cheese, allowing each of them a half, with an apple, because she knew the food she had packed would have to last them all the way to Rotterdam, and perhaps for some of the boat trip as well. Noah had explained in several letters that they would be given minimal food on the boat, and warned her that in the few hours they would have in the huge seaport before they decamped, she should buy bread and meat, but most important, she should find a produce stand and purchase lemons, bags of lemons, to protect them all from contracting scurvy on the long voyage across the ocean to New York City. Both Jules and Beck noticed that the third class cars were packed, as they had been from Buchach to Warsaw. It was with relief that they settled into their seats in the second-class cabin that their mother had purchased for them all. Even those were full, although there were many empty cars in first class. This they discovered when Jules and Beck dragged their larger trunks to the storage cars in the front of the train. Jules returned to check on their luggage several times, wending his way carefully down the aisles of the second and first class cars, amazed by the luxury he glimpsed within the private compartments as he passed by, visible through an open door or a raised shade. In one of the compartments a well-dressed woman wearing a hat in the latest fashion tugged at her husband's sleeve and pointed at him as he passed, and both broke into loud laughter. He wondered if they were laughing at his suit, stylish for his little village but clearly different from the clothes he noticed on the boys lounging in the first class area, or at his payos, which defined him as a Jew to anyone on the train. The woman and her husband were obviously gentile and wealthy, he with a neatly trimmed moustache, cleanly shaved face, and no sideburns whatsoever.

By the time Yetta had bought several loaves of bread as well as meat and cheese, and located the necessary produce stand, the Potsdam was already loading its first class passengers. She and the children waited at the edge of the dock with the other poor immigrants, too fascinated by the ship before them to feel shame at their circumstances. The boat rested low in the water, with one huge smokestack rising majestically towards the stern. When it was their turn to walk up the gangplank, little Min froze and refused to move although she had been walking for several years. Jules, who could usually charm his younger siblings into almost anything, was unable coax her into taking even one step. When he finally reached for her hand and tried to physically inch her towards the long walkway, which rose high above the dock to the deck of the ship, the little girl actually sat down. She looked like a tiny Buddha because of the many layers of clothing she was wearing due to the inclement weather, unusually cold for early May. Wearing layers of clothing had been the easiest way for all of them to bring as much as they could for their long journey. Finally Yetta turned around, saw what was happening behind her, and held her arms out to her youngest child; only then did Min rise, running as fast as her little legs could carry her, up the plank and into her mother's arms. Poor Jules had to apologize to several adults, emigrants like themselves, who had to step sideways on the narrow platform once Min had made up her mind to get to her mother despite her fear of the huge boat. And so it was, riding on Yetta's breast, that little Min saw both the upper deck of the boat that would carry them all to New York's Ellis Island, and the huge Port of Rotterdam behind her. The size of the other boats, as well as the length of the cavernous warehouses receding into the distance, overwhelmed the child and she again began to cry. Yetta continued to climb the steep plank, pressing Min even closer in her arms.

In her immediate and visceral reaction to the ocean liner, Min sensed something that was beyond the ken of the rest of them. The voyage was not one to be welcomed with open arms, but something else entirely. Though they knew they were not traveling in style, none of them had any notion of what lay ahead. Of course their passage had been booked in steerage where, along with hundreds of other poor travelers, they were squeezed together in a huge hold. They slept in layered bunks, when they could sleep, stuffed together like matjes herring in a jar, one atop the other. All of the females, including Yetta, became seasick within hours of leaving the dock behind. Jules was the only one to escape this misery. The boy persuaded his mother to lie down: he would prepare cheese and bread sandwiches for them with what remained of the supplies the family had carried with them from their humble little kitchen in Monasterzyska, saving the fresher food for later in the voyage. When each sister in turn, and then his mother, turned away from his offerings, Jules was not deterred. First he assured his mother that she must take a bite or two. With food in her stomach, he reasoned aloud, it would cease its endless turning, and eventually calm down entirely. Though reasonable sounding, it didn't appear to hold true. None of the girls was able to hold down the little they managed to choke down, although Yetta retained her small lunch. By the next day she stood side by side with Jules, soaking the center of Beck's homemade challah in milk, and feeding the soppy mess bit by tiny bit to each of her daughters in turn. She also convinced them to drink a bit of water, as she used to do when they fell ill in their tiny house in the shtetl. Though each of the girls was eventually able to walk up on the deck, Nell the last to recuperate, none of them ever became comfortable with the pitch and roll beneath their feet. It was little Min who persuaded them to rise and climb above deck. At least they would be outside, she told them, breathing in air that didn't smell of sweat, festering food, vomit and soiled linen. Nell sat down on a bench as soon as the air hit her face and closed her eyes. She smiled immediately, agreeing with her wise younger sister. "Yes," she sighed with relief the first day she had ventured above deck. "This is much much better."

One day Yetta was ladling out the lunchtime fluid that passed for soup that she had received in a huge pot from the below-decks cook when she heard a scream from the first class deck above her. "Land! Land!" She didn't have to be persuaded to set the pot down and stop what she was doing. Jules grabbed her hand, and she, Beck, and the three Unger's hurried above deck with everyone else. Beck impatiently stamped her feet as they waited for the immigrants in front of them to climb upwards. Nell and Min were already out on the deck. Nell had seemed rooted there even when it was raining ever since the day she discovered she felt better in the open air, despite her mother's warnings about catching a cold or worse. The passengers crowded around the railing closest to them when the emerged from below, so it was hard to see, especially for the shortest travelers, or those towards the back of the mob craning to get a clear view or pushing their way closer to the front. Yetta grabbed onto the sleeve of Jules' jacket, screaming so that she could be heard above the cacophony of voices doing the same, "What's that thing out in the water there?" Before he could reply, a cry went up from someone against the railing, "It's the Statue. The Statue of Liberty!" As first one, and then another began to scream "Hooray!" and "America", people hugging people they had barely spoken to throughout the journey, or hadn't even seen before – the Potsdam chugged into New York harbor.

"What an irony," Yetta thought, despite the fact that she could see nothing herself, "that the statue first appeared on our side of the boat. For once the upper classes had to stand behind us to see." And then a well-dressed man scooped her up in his arms, and held her aloft, and she, too, was caught up in the majestic sight of the green-tinged woman, who seemed to beckon to her personally with the torch she held aloft in the darkening sky. As he set her down, Yetta thanked the wealthy stranger for giving her the opportunity to see this icon she had already heard so much about from her husband. "Now I feel welcomed by our new land," she told him, beaming broadly. He told her he, too, felt the same, and gave her a quick hug before turning to find the rest of his own family. "The land of opportunity," he agreed, and was gone.

As Yetta and her children stood huddled together on the deck watching the amazing New York skyline move closer and closer, she could barely contain her excitement, from the rush of thoughts in her brain to her toes gripping the deck through her shoes as if to ground her so she wouldn't fly overboard to get to Noah now, right now. Jules, Beck and Nell had managed to bring their three trunks up the stairs to rest beside them, the bundled quilts and pillows, the three canvas bags stuffed to the brim with the items each of them has needed for the long journey, and even their dinner bowls, which he had carelessly stuffed into the top of one of the bags. The soup, of course, had been left below, forgotten by them all, even Yetta, in the excitement. It was only when they were lost in the crush of immigrants in the cavernous hall of Ellis Island that Yetta remembered none of them had eaten since breakfast, but by then it was too late. Fortunately little Min was so overwhelmed by all the new sights, she didn't seem hungry. As they were pushed from line to line Min turned back to look at the Potsdam, still moored to the dock.

"I am never ever getting on another boat again as long as I live!" she declared, making them all laugh in agreement, especially Nell.

The huge hall at Ellis Island was packed with immigrants. Three other boats had docked there, so the press of bodies was extreme. Yetta, who was a short woman, began to feel suffocated by the sweating people swarming on every side of her. Unable to see above them, she felt trapped, and desperately tried not to panic which she knew would distress all of her children, even the stalwart Nell and her competent son. Jules, who wanted to help speed their progress, slipped through the crowd until he was closer to the front of the room. Even though Yetta was afraid to let him out of her sight in this mêlée, she also wanted to get out of this room with its smells, people and horrible noise. He and his mother took their bearings before he disappeared in the throng so he would not get lost. Nell, the tallest of the girls, stood atop one of their trunks, and put a big hat on top of her head, watching her brother until he was swallowed up by the mass of people. All along the way he stopped to ask other immigrants already in queues what they were waiting for, and what was the meaning of the various lines. Since he had only learned rudimentary English, and many of the foreigners spoke neither Yiddish nor Polish, his progress towards this end was very slow. He was relieved to discover that fortunately his family was waiting in the first and correct queue, although he was dismayed to learn that they would all be examined for lice, an indignity he knew his mother would loathe: she had taken pride in having one of the cleanest houses in their village, even when one or more of her children were ill and unable to help with family chores. The final piece of information he managed to collect was that there was a separate queue for immigrants from the Ukraine who already had family living on American soil. This was the most important information because it would allow them to skip the longer, and more tedious lines set aside for newcomers. He found the 'family' line, which snaked all the way around one side of the huge hallway, and then bent back upon itself, and walked the entire length until he found the end. There he discovered a woman who had also crossed the ocean on the Potsdam. Although they had never spoken aboard ship, bunking at opposite ends of the hold, each recognized the other. She suggested she hold a place for Jules and his family, which came as a huge relief to the boy. He didn't tell her that all of them would have to make it through their health inspection before they could stand behind her because he wanted to secure the spot. It could save them hours or more, and get them to Elizabeth that much sooner.

When he turned back to the sea of humanity before him, he experienced a momentary panic. Disoriented by the vastness of the hall and this new location, he had to close his eyes to try to remember what points he and his mother had memorized: a clock on the wall, the double doors leading outside, two signs in the center of the shortest wall. When he felt calmer, he opened his eyes and located the clock, realizing immediately where he had to go. Although he had a terrible headache because of the constant din within the tightly packed room, he didn't allow himself to think about it. He merely lowered his head, and pushed past person after person so that he could find his family. By the time he managed to get back to them, they were not in the same place, causing another moment of panic, but the boy reminded himself that they had been inching forward along with everyone else. He located them because Nell was still standing on the trunk and spotted him first, waving her hat wildly so that he would notice her. Jules was delighted to see that they were near the long table upon which the immigrants were to stack their clothes as they removed them, so they could be searched for the dreaded lice. For once he was thankful that his mother was short and his sisters so young because they had no idea what was about to take place. He explained the procedure to his mother as it has been explained to him; she was quite distressed by the information, but like him, understood why this new country had to protect itself. Because she had forced them all to take daily sponge baths aboard the boat, she also knew that she and her children posed no threat: it was just an indignity they would have to endure. Jules could see her chin jut out as she accepted the news, and then his mother kneeled to explain what they were about to endure to eight-year old Beck, who began to cry. The usually feisty child was obviously exhausted and hungry and anxious to finally see the father she barely remembered. She was embarrassed to be behaving in such a childish manner, because she had come to think of herself as a diminutive mother to Min on their long journey. Besides, her mother hardly ever cried. Then the usually quiet and amenable Nell objected to stripping down to her undergarments in such a huge crowd because her body was just beginning its transformation. When Jules and her mother held up their coats to give her a ring of privacy she consented, appeased. Each of their passports was stamped with the requisite mark of approval, and then Yetta looked around in near panic because she could not understand where the woman was telling them to go next.

"We go over there, Mama. All the way against that wall," Jules explained, again relieved he had journeyed around the hall to find out the procedure they would have to follow so his mother wouldn't have to rely on the official's incomprehensible English. To give the woman credit, she was speaking the language of their new home – English - slowly. But it was not enough.

First Jules explained to all of them that he had already secured them a place in the line through Mrs. Leibowitz, whom both Nell and Beck knew. They had played with her daughter, whose age was between their own. He then ordered Nell and Beck to get behind one of their trunks and push, while little Min and her mother gestured people to move out of the way so they could get through; in this manner they headed diagonally across the room, a slow trek but efficient. The second line seemed endless to Yetta, still snaking around two sides of the hall. She could not understand why her son was smiling broadly, and found herself snapping at him as he rushed ahead.

"Jules, wait for us! Where are you racing off to? What would happen if I lost you?"

He screamed back, "I see Mrs. Liebowitz, Mama. She's almost at the center of the line, isn't that wonderful?"

All Yetta wanted to do was weep but she kept plodding forward, the children pushing the trunks along, Nell now moving first one, and then the larger trunk with the bedding, dishes and silverware which Jules had been maneuvering. Fortunately, Mrs. Liebowitz' daughters rushed to their side to help; with all of them pushing and tugging, they squeezed into the line behind the other family fairly easily. There were a few complaints about Yetta and her children usurping a spot in the long line, but mostly, people were too exhausted to complain for very long. Yetta immediately made a bed of sorts from their jackets in-between two of the trunks. Min fell down without any urging at all and was asleep in seconds. Even Beck lay down though Nell refused. Exhausted as she was, she felt that she, like Jules, must remain awake so she could help her mother. She didn't think about the fact that she spoke no English, or wonder how in the world she could help. At least she would be available. When Mrs. Liebowitz offered her a small piece of roll with butter, which she had saved from their far distant lunch on the Potsdam, Nell politely refused. Fortunately the other woman paid no attention and forced the bread into her hand, buttering another for the exhausted Jules, and then cutting and buttering three more pieces for Yetta and the sleeping children. By the time they reached the front of the line, Nell and her mother had taken a quick nap, too, and the younger girls had gulped down their small portion of bread, immediately thanking Mrs. Liebowitz, as Yetta had taught them to do. As she dozed off, Yetta realized she had never loved her children as much. They had each behaved with such dignity and honor on this long, difficult journey, that she promised herself she would thank them when she awakened.

Jules spoke for the family when they reached the officials' table, because he was the only one who was at all conversant in English. Unfortunately because of his thick Polish accent, neither of the women behind the table could understand him. The older, gray-haired one sitting behind her barricade of documents, papers and bureaucratic rule books, kept asking him to repeat his name, tell her where he was from, and where his father was living in America, which he did, though not in the order requested. The twelve-year old could not really understand what the woman was asking him, but since he was bright, he believed those were the details she would want to know. In frustration she finally pushed a piece of paper across the table at him and pointed to Yetta who needed to sign the thing since she was clearly the only adult present. Jules tried to read the document that had been set before him, but the English was much to complex. He did, however, recognize the name 'Elizabeth', which was where his father lived, but was confused by the word 'Young', which was also capitalized. The clerk patiently tried to explain, finally pointing to each of them in turn and repeating their first names, then adding the word on the paper before going on to the next. It was Yetta who grasped the meaning behind the woman's gestures: she was giving them 'Young' as a surname. Her consternation was obvious to everyone, including the couple behind her in line. The man spoke Yiddish, so she was easily able to explain the problem to him. He asked if she had any of her husband's letters in her purse. She understood immediately and rooted around in the thing, which was packed with Polish money, medicines, herbs, tea, and some dried fruit for the children, until she pulled out two of his letters, still folded inside their original mailing envelopes. She eagerly pointed to the writing on the top left hand corner of the envelope, where Noah had written his name and address. The two clerks engaged in a brief discussion during which the gray-haired woman tore up the paper she has been urging Yetta to sign, filling out a new one and handing it to her, along with her letters. There at the bottom, beneath the signature line, was finally the name even little Min could recognize because of her nightly studies with Jules: Unger.

As she and the children finally left the cavernous building in yet another long line that was headed towards the ferry to New Jersey, Yetta was startled to realize it was still daylight, having forgotten that the ship had arrived in New York as dawn was breaking. Because it was mid-May, the light hadn't faded by four in the afternoon. She found herself blinking with discomfort because of the contrast to the dim, dank atmosphere inside the hall, the only light coming from the high, dirty windowpanes on one wall, and the lanterns used by the clerks manning the tables. Before she could get her bearing, the family was herded towards a boat yawning open at the end of a dock already crowded with two horse-drawn wagons, one carrying huge metal canisters of milk, the other overflowing with clothing, and a mass of people all looking as confused as Yetta. Min began to bawl when she saw the ugly-looking vessel, followed in quick succession by both Beck and Nell. This almost silenced the toddler, because she had never seen her oldest sister in tears. Jules, who glanced at his mother and quickly realized that she, too, had reached a breaking point, picked the little girl up, raised her above his head and set her on his shoulders with surprising ease. He, himself, was not large, and certainly wasn't blessed with corded and muscular arms. After all, he had spent most of his young life seated at tables pouring over the Talmud, not laboring with cement block or raising walls of wood.

"Look, Matel," he urged. "There's a horse on the boat. Maybe you can pet him when we get on board. What do you say to that?"

"How do you know it's a 'him'?" she asked her brother, who understood his sister well enough to know she was not joking.

"I don't, little one. We'll check that out when we climb aboard, all right?"

Again, Nell and Beck were left to push the three trunks up the gangway, while Yetta carried the three canvas satchels. Two teen-age boys noticed the family's struggle and motioned the girls aside. Yetta had to run to catch up to them and not lose sight of their luggage, the girls racing behind her. In this way the family boarded the boat that would carry them across the river to New Jersey. Beck volunteered to stay with the luggage, which the boys had left near one of the horse-drawn wagons. Once Min and Jules ascertained the sex of the horse pulling the other wagon, and Min was able to pat the docile pack horse to her heart's content, she and her brother left eight-year old Beck behind and joined the rest of the family on the deck above. Because the wagon driver had offered Beck a cup of milk, she waved her brother on his way. "Boats don't make me sick. I'll be fine Jules. Go find Mama. She will be worried. You know she will."

As they watched Ellis Island recede behind them, Yetta reminded her children that soon they would be seeing their father. She was again rooting about in her large cloth purse looking for her hairbrush. Even though she wore a head scarf, which was only proper for a married woman, she could tell that many strands of her hair had escaped on this long day, and she probably looked like one of the poor souls who frequently passed through Monasterzyska on their way to some better place, begging for food, a warm jacket, or other supplies to use on their journey to nowhere. This was unacceptable. Nell and Min stood on either side of her so Yetta could remove her scarf in privacy. As her hands moved at their usual rapid pace, brushing and then pinning her long auburn hair in place, Min asked her a question so startling that she dropped several hair pins and had to bend to retrieve them.

"What does Papa look like? I don't remember."

"He's tall as a maple tree, Matel, but he has a moustache instead of leaves," Jules teased, making the little girl laugh.

"I know he doesn't have leaves, silly. He's a man," she giggled. "What color are his eyes?"

Surprised that he had to think about it before he could answer, Jules finally was able to reply, "Hazel."

"Is that like light green?" the little girl asked him, and he smiled his agreement.

"They are the warmest eyes in the world," said her mother. "When he looks at you, it makes you want to smile."

"I remember his hands," Nell mused. "When I had that awful cold before he left, he would come upstairs and stroke my forehead so I could go to sleep. My eyes must have been closed, so I can't remember what he looked like then, but I know how he felt."

"I can't believe we're going to see him in just a few minutes," Jules marveled. "Now I'm old enough to really challenge him in a game of chess. I'll be a real partner for papa, don't you think?" the boy asked his mother, sounding suddenly like the child he really was. Yetta had come to depend on him so much she had almost forgotten that he was not yet a man full grown.

"I'm going to be able to play games with Papa, too," Beck piped up.

With a grin, Jules asked her, "What games are those, Beck?"

Without any hesitation, she replied, "The ones you used to play when I was little."

Suddenly Nell's quiet voice interrupted their teasing.
"Isn't that Papa sitting on the wagon over there?" she asked no one in particular.

"Where?" Jules asked, his usually modulated voice rising in pitch.

She took his hand, raised his arm, and guided his finger so that he was looking where she was. "There!"

"Yes," Yetta gasped. "That is Papa. Is that Elias, sitting next to him, Jules? My goodness. He's shaved his beard. "

"I think so," the boy answered, although he hadn't seen his Uncle since he had been a boy of three or four.

"Oh my son, I'm sorry for asking. How would you even remember? Besides, he looks so different," his mother said, her arm around his shoulders.

"Pick me up, so I can see too," Min demanded. Jules again lifted her to his shoulders, but she had a difficult time finding him in the crowd waiting below. Finally Jules and Nell were able to pinpoint where he was sitting on the front seat of their uncle's wagon because of the white marks on the face of the horse pulling it. Min was quiet for several seconds, studying the two men.

"I'm glad Papa didn't shave his beard," she said, shaking her head up and down.

Finally, Beck, who had been silent since Nell had spotted their father, started to cry. The milkman had assured the child he would watch their things, and she had come up onto the deck to find her family moments before. Both Jules and Yetta turned to the little girl, stooping in front of her. "Sweet one, what is the matter?" Yetta asked her, truly baffled.

"I don't recognize him," Beck gulped in-between her tears. "I know you say he's my papa, but I can't tell."

Yetta enfolded her daughter in her warm arms, stroking her hair and her back. "Beck, you were only four when Papa left. Of course you don't recognize him. He even looks different to me," she agreed.

"Really?" Beck asked her mother.

"Yes. Really. If Jules hadn't seen him, I don't know that I would have been able to pick him out among all those people." She was relieved that Beck didn't ask her if this was true, because in fact, it was not. Her heart had begun pounding so hard at the sight of him that she couldn't believe none of her children could hear it. She felt weak in the knees when she looked at him, her, a grown woman with four children already. She was afraid to utter another word because she feared her voice would sound strange, as wobbly as her knees. When she finally managed to control some of the turmoil she asked them all, "Isn't he handsome, your father? Such a handsome man."

"He's certainly better looking than Elias," Nell agreed in her characteristic sober tone, adding, "But I'm not sure he would be without his beard."

"Look, Mama, he's standing up," shrieked Jules, taking hold of Min's hands and waving them wildly above his head.

The man with the beard sitting on the wagon seat was waving as well, and even from afar, they could all tell that he was smiling from ear to ear. They could also see his mouth move, but could not understand what he was saying, though he was obviously yelling at the top of his lungs along with almost everyone else on shore, as well as many of people standing at the railing around them.

"Papa, Papa, I'm your little Min," the little girl yelled as loud as she could from her perch on top of her brother's shoulders, though no one but her family and the other immigrants nearby could hear. They all began to laugh, though Yetta had tears streaming down her cheeks.

She had finally come home to her husband.

Min urged her brother to move away from the railing so they could all hurry back down to the milk wagon and their trunks, which were resting beside it. Then they could be among the first people off the ferry. Of course other passengers had the same notion, but the Unger's were still among the first families to reach the lower deck before the ferry docked and was secured. Suddenly Min, who was holding her mother's hand, ripped free and darted between the legs of the other departing passengers as she headed in a direct line for her father or where she presumed him to be. Noah had just climbed down from his seat next to Elias atop the wagon so that he could embrace each of his children, and then Yetta. My God, he couldn't believe how lovely she looked, despite the long journey. Nevertheless Noah was not ready for little Min, who hurled herself at his legs, almost knocking him over.

"I'm Matel," she shrieked. "Your little girl. Jules told me you're my father, but I don't remember you." When her father hoisted her up into the air, kissing her hair, her cheeks, and finally her eyes, her laughter was so exuberant that other immigrants, involved in their own reunions, turned to look at the father and his daughter. Like many of the men around him, Noah was smiling, but like them, he looked as if he was sleepwalking. Had he passed his son on the street, he would not have recognized him: the boy was no longer a boy; he looked like a man to Noah, albeit a very young one. And Nell. My-oh-my. Though plain, she had turned into a winsome young thing, slender and straight, watching everything unfolding in front of her with a clear and discerning eye. "Hello Papa," she said simply when it was her turn. Only when he had his arms gripped firmly around her lithe body did he realize that she was shaking from head to toe. "Besides you mother," he whispered in her ear, "I have missed you the most, my serious little woman."

Even though she could see that both father and daughter were crying, Yetta was impatient to feel her husband's arms around her, to taste his taste, to touch him and be touched. It felt to her as if there were invisible threads joining their two bodies, pulling at her to move closer, pulling, pulling. It was with great restraint that she allowed her daughter the moments she obviously needed with her father, but she managed. And then Noah turned to her, and the two stood apart, facing one another, staring. Yetta was vaguely aware that Min was jumping up and down screaming something or other, and that Beck, too, was running from their trunks next to the wagon to Elias, who had also climbed down to hug them all. And then everyone else disappeared as Noah took four huge steps and pulled her into his chest. The smell of him overwhelmed her in its familiarity as her mouth reached for his with a hunger that was shocking in its intensity. When his mouth found hers, Yetta melted with the relief of it: her husband was the same as he had been when she had last seen him in all the essential ways. Everything about him was still familiar, as familiar as her mama's kugel, or the breath of each of her children against her cheek.

"Mama!" Nell exclaimed, clearly embarrassed by her parents, who seemed to be embracing longer than any of the other adults around them. When they continued to kiss she started to speak again, but Jules stopped her with a hand on her arm, and a smile. "They love each other so much. It's wonderful, Nelly. Let them be," he whispered, urging her, "Come, help me with our baggage." As she turned in numb obedience, Nell realized that she was jealous, and suffered momentary shame. How strong her parents had been during the long years of their separation! How brave to have made this huge move so that she, her brother and sisters could have a better life. If they wanted to kiss for an hour, she decided, it was not she who would stop them.

It was Min, running around the couple in circles, who finally brought them back to earth. She tugged at her father's pants' leg, asking him, "Why are you crying, Papa? Aren't you glad we are here?"

Kneeling in front of her, Noah explained, "That is why I am crying, little one. Sometimes we cry when we are happy."

"That's silly," she giggled, dancing around him in a circle. "When we're happy we should laugh and dance."

She grabbed her father's hand, and without any hesitation he began to dance with his youngest child in the midst of the chaos on the dock, until first Beck, and then Nell, and then Jules, Yetta, Elias and one stranger after another were all dancing the hora in a line snaking through the crowds, watched from above by the ferry crew, who had just finished unloading the large vessel. One of the workers let out a cheer until the voices of the entire ferry crew above had joined together in song as they applauded the dancing immigrants below.

It was this spirit that had brought all of them to this shore, and it was this spirit that would enable them to survive and prosper.

* * *

Relishing this new creature he found himself married to, Simon urged Adelaide to dance with him every night on the ship back to New York once they were sure Holly was soundly sleeping. Again the neighbors in the next cabin assured the young couple that they would hear Holly if she awakened and cried out, both of them all but pushing Addie and Simon out the door. Although she didn't think she was a good dancer, she enjoyed those evenings moving to the music in her handsome husband's arms. Adelaide noticed the eyes of several of the single women, avidly watching Simon as they glided by. She had to admit to herself that part of her enjoyment came from knowing that the man they obviously coveted was her husband. Even though she lacked the ardor he craved, Addie believed she made it up to him in other ways. She was a good cook, and kept their home immaculate. She also realized she was a fortunate woman: Simon did not begrudge her the singing anymore, and even seemed proud of her accomplishments. This alone made up for their nightly fumbling for each of them.

By the time they were halfway to New York, Adelaide was quite sure she was pregnant again. Instinctively, she sensed that she could not tell Simon about this development. He might feel proud of her, but he loved nothing as much as he loved being a father. If she were to have this child, Adelaide did not know if she would have the energy or strength to continue with the Schola. She meant what she had promised Arnold: she would keep singing and she would improve. Parenting was not the center of her life although her husband wished it to be, especially now that she had experienced such success abroad. Odd as it might have seemed to other people, it was her voice that was her child, and her voice that she knew she must nurture. Walking alone on the deck one afternoon when Simon had taken Holly to the coffee shop for an ice cream soda, Adelaide mulled over what she could do about her situation. She remembered with shame some of the girls in the Schola whispering about a doctor, a doctor who could help a woman get rid of an unwanted child before the child was even born. Though the very idea made her feel sick to her stomach, Addie also realized this was something she needed to explore. That she would contemplate such an action was something she could never admit to a soul, other than the girl in the group who might be able to give her the information she needed.

Oddly enough it was with a much lighter heart and tread that she dressed for dinner that evening, braiding her little girl's hair and threading a ribbon through the braids much to the child's delight. Simon was thrilled, saying no man on the boat had such beautiful women as he. That night Holly begged to be allowed to stay up to dance with her parents. Addie, who was immune to the child's pleas, nevertheless acceded to her husband, who found it delightful that the little girl wanted to dance with them. He took turns with the two 'women', receiving a round of applause after he finished a waltz with his daughter, lifting her above the floor for most of it, and then bending down to hold her so that she could show off her foot movements, which were perfect. Once they were sure she was asleep, Addie was awakened from her own dozing by her husband's hand stroking her back, his signal that he wanted to climb on top of her. Perhaps from guilt about the secret she was keeping, or because his advances didn't feel as unpleasant as they had when they were first married, Addie reached behind her to take his hand and place it on her breast. The movement of his fingers across her nipple didn't arouse her particularly, but she had learned how to pretend with little sighs and whimpers in order to convince him otherwise. That seemed to excite Simon more than merely entering her to find his own release. As he moved into place on top of her, she idly wondered if other women felt more than she, or if this was just an act women endured when they were married. The only person she might have asked was her sister, but Sophie was far away. In Vienna Addie had been too busy with her rehearsals and shopping for such confidences.

For his part, Simon was relieved that she no longer lay beneath him holding her body stiffly in place as if what he was doing to her might break her in two. He was also proud of his wife. But he had also acknowledged to himself that she would never be the passionate woman he had longed for, a woman who would draw him into the boudoir with a look, a kiss, or a hand tugging at his. The enthusiasm that might have generated that kind of behavior in his wife seemed to be reserved for her music. He would have given anything to see the look of rapture she displayed on a stage beneath him in the privacy of their bedroom, but he had all but given up. Try as he might not to feel saddened by this reality, he was unable, spending many hours in the train on his way to his customers digesting the truth of his married life. What he might be able to do about it was another thing, and one, at this early stage of the marriage he was unwilling to dwell on. For now there were the concerts and the parties afterwards, which were really quite exciting; the joy of his daughter flying towards him when he opened the door to their apartment in the evenings, and the smile Addie gave him as she set his dinner down on the table. He prayed those things would be enough for him alongside the income he was generating at work, which was rising monthly. If he and Addie wanted to move to a larger apartment, they would be able to by the end of the year. For now, hiring a painter to freshen the walls of their current home, and purchasing the new sofa and hutch for the living room Addie had been coveting for months would have to suffice. If she again became pregnant, an earlier move to a larger place in the neighborhood could be considered. Simon understood that he had riches beyond the dreams he had held as a young man in Vienna, and a life more exciting than he had even imagined crossing the ocean. If he wasn't content the fault must be his.

The first night they were back in their apartment in the Bronx, Simon raced out while Addie prepared a simple dinner for the three of them, although he didn't tell her where he was going. As she browned the chicken with Holly at her feet playing with Addie's pots and pans, her favorite game by far, Addie couldn't dispel her irritation at Simon's absence, which felt like a defection to her.

"I'm making sliced potatoes, like you, Mama," Holly happily explained as she took a small chopping board and imitated her mother's hand motions on the counter above her head.

"And how are you going to prepare them," Addie asked her with a smile. Sometimes Holly did afford her some relief.

"With salt and paprika and butter, of course," Holly declared without a moment's hesitation, making her mother laugh aloud.

"That's just what I'm going to do, Holly," she agreed. Mother and daughter smiled at each other in a rare moment of shared intimacy. Then Addie heard Simon's key in the door, and frowned in irritation, confusing the small child at her feet, who had no idea what she had done to upset her mother. When Simon appeared, the little girl clapped her hands in excitement. "Oh Papa. They're so pretty!" she exclaimed, the pleasure in her voice making Addie turn at the sink.

Simon stood in front of them both holding a huge bouquet of mixed flowers. "I wanted to bring you something to let you know how much I appreciate all you do for us, even though you rehearse three times a week. I am so proud of you, Addie! Thank you for a marvelous trip." He moved first to his wife, whom he kissed on each cheek, and then bent to the child, who was already reaching her arms up to him so he could pick her up.

"They're very beautiful, Simon. Thank you for being such a kind husband, and for allowing me to take so much time away from you both," Addie replied, meaning every word.

Dinner that night was a very happy occasion. All three Liebman's fell asleep that night with ease, warmed by the memory of their trip and the contentment it had brought them.

CHAPTER EIGHT

On the ride from Hoboken, where the ferry from Ellis Island had docked, the sights along the way to Elizabeth silenced even Min. The houses they passed were larger than those in their little village, even the bigger homes of the balebatim, with enormous front yards and towering trees often creating an arbor above the wagon. The roads were all paved although it was obvious they were not in a major city. This was something none of them had ever seen. Beck interrupted the silence by piping up with the question, "Is everyone in America rich, Papa?"

He turned and ruffled her hair, explaining, "No, Beck. But the government here works differently than the one at home."

Even Jules was intrigued. "What do you mean, Papa?" he asked.

"Here, when people pay taxes the money goes towards maintaining the roads, and piping water into the homes, and street cleaning…" he replied. This last 'service' elicited peels of laughter form the children.

"Mama," quipped the usually serious Nell. "Here you will be a lady of leisure. When you get home from work you won't have to sweep the street in front of our house. And Beck and I will be home from school so we can prepare dinner!" Nell glanced at her parents, a huge grin plastered across her face. She couldn't believe she was going to be able to go to school.

"Where will we be living, Papa?" Beck suddenly wondered aloud. "Do we have a house yet?"

"You father found an apartment for you just around the corner from our house. But tonight we will all be staying together," their Uncle Elias explained to them all.

"I want to see our house!" squealed Min.

"What's an apartment, Papa?" Jules asked his father at the same time.

"Yes, Noah. What is that?" Yetta asked as well, nuzzling Min's head to quiet her.

"Some of these big houses we are passing have been divided into different homes," Elias explained.

"I don't understand," said Yetta.

The eyes of all the children were wide with curiosity, waiting for their father to explain this strange phenomenon.

"Sometimes there are four families living in one house, two downstairs, and two above," he began.

"Do they walk through each other's parlor?" Nell asked him, clearly disturbed.

Elias laughed, "No Nell. Each apartment has its own entrance."

"What a strange way to live," Yetta said, as puzzled as her children.

Noah gazed at them all with concern. He hoped they would adjust more quickly than he had. At least they would be in their own space, with the living room and kitchen downstairs, as well as a small bedroom for Jules, situated behind the stairs that adjoined their neighbor's wall. After an exhaustive search that had taken months he had found a duplex with an upper and lower floor, a real luxury for an immigrant family in Elizabethport. He and Elias had worked very hard designing and building the tiny room for Jules at the end of the hallway downstairs behind the steep interior staircase, so the young man would have some privacy. After all, how large a hallway would they need? The sisters would be sharing, but they had done so in Monasterzyska too, so this should not disturb them. The linen closet was larger than the wardrobe they had used in their village at home, and the upstairs hallway was quite spacious.

"Our building only has two families living in it," he told them, Elias chiming in immediately. "The Grossman's are a lovely family, and have been good customers for Noah."

"Can we meet them tonight?" Beck asked, suddenly as excited as her baby sister. Then as an afterthought she added, "Do they have any children?"

"Yes, little one. One of their daughters is nine. Just one year older than you," Noah told her.

"I want to see our house," Min declared again.

"Perhaps you should stay there tonight, Noah, so the children and Yetta can settle in. We could stop in as well before we go to our place for dinner," Elias suggested, sensitive to the family's need to finally reach their new home.

"Why are we going to stay with you tonight? Do we have beds in our ap…ap…." Min interrupted.

"Apartment. And yes we have beds," Noah chuckled.

"Wait until you see the place. It's really something," Elias added.

"Shhhh," cautioned Noah. "We don't want them to expect too much." He was worried because the apartment was smaller than their bungalow in Monasterzyska, but the kitchen was much more up to date, which he knew all of the girls would love. He hoped it would make up for not having their own house, as well as the other difficulties they would all soon be experiencing.

As they moved through the outskirts of Elizabeth, all conversation ceased. The houses there were closer together but still had front yards. The oak trees were tall and full, affording generous areas of shade as well as breezeways from building to building.

Nell was stunned by this new place. 'I didn't know you lived in a city, Papa. You didn't tell us," she murmured.

"This isn't a city, my child. Elizabeth is only a town," Noah replied.

"How many people live in a town?" Yetta asked him.

"I would think there are at least 20,000 people in the port alone," Elias mused. "I've never looked it up."

"That's as big as Buchach, and that's a city," Jules exclaimed. "How many people live in a city in America?"

"How many are there in New York, Elias? Several million?" Noah asked his brother.

"Oh yes. Easily." No one spoke very much on the rest of the journey, each one trying to digest all they had already been told.

When they finally arrived in front of the duplex Noah had rented and renovated for his small family, they were all speechless. "This looks very big, Noah!" Yetta, who was sitting on the bench between the two brothers with Min on her lap, exclaimed.

Noah reminded her that the building was home to two families, not just one, but he had to admit it did look imposing. He had become used to the size of the dwellings in this new country, and hadn't given much thought to what the buildings would look like to his family when they arrived. He climbed down from the wagon, holding his hand out for his wife.

The children raced through the rooms, exclaiming over the furniture, the size of the parlor, which was in truth smaller than the one back home. "Mama!" Beck called out. "Wait until you see the kitchen!" When Yetta followed Noah back to that room, her face broke into a smile. "Why I think even I could cook a meal on this stove," she sighed. "Oh no," her eight year old disagreed. "This room is mine!" All of the children burst out laughing, quickly joined by their parents. Elias, laughing as well, suggested they unload the wagon and leave everything stacked in the front room. Then they would have to drive over to his house, or Marlene would begin to worry about what had happened to them all.

Yetta and Noah were the last to leave the kitchen. For once she was silenced by all her husband had done to make this new place a home for them: the pieces of furniture he had restored; the table in the kitchen with its six matching chairs, painted white to lighten the room itself; the parlor couch and matching chair with mahogany frames and maroon velveteen cushions; and the book case lining one whole wall there, already filled with Noah's books from both the old and new country. All she had time to do was hold his face in both of her hands, look into his eyes and say, "Thank you, Noah. Thank you." Their kisses were short because they could hear the voices of their children calling them from outside, "Mama, Papa, hurry. Uncle Elias needs to go. Hurry."

Marlene had prepared a sumptuous feast for them all, but by the time she served the kugel pudding Beck and Min were both falling asleep at the table. The hug she gave Yetta as the Unger family prepared to leave was both long and filled with warmth. The two women smiled at each other, already sure they would have a deep and abiding friendship. A family picnic was arranged for the weekend, and Noah walked his family home. Although not a taciturn man, he was not one who moved through his days with a smile on his lips either. Nevertheless, on this day, on this evening, he could not keep his lips from turning up, or his heart from expanding in his chest in-between each breath. He had all but given up hope that this day would ever come, and now that it was here, it felt even better than he could have imagined in his wildest dreams.

The family joke that was passed down from generation to generation afterwards was that little Max was born nine months to the day of Yetta's arrival in Elizabeth. By the age of two he was speaking both English and Yiddish with a smattering of Polish words thrown in as well. Nathan, born a year after Max, toddled after his older brother, already bossing him around in a voice surprisingly loud for his tiny body. The two boys were adored by their older sisters from the moment they were born, and therefore soon expected anyone of the female persuasion to take care of them. Indeed, one of the girls or Yetta came running if either child let out so much as a peep; all of them attended to serious mishaps. Yetta knew the little boys were being spoiled, but these native sons of her new country held such importance for her that she could not desist from doing too much herself, let alone ask her daughters to do the same. Min, Nell and Beck had all become fluent in English, and all were excelling at school. But it was Nell who loved learning, utterly thrilled that school was not only permitted for girls, but expected. She dreaded the day she would be too old to attend classes, but didn't have much time to think about it, given the household chores she had readily assumed as soon as the family had moved into their apartment. Noah's old boss at the sewing factory hired Yetta the Monday after her arrival in Elizabethport. During her interview, conducted with Noah as the interpreter, the immigrant was able to correct a serious error by a factory seamstress, fixing a seemingly ruined garment without knowing a word of English. When Boiland realized that the seamstress who had made the error and worked for him for years easily comprehended the suggestions of the skinny foreigner, he hired Yetta on the spot. At first he asked her to work on the floor alongside the other piece workers, but within three months she had become a section supervisor, and within the year was running the entire floor.

Although she also took in piecework, and Noah's business was growing every day, neither of them believed they could afford to move to a larger apartment, although it was quite apparent to both that such a move was necessary. Jules was not averse to sharing his tiny room with his younger brothers, but it was too small for three beds. Max, as well as Nathan, was becoming too big for his crib, and Noah longed for the privacy of a bedroom he could share with Yetta. They slept in the parlor on a mattress they unfolded every night. One evening, after the younger children were all in bed, though Nell and Jules were still reading at the kitchen table, Yetta and Noah sat down to review their finances. Doing some rapid calculations on the pad in front of her, Yetta turned it to Noah so that he could see her calculations. If his workspace was large enough to hold more pieces of junk for him to turn into useable furniture, he could hire an assistant to do the scraping and hammering, increasing his profit three fold. With some publicity in the Elizabeth Daily News Yetta was convinced he could expand his business to the wealthier areas of Elizabeth, beyond the central downtown area. Two customers who lived in the Westminster neighborhood, a wealthy gentile area between North Avenue and Broad Street, had already heard of his skilled work and come knocking at his door. Neither seemed to mind doing business with a Jew from the port, and both had already returned to order a second piece.

After thoroughly digesting the financial implications of these figures, Yetta remonstrated in Yiddish, "Don't say no right away, Noah. Just listen to me first, and give it some thought."

"Uh oh. This doesn't sound like I'm going to have a choice," he replied, and the two smiled at one another. If it was possible, in America they had become closer and more dependent on each other than they had been in the old country.

"On my way home from the factory today I noticed an old building with a 'for sale' sign on it, so I got off the trolley. The realty office wasn't far away, and I wasn't tired, so I walked over there to find out about it," she explained, holding up her hand to silence him. "There was a huge room downstairs that was large enough for a salesroom in front and a shop behind. There are already two apartments above, and a small building in back that could be turned into another."

"Yetta, we're just making ends meet now. How could we possibly," he began, but his wife interrupted.

"We would qualify for a loan. The realtor knows your business, and also believes that it will expand quickly. He thinks they can arrange the loan so that we have six months before we have to begin to pay it off, and by then you will have the customers for us to do that."

The fact that she spoke with such assurance gave Noah pause. Finally he asked, "What if I don't. Then what do we do?"

"We make sure you do, that's what!" she replied, squeezing his hand. "I know Elias would help you with the construction. Jules is a fast learner, even with his hands. The girls and I can do the painting."

"Is either of the apartments large enough for us?" he asked. Yetta was delighted: he was not saying no.

"I think so. You would have to look at the larger one with me. You might have to knock down a wall here, add another there, but if that can be done yes, it would give all of us more room. Noah. We can't afford not to take this opportunity. Of course it is a risk, but how else will we prosper so that Jules and the boys can continue their education past high school?"

When Noah's responded with the question, "What about Nell?" and continued, "She so loves to learn and she is as bright as the boys," Yetta realized she would prevail, although she had no idea how to reply. She knew Nell would have to go to work at eighteen, but by then she would have had infinitely more school learning than her own mother had. It would have to do.

* * *

Sitting in the park watching her daughter climb the monkey bars, Adelaide could not tear her mind away from the appointment she had made with a doctor in Manhattan the following day, whose name she had gotten from her co-worker. She didn't think he would perform the operation that day, but she was very nervous about the appointment nevertheless. She loathed the exams she had been forced to endure when she had been pregnant with Holly and dreaded having to go through the same thing again. Nevertheless, she realized such an exam would be necessary. When she was a child, and her horrid uncle would pull her onto his lap, his big pencil sticking up into the folds of her skirt, she would pretend she was running in the park with her sister, throwing a stick for a dog. Of course her family didn't have a dog, but Addie and Sophia had always wanted one. Of course she had known instinctively that what was in the old man's pocket was not a pencil. What it was she didn't understand for sure, she just knew she hated both him and his horrid lump. Watching her child race over to the swings and wave to her mother to come push her, Adelaide wondered what she could imagine during the exam that would transport her someplace other than the doctor's office. As she stood she assured herself she would come up with something on the subway ride if she didn't have time that afternoon.

The following morning she could barely get out of bed because she was so nauseous. She ran the water in the bathroom to mask the sound, but was certain Simon could hear her throwing up. When he joined her in the kitchen for his breakfast, he even asked her if she was coming down with the flu. She told him she wasn't sure, but assured him she would bring Holly over to Fionella's if she got worse as the day progressed. He nodded absentmindedly, gulping down his hot coffee, a habit of his she had never come to understand, and ate his richly buttered bread standing by the counter despite her protestations.

"I'm in a hurry this morning. I have to go to Brooklyn to see a new client. It could be a very large account, for an entire factory," he explained with his mouth full, as he moved over to Holly's high chair to pick up a spoon she had just dropped. Despite his pronouncement about having to leave immediately, he fed the entire bowl of oatmeal to his daughter, kissed her on both cheeks, gave Addie a quick squeeze and deep kiss 'for good luck' he said, grabbed his briefcase, which his wife had already placed in the front hall, and slammed the door behind him as he hurried off.

Addie was relieved his mind was elsewhere.

Fortunately she had hired an Irishwoman in the building to watch Holly when they returned from Europe, because she knew she couldn't rely on the ailing Fionella, especially with the singing group's newly expanded rehearsal schedule. Weeks before she had explained to her husband that the 'Schola' would be preparing for several concerts in New Jersey as well as New York. Much to her surprise he acquiesced to her plan immediately. He said he understood the need for the new sitter, and Addie happily accepted his words without worrying about why he was being so agreeable. She assumed that even he felt embarrassed at the notion of asking their aging neighbor to watch Holly for additional hours. Of course he had insisted on paying Mrs. O'Reilly long ago, but she had retired a year before her husband died, and had explained to them both that she didn't need the income. Initially, watching Holly had given her something to do; but her varicose veins had made the trek to the park, and the lifting and holding, more and more of a problem. All of them knew Adelaide and Simon needed to find someone else to take over the job.

The day of the appointment the Irishwoman sent her little daughter to Addie's apartment to tell her she had a fever and couldn't watch Holly because she was afraid of passing on her sore throat. After offering her condolences and sending the child on her way, Adelaide became frantic. Just this once, she thought to herself, as she left Holly in her high chair and raced down the flight of stairs to knock on Fionella's door. There was no response. She realized Fionella must have already left to do her daily shopping at the local shops and stood in the hallway frozen in place. Telling herself she was being foolish and that she had to pull herself together, she raced back up to her own apartment to dress Holly as well as herself. She would just have to take the child with her.

Holly, of course, was thrilled to be going with her mother, especially when she was allowed to wear one of the new dresses she had been given in Vienna. The little girl chatted all the way into the City, down the stairs, and into the Schrafft's for her promised hot fudge sundae. When she dropped a dollop of fudge onto the bodice of her new frock, Holly burst into tears, and seemed inconsolable. Two of the waitresses helped Addie, one bringing salt to the table, the other, iced water. The older of the two women scooped up the crying child and carried her into the bathroom to show her that the offending spot was gone, completely eradicated by the salt and cold water. Only then did Holly stop crying. Adelaide had stood up but not moved from the table, so stunned was she by the tumult her child had caused as well as her own impending appointment. She smiled with relief when the waitress placed the placated child back in her seat. When the woman returned with an extra scoop of coffee ice cream, Holly's favorite, and a little pitcher of hot fudge, Adelaide didn't object. She and the laughing waitress covered the child's dress with at least ten paper napkins so that a second tragedy would not occur. When Adelaide paid her bill, the manager said the second sundae was on them. He stooped down to tell Holly to 'have a wonderful day in the big City', and was utterly charmed when the pretty little girl leaned up and gave him a smack on his cheek. Adelaide was exhausted by the time she and her daughter reached the doctor's office,

Fortunately the waiting area was well supplied with children's toys, which Holly spotted immediately, even before her mother had signed in and been given some papers to fill out. The receptionist assured Adelaide that many of their patients brought children to their appointments with the doctor. Before she even turned around another young mother suggested she watch the little girl when Adelaide went inside. It didn't enter Addie's mind that this other young woman would probably see the doctor before she did, and would have to wait until Adelaide was finished before she herself could leave. She was just grateful her child would be cared for, and would not have to go into the examining room with her. By the time the other mother returned to the waiting room, Addie was terrified. Noticing that she was actually shaking as she rose to her feet, the young woman told her that the doctor was a very kind man; she didn't have to worry.

Perhaps the other woman was used to being probed and prodded, but Adelaide was not. The exam was even worse than she had expected because the doctor was a young man, unlike her own obstetrician. Putting her feet in the ice-cold stirrups and spreading her legs for him was totally humiliating, despite, or perhaps because of, his gentle touch. She couldn't bear the thought of him looking at her 'down there' and was completely unable to retreat into her planned fantasy. When the good-looking doctor raised his head to look up at her over the sheet between her legs and declared with a broad grin, "You're pregnant, Mrs. Liebman!" Adelaide wanted to crawl into a hole and hide. She could not force herself to smile, but just stared back at him until she finally had to look away. When the nurse asked her if she would need help with the buttons on her blouse, she shook her head 'no'. She couldn't bear another moment in the room with anyone. She just wanted to be alone.

When she was finally seated across from the doctor in his office, and he asked her if she had any questions, at first she feared she wouldn't be able to say anything at all. Then she remembered Caruso, and plowed ahead, looking at her own hands twisting in her lap rather than at the doctor.

"I don't really know how to begin Doctor. Last year I began singing with the Schola Cantorum here," she began with some hesitation.

"Really! My wife has been after me to get tickets to see them. Now I'll have to," he interrupted.

Addie cleared her throat. "I'm sure I can get you tickets, if you let me know when you want to come," she said. "But you see, that is why this is not a good time for us to expand our family." Seeing the stern look that immediately pinched his mouth, Adelaide ceased to speak.

"If there was an illness in your family, or you had terrible financial difficulties," he mumbled, also embarrassed. Perhaps no woman had sought his services in order to be able to pursue a career.

Adelaide felt utterly shamed. She could barely breathe.

Finally the doctor continued, "I might try to help you terminate your pregnancy under those conditions. As it is, in any event the time has actually passed to safely proceed with such a procedure," he said, clearing his throat, and adding unnecessarily, "With an abortion."

It was such an ugly word. Adelaide's hands were clasped so tightly she could no longer feel them. She managed to stutter, "What are the dangers, doctor Platt?"

"To begin with there would be quite a bit of danger to you. If you lost your life, not only would you no longer have a career," he explained with a gentle smile, "But your husband would lose a wife, and the daughter who is waiting outside for you, a mother. It would certainly be a burden to her father to have to raise his daughter by himself, as he tried to build his own career, don't you think?"

"I don't know what to do," she murmured although in the depth of her being she knew what she wanted to do. She had whispered the words, surprised by the kindness in the doctor's eyes, but she had little hope he would help her.

"You will have the child and continue your life as a mother. As for the singing - who knows? Perhaps in time you will again be able to pursue that part of your life as well," he suggested. Despite the fact that he was not much older than Adelaide, his words made her uncomfortable. There was judgment in them – his, her own, and those of the society in which they all lived.

To her own amazement she blurted, "But I have been asked to sing with Caruso."

"I'm sure the great man will be willing to wait for you. What an honor that must have been," he agreed as he rose to show her to the door. Their conversation was at an end, at least for him. Addie did not think he had any idea what this pregnancy might mean to her, what she wanted from life, and what she didn't. Even worse, she knew if he had understood, he would not have approved.

Instead of going to the reception room, Adelaide fled to the bathroom, where she threw up the breakfast she had barely managed to keep down hours before. She sat on the toilet for several minutes before she could force herself to walk to the reception area. How in the world would she endure having to take care of yet another child? Even worse, how would she endure the necessity of curtailing her career? Why hadn't she asked the doctor what the dangers to her health might be if she stopped singing? The very thought took her breath away. At that moment she did not believe she would survive.

On the way to the subway poor little Holly came to a dead stop in the middle of the sidewalk, looking up anxiously at her mother. "What's the matter, Mama? You're … scary."

Only then did Adelaide pull herself together, take her child's hand, look around to get her bearings and turn around to walk back to the subway station, which she had passed in her state of acute distress. Once they were on the train she realized she felt better. If she continued to practice and perform until her belly was too large to continue doing either one, and she continued to lift Holly into her arms for the nightly bath as well as when the child was upset and begging to be picked up, perhaps she would lose this new child and everything would be all right. And that might occur even before Simon had a reason to object to her behavior.

* * *

After consuming a huge breakfast of hot cereal, a thick slice of Nell's homemade bread slathered with butter and jam, stewed prunes, and a large glass of milk, both Max and Nathan followed their father out to his wagon to ride with him on his morning pick-up route. They both adored these trips around the port with their father, Max at nearly four anxious to 'help' his father lift the larger pieces up into the wagon. When he could heft a chair, or small corner table all by himself, the look on his excited little face warmed his proud father's heart. Nathan was actually less clumsy than Max in the shop. He enjoyed pulling out rusty nails, although he had to hang on to the hammer with both hands, holding the piece of furniture in place with his feet. A humorous sight: Noah would never have humiliated the toddler by laughing, though several times he had to hide behind a wardrobe to conceal a smile. One slow day Noah took out his copy of the Talmud, determined that his boys learn to read in Hebrew as he had as a boy. He had collected several used children's books in English on his junk runs, because he also understood that his sons had to become fluent in English to be able to prosper in America as adults. The loneliness he had experienced during his initial four years in Elizabethport would not be in vain: his children would receive the education that had not been available to him. Jules, who was in his last year of high school, spent much of his spare time tutoring his younger brothers To honor his father. Little Max, especially, was a very quick learner, frequently asking Jules to find him 'new' books to read, since he already 'knew' the ones in their apartment. Indeed, Jules and Noah were surprised to learn that he wasn't 'reading' them anymore, because he had memorized every word within them. Jules knew his brother was special.

It was for this reason that one day, when he returned home from a full day at school, Jules slipped Max's arms into the sleeves of the heavy jacket Yetta had made for him, and then chased him all the way to the trolley stop, both of them laughing so hard they were out of breath when they got there. The child's eyes were huge when the trolley lumbered into view. The little boy had seen such vehicles, but never imagined he would ride in one. Jules swung him up the two steps into the trolley, paid the driver the fare, and, hanging on to the child so he didn't fall over, managed to slide them both onto the bench seat behind the driver before the trolley rocked into motion. Max wanted to stand on the seat with his back to the aisle so he could look out the window, which Jules allowed as long as the boy let Jules hold on to him. "It's for Mama," Jules explained. Max thought about this, and agreed, "Mama wouldn't like me to stand up because I could fall." When they turned onto Broad Street, the little boy faced his brother, pointing with great excitement, "Julie. Look at that. That building has so many windows!" Laughing, the older boy asked his little brother in jest if he could count them, but Max became silent immediately, and much to his amazement proudly stated several minutes later, "There are sixteen on the bottom floor, but the trolley was going too fast, so I don't know how many there are on the top floors. There were three more, can you imagine that!"

By the time they arrived in front of the new library, Max had turned himself around, sat down and inched his way off of the bench to a standing position so they could be the first passengers off of the trolley. Max looked at the grand, granite staircase leading up to the wooden doors of the library in wonder. When Jules grabbed him under the arms again to carry him up the stairs, Max's voice held a determination his older brother had never heard.

"No, Julie. I can climb them myself. I'm a big boy, you know!"

The steps were very high for the little fellow, but he half crawled, half climbed up them, eventually agreeing that holding on to his brother's legs to gain more leverage was acceptable. When he reached the top, he turned to survey the street below, his face suffused with light and his back ramrod straight.

"See. I told you I could do it!" he loudly declared, his pride in the accomplishment affording him the confidence that usually eluded him.

"I never doubted it for a minute, my little man," Jules told him, though in fact, he had wanted to pick him up and carry him the rest of the way several times, but couldn't figure out how to do so without humiliating him. Now he was grateful he had done no such thing.

The librarian already knew Jules quite well, since he often stopped by on his way home from school to take out a novel that was not required reading for any of his classes. Initially Jules had believed that reading American novels would enhance his understanding of American history and customs, which it did. Now he was reading the books largely for pleasure. That afternoon the librarian suggested a book by Nathaniel Hawthorne. Once the book had been found and checked out, she moved around the counter and bent down to Max, whose face was agog, looking at the stacks upon stacks of books within the main room.

"And what can we get for you, young man?" she asked.

"I need to find some new books to read. I've memorized the ones my papa has at home. I think there are enough here that I won't have to memorize any more," he replied seriously.

"I think we can take care of that," she smiled down at him, leading him into the children's section of the library.

Max turned in a full circle, obviously startled. "Are these books all for children?" he asked. As soon as she nodded 'yes', his face broke into an enormous grin. "Which ones would be good for me?"

"What do you like to do?" she asked him as she approached the shelves reserved for the smallest readers.

"I like riding my cousin's tricycle. I like to read. I like to help my father make furniture. And I like doctors," he said.

As he spoke the librarian pulled some simple, first grade readers from the shelves, most with pictures adorning each page with words below them. Max leafed through the first book, totally thrilled. Then he looked up and asked her, "These seem very good. Are you sure there will be enough?"

"I promise you will never run out," she assured him.
Jules had brought a canvas satchel to carry his own books, but had to persuade Max to let him put his inside it as well. The little boy wanted to sit on the floor, right where they were, and immediately begin to read the books. When his brother explained that he could take them home, and keep them for two weeks, Max could not believe his good fortune. Jules promised to bring him back to exchange the books spread around him for new ones. The librarian suggested she start to compile a list for him; she would have the first four books from the list waiting for him when he returned with his big brother in two weeks. Max could have flown home, but instead he allowed Jules to carry him down the library steps and onto the trolley. It had been a very thrilling, but tiring afternoon.

That evening, revived, the four-year old pulled the younger Nate up beside him on the parlor couch, opened one of the books on his lap, and began to read the words to him, pointing to the picture that corresponded to each word. Noah and Yetta peaked in at them, but the boys were so engrossed they didn't notice.

"Max is going to teach Nathan to read," Noah exclaimed with pride. Taking his hand in hers Yetta turned to her husband. "I think it may be time for you to teach me," she said. "What do you think?"

"We can begin tonight," Noah replied, adding, "If you learn to read, it will be good for the business, don't you think?"

Yetta laughed. "You mean I'll finally be able to keep your business accounts in English so you don't have to translate them for your customers anymore!"

The two older Unger's sat down at the kitchen table with one of their son's library books, and Noah began teaching his wife how to read in English. Jules, who had come into the kitchen for a glass of milk, suggested he pick out some simple books on sewing and other crafts, which his mother might enjoy more as she learned the new language. Towards the end of the lesson, Noah reached for his wife's hand.

"Do you really think we should buy that building, Yetta," he asked.

"If we want out children to have the education warranted by their intelligence, I don't think we have any choice," she replied in Yiddish. Then she laughingly asked, "Do you think I'll ever learn enough English to be able to say something like that in this new language?" Noah wrapped his arm around her shoulders. "I just hope our children will be able to speak English that well. I will talk to Elias tomorrow. He may have a suggestion about where we could borrow the money for a down payment on this building of yours," he replied.

"Don't you want to see the building first?" she asked him in surprise.

"If I look at it, that may make me even more nervous."

Yetta nestled into her husband's embrace. "This is a good thing, Noah. I promise you won't regret it. With the profits you will make, perhaps we will even be able to send Nell on to a teacher's college."

Husband and wife stood as one, Yetta carrying the business ledgers into the parlor where she put them on a shelf next to Max's new library books. "Our little reader will certainly be able to go to college by then," her husband agreed, pulling her towards him for a kiss.

At midday two days later Noah walked over to the realty office to make an offer on the building, although he had still not even seen it. Elias, who had persuaded Noah to allow him to lend them the $200 necessary for the down payment, had taken a walk through the building with Yetta the day before and approved the plan. The very next weekend Noah, Elias and Jules began the reconstruction, tackling the apartment first, the rental unit second, and lastly Noah's new shop and office in the huge space below the two apartments. They had decided the showroom could be small, leaving room behind the partition for a very large workshop. Since the pieces Noah acquired were often large, Noah would need this space to store them in until he could repair and refinish them. He and Jules also built a small shack in the yard where overflow could be stored. In the past Noah had often been forced to give up likely pieces because he had no place to store them, and knew the wood would have been destroyed by both rain and snow if he had stacked the furniture in Elias' yard, even covered in several tarps.

The spacious apartment where they would be living thrilled every one of the children. Max and Nathan would have a large room to share, while Jules would again have the privacy of his own space, albeit a small one. They were able to carve out a tiny, separate room for Nell as well, after a generous Jules suggested they divide his room in two. Beck and Min were delighted to be left to their own devices in their bedroom, with plenty of storage shelves for their games and books. Though neither girl was terribly interested in reading, both enjoyed the pictures in the books Max brought home from the library for them. Eager to help the men with the construction, Max wasn't terribly disappointed that he had to forego one of his monthly visits to the library. His ability with a hammer had improved, though no one was under the misapprehension that he would ever choose work that was dependent upon his muscles. Nathan merely toddled from one side of the room to the other, holding nails for his Uncle, or carrying a tool to his father. Because they worked around the clock, Elias racing over to his brother's building as soon as he closed his butcher shop each day, they managed to finish the major portion of the construction within the first two months. A young couple, expecting their first child, rented the second upstairs apartment as soon as Yetta pasted a rental sign in the shop window.

Because the Unger apartment was directly above Noah's shop, he wouldn't have to close for lunch. Beck, who at 12 had taken over most of the family cooking so that Nell could spend more time on her school work, was only to happy to run downstairs to bring her father a sandwich, or better yet, to send one of her little brothers. In the fall and winter seasons she would bring down the plate of food herself, not trusting either boy with the hot food she had prepared for their father's lunch. Min had been given the job of watching the boys, and was a happy little boss. Max, an unusually quiet boy, obeyed most of her pronouncements, tickled, nonetheless, by his younger brother's clever schemes to disobey the same rules. Sometimes he followed the younger boy, and misbehaved, but often he was too frightened of his mother's angry reaction when she would come home from the factory to follow Nathan. Besides, he preferred to spend those hours with his father downstairs, helping hold a piece of wood to be glued, or learning to read Hebrew by following along behind Noah when there were neither customers nor furniture for them to refinish. Although this was a rare occurrence, the little boy had managed to pick up a fair amount of Hebrew. One day he asked Noah a question about the page in the Talmud his father was studying, which completely shocked Noah. The only way the boy could have come up with such a question would have been by reading the page Noah was studying. That afternoon Noah brought Nathan downstairs to sit beside his brother, instructing Max so that he would be able to teach his younger brother the Hebrew alphabet. Noah was thrilled when his youngest son also proved himself to be a fast learner. He did not learn as quickly as Max because he was much more restless, frequently jumping off of his high perch by the front counter to explore all of the pieces being glued, sanded, or stained in the back room, and running around in circles in the yard between the shed and the workshop.

When Jules arrived home from school, he would relieve his father for an hour or so in the shop so that he could pursue his studies in the quiet of the upstairs parlor. Noah had brought a bible downstairs, which Jules urged Max to read aloud to improve his vocabulary and to teach both brothers world history. Within several months Nathan was able to take turns with his older brother, although his reading was slower and more hesitant. For someone so young, his ability was extraordinary. After all, he was only three and a half. Since both tykes adored their big brother, both were willing to do anything he asked of them. Several afternoons when Noah came back downstairs to the shop, he would stand at the foot of the stairs for quite a while watching his sons work together, amazed at his good fortune. He would then send his oldest son upstairs to study. A senior in high school, the boy was already preparing for a career in medicine, taking advanced chemistry to prepare. Like his brothers, Jules loved learning. His private dream was to attend college and become a scholar, but he understood that paying for so many years of higher education would make it impossible for his parents to help Nell. Since he did love science, he had set aside this dream, and rarely thought about them, except when he was able to soak in the tub where he had the luxury of both privacy and time. His mother was adamant that he be given this opportunity at least once a week as a reward for all the help he gave his father, his brothers, and his sisters, and guarded the bathroom door zealously. No one dared disturb Jules, even mischievous Nathan, because it would mean contending with Yetta.

Frequently at night when they climbed into their bed, Yetta or Noah would reassure the other that moving to this new land had been the right choice. Already, they were living a life beyond what they ever could have imagined in Monasterzyska. Noah had his own business again, but it was his business, not one he was sharing with anyone else. Yetta's worked at the factory from 8 in the morning until 5 in the evening, arriving home hours earlier than she had in the old country. It wasn't surprising that her private business was thriving because she had plenty of time each evening to devote to her local clients. Between them, they would be able to pay off their debt to Elias in another few months. Then they could begin to save for the college education of their children. Often, if they could but see each other, they would have noticed that they drifted into sleep in one another's arms with smiles on their faces. Life had been good to them.

* * *

Simon was thrilled when he discovered Addie's little secret, which infuriated the young woman. "How am I going to keep singing?" she asked him angrily, adding, "I thought you were proud of what I am doing." She ran from the living room, slamming the bedroom door behind her, which awakened Holly who was taking one of her infrequent late afternoon naps. Simon played with the child, and then made dinner. When she smelled the cooking roast, Addie emerged from the bedroom. Even Simon didn't try to speak to her. That night he slept on the living room couch. Unfortunately the child within her was as determined to be born as she was to prevent the event. Despite their huge fight, Addie was unwavering in her commitment to travel with the group to Boston to perform the following weekend, a long harrowing journey by train. She realized she was in her sixth month, and a miscarriage would be dangerous to her as well as the baby, but nevertheless she went.

The concert was well attended, but Adelaide did not sing a solo because it seemed inappropriate to the concertmaster for the young mother-to-be to come to the front of the stage with such a huge belly. It seemed safer to keep her hidden within the group of singers, blending her voice with the others. There was a huge blizzard the night of the concert, which meant the group had to stay an extra day in Boston because none of the trains were running. By the time she managed to get home, Adelaide was exhausted. When Simon heard her key in the lock and opened the door she burst into tears. He opened his arms to her, grateful to have his wife and the child in her belly home in one piece. She admitted that the company manager suggested she cease performing until the baby was born, sounding inconsolable. He merely stroked her head, her arms, and her back in response, knowing anything he might say would be misinterpreted. In his heart he felt joy: perhaps now Adelaide would begin to enjoy being a homemaker, having the time to walk over to the park, buy clothes for the new child and blankets for the crib without racing into Manhattan for a rehearsal. Together they looked at a larger apartment on the third floor. It was much more spacious than the one where they had been living since Addie's arrival in America. He assured her they could afford it. He was earning a good living, and would be able to support them until she was able to return to her work. Even before the words left his mouth, he knew he had to say 'until' rather than 'if', which would only fuel the flame burning inside his young wife. Of course he hoped the Schola Cantorum would become a memory, and that their life together would revolve around their growing family rather than her splendid voice. Proud as he was of her talent, and he was genuinely proud, what Simon longed for was a home filled with the smells of cooking stollen and laughing children. This, of course, he didn't tell her. Some things were best left unsaid.

The birth of their second child was long and hideous. Ruth was born breach, tearing Adelaide all the way through from her vaginal canal to her anus. When she roused herself from the fog of the anesthesia the pain she experienced made her cry out, horrified that she was screaming just as the woman in the next bed had screamed during her childbirth. The nurse raced into the room, followed by a frantic Simon who had rushed out to find the woman as soon as Addie awakened. Giving her a shot of painkiller, the nurse quieted Adelaide by stroking her forehead with a damp, cool cloth.

"I'll bring baby Ruth in to see you. I'm sure that will make you feel much better," she said as she hurried from the room.

Simon was not so sure. He felt a knot in his stomach that he couldn't explain. His wife looked so tiny and forlorn lying in the hospital bed. She wouldn't make eye contact with him, despite the fact that it was he who was now stroking her head, dipping the cloth into the bowl of cool water every few minutes. When their new daughter was settled at her breast, with Adelaide's arm holding her in place, Simon experienced a depth of despair he hadn't known was possible. Addie barely glanced at the infant, actually closing her eyes as the baby suckled. Telling himself that she was exhausted from the horrible ordeal of her labor gave him little reassurance because deep in his heart he knew this to be false. His wife did not want this child: the birth had obviously done nothing to change that fact. He had told himself her refusal to make love with him over the last few months related to her discomfort in sharing her growing bulk with him. But leaving the hospital that first night Simon was not so sure.

He longed for relief himself, but understood he couldn't have asked Adelaide to comfort him. After all, she blamed him for the baby and the life she would now be forced to live. He was concerned about Holly, and what she must have thought after awakening at Fionella's rather than in her own familiar bed. When the subway approached the stop where he would have had to get off if he was going to the apartment of his new, young mistress – a secretary at a firm where he did frequent business – he only hesitated for a few seconds. He sat back down, resigning himself to duty. For a fleeting moment he understood how life must feel to his wife, who now would be consumed by a mother's chores. He could not imagine staying home all day long, having no work to distract him, having no one to relieve his tensions. He no longer deceived himself that he fulfilled that role for Adelaide; it was only her singing that afforded her relief. No wonder she looked away from both him and her new child: now she wouldn't have even that to sustain her. As quickly as this realization came to him, Simon pushed it aside, his thoughts turning to his older daughter and his schedule for the remainder of the day. When he arrived at the apartment building, he could hear Holly crying from the foyer, his heart sinking yet further as he bounded up the stairs to fetch her. Racing into his arms, the little girl was inconsolable for hours, terrified that neither of her parents was ever coming home. She had never slept anywhere but their apartment, and never awakened without her mother or her father coming to lift her out of her bed. Even Fionella was concerned about her desolation, relieved that Simon had finally come home to appease her. One of her own labors had been unbelievably difficult she assured Simon, adding that it had taken her almost a month to be able to walk without discomfort. She added that 'everything else took even longer'. He knew she was urging him to have compassion for his wife, and he determined that this he would do. Inside, he didn't really believe his behavior would make a bit of difference to Adelaide, but he didn't tell his neighbor this for fear it would make him sound heartless. Holding his sobbing little beauty, he had no idea how to quell her tears. As he walked back down the stairs wondering what else he could do to comfort her, Holly's sobs lightened and then stopped altogether. He squatted down as he set her on the floor outside their apartment, chucking her underneath her chin as he kissed her nose.

"You have a little sister, my lamb. Isn't that exciting?" he said.

Her only response was to ask him, "Can we go to the park, Daddy so I can show you how high I can swing?"

Initially, Holly didn't show much more interest in the reality of baby Ruth than she had in her birth. The only time she seemed to notice her sister was when she was being held in her father's arms. Then Holly raced to his side, raising her arms to be picked up as well. At these times she could not be distracted. Simon became adept at juggling the two girls, often walking around the apartment with one under each arm. When Ruth began to toddle around the large apartment, he would hold Holly with his right hand and Ruth with his left, and stroll to the park with them. When the three went there together or to the market to pick up something Adelaide had forgotten, the girls often vied for his attention. In a way it was fortunate that both children were girls: Simon was as good with them as he had always been with the various women who had come and gone in his private life. The woman he had been seeing the last months of Addie's pregnancy had long ago departed, with great sturm und drang because he would not leave his wife for her. Another had soon taken her place. Although Simon and Addie had actually grown to like one another, their sex life was almost non-existent. At first he had assumed she didn't want him to touch her because it had taken so long to heal after Ruth's birth, and she was afraid. After several months, he no longer cared why. Since he had been getting those needs met elsewhere for almost a year anyway, his wife's lack of ardor didn't seem a problem to him. It certainly wasn't for Adelaide, who was greatly relieved by his lack of attention at night.

Her return to the Schola Cantorum was much more of an issue for them both. When Simon came home early from the office one evening and found the apartment empty, he was frantic. He raced down to Fionella's, although she had ceased to do any of the daytime baby-sitting chores long ago. The older woman gave him the name and address of a sitter she knew Adelaide used upon occasion who lived only blocks away, and that was where he found the girls. Ruth was coloring at the dining room table, and Holly learning to sew at the woman's heavy machine. His daughters shrieked with delight when they saw their father at the door, and both ran eagerly into his arms. By the time he got them back to the apartment Addie was inside unpacking several bags of groceries, a roast already floured and spiced, ready to slide into the oven. When her husband demanded to know why she had left the girls with a sitter when all she had needed was groceries, she stared at him for a few seconds. Then she led the girls to their bedroom where their toys were already spread out on the floor.

"I had a rehearsal," she told her husband quietly when she returned to the kitchen.

"A rehearsal of what?" he demanded, his voice rising with anger although he immediately realized what his wife meant.

"With the Schola, Simon. Grimaldi called me a few weeks ago, to ask if I wanted to prepare for another European tour," she replied calmly, not rising to the bait.

"How in the hell do you plan to go to Europe to sing with two children to take care of?" he screamed at her.

"I will hire a nanny with the extra money I earn," she calmly replied, which infuriated her husband.

"I didn't say you could do that!" he yelled even louder, which infuriated Adelaide though she seemed unruffled, outwardly, at least. Inside, she was of course seething as she replied with a quiet but now deadly calm, "I don't need to ask your permission!"

In their shared room the usually ebullient little Ruthie and her quieter, older sister lay huddled together on Holly's bed. Though Holly was usually sparing of affection where her younger sister was concerned, on this day she had no problem throwing her arms around Ruth, and pulling her little sister to her chest. She needed the warmth of her body as much as the younger child needed the comfort of hers.

"Mama and Papa fought like this once before. They didn't talk to each other for a whole day, but then it was all right. I promise," she whispered.

"Why do they hate each other?" Ruth asked, obviously distressed by the sounds coming from the parlor.

"I don't think they hate each other, I think they're just mad. Last time they didn't talk to each other the next morning, and then…and then…when Papa came home from work he kissed her 'hello' again," Holly explained. In truth, her parents' behavior hadn't made sense to her then and didn't now. But she had to believe that this time, like the last, her parents would make peace, and their life as a family would continue. After all, what else was she to think?

In the kitchen Simon demanded that his wife call the director of the singing group and tender her resignation, but she was adamant in her refusal no matter how loud he screamed. She continued to dice up vegetables and slice potatoes as they yelled at each other, which absolutely enraged her husband. Preparing their dinner made Addie feel somehow safer. When Simon stormed out of the apartment, slamming the door behind him, she was relieved. She found the children asleep in one another's arms, and tiptoed back to the kitchen. When she had their dinner ready, she carried the plates into their bedroom, awakening them with a kiss to the forehead. Neither child said a word because her behavior was so unusual. Adelaide sent them into the bathroom to wash their hands, and then allowed them to eat their dinner on the floor of their bedroom, a treat because she had never done this before. Halfway through the meal, Ruth, always the brave one, asked, "Where is Papa?" Both girls accepted their mother's response. "He's gone out," as if that were the normal state of affairs in the evening in the Liebman home. But once their mother had bathed them, put them each into their pajamas, and tucked them into their own beds, closing the door behind her, Ruth slipped from her bed and slid into Holly's. For the first time in their young lives, they slept together for the whole night.

When Simon returned at two in the morning, he found his bedroom door locked, and a set of sheets and blankets stacked on the living room couch. His anger spent, Simon fell asleep thinking about his marriage with a sadness that was becoming all too familiar.

CHAPTER NINE

Although their home was certainly not the sanctuary of Simon's dreams, the Liebman household settled into a peaceful routine. Both Simon and Adelaide felt affection for one another, and respected each other's strengths, even those they couldn't really understand. Simon had become a partner in the firm he had joined after spending several years making his mark as a salesman elsewhere. He and Robert Landers, the wealthy passenger he had met on the deck of the ship that had brought him to the shores of America, had spoken a few times over the years, even meeting for lunch at the other man's urging. Simon never spoke about work at those lunches; but when he was ready to approach Landers about a job, he called his secretary and made an actual appointment. "I have been waiting for this day for over a year, Simon," Landers said as he rose from his seat behind an imposing oak desk, reaching across it to shake the younger man's hand. The job he offered Simon had infinitely more responsibility than the one Simon had come to suggest to him. The immigrant from Vienna quickly moved up the corporate ladder because he was clever as well as personable. Landers' wife was a favorite of both of Simon's daughters, especially the rambunctious Ruthie. He and his wife came to every concert given by the Schola, in New York, delighted at the success of their young Austrian protégé and his talented wife. Landers, of course, also felt pleased by his own foresight, which had enabled him to see the unique qualities in that ambitious boy on the voyage across the Atlantic. The night of his promotion, Simon arrived home bearing gifts for 'his ladies', thrilling his daughter Holly with a new doll that was almost as tall as she, Ruth with a children's book with enough space on each page for the child's contributions to the story, and a delicate necklace of pearl, gold, and tiny amethysts for Adelaide. The necklace kept her from complaining about the book. Ruth was already precocious; she thought it wrong to encourage their daughter in a sphere not open to her gender. Simon just laughed at her, though he found it odd that she, of all people, would voice such an objection.

As for Adelaide, being able to perform had actually made her a better mother. She spent four afternoons a week in Manhattan, leaving Ruth with the Irish sitter who also picked Holly up from her school so Mama didn't have to shorten her rehearsal schedule. This year she would be singing two solo's, one a Mozart lieder and another by her old friend and mentor, Arnold Schoenberg. She had come to enjoy baking with the girls, laughing at the mess they made with the flour, although she was also quite strict about cleanup, forcing them both to help her in the kitchen once the goodies were in the oven. The more active Ruth found it torturous to wash the countertop and sweep the floor when they could all be racing off to Crotona Park, leaving the cleanup for later after the sky had begun to darken with the approach of nighttime. Nevertheless, she was more particular about her chores than Holly, sweeping the floor with such care that her mother didn't have to follow behind her with the dust mop. Because of this Adelaide sometimes relented, taking the girls to the park and doing the cleanup herself when they returned, exhausted, to the apartment.

Usually, however, it was Simon who played in the park with the children, often arriving home early to do so. On those mornings he left before they were even awake to be sure he'd finish his work early enough to be able to offer them this treat. When he came home one day with a pair of screw-on skates for each of them, it was the younger Ruth who couldn't wait to get to the park to try them out. She was jumping up and down with excitement in the hallway, her jacket on, ready to go, while Holly fussed with her hat, knowing this would elicit her father's attention. At the park Simon tightened Ruth's skates first, because she was clearly desperate to move. Holly watched Ruth with a deep scowl as she skated away from them without any hesitation, as if she had already done this many times before. To make matters worse, Holly started off with very shaky legs, and landed on her bum after just two tiny glides. Ruth skated in a circle around her, urging her back on her feet with the words, "It's really easy, Holly. Honest. Even I can do it!" Still kneeling by the bench where he had set down their things, Simon howled with laughter. In Holly's mind he was laughing at her, at her clumsiness; she had to fight back tears. Then her father was pulling her to her feet, holding one of her hands to keep her upright until she began to get the hang of it. By then little Ruth was doing figure-eights around her father and sister, making smaller and smaller loops as she became more adept on her new skates. Of course she was spurred on by the attention her father lavished on her for her easy expertise. Like Holly, she devoted a great deal of time and energy winning his approval. When he smiled down at her, she forgot how stern her mother often looked, and how much she seemed to disappoint her.

Despite her desire to appease her mother by helping in the kitchen, Ruth's longing to get out of the apartment and fly down the street on her new skates usually won out. Within weeks, she was leaving the apartment without admitting she was going to the park. She left with her skates tucked under her arms, a maneuver she could manage if she waited until her mother had started to prepare dinner in the kitchen. She could call her 'good-bye' from the front door, telling her mother exactly when she would come back upstairs from the stoop below, and then rush out the door and down to the park. Since she was only allowed to play on the sidewalk in front of the apartment building, and was forbidden to cross any streets, this was quite a brave, though foolhardy move, depending on your point of view. Ruth, fleet of foot and mind, had often watched her sister look both ways before crossing the street at the corner of their block, or walk the long way around to the park so that she could cross where there was a light. The little girl knew to cross when it was green, and this seemed the best idea to her the first time she was brazen enough to go there by herself. Soon she was making the journey at least twice a week, and no one, not even her sister, was the wiser. Holly often had a play-date with a girlfriend from her elementary school, and on those days, Ruth knew she would be safe.

One afternoon she ventured a bit further into the park in search of a hill she had spied when Simon had taken them to the ball field where he had been meeting some friends for a pick up game of baseball. At first she skated for awhile on the flat walkway, where she practiced her single-leg turns and a spin she had been concocting in her head and then on paper so that she could see it in a concrete way, not just in her mind's eye. Then she stooped, took the key from the pocket of her pants, loosened the wheels, removed the skates and hiked up the hill with a skate in each hand. At the top she stood, glancing down the long hill with a palpitating heart and gleeful smile. At first she was so thrilled by the feeling of flying, that she didn't think about how she would stop once she reached the bottom of the long slope. Once she did think about it, the trees bordering the trail as it circled around the small meadow to join the main pathway into the park, were almost directly in front of her. Before she could panic, one of her skates hit a stone, and she spun around, much as she had in her dreams at night, before sprawling across the hard ground, one leg beneath her in a weird, unnatural angle.

It took only a few seconds for the little girl to feel the pain, excruciating, sharp, and insistent. She began to scream in terror, more afraid of what her mother would say than how she would ever make it home. Unable to move her leg at all, she could only rise up on her elbows, fairly useless in terms of getting off of the pathway itself, let alone trying to get home. Her screams and tears intensified. Fortunately an older man had come to the park to walk his dog and heard her cries, although he was already all the way up on the field where Simon had played ball with his friends weeks before. At first he tried to comfort her, but she had been taught not to talk to strangers. He explained who he was and where he lived, and then described his own daughter, who had just had a baby he hoped would someday be as brave as Ruth. Finally she became interested in his story and stopped screaming. Without realizing she was still whimpering, Ruth asked him questions about the new child, whether it was a boy or a girl, and whether his daughter liked holding it. By the time the stranger had answered all her questions, she trusted him enough to let him try to move her into a more comfortable position. But his efforts only made her cry again, because every motion caused piercing stabs of pain, as if her leg was being poked with a very sharp knife that scraped along her shin up to her hip. The man did manage to half drag half carry her to the side of the pathway so that none of the boys on their bicycles would run into her. Fortunately Ruth remembered the name of the street she lived on as well as the number of her apartment building.

But she grabbed his arm and pleaded, "But you can't go there."

Totally startled, he asked her, "Why?"

"Oh, Mama's going to be so mad at me," she moaned, eyes filling again with tears.

The old man patted her head in a gesture of reassurance. "She may be angry at first, Ruth. But she will be so happy to know you're all right. And she'll want to take care of you."

'He doesn't know my mama,' Ruth thought to herself. Aloud, she explained, "She doesn't know I come here. It means I have to cross a street, and I'm not old enough to do that."

"How do you manage?" he asked her, intrigued by her daring.

"I go all the way to 138th Street, because there's a light there," she promptly replied.

"That's very wise of you. I will tell her that, OK? It will show her how cleverly you've thought all of this through," he suggested, adding "Your mommy will be more worried about you than angry. I'm sure of that." She nodded in mute submission, although she was not sure she agreed with him. "Would it make you feel better if I leave Rosa with you?" he asked. The dog had been quietly sitting by the little girl's side, nestled next to her hip. Again she nodded, watching the old man's back become smaller and smaller as he walked quickly to the main artery leading in and out of the park. By the time he disappeared, Ruth was in too much pain to worry about what her mother would say. Maybe the man was right and she would be too upset to be angry.

By the time Adelaide followed the dog walker back to the park, Ruth was again crying. Her leg throbbed with every breath. Even the warmth of the dog no longer helped mask the pain. She immediately noticed her mother's tight-lipped visage as she approached, but couldn't stop crying. Addie bent down to stroke her daughter's arm, telling her that her father and an ambulance were on the way. Behind her, the man was startled by the mother's dispassion, or as he put it to himself, her 'lack of female feeling'. Even he had tried to take the child in his arms. It was with relief he noted that this was exactly what the father did when he raced onto the trail from the street, obviously causing the little girl some pain; but her relief at being held by him was palpable. She hugged him tightly, not wanting to let him go even when the nurse from the ambulance had her on the stretcher and was ready to lift her into the yawning vehicle. It was the father who climbed into the back with the child. Thus began the first of many trips over the years to the hospital with the little daredevil, the child Adelaide had not wanted to have and had never really understood.

She offered to pay the man in appreciation of his time and effort, but he declined. He assured the woman he was only too happy to have helped the little girl, and hoped the break was not a serious one. He and Ruth became fast friends over the next few years. Like her father, he became a champion of her brave actions and athletic abilities. Often, after a ball game with the neighborhood boys, Ruth would sit down on the bench next to the old man, his dog at their feet, and talk to him about the game, or school, a teacher – her life – amazed that an adult would be interested in her thoughts about any of those subjects. Mr. Gross, who had lost his wife only months before he had come upon Ruth in the park, was charmed by this bright, brave little girl. The only disappointment he had ever experienced in his thirty-year marriage was its childlessness, though it certainly hadn't been for lack of trying. Over the years had he dreamed about what their child would have been like, Ruth would have more than met his expectations. He knew his wife would have adored her.

That evening, after settling Ruth into her bed with her leg in its cast sticking out of the comforter, Simon and Adelaide managed to get her into her pajamas together by ripping one of the legs from hip to cuff. Holly watched them wide-eyed. She would never have had the courage to defy her mother by going to the park to play by herself. Though she skated with her sister when they were there with their father, she didn't really feel comfortable sliding. Walking to the top of that steep hill and then choosing to skate down it was totally beyond her comprehension. The eight-year old had no idea whether to feel admiration for her younger sibling, or scorn. When their parents began to fight about what had happened that evening, Simon defending the bravery of their youngest daughter, both girls were still awake. Holly felt jealous that Ruth was again the center of attention, even though she would have been distraught to hear her parents screaming at each other about something she had done. Ruth was terrified. Until she heard her father scream, "She is such a fighter, Addie. How can you not realize this? She is as determined as you!" and she suddenly realized her father approved of her. Despite the constant throbbing in her badly broken shin, she positively glowed. By the time their mother shrieked, "Fine. I'll leave her be. But the next time she breaks something you can go get her and take her to the hospital. I'm finished!" Ruthie didn't care. Although her mother had stormed out of the room, she knew her father would never desert her. The slam of her parents' bedroom door reverberated throughout the apartment. The sisters stared at one another, but neither said a word.

Both little heads turned towards their bedroom door when it opened. Simon entered the room with a bowl of warm water and a washcloth, sitting down gently on Ruth's bed. As he spread the cloth on her forehead, he said, "I am sorry you girls had to hear that. You mustn't mind your mother. She is just frightened for you both."

"Does she hate me, Papa," Ruth forced herself to ask him, although she feared what his answer might be.

"Liebchen, no. How can you think that?" he stammered. Although he believed his wife did not hate their daughters, he was not sure she loved them either, at least in the way other women seemed to love their offspring.

"She is grumpy a lot," offered Holly.

"And she doesn't hug as all the time like you do," Ruth added.

"Some people don't show the love they feel as easily as others," he told them, wondering if that was true. Perhaps his wife could only love her singing. It was he who wanted children, not Addie, and it would be him who would shower them with all the love he had in his heart. Of course these were thoughts he voiced to no one, and rarely even allowed himself to think. This was the family he had; what would have been the point? When he was certain both children had drifted into sleep, he tiptoed out of the room, not the least bit surprised to find sheets and blankets again piled on the living room couch. Truthfully, he was relieved to be sleeping by himself. Sometimes he found his wife's behavior chilling.

* * *

The Unger children adored their new apartment. Jules was thrilled to have his own room again so that he had a quiet place to study. Though he spent a great deal of time with his younger siblings – reading with the girls, explaining higher math to Nell, who was far ahead of her classmates in school, and playing games outside with the two little boys – having his own space was a thrill. Nell was no less excited than he by this new apartment. It was the first time in her young life she would be able to have a private moment. Now, when she had finished helping her mother and sister in the kitchen, and had completed her homework, she could lie on her own bed with the light on and read until her father came in to say goodnight. Like Jules and Max, she loved to read. And in America it was not considered a pastime that was wasted on girls. Of course she had to finish all of her chores and family duties first, but in Elizabethport she had both the time and right to pursue her intellectual interests as well. Beck and Min shared a bedroom next to their parents, which Noah had managed to create by making the master bedroom smaller. He and Yetta barely had room for a dresser at the foot of their bed, and he had to remove the doors from their closet, hanging a curtain in its stead so they could use it. These changes made little difference to them both because they could see the excitement of their children, which meant a great deal more.

Yetta had persuaded Noah to close the shop for forty-five minutes at dinnertime. Often, he climbed the stairs with either Nathan or Max in tow, since both of the boys loved 'working' in the shop with their father, either puttering around in his shop, learning how to glue a leg in place, or how to hammer without damaging a finger. Nathan enjoyed sitting beside him at the counter when he talked to customers, often making up imaginary conversations later at night in the bedroom he shared with Max, as if he, too, was a business owner who had to reason with a customer. One night Yetta overheard the little boy, and was totally nonplussed by the depth of his analysis of all the uses the make-believe man would have for the wardrobe his father would make him. When she tried to repeat the conversation to Noah later after they were in bed, he laughed, saying, "I wondered what he was thinking when he sits there day after day. Max just reads, totally engrossed in his books. We may have a little lawyer in our midst with our younger son." Little did he know how prescient this remark would prove to be over twenty years later.

At dinnertime the girls brought platters of food to the table every night, Noah saying 'kaddish' over it before the entire family sat down to their dinner. Yetta was always busy at her sewing machine, sitting at the table Noah had refurbished for her in the corner of the parlor beneath one of the windows. Conversation at their dinner table was often raucous, one child overlapping the other with the stories they wanted to share about their day's adventures. Yetta, in particular, loved these meals. Her daughters were already much better cooks than she, which made her extremely proud. It was Nell who mixed the ingredients, and Beck who did the lion's share of the preparations. Each night at dinner she thanked God for allowing her little family to travel so far from home so they would all have a chance for a better life.

One evening the children were all consumed with the story of Henry, a skinny little third grader who often endured taunts and worse from the neighborhood bully, John Bates. The well-muscled fourth grader loved picking on smaller, younger children, whom he forced to do his bidding: carrying his books, completing his math homework, sharing their homemade lunches with him or worse, giving him the whole lunch if it was one that appealed to him – any whim that came to mind day by day. Apparently, little Henry had been planning his revenge ever since his first, unpleasant encounter with this schoolyard tyrant. Instead of waiting for John's second approach, during the morning snack break Henry approached Bates with an offer. If the older child would agree to leave him alone, he, Henry, would help him collect the booty from the game of pennies the sixth grade boys played every day. Although gambling was frowned upon by the teachers, and expressly forbidden by the Principal, boys would still be boys. Excelling at this game meant that by the time you were in your last year of grammar school you could win yourself extra money for candy and ice cream, which in this poor neighborhood of immigrants, was nothing to sneer at. At first John just laughed. "Yeah right kid. Dream on!"

Henry removed a penny from his back pocket and threw it against the wall. He repeated his move three times. The coin landed in almost the same place all three times. Suddenly John was interested. Henry explained how he had weighted the coin, which you couldn't see, so that it would fall in the same spot every time. Henry, of course, was the best student in his science class, perhaps in the entire school. John took the proffered coin and tried it himself, achieving the same result. He became quite excited. Although he hated losing one child he might later torment, his greed for the daily kitty was even greater than his need for dominance. "You got it kid," he said, standing. He sauntered over to the cement wall against which the older boys played their game.

What he didn't know was that the day before, Henry had told the older boys his plan. He had fashioned a heavier coin for them, one that would always, without fail, fall closer to the wall than the one he had made for John. The boys were delighted. They rarely made an effort to protect the younger and weaker children in school. Like the boys who had come before them, they had been taught that learning how to survive boys like John was part of the education received at the school, albeit on the playground. But no one liked John much, and he had tortured the younger siblings of several of the sixth grade boys. They loved the idea of humiliating him. There was one part of Henry's idea they didn't much like. They didn't want him to lose right away. First they should let him think he was beating them, several pretending they were angry and upset. Then they should up the ante, each pitching two pennies a game, until the bully was crowing with his approaching victory, lording it over the older kids as he surely would. Only then would one of them replace the two 'fixed' coins Henry had made for them.

Even Noah was surprised by the well-constructed details of Henry's plot. His children told him with some excitement that it had gone without a hitch, more and more children surrounding the game until even the teachers came outside. Henry quietly begged them not to close down the game. The older boys had just switched coins, which he didn't tell them. When these new coins hit the wall, the science teacher looked at Henry oddly, but the boy managed to keep his face blank. Suspicious, although he was unsure what exactly was happening, the man let the game continue. By the end of recess the growing frustration and anger in John's face was obvious for all to see. When he turned to look at Henry, the boy pretended to be very distressed. John could not back out of the game by this point, and was slaughtered, of course. Once he started to lose, all the boys started to laugh at him, and point and ridicule the prowess he had been gloating about only moments before. He left the playground in tears and ditched school the rest of the day. Even the girls were hoping he would transfer to a different school. When the older kids picked up the diminutive Henry and carried him into the school, even the teacher laughed. A short, skinny third grader who wore thick glasses had managed to defeat the biggest bully in the school on the strength of his brain.

Noah liked the story as much as his children.

Jules, who was a junior in high school, had decided to go to dental school at the urging of his guidance counselor. Since it was only a two year program, he would be able to earn a portion of the tuition with an after school job before his first year of study even began. And because he was such a stellar pupil, the guidance counselor was quite sure he would receive a partial scholarship as well. When Noah expressed disappointment at this choice, since dentistry would not utilize his son's prodigious intellect, Jules explained that by the same token it would leave him with enough energy to pursue those needs in his spare time, reading widely every night when he came home. He was also excited by the prospect of helping his parents with certain expenses. Dentists earned a decent wage, even when they worked for someone else. Until he started a family of his own, his financial support might enable at least one of his brothers to take a four-year college course, or in the case of his sister, Nell, to go on to a school of higher learning in the first place. When Yetta told her eldest in no uncertain terms that she did not want him postponing marriage on the family's account, all of the girls teased him about his 'way with women'. This was the first that Yetta had heard of her son's flirtations. Everyone laughed uproariously as Jules tried to explain that a group of girls at the high school kept flirting with him for some reason he couldn't understand. In the midst of the laughter, blushing mightily, he weakly protested, "Really. I just don't know what to do about it."

That night as she was preparing for bed, Nell allowed herself to think about the possibility of going to college. She knew one senior girl who was planning to apply to Douglas College, the women's branch at Rutgers University, the state school for men. But the senior at Battin High came from the other side of Elmora Avenue, where the wealthy people lived. More significant was the fact that she was a gentile. Although Nell was only a freshman, she was the most organized of the Unger children, and had been helping her mother with their books for several years. She knew that sending both Jules and her to college would put a huge strain on the family budget, even though her father's business was doing well and her mother had been given a raise at the factory because of the increasing productivity on her floor. If Jules became a dentist she knew he would help as much as he could, but she was afraid to count on him because he was handsome and girls really did pursue him. Eventually one of those girls would succeed. She sighed as she twisted strands of her hair into circles against her head, crossing each tight roll with two bobby pins so her hair would fall in simple curls the next day. She longed to continue her education, but in her heart didn't believe that would be fair to the family. After all, her two little brothers would only be several years behind her, and they would both be expected to go on to college, given that each of them already devoured several books weekly.

By the time she talked to Yetta about her plan, she had made peace with herself, and was able to do so with a smile. As the two stood side by side at their kitchen counter, Nell kneading the dough for blintzes, her mother stirring the apples cooking on the stove for the applesauce that would compliment them, she began to speak quietly.

"Mama. They offer a secretarial course at the high school, and I thought I would enroll next year," Nell said.

Yetta turned to look at her daughter, startled. "But Nell. Your father and I are working very hard so that we will be able to send you to college. In this country you could be more than a secretary." As an afterthought she added, "Even a teacher."

Nell would have loved nothing more than to do just that, but she knew what she knew, and therefore she persevered. "I know that, Mama. And being able to teach would mean more to me than I could ever tell you. But there is Max and Nate, and, well...."

Yetta gave her arm a pat. "We will deal with the boys when we get there. That is many years away."

"Yes, I know." Nell continued, "But if I take this course next year, I can perfect my skills so that by the time I graduate, if it is what the family needs, I will be able to get a good job. Even if it means postponing my own education for awhile, it might be a good idea for the family if I was prepared." She hoped her mother could not see how heavy her heart felt, because this was not what she wanted to do.

But she had long accepted she would have to put the needs of her brothers before her own.

Despite herself Yetta was impressed by the wisdom in her daughter's plan, although it was not one she wanted to see unfold. "What classes would you have to give up to take this course, Nellie?" she asked her.

"Social studies."

"If you don't take social studies, would you still be able to go to college if we can afford it by the time you graduate?" she asked.

"I don't know, Mama. I could ask the guidance counselor," Nell replied. It was a good question and one she hadn't considered.

"If you take this secretarial course, I would want to make sure it would not make it impossible for you to continue your education, and I'm sure your father would feel the same," Yetta explained.

Nell shook her head in agreement, the unusually calm young woman afraid she would start to cry if she spoke. It was amazing to her how happy she felt at this brief reprieve. As usual her mother had thought of something that hadn't crossed her mind, focused as she has been on what she needed to do for the good of the family. Perhaps there was another course she could drop that would leave the door open, and she wouldn't have to give up her dreams quite yet. She worked quickly with her slim hands, rolling out the dough and then folding the rectangles she had cut for the seasoned cottage cheese filling, one right after the other.

Yetta glanced sideways at her daughter, amazed, as always, at the skill this daughter exhibited at almost everything she did. Beck might be more creative in her cooking endeavors, making savory sauces to smother the roasts she cooked so that the meat melted in your mouth, but Nell was consistent and reliable. Tonight, when dinner was done, Beck and Min would clean the kitchen so that she and Nell could repair to the parlor, along with Max and Nathan. The 'girls' would work on the ledger for Noah's business, Yetta entering the figures for the week, Nell responsible for the addition and subtraction. The 14-year old had been helping her mother with this task back in the old country, teased by the seamstresses in Monasterzyska for her 'mathematical mind'. She had only been eight when she had asked her mother if the could help her in this way. Yetta was aware that her daughter's mind was capable of more than addition and subtraction, and was determined she explore its depth. Nevertheless she realized the plan Nell had devised was a good one. With business, one never knew what would transpire. Should disaster strike, if Nell had taken this course, with her book keeping skills and experience, along with the secretarial ones she would be learning, she would never lack for employment. If she didn't find a mate in those first years after graduating from high school, she would not only be able to support herself, but to contribute to the household along with Jules.

One way or another the family would prosper, of this Yetta was convinced. She and Noah had raised marvelous children. They had been blessed by God, there was no denying it.

* * *

By the time Ruthie was old enough to go to school, Holly had become a star there, even in the third grade. Not only was she admired for her beauty by her teachers as well as the older boys, her dramatic talent, even in such a young child, was astonishing. She transformed the small school stage at every performance, causing her father's chest to fill with pride at his beautiful china doll. For this was what Holly most resembled. The first day he walked both daughters to school that fall, he had to assure Ruth that she, too, would shine; for once the little adventuress was frozen, and could not get her feet to carry her up the stairs into the school building. Holly had already rushed off to join her girlfriends, leaving her sister and father behind without a qualm.

"Your smile can win over the most grumpy person, little one. There is no one here who will not love you," he promised her, adding, "By the time you come home, you will have learned to jump rope with the older girls, and then you will teach all the friends you will make in your own class how to jump with you."

All Ruth could hear was that she wouldn't win friends or the affection of her teachers because of her beauty. Her father hadn't even told her she was pretty, or called her his pretty little girl, a phrase she had been willing him to say ever since she had understood what it meant. He frequently said those words when he was kissing Holly good night. It wasn't that he didn't love her – she knew from the depth of her little being that he did – but she longed for the look he lavished on her older sister nonetheless. Ruth performed a nightly ritual before she fell asleep, holding on to the end of her nose and pinching it closed so that it would not grow any bigger. And every morning she awakened disappointed to discover that her arms were flung wide and her nose still seemed too large. Even on this day, her entry into the grown-up world of school, when her sister Holly went racing down the hall dragging her school satchel behind her, their father had grinned, saying, "I don't think she'll ever learn to be on time, my little beauty," and Ruth's heart had stopped beating in her chest.

"Ruthie, my sweetheart, where are you," she heard him ask and realized she was still standing outside the school building, her father kneeling at her feet.

"I'm standing in front of school, Papa. Don't you see me?" she asked him.

Laughing, he stood up, brushed off his trousers, and smiled down at her. "Do you want me to walk you all the way inside, or do you want to go by yourself?" As she was thinking about her answer, Ruth noticed a little girl she often played with in the park. Breaking away from her father, she turned and raced forward, calling out, "Nomi. Nomi. Wait for me."

Simon saw the other child turn, and proudly watched as the two little tykes joined hands, swinging their arms in a wider and wider arc as they trotted up the front stairs to the school entrance together. 'Nothing will stop this child, even if she isn't a beauty,' Simon thought to himself as he hurried to the subway kiosk to get to his first sales meeting on time.

Ruth loved school. She did learn to jump rope, though not the first day, and happily taught the more adventurous girls in her class how to do so too. Not only did Nomi count on her when their class was sent out to the playground, but Stella, Rachel, and Leah did as well. The four girls shrieked and ran and jumped and swung together, a happy band of banshees, as the playground monitor labeled them. They didn't understand what the word meant, but it sounded just fine to all of them.

In the classroom the teacher had already come to depend on Ruth as well, because she and Nomi were the only two children in her class who could already read. In the half hour before naptime, the two girls helped the teacher set up cookies and milk because both had easily completed sounding out several words from the blackboard before any of their classmates. Ruth asked if she could take home the two books on the shelf that she hadn't yet read; the delighted teacher saw this as an opportunity to teach the children about libraries, writing out three-by-five cards with the names of every book on the shelf above her desk so her students could have a mini-library within their very own classroom. Ruth was even able to help another little girl learn to sound out her words, much to the teacher's satisfaction. In return the girl, who was better at double-dutch than Ruth, worked with her during recess until she too could race in to the swinging ropes as they arced together high above their heads. In that way the banshees became a group of five, happily adding Sally as the newest member. By the end of the first month of school Ruth was no longer thinking about Holly's successes because she was so happy.

"Mama, Mama. I'll help you cut the carrots," she said as she ran into the kitchen one afternoon when she had finished her 'homework'. Kindergartners didn't usually have homework, but Ruth's teacher had assigned her a book to read, and asked her to tell the rest of the class about it the next day, feeling it her duty to encourage this bright little child to excel.

Addie turned to look at her, nonplussed. Neither of her daughters seemed to enjoy working alongside her in the kitchen, although that might have been because she found them too slow and usually took over before they had finished their assigned task so she could be done. "Are you sure you want to stay inside?" she asked, the surprise apparent in her voice.

Ruth stood in the kitchen looking at her feet, and shuffling from one to the other.

"What do you really want, Ruth?"

Still staring at her feet, Ruth mumbled the question, "Do you have any extra clothesline, Mama?" Her voice quivered, because she was frightened her mother would not want her jumping rope any more than she had approved of her skating once her leg healed.

"And what would you need clothesline for?"

"We play jump rope at school during recess, but the only rope at the school is used by the bigger girls and they don't like it when we play, because there are too many of us."

"Why does that matter?" her mother asked, genuinely curious.

"Because they don't get as many turns if they let us play with them," Ruth replied as if it were the most obvious thing in the world.

If the older girls played jump rope, this was a game Adelaide wanted to encourage. It had to be an accepted sports activity for female students. "I need to go out and get some onions," she said. "Why don't you come with me and we can stop at the hardware store so you can pick out the rope you want." When Ruth smiled in response, Adelaide thought to herself, 'her nose doesn't look quite as large when she is happy'. On the way to the store Ruth asked her mother if two of her friends could come over to play one afternoon. Adelaide was amused when Ruth explained, "Your brisket sandwiches are so much better than the ones their mothers make. I know because we've shared our lunches with each other; your stollen will be better as well."

The first time Nomi and Sally came to the apartment after school, they were indeed very complimentary about the little cakes Adelaide served them. It was obvious to her that their remarks were not merely polite: they each ate several pastries and didn't turn down the extra one she placed on each of their plates. After the girls had followed Ruth to the sink with their plates they raced from the room. When Ruth turned to look at her mother at the doorway to see if she was expected to dry the dishes, Adelaide sent her on her way. Within seconds she heard the chatter of childish voices coming from the bedroom Ruth shared with

Holly. By the time she had washed and dried the dishes, putting them away in the cabinet above the sink, they were all laughing, having a grand time apparently.

Suddenly Adelaide realized what a boon it was for her that Ruth had invited her friends over to play. Ordinarily she either would have taken the child shopping with her, which was not at all pleasurable since Ruth's little body overflowed with energy ill-suited to walking from shop to shop with her mother, or to the park where she could run it off. With other children in the house, Adelaide was suddenly free to sit down at the piano and practice. At some point in the middle of practicing her scales she realized all three girls were standing in the doorway to the living room, but was so concentrated on what she was doing that by the time she was ready to ask them what they wanted they had disappeared. Much to her daughter's surprise and obvious delight, before Adelaide walked the children home on her way to the shops with Ruth, she invited the girls to come again, even that very week if their mothers approved.

Before she drifted off to sleep after allowing Simon his due, she felt happier than she had since Ruth had been born. Now she wouldn't have to wait until Ruth was in first grade attending school until 3 PM every day to return to singing full time. If she encouraged her daughter's friendships she might be able to practice enough each day to perform again. As soon as her voice was back, she would call the choirmaster and arrange a trip into Manhattan to attend a group practice. She was sure she would be invited to sing full time with the group, even though another singer had taken her place during the last month of her pregnancy. When her mentor realized her voice was ready, someone else would be asked to be the alternate. She was startled by her own confidence. She was no longer the shy, innocent maiden who had walked down the boat plank into the arms of her fiancé less than ten years before. She didn't feel the least bit ashamed of the change.

As for Holly, she was again performing in every school production despite the fact that she had to race to the girls' room before each performance to throw up. Her anxiety about being center stage had certainly not abated, but the fourth grader gave no thought to giving up performing. Her father came to every recital, even when her mother was in another city singing with the Schola Cantorum. The Irish woman on the floor below theirs always agreed to babysit her younger sister, sometimes even asking her own daughter to stay with Ruth so that she, too, could see Holly's plays. Both the Christmas and Easter pageants were performed for the children during the school day and for their parents at night. Holly's father was one of the few parents who managed to attend every showing, even during the day. Of course he worked fulltime, but he always arranged his appointments on the day of a performance so that he could attend. That was what Holly lived for.

Now that Ruth was gaining a reputation throughout the school as a clever student and positive leader even though she was a mere first grader, earning their father's attention was still paramount in the minds of both girls. When the younger child brought home a mimeographed copy of the school magazine she had started, filled with poems, pictures, and little stories by children from every grade in school, Holly was miserable for days. Her father couldn't hold back his praise; it overflowed from the dinner table to the parlor, and even continued the following morning at breakfast. That day Holly signed up for another play, garnering attention of her own at the dinner table that evening. There was no way she would abnegate her perceived role as Simon's favorite without a fight. Simon was oblivious of the competition for his favor that consumed both of his daughters. Adelaide, who noticed, couldn't see any harm in it. The activities of both girls kept them extremely busy at school; she was back to full time membership in her singing group, and again rehearsing four afternoons a week.

Though the sisters sometimes still snuggled at night after their mother had scolded one of them, neither girl was willing to depend upon the other anymore, even Ruth, who despite her jealousy had looked up to Holly. Now she felt on equal footing, a reality that Holly unhappily experienced as well. This rift, begun in their early years, was to grow wider and wider with time. Had either parent noticed, discussed it with one another, or even talked to the girls themselves about it, perhaps this divide could have been crossed. As it was, each child turned to friends rather than each other. And neither ever really trusted the other again.

In later years, when Ruth thought about her sad relationship, or lack of one, with her older sister, she always returned to the same day in her mind. One of her teachers had called her mother to suggest she and her husband come in to school to discuss Ruth's work. Ruth had of course been terrified, since she was attempting to achieve perfection. As it turned out the teacher had suggested the meeting to let the child's parents know what a clever girl they were raising; Ruth, she told them, not only had a very quick mind, but a winning personality as well, her tinkling laugh utterly contagious. She should be encouraged in her learning, the teacher told them, and praised for her intuitive gifts with adults as well as with children her own age. When her mother and father returned home from the conference, Simon lifted his younger daughter into the air with a huge smile, telling her how much her teacher liked her, adding, "That doesn't surprise me one bit!" The teacher had given him three extra books so that he could read with his daughter at night. Did she like that idea, or would it be too much of a burden, piled on top of her chores and other schoolwork. Ruth could have crowed aloud: what a silly question!

Holly, who had come home just moments before from her rehearsal, was standing in the hallway and heard the entire exchange. She was devastated, convinced she was losing the battle for their father's attention, and furious at her growing feeling of helplessness. After dinner that night she locked the door when she went into the bedroom she shared with her sister, turning on the radio and flopping down on her bed. As usual, Ruth was working on a school project at the dining room table and her mother was practicing scales at the piano. Their father had gone out for a late-night business meeting. Holly stared at the ceiling, waiting for her sister to try to get into their bedroom. When she heard the handle shaking, she looked at the door and smiled broadly. 'Ha' she thought to herself. 'You can't get in. What are you going to do now, special one?' First Ruth knocked, fairly quietly so she wouldn't disturb her mother. Then she called out to her sister, with no result at all. She was tired, and angry at being kept from her bed, and started to bang on the door to be let in.

Adelaide was beside her in seconds, yelling at Holly to open the door and at Ruth to stop her horrid banging. When Holly opened the door she acted as if she had been unaware it was locked, which Ruth didn't believe for an instant. Because she wanted to return to the piano, their mother accepted her explanation, ordering both girls to get ready for bed. She didn't want another interruption, and made it clear that if they bothered her again there would be a price to pay. When she left the room, Holly smiled at her little sister with utter malice as she swished past her into the hallway on her way to the bathroom. Ruth went right to bed, not even bothering to brush her teeth. She lay awake for a long time, devastated by her sister's behavior. Although she was desperate to attain and hold onto her father's love, she didn't think she wanted her sister to cut her out of her life. But she now believed that was what Holly wanted. Not only didn't she have a clue what to do about it, Holly's retreat felt overwhelming. She never knew if her mother told her father what had happened and was afraid to ask either one of them lest she make the situation worse.

As for Adelaide, that was the evening she reached her limit as far as her husband's evening 'business meetings' were concerned. She was so furious at him for his utter disregard for her feelings as well as her intelligence, that she was already pretending sleep when he returned to their apartment at 10. She most certainly was not going to offer herself to him as 'seconds' that evening, certain that he would be more than happy to accommodate her. She remembered hearing one of her mother's friends years ago say, "Men are animals" which she hadn't understood at the time. Simon's behavior would probably have even shocked that woman, Adelaide thought as she lay in their bed waiting for his key to turn in the front door lock.

She said not a word about the girls' fight precisely because she knew he would want to know.

CHAPTER TEN

By the time she was in sixth grade Holly had started to watch the older girls on the block to see how they moved their bodies when they walked. In the afternoon when she came home from school she would go right to the bedroom she shared with Ruth, usually arriving before her younger sister, despite the fact that her younger sister usually ran a race to their apartment with her tomboy friends who lived nearby, bursting through the front door, breathless. Holly would practice rolling her hips in front of the mirror before the younger girl's arrival, stopping as soon as she heard the front door slam. The last thing she needed was to be caught by Ruth, who would surely have teased her about her efforts, and perhaps even told their parents what she was up to. Holly was determined to alter her entire walk so that her hips rolled, not merely for the boys in school but to attract the attention of her father. She would never have admitted the last part of her scheme to anyone under any circumstances, and didn't even think about it herself. Adelaide, who had become more prudish with each passing year, was totally discomfited by this change in her oldest daughter's gait. Having no idea how to talk to Holly about it herself, she relegated the task to Simon, who was actually equally disturbed. He didn't admit this to his wife, but as a man about town he knew how unscrupulous men in the five burrows could be: he didn't want his own daughter to become easy prey. Holly was not only stunning but well-developed for her age. Concerned that her burgeoning sensuality could actually be dangerous, one Saturday he suggested a father/daughter excursion to the Zoo. For once Ruth, who had organized a meeting with her school magazine staff, didn't object. It was their first meeting outside of regular school hours, and as far as she knew, the first elementary school publication of its kind in the Bronx.

Though Holly's demeanor was aloof, inside she was afire with excitement. As she walked hand in hand with her father towards the zoo, Holly barely heard what Simon was saying. She understood his concern that men might begin to look at her, which, rather than frightening her into more cautious behavior, excited her fancy. As he talked, she tried to remember how much money she had saved from her small weekly allowance, newly determined to buy a pair of silk hose, and perhaps a perm kit from the pharmacy if she had enough money left over. She was thrilled to have this opportunity to spend the entire afternoon with her father. Once he stopped trying to explain why he was worried about the way she was beginning to walk, she was free to talk about the new play, her thoughts about the junior high school she would be attending the following fall, a new department store she was dying to visit in Manhattan, and to laugh with him about an older tenant's dog, which kept peeing in the downstairs hallway. The dog infuriated Addie; Holly's stories about her mother's efforts to talk to the neighbor actually elicited a belly laugh from her father. They sat down to eat lunch together like grown-ups at an outdoor café near the zoo. The entire experience increased Holly's resolve to become more 'womanly' so her father would spend more time with her, an outcome that would have horrified Simon. He actually assured Addie that he had 'gotten through to her'; he was sure of it.

When Holly stepped into the kitchen one evening the following week, her hair curled in fashionable tight curls close to her scalp, Adelaide turned to stare at her, tight-lipped. It made not a whit of difference to the 12-year old. Her father twirled her in the air although she was almost grown, telling her that her new 'do' was adorable. He didn't connect the style change with Holly's new manner of walking, or he might not have been as sanguine about it.

"Your eyes look red and puffy," was Ruth's only comment. She never even contemplated trying a perm herself, though she found her father's behavior upsetting. She had learned it wasn't her looks that inspired his attention, and had resolved to become a better ball player, and to launch her little magazine no matter what obstacles had to be overcome to do so.

That evening neither girl said a word to one another as the apartment erupted in another quarrel between their parents. They no longer cuddled during these battles, but kept their own counsel. Ruth was relieved that her behavior no longer seemed to incite these incidents, since a pitched battle between her parents was not the sort of attention she craved. When she glanced over at her sister before Holly turned out the light, she wasn't surprised by the smile on her face. Both girls had heard the words their father shouted as he slammed the door and left the apartment, but neither said a thing about that either.

"Not all members of the female sex are repelled by the idea of looking lovely for the men in their lives," he screamed, the sound of the door banging shut reverberating throughout the apartment.

Ruth fell asleep wondering if perhaps she should do something about her own hair. She certainly didn't want to turn out like her mother, although her mother's attire and hair-do seemed perfectly acceptable to her. She didn't really understand what her father meant, but she knew his words were important. Her last thought as she drifted into sleep was that she would discuss them with one of her friend's older sisters who was not nearly as close-mouthed as Holly, and certainly not in competition with her for her father's attention.

She never got the chance because the very next day her mother took her to the local barber and had her hair trimmed to forestall the possibility that she, too, would try to curl her own hair, making a mess in the bathroom. When her mother told her to put on her coat so she could take her to the barber, Ruth sat down on the floor of the foyer, and began to stamp her feet on the floor.

"No no no! I won't go. You can't make me!" she kept repeating in a voice that was totally bereft, but Adelaide paid no attention. She stood there staring down at her hysterical daughter until she was spent, and then repeated her demand. "Put on your coat, Ruth." Exhausted, the child rose to her knees, head hanging between her arms, and took the coat from her mother's proffered hand. When the barber cut off her braid almost at its base, the tears streamed down her cheeks although she didn't utter a sound. She refused to give her mother the satisfaction.

When her father came in the door after work, he called out to her as he usually did, surprised that she wasn't racing to greet him. He walked to her room and opened the door. At first he thought one of her friends was sitting at her little desk doing homework, but then she turned to look at him with eyes puffy from crying. Unable to think of anything comforting to say, he held out his arms and she rushed inside the warmth of his embrace. They both knew the haircut was hideous. Even Holly hadn't teased her sister when she had come home late from her rehearsal for a new play. That cruelty would have been beyond even her. When she gave her younger sister one of her infrequent hugs, it actually made it worse because Ruth fully understood the hug meant that her hair looked as awful as she feared. Later when she heard the raised voices of her parents, Simon's words clear as a bell – "What have you done to the poor child?" – she grabbed her coat and raced outside to play ball with the boys despite the late hour. She played particularly hard that evening, belting a ball over the benches bordering the outer edges of the field. After she crossed home plate, she heard one of the boys say to another with a laugh, "She even looks like us now."

Distraught, she ran from the field, the only place she could think to go the bench where her friend, the dog walker, usually sat, but he had already left the park. Ruth sat there until the streetlights flickered on, and then slowly walked home because she was afraid to stay out in the dark. When she slipped in the front door, it was her father who was waiting there for her. He helped her out of her jacket without a word, stroking her back as the two walked into the dining room for dinner. The look he leveled at his wife would have frozen water. For once Adelaide didn't scold her daughter for staying out so late. Dinner was a silent affair. Holly offered to wash the dishes, although it was Ruth's week to take care of that chore, and no one objected. Ruth didn't bother to brush her teeth, sliding beneath her comforter and huddling there in a ball, which is how her father found her moments later. He all but lifted her onto his lap, whispering into her ear.

"My little sweet, the good news is that hair grows. At your age it will fill out in no time." All Ruth heard was that she was now even less attractive than she had been that morning. "Trust me, Ruthie. You will be my wonder girl in no time at all," he continued when his daughter remained silent.

Not 'my little beauty': he would never call her that, even if she still had her long hair. What she didn't understand, or know how to ask again was why her mother hated her. Why else would she have forced her to chop off her hair? A new goal was born in Ruth's heart that day: to leave home as soon as she was able. It was not a goal that receded with time, but one that intensified.

Nevertheless, when her mother came home months later to announce that the Schola Cantorum was again planning a summer tour, Ruth was not averse to going to Europe with the family. Since she had been barely two at the last crossing, she had no memory of the trip or her mother's family. She had heard the tales about her cousins from her sister, about the shops, the clothes, the fashions, and wanted to see al of it for herself. Apparently her aunt had a sense of style, and perhaps, could help. Her hair, though still ragged, was growing as her father had promised it would, so she no longer looked like a boy. She steadfastly refused to go back to the offending barber, and no one had suggested finding another, even her father. Ruth trusted that her aunt would know a salon in Vienna that could shape the disaster atop her head so she would at least look stylish as her hair grew back. When her sister expressed the same thought, Ruth felt enormous relief. On this, at least, they agreed. When Simon said he welcomed the opportunity to show off both his girls, for once Ruth believed him. He had held aloft several copies of her school magazine moments before, telling his wife he was bringing them in the bottom of one of their trunks. Adelaide's brother and sister might not be able to read the English easily, but he could translate Ruth's articles for them. He told Holly to pack her two new frocks, and demanded that Adelaide go shopping for one or two dresses for Ruth, so that she wouldn't look like a poor relation. When she protested, the look Simon leveled at his wife was enough to silence her. As he passed behind his daughters who were doing the dishes in the kitchen he whispered that he would pay for a Viennese dressmaker to make them each two frocks in the latest European style. For once the two sisters looked at one another, both of their faces shining with equal delight.

Ruth resolved to complete a masterful June issue of the magazine, including a non-fiction and fiction piece of her own, as well as drawings by two of her fellow students whose artwork was special, even to an untrained eye. This she had heard her art teacher telling her social studies teacher on her way to the cafeteria the month before. She was determined that her father would have something splendid to both show and translate for her cousins in Vienna. Holly was equally determined to stay in the Bronx, a thought she shared with no one, not even her sister, despite knowing that Ruth would have been delighted to have her father to herself for the entire crossing. Holly was experiencing her first crush, the recipient of her ardor an eighth grade boy in her new school and couldn't risk what might happen if she were to be away for the entire summer. For the first time in her young life, capturing the heart of the eighth grade boy seemed more enticing to Holly then being squired around the boat deck by her father.

On Thursday when Holly knew her mother had a rehearsal in Manhattan and Ruth would be working on her silly magazine, she left school as soon as the final bell sounded, forgoing her usual fifteen minutes of gossip with her girlfriends, and raced home to the apartment. Stopping at Mrs. O'Reilly's door, she collected herself before knocking. Fionella was delighted to see Holly, whom she had adored since the day of her birth, not solely because of that long bus ride all those years ago with Adelaide. Holly had been a pleasant child, her beauty enticing; now that she was turning into a woman, that beauty was a bit daunting. Nevertheless, Mrs. O'Reilly beckoned her inside with her hands, which she wiped on her apron to rid them of the flour that coated them.

"What are you making, Mrs. O'Reilly? Something for us, I'm sure," Holly teased. This sisters' favorite neighbor was forever talking about some diet or other, although her hands were forever dipped in flour as she made her favorite doughnuts or cookie bars. Today, it seemed, was no exception. The entire apartment was filled with the scent of baking. Fionella laughed aloud.

"You've caught me, girl. But I'm sure I can convince you to have a bar with me before you go back upstairs, can't I?" she asked, turning her smiling face back towards Holly, who was following her into the kitchen.

"I shouldn't," Holly hesitated. She loved Mrs. O'Reilly's cookie bars, so different from anything her mother made.

"Nonsense!" declared Mrs. O'Reilly. "You're still a skinny little thing. If anyone has a concern it would be me, and you don't see me turning down the offer, now, do you?" Indeed, she had a half-eaten bar on the counter in front of her.

Even before Holly was seated at the kitchen table, the woman had managed to produce both a glass of milk from the icebox and two bars from the cookie sheet she had just removed from the oven, the heat as well as the scent of chocolate still wafting off of them. Holly bit right into the soft dough, quickly licking away the melted chocolate oozing out the sides. "Oh, these are so delicious, Mrs. O'Reilly. You know I can't turn them down, though I wish you hadn't given me two."

As Mrs. O'Reilly slid another cookie sheet filled with bars into the oven, she asked, "And what brings you to my door, sweetheart. I haven't known you to come home from school so early since you started at that new school of yours."

When Holly again hesitated, the woman reminded her, "You don't have to be shy with me, of all people, Holly. What is it you want?"

Taking a very deep breath Holly blurted, "I don't want to go to Europe this summer with my family." Across from her the older woman's face creased with concern. "My goodness, child. Don't you realize how lucky you are to be able to travel all the way across the sea?"

"Yes, I do. But I have a life here now, and friends. I don't want to be separated from them for the whole summer," she said with such earnestness Mrs. O'Reilly couldn't bear to smile. Suddenly, she understood. "You're wanting to stay here with me, aren't you child?" All Holly could do was nod her head. Her mouth was stuffed with the remainder of her first chocolate-almond bar.

"I would love to have you here with me, Holly. But even if I tell your Mama and Papa that, I don't think it will get you what you're looking for," she explained. "Your papa isn't likely to leave you behind."

Holly refused to hear her. "But that means you would be willing to look out for me?"

"You know I would."

By the time Holly left her neighbor's apartment for her own, she was carrying a bag of chocolate bars for the rest of the family. Ruth and her father loved them as much as she did, though her mother rarely ate them, saying they were too 'sweet' for her taste. Holly could have cried with relief. Now there was a slim ray of hope for her plan. After dinner when she was drying the dishes her mother had set atop the drain board, her father lingering at the table over his second cup of coffee with Ruth, who was working on her silly magazine, Holly decided to broach the subject.

"Mama. You know I have a large circle of friends now," she began, the words causing Adelaide to turn away from the roast she was wrapping to put into the icebox.

"Yes…"she agreed, though she had no idea where her daughter's words were leading.

Holly plunged ahead despite the wary look on her mother's face. "Social life is very important for a girl at this time of life. They're always telling us that in our home ec class, Mama."

By this point, Simon was also listening to the conversation. He winked at his wife over his daughter's shoulder. "Tell us where this is headed, my girl," he suggested.

"I would like to stay behind this summer, so that I won't fall out of the loop. The girls are planning to swim together every day in the lake, and to take one or two trips into Manhattan to buy clothes for the fall," she explained.

"Holly, this is a yearly family trip," her mother said, but her daughter interrupted before she could complete her thought.
"I've already spoken to Mrs. O'Reilly, and she said she'd be delighted to have me stay with her. So you wouldn't have to worry at all."

Both parents were so shocked by this revelation, that for a moment they were speechless. Then Simon held up his hand to silence his wife, pulling Holly onto his lap with the other. "Pretty one," he said quietly. "I understand how sad it will be for you to be left out of these activities. But both your mother and I would worry about you constantly, and that would be a very unpleasant way to spend two months, don't you think?"

None of her wiles worked on her father that night, and using them on her mother, was of course, useless. Ruth gave her a little kiss goodnight because she realized instinctively how upset her sister must be, and Holly quietly cried herself to sleep. She didn't mention the idea again, not to her sister, her parents, or Mrs. O'Reilly. But her family's intransigence did heighten her resolve to see what 'kissing' was all about before the end of the school year. Holly had overheard several of the ninth grade girls talking about it in the girls' room. Although she couldn't imagine what saliva had to do with the act, she obsessed about the boy, whose name was Roger, staring at his lips during math class instead of listening to the teacher. Once, when he called on her, she didn't even know what page they were working on, and was mortified. She found ways to attract Roger's notice: dropping a book beside his desk as she left the class; sitting down with her girlfriends at the far end of 'his' table in the cafeteria; playing tag near the boys' baseball diamond so that she could run around him in the outfield. Her actions paid off: twice he followed her home from school. The third time she asked him to carry her books if he was going to walk that way. The fourth time he asked her if she would have an ice cream soda with him, but she turned him down. She had also heard about being 'easy' in the girls' room, and certainly didn't want to be seen as that sort of girl. The fifth time they left school together she let him lead her into an alley, heart pounding in preparation for the big moment.

It was much less riveting than she had expected. Their lips smushed together, hers mashed down like her hair at night in its tight little curls. It wasn't even comfortable. When he tried to poke his tongue into her mouth she shook her head and waved her hand around it as if a fly was bothering her. The movement created the effect she desired: he moved away. Nevertheless they left the alley hand in hand. When they reached her front stoop he shoved her books into her arms and ran around the corner, embarrassed. She was the first girl he had kissed. The next day she waited for him, in case he was suffering from shame or remorse, and they again sauntered into the alley. This time he didn't press quite as hard, and she was more willing to open her mouth a little way. As his tongue played with hers, she realized this was what the girl in the bathroom had been talking about vis-a-vis saliva. She decided then and there that no matter how hard a boy pressed her, she would never open her mouth very wide. That way saliva couldn't dribble out of his mouth or hers.

When she finally told Ruth about it weeks after the initial 'kissing' incident had occurred, her younger sister's eyes opened so wide Holly thought it must have hurt. Holly and Roger had gone to the park where they had actually run into Ruth, who was sneaking home after playing a game of basketball with a group of boys there. Now that her hair was growing out, Ruth hadn't heard any more nasty comments, so she had started playing in the park again. Holly had to admit that Ruth behaved with remarkable reserve when they passed her, merely saying 'hello' and then continuing on her way. That night as they prepared for bed, Holly decided to reward her with renewed intimacy. The older girl was actually relieved; she needed someone to talk to about her adventure.

After listening quietly for some moments until Holly ran out of steam, Ruth asked, "But what about infection? Mama always tells us not to put strange things in our mouths because of bacteria…."

Holly hadn't thought about that, and was actually stymied. "I don't know. It never crossed my mind," she admitted.

"I could look up kissing in the encyclopedia and see what it says," Ruth suggested, adding unnecessarily, "I'm always in the library."

For once Holly was grateful for her sister's facility with language. The next day after school she told Roger she had to meet her sister, and raced to the elementary school to see what Ruth had discovered. Since neither the encyclopedia nor the dictionary mentioned the danger of bacteria, the sisters assumed Holly didn't need to be concerned if she kept going to the alley with Roger. They continued to walk home from the junior high school together until the first snowfall, when even Holly's need for male attention paled in comparison to her dislike of wading through dirt encrusted snow. Besides, for some reason kissing Roger for two months had dampened her enthusiasm for him. When she watched him in school, she noticed how silly his laugh was. His mouth was crooked, with lips too large for his narrow face. Another boy, Charles, began to interest her instead, but she didn't think pursuing him would be a good idea. Everyone knew she was 'going' with Roger. It would take weeks for the rumor mill to make it clear they had broken up. The twelve-year old was aware that some months should intervene before she even considered walking home with Charles, or the kind of reputation she feared would attach itself to her like a spider's web, until there would be no way for her to disentangle herself.

One afternoon when Ruth found her sister crying in their bedroom 'just because', she finally admitted that their mother had found a love note she was preparing to send to Charles. The older girl was told to come right home from school every day, no longer allowed to play with her friends at their apartments. Adelaide was holding the tryout for the next school production in abeyance as well, depending on Holly's behavior over the following weeks. Sitting on her older sister's bed, Ruth found herself telling her about her friend Rosalie's mother, who often grabbed her daughter in a huge, jolly bear hug in the middle of the afternoon when the two girls were playing in the living room. Sometimes, Ruth said, she even included her in these extravagant displays of affection. On those days Ruth walked home like a sleepwalker, overwhelmed by her longing for similar manifestations of love from their own mother. Instead she usually found herself facing some complaint – or worse, a wordless sense of her own incomprehensible failings. If it would make Holly feel better, Ruth suggested to her sister, she would try to get home earlier from school over the next few weeks, which she should be able to accomplish at least three afternoons so she could be a comfort to her older sister.

Like guilty, but happy conspirators, the two girls snuck into the kitchen, relieved to discover their mother had gone out to shop for the family dinner. They made a beeline to the icebox to find something to assuage Holly's misery. It was Ruth who discovered the cooling rice pudding, obviously prepared for their evening dessert, lifting the huge bowl from its hiding place behind the enormous chunk of cheddar that rested in front of it. She almost dropped the bowl on her way to the kitchen table, but was saved by Holly, whose arms rapidly snaked underneath it so the bowl couldn't slip to the floor and shatter into thousands of sticky pieces.

At first Holly decided they should skim the top of the pudding so their mother wouldn't be able to tell that they had eaten any. She was practiced at skimming off the top with a large cooking spoon, which no one in the family had ever noticed. Ruth held a small bowl at the ready, each spoonful plopped into the smaller bowl for them to eat. It was absolutely delicious. Before they realized what was happening, they had eaten at least half the pudding in the large bowl, although on top the pudding looked undisturbed. Ruth was terrified. "There's no way mama won't know there's pudding missing,' she screamed at her sister in a panic. Holly looked down at the bowl and started to laugh. The younger child found her peels of laughter contagious despite her fear, and soon both girls were doubled over the large glass pudding bowl, which they were eating from directly by then. Just before they reached the bottom of the bowl with their spoons, Ruth dropped hers and made a beeline for the bathroom. Unfortunately she wasn't able to reach the toilet before everything she had eaten over the course of the day was expelled. Gobs of goop landed on the shower curtain, the outside of the bathtub, the sink, and the floor, miraculously missing the outside of the toilet completely. Holly stood, spoon in hand, watching her sister from the doorway, the sight before her putting a stop to her hilarity. Then Holly heard her mother's key turn in the lock, and momentarily froze in place. Ruth heard nothing, because she was now kneeling on the floor, surrounded by vomit, still heaving.

"What in the world?" stammered Adelaide who could hear Ruth's retching from the front hallway. When she opened the bathroom door she saw Holly holding Ruth's head from behind in a desperate attempt to comfort her. Their mother hesitated at the doorway when she noticed the spoon still clutched in Holly's hand.

"What is going on here, Holly," she asked, her voice much more gentle than either child could ever have anticipated.

"I'm so sorry, Mama. We wanted something to eat when we got home from school…." Holly paused.

"And you found the pudding," Adelaide finished the sentence for her. Holly, still holding her sister's head, nodded in agreement. "How much did you eat, Holly?" Adelaide asked.

"Almost all of it," her older daughter replied, and then started to cry. Ruth was still vomiting, though nothing much was coming out anymore.

"No wonder she is so sick. Are you feeling sick too?" Adelaide asked, dropping her purse and bags on the hallway floor. When she saw Holly shake her head 'no', she turned away. 'I'm going to get some rags," she said. "Will you be all right?"
"Yes," Holly said. By now Ruth was crying, cradled by the older girl.

Adelaide was so startled that Holly and Ruth had transgressed together, and so pleased, she hadn't the heart to scold either of them. The cool silence that had grown up between the two girls over the past year had not only made it more difficult for her to care for them, but had actually caused her grief. Though she had shared none of this with her husband because they lived in a silence of their own, the only truly happy memories she had of her own childhood in Vienna revolved around her sister.

By the time Simon got home from the office, Ruth was in bed, bathed and clean but miserable, Holly sitting at the foot of the bed with Adelaide next to her, holding a cold compress in her hand. She motioned for her older daughter to take her place, and went into the front room to explain to her husband what had transpired. Both girls heard their voices, looking at one another with great trepidation: now their punishment would surely begin. But instead they heard their father break into raucous laughter, joined by their mother. This was such a rare occurrence both girls were stunned into silence.

Simon composed himself before entering their room, however, asking Holly to scoot over so that he, too, could sit on the bed. First he leaned over and gave sick little Ruth a kiss on the forehead, one hand resting on Holly's back. Ruth noticed, but didn't mind. After all, without her sister, she had no idea what would have happened to her. She would have hated being alone in the apartment when she got sick, alone in the bathroom surrounded by her own leavings.

"I suppose you won't be wanting rice pudding any time soon," he joked.

Ruth turned her face to the wall and grimaced, as did her sister.

"Don't worry," he said with a grin. 'I'll tell your mother not to make any for awhile."

Ruth looked up at him. "But it's your favorite, Papa," she managed.

"No little one. You and your sister are," he replied, making both of them smile inside and out. After Ruth fell asleep, Holly sat down to dinner with her parents. Neither commented when she set down her fork after only a few bites. She was allowed to excuse herself without demur. Both girls were sound asleep by eight, allowing their parents a rare night to themselves. For once, they even enjoyed one another's company, sharing stories of their own childhoods until after ten.

They made love that night for the first time in months. All because of a bowl of rice pudding.

When preparations began for the family's summer tour of Europe, Holly was expected to help her mother pack because she was already 12, old enough to start to take on the chores of a woman. Initially she placed the shirts, and skirts and dresses on the ironing board and held them in place for her mother. But after an hour Adelaide suggested her daughter take her place at the board and iron her first blouse. Holly was actually excited to be given such a grown-up task, taking the iron from her mother with shaking hand. Although some of the wrinkles didn't miraculously disappear as they did for her mother, it was a relief to Holly that the blouse didn't burn. Adelaide made her iron one of her own blouses first; it was a new one, and very dear to Holly's heart. As she pulled the lovely white linen shift off of the board and handed it to her mother to fold and place in the pile ready to be packed, she found herself laughing with relief.

"I'm not sure I find ironing amusing, Holly. But it is good you didn't burn a sleeve on this first attempt like I did," her mother said with a smile. For once she totally understood her daughter's feelings; she could see the laundry room in the basement of her house in Vienna as if she had been in it the day before, and could still smell the starch permeating the room from the wet items waiting to be ironed in the basket at her feet. When her new slip lay before her, a huge burn right across the bodice, she had been inconsolable. Even though they had had a maid, her mother had believed that every woman should know how to iron, and iron without mishap.

"Oh Mama! What happened?" Holly blurted, interrupting the vivid memory. Ruth sat at the kitchen table watching the procedure with open mouth, also urging her mother to elucidate. Adelaide looked at her two daughters; instinctively she knew this was a time to share a part of herself with them. It was not something she found easy to do.

"Nanny had a maid who did all the family ironing, but she still thought it was a woman's duty to learn how to keep the family's laundry in order, should we fall on hard times," Addie explained.

"Did that ever happen?" Ruth asked, wide-eyed.

"No, it didn't," her mother replied. "But in America only the very wealthy have maids; so it was a good thing Nanny taught me how to iron and how to cook, don't you agree?" Both girls vigorously shook their heads 'yes'.

"Does that mean the maid will be ironing our clothes when we are in Vienna?" Holly then asked.

Her mother shook her finger at the older girl. "While we are there, yes, we won't have to take care of this task. But we certainly do now, before we pack our things," Adelaide answered, her demeanor and tone becoming stern again.

Holly took the iron that her mother had heated on the stove and began to iron another blouse that Ruth was beginning to outgrow. Ruth, who couldn't bear it that her mother thought she was too young to help with the preparations for their trip, stood beside her mother so that she could fold the blouse when Holly finished with it. Adelaide watched Ruth fold the blouse exactly as she had, surprised that such a young child could be so meticulous. When Holly was finished ironing the next piece of clothing, one of Simon's shirts, she actually handed it to her sister, who beamed up at her with obvious pride as she reached for it.

"You are doing a very good job, Ruth," Adelaide told her as she set Simon's folded shirt on top of his growing pile. "Holly," she turned to the older girl. "Do you realize there were no wrinkles on your father's shirt?"

"Ironing isn't as hard as I thought at first," Holly agreed, although she didn't enjoy the process of ironing and folding the family clothes as much as her sister, who was humming happily as she folded each item.

"Do you think I could go into the bedroom to prepare our toiletries, while you both work out here?" Adelaide asked her daughters.

"We'll be fine, Mama," Ruth immediately replied. "This way we'll be done by the time papa gets home for dinner," she added wisely. Which, indeed, they were. When Simon opened the front door he heard the laughter of all three, which came as a complete surprise to him. He found them all in the dining room, his oldest daughter actually holding her sides as she pointed to the strange little birds Ruthie had fashioned out of their dinner napkins. He took in the merry scene, including his wife who was smiling broadly at both girls, with utter amazement.

"What have we here?" he asked in obvious surprise.

"I'm making birds for our dinner," Ruth explained in-between infectious giggles.

"So I see," he said. "But why are you doing that?"

"Because Mama let me fold all of our clothes for Europe, and I got good at it," she told him.

"Holly did the ironing and Ruth the folding. All that remains is packing everything into the trunks," Addie agreed. "We're a day ahead of ourselves, Papa. Perhaps the Cunard line would agree to leave a day early!"

Both girls broke into peals of laughter, Simon staring at all three. He had never seen such a sight.

Dinner that night was atypical to say the least; it seemed an almost joyous affair. If Simon still entertained dreams about what his family life might include, this evening would have exemplified his most outrageous fantasies. Because he didn't want the evening to end, he walked to the dining room hutch, took down the bottle of sherry he kept there for special occasions, and poured both himself and Adelaide a glassful.

He wasn't terribly surprised when Addie suggested he pour Holly a half glass because she had become such an accomplished ironer. It gave him pause however, when Holly asked that Ruth be given some as well, because of 'how hard she worked'. Adelaide merely nodded at him. It was surprising enough to have his older daughter speak up for his younger one, but to have his wife not only acquiesce but smile at the idea of serving wine to them both was unheard of. As Simon fell asleep holding his wife in his arms, his last thought was how marvelous it would be to come home from work to such an atmosphere every night. If his home was filled with laughter, perhaps he wouldn't have to look outside of it for comfort.

When the family trooped up the gangplank together a few days later, following the porter who was wheeling their trunks ahead of them, he watched the girls chatting happily together like fast friends, and marveled at the change. Neither he nor Adelaide had commented to one another or the girls about their renewed friendship. Simon hoped that if he said nothing their closeness might continue. Addie, too, would have welcomed such a thing, but more for herself than for her daughters. A freely functioning household would have made her world flow with greater ease, and this would have been a wondrous thing.

The night before, although she didn't yet understand what had happened, she had felt a tingling in her body when Simon began to stroke her breasts, and a quickening in her belly when his fingers moved downward, sliding between her legs. Usually she dreaded the moment when he touched her most private places: it felt an invasion, unwelcome and unbidden. But the night before she had made no effort to stop him, and actually opened her legs a fraction to make it easier, shocked by her own wanton behavior. When Simon moaned with pleasure she wasn't appalled, and even waited with some anticipation for him to mount her. Afterwards he fell asleep almost immediately. She was sure that had she been able to see him in the dark, his face would have been wreathed with a smile. Sleep for her came much later, after she had convinced herself that as a wife it was not shameful to have felt such things.

* * *

Noah was inconsolable once he had he agreed to Nell's plan for her to sign up for the secretarial course at Battin High School. Nevertheless, he had to agree with Yetta that the likelihood of them being able to help Jules with dental school, and also come up with extra money for even a two-year college course for their daughter by the time she graduated from high school, was extremely unlikely. At least with the secretarial course under her belt, Nell would be able to find a decent job and earn good money, should the funds for a college education for her be lacking. Perhaps in time they would be able to send her to a teacher's college, where she would be able to more fully utilize her prodigious mind, or so he told himself. Noah never doubted for a second that his oldest daughter was fully as bright as his sons, nor that she deserved to explore this gift. It was for the education of all of his children that he had endured those four long, lonely years living in his brother's cramped bungalow. He found it deeply disturbing that even now, three years after the family's reunion in America, he did not believe he would be able to help his oldest daughter. He was also concerned that he would not even be able to come up with sufficient funds to send his two American-born sons to college, but this he admitted to no one. Not even Yetta.

When he sat down at the kitchen table to talk to Nell and Yetta after closing the shop one night, it was with a heavy heart that he agreed with Nell's assessment of her choices. None of them talked with one another about how they felt about this decision, Nell behaving with an adult resolve that was astonishing in one so young. Her attitude buoyed his spirits, which itself shamed the man. The three reached agreement and went to bed.

Nell revealed nothing she was feeling to her parents either. No one but she knew the toll the evening had taken. When she climbed into her bed that night after preparing the food her sister would cook for their breakfast the following morning, she lay there trying not to cry. Tears were not familiar to her: Nell was used to rising each day and doing what lay before her without allowing herself to think about how her life felt. One of the ways she had managed to cope was to dream, in her heart, about the time when she would be able to attend medical school in America. Although she realized this was an unusual choice for a woman, and unlikely in a family as poor as hers, from the time she had learned as a young child that her parents planned to move to this new country where opportunity for all was an abiding principle, this dream had allowed her to move through day after day of the drudgery that actually made up her life. She was bereft at having to give it up, but knew she could reveal her feelings to no one. Nell understood her parents had no idea that continuing her schooling had been her deepest desire, nor did any of her siblings. There was no one to share her distress with, because there was no one she dared to tell. Beck would think she had been foolish to dream such a thing, and Min, sweet Min, would try to comfort her. But she, too, would be shocked that her older sister could have thought there was a chance she could become such a thing, a doctor. None of them had ever known a woman who had been anything but a homemaker or shopkeeper to help support her family. Although the value of education was certainly stressed in this new country, no one in the Unger family actually know a woman who had gone on to college, even a two-year teacher's program. So Nell lay in her bed as tears quietly dripped down her cheeks, wiping them away quietly with the sleeve of her nightgown so she wouldn't awaken anyone in the apartment. The walls were thin, and no one would know what to do with a weeping Nell. By morning she was again ready to do whatever needed to be done.

Fortunately Noah's business flourished, and although it did not allow him to save enough for Nell's schooling, he and Yetta were able to pay off their loan from Elias within the first year. Because of Yetta's prodding, Noah attempted to attract business from the wealthy areas of Elizabeth, including a gentile neighborhood near Westminster Avenue. He placed an ad in the local newspaper for several months, until he had a good number of customers from outside the ghetto; many of them sent friends and neighbors to him after he had repaired a settee or hutch. He was so busy that he sometimes worked on Saturdays, the Jewish holy day, after the family returned from shul. On Saturday afternoons the boys were torn between working with their father on a piece of furniture or going off with their older brother to the baseball field, where he was teaching them to throw, catch and hit the ball like real Americans. They loved to go to the park with Jules, and often sat in the bleachers cheering for the team he had joined in the beginning of the spring season. When Jules became the pitcher on his team for the summer tournament of immigrant teams from the northern part Jersey, both boys were beside themselves. Much to his mother's dismay Nathan actually lost his voice screaming at one of the closer games.

The younger of the two brothers had an amazing arm for such a small child, impressing both Jules and one of his teammates who had come along one day to hurl the ball for the little boys. It was humiliating for Max that his baby brother could throw the ball farther than he could. The incentive was great for him to practice in private, but he was also afraid of crossing the large street between his home and the park. The first time he snuck out by himself with Jules' baseball, he couldn't get himself to step off the curb, standing there for almost an hour and then slinking home in ignominious defeat. Like the other Unger children, he kept his distress to himself, more determined the second time he ventured to the corner to overcome his own cowardice. He had decided that even if he found no one to help him cross the street and had to brave the intersection by himself, he would get to the park. Once he had gained the courage to race across the street, he didn't stop running until he was inside the park, and then stood still shaking from head to toe. When he had his body under control, Max threw the ball towards first base as hard as he could, over and over. An older boy he had seen on several occasions when he had been in the park with his brothers, gave him pointers, agreeing to meet him the next day to help him. The other boy wanted to practice his catching skills, so the two discovered they could actually be useful to one another. On the third day, although his throwing had improved, and he no longer looked 'like a girl', the other boy persuaded him to hit a few for him so that he could practice catching fly balls. Much to the surprise of both boys, Max could hit.

By the time he returned to the field the following weekend with Jules and Nathan, Max could not wait until his older brother suggested he and Nate step up to the plate to learn a new skill: batting. That Jules was impressed by his newfound ability to throw the ball without having to hide in embarrassment because it didn't go further than a couple of feet meant nothing to Max. He would never be as good as Nate. But from his forays into the park he had learned his talent lay in connecting bat to ball. When it was his turn, he calmly took the bat from Nathan, who had a hard time even holding the thing up in the air, and immediately stood in the correct position. He felt ashamed that he was pleased at his younger brother's inability to hit the ball, but it did please him, enormously. When Jules pitched the ball to him, he slugged it over the mound way into left field: both Jules and Nathan stared at him in utter amazement.

"Wow, Max! That was amazing," his big brother exclaimed. "Let's try it again."

If Max could have put words into Jules' mouth, those were the ones he would have chosen. He knew his brother wanted him to bat a second time to see if the first slam had been an accident. Again he slugged the thing over the mound, this time aiming for right field, and hitting it even farther. Nathan clapped his hands together in glee, obviously excited by his brother's ability at bat, shaming Max for the secret delight he had taken in the boy's poor performance earlier. To make up for his evil thoughts Max ran up to Nathan and clasped him in a hug.

Jules exclaimed, "You are really good at this, Maxie. Do you want to come here with me on Wednesday's to practice?" Max was utterly thrilled. Terrified as he had been crossing the street on his own each day, he was discovering that overcoming fears held obvious rewards. Even better, he would now get to come to the park alone with Jules. If he continued to improve, he, too, would be able to join a team, and then the whole family would come to see his games. Timid Max could not believe his good fortune. He wouldn't even have to walk to the park alone anymore.

Since her younger children were spending so much time in the afternoons with Noah or their older brother, and Beck and Nell usually prepared dinner because their cooking was so much better than hers, Yetta had leisure time when she got home from work in the afternoon. She had no idea what to do with herself. Within days, she was discussing starting her own small sewing business for their community with her sister-in-law. Marlene thought it was a marvelous idea, since most women in this new country were so busy with children, cooking, school activities and improving themselves, they often didn't have time for mending or doing alterations. Even better, some of their neighbors were doing well enough financially to afford the luxury of hiring someone to do those tasks for them. After Noah accepted the fact that his wife didn't want to lie around their house reading, or go to 'tea' with her friends, he agreed to partition a small space for her new business venture behind his shop. Within a year her business was thriving. Instead of hiring someone else to do the mounds of sewing awaiting her nimble fingers in her 'shop', Yetta quit her job at the factory and again became her own boss. One day Beck found her mother singing a popular American song, which she probably didn't even understand, as she bent over the used sewing machine her husband had found and repaired for her. The Unger family, though still not wealthy by American standards, was flourishing on almost every level in their new country, a mere three years after Yetta and the children had disembarked from the Hoboken ferry.

* * *

Within days of arriving in Europe, Ruth overheard her Aunt Sophia ask her mother why on earth she had allowed her daughter to walk out of a salon with such an unattractive haircut. She felt devastated, and didn't stay in the hallway to hear the answer. Racing to her room and flinging herself on the bed she had been given for their stay in her Aunt's home, she quickly had to dry her eyes when an unexpected knock interrupted her tears.

"Ruthie, my sweet. Can I come in?" she heard her Aunt ask as she wiped the tears from her cheeks. Thankfully her Aunt was too polite to ask why her eyes were rimmed with red, or even more directly, what she had been crying about. Instead she had a suggestion, which she made as she brushed the hair from Ruth's forehead and stroked it gently with her cool, slender fingers. "How would you like to go to the Salon of Beauty with me?"

"What for?" the child asked, by now utterly suspicious of any place with 'beauty' in its name. She knew she didn't belong in such an establishment.

"To get you a stylish, European haircut, sweetie," Sophia replied, not for a moment chastising her niece for her impolite question. Ruth felt a tingle of excitement. Her cousins, even her younger cousin, Dorothy, looked so sophisticated. Could a haircut by a European stylist actually change what she had come to accept as her awkward and certainly not pretty, appearance? Whatever would the beautician do to hide her large and ungainly nose?
Moments later, as she watched him clip away at her horrible hair, and then accepted her seat under the hair dryer next to a women who

hadn't looked particularly sophisticated before she came under the shears of the same hairdresser, Ruth anxiously awaited her own transformation. She knew, even before she saw the expression on her Aunt Sophia's face, that she looked utterly different. Her hair was cut in a bob, one that framed her face with a sleek little cap, the hair falling forward if she leaned forward, and swinging side to side as she walked. She knew she didn't look beautiful, but the little girl realized she did have style. When she and Sophia walked in the front door of their two-story apartment, Simon was standing by the coat rack, having just returned from a clearly successful business meeting. He turned to his sister-in-law and daughter to say something but the words never came. His mouth fell open for a second, before he scooped his daughter up in his arms and began twirling her around the narrow entryway.

"Daddy," she squealed in obvious delight. "Put me down. I'm not a little girl anymore."

"Pumpkin you will always be my little girl, and you better accept that," he whispered, nevertheless setting her down on the tiled floor. "My God, Ruthie. You look stunning. You've got style, my girl, and don't you ever forget it," he beamed.

The word 'beautiful' would have been better, but stunning wasn't bad, and would have to do. In truth, it was more than enough, because Ruth realized she had found her place. She could nurture her 'style, and this she vowed, at only nine, to do.

"What is all this commotion about?" Adelaide asked as she, too, entered the foyer. "My oh my. What an amazing hair cut!" she blurted, staring at her daughter. "You look lovely, Ruth," she added, turning next to Sophia. "You were right, as usual. And thank you."

Sophia, never a reticent person, and certainly not where her younger sister was concerned, immediately ordered, in no uncertain terms, "Now apologize to your daughter for the abysmal hair cut you subjected her to, Addie."

Ruth watched this interchange with some surprise along with Simon, who realized he had something to learn from Sophia in his dealings with his wife. In amazement he watched as Adelaide digested her sister's words, and then admitted, "I'm sorry, Ruth, for taking you to that barber. But I was worried you would try a box of home perm, like Holly did, and I couldn't handle the thought of that."

"Just promise me you'll find me someone who can cut my hair like this at home," Ruth requested, emboldened by her Aunt, but surprised by her own audacity nevertheless. "And thank you, Mama, for apologizing," she added. She had never heard her mother say she was sorry to anyone.

Later in the day when Simon took his daughters to the museum so that Adelaide could practice in the quiet of the apartment by herself, for once Ruth didn't mind that people turned to look at her beautiful sister. It was she who had her father's heart because of her quick mind and creative endeavors, and now, he also thought she possessed style. The following day he persuaded Adelaide to join them at another museum, and she came, to the amazement of both girls. As she described the architecture of the Borse Palais, Ruth realized how bright her mother was, and how knowledgeable. Her father looked proud of them all. In later years she often wondered whether the pleasure of that experience was what had endeared museum visits to her forever, and made visiting them a regular part of her life. When Holly linked arms with her as they strolled from room to room, Ruth realized her sister was enjoying this rare family outing as much as she. Neither girl wanted to leave the museum, Holly even begging to be shown another wing that had been described by their tour guide, but hadn't been included in the tour.

By the time they took the tram back into the center of Vienna, all of them were exhausted. Both girls stared at the furnishing in the lobby of the Hotel Sacher, entranced by its elegance and old world charm. At first they all shared two pieces of the Hotel's famous torte, but no one, not even Adelaide, objected when their father ordered two more. Adelaide even made a joke when every morsel had been eaten, complaining that she 'would have to waddle back to Sophia's apartment'. "After eating a whole piece all by myself Daddy certainly would not be able to carry me!" she concluded. They all laughed, Ruth thinking that the other café patrons must think they were a normal family. The very idea made her glow from the inside out.

After Simon asked for the bill he bent over to wipe a smear of chocolate from Holly's chin. As he leaned back he glanced at his wife, and, wiping her nose said, "Your turn, Addie," which caused even more hilarity at the table.

Ruth wanted the day to go on forever, and wasn't even jealous of Holly.

Several nights later, the Schola gave their first concert of the tour in Vienna. Ruth loved the frock she wore, and knew it hung well on her slender frame, complementing her new hairdo. Adelaide even let Sophia smear her lips with color, which was absolutely thrilling. Of course everyone ooh'd and ah'd over Holly's hair and dress and beauty, but for the first time they also complimented her. Ruth floated into the concert hall and only awakened when thunderous applause erupted for her mother. For the life of her, Ruth couldn't remember her mother stepping forward, or a single note she had sung. Later, in the dressing room, one of the other singers commented about how 'smart' she looked, even asking the little girl where she had found her hat, and telling her how stylish it looked perched atop her new 'do'. By the time Enrico Caruso came to the door, Ruth wasn't even nervous about being introduced to the famous man. She was, however, overwhelmed by his girth, and his voice, which even in conversation seemed to fill the large dressing room. She and Holly glanced quickly at each other when he reached for their mother's hand and brought it to his lips, both riveted by the display enfolding in front of them.

"I cannot believe you did not tell me you were coming to Europe again, Adelaide. I had to read about this concert in the paper," scolded the great man with a warm smile.

"I…I…I didn't want to disturb you," Addie stammered, a flush blossoming across her face from collar to temple. Neither of her daughters had ever seen her this flustered.

"My dear young woman. I meant every word I said the first time I heard you sing. As a matter of fact, I am singing in Berlin in a week," he mused, continuing with the remarkable question, "Would you like to join me for a few numbers?"

Although she was not convinced she would even be able to breathe, Adelaide heard herself reply, "I would love to sing with you, sir. It would be an honor."

"I would not want to intrude on the schedule your choirmaster has already arranged," the great man said with a simplicity that was genuine and totally endearing in one so famous.

"We don't sing again until our Munich concert, and that isn't for a week and a half," Eleanor, a friend of Adelaide's from the choir, blurted.

"How marvelous! Would you like to speak to Mr. Gordan, or shall I?" he asked the young woman. Gordan was the tour manager. Caruso reached into his pocket for a piece of paper, searching for a pen to write with. Another chorus member brought him one. "This is my number in Vienna. Perhaps we can arrange a bit of rehearsal time here before I leave. Or we can find time in Berlin, the day after tomorrow."

Before they could discuss the arrangements, Gordan, who of course had heard that the great man was again visiting his star performer, appeared. Arrangements were made, Addie agreeing to arrive in Berlin two days before the concert to rehearse, after Simon assured her caring for their daughters in Berlin would not be a problem for him. As Caruso turned to leave the room, he stopped and turned back to the people crowded into the group's dressing room.

"How could I be so thoughtless? Your daughters are both quite beautiful," he boomed, and then asked, "And so, my little beauties. What are your names? And do either of you have the voice of an angel, like your Mama?"

"My name is Ruth, and I write," Ruth replied without any hesitation whatsoever. Years later she believed that was because she had no real sense of how important the man was, so she wasn't afraid of him.

"Ruth is a fine name for you," he smiled. "And you?"

"I'm Holly. I…go to high school." Praying the ground would open up and swallow her, this was all Holly could think of to say.

"Do you do well there?" he asked her.

Neither Adelaide, nor Simon, nor Gordan, nor the other members of the singing group could believe such a mundane conversation with this illustrious celebrity was actually taking place before them.

"Yes," said Holly with some reticence. "Papa wants me to go to college when I graduate."

"A fine idea," Caruso assured her. "Although I'm quite certain you will be besieged by many suitors by that time."

And with that, he was gone, leaving a total vacuum in the suddenly silent dressing room. Finally Adelaide spoke, her voice trembling.

"Simon, I don't know if I can sing with Enrico Caruso. I really don't."

With everyone watching, including the girls, Simon took his wife's hands into his larger ones, and brought both of them to his lips, kissing each finger gently. "Adelaide. You were made to sing with this great man. If you truly don't know that, you will have to trust me."

"Are you certain?" the usually confident young singer asked her husband in a near whisper.

"Utterly," he replied, smiling down at her.

The entire dressing room erupted in applause. Both girls watched their parents in awe, thrilled to see the love between them, especially because it had never been apparent to either of them before. Somehow these weeks in Vienna had dissipated the chill that usually permeated their family relations.

That night Adelaide initiated lovemaking for the first time in her marriage to Simon, welcoming him with an abandon neither of them had ever believed she possessed. Simon asked no questions, but accepted her advances with relish as well as inner relief. Disappointed that he couldn't bring her to climax, nevertheless he was thrilled with the way her legs wrapped around his back, holding on tightly until he had come. "My pet, my sweet voiced Adelaide," he murmured, holding her to his chest until her breathing had become even and he knew she was asleep. He lay there in wonder, grateful that he had not forbidden his young wife to sing for fear that her career would tear them apart. In truth the only closeness they seemed to experience revolved around her singing. For the second time in as many weeks, Simon fell asleep with a smile on his lips and didn't awaken until morning.

Neither of the girls remembered Berlin from the family trip the year before. Because their mother was so busy rehearsing by herself to prepare for her two practice sessions with the famous man, they had the rare opportunity to explore a foreign city with their father. The first day he took them to the Neues Museum. After several hours even Ruth told her father she was 'a little sick of looking at pictures', much to his amusement. After controlling his laughter, which clearly irritated the other museum patrons, he grabbed each of his daughter's hands, and swinging them by his side, strolled outside with 'his two beauties'. Because it was only 11 in the morning, and too early for lunch, the three stood on the sidewalk outside the museum as Simon pondered where next to take them. Ruth was sure she was really floating.

With a huge smile her father looked down at his younger daughter and said, "I've got a treat for you, Ruthie. Wait till you see where we're going!" And off they went. As soon as they reached the Freizeitpark, Ruth understood the 'treat', and broke away from both father and sister to race headlong into the field in front of her. It was huge, with several different games in progress at the same time. One group of men was playing soccer, another curling, which neither girl had ever seen before, and a group of high school boys playing a game of American baseball, just catching on in Europe. Holly happily sat on the grass after their father laid down his jacket for her to sit upon; he then strolled over to the boys to see if he could borrow a ball, tossing the borrowed ball to his talented athlete on his way back to his older daughter. Ruth ran beneath it shrieking in delight, catching it on the first try. After seeing her catch three more fairly difficult throws, the boys called out to both father and daughter to join their game. Even though she was tagged at second base, Ruth hit the ball way into left field, a feat that made her father extremely proud. When she slid across the muddy field to get beneath a fly ball in center field, Holly couldn't contain herself and screamed in an effort to make her sister stop. But it was too late.

Standing open mouthed at the edge of the playing area, Holly began to clap in absolute glee because her sister had caught the ball, no longer thinking about what their mother would say about her ruined frock.

Before they left the park to go back to their hotel, she even tried to brush the dirt off of it. When it was clear to both father and daughter that Ruth's dress would have to be laundered, perhaps twice, to remove the offending patches of mud, Holly linked arms with her younger sister and assured her she would tell their mother "it was worth it". She continued, "You have such gumption, Ruthie. I would have seen that ball flying towards me and had no idea what to do to catch it. I might even have run away. I certainly wouldn't have slid in all that mud!"

"You're a trooper, all right, my girl," added Simon as two of the boys screamed after them, "Are you going to come back tomorrow?"

Before Ruth could even look at her father for his approval, Holly had screamed, "Oh yes. We'll be back. Same time?"

At that very instant Ruth decided that their first day in Berlin had turned out to be even more rewarding than the day of her haircut in Vienna. Even her sister approved of her now.

CHAPTER ELEVEN

Ruth never forgot that trip to Berlin with her father and mother, not only because she and Holly spent most of their time with Simon while her mother rehearsed with the famous Enrico Caruso. The great man had booked them into the Kempinski Adlon Hotel on the Unter Den Linden. When she stepped from the cab onto the stool the doorman had whisked into place upon their arrival in front of the white awning, the liveried young man smiled broadly at Ruth as he bowed in front of her, holding out his hand to assist her. He looked very handsome to her in his full dress uniform, and he was smiling directly at her. She knew he had probably smiled at Holly and her mother as well, but the look he gave her as he helped her step down from the stool thrilled her to the tips of her toes. She followed Holly into the lobby, the door held open for them by another equally well-dressed man, this one close to her father's age, but handsome nevertheless.

The lobby was magnificent, the domed white plaster ceiling arcing above their heads, an enormous staircase rising into the heavens before them. The hotel desk was carved wood, and so high from the ground that Ruthie could barely see the three men standing behind it as they completed their registration and attended to the disposition of their luggage. There were mirrors everywhere, and Ruth was surprised to see that she did look 'smart' as her adored Aunt Sophia had suggested, with her new haircut and the navy blue suit that had been purchased in Vienna for her travel days. Holly looked ravishing of course, but Ruth realized she no longer felt embarrassed to be standing next to her. They were different, and her sister would always receive the first glance, but now, she, too, knew she was worth studying. She stood behind her father, feeling utterly amazed. Europe was surpassing whatever notions she had held about it. Plush velveteen couches were placed at strategic locations around the lobby: some were empty, but in many sat other visitors to Berlin, all elegantly dressed, all conversing with one another, though she noticed one lone man seated in the middle of a welcoming arrangement of a couch and two wing chairs, sipping coffee and reading his morning paper. The attentive staff seemed to anticipate a guest's every need without a word being spoken. A young woman in a black maid's uniform with full white apron whispered into her sister's ear. Holly took her hand and the two followed her mother through the lobby to a ladies' room, a long room with sinks on one wall, mirrors above, and elegant private stalls for meeting your needs opposite them. Their mother even gasped when she saw the splendor within; the housekeeper, whose only job seemed to be opening the linen hand towels for the female guests, held theirs in front of her as they left their individual cubicles. The water in the sink was already flowing, warm and inviting, and the bar of soap smelled heavenly to both girls. Holly seemed as impressed as Ruth, returning her grin as the same woman took her towel from her hand to drop it into a hamper to the right of the sinks. By the time the three 'women' returned to the lobby, the bellman had their luggage on a cart and led the way to their suite.

The rooms the great man had reserved for Adelaide and her family were breathtaking. Even Holly, who was usually calm because she believed that showed her sophistication, gawped as they entered the first room of their suite. As soon as the bellman had unloaded their bags into their respective bedrooms – there were two: one for Adelaide and Simon, the other for the sisters – and left them to their own devises, she exclaimed, "I think this room is larger than our whole apartment in New York."

"Simon, this is too much," her mother agreed. "You must speak to the desk clerk."

Simon disagreed. "Adelaide, you cannot insult Mr. Caruso. It is he who reserved these rooms for us, and it is he who is paying for them," he explained. This did nothing to assure his wife, who because even more distressed.

"Why would he do this?" she asked him, dumbfounded.

"His actions show that he is a true gentlemen," her husband suggested.

"Will we meet him again," Ruth asked, giddy with the excitement of it all. Even her mother was touched by the glow in her daughter's eyes and the flush suffusing her cheeks. She looked as if she were ready to fly, if only they hadn't been situated on the fifth floor of the hotel.

"Yes, little Ruthie. I am sure you and your sister will be allowed to come to one of our rehearsals, if you promise to sit still," Adelaide assured her.

"And don't ask any questions," her sister added, sounding as stern as her mother usually did, which made both of her parents laugh aloud. Then their mother repaired to her bedroom to freshen up. She was due at the rehearsal hall within the hour. Holly sat on the living room couch, sinking into the cushions with a sigh. Her sister wandered into their bedroom, but was out again in just seconds.

"We have our own bathroom, Holly. And it has a huge huge tub in it!" she screamed. Even Simon went to look, almost as impressed as the girls by the large lavatory. "It has a sink for each one of us," Ruth pointed to the shiny, white, countertop and its double-sinks with great excitement. Even their father had never seen one like it before. Laughing, Holly added, "There's even a chair by the tub for our underthings," and then blushed to be talking about intimate apparel in front of their father.

The first day their mother rehearsed into the early evening, but their father urged them into their party dresses after they had all taken a nap and ushered them downstairs to one of the better restaurants, in a hotel already famous for the quality of its eating establishments. The elegant room contained several round tables covered in cream-colored linen cloths, crystal glassware, Limoges dishes, and gleaming silverware, noticeable even from the entryway. This huge, stylish room was more impressive than their suite. It's walls were carved mahogany, shiny with varnish, the carpets plush oriental, laid wall to wall although probably made in Berlin rather than the Orient, Simon assumed as they followed the maître d' to their table. "You ladies look lovely this evening," the man said with a slight smile on his otherwise serene face as he led them to a booth along the wall. Ruth was thrilled that their booth was close to the fire roaring beneath the carved mantle to their right. She assured her father she could hold the menu herself, although it was rather large, and perused its pages with awe. She had no idea how a dollar might translate into a deutschmark, but understood immediately that this was the kind of restaurant she and her parents rarely frequented. When she looked up at her father, he, too, was smiling at her. "A treat for us all, my little Ruthie. Don't you think?"

Holly asked if they could have anything on the menu, or did their father want to order for them. Ruth wished she had thought to ask him the question, so that he would bestow upon her the look of appreciation it elicited for her older sister. He told them both that they could order as they pleased, this once, if they didn't tell their mother. All three giggled conspiratorially. Ruth began to read the entrées aloud, asking her father what ingredients were in each dish, though some she recognized because her mother made them. When he told her that the hotel was famous for steak smothered in thinly sliced potatoes, she asked him to order it for her. Holly chose roast pork, served with applesauce and mashed potatoes as well as a serving of sweet, pickled beets, which would be served in many of the restaurants they frequented with their father while they were in Berlin. He ordered trout for himself, with julienned vegetables and a baked potato. After the waiter had departed with their order, and returned with their father's scotch, Ruth asked him what 'julienned' meant. For once the look of admiration was focused on her, and she basked in it. Their mother chunked their fresh vegetables in the summer, and although Ruth didn't see the point in cutting them in thin strips, asked if she could taste some of his, which also seemed to please him.

By the time their salads arrived, their father had ordered a second drink for himself and another ginger ale for each of his daughters. Ever curious, Ruth asked him what they were going to do the following day.

"We'll have breakfast in the room," he began, amused by the shocked look on the faces of each of his daughters. "We can order whatever you want when we go back upstairs," he added.

"Do the hotels in New York serve breakfast in your room too?" Holly asked her father, who nodded his reply.

"I didn't know…" she replied, obviously intrigued by the notion.

"You can eat any of your meals in your room at the more exclusive hotels all over the world," he explained to his wide-eyed daughters, who hung on his every word.

"Can you order the same food in our room that we're going to have at this restaurant," Ruth asked, ever the practical one.

"No. Most hotels have a separate kitchen to prepare the food for the rooms," he replied, amused at his little girl's curiosity about almost everything.

"I'd love to see such a kitchen. It must be huge," she marveled, just as their waiter appeared with their dinners.

"Ruth!" Holly exclaimed, appalled that her sister would want to descend to the dungeons of the hotel, convinced that was where such a place would be.

"It's alright, Holly. You don't have to go with us if I can arrange a viewing for your sister," their father chuckled as he took a bit of the delicate trout on the plate before him.

With her mouth full of thinly sliced beef, Ruthie could not contain her excitement, and exclaimed, "Really Papa? You think the hotel might let us see the kitchen?"

"Don't talk with your mouth full, liebchen," he cautioned, brushing her hand with his to lessen the impact of his words.

When she had swallowed the piece of meat she had been chewing, the little girl apologized immediately. Almost at the same time she and Holly both told their father their food was delicious, Ruth adding with a grin, "It might even be better than Mama's cooking," which made them all laugh.

"I won't tell your mama you said that," Simon said with a chuckle.

When he ordered a half bottle of wine for his meal both girls were surprised, but neither said a word. They rarely saw their father drink, but it was a special meal, so there was no reason to tell their mother about the wine either. When their father ordered a piece of cake for them to share, neither girl complained. Ruth was so full she was grateful she had worn one of the dresses her Aunt Sophia had bought her in Vienna. It was looser than the chemises she had brought from

New York, in the new style popular on the Continent. But when the amazing confection arrived at the table – layers of chocolate mounded with whipped cream on each layer as well as fresh, baked coconut, she didn't give a thought to declining her portion. Simon offered Holly a bite first, and then the younger child, who closed her eyes in ecstasy as she savored the flavors filling her mouth. Because she didn't want to speak again with her mouth full, and Holly had tasted first, it was her sister who sighed, "Oh Papa. This is divine!"

"We will have to buy your mother some German chocolate at the KaDeWe," their father agreed. "If we describe this cake to her, perhaps she can duplicate it."

"We must buy her a piece, so she understands how wonderful it is," Ruthie suggested and then took another small piece on her own fork. She had been trained to eat like a lady, and that she was determined to do.

"That's a good idea," Holly agreed, which totally silenced Ruth, who couldn't remember her sister ever acknowledging anything she had said or done as worthwhile. Amused at his daughters' concern for their mother, Simon ordered a piece of the cake to be wrapped for his wife, paying the bill as he waited for the task to be completed. When the girls saw the amount of money he was placing in the little tray the waiter had placed on the table for that purpose, they glanced at each other in concern. But their father was busy counting out the change and failed to notice their exchange. On the way to the elevator Ruth whispered to her sister, "We can share something for breakfast," a suggestion that seemed to relieve Holly as well.

After they deposited the cake on the coffee table in front of the couch in their suite upstairs, Ruth stood in the middle of the room and groaned, "I am so full, Papa, I don't know what to do."

He scooped her up in his arms and swung her around the large room. "Papa, stop! I'm going to be sick," she squealed, and though she was laughing, she also meant it.

"How about going for a walk," he suggested as he gently set her down on the carpet.

"At night, Papa?" Holly exclaimed in wonder, adding, "That would be very exciting,"

"And I know it will make my tummy feel better," Ruth agreed, even more excited than her older sister about this unexpected nocturnal adventure. She managed to keep her countenance calm, though inside she was filled with butterflies.

When they walked through the amazing lobby with its arched ceiling, both girls couldn't help but stare at the glamorous women being escorted into the restaurant they, themselves, had left only minutes before. One in particular, who stepped daintily down from a hansom visible through the glass of the lobby door, wore a tiered dress in a chiffon that seemed to float all around her, adding grace to her already amazing appearance. "Oh," Holly sighed. "What I would give for a dress like that." Ruth said nothing because she knew she would look ridiculous in such a diaphanous thing, but she felt the same way even so. The hat the woman wore was tightfitting, complementing the short new European hairstyle. Most of the women still wore their skirts calf length, but the sisters were able to glimpse slender ankles sheathed in silk and elegant heeled shoes, often with straps across the instep. The elegant woman was not lost on their father, although he was more circumspect in his perusal. When Ruth saw his eyes follow her all the way into the restaurant, her tummy felt an uncomfortable flutter but she paid no attention. She didn't want the evening ruined by anything, especially something she didn't understand. Holly longed for a pair of shoes like the strappy ones the lovely lady wore, but knew it was futile to ask. Her mother would think she was too young to wear such shoes, so Holly would never have dared voice her desire aloud, even to her father. Especially after their conversation about the new sashay in her gait.

Out on the street Simon declined the offer of a taxi, preferring to walk to the Deutsche Staatsoper with his daughters, where Caruso and Adelaide would be singing the following evening. He intended to show them where their mother would be performing in a few days; she had told him that afternoon when she had called the hotel that a poster was already in place in front, with both her picture and name below that of the famous man with whom she was to sing. The concert hall was not that far away, the Unter den Linden one of the most famous streets in Berlin because of the trees lining the sidewalk along its length. Holly ogled the shops, and Ruth asked questions about the park beyond the trees, and the buildings along the long avenue which all seemed massive to her, much larger than the ones in their own neighborhood in New York. Some were old – she could tell from the coal dust covering the stones – but most were newer in this neighborhood. She agreed with her father when he explained that the city seemed to be undergoing a rebirth, with quite a bit of construction in progress. Even Holly didn't complain about the length of the walk, fascinated by the shops, the pedestrians, and the hansoms, with their snorting horses and whip wielding drivers.

Of course it was Ruth who spotted her mother's picture as they approached the opera house. Although she already needed glasses for reading, she was farsighted and could easily read the larger words on the poster from almost a block away. "Look. Mama's on the picture in front of the theater!" she whispered, as if this was something she had to proclaim quietly, or be thought un-ladylike.

Amused, her father asked, "Why are you whispering, Ruthie?"

Startled, she replied, "I don't know. I didn't realize I was whispering."

"You still are," he whispered back.

"You're being silly," Holly complained, but even she was impressed. "It's a very good likeness," she sighed. "I wonder where he got it…."

Simon wrapped an arm around each of his daughters. "The Scola had a special photography session with your mama, and then sent several likenesses to Mr. Caruso."

"You never told us!" Ruth scolded, but her father interrupted. "Isn't it better this way, sweetheart?"

And it was.

They were still standing in front of the theater, under the lovely, fawn-colored awning, when their mother stepped out of the double entry doors, followed by the great man himself. He was very large, both tall and broad, his face almost hidden by the large mustache atop his lip. Ruth wanted to ask him how he managed to sing through that forest.

"Oh Mama, your photo is lovely," Ruth blurted instead, covering her mouth in embarrassment when she realized Mr. Caruso was looking down at her.

"Yes, indeed it is," he said to her, voice booming though he was not speaking in an overly loud tone. His facial hair was obviously not a problem. Then, to her mortification, he knelt before her. "And you are....?"

"Ruth. My name is Ruth, though people who know me well call me Ruthie," she said, mortified by her complicated answer.

"Then I will call you Ruth until I know you better. But by the time you leave, I hope you will be comfortable with Ruthie," he suggested, turning to Holly with raised brows. "And you are…?"

"Holly" was all she could manage.

The next morning after breakfast, which their father persuaded them he could afford, Adelaide suggested they stroll the Unter den Linden together to see if they could find a stylish outfit or two for the girls, since they were not rehearsing until two that afternoon in order to preserve their voices for the evening concert. Ruth could not believe her ears: her mother was expressing interest in finding clothes for her as well as Holly, something that had never happened before. Her father winked at her behind Adelaide's back, Ruth beaming back at him with absolute delight. The first shop they visited actually had a frock similar to the chiffon dress the glamorous woman had worn into the restaurant at the hotel. Before her mother could suggest she try one on in her size, Ruth demurred, saying that Holly's features were much more suited to such a dress. She would wait for another shop, or another day.

When Holly stepped from the dressing room she looked utterly ravishing in the dress, the expression on her father's face enough to have made the entire European trip worthwhile for her. The boy –

what was his name? – Holly had been dreaming of kissing the entire time they had been away – had already receded into a distant past. When she returned to New York with the new clothes she had bought in Europe, older boys would certainly notice her; whatever-his-name-was would just have to find a girl his own age although she would certainly be less lovely than she. Of course she shared these thoughts with no one, aware they were shameful even as she thought them.

At the Wertheim department store, an amazing new and enormous shop of several stories with a department for every need, their mother pulled two skirts from the rack in the young women's section for Ruth, as well as a belt that would suit both, and two blouses, one with a square neck, the other softer, and more feminine. Ruth preferred the square-necked one with the red trim, but was willing to try on both, sensing her mother was set on the cream-colored blouse with the layered frills. Her father loved both, taking her in his strong arms to tell her how marvelous she looked now, with Aunt Sophia's new haircut. The two chemises, the belt and both blouses were purchased and then they all strolled over to the Café Uhlandeck, a new restaurant recommended by the hotel staff for luncheon. When they walked inside it was again Ruth who was stunned by the décor. The ceilings were fluted, rising in an arched fan above their table, with insets of modern and attractive sculptures that even their mother admired. The meal was almost as marvelous as their dinner had been the night before, Simon talking both girls into trying the famous Berliner sausage sandwich. Ruth surprised everyone by finishing every mouthful, and then asking if they could share a piece of the cake they had eaten at the hotel restaurant. As her father protested, "But Ruthie, sweetheart, this is a different restaurant," he paused as she pointed to the counter at his back. And there behind the glass on the second shelf was an exact replica of the splendid chocolate layer cake. He ordered two whole pieces even though Adelaide protested. She would be unable to indulge, even though she had only eaten a salad for luncheon, because a full stomach would impede her rehearsal.

When the waiter brought the pieces to the table, Ruth asked him, "Could you wrap the second piece for my mother, so she can eat if after tonight's concert?"
"The only concert in Berlin tonight is the great Caruso. No other performer would want to compete with that man," he said.

"My mother isn't competing with him. She is going to sing *with* him. He invited her when he heard her sing in Vienna," Ruth declared much to her father's amusement and her mother's embarrassment.

The waiter's eyes grew as wide as the plate he held in his hand. "I read an interview with Mr. Caruso in the Berliner Tageblatt. He spoke of the young woman he had invited to sing with him" he gushed, adding, "I cannot believe I have been waiting on you." With those words he turned and went behind the counter, pulling out an additional chocolate cake, settling it into a cardboard box, and bringing it back to the table with a flourish. "Please. You must all enjoy this later in the evening. It is an honor for this restaurant to serve you." When their bill came, they hadn't been charged for the extra piece of cake.

Holly wanted to wear one of her new dresses that very afternoon, agreeing to wear the chiffon frock to her mother's concert that evening, while Ruth put on her favorite blouse with the wine-colored skirt and belt. That evening she would wear the dress her Aunt had purchased for her. Adelaide left for the concert hall and the girls followed their father along the Unter den Linden onto the Charlottenburg Tiergarten Chaussee into the Tiergarten itself. Despite living near a very large park in New York City, and one Ruth knew from end to end, the size of the German park amazed both girls. They could have walked for miles, viewing lines of sculptures, small ponds, and, to Ruth's obvious delight, playing field after playing field. Holly was tired by then, and asked her father if they could sit on a bench, but Ruth was too excited by the shopping, the clothes, the luncheon, and the playing field across from the bench her father had chosen to be willing to sit for very long. She finally walked to the edge of the playing field and was fidgeting in her new shoes as she watched the boys kicking a round ball back and forth. When it shot off the side of one of the younger boy's foot, and rose into the air heading straight at Ruth, she shocked all of the boys on the field by running towards the ball, catching it on her calf in mid air, and shooting it back at them. Several of them burst into laughter at this tourist who had kicked the ball as well, or better than, most of them. One of the older boys raced across the field, grabbed her hand and urged her to come play with them. Without a backward glance at either her father or sister, Ruth ran onto the field after him. She could hear Holly speaking in a shocked voice to her father – "Papa, oh no. You won't believe what Ruthie's doing!" but was too far away to hear his reply.

She had only been playing for a few minutes when one of the boys kicked the ball just outside her reach. She sprinted backwards anyway, in an attempt to retrieve it, but lost her balance and slid across a muddy section of the field. Several of the boys helped her up, but she stood there in shock, unable to understand what any of them were saying. All she could do was look down at her new skirt, a long streak of wet, squishy mud going all the way from the hem to the bottom border of her blouse, which had gotten muddy as well. Before she could utter a sound, or begin to cry, her father was beside her, having run in great haste towards the calamity he had witnessed seconds before. He knelt in front of her and tried to brush the mud from her new skirt, but it was obvious this was an impossible task. Ruth looked down at her ruined clothes and began to cry. The boys had no idea what to do, and were even more surprised to discover they had been playing with an American. Simon spoke flawless German, so they were able to communicate. Even the boys who had laughed initially at the young female firebrand, were upset by her distress. All of them told her father how well she played, and how much she had impressed them. When they asked if she could return the following afternoon in more suitable clothing, they were clearly disappointed to learn they would be leaving the city the next day. Ruth was inconsolable, even when her father translated what the boys had been saying, even after he had brought her back to the bench and Holly had said how sorry she was about the accident.

"Mama will never forgive me. She finally wants to take me shopping and I ruin my new skirt. Oh Papa, I want to die," she sobbed, unable to sit, unable to stand still. When he said, "Ruthie. We will go back to the shop and I will buy you the same skirt and the same blouse. Your mother will never know," she sobbed two more times and then was silent. She stared at him with wonder, not knowing whether to object or cover him with thankful kisses.

The shop had another skirt in her size, and the exact same blouse. The owner of the shop offered to throw away the ruined clothes, and let Ruth wear the new set out of the shop if she promised to forgo athletics until she was back in New York City. Adelaide never discovered the ruse, even shortening the skirt the following spring when styles permitted, so that Ruth could wear it for one more season.

The evening of the concert they all ate in the room so that Adelaide could relax beforehand in her robe, and bathe before the food was delivered. For once Holly was more excited than Ruth about the evening before them. She could not wait to don her new dress, picturing herself on her father's arm like a grown-up. Ruth did not even appear in her sister's fantasy; when she started to chatter about her shoes Holly became snippy because she realized her sister would have to be included in the evening's events. Holly wondered if perhaps her sister could walk behind them, but knew enough not to suggest such a thing to either parent. When they reached the Deutsche Staatsoper Ruth was so awestruck by the elegant crowd milling outside before being admitted to hear her mother sing, she actually stood on her toes to see everyone better as they walked up the majestic staircase. Holly slipped her arm through her father's, who glanced down at her with a radiant smile, as pleased as his youngest daughter by the crowd outside, and then he took her hand in his. When Ruth whispered, "People are looking at you, Holly. Your dress really is lovely," she was startled – Ruth rarely complemented her – and immeasurably pleased. Ruth was so excited by what she was seeing she didn't seem to notice that her father was squiring Holly, or so Holly believed. In actuality Ruth's heart skipped a beat when she saw her sister's arm slip into the crook of her father's elbow. She longed to be the girl her father was escorting, walking through the lobby to the stares of the well-dressed women of Berlin, but knew this was not to be her lot in life. Her antics would amuse her father, and even at times, impress him, but Holly was the beauty he would always dote on.

Still it was an evening to relish. They were seated in a private, center box, the spot always reserved for the great man's guests, and thus were on view for the entire audience below. Ruth realized she was enjoying the attention because she no longer felt unattractive. The women might glance at her sister first, but they didn't ignore her anymore. She believed her Aunt Sophia, and knew she looked 'smart' in the dress her aunt had bought for her a few weeks earlier. Her mother had washed her hair before she had taken her own shower, and for once she hadn't complained about having to brush it dry. She could tell it glowed with life as she stood in front of the hallway mirror with her father, waiting for Holly to join them. How a human being could take more than an hour to dress was more than little Ruth could comprehend, but she didn't complain because it gave her a few precious moments alone with her father. When he stroked her hair and told her how 'smashing' she looked with her new 'do' and new dress, the wait became a blessing. Though her sister tried to get her to sit down and not stand so that she could look down at the audience below them, she was unsuccessful. Ruth loved looking at all the women in their finery. For once she wasn't overawed by them, and was even able to find women she could emulate, smart and stylish, their personalities enhanced by their hairstyle or choice of dress, who obviously commanded the attention of the people surrounding them. When Holly pointed out the flowers in one woman's hair, or the elegant dress of another, she nodded in agreement, but they were not the women who demanded her attention.

It was at the concert in Berlin, where her mother actually sang with Enrico Caruso, that Ruth realized she would have a place in the world of women and not be relegated to the role of outcast. For the rest of her life she could bring back some of the women she had seen that night at the concert hall by merely closing her eyes. The hall was lovely with its plush seats, high ceiling adorned by obelisks carved within its panels, and elegant boxes lining all three walls above the orchestra. Directly in front of their box the huge modern chandelier with its hundreds of glass lights hung from the center of the ceiling above the orchestra. Even Holly stared at it as the curtain on the stage below began to rise.

Although each of the girls enjoyed the first half of the concert when Caruso sang several arias alone on the enormous stage, it was the second half that neither ever forgot. During the intermission their father took them out to the mezzanine where he ordered a glass of champagne, allowing each of his daughters a small sip. All three were too nervous to enjoy the bubbly, or to watch the amazing outfits of the other operagoers encircling them. Once again they made their way to their seats. Again Ruth stared at the chandelier in amazement. And once again the famous man walked onto the stage. Then he stepped forward and spoke without any enhancement, even though he was not singing but speaking. He told the audience that he had been visiting some friends in Vienna where an a cappella group from New York City had come to perform. They had all gone to the concert together, thoroughly enjoying the singing. Then a young woman stepped out from the front row of performers, the conductor raised his baton, and she began her solo. It was a wondrous sound, clear, with just the right amount of vibrato and it soared above the audience. He was mesmerized and found it difficult to believe that such a tiny woman could produce such a large sound. After the concert he made his way backstage to meet the little singer. When he discovered the group had a three-day respite before moving on to their next engagement in Strasbourg, he asked the young woman if he could persuade her to sing with him during this break. He was delighted when she said 'yes'. He asked the audience to forgive them for only having that day to rehearse their duet and then turned to usher their mother onto the stage. Ruth's heart lurched in her chest as Holly reached for her hand, clutching it so desperately that Ruth feared she would lose the circulation in her fingers. Their father looked proud and stern, and then Holly pointed at his knees, which were shaking. Adelaide wore the silk dress Sophia had persuaded her to purchase, scooped down in the front in a style even Holly could not believe her mother would wear. It was difficult to see how low-cut it was from their spot in the great man's box, but they all knew. They had seen her leave their suite at the hotel only hours earlier. She looked tiny standing in the center of the huge stage next to the large tenor as he motioned for the orchestra to begin.

Ruth felt terrified: singing with no accompaniment was one thing, but how would anyone be able to hear her mother's voice above the sound of so many instruments? Much to her amazement when her mother opened her mouth the most amazing sound permeated the enormous hall, filling the space without any difficulty. When Mr. Caruso joined her he modulated his voice to hers. Together they were magnificent, their two voices dipping and soaring in glorious harmony. Ruth held her breath during the first number, and when it was over, realized both her father and sister had done the same. The applause was thunderous. Caruso had to hold up his hand to quell the noise. He began a second number, the spectators utterly silent as their mother's soprano joined his remarkable tenor. The audience would not let the two singers leave the stage, even after they had sung two encores. When he protested that they hadn't had time to rehearse any other numbers, the audience was quiet for a few seconds and then began to cry out for more anyway. The great tenor leaned down to whisper something to their mother, who nodded, walked over to the conductor, again whispering a few words, and then moved back to his original position next to Adelaide Liebman, explaining that she had grown up a short distance away in Vienna, but now lived in New York City where she and her husband had become citizens several years before. As her melodious voice again filled the Deutsche Staatsoper as if she had been singing there for years, Ruth felt her father raise himself to a more upright position, which she would not have believed possible moments before. She glanced at him, shocked to see tears wetting his cheeks and dripping into his mustache. When she reached for her hanky, he shook his head. She turned back to the stage and watched in wonder as her mother and Caruso sang a piece by Mozart together as if they had done so hundreds of times before. During the last few bars his voice fell away, the only sound their mother's soprano accompanied by a single violin. No one in the entire Staatsoper was breathing when the last note died away. Their mother stood there with Caruso's arm around her shoulders, a rapt smile on her face. It felt like hours before the audience allowed the two performers to leave the stage. When they did depart, they left arm in arm.

Simon sat still, unable to move. He felt a deep love for this woman who had persevered against all odds to experience such a moment, through immigration, marriage to a virtual stranger, and bearing two children she had not truly wanted. She had prepared sumptuous meals for him and later, their two children, without complaint since she had married him and moved into his apartment, chosen his suits, pressed his shirts, cleaned their apartment. This talented creature had taken the girls to the park almost every day, and still found time to travel into Manhattan for her singing lessons. He felt ashamed that he had not been more supportive, realizing he had allowed her these 'little trips' on sufferance. Even though he had heard her sing with the Schola Cantorum and in the restaurant at their wedding, he had not realized the extent of her talent. He felt Ruthie tug at his sleeve, but he remained in his seat. At that moment he vowed to himself that he would work harder to make their marriage more manageable, and perhaps if he became more thoughtful, it might even become a haven for them both. The night he heard her sing with Caruso Simon truly believed that was possible. He would make it so.

* * *

The first year Yetta's shop was up and running Elizabethport suffered a severe flu epidemic, one that was killing thousands of people all over the country. She decided to keep Max and Nathan home from school, where germs were more likely to spread from child to child. They could study in Noah's workshop, or on the floor next to her sewing machine. Because she was in her last year of high school, Min refused to stay home. Like her older sister Beck, she realized she would have to work when she graduated, but she was determined to be fully American and as an American girl, to get her diploma. Beck was working for an insurance broker as a secretary, but she, too, had graduated from high school. Nell was working in the shop with her mother, and taking two college courses at night at the local teacher's college on the outskirts of Elizabeth. She would have preferred attending the new women's college attached to Rutgers in central New Jersey, but would never have suggested such a thing. Her parents would have a hard enough time sending Max and Nathan to college without having to worry about the higher education of any of their daughters. If she was determined, she believed she would eventually receive a teaching credential; once she was teaching, perhaps some of her female students would be inspired by her to complete a four-year course she, herself, had been unable to afford. All of the older girls continued going to work despite the epidemic because the family needed the income; besides, life couldn't stop because of the dangers of illness. Illness was part of living, in both American and back in Poland, where many children often didn't reach adulthood.

The second week of the epidemic Max became listless and Noah sent him upstairs to lie down. He ran up and down the back stairs to check on his son several times during the afternoon, but didn't go into Yetta's shop because he didn't want to alarm his already worried wife. Towards six o'clock, when she usually emerged from the shop to help her daughters set the table for dinner, Noah knew he could hold back no longer. Max had a fever, and it was steadily rising. This he had been able to tell from resting the inside of his wrist on his son's forehead.

None of them ate much dinner that night. No matter how often Yetta bathed her son's face, arms and legs with cool water, his fever continued to climb. Nathan ran over to Elias's house to ask for the name of a doctor. The man they had used, only when it had been absolutely necessary during their first few years in Elizabethport, had long retired. Miraculously none of them had needed to consult a doctor since that time. 'Now we are paying for that good fortune," Yetta thought to herself as she dunked the wash cloth into the clean water Noah had just set beside her on the bed stand.

By morning Max's fever had climbed to dangerous proportions, the skin on his forehead burning Yetta's fingers each time she placed the cool clean cloth there. Her hand shook so that Min, who had stayed home from school to help her mother and was hovering in the doorway despite the parents' warning to not come into the room, ran to get Noah in his shop. Nathan stood at the top of the stairs crying because he loved his older brother, but wasn't allowed anywhere near him lest he contract the dreaded disease. Noah raced past the little boy and into the room Max usually shared with his brother, brushed his son's hand with his own, and, terrified, raced over to the butcher shop. Elias waited on the customer standing at the counter, but told the woman who had entered the shop before Noah arrived, breathless, that she would have to wait until later: he had a family emergency. On the way back to Noah's apartment, Elias gave him the name of the doctor they had used when Dottie had contracted the horrible disease. It was only with the unguents he had prescribed that her temperature had lessened, and she was not out of the woods by any means. He and Marlene waited for his nightly visits, though it was Marlene who was clinging to the belief that if he came every night, their little girl would survive. Elias offered to run to the doctor's office, only blocks from their homes in the port, so his brother could help Yetta with Max.

The doctor's demeanor became more and more grave as he examined the boy. Elias had not thought to tell them to immerse the boy in a tub of cool water because he had been wrapped up in his own concern about his daughter. Noah tried to console his brother as best he could as they raced downstairs to the bathroom to fill the tub that had been installed when Yetta and Noah had remodeled the upstairs apartments. Noah held nothing against Elias; most families had a family member who had been felled by the virulent flu sweeping the Port, and most, like Elias and Marlene, were overwhelmed with their own worries. He and Elias carried the boy downstairs, though he was already so light from weight loss, Yetta could have done the job. Min held Nathan in her arms; both were crying openly. They looked as terrified as their parents felt, though the adults were trying to appear calm despite the haste with which they were working. When Max felt the cool water on his limbs, he flailed his arms and legs so much that his father could barely hold onto him. He groaned loudly, begging to be left alone. As his body was immersed in the water, he began to cry.

"My brave little Maxel," Yetta crooned to him. "Hold on, little one. This cool water will make you feel better, my son. Trust me." Only Noah could see that his wife was at the end of her tether, barely hanging on to her composure.

Elias raced back to his own bungalow, distraught to discover his own daughter Dottie's body was again raging with fever. Ordering his exhausted wife to fill their tub again, he carried the four-year old to the cooling water and gently lowered her into the tub. It broke his heart to hear her cry out, "No, please. Not again," but he didn't listen. The cool water was the only thing they had; there was no medicine to quell the fever.

As it had the entire day before with his cousin, the cooling waters brought Max's fever down. He felt warm to the touch, but no longer hot. When his body temperature had held for several hours, Noah sent his wife to their bedroom to sleep, carrying a rocker into the room his two youngest sons shared so he could sit beside Max to monitor his condition. Nell and Min prepared dinner for the family though no one wanted to eat. Yetta would not go back to bed until they agreed: they had to eat to keep up their strength or one of them might succumb to this dread disease as well. Just as Noah was sitting down at the table with Nathan and the girls, he heard his wife scream from above. All of them ran for the stairs. Jules had fallen asleep in the rocker, which he had offered to man when he had gotten home from work so his father would be able to eat. Max was again burning with fever; Jules was distraught, because he had no idea when the fever had begun to rise again. He pushed his father aside and carried his brother down the stairs, where Beck was already filling the tub. Max was so exhausted, burning with a fever of such intensity he could not even object or moan when he was lowered into the cool water.

Within minutes his fever again began to drop. Yetta toweled his body gently, as he moaned in his father's arms, muttering, "I'm thirsty mama. And I'm so tired." Min appeared with a cup of water, which Yetta fed him sip by sip as he rested in his father's arms. Only then did Noah carry the boy back to bed, where he immediately fell into a fitful sleep. After Yetta had eaten a few mouthfuls, Noah ordered her to sleep, taking the shift beside their son's bed himself. It was clear someone had to be in the room with Max continuously, and it couldn't always be Yetta or she would be sure to fall sick herself. Min brought her father a plate of food, which he quickly finished, much to his own surprise. Beck told Noah that Nathan was inconsolable because he had been the only one in the family who had not been allowed into the bedroom. Noah suggested he stand in the doorway for a few seconds to look at his brother, and then gently told him he must go back downstairs where Nell was making a bed for him in her room. Earlier he and Jules had carried the little boy's mattress there so he would have a place to sleep. Then Noah prepared a schedule so each of the adults could take two-hour shifts, allowing the others to sleep for a few hours at a time. During the day the older girls would be at work, so they each were assigned a nighttime shift, as was Jules. Noah allotted himself and Yetta the most hours in their son's room, since their presence seemed to ease their Max's mind, affording him the little relief there was for his suffering.

Fortunately both Yetta and Max were asleep when Elias arrived, banging on the front door of the apartment, too distracted to think about who might be sleeping within. His sobs filled the parlor as he told them in barely distinguishable phrases that little Dottie had succumbed, dying only a short while before. Her breathing had been so labored and so intense the last two hours of her young life he had actually found himself praying for her release, Elias told his younger brother, again breaking down in wrenching sobs at the admission. During that night Max also began to have trouble catching his breath, until Noah feared he would have to breathe directly into his son's mouth to help him. But then he rallied, and Noah neither had to breathe for him, or awaken his wife. The boy's fever spiked and broke, spiked and broke, again and again over the next two days, but never did it go as high as it had on the very first day. Noah waited until it was obvious their boy would survive to tell his wife that Dottie had died. She immediately donned her coat without a word, furious that her husband had kept this horrible news from her, but understanding his reasons for delaying. Noah could not stop her, even with dire warnings about entering another infected home.

"Marlene will have scoured every surface by now. I will not be in any danger, and she will need me," Yetta told him as she tied a headscarf beneath her chin. She didn't remind him to keep up his vigil for their son, even though his fever had abated. They would watch him carefully for months, even after he was outside playing with Nathan, who never let his older brother out of his sight.

The burial took place the day after Noah had told his wife of their niece's death. Because of the number of deaths in the area and Max's illness, the rabbi had given the family dispensation to wait longer than the twenty-four hours required by Jewish law. Dottie's funeral was not the only one held on that day in Elizabethport. Many residents were dying, or ill, so attendance was not great. The little girl's kindergarten teacher came, unable to hold back her tears. She had lost many students, and her own sister, a teacher as well, had passed away weeks before. Min was inconsolable. She had been little Dottie's most frequent babysitter; it felt like losing a sibling, or a child of her own. Max was alert enough by then to see that his father and mother were wearing their Shabbos clothing, and to understand what it meant. Noah was forced to tell him that someone had died, and Yetta, when he demanded to be told 'who' with the little strength he possessed, whispered that it was his little cousin Dottie. Max and his little cousin had shared a love of reading. As Jules had done with him, Max had been the person to take the little girl to the public library in downtown Elizabeth, pulling her up each step until they stood in the large foyer, looking at the shelves of books spread before them. The boy was more distraught about his cousin's death than his older sister had been. Frightened by the depth of her brother's sobbing, Min ran to the train station to intercept Jules, who had just left to catch the train for his afternoon classes at Rutgers. He had skipped so many classes during his brother's illness that he had been forced to heed his Uncle's admonition to miss the funeral. He would sit shiva with his cousins when he didn't have to be at Rutgers. Jules raced home without a thought to another missed class and sat with Max while his siblings prepared for the funeral.

"Are you sorry you were the one to survive, Max," Jules asked his brother without preamble. They had already developed a relationship based on honesty and directness.

Max could only nod his accord. He could not stop crying.

"We cannot begin to understand what God has in mind for us," Jules continued with a gentle tone unusual in such a young man. "He did not think it was your time to go."

"Why would he take someone as little as Dottie," Max asked his older brother, adding with a sigh, "She was so intelligent."

"Sometimes it is very difficult to believe, isn't it?" Jules replied.

"For you too?" the boy asked him.

"Of course. It feels unnatural to me, too" he said. "The death of such a young child, who hadn't begun to know what life might be."

"Where do you think her soul has gone?" Max asked him.

"Why don't I get Papa's copy of the Talmud and we can see what it has to tell us about that," Jules suggested. The two sat in Max and Nathan's room reading sections of the tome together, affording both brothers great relief. Then Jules walked to the closet, took Max's suit from its hanger, and dressed him. His mother was furious when he carried the boy into the parlor, but relented when she saw the determined look on the boy's face.

"She was my friend, Mama. And I survived," Max explained.

She stared at them both, and sat down heavily on the couch. Neither said a word, waiting for their mother's verdict. Both knew she was a very fair human being, more so than anyone else either of them had ever known.

"Alright. You can go to the cemetery. But then Papa will bring you back in the wagon and you will go to bed. Going there and then to shul would be too much for you, Max," she reasoned. The three nodded in agreement, and so it was decided.

That evening when their father returned from sitting shiva, Nathan sat beside him on the couch. At the age of eleven he could not imagine life without his older brother, even though the two were only a year apart. "Is there a chance that Max won't recover, Papa?" he asked, only partially reassured by his father's words. Though Max was older, Nathan was the adventurous one, crossing the street at an earlier age than Max but urging the older boy to follow him; riding the old bike their father had found long before Max, but never giving up his efforts to get his older brother in the seat as well; being picked by the neighborhood boys for the stick ball team, but refusing to join without his older brother. On the other hand, it was Max who pushed Nathan to think about more weighty matters: the state of affairs in Europe; the value of literature in both English and the native language of their parents; the beauty of music. The older boy's mind was more curious and wide-ranging, though both were obviously bright. Max had helped Nathan with his math homework since the younger boy had started school as well as with the short paragraphs Nathan was assigned from the stories he had to read in English class.

"His fever has broken, Nathan. But this influenza is a dangerous disease. I can't promise you, but I can tell you that your mama and I both believe your brother is over the most serious hurdle," Noah quietly replied, trying to sound as reassuring as he could.

Nathan thought about that for a few minutes, sitting silently beside his father on the couch and than quietly said, "I want to sleep in our room tonight, Papa. If anyone can keep his spirits up it is me, and you and Mama must know that."

Noah didn't even have to glance down at his son to know how important this request was. "Let me speak to your Mama," he replied, squeezing Nathan's knee as he stood.

Moments later Yetta followed her husband back into the parlor. "You have to promise me that you will not get into his bed after we are asleep," his mother cautioned Nathan, her face stern, lips set.

"Of course I promise, Mama. I know it would be unwise for me to be that close to Max," he replied with equal equanimity.

And so it was that after Beck, Min, Nell and their mother had scrubbed every inch of the room Max and Nathan shared, that Nathan moved back into his twin bed in their bedroom. Yetta found them with their arms outstretched, hands clasped, when she came in with the tray carrying Max's breakfast of farina and warm tea the morning after the doctor's visit. She stood there for some time staring at her two sons, grateful beyond belief that she had not lost either one of them.

* * *

That night in Berlin when Simon and Adelaide were finally able to tear themselves away from the theater and all the well wishers there, and return to the hotel with their daughters, all of them were too excited to fall asleep. Adelaide didn't even object when Simon lifted the torte from its box on the coffee table in front of the couch, and cut each of them a piece of the rich confection. For years Ruth would look back on those late evening hours on that momentous evening as among the best in her childhood. For the first time it felt as if she belonged to a family with shared moments, history, ideas, likes and dislikes. All of them had eaten every crumb on their plates, even their mother. They chatted about the Berlin museum, and the Tiergarten, the dress shops, how Berlin food differed from Austrian, and the other cities and towns they would be visiting on their mother's tour until both girls began to yawn and nod. No mention was made about the ball game, which Addie never did learn about. It was Simon who brought them into their bedroom, and Simon who undressed them and put them to bed. Ruth was asleep before he had even tucked Holly into the fluffy down comforter provided by the luxurious hotel.

He and Adelaide sat and talked on the couch for quite awhile afterwards. Simon felt compelled to speak to his wife, and she, to listen. He told her how thrilled he was by her courage in standing on that stage with such a great and famous man and sing beside him, looking as if she belonged there, her voice entitled to share the stage with his.

"I have never heard such a sound before, Addie, as your voice soaring above his, the two of you joined in a way that amazed everyone in that hall," he continued as his wife slipped her heeled slippers from her feet, and curled them beneath her on the couch. She sipped at the tea he had ordered from room service and watched him. It was clear to her he was not finished.

"I ask you with all my heart to accept my apology to you," he said in a burst and then stopped, as if he had no idea how to continue.

"For what, Simon?" she asked him, actually curious about what he would say. She was not sure, although she hoped she understood.

"For making it so difficult for you to take your classes when you first came to this country, and objecting to you continuing with them after Holly's birth. I knew you were talented, but I had no idea…the depth of that talent," he replied, taking her hand in his and holding on to it.

"Thank you Simon. I never thought I would hear you say these words, though I hoped I might," she sighed. "You have no idea what they mean to me."

The two sat side by side on the couch, holding hands in a silence that was comfortable to them both.

"You will have to tell me what I need to do to make it easier for you to continue your career," he finally spoke. "We must look for a girl to clean for you, and even to cook if that would help."

She smiled at him with all her being. "I think I can manage the cooking Simon. I know how much you and the girls enjoy what I make."

He smiled back at her and sighed. "I am very glad. I do love everything you make for us."

She wanted to shout out her relief and to run around the room in absolute glee, but neither action would have felt comfortable to her. She hated to behave in an unseemly manner, her mother's daughter in almost every way, despite her determination to sing. But she had never felt as happy in her life. First the amazing concert, and then the applause, and then the great man's words, and finally, the delight of her daughters, and the words of her husband. For the first time in her young life, she was free. She would be able to rehearse for longer hours, go to Schrafft's with the other women in the group, and even visit a museum or two, something she had been longing for without any hope of accomplishing. She thanked her husband quietly, saying she would think about what they might both do for one another, although she suspected what he would want.

After he mounted her and was spent, she lay beside him in their huge hotel bed staring into the darkness. She was already forming the words for an ad to place in the Bronx newspaper for a maid, and figuring out how to get Ruthie to school in the mornings. Holly could walk herself, and although Ruth would demand she be allowed the same privilege, this was not something her mother was yet comfortable with. Perhaps the young mother who had moved into their old apartment, and had a son a year younger than Ruth would be willing to walk both children to school for a small stipend. The girl they hired to do the cleaning and food shopping would be able to pick her up. Already Adelaide was expanding her notion of the chores she could assign to this as yet imaginary person. She sighed with contentment, quietly so as not to disturb Simon. She truly didn't mind cooking for her family, and found the creation of new dishes another outlet for her abundant inventiveness.

She wanted to thank him again, letting him know the significance of his words for her, but did not want to revive him because she had no desire for any more caresses. She realized suddenly that if she rehearsed longer hours, and stayed in Manhattan later in the day, she would be tired at night, and unable to perform her wifely duties as frequently. She held her breath and closed her eyes, startled at what a great relief this was to her, despite her suggestion that they both find ways to please one another. Though she no longer hated his advances, she didn't look forward to them either. It would not upset her in the least if her husband found enough succor from other women more amorous than she to be willing to leave her alone. The very notion increased her sense of freedom. How she might lead her husband to this most obvious and relieving solution to the one problem that still plagued their marriage she had no idea. But there was ample time for a resolution to be revealed to her. To her surprise she realized that she felt compassion for her husband's need. Now that he accepted who she really was, she had no compunctions about acknowledging this aspect of him as well. She vowed to become a more satisfying partner.

As Adelaide closed her eyes and drifted into sleep, her last thought 'how odd it is that I have found the life I have always wanted in America, with a man my parents chose and whom I never thought I would ever come to love. Isn't life strange…' and then she slept.

CHAPTER TWELVE

After dinner one evening Nathan sat down beside his mother at the dining room table where she had just opened her accounting books. Surprised, she glanced at him, quickly realizing he was afraid to speak.

"Tell me what you need, Nathan," she gently suggested. "Please."

He sighed and then quietly said, "I would like to be able to sleep in bed with Max again. He will heal quicker if he knows I am there."

Although she would have preferred waiting another week, she knew Nathan was right. The need to protect Nathan was hers, and not the best thing for either of her sons. Noah, who had just come in from his shop, awaited her response as well.

"Please Mama. The doctor said that the danger was passed," Nathan urged, unwilling to be deterred. And so it was that the younger brother slipped into his brother's bed that night. The healing boy fell asleep with a smile on his face. The next morning he had a healthy glow on his cheeks, one not caused by the fever that had been raging just a week before. Both Noah and Yetta could see the improvement when they entered the brothers' room to bring him his morning breakfast of farina, even before Max accepted several bites of the warm cereal, something he had been unable to do the morning before. Every day brought another improvement.

By the second week Noah was taking the boy down to his shop, where he was allowed to pull apart some of the pieces his father had collected in the alleyways of Elizabethport. His father kept him far away from the stains and waxes he used on the furniture once he had rebuilt the pieces because he was concerned the fumes might be hazardous to his son's steadily improving health. Max loved being in the shop with his father, begging Noah to allow him three hours, rather than the prescribed two. Noah relented once the boy promised he would not tell his mother. This was easier to do than to pretend he was not tired when his mother brought him his dinner that evening, but he managed, and she left his room with a smile on her face after he had eaten every mouthful she had prepared for him. Her son was getting stronger.

That night Max tried to remain silent until Nathan fell asleep, and then cried quietly to himself. Because of his improving health he was able to fully experience his losses, especially school and all he had been learning there. He missed his friends, who were as yet unable to visit him, but more serious was his fear that he would fall so far behind in his studies that he would be held back. Max had no idea how to prevent this from happening. Fortunately Nathan was not yet asleep, and again crawled into bed with Max and lay there quietly until his older brother was able to share his distress. They talked for quite awhile before they fell asleep.

The next day Nathan left for school a good half hour early, explaining to his parents that there were some tasks he had promised to complete for one of his teachers before the school day began. Although he wasn't the student his older brother was, both parents believed him. When he arrived Nathan sat down outside the door of his brother's English class. A few moments later the teacher walked down the hallway towards him, taking out her key as she reached the door. Nathan explained who he was; she was delighted to accommodate him since Max was one of her best students. She pulled several sheets of assignments from her desk drawer, along with paper and two pencils, explaining that Max would have two months to complete them before the end of the school year. If he handed in the assignments by that time, she would pass him on to the next grade. She offered to talk to his other teachers, sure they would be equally willing to help so that Max could graduate with his classmates even if he couldn't attend the ceremony. Nathan put the papers into his book bag and climbed the stairs to his own class, feeling better than he had the night before. Though he had assured Max his teachers would want to help him, he had not been so sure. If the English teacher, who clearly enjoyed his brother, had not been helpful, he had no idea what he would have told his brother. Now he could run the five short blocks to their apartment with the good news once the dismissal bell rang.

After Noah had helped Max to the kitchen so he could eat dinner with the family, Nathan withdrew the papers from his pack, revealing what he had been up to that morning. Everyone at the kitchen table stared at Max, whose entire face all the way to his forehead, radiated joy. This was the first smile Yetta had seen on her son's face since he had been struck with the hideous flu months before. Gruffly she told him that he could only read for an hour each day, until she was convinced the effort would not exhaust him. He readily agreed. "Don't worry, Mama. I won't do too much because I know I have two full months to complete the work. It never takes me very long to finish the assignments once I've done the reading and the math has been explained." That silenced everyone because no one in the family was good at math, until Jules walked in the door from his late afternoon class and asked them what was wrong. When Max explained, his older brother laughed with relief. One of his Rutgers friends was a math whiz; he would bring the young man home with him with the lure of his sisters' cooking skills and then pounce. The young man was 'a good guy' and would certainly volunteer to teach Max all he needed to know, even without the promise of a marvelous meal. When they went to bed Nathan helped Max set up the lamp beneath his covers so he could read a few pages before going to sleep. The younger boy forced himself to stay awake until Max was ready to stop. The last thing the boys needed was to start a fire by falling asleep before they had pulled the lamp out from under the covers. Max may have been exhausted when he finally closed his eyes, but he was also content.

The household fell into a comfortable routine. Max would help his father in the shop for a couple of hours and then be carried back up the two flights to his bedroom. He would sleep until lunchtime, and eat his sandwich and soup in bed, drifting back into sleep again for a little while. Then he would read a few of his assignment pages, or a chapter if he had enough energy to complete such a task. His sister Beck would come to get him at around four PM so he could sit at the kitchen table and work on another assignment while she and Min or Nell prepared the evening meal. Sometimes he would read the pages he had written aloud to them, which they all enjoyed. Neither Beck nor Min had read the books he had been assigned, so this activity was educational for all of them. When the girls had the time they would make apfle kugle or yeast cakes, eagerly setting a plate before their recuperating brother. He would usually be totally concentrated on his schoolwork, but would absently reach for a piece of cake, and then another, until the plate had been emptied. The girls were delighted. Sometimes Nathan sat with Max too, asking him to explain his answers to the social studies questions as well as the ones from his history teacher. Nathan especially loved the history lessons.

When he would drop off his brother's completed assignments to the history teacher, Nathan enjoyed asking him questions about what the class had been reading. He was especially interested in the checks and balances of the American constitutional system and how they were supposed to work, as well as the reasons the founding fathers had set up three separate branches of government. He loved the symmetry of the constitution and could easily talk to the man for an hour. Sometimes, because it had become dark outside by the time they had wrapped up the day's discourse, the teacher would walk the boy home. Several times he came inside to talk to Max, meeting Noah, Yetta and the girls, who began to bake with more frequency so there would always be something warm in the kitchen for the teacher. In turn he was greatly impressed by this immigrant family, the intelligence of the brothers and their parents, and the quick repartee between the siblings, including the girls.

One day he told the sisters he was sorry none of them had taken his class, an elective in those days, at least for female students. Min giggled about that for some time after he departed, but Nell was fairly quiet as she mixed the filling she was making for the blintzes. Min assumed she was too busy to have noticed the man's remarks, but of course that was not the case. Nell would have loved to ask him some questions of her own about the material, which she and Max had been discussing for days, but didn't want to intrude upon Max's time with him. That evening she took his history book into her bedroom and continued reading. From then on when Nathan and Max were talking about the books she joined their lively discussions, often contributing as much as her brothers. In an odd way Max's illness contributed to the education of his siblings. By the time his class graduated from junior high school in the spring, Max was able to attend the graduation, though he was not allowed to walk up the aisle or onto the stage with his classmates. Nathan climbed the stairs for his brother's diploma, and when he turned, the entire audience began to clap. Max was the only student who had been struck down by the influenza epidemic of 1918 but nevertheless had managed to complete his studies for the year. When some audience members turned in their seats to look at him, the 12-year old blushed to the roots of his red hair. Min laughingly told him the two reds clashed, causing much laughter at the dinner table that night.

The following fall Nathan was bereft because Max began his first year at Battin High School. He resented that his brother had been unable to walk to the lower school with him for more than half the preceding year, and now had moved on to the high school without him. Max was always better at schoolwork, and Nathan at gathering friends for them from his own grade as well as his brother's. If he was having a difficult time those first few weeks, his misery did not compare with that of his brother. Max was very shy. Instead of being relieved at having returned to school, Max was dejected. Even though some of the friends he had made with Nathan in junior high and elementary school had moved over to the high school with him, there were students in this new school from the other side of Elizabeth, the wealthy Jewish and Gentile areas. Those boys had a confidence he couldn't ever imagine possessing, laughing and joking and walking to and from their classes with a swagger he knew he'd never attain, even if he had wanted to. Because he had spent so much time inside for the past six months recuperating and working in his father's shop, Max looked wan, and tired. He also wore glasses. The girls in this new school were even more terrifying than the boys. They stood around in clumps and laughed when he walked by them. He quickly noticed they laughed at all the boys, so he stopped worrying that it was something about him that drew their looks and their laughter. He rarely talked in class because he was afraid of sounding more ridiculous than he already felt, though he handed in all his assignments on time and thus far had received nothing but A's.

One night when he was sitting at the kitchen table as Yetta and Nell washed and dried the dinner dishes, Jules motioned to him from the back door. Max closed his book and followed his brother outside. He had no idea what Jules needed, but he would have done anything for his big brother. He certainly wouldn't have told him he had schoolwork to finish, though that was true. He sat down next to him on the back steps.

"What's wrong, Max'l?" Jules asked him. Max had never been a voluble boy; he had no idea how to explain, even to his beloved older brother, because at that moment his entire life felt wrong to him. He just shrugged.

"If you tell me a little, I'll at least know what questions to ask you," his older brother suggested.

Max hesitated and then said, "I'm doing well at school, but…" He stopped, unsure how to explain himself, when Jules interrupted.

"All those new rich kids," he said, completing his younger brother's sentence. When Jules saw the expression on his Max's face, he laughed. "I felt like such a bumpkin when I entered the high school, and I was. I didn't even talk like the rest of them."

This Max found hard to comprehend. His brother no longer had a trace of an accent. It struck Max for the first time how hard his brother must have worked to sound American. "How did you lose your accent?" he asked with genuine interest.

"The librarian you like so much, the one in the children's section downtown. She sat with me every day after school and coached me. It was pretty awful," Jules replied.

"It would be worse to sound like a foreigner," Max agreed. "Still, I don't think I'll ever fit in with people…who aren't immigrants. I'm even terrible at sports."

"You have to practice at everything, like I did. And I think you're wrong about the sports thing. The few times you played baseball with me and the guys, you hit pretty well for a little kid."

"That was years ago. Before I got sick," Max sighed.

"You're going to have to give up that tired old excuse," his brother advised. "Tomorrow I don't have to go down to Rutgers. I'll pick you up at school and we'll go over to the park and see what you can do."

Max didn't have the heart to argue. After all, the only one who would see his miserable performance would be Jules. "We have to find a field where I don't know anyone," he told his brother nevertheless.

Jules patted him on the back. "Agreed," he said as he stood up. Max couldn't see the smile on his face, but he could hear it.

The next day in geometry class Max noticed that one of the Jewish boys from the other side of Elizabeth also wore glasses. He was popular despite this defect, and very smart. When he noticed Max looking at him, the boy suggested they walk to their chemistry lab together. Max hadn't realized the boy was in two of his classes. He had no idea why he had even noticed him walking up the aisle towards the door; perhaps talking to Jules had allowed him to let go of some of his fear and self-doubt. For the first time since he had set foot in the hallowed halls of Battin High School he was not shuffling from class to class alone. He was walking beside a boy with many friends and didn't have trouble talking with him, although he was startled to discover they had both been going to the downtown library since kindergarten. Samuel had also been taken to the library by an older sibling, a sister who loved to read. Unlike Nell, his sister planned to go to Douglas College because her parents could afford to send her. Their parents, like Noah and Yetta, believed in the value of education for all of their children. Samuel told Max he would ask his sister if she knew Nell. As it turned out, they had graduated in the same class. As Max waited for Jules outside the school at the end of the day, he realized life could be full of surprises. Of course it was also possible that Samuel would not talk to him the next day or the day after that, pretending their conversation had never taken place. That wouldn't have surprised Max at all, though he hoped it wouldn't be the case. He longed to talk about the books he devoured with someone other than Nathan, who didn't read as widely or with as much interest as he did.

When he saw his older brother striding up the block towards the high school, his head held high, a smile on his lips, Max ran towards him without thinking that this might make him seem like an elementary school child until after he and Jules had turned the corner together. Somehow it didn't seem worth worrying about, a surprising realization. Max tended to worry about most things almost every day. He followed his brother into the park, trudging behind him across several unpopulated fields until they came to one in a far corner that had been much used and was more dirt than grass. No one was nearby, not even any of the young mothers who frequently strolled through the pathways with one another, pushing their prams side by side. Max put his book bag next to his brother's behind the chain link fence bordering third base, and took the bat his older brother held out to him. Even though practicing baseball meant he would be spending several hours alone with his big brother, it didn't make the prospect more enticing. Max really did not like playing games, at least physical ones.

He missed the first few balls Jules threw at him, but finally connected on the third. He watched with some surprise as the ball bounced in-between second and third base, landing in the outfield. The fourth ball skidded past Jules, just out of his reach.

"You did that on purpose, Max'l," the older boy laughed as he lunged, missed, and chased after it across the field.

"I did not. I wouldn't do something like that," Max yelled after him, indignant.

"I was just teasing, kiddo," Jules replied, sending another ball flying his way that Max also hit with some aplomb.

"You're not half bad at this, little brother. Why don't you throw me a few?" Jules suggested.

It took a few weeks for Max to develop a throwing arm, but he did, at least a good enough arm to forestall the possibility of anyone calling him a sissy. Catching was another matter. He was a very good catcher. He made excellent calls when he took the plunge and actually played the position in a few games with Jules and his friends. He had no trouble catching fly balls, or confusing the boys at bat with the signals he sent the pitcher. Max loved the attention the older boys showered upon him, and the approval, and after playing with them several times, realized he was starting to enjoy the game itself. Nothing could have surprised him more.

"So. It seems we have a true athlete in the family," Jules declared when they were on the way home after a long, but exciting game, where a catch by Max had turned the tide in favor of their team.

"You promised you wouldn't tell anyone," Max warned him, suddenly worried about what his siblings would think of this foolish endeavor.

"I won't if you don't want me to, Max. But I think you should invite Papa to Saturday's game," Jules replied, adding, "He would really enjoy it."

Max sighed, because he knew Jules was right.

"Everyone would be proud of you, even Mama," Jules continued. "It's not as if you're a lousy player. You're much better than I am at bat, and everyone's come to my games for years."

"I'm not better than you," Max muttered, frowning.

Jules cuffed him on the arm. "You're an idiot," he laughed.

That evening after dinner, Max went down to the shop to do his homework while his father sanded a hutch he needed to finish by the weekend, and told his father that Jules had been teaching him how to play baseball.

"Max'l, what a marvelous idea," his father beamed at him. "Baseball is a fine sport. And very American!"

"Baseball is a game, poppa," Max couldn't keep himself from correcting his father.

"Yah," Noah agreed. "A good game." He seemed comfortable with his son correcting his grammar, or perhaps he didn't realize that was what he had been doing.

"I like playing," Max told his father.

"That is good, yes?" Noah asked him.

"Yes," Max agreed. Then he added, "And I am good."

"Isn't that amazing!" his father declared, which made Max laugh.

"Yes," he agreed once he could contain himself. "It is. Would you like to come and watch us play. I'm catching for Jules' team on Saturday, at least for the first few innings."

"Of course I would come," said his father. "Aren't the other boys on this team already in college? They don't mind a young squirt like you playing with them…?"

"Their regular catcher hurt his elbow at work, so I guess I came along at the right time. He'll be able to play by next week, but the coach agreed to let me sub for him Saturday," Max explained.

"What means 'sub'?" Noah asked him.

"Take his place."

"Ah. For just this game… Can your mother come with me, Max'l? She would be very proud to see this one game also."

"She won't understand what's going on," the boy objected.

"What's to understand? You hit the ball, you catch the ball, you run around the bases," Noah shrugged.

Max returned to his homework to give himself time to decide, answering another question he had been given by his history teacher first. Finally he touched his father's arm. "Mama can come. And if Beck, or Nell, or Min want to come, that's alright too."

"You left out Nathan," his father said with some dismay.

"Oh. I just assumed Nathan would come with you and Mama," Max replied.

And so it came to pass: the entire family came to watch Max play on his older brother's baseball team one blustery Saturday in November. At first he felt self-conscious, which inhibited his play. He fumbled a ball, and failed to catch a strike as it flew past the batter, missing his mitt completely. But the pitcher slapped him on the back after the first inning, quietly suggesting he pretend he was at a team practice with no one from his family there besides Jules. The pitcher admitted to Max that he was especially nervous if his girlfriend was in the stands. Jules encouraged him to ignore the bleachers too while other team members took their turn. Fortunately, when Max came to bat he slammed the ball past the short stop, easily reached first base, and scored before the inning was over. By the time he again took his place behind home plate, he was no longer worried about his audience. For the first time in young Max's life, he knew how it felt to believe in himself: he could play baseball, and play it well. The team lost the game, but he had continued to play well so he wasn't upset by the loss. His major disappointment was that the real catcher would be returning to the team the following week, and he would no longer be needed.

On Monday he left for school even earlier than usual, but Yetta didn't ask him to explain. She was preoccupied with finishing her own chores before she crossed the yard to her little workshop, and didn't give it much thought. Max climbed the steps to the school entrance and went inside. He then had to descend an interior staircase because the athletic offices were all in the basement. The baseball coach was already sitting behind his desk collating lists when Max knocked on his door. The coach looked up, startled that someone was knocking at such an early hour. Most students didn't arrive at the school for another thirty minutes. When Max explained that he was a freshman, and wanted to enquire about joining the baseball team, the man smiled at him with surprising warmth. This Max found startling since he had never met the coach.

"You're the boy who pitched in the park on Saturday," the man exclaimed with delight. "I wondered if you were a student here!"

"Yes, I've been a high school student since September," Max replied, embarrassed that this man had been in the bleachers.

"Why didn't you come to see me then?" the coach asked curiously.

"I didn't know how to play baseball in September. My older brother, Jules, has been teaching me," he said with disarming honesty.

"How lucky for us," the coach laughed. "We practice five afternoons a week. How about starting today?" he asked.

"I didn't bring my mitt to school, or my knee pads," Max replied with obvious consternation. The last thing he wanted to do was disappoint this man before he even got a chance to play on the team.

"We've got extra's. You can give yours back to your brother. I'm sure his team could use them."

This suggestion was even more surprising than the fact that the man knew whom Jules was. Most teachers didn't understand what it meant to be poor. Sports equipment was not a necessity; therefore most Port kids didn't own any. The sensitivity of the coach gave Max the courage to ask, "Why were you at the game on Saturday?"

"I love baseball. Some of the boys on your team played for me. I go to their games whenever I can," the coach answered.

"I can't believe you saw me play!" Max blurted, utterly nonplussed by the idea. He wasn't as good as the college boys and knew he wasn't good enough to play for their team permanently, though he also understood that he played well for a boy his age. His hope had been that the Battin High School coach would see his potential and teach him how to become a 'real' player.

"Yup. How do you feel about starting? You're better than the kid who's been playing that position this year. He prefers shortstop, anyway," the coach explained.

Jules and his father came to the first game Max played for the Battin High School baseball team; Yetta and the girls were working, and Nathan had a terrible cold. There had been no point in any of them arguing with Yetta about allowing Nathan to go to the game and then returning to his bed at home: since Max had almost died in the influenza epidemic, she had become even more vigilant about the health of her children. She wouldn't even hear of one of the girls going to work with a bad sore throat or cold. After Yetta went to Nell's office at the Singer factory to explain her position, no one dared argue with her again, even the men who ran the business that employed her daughters. The Unger's stayed home if they were sick, and they stayed in bed until every last sniffle had disappeared. Yetta was the only family member who worked when she was ill; she told Noah she was an ox, and had worked through worse things than a little cold. No one argued with her about that either, including her husband.

Samuel, the boy from the 'other side of town', didn't ignore Max in school the day after their initial conversation, and seemed to relish their growing friendship as much as Max did. Somehow this miracle became linked in his mind with being asked to join the baseball team, although they weren't related in any way. The boys would often walk to the public library from school when Max didn't have a baseball practice, and would share the knowledge they had acquired from the books they were reading. The librarian, who had nurtured both boys since they were small, was delighted by their friendship. She introduced them to a third boy, a gentile from the Westminster section of town who also devoured books. Though the two Jewish boys were uneasy at first about Joe, his love of reading soon dispelled their doubts and the three became inseparable. Of the three, only Samuel felt comfortable around girls. He was handsome and muscular, taller than the other two, and had been followed home from school by girls when he was still in elementary school. He tried to convince the other two that talking to girls was not a big deal, but neither heeded his advise. Max would turn scarlet if a girl even looked at him; he was sure he would pass out if one actually said his name. Samuel laughed at his two friends, hoping they would come around eventually. He couldn't have imagined a life without girls though he hadn't yet given his love to just one. The attention he received from the Port girls, who were as interested in him as the girls from his own neighborhood, was too enjoyable to give up for just one girl to the exclusion of any of the others. The teasing he endured from his two friends created parity between them all. Joe and Max watched his successes from afar with nothing but awe and admiration. Amid his practices, homework, the work he did for his father in the shop, and the educational adventures he was embarking on with his two friends, Max wouldn't have had time to expand his horizons to the opposite sex anyway.

Nathan entered Battin High as a freshman the year after Max. Despite the urging of both of his older brothers, Nate refused to try out for any sports teams. His ability in that arena was even more woeful than Max's had been, and he had no interest in practicing because he didn't believe he would improve. Besides, his personality more than made up for his lack of physical dexterity. Unlike Max he was quite outgoing, easily talking to the boys he met in his new high school classes. He didn't give a thought to where they lived, but still felt more comfortable with the Jewish boys. He quickly made a best friend, a boy named Philly he met on the debate team. It was surprising that the two boys became friends at all, since they were in obvious competition with one another from the moment Nathan joined the club. Philly, who was a sophomore, had been the star of the group before Nathan arrived on the scene, but he had been longing for a friend who loved discussion and debate for several years. At first he merely enjoyed the challenge Nathan represented, but within a few months he had also come to respect his arguments during their debates. The boys would stay after school longer than anyone else to continue discussing the assigned topics because both quickly realized they had much to learn from each other. Like Max and Samuel, Nate and Philly often walked to the public library together after school to find additional material about a subject that interested them both. The four boys would often run into one another and walk to a local coffee shop to talk once they had checked out their books. Nathan and Max usually ordered plain water. The two other boys would order coffee. As soon as they realized the brothers were only drinking water because they couldn't afford the coffee, four cups were ordered for the table. Neither Samuel nor Philly paid any attention to the brothers' objections. Sometimes they would even order donuts, which all of them would devour. Donuts were an American invention as far as the Unger boys could tell; Yetta never made such things, and neither did any of their sisters. Nathan loved the sweet, sugary things more than Max, but both boys finished what was set before them without complaint. They were equally careful to eat them early enough that they wouldn't lose their appetite for dinner. Yetta would have forbidden them to indulge if they had, and Max knew that Nathan would have been very disappointed to have to give up those extremely American confections.

* * *

By the time Ruth entered Evander Childs High School, Holly, two years her senior, had been welcomed into the popular crowd and had neither the time nor the inclination to introduce her sister to the in's and out's of the school. She didn't particularly care about the teachers, and didn't believe her smart-mouthed sister would fit into the crowd she had easily joined because of her looks. Ruth was left to her own devises; because she was ashamed of her large nose, and uncomfortable with the clothes her mother forced her to wear, as if she was still a child, she kept a very low profile. Her friend, Doris, who had shared the duties of editor on their junior high school newspaper, had moved to New Jersey, which made the transition even more difficult. The first month in her new school Ruth went to her classes, sat quietly, completed her assignments and kept to herself. Adelaide, who was rehearsing for another tour with the Schola Cantorum, didn't notice that her usually voluble daughter had become fairly quiet, even withdrawn. Simon, as usual, was swamped with his customers, and was also struggling to come to terms with the truth of having a wife who did not share his love of touch or physical pleasure. He was exhausted, and less attuned to his daughters than he usually was. Oscar, the man in the park who had rescued Ruth when she had broken her leg, suggested she join some after-school clubs as a way to engage her mind as well as find friends, but she had thus far resisted his advise. Her parents didn't know that she still met him in the park, or that she shared her most intimate feelings with him. She had never told them because she believed they would not approve, which would certainly have been true of Adelaide, who had a deep and abiding distrust of most of the male members of the human race.

One day, shortly after Oscar had made his suggestion to her, Ruth's English teacher asked her to stay after class for a few minutes. As she waited for the room to clear, Ruth nervously stood beside the teacher's desk, wondering what she could have done to receive this unwanted attention, but could not come up with a thing.

"Ruth, Mrs. Levy tells me that it was you who created 'The Junior Times'. I had no idea," the teacher exclaimed.

Ruth shrugged. "It was my idea, but my best friend helped me, and so did my English teacher."

"Your writing is wonderful, especially for someone so young," the woman continued. "Have you signed up to work on the paper here?"

Ruth felt embarrassed because she hadn't even considered it. She had felt comfortable at the junior high, and had known she could create a paper there where she would have some control over the content and issues presented within it. At Evander Childs, she was just one small person in a sea of popular and bright students; she didn't believe herself qualified to work on such a well-known and popular paper. She mumbled something, and stood in front of this new teacher, shuffling from foot to foot.

"Our school paper needs students like you Ruth, with talent as well as convictions. If you don't mind, I would like to talk to Mr. Hunter, who is the staff advisor for the paper," she gently suggested, although she had no idea why this student who had been such a firebrand at the junior high seemed so shy and self-effacing here. High school was a huge transition for some students, she supposed, though this was a student she would have expected to have done very well with it.

Hesitantly Ruth replied, "I was told there are no freshman on the paper, so I thought I should wait until next year."

"Nonsense. Harvey Hunter is always looking for kids like you. He doesn't care what grade you're in, just that you can write and have good ideas. Have you lost yours over the summer?" she asked with a huge grin.

Even though it was obvious her new teacher was joking, the suggestion had its intended effect, reviving Ruth's natural spirit. "I always have ideas," she said with indignation, adding as an afterthought, "Which seems to irritate my mother" with a wry smile.

"My mother didn't understand me very well either," Mrs. McCarthy said. "But I've turned out fairly well, and I'm sure you will too. There will be even more opportunity available to you by the time you graduate from Evander and move on to college, especially if you utilize your very special gifts, Ruth. Why don't we walk down to the 'Evander' office together right now?" With that she stood up, put her hand on Ruth's shoulder, and before the girl could even begin to object, steered her out the door and down the hallway. By the time she left school a half hour later, Ruth had signed on as a student reporter, even suggesting an article on the difficulty of moving from junior high to high school to the advisor. Mr. Hunter thanked Mrs. McCarthy with heartfelt enthusiasm, assuring his new recruit that he would anxiously await her article.

For the first time since she had started the school year at this huge new school, Ruth walked home with a swing to her step. She detoured to the park to see if Oscar was sitting on his usual bench, delighted to find him feeding the pigeons while his dog chased birds on the field in front of him.

"I told you so!" he exclaimed with glee when she told him her news. "How will you prepare such an article?" he asked immediately.

"I guess I'll have to find some other freshman to talk to," Ruth replied. "Everyone in my classes has come from one junior high or another, so it shouldn't be too difficult…if I can drum up the courage to talk to some of them."

"How can I help?" he asked her. This young girl had become the joy of his days, the daughter he had never had, a challenge to all of his long suppressed notions of parenting.

Ruth laughed. "Just talking to you about it helps. I was so hoping you would be here so we could discuss it, and here you are." She then dropped her books and raced onto the field to throw the ball Oscar always brought for his dog, though lately his legs had been bothering him and he had been unable to throw it very much himself. The unlikely friends said good-bye to one another an hour later, parting at the entrance to the park after Ruth had promised to meet him there the following day to report on her progress with her fellow students.

Writing the article changed Ruth's experience of high school completely. First of all, it gave her the courage to approach the students in her classes she hadn't known before because they had attended different junior high schools. Thanks to her natural curiosity about what made people do and feel what they did, she thoroughly enjoyed interviewing her peers. Two of the girls became friends, one from her US History class, and the other from her Algebra class. The three girls became inseparable. When Ruth asked if she could play baseball with one of the boys she had interviewed, he was intrigued rather than shocked, and happily took her to one of his practices. It was a pick-up team, not one sponsored by the school, or he wouldn't have been able to bring her along. Several of his team members weren't terribly welcoming, but once they saw how well she could throw a ball and hit, they stopped complaining. Going to their practices was a highlight of those first months, even though she couldn't go very often because of her commitments at the school paper. Of course when she told her parents what she was doing, she omitted any mention of baseball. Hearing the stories of her classmates, and realizing how similarly they felt about the move from their junior high schools to Evander Childs – lost, inferior, unpopular, shy and basically incapable although this was clearly far from the truth – helped Ruth shed her own feelings of inadequacy. When the article appeared it had the same effect on the student body. In the cafeteria everyone was talking about it. Kids were talking to one another how they felt, which helped to dissipate their fears.

When Greg, the senior editor of the paper, approached Ruth in the cafeteria as she was carrying her lunch tray to the table where her two new friends were waiting, she didn't have time to become anxious. Her tummy turned over, and she experienced a tightening in her chest as if the air wasn't flowing properly.

"Hi Ruth," he grinned at her. "Now that you're a star at Evander, would you be willing to drop by the office this afternoon to talk to me?"

"I'm not a star," she scoffed, deeply offended. After all, it was only the first piece she had written for the paper.

He patted her on the arm. "It's not something to be ashamed of. Hell, none of my pieces received any kind of attention until I was a junior. You should be proud of yourself."

She mumbled something in return, having no idea how to respond, but he didn't seem to notice. She couldn't believe he had used the word 'hell' in front of her, and was very pleased. It made her feel sophisticated.

"Mr. Hunter showed me some of the pieces you wrote in junior high. They were terrific. I'm really glad to have you on board," he declared.

"Thank you," Ruth managed to stammer. She didn't even say his name: he was a senior, and popular. She thought he might have known Holly, but certainly didn't want to pursue that line of inquiry.

"So. I'll see you at 2:30, OK?" he continued. She nodded her agreement, having no idea what he wanted but afraid to ask, especially in the middle of the crowds milling around them in the cafeteria.

Her friends were wide-eyed by the time she reached their table. Everyone in school knew who Greg Ingram was. That he had stopped their friend in front of everyone in the cafeteria seemed absolutely amazing to them. Both girls agreed to wait for Ruth outside of school that afternoon so they could walk home together, which they usually did.

"He asked me if I'd write a weekly column on student issues," Ruth shrieked as she approached them. Her face looked glazed, though she sounded excited beyond belief.

"Now you really will be a star," Dottie gasped, silencing all three of them.

Finally Ruth blurted, "Oh gosh. What's Holly going to say?"

Neither girl replied. Both of them were in awe of Ruth's stunning older sister. They knew she and Ruth had an uneasy relationship but not much more. How ugly their competition sometimes became was not something Ruth had shared with them. She really didn't want to anger Holly, or stir the pot. Ruth was genuinely frightened of her sister's response. Holly could be vicious, both at home and in school, her words barbed, and her actions – laughing with her friends whenever Ruth was near – brutal. The last thing Ruth wanted was for her to become a topic of conversation for the popular crowd, especially Greg, who must have attended to the same parties Holly did. Ruth admired him, and quietly basked in his attention. Her sister could so easily poison the easy camaraderie she hoped to develop with him.

For that reason she was low-key about this new development at dinner that night. To make matters worse, Holly had always loathed the attention their father bestowed on her younger sister because of her writing talent. Even though she said she had been asked to write some weekly 'items' for the school paper, downplaying that they would be in column form with a little picture at the top with her name beneath it, her father's ears perked up.

"What kind of items?" he asked with interest.

"Oh, I don't know yet. Mr. Hunter hasn't decided," she replied. She was certainly not going to tell anyone that the whole thing was Greg Ingram's idea.

That seemed to satisfy her father for the moment, and no one else asked her anything else about it. Her mother was still bringing food to the table, and Holly, of course, had no interest.

"Well, just make sure you tell me once you know," her father said, digging into the bowl of sliced potatoes Adelaide had just placed before him. He held out his hand for his daughters' plates, serving them first and then happily giving himself a very large pile.

"I really love pritchen-kartoffel," he told his wife, smiling up at her with genuine relish. Her cooking, and his love of it, was one of the things that made the marriage bearable for them both. Addie kissed the top of his head, embarrassing both of the girls, and then set the platter with the meat on the table for Simon to slice. By the time she sat down, all of them were eating and Ruth's announcement about her meeting with Mr. Hunter was forgotten, much to her relief. Even Holly was friendly when they were helping their mother clean up in the kitchen, laughing with Ruth about the horrible lunches served by the school cafeteria.

By the time the Thanksgiving holiday was upon them, Ruth's column had become the talk of the school. One Saturday Holly could contain herself no longer. Before either girl left their shared bedroom to help their mother with breakfast preparations, she launched her attack.

"How could you write about the girls' shower, Ruth? Don't you have any sense of decency?" she hissed, wanting to scream at her sister but unwilling to let her parents hear her.

Blithely Ruth replied, "I wrote about the boys' shower too."

Holly lost all restraint. "That was even more disgusting. How could you know what happens there?" By this time her voice was raised, which pleased Ruth enormously even though she wasn't certain that she wanted her parents to read the aforementioned article.

"I had a spy from the paper take notes after his own gym class. It wasn't so hard," she explained with a shrug.

"You said that girls stand three deep waiting to get under the water," Holly continued, her volume rising with every word. She was obviously distraught. "Everyone must have known that meant we were naked in that room and could see each other."

At that Ruth just shrugged again, and then there was a knock on the door. "Girls. Whatever is the matter?" their mother asked through the closed door. She believed in privacy for herself and her daughters and wouldn't have dreamed of entering their room if they hadn't invited her inside. Before Ruth could object, Holly grabbed the door handle and flung it open.

"Your daughter has … she's… she has no sense of decency," she announced, totally flustered.

"Holly, making an accusation like that is really a bit extreme," Adelaide suggested, having no idea at all what else she should say.

Holly spun around, grabbed the school paper from the night table and shoved it into her mother's hands.

"Ach, the paper again," Adelaide sighed, and opened it to her daughter's column. "I know it is an honor for you to be doing this, especially your first year in the school, but it does seem to cause problems."

By this time Simon had heard the commotion from the bathroom where he had been shaving and appeared in the doorway, wiping the shaving cream from his face. "What's all the ruckus about?" he asked.

His wife was reading, the frown between her brows increasing as she read. Wordlessly, she handed the paper to her husband. Ruth decided it was better to stand mute, rather than try to defend herself. After all, neither the staff advisor nor the editor seemed to have felt the article was inappropriate. When her father started to laugh, she exhaled.

"You are a very witty writer, Ruthie. I didn't realize," he smiled at her.

"Do you really think it is … proper for your thirteen-year- old daughter to be writing about the boy's shower?" Adelaide asked her husband.

He read, "Seventeen year old boys snap their wet towels at thirteen year olds waiting for their turn under the nozzle, aiming for the legs of the younger boys, though often missing their intended target. Whether this is purposeful or not has not been revealed to this writer." Simon's face filled with amusement as he demanded, "And what do you know about 'their intended target' my little one?" chuckling at the end of the question.

"Simon!" Adelaide objected. "You mustn't encourage her. It is very unladylike, and she is only thirteen! Ruth, this is not a good idea. I can certainly understand why your sister is upset."

"You might try less…sensational subject matter, little one, but don't you even consider giving up your writing," Simon continued. Then he turned to his wife. "You, of all people, should understand her creative urge and support it," he added and left the room. The three females stood uneasily between the twin beds, not knowing what to say.

"My advisor thought it was funny. And he didn't think there was anything wrong with it," Ruth explained in a very quiet voice.

"Well, I do. And I want you to promise me that you will take more care with your choice of subject matter. I know you understand what would be embarrassing to either your sister or me, and I want you to respect that," Adelaide replied, looking sternly at her younger daughter. Ruth thought to herself 'she's not asking me to give up the paper' with utter relief. Saying "of course Momma" was much easier than she thought it would be because she could keep working with Greg; that mattered to her more than the column itself, although she also loved coming up with ideas and talking about them with the older editors at the paper.

Holly left the room in a huff, saying, "I still don't know how you could have written something like that!"

Almost to herself, since she didn't think her mother cared, Ruth replied, "The article was about the lack of privacy in the locker rooms. I was only describing what we all have to endure." Her mother merely sighed again, put the newspaper on her daughter's bed, and left the room. Ruth quickly braided her hair and left as well, knowing preparations for their breakfast would be well underway.

On Monday Holly joined the committee organizing the winter dance that would take place the Saturday before their Christmas vacation. This was an activity she could do with total enjoyment, knowing her sister would not be attending. Ruth was clumsy on a dance floor, and rarely received any male attention. Of this Holly was quite certain. Aside from her nose, Ruth's sharp tongue frightened most of the boys she knew. They liked a girl to be clever, but not too clever. And a girl who made her reputation with her wit before the entire school on a weekly basis, well, what boy would take on someone like that? Ruth, busy with her chores at the paper, and her secret athletic endeavors, knew what her sister was doing but didn't give it much thought. None of her fellow athletes would invite her to a dance, and who else was there? She longed for Greg to take an interest in her in that way, and would have taken dance lessons if she had thought it would help, but she didn't give that much thought either. Such a notion was beyond her dreams regarding what might be possible in her nonexistent romantic life.

When Greg asked her to stay behind one day in early December, she assumed he wanted to talk about the column she had just turned in, though she had no idea when he had found the time to read it. He waited until everyone had left the office before he said, "Ruth. I wondered if you'd be willing to go to the school dance with me? I know your sister's on the committee, so it's going to be great fun." She was so startled that she didn't respond immediately, but stood there in a silence unusual for her. Confused, Greg continued nevertheless. "I'm not the best dancer, but I think we could manage."

This gave Ruth the time she needed to compose herself. She finally was able to thank him and say she would love to attend the dance with him, heart hammering in her chest. She could barely get her breath, so shocked was she that this boy, this popular boy, was asking her to go to a dance with him. It wasn't until she was walking home that she thought about her wardrobe and groaned with distress. She didn't have a single dance frock because she had never needed one. The dress her aunt had bought her long ago had been given to a charity years before as soon as she had outgrown it. She knew she couldn't talk to Holly about it because her sister would be enraged that she was going to 'her' event, let alone going with Greg. After dinner she knelt at the foot of her father's ottoman but didn't immediately say anything.

"Tell me, my sweet. There isn't anything you could say that would shock me," her father suggested, reaching out to ruffle her hair. His eyes filled behind the sports page when she explained – he had been worried about Ruth's ability to attract boys, and felt a swelling of both relief and pride that his younger daughter had found her own avenue – and immediately told her he would happily give her ten dollars so she could find a dress with shoes to match. The joy on her face was enough to make him happy with the offer; if he had to work an extra hour to be able to afford it, he didn't mind at all. His girls really were the centerpiece of his life.

THE TEACHER: THREE

Jen invited Hillary to spend the weekend in New Jersey with palpitating heart. She was quite excited about being able to show her all the research she had collected about her own family as well as Ernie's. She suspected the young woman would be as interested as she in all the information that was available on line about eastern European Jews and Jewry. They might even be able to go to the Elizabeth library together and see what was stored on microfiche there. For the first time she found the photo albums that her mother had passed down to her fascinating. They weren't a flat depiction of relatives she had never known anymore, but a pictorial history of an era, as well as a history of her son's heritage. She decided to initiate a Skype call with him while Hillary was there to serve as an introduction of sorts, which also seemed exciting. Jacob would finally understand what she was doing and why, and perhaps even become interested in helping her.

Although she didn't think her dinner would be the culinary treat that Hillary's had been, she knew her buttermilk chocolate cake would outshine the bakery confection her former student had served. It would also get them through the weekend, hopefully not adding pounds to the hips of either of them during the process. When she picked Hillary up at the train station, she could barely repress her enthusiasm. The younger woman was delighted.

"I'm reading 'There Once Was A World' the second time, and finding it even more intriguing than I did on the initial go-round," Hillary exclaimed as she climbed into the passenger seat.

"Wait till you see what I've found. All my papers are spread out on the dining room table, so we'll have to eat in the living room at my coffee table," Jen explained.

Hillary grinned from ear to ear. "I don't know which one of us is more excited by all of this!"

They deposited her suitcase in the guest room and raced downstairs to the dining room. Papers were everywhere. Jen pointing out the pictures of the shtetl her grandparents had emigrated from first. They poured over the shots together, side-by-side.

"I wonder if we could find more information at the library. More pictures," Hillary mused. "I'd love to see the inside of the homes…"

"Shacks, really," Jen interrupted. "No wonder my grandparents were willing to take the risks they did, coming here. We could go to the library tomorrow," she proposed.

"Let's look at the other stuff you have and then go now," Hillary declared with as much excitement as Jen had been feeling the night before.

In the library Mrs. Gold was immediately enthusiastic about their proposed search, and found quite a few websites on line for them to peruse as well. They were both thrilled when the librarian found a rash of pictures depicting the cottages that lined the dirt streets of eastern European shtetls, though not one for Monasterzyska, where Jen's grandparents had lived, or Bircza, the village most often mentioned by Hillary's grandparents. When the librarian pulled up a map, they were amazed to see that the two tiny towns had not been that far apart.

"We could go up to the Bronx next weekend, if you want to take the train into the city, and see the albums my parents have saved. Maybe they'll have pictures of the interiors of some of the buildings," Hillary proposed.

"I could make another cake," Jen said without even thinking about it, making Hillary laugh.

"We are both so Jewish," she giggled.

"I never even realized that before," Jen said with a grin. "Imagine that!"

They shared all they could remember from their familial stories until almost two in the morning, when Jen finally said they had to get some sleep. The library website listed its hours: it opened at nine on Saturday morning. If they didn't have breakfast before they left the house, Hillary said she'd become a grouch. With great reluctance they left the living room, carrying their cups, the cake, and their plates into the kitchen, Hillary insisting she wash them before they went upstairs. Since that meant they could continue their conversation about shtetl life, Jen didn't object.

"What I found most amazing were the values that were significant in shtetl life. They were so similar to ones I was raised with, I couldn't believe it," she shared.

"Me neither. Do you think our parents knew where so many of their beliefs came from?" Hillary asked her.

"I doubt it. My grandparents weren't religious on either side, although my father's mother did make her children go to Temple every Saturday", Jen replied.

"My mother made us go too, even though my brother and I complained bitterly about having to get up early on Saturday," Hillary admitted with some guilt.

When she asked Jen where her mother's parents had emigrated from, she was stunned by the answer, exclaiming, "Mine lived in a small town outside of Vienna. My grandmother used to always talk about going into the big city to hear the philharmonic."

They both crawled into their respective beds, startled by how similar their backgrounds were. Perhaps that was part of the reason they enjoyed each other's company so much and had found it easy to discuss almost everything from the first time they had talked. Each felt familiar to the other.

A few weeks later, Jen took the train into the city and the subway down to Hillary's apartment in the west Village. Instead of preparing breakfast, which she said 'couldn't have competed with Jen's anyway,' Hillary took Jen to a favorite breakfast haunt. They quickly decided to share, Jen ordering a vegie omelet and Hillary blueberry pancakes, 'for desert' quipped Jen. By the time the food arrived they were so engrossed in their continuing conversation about their research into various aspects of shtetl life that they didn't even notice the waiter patiently waiting to deposit their breakfast plates on their small table. Jen absentmindedly moved her purse to the floor, Hillary mimicking her action.

"I didn't think I was hungry, but this food really smells divine," Jen said with relish as the bemused young man hurried off to continue serving his other customers.

Shaking her head in agreement, Hillary replied, "Let's eat!"

After a few mouthfuls they were sated enough to continue their intense conversation. Jen was amazed by the practice in the shtetls of leaving a small bungalow open for visitors who were passing through in almost all the small villages. Hillary's parents had always had a steady stream of visitors from their past, or from Europe, or by request from friends in the Bronx, never turning away anyone. Both Hillary and Jen had continued the practice throughout their lives, once they were living on their own. Ernie had thoroughly approved, and often helped with both preparation and cleanup once the visitors were again on their way.

"Was your husband always helpful?" Hillary asked, her tone wistful.

Jen resisted the impulse to reach for her hand. "When we were young, he resented my visitors, saying he 'wanted me all to himself'", she admitted, seeing the relief on her new friend's face immediately.

"What made him accept it?" Hillary asked.

"Time. And I think he grew to really enjoy the lively conversations we would have with visitors, or most of them, at least."

"My parents friends always seemed very smart to me, even when they didn't have a terrific command of English," Hillary agreed. "Sometimes I would hide in the hallway to listen to their conversations. I learned a lot about village life in Poland, and life in general, that way."

"I hid on the stairs as a kid. Heard my first dirty joke that way," Jen laughed.

"Do you remember it?" Hillary demanded.

"Not really. It was something about a pussy," Jen replied, brow furrowed in concentration. At that, they both started to laugh. "I repeated the joke the following morning to one of my mom's friends who had stopped by for a cup of tea," Jen added with a mischievous grin.

"Oh my God. What did your mother do?" Hillary asked.

"She asked me if I knew what 'pussy' meant. I said 'of course, a little cat' and they both howled. I didn't feel insulted. I thought I had been very sophisticated and had pleased them," Jen chuckled, surprised when she noticed that Hillary suddenly seemed overly involved with the eggs remaining on her plate. "Do you want to talk about it?" Jen asked her.

Hillary sighed. "Bruce didn't even understand why I had to meet you at a restaurant tonight when we could have had dinner at our apartment."

"I think a lot of men have a hard time with women's friendships, and how intimate they become," Jen agreed.

"Especially because it happens so quickly," murmured Hillary, Jen shaking her head in agreement.

"Ernie and I were so much more innocent than your generation. We had no idea what to do beyond the stroking through the blouse syndrome," Jen admitted, surprising the younger woman with her honesty. Jen had never been particularly reticent when it came to sexual revelations.

"Were you both virgins?" asked Hillary.

"Yup. He's the only man I've had sex with. Aint that a kick in the teeth!" Jen laughed again.

"I presume you learned?" Hillary said.

"I actually had an orgasm the first time we 'went all the way', which is what we called it back then."

"If we're being polite we say 'made love'. With close friends we feel comfortable asking, 'Did you fuck?'" Hillary shared, her tone conspiratorial. Jen knew she had not misheard her.

"So my son tells me, when he tells me," Jen sighed.

"It doesn't mean we didn't have a lot to learn in the beginning," added the younger woman.

Jen repeated, "So my son also tells me."

CHAPTER THIRTEEN

It had been very painful for Nell to give up her dream of going to college, but she kept her feelings to herself. She knew her family needed the income she would bring home from the Singer Sewing Machine Factory, and Nell was nothing if not responsible. She disliked the painstaking work, fitting each machine with the needle and presser foot that held it in place – she had been doing this task since she had been hired almost two years earlier. But she was proud of the money she brought home for her parents, and glad that her labors relieved some of the financial burden her parents carried, especially after the expense of Max's illness. She did enjoy the friendships she had forged with some of the other women who worked alongside her. When one of them suggested introducing Nell to her older brother, her face flushed pink from the roots of her hair to the collar of her starched cream-colored shirt. She had never been on a date.

It was Yetta who persuaded her to say 'yes'. Since she already knew quite a bit about the family, their journey from Germany to the new country, the struggles of both parents to find work, and their joy when they had been able to purchase the small house they had been renting for years, a few blocks from the Unger house, Yetta suggested to Nell that it would not be difficult for her to come up with subjects to talk about.

"You can ask him some of the same questions about their journey to Elizabeth that you asked Rose when you first met her," Yetta assured her. "Even if you already know the answers, conversation won't flag and you'll do just fine."

What Nell did not tell her mother was that she had met a man at the Singer Factory she really liked, but he was almost ten years her senior. She was afraid her parents would disapprove, and besides, their friendship had certainly not reached the point where she felt a need to talk about it. They had begun talking at lunchtime months before, standing next to each other at the coffee machine; it had felt perfectly natural to the young woman to sit beside him at one of the long lunch tables the next day when he suggested it. They had no problem at all talking with each other, because they quickly discovered they had many things in common. Both had large families; Abe's younger sister had almost died from the same flu that had felled little Max, and his Aunt, not a favorite, but an aunt nonetheless, had fallen sick and never recovered. It had only been in the last year that his Uncle had begun seeing one of his deceased wife's friends, who had also lost her husband in that flu pandemic, Abe had explained. They had yet to go on a date, but news spread like wildfire in the little factory; Nell was sure Abe would soon learn that she had 'gone on a date', which seemed fine to her. Maybe the news would give him the impetus he needed to actually ask her out.

Noah was still distressed that he could not afford to send his bright eldest daughter to the teacher's college at Rutgers. Understanding his disappointment, Yetta had suggested putting aside several dollars a week from her own earnings, adding to the three dollars that Noah had been setting aside, at first over her rather vigorous objections. Both husband and wife were amazed to discover they had amassed enough money to pay for the two years of teacher's college Nell had always dreamed about. Although Min was now a senior in high school, both parents felt it was only right to offer the funds to their oldest daughter. Min could take Nell's place at the sewing machine factory, and they would continue to save. Yetta was not even sure Min would want to attend college; she was not nearly as studious as her older sister, although she loved reading novels.

The next afternoon Noah was waiting outside the Singer factory when Nell and all the other workers streamed out of the front door at the end of the day. Surprised to see him, but pleased to have the chance to talk with him alone, she immediately asked, "Papa, what's wrong?" fearing her mother or one of her siblings had fallen ill. She certainly did not expect him to offer to pay for her college education as soon as they crossed the street to begin their walk home. Had the offer come even a month before, she would have been hard-pressed to turn it down, but now that she had met Abe, she was loathe to accept it. Seeing the disappointment and confusion on her father's face, she told him she would think about it and give him a response the following day. She wanted to talk to Abe about it, though even if he urged her to accept the offer, she suspected she would not. If she wasn't at the factory, she knew her shy male friend would not stop by her house to see how she was doing, or to try to deepen their friendship, which was what was most important to her. If they married, which she was determined to facilitate one way or another, she knew she would soon become a mother and have no time for schoolwork, let alone her classes. Once they had had their first child, she was also determined to return to the factory. Her mother, Beck, and Min could watch the little boy or girl. After all, she was quite certain she and Abe would live with her family until they could afford to rent a place of their own. All of these thoughts swirled in her head as her father was talking to her, but she was not ready to share any of them, even though they would have explained her reticence, which she could see was hurtful to her father.

That evening as they prepared for bed Noah told Yetta that Nell had not accepted their offer, but instead asked for time to think it over. At first Yetta looked distressed, and then smiled broadly, much to her husband's surprise.

"She's met a man!" Yetta blurted.

"No", her husband demurred, but then he tilted his head to the side and shrugged. "Do you really think so?"

"Why else would she turn us down? She's wanted to go to college since she was a freshman at Battin High," his wife replied.

"I will meet her again tomorrow, and ask her," Noah declared. This surprised them both, since he had not left his shop for any reason for many years except to come home for supper. He often worked late into the night in his efforts to support their family.

The next afternoon Noah was again waiting outside the factory so that he could talk to Nell as they walked home. She was happily chatting away with two other young women who were close to her own age. This too came as a surprise to her father, who had never seen her as animated, or comfortable in her own skin.

Mid-sentence with the black-haired girl to her right, she noticed her father.

"Papa!" she exclaimed.

"I'm sorry to interrupt you, Nell. We could talk when I come in from the shop this evening if you'd prefer," he suggested, embarrassed.

"Don't be silly. If you came all this way, and interrupted your workday, I know it must be important," she replied. As she turned away from her friends to walk beside her father, she gave them a happy wave of her hand, which they both returned.

The dark-haired girl called out, "We'll see you tomorrow. I'm looking forward to sharing our sandwiches again!" This came as a surprise to Noah as well. Beck made very good sandwiches for all the girls, and was quite famous in their neighborhood for the concoctions she created.

"What is it, Papa? What do you want to talk about," Nell immediately asked with some concern.

He didn't speak right away, and then cleared his throat.

"Uh oh. It must not be an easy subject," she paused. "What does Mama want you to do?"

Noah put his arm around her shoulder and actually chuckled. "My being here again today is because of her reaction to the conversation you and I had yesterday, but I'm the one who said I would ask you."

"Ask me what?"

"Nelly, have you found yourself a beau?" he inquired, noting the flush that spread across her cheeks.

"I don't know if I'd call him that yet, Papa, but I like him very much," she replied.

"Will we like him" her father asked her, which was not the question she expected. The afternoon seemed to be full of surprises.

"You will love him, Papa," she grinned. "Mama will be a harder sell, just because...she will be." Her father shook his head with understanding. Nell had always been prescient about the character traits of their family members.

"He works at the factory?" he asked.

"Yes, he does. He repairs the machines, all of them!" she said with pride.

Her father smiled warmly at his spinster daughter. That was how he had come to think of her, and he had been wrong, and couldn't have been more delighted at his own lack of foresight. "I wonder if he knows how to fix wood-working machines when they break down," he mused with a smile on his face.

They walked home together, talking about Abe, whom she hoped would become her husband. Noah described his first sighting of Yetta, and although Nell had heard this tale many times before, she loved hearing it. On this particular day, the tale had a very special meaning for her. When he said that he had known the moment he saw her across the town square that he must meet her and talk with her and make her agree to be his wife, Nell shook her head in agreement.

"I really haven't noticed men very much, even at the factory," Nell admitted. "I didn't think anyone would notice me so there didn't seem much point. And then Abe stood behind me at the coffee machine, and we started to talk."

"I imagine he started to talk and you listened. What gave you the courage to respond?" he asked with a smile.

"That's what's so amazing, Papa," she said with great enthusiasm. "I never had a problem. He is the easiest man to talk to, and so responsive."

Noah and Yetta had both been concerned that Nell would never find a mate. Noah was glad that Nell thought he would like the young man, which he did, when they met the very next Friday. Though he was happy for his daughter, he was disappointed that she would not become a teacher, since he had always known she would make a very good one. Instead she would adjust to the roles of helpmate, and eventually, mother. He knew his wife would coach her, and she would learn quickly.

"I could invite him to the Sabbath meal on Friday after work next week if you and Mama would like," Nell suggested.

"Why not ask him to come this week," said her father.

Nell took a very big breath. This was moving awfully quickly for her, but she knew Abe would be delighted with the invitation. "Do you think Beck would make kugle on such short notice, and Min a roast chicken?" she asked, adding, "I can prepare the blintzes the night before."

"I'm sure your mama will make a challah too, if she has the time," he agreed.

Her smile could have lit the street. Noah was startled, and realized he had rarely seen her smile since she had left the high school. "You don't think they will find all of this an imposition?" she asked him.

"All of them will be as excited for you as I am," he assured his ungainly eldest daughter.

"This may not be what you hope it is," Nell nervously explained.

"Do you feel you have known this man your whole life," her father asked, Nell quite startled by the question.

"Yes, Papa?" she replied. "How did you know that?"

"Because that is exactly how I felt when I first talked to your mama. And later, I learned that she had felt the same way about me, and that is what I want for you." Then he added, "And I wouldn't want you to give up the chance to do something you've always dreamed of doing for someone who doesn't make you feel that way."

"Abe is a very special sort of person," Nell turned to look at her father as she spoke these words. "He's loyal, stalwart, treats the men he works with compassionately..." she paused as the thought how best to describe this man she hoped to marry.

"Do you love him?" her father asked her.

"I think I could make a good life with him," Nell quickly replied.

Noah's heart contracted. Perhaps this was all she expected for herself. Perhaps love would come along with the children they would have. He certainly hoped so. He wanted so much for all his children, but certainly that they should experience the same sort of warmth, support and succor – that was the only word for it – that he had experienced all these years with Yetta.

"Papa, we have to be realistic," Nell interrupted his train of thought, ever his thoughtful, practical girl. "I never expected to find a man who would want to be with me, let alone one I thoroughly enjoyed. But he and I have yet to talk about the future, or about what work I might do. He is fairly traditional in that regard, and, I assume, believes he will support his wife and family."

Noah took his daughter's hand. "I am glad he is that kind of person, Nelly. But it might be possible, at least those first few years, for you to still attend college. Your mother has always contributed to the family's finances, but I think she has also regretted that we arrived in America too late for her to pursue a life of the mind. Poland certainly didn't offer her that possibility."

"I think if he were to ask me to marry him, I would want to have a child as soon as possible. I know it's a little late for me to start that part of my life, but not too late, I think," she murmured. Father and daughter walked companionably side by side for a few moments.

"Papa, perhaps you should offer this opportunity to Min, since Beck and Morris are already planning their wedding, and will probably move closer to his family since he works with his father in their pharmaceutical business," Nell suggested.

"Do you think she would have an interest in going to college?" Noah asked with some surprise, because he certainly didn't think so.

"No," Nell replied with a smile. "But if that is what she decides, then you could save the money you already have for Max or Nathan when they are ready. They are both very bright boys. Max reads everything he can get his hands on."

"That he does," Noah agreed. "I can't imagine him not going on to college, or some other kind of advanced education."

"He would love to become a doctor," Nell shared with some hesitation, not believing this fact was hers to reveal. But she also realized her father deserved to know.

Her father was nonplussed, since no one had told him that Max harbored such a dreams. He was not sure medicine would be the best choice for his quiet, shy son.

Nell was watching her father's face, and began to laugh, startling him. "He will have to do something about being able to look his patients in the eye," she agreed, still laughing. "He is not the most communicative person. I know how much I appreciate it when a doctor can talk to me easily about what's wrong. I still remember how Doctor Gelb talked to you and mama when Max had that awful flu, and how relieved you both seemed after your conversation with him."

"That we did. He seemed to know what we needed to hear, but he also didn't minimize what was happening. I certainly understood the danger Max was in, but I also believed the doctor knew what he, and we, had to do. Your mother actually looked forward to his visits," Noah told her. "Everyone has a dream, eh? And what are yours my smart, practical little Nelly?" he asked.

"To be a wife and mother," she answered without any hesitation at all.

Her father wondered if she would still feel that way after there were one or two little ones running around. Yetta loved her children one and all, but she was very relieved to be able to continue working, even if most of what she accomplished with her business she accomplished at home. Handing over some of the 'mothering' chores to both Nell and Beck had been a big relief for her.

* * *

One day Ruth was walking home from school, anxious to be home so she could go over the proofs for the next edition of the school paper. Her stomach had been bothering her all day, but suddenly it felt much worse. A sharp pain knifed all the way up her right side, and she could no longer stand up straight. Bent over at the waist, she continued through the park until she came to the hill where she had broken her leg as a child. Looking up the rather small incline she realized she might not be able to make it home. Elena, a girl who was a grade ahead of her at Evander Childs, passed Ruth and started trudging up the little hill. Then she turned and asked Ruth what was wrong. She told the younger girl to sit down on the path and hurried off, shouting that she would call Ruth's mother as soon as she got home. Her family shared a hall phone with the other tenants on their floor, but she was sure her mother would let her use it for something like this. If Ruth's mother did not answer, Elena promised to walk the three blocks to their apartment, and wait there until her mother came home.

Several minutes later Elena again appeared, out of breath from running all the way to their apartment building as well as the entire way back.

"My brother's coming too. We're going to bring you to our apartment. My mama stayed home to call the doctor. He was on a house call and she thought she should stay and keep trying," Elena explained, the words coming out in bunches, in-between the deep breaths she kept taking to fill her depleted lungs.

By this time, Ruth was sitting at the bottom of the hill, collapsed upon her belly. "It really hurts," was all she could groan. As soon as Elena's brother arrived, the two siblings managed to stand her on her feet. With one arm wrapped around each of them at the waist because she still could not stand up straight, they managed to drag her back to their apartment. A neighbor's son helped them get her up the three flights of stairs to their apartment.
Their mother had prepared a pot of tea for the wounded Ruth, which thankfully, she declined. Had she taken even a sip of the hot liquid, her appendix might have burst in the apartment. She thanked them all, but

explained that she really wanted to go home. Her hope was that her father would already be there, his workday usually finishing at the same time she left the journal office. Although she found the ever-increasing pain in her abdomen frightening, she declined the young man's offer to help because she was embarrassed. Being ill was not something she experienced very often, and when she did, her mother was not the most compassionate of parents. Ruth had long ago learned to fend for herself.

By the time she again reached the infamous hill, she was in agony. An older gentleman in suit, vest and bowler hat was watching her climb the hill with concern. When she reached its crest, he stopped her to ask, "Are you alright, my dear? Is there anything I can do to help?"

Ruth burst into tears, despite her best efforts to contain herself. The man put his arm around her shoulder and helped her sit down on a park bench. She was too exhausted to protest; he had a kind face, but she nevertheless worried that he could be the dangerous kind of fellow her mother was always warning her and her sister about. When he asked her where she lived, she told him anyway because she had told Elena's brother the truth: she wanted to get home to her father. They exchanged names on their halting route to the Liebman apartment. It turned out the man loved classical music, and had heard Adelaide sing with the Schola Cantorum at Carnegie Hall several times.

"I hope she's home so you can meet her," Ruth managed to mutter through clenched teeth.

When she and Mr. Cohen reached the steps to Ruth's apartment building, she thanked him for all his help, but assured him her family's apartment was on the first floor and she could make it inside by herself. With obvious concern, he watched her struggle up the two steps to the building, take out her key, which took quite a bit of effort, open the door, and limp inside.

As soon as she entered the front lobby, the pain became unendurable. She contemplated asking Mrs. Baker, on the first floor, if she would mind hiking up the five flights to the Liebman flat to get her mother, but refrained, again because of embarrassment. She was afraid the woman would think she was exaggerating, and didn't have the energy to explain what was happening to another adult anyway. She hauled herself up one flight after another, groaning loudly with ever step, and collapsed in a heap in front of their apartment door. Fortunately, Mrs. Baker had heard every clumping step she made as she crawled, moaned, and hauled herself upstairs one step at a time. After squeezing the water out of one last garment from her afternoon laundry, the woman climbed the stairs to see who had made all that racket. Startled to see young Ruth in a heap on the landing, the sight galvanized her into action and she banged on the front door of the Liebman flat. When no one came right away, she banged again, this time loud enough for anyone in the building to hear.

"For goodness sake," Adelaide said as she jerked the front door open. "Have some…." And then her daughter crumpled on the floor at her feet, the downstairs neighbor looking terrified.

"I will go downstairs and call police emergency, Adelaide," Mrs. Baker shouted as she raced for the stairs.

"Thank you," Adelaide called after her, finally bending down to touch her daughter.

"Ruth. What is the matter?" Then she screamed, "Simon. I need you!"

Finally Ruth's father appeared, and Ruth knew everything would be all right. By that time Adelaide was cradling their younger daughter in her arms, stroking her hair, whispering in her ear, and for the first time in her life as a mother experiencing guilt at how infrequently she had done anything like this before. Simon squatted before them.

"Can you tell me what is wrong?" he asked his daughter.

"My tummy!" was all she could manage, tears streaming down her cheeks.

Simon turned to his wife. "Make sure Dorothy calls an ambulance. We need to get Ruthie to the hospital." She obeyed without demur. Their daughter was not a complainer. They both knew that whatever was wrong was serious.

"Breathe, my child," he ordered her. "In, out, in out…that's it." As soon as Simon could see that she was beginning to relax, though she could clearly not stand, he told her he was going to take her in his arms and carry her downstairs. By then, he assured her, the ambulance was sure to be there.

Ruth never forgot that day, even when she was older than either of her parents had been. She could summon the feel of her father's arms around her, enfolding her, carrying her down the five flights, and often did so in times of stress. Indeed, he had been right. The ambulance attendant was opening the back door as her father carried her through the front door that Adelaide was holding open for them.

"Please let me keep my knees bent," Ruth begged as her father laid her down on the gurney. The attendant glanced at her father, who nodded in agreement. Even the attendant could see how much pain the girl was in, and said he would do his best. With a great deal of effort he managed to thread the strap between the girl's chest and knees, before he lifted the gurney back inside the ambulance. In this unusual fashion, Ruth would be transported to St. Barnabas Hospital the newest hospital in the Bronx.

As the ambulance attendant was raising the gurney to slide it into the ambulance, Dorothy Baker appeared, running up the block with a bouquet of flowers, which she hurled at the gurney. As the flowers landed all around her, Ruth noted their lovely scent. "I feel like I'm going to my own funeral," she murmured, her father's laughter the last thing she heard before she passed out in the ambulance.

"I'm right here, Ruthie. I'll be with you all the way to the hospital," he cooed as he stroked her forehead. The ambulance attendant hadn't even attempted to suggest he ride in the front of the vehicle. He, too, had a daughter at home, and knew instinctively that this was what his own child would have wanted. Ruth never heard Simon's words, but she had always been certain that she had felt him beside her on that ride, even though she hadn't been conscious. When Ruth awakened later that evening, her father's was the first face she saw. He smiled at her, and she smiled back. When she started to cry, he did as well.

"You're fine, my amazing daughter. It was your appendix, and now you don't have one anymore," he explained.

"I guess that's why it hurts," she groaned. "But the pain's not the same."

"Would you like me to ask the nurse if she can give you something for the pain?" he asked. Ruth nodded, but when he started to rise, she added, "Wait until she comes. I don't want you to leave." Fortunately the nurse rushed into the room at that very moment, gave her a shot, and as Ruth drifted back into dreamland she managed to smile at her father. Simon remained in the hospital for two whole days and nights, the nurses finding him a razor as well as calling Adelaide for him to ask her to bring him a change of clothing.

This Ruth never forgot either. Years later she would think it had been a hell of a way to get her father's attention.

* * *

Although he didn't usually help Yetta with meal preparation because it would have taken time away from his work and the income it provided, he and Yetta were both so nervous about Nell's suitor coming to their home for the evening meal to meet them that Noah found himself chopping carrots at the kitchen counter next to his wife. By the time they got the roast into the oven, and the vegetables into a pot on top of the stove so they wouldn't have to deal with them once Abe had arrived, they were surprised that a whole hour remained before the momentous event was to take place. Noah suggested he help Yetta with the family laundry, another unusual event in their household. Noah had only taken charge of the laundry, supervising his daughters at the task, after Yetta had given birth to one of the younger children. By the time the hour approached they were as nervous as Nell, although they tried to hide their anxiety from her. They knew she cared about this man, and feared this would be her only chance to marry anyone or have a family. Neither parent knew what they would do if they found him unsuitable.

When Noah opened their front door at 6 PM, the man who stood there was tall, thin, and balding, his back somewhat stooped from the work he did at the factory. At least that was what Noah assumed. Max and little Nathan were jumping up and down behind him, each boy grabbing one of his legs and peeking around their father to see this important and significant man. Once Noah had ushered him into their sitting room, Max pulled his father back into the hallway.

"He's almost as old as you are, Daddy," he said with obvious surprise. "He can't be the man coming to ask for Nelly's hand!"

"Shhh," warned Noah. "He might hear you."
Yetta grabbed both of her youngest children and dragged them all the way to the kitchen. "Joe is a very important man at the Singer factory," she told them. "He is an assistant to the general manager, and is being groomed to take his place when the older man retires."

"Older than him?" blurted Nathan. By the look on his mother's face, Nathan realized he should have kept that thought to himself, and ducked below her arm that she had raised so she could swat him on his back for the impertinence. He raced out the back door, followed by Max, who certainly did not want to incur his mama's wrath either. Yetta sighed, picked up a platter of pickled vegetables from the counter, and slowly headed back down the hall to the front of the house. She, too, was concerned. The man did look awfully worn, if not old.

Although he was usually a quiet person, Joe warmed to Noah. When Yetta returned the two were already deep in a discussion about woodworking, which the younger man often pursued on his one day off each week. He had made a cabinet for his mother so she could move her good dishes into their dining room, and was presently working on carving a shelf at the back of his father's worktable for their tools. Even Yetta was impressed, thinking to herself that he might, indeed, be a good choice for her hardworking, capable daughter. Both she and her husband could see how anxious Nell was, sitting on the parlor couch next to Joe as the two men discussed the benefits of different kinds of wood. Her back was as stiff as chestnut, the hardest of the woods the two men were discussing. Joe had saved for months to be able to buy, and then use that wood for the chest he had made for his mother. He wanted it to last, he explained, since the Shiffman's had seven children, all of them younger than Joe.

When Max and Nathan were called to the dinner table, they both entered the room meekly, on their best behavior. Max in particular adored his older sister. She had been the one who had spelled his mother so that she could get some rest when he had been so sick, changing the cool, wet rag on his forehead often, laying the cloth down gently to not cause him any more discomfort. She would then open her own high school reader, picking a story she thought he might like and read it aloud to him. She knew how much he loved to read, and always chose a story he found interesting. Beck was too busy with other household chores to read to him when it was her turn to sit beside his cot, and Min didn't enjoy reading. She wasn't particularly gentle either. Although Nell was the most serious of the sisters, she was kind. She watched over her little brothers with concern and actually seemed to enjoy the task, even smiling upon occasion, and sometimes laughing at their antics. Nell's laughter was infrequent, but it gave both boys inordinate pleasure when it did erupt. They felt that somehow they were easing their older sister's burdens, which they could see even at their young age.

And though he wanted Nell to find a husband who would cherish her in the way he and Nathan already did, he was really worried. He wanted to ask her why she was agreeing to marry this old man. Didn't she realize she didn't have to marry someone she didn't love? He and Nathan would always take care of her so she would never be alone. When he tried to talk to Beck about this, she smiled and patted his head.

"You're just too young to understand," she told him, which of course, felt terrible. He was always being told he was 'too young' for this or that. He wondered when he would be the right age, but didn't dare ask Beck or anyone else that question because it would prove that he was inadequate in his understanding: i.e.; too young.

* * *

When Ruth awakened in the hospital the next morning, it was her mother who was sitting by her bedside. She hoped her face did not show her disappointment as she tried to speak. Then she realized that her mother was asleep. Ruth started to cry, quietly, so as not to disturb her. Her mother looked exhausted even in repose. As quietly as Ruth tried to be, eventually she had to take a huge breath, gulping in the air being blocked by her quiet crying. Adelaide's eyes popped open. When she saw that her child was trying to comfort herself with hugs as much as she could, given the bandages around her belly and the tubes attached to her arms, Adelaide reached for her hand and clutched it gently within her own.

"What is the matter, Liebchen?" she asked.

"It hurts," Ruth replied, obviously ashamed by her inability to handle the pain.

"Of course it hurts, Ruth. You just had surgery," her mother explained.

"What does that mean?" the girl asked.

At first her mother hesitated, unsure how to explain what surgery meant without frightening Ruth. Then she shrugged and said, "The doctor had to go into your belly and take out your appendix. It was infected, and that was why your tummy hurt so much."

"How did he get it out?" Despite her discomfort, Ruth was still the curious child she had always been. "You can tell me, mama. It's already been done, so it can't frighten me," she said with more insight than most children her age possessed.

Taking a deep breath, Adelaide replied, "The doctor used a very very sharp knife, and cut along your lower belly so that he could get inside and lift out your appendix."

Her father's gentle voice added, "You were out cold, my sweet. The nice doctor gave you something so you wouldn't feel anything."

"Well, that worked," came Ruth's wry response.

Her father continued. "Under all those bandages you will see that he stitched you back together."

"Take them off so I can see!" she ordered, and then immediately asked, "He sewed me up, like Mama does when she's fixing one of your shirts?" Adelaide and Simon glanced at each other in utter amazement.

"It's not quite the same," her father replied, trying to contain himself so he wouldn't laugh and make her feel silly. He didn't think his daughter was trying to be humorous.

"No," Ruth agreed. "Your shirts don't hurt afterwards."

Her parents could no longer keep from laughing. Ruth was delighted; her humor had been intentional because she loved making her father laugh. But this time her joke had unintentional consequences as well.

"Stop, please. I can't laugh, it hurts too much," she managed to sputter, hands on her belly in an effort to stop it from jiggling.

"Take little breaths, Ruth, and the pain will stop," her mother suggested. Ruth was able to curtail her laughter so she could follow her mother's advice. Both parents were staring at her. "Yes," she finally managed. "That's better."

Her father's hand again stroked her forehead, his love for her obvious even to his wounded daughter. "I can't imagine telling a joke if I had just had my appendix removed," he told her.

"Have you ever had your stomach cut open for anything?" she asked with curiously.

"No, knock wood." With his other hand he lightly rapped his knuckles against the small bedside table. "You still look pretty uncomfortable, little girl," he added.

Ruth didn't bother opening her eyes, as she replied, "I'm not a little girl, Daddy. I'm a freshman in high school."

"You're right, my sweet. I don't think either your mama or I could have handled this any better than you have."

"Maybe you better find the nurse," Adelaide suggested.

"Yes, that's a good idea. There must be something she can give this little woman," he agreed. The smile on his daughter's face was immediate, although she didn't open her eyes.

"That's right, papa. That's what I am."

By the time her father returned with the nurse, Ruth had drifted into sleep again. Adelaide was still holding her hand. The nurse suggested they come to get her when their daughter again awakened; if she gave her a shot to ease the pain now, she would awaken. Simon grabbed the chair on the other side of his daughter's bed and carried it around the bed so he could sit beside his wife. He took her hand, and that was the way Ruth found them when she stirred a few hours later. Her father was holding her mother's hand, and her mother was holding hers. All three of them had been asleep.

CHAPTER FOURTEEN

A week after the surgery, the day Ruth was to be released from the hospital, she was totally prepared. Her father was sitting next to the bed, her mother standing by the doorway. Instinctively Ruth understood that her mother was afraid to see the nurse peel away the dressing covering her stomach so she could remove the stitches before the doctor examined her and let them all go home. As soon as the nurse had dropped the dressing into the bin she had wheeled in for just that purpose, Ruth put out her hand to stop her.

"Before you take the stitches out, I'd love to see them, " she explained. "I can't really believe I was sewed together like a piece of cloth."

Startled, the nurse said, "I don't think you'll be able to bend over to see them. I imagine that would really hurt."

As Ruth expected, her father was totally in her corner. "What if we get a mirror?" he asked the nurse.

She looked concerned. "Most people can't watch this procedure," she said. "She might faint."

"Our little Ruth is quite an amazing young woman," he assured the nurse. "She walked herself all the way home from her friend's apartment bent over double. If she had known where the hospital was, I think she would have come here instead."

"If you're sure she can handle it...."the nurse replied with some hesitation.

From the doorway Adelaide said, "If anyone can handle it, Ruth can. She is amazingly brave."

Though Ruth had been a bit surprised by her father's words, her mother's comment totally amazed her.

"I don't want to watch you take them out. I just want to see them before you do, so I can remember," she explained.

"Let me get a mirror from the nurses' station," the nurse finally agreed, adding, "I'll be right back." When she returned, she carried a small cosmetic mirror in her hand. "Tell me when you can see your belly," she said as she angled the mirror over Ruth's stomach.

"Stop. I can see them. I don't believe it. He used little stitches, just like you do Mama!" Ruth exclaimed. Then she closed her eyes. "OK. I'm ready now."

"This is going to smart, Ruth," the nurse explained. "But I'm sure you'll be able to handle it. You are one patient I will never forget."

Ruth gripped her father's hand, but she didn't make a sound during the entire process. It was obvious to both of her parents that 'smarting' had been an understatement. Ruth's eyes were squeezed shut and her mouth clenched. When the nurse stood straight and said, "I'm done. They're all out," Ruth let out the air she had been holding with a whoosh.

"Don't tell anyone what it really feels like or they'll never let you take out their stitches," she mumbled, to the amusement of all concerned.

Ruth leaned on her father as she made her way up the hospital corridor although she believed she could walk on her own two feet. She had always loved physical contact with her father, so she had immediately agreed when he suggested helping her. He carried her small suitcase in his other hand, and Adelaide walked beside her on the other side.

"Daddy, do you think the stitches were made of silk?" Ruth asked with some excitement.

"Yes," Adelaide replied. "But I think it's ghoulish to keep talking about it."

When Simon suggested he and his daughter talk about it after they got home so her mother wouldn't have to listen, his wife glared at him. "She is a girl and it isn't appropriate at any time for her to talk about these things."

"You do realize that someday we will have female doctors," her husband replied, his wife throwing up her hands in disgust. He was incorrigible.

Getting in and out of the cab her father had flagged down was extremely uncomfortable. Ruth didn't think she would be able to do it on her own, so she happily accepted her father's help with that as well. Her mother took his hand too, but wasn't nearly as gracious as her daughter about his assistance getting into the yellow cab. Or at least that was the way Ruth viewed it on that day, and in her mind's eye for the remainder of her life. In later years she often told the story of the entire misadventure to her children and at parties when she and her husband entertained their circle of friends.

The most memorable part of the experience was when they alighted at their apartment building, and her father took one look at the front stoop, swooped her up into his arms, carefully so as not to cause undo stress on her tummy, and carried her through the front door and up the stairs to their abode.

"At least Mrs. Baker isn't throwing flowers at me," Ruth joked as he climbed the stairs with her. Even her mother had to laugh at her remark, and thus the three arrived on the fifth floor outside their apartment. Holly was standing in their doorway looking frightened, and immediately blurted, "They wouldn't let me come to the hospital, Ruthie. I wanted to!" Ruth's eyes were glued to Mrs. Baker, who was also standing in her doorway, a vase filled with flowers in her hands. Simon noticed her too, and motioned Holly to step aside with Ruth's suitcase as he lunged through their door. Once it was closed behind them all three broke into howls of laughter, Holly watching them with her mouth hanging open, the base clutched in her hands.

"I hope she can't hear you," she said, which made them laugh even harder.

* * *

When Max was fifteen and Nathan thirteen, their brother Jules instigated one of the most momentous occasions in both of their young lives. He came home from dental school at Rutgers to have a longed-for Sabbath meal, cooked by his sisters, of course, and not his mother, who remarked that he looked too skinny even by her rather lax standards. Yetta had always been too thin, so she certainly couldn't berate any of her children for the same condition. After the meal of gefilte fish, roast chicken with onions, carrots and browned potatoes, and homemade cheesecake, he asked the boys if they wanted to go for a walk.

"Jews don't go out on the town after the Sabbath meal," Yetta complained with distress.

Her oldest son patted her on the back and reassured her by saying, "No one we know we are out on the street, Mama, so you needn't worry. Besides, everyone knows we aren't a very religious family." And out they went, although their mother did not look at all pleased. As the front door closed behind them, Nathan piped up, "Mama didn't look very convinced."

"I'll talk to her about my studies when we come home and that will appease her, don't you think?" Jules asked. Both of his brothers nodded their agreement. According to their mother Jules rarely did anything unforgiveable, and certainly his entrance into dental school had enhanced this belief. That he was also married now, with a baby on the way, made him seem special to all of them. Beck already had one son, and Nell a child on the way. But it was the issue from her first son that had true value for their mother. Noah adored the issue of all of his children, spoiling them because he could. Even Yetta didn't complain, because she understood the pain her husband carried about how little he had been able to give their own children when they had been young.

"So, Max. What do you know about babies?" he asked as they rounded the corner.

"They cry a lot," came the succinct and witty response.

"Shhh," said Nathan, who was anxious to hear what his older brother had to say. "I don't think he knows anymore than I do," he added.

"Which mean you don't know how ... you would make a baby," Jules suggested.

"Hopefully we won't be doing whatever that is just yet. Mama would kill us," Max joked, although he wanted to learn about sex as much as his younger brother.

"Do either of you know what a vagina is?" Jules asked them.

"Julie!" Max moaned.

"I guess you don't," the young man smiled. "Dad took me aside the night after I asked Lil to marry me. I didn't tell him we had already begun to explore the 'wonders' he wanted to tell me about."

"I think I'm going back inside," Nathan groaned, flushing scarlet.

"Don't you dare, Nate. Otherwise when the time comes you'll be completely unprepared, and I know you like girls," Jules teased. When neither of his brothers said anything else, he continued.
"A vagina is the female counterpart to the penis," he began.

"Beck and Nell never have a bulge in their pants," Max joked, making Jules laugh aloud.

"Vagina's are a nice, warm cave. Women don't have anything that sticks out," he explained.

"Except breasts," quipped Nathan. Both of the youngsters were beginning to enjoy this discussion.

"When they're loose and free they don't stick out," Jules explained, causing more groans. He continued anyway. "So I know by now your penis gets hard sometimes, and you probably touch it." More groans. "What's nice is, when you have a wife, or a girlfriend, she can do that."

"No!" Max gasped, utterly serious.

"Oh yes, and it feels…unbelievable," his older brother assured him.

"I would turn red as a beet," Nathan muttered.

"So would your dick," quipped Jules, and they all broke into embarrassed laughter.

"Go on," urged Max, and so he did. He explained the basic facts of life, but was not content to stop there, much to the relief of both of his younger brothers. Max often wondered what he was meant to do if he ever got the courage to approach a girl, let alone kiss one. 'Then what?' had been beyond anything he could have even imagined thinking about let alone asking. When Jules stopped talking, neither of his younger brothers said a word. It was clearly still up to Jules. So he continued.

'That's the barebones," he said. "Do you want to hear more? It's the 'more' that's significant, if you ask me."

"Yes," both Nate and Max immediately declared, amusing their brother. He didn't laugh or even chuckle aloud, since he didn't want to embarrass either boy.

"Kissing is the beginning, but what's great about kissing is touching tongues!" he told them.

Neither of the brothers uttered a thing, though Max made a face.

Jules resumed, "Touching a woman's body feels wonderful to us, and to them too. Nipples are very sensitive. You can kiss them too."

"I bet biting's out of the question," Max again joked, obviously uncomfortable with all this information, but not wanting his brother to end the conversation either.

Jules smiled, understanding his brother's need to joke about the information he was imparting. "But it's the area below the waist that's the most wonderful. "

Max found himself holding his breath, not having the courage to glance at Nathan, but imagining he was doing the same.

"There's a little spot, a bump almost, above the opening of the vagina. If you rub it with your fingers, a woman becomes aroused. It's much more fun if your partner is aroused," he added.

"Why?" blurted Nathan.

"When your wife is aroused, she gets very wet, and it's easier for you to…." Jules began, at which point Max interrupted.

"OK. I get it."

Again Jules smiled at the two young men. "Trust me. This is a part of life you are going to like a lot."

All three were quiet until Max spoke again, this time with some hesitation. "Nell doesn't…laugh much, even now that she's married," he murmured, not sure how to continue.

"That's true," Jules replied. "But that doesn't mean she and Joe don't enjoy one another. Joe is very quiet as well, which may be what drew them together. We can never know what anyone else feels. Not everyone is as open and lively as either Beck or Lil."

Nathan did not look convinced. "Do you really think she loves Joe?" he asked his big brother.

"Actually I do," he replied. "You know, they are both pretty tired when they get home from work. Joe is a supervisor at the factory and works ten or twelve hours a day, and Nell does too."

Jules hoped his words reassured his brothers, although he wasn't completely convinced by them himself. Nell never looked at Joe the way Lil looked at him. His wife's expressions of affection, both verbal and physical, had become a necessary part of his life, and he certainly wanted his older sister to experience a love that was both expressive and full as well. It might have been that she and Joe were quiet, and worked hard, but Beck and Morris also worked long hours, and were very affectionate with one another, even when they were tired. Of course Beck was much more effusive about all of life than her sister, but still, Jules would have preferred hearing Nell laugh more often.

"Maybe because they're both so quiet, they don't feel comfortable throwing their arms around each other," mused Nathan, a wise assessment for someone so young.

"They may also be more affectionate when they are in their own room," Jules added, though again, he was not sure he believed that was so, which made him sad, a feeling he hoped he was hiding from the boys. He, too, wanted more for Nell, but perhaps just being married and knowing that children would follow was enough for her, and more than she had ever expected from life.

"I think Papa is expecting me to read the evening paper to him," Nathan explained as he turned to go back into the house.

"He can read most of it himself," Max told Jules, "But he enjoys it if we read him the longer articles so he's sure he's understood them."

When the fifteen-year-old was certain Nathan had closed the kitchen door, he put his hand on his brother's arm. "Jules..." he began, although he was again not sure how to continue.

"Whatever it is, Max'l, I'm sure I've experienced it," Jules assured him.

"There's a girl in my English class named Teresa," Max mumbled.

"Pretty name," Jules said.

"Pretty girl too," Max agreed, and then added, "But she's Catholic."
"I see."

Jules suddenly looked more serious, which did not bode well for the conversation Max wanted to have with him.
"I know Mama and Papa would not be pleased about our friendship, but we talk about books, or that's how we started to talk to each other. Our teacher put us in teams a month ago, and we were paired," Max explained with obvious discomfort.

Jules, who was not considered slow by anyone, added, "And now you've found you have other subjects you enjoy talking about."

"Jules, she's the only girl I've ever talked to, let alone talked about books with, or the articles I read in the paper about what's happening in Europe," Max told him. "I don't want to stop talking to her, even though I know that's what Mama and Papa would want me to do."

Jules put his arm around his brother's shoulder. "When we get older we sometimes take a path our parents don't understand. We're meant to do that, Max. But I think we're also meant to respect our parents and I think you're right about how mama and papa would feel about this friendship."

Max, who was usually shy and reticent exploded, totally startling Jules. "So that means I should stop talking to Teresa?"

"Not at all," Jules replied, somewhat flustered by this outburst but persevering anyway. "I also think you should keep your relationship to yourself. You are entitled to choose your friends, even friends Mama and Papa might not like, and I think you can do that without flaunting your worldview to them."

At that Max had to laugh. "I don't think I ever thought anyone would say I flaunted anything."

Jules laughed as well. "No, that wouldn't be likely, would it?"

They sat companionably side by side on a bench outside Noah's workshop until Max asked his brother, "Would you like to meet her?"

Of course Jules said he would like that very much indeed, and the following week met Max and his new friend at the park near their house. It took awhile for them all to become comfortable with one another, but within fifteen minutes they were talking non-stop about the changes in Elizabethport, Battin High and its intellectual limits, and what both Teresa and Max planned to do when they graduated. Jules was surprised by how much he liked this young woman, as well as by the depth of the relationship his shy younger sibling was having with her. He realized he was also pleased. For the first time in years Jules believed he could stop worrying about how Max would fare in the outside world.

* * *

By the time Max became a junior and Nate a sophomore at Battin High School, Nathan had begun to show an interest in girls. He was not sure how much he should talk to his older brother about his amorous thoughts or the stirring inspired by them in his nether regions because he couldn't imagine Max harboring such forbidden feelings. Max had never told Nathan about his friendship with Teresa, let alone the burgeoning romantic aspect of it. Both boys, who had always been close and shared almost every aspect of their young lives with one another, were suddenly becoming more circumspect. Each missed the other but neither had any idea how to bridge the gap that was developing despite their best intentions.

Although he rarely thought about his cousin who had died several years before, and been his closest friend throughout his childhood other than Nathan, Max often found himself thinking about her now. He would have loved to be able to tell her about Teresa, to introduce them, to share what he was feeling about his new friend with her. He knew she would not have judged him, either for his feelings, or because of Teresa's religion. Jules was almost always in New Brunswick, where he and Lil had settled with their new little baby because he had opened a dental practice there. When the family did travel to New Brunswick, they were always together as a group with rarely a private moment for anyone.

Max wanted to ask Teresa to have a soda with him after their final class of the day, but was hesitating because he wasn't sure how to go about it. His friendship with her had become one of the most important parts of his life, and he certainly did not want to jeopardize it by attempting to take it to another level. He had no idea if Teresa was harboring the same dream, or if she was satisfied with what they already shared.

Sitting in chemistry class, Max decided he would ask Teresa to walk home with him the following day, and he would ask her then to go to the soda shop with him. The only problem that remained was Nathan. They always walked home together: what possible excuse could he give his brother so he wouldn't wonder why Max could not walk home with him. He was still pondering the problem when he and Nate were already halfway home.

Much to his own surprise Max suddenly blurted out, "I have a meeting with the baseball coach after school tomorrow, so I won't be able to walk home with you."

Nate, who had been totally focused on the derriere of one of the girls walking in front of them, replied, "That's fine, Max. I'm a big boy now, and can find my way by myself."

Max laughed at Nate's teasing words, relieved that his younger brother hadn't asked any questions about his supposed meeting. It was November, and baseball season did not even begin until early in March.

Nathan was just as relieved. Without his older brother trailing along, he would be able to walk home with Dorothy and Holly Welch, Holly of the appealing behind. He had no doubt that if he suggested the three of them walk together since they went the exact same way for blocks, the girls would all agree, probably in a gale of giggles. The Welch's had known his parents for years, although the two families rarely got together for social occasions. Holly had played with Min when they were little, but upon reaching high school that friendship had withered on the vine, which had not surprised Nathan. Holly was one of the popular girls, and Min was both shy and more serious. She didn't have time for frivolity, she often declared when Nell or Beck asked her why she didn't sign up for any after school activities. Although both of her sisters realized the real reason: she feared the girls who regularly participated in those activities would not accept her; neither questioned her further because they didn't want to make her more uncomfortable about her status than she already was.

"Let's catch up with the girls," Nathan suggested, already quickening his pace, leaving Max no choice but to follow. He couldn't tell his younger brother that none of these girls held his interest. Teresa would be his 'secret' for as long as it was necessary. Still, when Nate reached for Holly's books to relieve her of her burden, Max swooped the books from both Lillian and Dorothy's arms.

Completely startled Dorothy quipped, "He doesn't look strong as an ox, does he?" which sent all three girls into gales of laughter. Even Max had to join in the hilarity. If the word had been in vogue back then, Max would have been called a geek. Not Nathan. Although it was clear the two young men were brothers, Nathan's personality precluded the use of that word or any other 'intellectual' moniker despite his very obvious smarts.

"We both move heavy furniture around in our father's shop," he explained which made the girls laugh even louder.

Racing ahead of them all Max pulled up his shirtsleeve and made a muscle, jumping from side to side to show off his pectorals. They were actually surprisingly round for someone so skinny. Everyone was laughing with total abandon including Max. He realized with some surprise that it was easy for him to fool around with girls he saw as mere friends. He would never have behaved this way with Teresa, even if she had enjoyed his sense of humor. It would have felt humiliating.

The following day Max could barely concentrate in any of his classes, and even flubbed an answer to a chemistry question, which surprised the teacher more than it did his student. Max had to ask his teacher to repeat the question, turning scarlet, but then answered it correctly. Field hockey passed in a blur, which actually was a relief given his awkward performance on almost any athletic field. He managed to pass the puck twice, but by the end of the hour barely remembered either shot. When his teammates clapped him on the back at the end of class, he almost asked them why. He loathed being mocked during gym, which he often was, and could easily imagine their reaction to that question. Although the day passed at a snail's pace, the final bell finally rang, and Max headed for his locker, startled as well as irritated to see Nathan already standing beside it.

"I have an English assignment I hoped you could help me with," Nate announced.

"We can do it at home," was his brother's short and rather abrupt reply. Nate opened his mouth to begin to explain the problem despite his older brother's tone, but then noticed his anxious demeanor.

"Oh. You're meeting the baseball coach," Nate suddenly remembered. "Sorry, I just forgot. I didn't want to bring my book home, but I will."

Relieved, Max assured his younger sibling that he himself had little homework, and would certainly be able to help Nathan with his. English was a subject he was good at, given his long-standing love of books.

Max and Nathan parted ways at the entrance to the school, Max supposedly on his way to meet with the baseball coach, who was probably not even in his office at this time of year. Nathan did not think about the season, or wonder about his brother's lame excuse. He had other things on his mind. Maybe, if he hurried, he would be able to spot Holly and offer to carry her books again. If the other girls had any sense at all, they would move ahead so he and Holly could walk side by side. Of course he had no idea what he would talk to her about, and was therefore relieved he would have a couple of minutes to compose his opening riposte.

As soon as Nate ran down the steps outside the main entrance to the high school, Max closed his locker and hurried outside as well. He ran all the way to the soda shop down the block where he was supposed to meet Teresa, gasping to catch his breath when he got there, grateful that he was the first to arrive. In a bit of a panic he shoved his hand into the left-hand pocket of his lightweight jacket, afraid the money he had brought with him for this momentous event had fallen out during his frantic run. The coins were still there, in the bottom of his pocket. Twenty cents was a lot for him to spend, but he had decided that if he was going to behave like a man, on special occasions he needed to take money from the little he had saved working for his Uncle on the weekends. Ten minutes passed, long enough for Max to regain his composure and the ability to breathe like a normal human being. When another few minutes passed, Max's heart sank. Teresa had forgotten, or perhaps their first 'little' date did not mean as much to her as it did to him. Or maybe, he silently prayed, Mrs. Halloran had changed the day she did laundry and needed her daughter to run home to help. Teresa had raced out of their English class, and he hadn't had an opportunity to remind her that they were meeting after school. He sat down in the curb and waited for quite awhile, reading a short story in his English book to pass the time. If she had seen him sitting there, surely she would have spoken. Despondent, Max gathered his things and stood. As he turned to walk home, he happened to glance into the soda shop, and there she was, sitting at the counter only several feet from the front door, glancing around as nervously as he.

As Max burst through the door he blurted, "Have you been waiting long? I was doing homework at the curb." His face was scarlet because the door had made a horrible loud sound when he wrenched it open. He was certain it could have been heard around the corner and all the way up the next block.

Teresa was smiling with relief. "Oh no, just a few minutes." She was clearly uncomfortable. "Actually I've already finished one soda. I didn't think you remembered."

"I was sitting outside doing my English assignment. I just didn't see you get here," he explained, unnerved by how lame his words sounded.

"Well, it's alright now, isn't it?" she smiled at him. "Next time we better decide whether we're meeting outside or inside!"

Next time! There was going to be a next time!

"Who do you have for geometry?" he asked, though he wanted to kick himself around the block for asking such a boring and silly question. "Since you've already had your tea, what else would you like to try?" he then asked to try to cover his own foolish opener.

Hesitantly she looked at the chalkboard on the wall in front of them and replied, "I love vanilla ice cream, but we hardly ever have it at home. My mom says we can't afford it."

"Sure, that would be fine," Max replied, although his heart was pounding. He, too, looked at the board of offerings to make sure he had enough money to pay for vanilla ice cream. He was frantically looking for a way to say he didn't want anything, so he could meet her simple request. Then he breathed a sigh of relief: he could pay for the ice cream and still have enough for a cup of tea. Watching the smile spread across her entire face when she put the first spoonful of ice cream into her mouth was more than enough reward for spending the twenty-five cents he had taken from his hard-earned savings. Teresa was much prettier than he had noticed when they had first become friends.

"Oh," she sighed. "I really do love vanilla ice cream."

"My sister, Beck, makes ice cream for us during the summer. But it's too cold outside, even in the fall, for her to make ice cream the rest of the year," Max said, wondering if she would think him foolish for talking about making ice cream.

"So does my mama!" Teresa eagerly agreed. "Our ice cream maker is already up in the attic. We don't have room for it in our kitchen."

"We don't have an attic," Max explained. "We keep ours out back in my father's workshop, behind the wood he uses to repair furniture." He took a sip of his soda because he had no idea what else to say.

"I told my mama I want to add some of the strawberries we grow in our garden to the ice cream next summer," Teresa told him, agonized because she couldn't think of anything to talk about besides ice cream. Then she remembered his question about her geometry teacher. 'I have geometry fifth period with Mrs. Demarco," she blurted, her mouth still full from her second spoonful of the wonderful ice cream.

"I have Mr. Holmes fifth period, for history. My geometry teacher is Mr. Hayes, but I've heard Mrs. Demarco is much better," Max said, greatly relieved they now had something to talk about, and indeed they did. Both of them loved to read, the librarian having recommended 'Main Street' to them both, which neither of them had realized. They talked about the novel, and what it had meant to each of them. Teresa totally identified with Carol, the main character, explaining that she wanted more from her life than just being a homemaker, which was quite surprising to Max. Although he didn't say so, the book seemed a wonderful fiction to him, and though he really admired Lewis' heroine, the notion that anyone he knew might have championed her causes had never entered his mind. Since he dreaded the thought that this young woman would find him lacking, he decided to ask her what she envisioned for herself.

"I don't want to be a secretary I don't think. My older sister is working for Singer in their main office. I can tell she's not happy." When Max didn't respond immediately—he had no idea what to say that wouldn't sound judgmental— she continued. "I was thinking about nursing school, but I have no idea how my family would pay for that." Suddenly she sounded very sad.

"I've been saving money from my allowance since I was in elementary school, and the little my father's able to give me when I work in his shop after school or on the weekends because I want to go to medical school," Max admitted shyly. No one outside his family knew about this dream.

"What will you do until you've saved enough," Teresa asked him with obvious excitement. Maybe her dream was not out of reach.
"I've talked to Mr. Groves at the pharmacy. He said he should be able to hire me full time this summer. I started working for him last summer because my father knew I needed to earn more money than he could pay me," Max replied, adding "I only work for him during the holidays now, because my Papa needs me in his shop when he's out back repairing furniture."

"If I think about being a secretary only until I save enough to go to nursing school…well, that wouldn't be so bad," Teresa mused aloud, although it was obvious this was a totally new concept for her. Max was thrilled that he had given her the idea, even if he wasn't sure he wanted to marry someone who worked outside the home.

"I'm terrible with my hands, putting pieces of wood together for my father," Max laughed. "He's always known I wouldn't be joining him in the shop when I graduate from Battin High!"

"He doesn't mind?" she asked him, somewhat surprised. Her parents would not be pleased to learn that she had plans beyond a wedding and raising children. But of course Max was a boy, and boys worked when they became men, and often before that, like Max had been doing.

"Oh no. Both of my parents want Nate and me to have a better life than they do. Nate wants to be a lawyer, and started working for one of my father's customers last year."

Teresa sighed. "I wish I could tell my parents, but I don't think they'd approve. They think I'll work at Singer, like my sister, until I get married. She's already engaged, so I could probably take her position when she starts a family."

Max thought about his response before saying, "By the time you've saved enough for nursing school, they may feel so proud of what you've accomplished, their response may surprise you."

"Maybe," she said with evident doubt.

With shocking bravery, Max reached for her hand and gave it a squeeze. He certainly didn't want her to think he held the same views as her parents, though he wasn't at all sure that he didn't.

They both fell silent, relieved to have shared their dreams with someone, and in particular, with one another. Neither had any idea that both had doubts about the other's dreams. Still they felt a closeness that was new to them both, and in this, they were both comfortable and united. When they reached the turn-off to Teresa's block, they stood close together, smiling at one another.

"When can we do this again?" Max asked, heart pounding to beat the band in his chest.

Again he was graced with her magnificent smile. "When can you take time off from your papa's shop?" she asked him.
"Tuesday is the day I usually study after school. My father wants me to do well in my classes so I can get into college," he replied. "I'll have to figure out what to tell Nate—he won't believe I'm meeting the baseball coach two weeks in a row."

Her laugh was infectious. "Me too," she agreed once they stopped laughing. "I'll probably tell my mother I'm going to the library, though I really don't like lying."

"Next week let's figure out how much to tell them," Max suggested and Teresa readily agreed. Both of them walked home without a thought about where they were going. Teresa felt as if she were walking on air, not through it. Max knew he had to compose himself before he arrived at his front door, or his mother's eagle eye would spot something and be sure to ask him questions about 'what was wrong'.

Instead, when he walked into the kitchen, his mother and father were involved in a conversation that was obviously significant for both. Curious about what they were discussing, Max opened the cupboard where his mother kept the snacks his sisters made on a weekly basis. Munching an oatmeal cookie, he stood by the counter as he poured himself a glass of milk, not because he wanted one particularly, but because he wanted to stay in the kitchen to make sure no one had spotted him with Teresa in the soda shop.

"Don't argue with me, Yetta. It isn't only the woodworking people want," Noah patiently explained to his wife.

Her lips were set in a line familiar to everyone in the family. Her heels were making a groove in the linoleum of the floor beneath her feet. "No one needs cushions," she said, repeating what his father had already heard before.

"Yetta. I talked to Mrs. Barlow today, and she mentioned how wonderful it would be for her husband to have a soft cushion to sit on when they brought their repaired rocker home with them," he replied with a sigh.

"You must have brought it up," Yetta argued even more stubbornly.

"Yetta-la. It would be a wonderful way for you to increase your sewing business, and would be profitable for mine as well," her husband suggested. "If I tell her you are willing to make her a cushion for the rocker, I'm sure she'll tell all her friends."

"You'll probably ask her to," she grumbled.

"That's a good idea," her husband said with a smile. Noah didn't ask her why she objected to the plan, because he believed that such a discussion would only increase the wall she had erected between them.

"I'll think about it," she told him before turning back to the counter to prepare the pot roast for their dinner. Of course there was nothing for her to do, since Beck had long since filled the little slits she had made all along the outside of the roast with garlic. Yetta picked up the salt container, but didn't actually use it since she was sure that had also been done. She didn't turn around until she heard her husband's heavy tread cross the room, and the back door open and slam shut behind him. He was very irritated. He rarely slammed a door or raised his voice. Yetta knew she was wrong, but such an admission was as rare for her as a slammed door was for Noah. She would ask Min, who had already come home from the factory, to whip up his favorite cake for desert. Noah would know the suggestion had come from her, so they would be able to repair to their bedroom at peace later in the evening.

Max finally sat down at the kitchen table and removed his history book from his school bag, hunching over the book as he began to read.

"Don't hunch your shoulders, Max. I've told you that before. It will give you a hump when you are older," Yetta ordered.

"Yes Mama," the boy mumbled, though he continued to read, his back a bit straighter.

"No young woman will want you for a husband," his mother teased. It took everything he had not to say that one already did. Teresa's family was Catholic; talking about his newfound girlfriend was not a topic he intended to ever tackle.

Nathan came in the back door and sat down beside his brother. "Papa doesn't need our help today," he said adding, "There is room behind the counter for the piece of furniture he is repairing, so nothing needs to be moved."

When he opened the Torah, Max glanced at him with a raised eyebrow.

"All I have to study today is a little geometry," Nate whispered. "Papa told me that this section of the Torah relates to the law, and could be useful to me when I apply to law school, especially if they grant me an interview."

"We can talk about it after dinner. I'd actually be interested in what you learn," Max told him. Then the two boys bent their heads over their books, careful to keep their backs as straight as they could for their mother. Of course by the time Beck shooed them aside so she could set the table, both boys were bent over their books, totally concentrated on the words they were reading.

When Noah returned to the kitchen to study the Torah beside his son for an hour before dinner would be served, he put his arm around his wife and brought her close to his chest.

"You know, Yetta, we'll save much more quickly with you doing this extra work, and with me working on Sundays. You will have a much bigger garden once we move to the other side of Elizabeth," he suggested.

"The yards are much bigger over there," she agreed, not quite ready to smile as well.

"Even if we have to build a shop, like we did here, there will be more room for you," Noah whispered into her hair as he held her close. Yetta could not resist sighing with contentment. She did love being held in her husband's arms.

Looking up at him she finally grinned. "I promise I will plant more tomatoes for you and the boys!"

"When are we moving?" Nathan quipped even though that meant his parents would realize he had been listening to them and not studying Torah.

"Once you have learned all you can learn from Torah!" his mother replied with a gentle slap to the back of his head.
"I was joking," Nate said. "But I'd really like to know anyway, if you have any idea."

Husband and wife glanced at one another, Yetta's assenting nod impossible to see unless Nate had been looking at his parents. He was still bent over his book. Asking the question was all the bravery he could muster. Watching for the answer would have been beyond him. His father's response came as a surprise to both him and to Max.

"Your mother and I are hoping that we can begin to look for a new house sometime in the next six months," Noah replied. Beck, who was sliding the roast from the oven, looked over at her parents with obvious surprise. But she didn't utter a word either. Each of the siblings knew that their father had said more than any of them expected, and that would have to suffice for the time being.

"I would like to have more fresh tomatoes," Noah continued, as if the other subject had never arisen.

"Me too," Max chimed in. "Would it ruin our appetites to have a small tomato sandwich with Papa before dinner?" he asked, certain the answer would be a resounding 'no!'

"I think that's a wonderful idea," Noah replied, moving over to the pantry where he grabbed a loaf of fresh rye bread wrapped in a linen towel. Even Yetta didn't have the heart to berate him. Both boys jumped up, Max getting two tomatoes from the icebox, and Nate, the butter, which his father liberally slathered all over three slices of the rye bread. Father and sons stood at the kitchen counter happily chewing on the rich treat, wiping away the tomato juice with their left hands. They didn't utter a word until they had each finished consuming the juicy sandwiches. With his mouth still half full, Max grinned at his father. "Thank you Papa. I'll make sure to eat everything on my plate for dinner," which sent all three into gales of laughter. No one ever left a crumb on his plate in the Unger family.

"Did your mama have a garden in Monasterzyska, Papa?" Max asked his father as they cleaned up the mess they had made on Yetta's kitchen counter.

"We all had gardens," Noah replied. "It was much too expensive to buy vegetables at the local market, and my parents were way ahead of the times: they wanted us to eat healthy food, and vegetables were the most important."
"Then why did you fight with mama when she wanted to plant her garden in our yard?" Nathan asked him.

"Because he likes arguing with me," Yetta interrupted. Both boys turned to grin at her. They knew from first hand experience that this was not so. Their quiet, contemplative father didn't like to argue with anyone, especially their feisty, opinionated mother.

Noah ruffled his son's hair with a smile on his face. "I wanted to have enough space to store the junk I collect so I could turn it into furniture our neighbors would buy," he explained, adding, "Our yard here is very very small."

"But her tomatoes make stacking it worthwhile, don't they?" Max asked, mostly in jest.

"I think these 'Jersey' tomatoes are better than the ones I grew in the old country," his mother agreed. She had sliced herself one, and was eating it without bread, salted, her preferred approach.

Before Noah sat back down with his sons at the kitchen table to read Torah, Yetta whispered into his ear, "I will make a slip cover for the cushion. We can probably even find some old cushions in our neighbors' trash bins that we can refurbish." Surreptitiously both teenagers watched their parents. Public affection was not typical in their home, though both sons knew how much their parents loved and depended upon one another. When their father bent over and kissed their mother on the lips, Nate almost gasped. Max had grabbed his brother's knee beneath the table, so he managed to keep mute. He loved seeing his parents kiss, and often wished they would do so more often.

When Noah sat down he found it unusually difficult to concentrate on the Hebrew words in front of him. Even though they struggled financially–not to put food on the table, or clothe their children, but to afford the few extras, like a new coat when an old one had holes at the elbow, or tickets to a concert Yetta would have loved–their lives were much better than the life they would have shared in their little Polish shtetl. He still could not believe their good fortune. Despite the first lonely four years when he had been in Elizabeth without his wife living with Elias and Marlene, Noah had known the move to this new country would be worth those struggles. Even though he still suffered from nightmares about that time, and his first attempts to make something of the junk he managed to find in his brother's wagon that first year were not up to his standards, he had known that the choice had been the right one for the wife and children he had been forced to leave behind. Any doubts he might have held vanished when his family arrived in the New World, and that family had begun to grow in this strange new world. Because he didn't want to cause his wife even more worry he never told her about the nightmares, which frequently followed him for days, the pictures as clear in his mind as if they were real. Eventually the troubling images would recede, especially if he forced himself to bend over a piece of furniture, creating beauty from the broken, shattered pieces spread out before him.

He had one married daughter, and another who had found a good man and was sure to marry before the year was out, and two bright young sons he was determined to help receive an advanced education. These were notions he could never have imagined even ten years earlier, when they had decided to embark on a life in this new place. Through hard work and perseverance, as well as their mutual belief in the importance of their family's spiritual life, he believed he and Yetta had wrought a miracle. The words swam before him, but what he felt was joy. They had a good life, all of them, and he was grateful for his part in it. He was also relieved that none of them could see the tears he was holding back. It would have been beyond his ability to explain them, even to his wife. He sighed, and then began to read. Life was a marvelous thing.

CHAPTER FIFTEEN

Greg, the boy who had created the school magazine with Ruth, had stopped by Evander Childs on his way home from Hunter College, where he was now a freshman. He quickly realized she needed a break from the grueling work of putting the fall issue to sleep. After pitching in to help her finish the task, he suggested a walk through Crotona Park, and even offered to buy Ruth a soda and hot dog. Since her successes in the dating were limited, to say the least, she was quite pleased by his suggestion, even though she had no romantic interest in Greg. This was not true for Greg, who kept his passion for the young girl hidden, and had done so for more than two years. Because he was tall, thin, and very shy, he knew he had no hope of winning the exuberant Ruth, and told himself he was content with being one of her best friends. Nevertheless, after one of their infrequent meetings at his former high school, he would go into his room in his parents' apartment, shut the door, lie down on his bed, and dream of another time and place where he and Ruth were married, working together on some kind of news journal in the adult world, and thinking of starting a family. These reveries always put him to sleep, which aggravated his mother who depended upon him to run out for needed groceries and the like.

Though Ruth understood that without Greg at her side the preceding year, her dream of having a school magazine would never have born fruit, she also realized that the young man, who found almost any excuse to drop by the school to see her now that he was attending Hunter, would have loved them to be more than friends. She pretended innocence. The very idea of kissing him made her feel slightly queasy, though she longed to be kissed. Just not by him. Holly had told her how 'lovely' kissing was, and had kissed several different boys, but Ruth remained mute on the subject. She would have loved to ask questions about how each boy kissed: did Sheldon mash his mouth so tightly against hers that her teeth felt funny; was Ruth supposed to open her mouth or keep it closed; should she purse her mouth when she leaned forward for her kiss, or leave it au naturel? She had no answers to any of these questions, or the many others that swirled through her very active mind, but knew her sister would not be a wise confident, let alone mentor. They still didn't get along very well. Ruth was the 'creative' one, who had found her place with the avant-garde crowd, and Holly the popular sibling, who easily moved into a leading role with the high school's trendsetters. Neither sister particularly liked the other. Still, despite her lack of interest in her former assistant as anything more than the good friend he had become, Ruth's heart raced when Greg made his suggestion.

She was surprised by how spicy the hot dog tasted; she had never had one before because her mother didn't believe hot dogs were a healthy food. For that reason alone, Ruth enjoyed the funny little meat stick, and loved the mustard Greg slathered all over it. He was shocked she had never had one before, and suggested she add sauerkraut to the bun before she bit into it again. Ruth liked sauerkraut; their downstairs neighbor often made it, and gave them a bowlful when she did. Her father loved the stuff too, which gave her another reason to drop a rather large blob onto her bun. She and Greg walked over to a bench some distance away from the hot dog wagon so they could have a quiet conversation about the journal, both relishing every bite of their hot dogs. Just as they sat down, Ruth heard the distinct sound of a motorcycle, which she recognized because her father had bought one years before. She loved riding behind him, which was a rare occurrence because Adelaide was terrified of the contraption.

As the large machine roared past them on the street side of the grass border in front of the bench they had chosen, Ruth was shocked to see her father on the bike. Not because she thought he was at work, or in Manhattan, where he often visited his company's factory to pick up supplies, but because there was someone on the bike with him, and it was a female someone. The woman's bright red hair was streaming behind her, and she was holding Ruth's father tightly around the waist. Ruth was truly shocked. She thought she might burst into tears, and felt humiliated in front of Greg. She certainly didn't want him to know anything was amiss, especially something that personal. Although she had long understood that her parents' marriage was not a happy one, it had never dawned on her that either one of them would choose to be with someone else. It felt like a betrayal to her, even though it was her mother who was being betrayed. She found herself wondering if it would bother her mother as much as it bothered her; perhaps she would be relieved. Even though sex was something Ruth had thought about a great deal, and longed to explore just a little, she was not sure her mother would feel the same interest.

Greg could immediately tell something was amiss. He had spent more than a year watching her every move and mood, and understood her better than anyone in her own family, except perhaps, her father. Greg knew Ruth was trying to hide her distress, so he quickly acceded to her request that they leave the park because she had a great deal of homework to do before she helped her mother prepare dinner. In truth dinner preparation was Holly's task that week, but there was no way for Greg to know that. He was disappointed when she turned down his suggestion that he walk her to her apartment building. She explained that she was not afraid to walk home herself, something she did regularly when she had to work late on the journal, even after dark.

Ruth was completely distracted as she walked the three blocks herself, and only remembered to stop at each corner before stepping into the intersection because she sensed that the people around her were stopping. When they moved again, so did she. By the time she had reached her front stoop, she had decided she would wait for her father there so that she could ask him who the woman was before he came indoors. If he was willing to give her a ride, which she knew she could talk him into, she believed it would be easier to ask. Her arms would be wrapped around his body, her face leaning against his leather jacket so he couldn't see her face, and she would just ask, and then wait to see what he said. She knew her mother was attending a rehearsal in Manhattan, and that Holly was rehearsing a new school play at school, so neither of them would interrupt. Ruth raced upstairs, took out the cooked pot roast her mother had left in their ice box, sliced it, shoved it back inside, and speared four potatoes, putting them in the oven, which she turned on so they would be ready for dinner. She decided she could snap the beans after she had spoken to her father. They didn't take very long to cook. She knew her sister would be relieved when she reached their apartment, because her rehearsals often made her late. Now when Ruth needed help, her sister would not be able to turn her down. She took one last look around the kitchen to make sure she had everything under control for the family's evening meal, and then raced back downstairs. She had to wait five more minutes before she heard her father's motorcycle roaring around the corner.

Though he was a little surprised by her request for a ride so close to the dinner hour, Simon couldn't deny his little sparkplug's request. She was so responsible, and so spirited, his little Ruth. He often gave his younger daughter rides on his motorcycle when his wife was rehearsing in the City, which would have appalled Adelaide. 'What she doesn't know won't hurt her,' he told himself, and again helped Ruth climb up on the seat behind him. Feeling her slim arms around his chest, and her head leaning against his back, gave him a great deal of pleasure. Now that his girls were both in high school, he didn't think it appropriate to wrap them in his arms. Simon had come to depend upon the affection of his daughters, and missed their easy affection. As they entered Crotona Park, he heard Ruth yelling something, but couldn't make out her words. He turned his head quickly, asking her to repeat whatever it was she had said. He was totally nonplussed by her question.

"Who is the red-haired woman," she yelled this time, and then became silent.

Simon has no idea how to respond, or what to say. His silence made Ruth very uncomfortable, so she continued with an explanation.

"Greg and I went for a walk after I put the magazine to sleep," she screamed.

Again silence.

"I saw her on the bike with you, but I didn't say anything to Greg," she finished, feeling lame and foolish, but needing an answer from her father nevertheless.

Again her father said nothing, so she yelled, "We were walking near the baseball field."

When her father completed his turn back into the park, Ruth was not surprised that he pulled over to the curb. He turned to look to her, his eyes unutterably sad.

"Oh Ruthie," he sighed. "I am so sorry you saw us."

"I don't understand," she mumbled.

"Your mother and I have not lived as man and wife for years," he began, immediately sensing his daughter's confusion. "Do you have any idea what I mean?" he asked her.

"I think so," she muttered, adding, "You don't kiss anymore...."

"Men and women do more than kiss, my sweet. Hasn't your mother talked to you about this?" he asked. "Never mind. We can talk about it another time."

"Why not?" she asked him. Her question clearly necessitated a reply, though Simon dearly wished he could change the subject.

Again he sighed. "I suppose your mother would say it's because I am a brute," he began.

His shocked daughter interrupted. "But that's not true!"

Neither father nor daughter knew how to continue so Ruth asked, "What would you say?"

"That your mama does not like that part of married life," he replied.

"I would like it!" she declared, feeling a traitor to her mother, though she wouldn't learn for many years what she and her father were really talking about. At that her father ruffled her wind-blown hair. "I truly hope so, Ruth. It is a wonderful part of adult life." Although she was dying to ask him what that part entailed besides kissing, her instincts told her that having such a discussion at the side of the road was not the best idea. She didn't object when he cranked the motor with his foot, and again took their familiar route through the park and back to their apartment. No one was home when they entered their foyer. Ruth immediately headed for the kitchen to slide the sliced roast into the oven above the potatoes, surprised when her father followed. He usually read his afternoon paper after work and rarely helped prepare a meal, although he did often dry the evening dinner dishes, or scrub out a particularly nasty-looking pot.

When he was standing beside her, and had handed her the tomatoes, radishes, and red onion for their dinner salad, Ruth's next words almost brought him to his knees.

"I suppose that's why Mama wanted to abort me," she said.

"Oh Ruthie! Did Mama tell you that?" he asked her, unable to keep his voice from trembling.

"No," she replied, staring into his eyes. "I overheard her yell those words at you when you were fighting, a long time ago."

"Do you have any idea what that means?" Simon asked. He couldn't even bring himself to repeat the dreadful word. That his wife would have wanted to subject herself, and him, to such a thing had been horror enough.

"Not really. Just that I wouldn't have been born," Ruth sighed.

"I am so glad you were, Ruthie. You are the light of my life," her father told her. "You do know that, don't you?"

Her smile spread from one side of her face to the other. "I'm glad, Papa. You are my light as well."

Her words and the look in her eyes, given the topic of conversation, were too much to bear. Simon could not remember the last time anything had brought him to tears.

"I'm sorry Papa," Ruth whispered, her distress palpable. Simon wrapped her in his arms, not giving a thought to the appropriateness of the gesture.

"You don't have to be sorry for anything, Ruthie. It is I who should be apologizing for causing you pain. That is the last thing I wanted to do."

They held each other for some minutes, and then Simon asked her how he could help her prepare the salad, because Adelaide was due home in fifteen minutes. Since Ruth had heard her mother say the same words many times over the years, she, too, said, "Go read your paper, Papa. I can finish this in no time."

Before he left the kitchen, Simon turned to Ruth, whose back was to him as she bent over the cutting board. Holly would owe her one huge favor, she was thinking as she peeled and sliced the cucumber.

"Ruth. That fight had nothing to do with you. When Mama thought she didn't want to have a second child, she had no idea how wonderful you would turn out to be." That was all he could manage as he grabbed his paper from the kitchen table and stumbled down the hallway to the living room. By the time Holly burst into the apartment after her rehearsal, the table was set, and dinner was in the oven waiting for Adelaide to come home as well.

That evening Simon told Addie that he wanted to tuck his daughters in, a nightly ritual she usually performed, especially when one of the girls had to prepare their evening meal because of her rehearsal. He said goodnight to Holly first, listening to a story about her rehearsal and the play her drama group would be presenting. Usually he relished Holly's stories, but this evening he was anxious to make sure their earlier conversation had not upset Ruth. She was sitting up in bed when he entered her room. By the time the girls had become teen-agers, Simon and Addie had moved to a larger flat in their building, one flight farther upstairs. Both parents were more than willing to walk the extra flight since it meant that each of their daughters would finally have a room of her own. Simon had talked his wife into allowing each of them to choose a paint color, and to otherwise decorate their rooms to suit their individual style. Ruth's room was covered with posters of her favorite writers as well as the covers of several contemporary magazines.

When he sat down beside her Ruth grinned the mischievous smile that had always made his heart sing. "Mama would have made a good nun," she quipped. Both father and daughter could not keep their laughter from erupting, though Simon had no idea what he would tell his wife they had been laughing about. "If she wasn't Jewish," he grinned. This set them both off again. When the last of the giggles had receded, Simon leaned down and took his daughter in his arms. "I wish I didn't agree with you, my sweet. But I suppose I do," he admitted.

"It's a shame women can only be homemakers, Papa. Mama would have been so much happier on her own," she suggested. Simon was amazed at the wisdom this sixteen year old possessed.

"Yes it is," he readily agreed, although he had never thought about it before. He could imagine Adelaide singing with more than one group, building a career of her own, singing at Carnegie Hall, and earning a living. He was startled to realize that his wife would have been a much happier person if this had been her life. "Perhaps by the time you are a woman, there will be more opportunities for women like your mama," he mused aloud. "Women with either brains or talent."

"Or women who have both," came his daughter's quick response.

Again he enfolded her in his arms. "Yes," he smiled. "Women who have both. Like you."

"I don't have talent," Ruth said, looking up at her father with some surprise.

"What do you think your writing is?" he asked her.

Ruth looked genuinely surprised. 'Oh. I hadn't thought about that."

"You should," Simon found himself suggesting. "And you should pursue writing as a career when you graduate from college."

"I thought I might have to go right to work when I graduate," Ruth murmured with some sadness.

"Not on my life!" her father replied. His heart ached as he saw her glance at him with absolute longing.

"I'm a junior. I guess I could look at some City College catalogues in the library," she said, looking both serious and excited at the same time.

"Why don't you see if you can bring some of them home so we can go through them together to see what they offer," her father suggested.

The feelings this suggestion aroused in her were wondrous. It meant she would be able to spend hours with her father, just the two of them, pouring over the catalogues. At the end of the process she would ask the school guidance counselor for some applications and bring those home as well. That would mean even more time with her father as he helped her fill out the applications, rereading her essays and making suggestions. A world was opening up for her that she had never imagined. Both college and a life with her father that was separate from anyone else in their little family. She found herself hoping that her sister would be so busy with her own life at school as well as her rehearsals that she wouldn't notice.

"Daddy," she began and then plunged ahead, the only way she knew she would be able to ask the question. "Are you happy?"

His daughter could not have asked a question that would have surprised Simon more. He knew his answer would not satisfy her inquisitive mind, or quell her concern for him. "I haven't thought about it," he replied anyway, and then continued. "I am very happy to have both you and your sister in my life, and have been since you were each born."

"Papa!" groaned Ruth.

"It's true. Nothing gives me more joy than an afternoon like this, Ruth. Both the conversation and watching you begin to prepare our meal, though I still think I could have helped," he added with a grin. "I bet I would have been good at it."

"I think you're good at everything you do, Papa," Ruth blurted.

"Would that everyone in my life thought that," her father quipped, and then noticed her expression. He had not been thinking about Adelaide. "Sweetheart. About your mother," he began.

"You don't have to explain anything, Papa," Ruth interrupted him, afraid, perhaps, of what he might say. Her voice trembled, which irritated her no end.

"Actually there is a great deal I love about your mama, my sweet."

Ruth was too startled to interrupt, and besides, she wanted to know what else her father would say.

"She has an amazing talent, Ruthie. If we lived in a different time, she would be giving concerts in Carnegie Hall. She has convictions about many parts of life, and is actually looking for a church…well, not exactly a church, but a place we could go as a family to look at the spiritual parts of life. Certainly for a singer spirituality is an important part of performing, or so your mama says, and she's found an organization called The Society for Ethical Culture in Manhattan."

Ruth could not help but comment on this last piece of information. "God has never been important to us before!" she said, which made Simon laugh aloud.

"I don't think Ethical Culture is about God. It is about how human beings treat one another, and how they connect with spirit, their own and the spirit that resides in the people they love," he explained.

When Ruth didn't respond for several moments, he said, "That seems interesting to me, my sweet. How about you?"

"Yes, it does in a way."

"Is that so hard to admit, Ruthie? That Mama might have a good idea here and there?" he teased.

Ruth looked away from her father, because she felt ashamed.

Simon put his arm around her shoulders and suggested, "It might be easier to be around your mother if you could acknowledge the parts of her you admire."

She nodded, and then closed the book she had been reading, and stuffed it back into her book bag. "I know you're right, Papa, and I will try. I just want more for you, more for us all." She turned to look at him, clearly embarrassed by what she had just said.

"I have tried to make up for some of what's missing," her father replied, sighing. This was such a painful subject that he had never broached it with either of his daughters before.

"The redhead makes up for some of it for you," Ruth quietly suggested with newfound understanding as she moved over to her bed, and turned down the covers.

Simon felt his heart expand. This daughter was truly an amazingly insightful person. "We have to accept what we have been given, and find ways to make up for what we haven't," he replied with some hesitation. "I don't know if that is right, but it is what I have come to believe. And you may be too young to truly understand it."

"I think I do understand, but it still makes me sad."

"Me too," he agreed, adding. "Marriage is a funny institution."

"Do you think anyone finds all that they need with one person?" Ruth asked him with quiet intensity. "I really enjoy Greg, especially our conversations, but kissing him is out of the question. The idea kind of makes me queasy."

"Then he is definitely not the one you should be kissing, especially if you haven't kissed anyone else," he replied, smiling as he gently stroked her arm.

Then Ruth, ever the imp, grinned up at him. "I think I'll start looking around Evander Childs to find the right person for that."

Father and daughter were still sitting on Ruth's bed grinning at one another when Adelaide knocked on the door. When her mother complimented her on the brisket she had prepared, saying, "It's almost as good as mine, Ruth. You will be a fine cook some day," Ruth could not believe her ears. Then her mother continued, "The potatoes were crisp on the outside and soft inside, which is not easy to do. I am very pleased." Ruth was so startled she could only mumble her thanks. Her father gave her foot a little nudge and smiled at her, so she told her mother she had learned it all from watching her. Adelaide seemed very pleased, but Ruth hardly noticed. What was transpiring with her father was something she wanted to hold on to, hoarding it like a particularly juicy piece of fruit.

Before she left Ruth's bedroom, Addie said, "You know, I think it's time for you to learn how to make yeast cake, and I was thinking of making some on Saturday because we don't have a rehearsal."

Simon could tell that his daughter was thrilled. She had wanted to learn how to bake for several years, and had even asked her mother, but Adelaide had always told her she was too young. "Oh Mama, that would be wonderful. I would so like to learn how to bake, and eventually, become as good a baker as you are!"

Adelaide, who was not used to receiving compliments from either of her daughters, awkwardly patted Ruth's shoulder. "Then we can begin that task on Saturday."

When Holly piped up from her own bedroom, "I want to learn too!" Ruth blurted, "Don't you have a rehearsal?" and then felt ashamed. She really didn't want to share either parent with her more popular sister. That stopped Holly in her tracks.

"Well, yes," she remembered. "But I would be home by one o'clock. Couldn't you wait till then?"

When Adelaide said she didn't think that would be a problem, Ruth was disappointed but thought she hid it well. When her father squeezed her shoulder as he stood up, she was afraid she would start to cry. He understood! Her father understood what she was feeling, and he cared. What an absolutely marvelous day Wednesday had turned out to be. A day she would remember for the rest of her life, and relish whenever she felt blue.

* * *

When he had become a sophomore, Max had stopped by the only drug store within walking distance of Elizabethport, and asked the pharmacist if he could apprentice with him after the end of his school day. The boy had known he would have to save money of his own if he were going to ever fulfill his dream of becoming a doctor, and believed that working for the old man who had been the family's pharmacist for years would serve a double purpose. He could earn money, and also learn about the medical profession. Of course Noah and Yetta had said they would help him as much as they could, but Nathan was only a year behind him, and he had made it clear that he very much wanted to attend law school.

When Nathan became a sophomore he asked his brother if he thought he should get a job too. Max told him that was a good idea so he also could save money to help with his college tuition. If both boys were able to pay for their first year of advanced schooling, it would be an amazing boon to their younger sisters. Nell would have loved to attend teacher's college, which was out of the question now that she was married, and although Beck seemed content to work at the factory, she was quite bright. Min, who was not yet in high school, might want to attend teacher's college. If the remaining Unger children could attend a college of some kind, the brothers knew it would mean the world to their parents. When Noah objected to his younger son looking for a job, the boys sat him down and talked about why they both had agreed this would be a good idea. If Noah hadn't acquiesced, they would have brought in the big gun: Jules. Both Noah and Yetta had kept their dreams for their daughters to themselves, but they had certainly discussed them with one another. Noah could not disagree with his sons' reasoning. He and Yetta knew they had raised good, responsible and caring boys. They could not have been more proud.

Nathan found a job easily with a man who practiced law in downtown Elizabeth. He had a number of clients from the Port, and was pleased to have a young man working for him who lived there. He believed the boy would bring him more clients, which he did. He also admired Nathan's swift mind and keen intelligence, and within a few months was asking the young man his opinion on many issues, including some knotty legal ones. Without being asked, the attorney offered to write Nathan a recommendation for Rutgers, his own alma mater. Given the boy's high school grades as well as the attorney's letter, his entry into law school was all but assured. Max had told his parents that he had already saved enough from his part time job to pay for his first year of medical school. Though Yetta offered to make a celebratory meal for her sons, Beck and Nell shooed her out of the kitchen, suggesting she put her feet up instead. She had already finished a 10-hour workday in her shop, but still needed to allow her daughters to pick up some of the household load. Noah poured a rare glass of sherry for himself, Yetta, and the two boys, telling his daughters that they, too, should join them in the parlor when the meal was in the oven.

Max's relationship with Teresa was even more complicated than it had been the year before. The previous week Teresa had taken his hand and placed it on her breast, which had come as a total shock although it was something Max had been longing to do for months. Their kissing was marvelous, but it was not enough, a fact that shamed Max and made him think he must not be a good person, the person his parents had raised him to be. What had happened that week had been so troubling to Max that he had not yet tried to talk to Teresa about his feelings. Of course he had left his hand there, and even squeezed a little bit. When her nipple rose to meet his fingers through the fabric of her blouse, he quickly removed his hand and Teresa looked down at her feet, utterly mortified.

The following afternoon Jonah, the co-captain of Max's baseball team, sat down beside him in the school cafeteria. He, too, was dating a Catholic girl although his family was Jewish. His parents were even less religious than Noah's, who rarely went to shul except for Passover, Chanukah and other significant holidays. Jonah said he thought he and Max should talk about their situations, since they were so similar.

"Even though my folks are free-thinkers about issues like this, I know they would not be happy about my dating a shiksa," he said with a smile that belied the feelings beneath it. At first Max pretended ignorance–he and Teresa were just friends–but Jonah shook his head and sighed, "That kind of attitude isn't going to help any of us, and besides, it isn't true." Apparently Teresa had confided in his girlfriend. Max was startled at the revelation because he and Teresa had spent so much energy keeping their relationship secret all year. Jonah explained that 'women needed to talk' and neither girl had had anyone else they could confide in. It was good, he explained, that they had found one another. Max, who realized this was true, relaxed a little bit. Then Jonah brought up the issue of sex, which Max was concerned about as well, although he wouldn't have acknowledged that aloud. He couldn't believe that Jonah, whom he didn't even know that well, would bring up this subject and bring it up that afternoon.

Jonah thought that Max looked like a deer caught in the headlights although he had never even seen such a thing. He had read the phrase in a book his English teacher had assigned. "Max," he said quietly. "I'm not comfortable talking about this either, but like the girls, I have to talk to someone."

"I don't know how to talk about it," Max whispered, close to tears. It was shameful enough that he and Teresa had progressed as far as they had. Talking about it to anyone, even her, had been beyond his capabilities until now.

"Me neither," the other boy agreed. "But are you willing to try?"

Max thought about it, and realized it was a good idea. He also knew he had to give it some thought before he agreed. "Let me talk to Teresa first. I can't say anything to you without doing that."

"And I will talk to Cynthia. I was so nervous about doing this I didn't even think about that," Jonah replied. Then he took an enormous breath, as if his life depended on it. "I can't believe I did this."

Max looked the other boy directly in the eye, "I'm glad you did. I think I'll tell her I need to talk to someone because I know so little, which is true, and that I won't say anything directly about her," he told the other boy.

"That's a good idea. I'll do the same thing. She would be mortified if she thought I was talking to you or anyone else about her, especially about … well, you know."

"Yes, I certainly do," agreed Max, letting his breath out in a whoosh. He hadn't even realized he'd been holding it.

"Let me know when you're ready. There's so much I don't know and I feel so inept," Jonah then admitted with some embarrassment. "I don't know who else to ask."

As soon as Max nodded, Jonah picked up his lunch tray, threw away his garbage, deposited the tray on top of the others already piled at the end of the food line, and left the cafeteria. By the time he disappeared around the corner, Max had decided to approach his older brother Jules, who would certainly have advise to give about this troubling new problem. He would also be able to explain some of the rudiments of sex, which their father would never have been able to discuss in a million years. On his way to Jules' office, Max began to wonder how Teresa would feel about his speaking to his brother about the progression of their sex life, and decided he could not take that kind of liberty with Teresa's privacy. Jules would have known immediately why Max was asking him these questions, and understood that their relationship had progressed further than he had imagined. Max did think he could talk to Nathan about some of the problems surrounding the issue, and do so without breaching a trust. He might not have had a steady girlfriend yet, but his exploits must have taught him something. And then there was Holly, the girl who had caught his fancy more than a year before. Max had been so preoccupied with his own problems, he hadn't thought to ask his brother if he had even asked her out.

He headed back the way he had come, but before reaching the high school, turned down the side street where Nathan's law firm was located. Although his younger brother loved to call himself a researcher, Max knew he was really a glorified clerk. Of course he had never said this to Nathan because he felt no need to puncture his brother's fragile ego. Despite the fact that Nate often bragged, especially about his job, Max knew him too well not to understand the insecurity that lay beneath his bravado. If Nathan was not admitted to Rutgers law in the spring with at least a partial scholarship, he would not be able to attend beyond the first year. His classes, and the studying he would have to do to maintain a superior school record, would more than take up every waking hour of his day and preclude even a part time job. Max hesitated before entering the law firm's lobby, but then pushed open the door. If Nate was too busy, or one of the senior partners was working with him, Max would wait until the evening or the next day to talk to him.

Max found Nathan filing papers in the storage room at the end of the long hallway where the five partners had their offices. Nate seemed surprised to see him, but also pleased.

"Max'l! What are you doing here?" he blurted, and then didn't give his brother a chance to respond. "I'm working on the most interesting case," he continued, and then launched into a description of voir dire, habeas corpus, and other legal matters he had been learning about. Nate possessed a quick, curious mind, and listened to everything that went on around him as he moved from one partner's office to the next, delivering the papers they needed. In this way he had already learned a great deal about how the legal profession worked, things most first year law students would not know. He assumed this knowledge would hold him in good stead in law school and beyond and was, of course, correct about this.

The brothers filled two paper cups with coffee and sat down in the small courtyard in the center of the office building. Although any of the partners could have seen him taking this small break, Nate was not concerned. He was the hardest worker that had ever filed papers for the firm, and had been told so numerous times. If anyone saw them, they would know something important was transpiring or the young man would not be sitting in the courtyard with his brother.

"I haven't told anyone this, Nate, but I think I need to talk to you about it now," Max began. Nathan looked curious, since he and his older brother usually told each other everything.

"OK," he said.

"I've been seeing Teresa McNally," Max began. When he saw the startled look on his brother's face, he almost lost his courage. "We've been meeting after school and going to that coffee shop that no one goes to 'cause it looks kind of seedy…."

"Off of Broad Street," Nate replied.

"Yes, that's the one." Max was stumped. Even with Nate, who was closer to him than any other human being, he had no idea what to say next. He knew what he wanted to say, and ask, but not how to begin such a conversation.

"How long have you been seeing her, as more than a friend?" Nate asked him.

"I don't know…all year?" Max admitted, almost stuttering, it was so difficult for him to get the words out of his mouth.

"And you've never told me?" Nathan was so shocked he rested his right hand on his chest, as if he needed to protect his heart.

"I'm so sorry. Neither of us told anyone, because we were both so afraid of our parents finding out," Max tried to explain.

"You know me better than that!" Nate turned to his brother, clearly furious.

"I really am sorry."

Both young men sat side by side, both now at a loss for words.

"I want to take her to the prom!" Max blurted.

"Oh. Wow. I don't think you can do that without Mama and Papa finding out," Nathan said with dismay.

"I know. That's why I said I needed to talk to you. Or one of the reasons," Max said, feeling as if he would never be able to take his next breath.

"What else do you need to talk to me about?" Nathan asked, obviously surprised there could be anything else. He waited with some impatience for his older brother to explain.

"We've been kissing in the park for awhile now…" Max began, Nate interrupting despite himself, "Awhile?"
'Yes. For months. But last week she took my hand and put it…she put it…." Max was again at a loss for words.

"I get the picture," Nate groaned. "And?"

"I can't ask Papa about sex," Max said.

"Max!" Another quick groan, then, "I probably don't know much more than you do."

"Any little bit would help," Max tried to smile to lighten the mood.

"Girls like to have their nipples rubbed, but very gently," Nate offered. "I can't believe we're talking about this at all, let alone here."

"I can't either. Have you ever reached under a girl's sweater?" Max asked, feeling very brazen.

"Once. It was pretty thrilling!" Both boys grinned from ear to ear.

"I still don't know if I would have the courage to try that," Max admitted.

Nate came back with a quick, and sensible rejoinder. "She put your hand there. Imagine how scared she must have felt doing that!"

"That's true...."

"I can see why you couldn't talk to Papa about this," Nate said, poking his brother in the arm.

"Well, that brings us back to the biggest problem: the Catholic part. You know, she doesn't go to church every Sunday because sometimes she has to babysit for her cousins."

"I don't think that would make a very big different [once] to Mama and Papa," Nate replied with some asperity. "Do you want the truth?"

"Yes, of course I do," Max quickly responded.

"I think you should stop seeing her. You'll both get over it by the time the prom even rolls around. It's months away," Nathan said, the compassion in his demeanor softening the actual words.

"No. I can't do that to her. She's a really decent person, and I think she'd be devastated. We've already started talking about the prom," Max replied with more determination than his younger brother had ever even suspected he possessed.

That silenced both boys, who were obviously distressed by the tenor the conversation had taken. Nate tried to feel what his brother was feeling, or what he, himself, would want to do in the same situation. His parents had immigrated to this country so they would no longer be persecuted. No one in the family had given a thought to the nature of the country their parents had chosen as their final destination, or its unspoken rules. America was truly a melting pot, Irish, Catholics, Jews, Gentiles, and immigrants of every denomination residing in Elizabeth alone. How could Nathan urge his brother to give up someone he was more than entitled to date, or even love, in the land where they had both been born?

"Maybe you should ask Mama if you could invite a friend to dinner. Neither of our parents would ask her about her religion, not at the dinner table, and not the first time they meet her. At least I don't think they would," he suggested.

"She would be a nervous wreck!" Max exclaimed.

"Probably. But we could figure out some topics we could talk about that Mama and Papa would enjoy, and tell her beforehand what they might be," Nate proposed. "At least if you're hell bent on continuing with this."

"I am. She's really a wonderful person," Max replied.

"Maybe she'd convert," Nate quipped.

"Very funny."

Nate put his arms around his brother's rather narrow shoulders. "I will give this some thought and see what else I can come up with. You too, and then we can put our heads together tonight."

"The prom is in a few months," Max moaned.

"Then you better start thinking! If they've gotten to know her by then, maybe it won't be an issue if you want to take her to the prom. And I have to get back to work. My bosses will start to think I'm a slouch," Nate said, using a joke to ease the tension between them.

The next afternoon Max met Teresa at the coffee shop. She could tell immediately that something was bothering him and asked him what was wrong.

"I had a long conversation with Nathan yesterday. I went to the office where he works so no one in the family would see us talking," he began.

"You told him about us!" Teresa interrupted with some distress.

"Yes, I did. If we are going to keep seeing each other, I think it's time we figured out how to tell our parents," he replied quietly, his tone making it obvious that this was something he had been thinking about for some time.

Teresa looked miserable, but she agreed. "I don't like sneaking either. I haven't been sleeping well for more than a month."

Max took Teresa's hand, and was quiet until the girl behind the counter took their order. Both he and Teresa ordered strawberry ice cream this time, his with hot fudge, hers without. Both knew they needed sustenance if they were going to discuss telling their respective parents that they had been 'stepping out'.

When the waitress walked back behind the counter to fill the order, Max continued with some embarrassment, "I have no idea how to do this. But Nathan thinks that if my parents get to know you, they won't be as upset when I invite you to the prom," he stammered. Then he added, "He suggested I ask Momma if I can invite a friend to dinner."

When Teresa looked horrified, Max said, "They'd never ask about your religion at the dinner table!"

"That's true. But when would we tell them, and tell my parents, that we're actually dating? And that I'm Catholic," she asked.

Max paled. "I have no idea. We could try the dinner invitation first, and then go from there."

"I could ask you to dinner too. I have told them there's a smart boy I have great conversations with about school stuff," she mused. "I could also write down some possibilities on how to broach the religion part with our families on paper tonight, and bring them to school tomorrow."

Max sighed with relief. Teresa did write well. "That's a really good idea," he agreed. Then he asked if she wanted him to do the same. Even if his writing style was not stellar, some of his ideas might be worth a look. Both were relieved when they left the coffee shop that afternoon, although they both did so with heavy hearts. Neither looked forward to the task awaiting them, or the distress their revelations would be certain to cause their parents.

* * *

When Adelaide asked Ruth to go the corner store to pick up a few things she had forgotten to get at the vegetable stand, Ruth was surprised that Holly grabbed her jacket saying, "We'll go together Mama. It sounds like there might be too much for Ruthie to carry on her own," although that was not true. Both mother and daughter were so startled by Holly's suggestion, neither thought to say so.

"Al has been kissing me when he walks me home from school, and it's very sloppy," Holly blurted as soon as they reached the street. "It doesn't happen every day because Tuesday and Thursday he has a history class at Hunter." She almost added, 'thank God', but refrained. Sharing these things with Ruth was not something she had ever considered before. But her need to know prevailed this time. "I know there's a way to kiss that would feel better," she added.

Ruth turned to her in total dismay. "I don't know anything about kissing," she frowned.

"But you've been seeing Greg for over a year," Holly argued. "You have to know more than I do."

"Greg and I are just friends," Ruth explained, although he had kissed her a few times. She had liked it, and wished he would continue. But this was not something she wanted to share with her sister, who she suspected would find a way to hurt her some time in the future with whatever information she imparted when she was angry with Ruth, and not in need of any help.

Holly sighed. "I should at least get to enjoy the experience. Especially since he's pressuring me to sleep with him." Holly sounded more exasperated than distressed, and didn't notice her sister's startled expression. She added, "I like it when he strokes my breasts," which completely shocked Ruth. She was very good at keeping her feelings from traveling all the way to her face, which rarely showed what was going on inside of her, except, perhaps, with their father. When she could compose herself Ruth finally replied.

"I bet it's something he's learned about at Hunter," Ruth mused, almost as if she were talking to herself.

The very idea horrified her sister. "Do you think so? That would mean he's talked to someone about me! How could he do that," Holly moaned. It never entered her sister's mind that Al might have been learning in a more direct way, which amused Ruth.

"Have you talked to Gloria or Judith about any of this?" she asked her. Gloria and Judith were Holly's best friends, popular girls who would have nothing to do with the intellectual Ruth.

This idea was even more distressing to Holly. "Are you kidding? No one in that crowd goes past kissing, or if they do they don't tell anyone. If they talked about it, they sure wouldn't be in the popular click anymore!"

Ruth should have realized this. She well knew that the line between popular kids, athletes, smart kids, and the 'fast' crowd were drawn in oil paint and couldn't be altered in any way.

"I don't have anyone else to talk to, Ruth. I promise if you and I start to talk about the issue of sex with our boyfriends – don't' deny it; I saw you and Greg kissing when I walked through the park a few days ago – I won't be mean to you anymore," Holly begged.

"I don't think I believe you," Ruth replied. She honestly could not imagine her sister treating her with respect, let alone kindness.

Holly grabbed her arm. "I know I've been awful. I've been awful for years. But I can change. I promise. Please!" she begged.

The two paid for the items their mother wanted and slowly began the two-block walk back to their apartment, staring at each other.

"OK. If we're going to try this, we have to come up with a set of rules about how to talk to each other, what we say and what we can share with anyone else about these conversations," Ruth suggested. Holly readily agreed. Then Ruth said, grinning, "And now you have to tell me what it feels like, what you're doing. If I knew a little bit more, I don't believe I'd be so frightened."

"What are you frightened of?" Holly asked, her curiosity aroused.

"I'm not really sure. Maybe that I won't like it, but I'll end up feeling bad about myself anyway. Or, maybe it would hurt, if…." Ruth mumbled, speaking so quietly Holly could barely hear her.

Finally she figured it out and replied, "Whatever we've done certainly didn't hurt."

Ruth persisted, "And that was…?" When Holly didn't respond immediately, Ruth continued. 'Now that I know you've been petting, I think you might have done more than that!"

"We have not slept together! If we had, why would he be pressuring me?" Holly demanded with absolute fury.

"Oh. I'd forgotten that's how this discussion began. Well, I still bet he's touched you…down there and I want to know what it's like. The very idea of it makes me clench my knees," Ruth blurted.

Holly started to laugh; finally Ruth joined her. "That is a very funny image," Holly managed. "Do you mean when he might try it or when you're thinking about it?" she asked with a grin. That set both girls into gales of laughter, which only stopped when they reached their front door, which was opened by their father, who had just gotten home.

"Whatever it is, it sounds pretty funny. Let me in on the secret," he quipped.

When he saw the horrified expression on the faces of both girls, he added, "Just kidding. Dinner will be on the table soon," and closed the door behind them. He was delighted that his daughters were enjoying one another. That was a rare occurrence, something he had never understood. He thought both of his daughters were unusual, and could actually benefit from sharing their very different perspectives on life with one another.

As soon as he had retreated to his favorite chair in the living room, Ruth insisted, "Quick. Tell me. Please."

Holly believed their father would be horrified if he learned what she and Al had actually been doing. Though Holly, as well as Ruth, had suspected for a long time that their father had dalliances with other women. That did not mean he would want either of his daughters to experiment with sex beyond simple necking before they were married. Still, there was a lot she wanted to learn, and she knew she couldn't do so from either one of their parents. Talking with Ruth might really be the only solution to her own problems in that arena. So she whispered, in case their father was listening behind his newspaper, "At first he would stroke my breasts on the outside of my sweater. It made my nipples all tingly."

"Was that good or bad?" Ruth whispered right back.

"*I* liked it," Holly giggled, adding when she could stop, "It certainly beat kissing him!"

Ruth grinned, and replied, "It sounds like I'd like it too. I can tell there's more. Come on. Give."

With a very broad smile Holly replied. 'It felt even better when he took my sweater off."

"What about your bra?" Ruth hissed.

After a slight hesitation, Holly hissed back, "That came off too."

"Oh my," Ruth sighed, adding, "I still don't know if I'd want Greg to do any of that."

"Do you like the way he kisses?" Holly asked.

"Yes. It's very soft and gentle and not sloppy at all," she replied, her smile at the memory indicating that she had enjoyed the experience very much indeed.

"Does he shove his tongue into your mouth?"

Startled, Ruth replied, "He doesn't ever shove it into my mouth. He kind of teases my lips with it, and then I open my mouth a little and then his tongue kind of plays with my tongue."

"That sounds wonderful," Holly sighed.

"Maybe you can teach Al," Ruth suggested.

"How would I do that?" Holly asked her. Ruth had to think about her answer.

"Well, when he pushes his tongue into your mouth, you could pull back and tell him you've been thinking about this kissing business and want to try it another way, and then suggest he do what Greg does," Ruth suggested.

> You wrote earlier that they each have their own bedroom!

"That sounds scary. It might make him angry." Holly paused and then actually gave her sister a pat on her foot, the only part of her body she could reach across the divide between their beds in their bedroom. "But that's a good idea. I think I could at least try it."

Ruth grinned at her. "Then you'd like both things you're doing and wouldn't that be nifty. Besides, he doesn't go to Evander anymore, so how would anyone know?"

"If anyone does find out, I'll know how," Holly warned her sister.

"I would never do that, Holly. Never. This conversation is great, and I hope we can have more of them," Ruth said with utter seriousness.

"Me too, " Holly admitted. Both girls were wondering if this sister thing wasn't so bad after all, though neither ever learned what the other had been thinking.

"I'm not attracted to Greg, but I sure like him a lot, maybe even love him," Ruth haltingly explained.

"Do you think that kind of feeling could grow, the more you get to know someone," Holly asked her.

"I don't know. Maybe. I wish there was someone we could ask." Suddenly Ruth looked sad.

"That's something I could ask Gloria," Holly offered.

Ruth's smile was immediate. "That would be great."

"I'm attracted to Al, but I really hate kissing him, " Holly admitted very quietly, not as much because their father might still be outside their door, but because it felt like a terrible thing to say out loud.

"Being attracted to someone is that fluttery feeling you get when you look at him, right?" Ruth asked her.

"I think so. And that you just feel drawn to the person, almost like a physical pull," Holly concurred. "I'll write down some of the rules for these conversations during my study period, and I'll give them to you tomorrow night."

Shaking her head in agreement, Ruth said, "I can do that too. Wow, can you believe we're doing this?"

Both girls were shaking their heads 'no', but both wanted to keep having conversations like the one they had been having. "I am glad we talked like this Holly, and that you want to do it again."

"Me too." Then Holly added, "You could try letting him go under your blouse to see if you like it. And Al has touched me down there, but never without my panties on."

"And?" came Ruth's breathless reply.

"That felt pretty good too," her sister giggled. Both girls were still smiling at each other when Simon knocked on their door and came in to say goodnight.

"It actually feels steamy in here," he said, cocking his head to look at each girl in turn. At that, both sisters burst out laughing. Simon joined in, with a pretty good idea what they had been giggling about. He was relieved. Sex was not a subject his wife would ever be able to broach, and Simon was not sure it was something he should be talking to daughters about either. Neither could know very much about the subject, but if they were talking about it, he was sure they'd figure out a way to learn more. At least he hoped they didn't know very much yet.

If they knew more than he suspected, he hoped they'd have the courage to come to him for advise or needed help, but had no idea how to suggest that. Neither Holly nor Ruth fell asleep quickly that evening. Both had much too much to think about, especially opening up to one another in the way they had. Ruth thought it was a miracle. Holly was just surprised, though pleasantly so.

CHAPTER SIXTEEN

On Saturday Adelaide found Ruth at her little desk in the bedroom she shared with her sister and suggested she come into the kitchen. When she asked where Holly was, Ruth explained that she was doing schoolwork in the living room. The older girl liked to listen to music when she did her homework, but Ruth did not, so they rarely completed their assignments in the same room. Adelaide was a bit surprised that she hadn't known this, but didn't give it much thought. How her daughters completed their school assignments was not her business, unless a teacher told her or Simon that one of the girls was developing lax study habits. She assumed both daughters feared the wrath of their parents if they fell behind in school and that neither would tempt fate, at least in that way.

Ruth was delighted to discover that her mother was preparing to make yeast cakes, famous in their neighborhood for melting in the mouth. Every year when she had asked her mother if she could help, Adelaide had told her she was too young for this task. Holly had been included a couple of years before, which had been a bit galling since she had never volunteered to help with kitchen tasks, but Ruth pushed that ungenerous thought from her mind. Holly didn't look particularly pleased by their mother's invitation, which was a plus, and another ungenerous thought. As Adelaide prepared the dough, which had been rising in the refrigerator overnight, Ruth began to mix the various fillings, with Holly supposedly assisting her. In truth the older girl stared into space absent mindedly, sometimes contributing if Ruth asked her directly to measure out two teaspoons of cinnamon for the cottage cheese filling, or take out a lemon from the ice box. Holly finally poured the pureed prunes, which their mother had already boiled, strained, and mashed, into a bowl so the mixture could easily be spooned into the little pastry squares and then folded. Adelaide's poppy seed filling was already in its own bowl on the kitchen counter. Ruth didn't like mohn, but her father did, so Adelaide usually used the poppy seed concoction in a quarter of the yeast cakes.

When Adelaide asked Holly to kneed the dough she had been working with at the kitchen counter, Ruth couldn't help but feel annoyed again. That's what she got for being helpful and asking how she should prepare the cottage cheese; she was obviously already busy. Holly, who was not, was the logical choice for this new task. Of course Ruth would have preferred to knead the dough, which seemed a much more difficult and essential job. Noticing her frown, Adelaide patted Ruth on the back, assuring the younger girl that she and her sister would be taking turns with the dough, since kneading was tiring work. Within seconds, Holly was groaning with the effort, so Ruth pushed her aside and took over. Startled at how hard it was to push the dough down and around the large bowl, she nevertheless was determined to work the dough longer than her sister had, and not to utter a sound. When Adelaide pushed her aside to take over, she burst out laughing. At first Ruth was insulted, but then Holly managed to sputter, "Your face has flour all over it!" Adelaide pulled her compact from her purse, and opened it for Ruth to see; she could not keep from laughing either. Wiping the flour from her face with the towel their mother always kept on a hook above the sink made the situation worse. After Holly tried to remove the offending spots, Ruth took the towel to her sister's face. Within seconds, all three of them had clown faces, as Adelaide called them in-between guffaws.

Simon came home in the midst of their hilarity, totally bemused by the site of all three of his 'women' covered in flour and laughing together uproariously. Such camaraderie was not a staple of the Liebman household. First last night, and then today: amazing! When Adelaide saw her husband standing in the doorway, she sprang back into motion. "Ruth, wipe down the counter. Holly, put the bowls in the pantry, covered with linen napkins."

"Don't hurry on my account. I can eat dinner whenever you're ready," Simon told them. His smile showed his clear approval of the scene before him. He would have been content to eat after nine if his wife and daughters continued to enjoy their time together.

"The dough will have risen and be ready to cut once we've eaten and cleaned up the kitchen," Adelaide explained to them all. "There's sliced brisket in the pantry, with potatoes and carrots. All we have to do is heat the pot on top of the stove." Keeping her husband waiting, even if he didn't seem to mind, was beyond her capabilities, a trait that her younger daughter carried into her own married life years later.

Their conversation at the dinner table that evening was more lively than usual, even Holly joining the discussion about Ruth's school magazine, and suggesting two topics for future articles, both of which Ruth and her father thought worthwhile. Adelaide's pronouncement that 'Your principal asked me to meet with him last week' came as a complete surprise to everyone at the table.

"Doesn't he like the magazine?" Ruth asked, her voice shaking. She had wanted to be more controversial with the stories she used, but had been persuaded by the other editors to be politic, at least until their journal had become a school staple, one that would continue long after they had all left Evander Childs.

"He thinks it's an amazing accomplishment," Adelaide declared with pride. "I only went to see him yesterday, and both of you disappeared with your homework right after you came home," she continued. Truthfully, Adelaide had become involved with her dinner preparations and completely forgotten about the meeting by the time they had sat down at the table the night before.

"Smart man!" Simon declared, displeased that it had taken a full day for his wife to share this amazing news, but unwilling to tarnish the moment for Ruth. "You've created a marvelous thing, Ruthie, and I'm glad he agrees with us."

Even Holly couldn't help but concur. "My friends are already looking forward to the next issue, and can't wait to read the columns on our school clubs, especially drama!" Of course Holly couldn't keep from touting her own accomplishments in her compliment, but still, no one could deny it was praise.

Blushing profusely, Ruth murmured, "It's something I really enjoy doing."

"I enjoy singing, but that doesn't mean being asked to join the Schola Cantorum wasn't an honor," Adelaide declared. Then she asked, "Have you already written the article for this month, or do you have to write it tonight?"

"I wrote it after school, Mama, before I came home, " Ruth replied, puzzled by the question.

"Good. Then I think we should all go to see that new talking motion picture tonight. The Jazz Singer," she added. Simon, Ruth and Holly all stared at her as if she might need to be committed to a loony bin.

"Don't look at me that way," Adelaide laughed. "It's only 25 cents for a ticket, and tickets for the girls might be less."

"I think it's a fantastic idea," Simon declared. "Do you have any idea when the show begins?"

"Yes," his wife replied, at which point Holly's mouth actually dropped open. "I noticed when I came home this afternoon, but I didn't believe we'd be able to go. It begins in a half hour."

Ruth jumped up from the table. "I can do the dishes in a jiffy."

"What about the dough?" Holly asked, dismayed.

Adelaide airily replied, "I will make the yeast cakes when we get home," laughing at the shocked faces surrounding her at the dinner table.

Her father suggested that if they all helped with the dishes, they would be able to leave the apartment more quickly, a suggestion as surprising as his wife's. They all followed him into the kitchen. By the time they all left the apartment, they were laughing about Ruth's description of the chaos that had accompanied preparation of the first edition of the school paper. Her account was so vivid, all of them felt as if they had actually been in the tiny room allotted for the paper's production.

By the time they all poured out of the subway car and raced up the steps in Manhattan, there was already a long line in front of the movie theater on West 50th Street where the movie was showing. Adelaide declared, "Don't worry. The attendant told me this afternoon that the theater is quite large. I'm sure we'll get in," adding to the amazement the other three felt about this new side of Adelaide.

And indeed they did. The sisters were mesmerized by the singing, their mother by Al Jolson's voice. Simon's pleasure was enhanced by the rapt attention of 'his women' as the movie progressed. But an hour into the amazing spectacle, his attention was also drawn to the screen in front of them.

"Do you think the next talkie will also be in black-face," Ruth whispered quietly.

"Oh no," her mother replied. "That was something that was appropriate for this film. Jolson doesn't always sing in black-face."

"I didn't know you'd even heard of him," Holly declared with some amazement when they left the theater.

"Oh yes. Several of the members of the Schola went to see him in Sinbad years ago," Adelaide said, turning to her husband. "The girls were way too young, and you work so hard I didn't want you to have to give them dinner and put them to bed, so I didn't go with them."

"I wish I could have seen him in that too!" Ruth gushed before her father could respond. "Was he wonderful?"

Holly agreed, and the girls began dissecting all the details of the movie they had just seen as they walked to the subway station. By the time the family was disembarking in the Bronx, they had all replayed the film by talking about it, and had agreed that as soon as another 'talkie' was shown in Manhattan, they would all go to see that one as well.

When Adelaide sighed, "I do hope it's a musical!" the rest of them burst out laughing. "I love music of any kind," she declared, which set them off even more. Finally Holly managed to sputter, "We know that, Mama," which even made Adelaide chuckle. Simon was so engrossed in his own thoughts about the reception he might receive from his wife that evening, given her frame of mind, even he failed to notice that his daughters were vying for his attention with their comments. Nonetheless, when they arrived home everyone was still in very good spirits. And Simon was not disappointed in the boudoir later in the evening.

Several weeks later Ruth was daydreaming in her algebra class, the one class that didn't hold her attention with any regularity, when the office secretary opened the door to the classroom, gesturing to the teacher who quickly stepped to the doorway. "Ruth," she called out. "Could you please come here." Startled, Ruth stood up and began to make her way there when the teacher again raised her voice. "You had better pick up your books, Ruth." Puzzled, Ruth returned to her seat and quickly collected her papers, notebook and books, again making her way to the women waiting in the doorway. When the secretary ushered her outside the room, she was even more startled to find her sister already standing there, holding her own pile of books and papers. Her heart started hammering in her chest: something was clearly wrong, and it must be serious if they had both been called out of their classrooms. The look on Holly's face confirmed her fears.

"Your father has had an accident girls. Your mother would like you both to go to Montefiore Hospital. I'm to give you money for a cab," the secretary explained.

"What kind of accident?" Holly demanded. Ruth was surprised she could speak at all. She certainly would not have been able to utter a word. She was not even sure she was breathing because her chest felt gripped by a vise.

The secretary shook her head. "I'm sorry, Holly. Your mother didn't say."

By the time she called a cab for the girls, and held open the door so they could both slide across the backseat, the sisters were holding hands. Once the door closed, and the cab pulled away from the curb, Holly murmured, "Don't cry. If you start, I will and then I don't think I'll be able to stop."

"I know," Ruth agreed.

"I'm thinking something so horrible I can't believe it," Holly added. At first Ruth is silent, and then she whispered, "You wish it was Daddy who had called…"

"Oh, that's horrible," Holly shuddered, but didn't deny it.

Adelaide was waiting outside as the cab pulled into the space reserved for taxis in front of the hospital, which was somehow even more frightening. When they were both on the sidewalk next to her, she put her arms around their shoulders and pulled them close. Ruth glanced at her sister, the terror she was feeling mirrored in her sister's face. Something was very very wrong.

"Please mama, tell us," Holly demanded. Ruth still felt unable to speak. Whatever would she do without her father?

"Your father has had a heart attack," Adelaide began. Neither of them had any idea what a heart attack even was, though it sounded terrible. Adelaide continued, "The heart stops beating and it can be very painful. If the pain continues, that is a good thing," she added as an afterthought.

"Did Papa's pain last a long time," Ruth asked, finally unable to keep the words back, as if they had a life of their own.

At first their mother did not respond, and then she just shook her head sadly. Holly realized she was holding her breath. 'This could not be happening. It could not,' she thought. Her mother was a stranger; her father, the only parent she had long depended upon. What would she and Ruth do without him? Ruth thought their father must be very seriously ill because they had been told to come to Montefiore. If he were dead, they would have been told to meet their mother at their apartment.

"Daddy must have died instantly." Adelaide spoke so quietly, neither girl was sure she had heard her correctly.

"No!" they cried out in unison. Ruth immediately added, "He can't be dead!"

"It would not have been painful," Adelaide plowed ahead, knowing she had to maintain her composure for her daughters, though inside she was seething. Her husband had collapsed on top of the redhead who was his latest mistress, the same woman the girls had seen on the back of his motorcycle earlier in the fall. Of course since that was something neither daughter had ever shared with her, the park sighting was an insult unknown to Adelaide. Neither Holly nor Ruth realized their mother had been aware of their fathers' peccadillos, and didn't learn that she had until they were adult women themselves.

The next few days passed in a blur for all three of them. Adelaide took care of the funeral arrangements, invited all of their friends back to the apartment afterwards for her famous apple cake and coffee, cleared out her husband's clothes and sundries from their bedroom and bathroom, and arranged for a male cousin to transport them to a local church resale shop. Keeping busy kept her feelings, which were confusing to say the least, at bay, at least for awhile. Even in the midst of all her activities, she was nonetheless surprised at how much she missed Simon. He had always held her at night; she found it difficult to sleep despite her exhaustion because his arms were not soothing her into sleep. They had always discussed important family issues, as well as problems her husband was facing at work because he valued her opinion, acerbic as it sometimes was. Now she realized how significant that part of their marriage had been. She had relied on those late night discussions as much as he had, another surprise. Their sexual life was the only aspect of their marriage that satisfied neither one of them. She still loathed the red-haired woman, and would not have dreamt of inviting her to the funeral. Neither did she have any interest in giving much thought to any of it. After all, what good would it have done at this point to admit how much she had actually loved her husband, and how unwilling she had been to meet him even halfway in their bedroom.

Ruth walked around in a daze. Her father had been the only person in her entire life who had made her feel 'right' and not 'wrong', from the time she had been a boisterous little tomboy until she had entered high school two years before. He had often told her she wouldn't always frighten away the boys because of her intellectual curiosity, but she hadn't believed him. Even the boys she had played baseball with for years still turned away when she passed them in the hallway.

Finally Greg, who was still her closest friend, put his arm around her shoulders as they wandered through Crotona Park and implored her, "Ruth, you can't keep on like this. You have to feel. That is who you are!" At first she just stared at him, and then everything loosened inside her, as if she was exactly like the turbulent stream she and her father had always dipped their toes into when they were at Smith's Farm. Greg led her to a grassy mound in the park, where she sobbed and sobbed uncontrollably, often unable to catch her breath. He held her for what felt like hours. Later he assured her they had only been sitting there for thirty minutes. Although all of her emotions were spent, once the tears stopped she still carried a deep sadness within. Her eyes were the only sign that this was so, and only someone who knew her well would have understood.

"It will take time, sweet Ruth. You have lost the fulcrum of your life. Your father's judgments and feelings informed every action you have ever taken. Now you will learn to rely upon yourself," he suggested with a gentleness that immediately reminded her of her father. Perhaps that was why she had been drawn to Greg in the first place, and not because of shared interests.

"Will I ever feel alright again? And if I do, what will that make me? I can't just give him up with a snap of my fingers, or by rushing around the apartment with a dust mop like my mother, who seems like a madwoman," she mumbled.

"It is what your father would want you to do, Ruth, and you know that," Greg replied.

She took a deep shuddering breath in his arms, and then was still.

"How will I survive until then?" she asked. Although the question sounded ridiculous to her, the feelings behind it were very real, and Greg responded as if it was sensible.

"By going to your classes, putting out another issue of the magazine, by helping your mother, by talking to Holly, though I know you don't want to do that," he said. "I understand that you have a very hard time with her, but Holly has lost her father too. You might actually be able to help one another."

"Yes. I suppose that's true." She paused, and then continued. "Do you think my mother actually loved my father? She really seems to be grieving," Ruth mused with some surprise.

"I suspect your mother is asking herself the same question. From what I've seen, human beings don't understand love very well," he replied.

Ruth took another shuddering breath. "I do love you, Greg. But I also don't know that we will be together forever."

"Don't worry about that now, my sweet. I don't know that we will either. We're both very young, at the start of the journey that will teach us about love," he sadly replied. Greg knew he could have committed to Ruth right then and there, but that she did not feel the same way. As she let go of her father, he would have to try to let go of her, at least inside.

"I'm not sure I know what love even is," Ruth said. "But whenever I talked with my father, or he teased me or we laughed about something we both thought was hilarious, my heart felt so full and…big in my chest."

Greg would have liked her to include him in the list of things that affected her heart in that way, but he told himself her father had just died, and for the time being Simon's loss claimed her heart. At least he could be there for this girl who affected him so deeply, and that would have to suffice. Even if he wanted their relationship to continue, he knew that in time she would move on. He was more conventional then she, and that would be a stumbling block for the remainder of their high school years. This, too, he knew he had to accept.

"I should go home to help my mother. Holly stays locked in our room when she comes home, and she stays there later and later," Ruth explained.

Greg stood and reached out for her hand, pulling her to her feet. For a few seconds she clung to him, and then turned in the direction they would have to take to return to her apartment. She did hold on to his hand, and for that he was grateful. Neither gave any thought to kissing, even when they said goodbye to each other in front of her apartment building.

Holly feared she was losing her mind, especially when she thought about going into the living room to talk to her sister about their father's death. She rarely talked about anything serious with Ruth. If she were honest with herself, she would have admitted that this was because she had long feared her younger sister was smarter than she, and might even have cracked a joke about whatever subject Holly raised. Talking about sex had been different. That was 'girl' stuff, and OK. Of course they didn't have conversations like that very often either. Holly sniffled in hopes that would staunch the endless flow of her tears, at least for the day. But that was not to be; she couldn't seem to stop crying, and had spent every afternoon since the funeral huddled under her blankets with a pillow over her head so no one in the rest of the apartment could hear her sobs. She also tried to control them, so they came out like gulps. Gulps weren't loud. None of her friends wanted to hear about her father's death. Probably it frightened them, but the end result was that she had no one to talk to at all. Her mother was being a stoic, cleaning the apartment over and over though there was no longer a spot of dust anywhere. Finally, in desperation, she went into the living room where Ruth had already opened her algebra book, and asked her if she would mind coming into their bedroom. There was something she needed to talk about, but didn't want to do so in the living room, in case their mother came home from her rehearsal early.

"I don't have anyone else to talk to," Holly began, totally unaware how insulting this might have sounded to her sister. "As you may have noticed, I can't seem to stop crying, and I don't know what to do."

"I've been talking to Greg about it, and I even started a diary," Ruth said, adding, "You might do that too. It's helping me...."

"Well, you're a good writer and I'm not!" Holly pounced.

Because it was obvious from Holly's reddened eyes, so puffy they looked like they weren't even open, Ruth didn't try to defend herself, which she usually found herself doing when she was talking to her. "You don't have to show it to anyone. It's for you. So you can get out your feelings," she suggested in a tone more caring than her usual blurts to Holly.

"Maybe that isn't a bad idea," Holly sighed. She then asked, "Don't you cry anymore", clearly wanting to know.

"Sometimes I go into the park behind the baseball diamond and sit and cry by myself. So far no one has seemed to notice," she admitted.

"Oh. I couldn't understand why I seemed to be the only one in this family who was still upset," Holly said, sighing yet again.

Although she wasn't sure this was what she wanted to do, Ruth held out her arms to her sister, and Holly, hesitating for only a few seconds, gratefully moved within her embrace.

"If Momma comes home she's going to find us this way and might die from shock," Ruth said, trying to be funny. Neither she nor Holly even smiled. "Maybe we should go into our room. I think you're crying again. At least you're shaking."

And so the sisters, who rarely had given one another comfort throughout their childhood, sat on Ruth's bed holding hands, both of them crying. When their tears had subsided, Holly asked, "How are we going to survive without him?"

Ruth couldn't help but smile. "I think Daddy would say, 'You might begin by being nicer to each other.' "

"That would be novel," Holly agreed. "We could try to be nicer to Mama, too."

"I don't think that will make her treat us any differently," Ruth muttered.

"No," Holly agreed. "But it might make us feel better."

"We could start by getting the roast in the oven, and cutting up the potatoes," Ruth suggested. "That would certainly surprise her."

"I don't know what she does with the roast," Holly admitted.

"I do. I've watched her prepare pot roast a thousand times and even helped once or twice. Do you want to cut up the onions, or peel some garlic cloves?" Ruth asked her.

"I hate the smell of garlic. I'll do the onions."

The sisters walked into their mother's spotless kitchen, and then worked side-by-side preparing their dinner. Both of them cleaned up the mess they had made, and Holly even mopped the kitchen floor. By the time the roast was in the oven, the kitchen looked as clean to the girls as it had when they entered it. As they were doing one last survey, they heard their mother's key in the front door lock.

"What am I smelling?" Adelaide called out from the hallway. She hurried into the kitchen, looking around for crumbs, a dirty counter, peels on the floor, but could find nothing out of place. She turned to her daughters in amazement. "Did you prepare the roast and put it into the oven?"

"With garlic in the little slits I made in the top and bottom," Ruth began, quite proud of them both. Holly chimed in, "And I sliced onions and spread them all around the bottom of the pan. The potatoes are boiling on top, but when they're partly cooked, we can add them to the roasting pan."

"And where did you learn that?" Adelaide asked, not believing her ears.

"From Ruth. She's watched you do it a lot," Holly explained, grinning broadly. She was surprised how good it felt to give her younger sister the credit for the meat cooking in the oven, just as if it had been prepared and placed there by their mother.

The final shock of the afternoon was when Adelaide opened her arms and pulled both girls to her side. When she spoke, her voice sounded very strange to both of them, almost guttural. "I am really grateful. Thank you girls." Then she offered them each a glass of sherry from a bottle their father had opened only on special occasions. Perhaps the evening was special, Ruth thought to herself: all three of them were trying to comfort one another, which would have delighted him.

All three of them returned to their daily lives. Adelaide did not share her feelings, which she didn't understand, or any information about the redheaded woman for years. She attended even more rehearsals in Manhattan, leaving instructions for Ruth about when to put this or that into the oven. At first Holly helped her sister with these preparations, but eventually she began to stay later at school so she could spend time with Al, who was more than happy to give her comfort in the only way he knew how. She was a 'plum' and he was happy to have been able to land her. This did not mean that he stopped noticing other girls at Evander, or stepping out with them upon occasion. He just kept those activities private, not acknowledging his roving eye and hands to Holly or anyone else. Much to his surprise, he discovered he was a good sneak.

Ruth quickly realized that she could do the dinner tasks her mother left for her in fifteen minutes so dinner would be ready for them all later, as long as the roast or chicken was in the oven an hour before they were to eat dinner. She started to stay later at school as well, to work on the magazine, churning out articles it would take the journal months to have the room to print. But she enjoyed the topics she chose; best of all penning them took her mind off her grief about the death of her father. When she felt pangs of guilt at how many hours would go by without giving him a thought, she prayed that Greg was right, that this was what her father would have wanted her to do. She never got over his loss, and never found a man who made her feel as he had, except once, and that man she turned away because the feelings he evoked in her were terrifying. She was determined to never feel overwhelmed by her feelings for a man ever again, and she never did.

* * *

Max left a note in the hidey-hole he and Teresa had been using as a way to contact one another. They were afraid to use the phone, an invention that neither of their families had been able to afford until that very year. Both feared that if they were overheard, they would stumble around too much trying to explain whom they were talking to, agreeing that was too dangerous. Max had yet to ask his mother if he could invite a friend to dinner, walking with head hanging to their coffee shop. He waited and waited for her to come through the door, feeling guilty that he was still deceiving his family, especially Nathan, but also unwilling to stop seeing Teresa. Usually, if she was late, he would finish his English homework, his least favorite assignment, but that day he couldn't get himself to even take the book out of his book bag. Without his conversations with Teresa, Max had no idea how he would get through his last year of high school. How he would he handle Rutgers without her advise, to say nothing of medical school, if he managed to save enough money to attend such a place, he had no idea. No one else took the time to listen to him; he was so shy that he needed months to begin to open up and by then most boys his own age had given up on him.

His stomach was in a knot. Teresa must not have checked the hidey-hole, or she had a chore to do for her mother and hadn't had time to look there. He was collecting his books, about to pay for the soda he had ordered for himself, when Teresa came racing through the door, her scarf catching in the jamb as it slammed shut. Max jumped up to help her, but she was laughing as she extricated herself and her scarf.

"I'm so sorry. My math teacher asked me to stay after class so he could talk to me about my test score," she exclaimed breathlessly.

"Was there a problem?" Max asked, immediately concerned.

"Oh no. I did very well, which he said was quite unusual for a girl. He wanted to talk to me about courses I could take in college, and what careers might be open to someone like me, who 'has a head for numbers', as he put it," she explained, smiling broadly.

"That's wonderful!" Max exclaimed.

Teresa knew him well enough to tell his heart wasn't in his words. Actually, she realized he looked quite worried.

"What's the matter?" she asked, adding, "And don't say 'nothing'. I know that isn't true."

"I don't even know how to begin," he mumbled.

"Just tell me the truth. I can handle it, whatever it is," she promised, although her heart was pounding and she wasn't sure she could.

Max took a very deep breath and said, "I still haven't asked my mother if I can invite you to dinner," he admitted.

Quietly, almost as if she had turned inward, Teresa started to cry. Dismayed, Max reached for her hand.

"My parents would be devastated if they knew I was dating a Jewish boy," she admitted, barely able to get the words past her tears. "I couldn't tell anyone in my family, but it is getting harder and harder for me to keep our secret too," she said, understanding immediately.

The two stared at each other across the table, the divide seeming more and more a chasm to them both. Then Max drew her to her feet, and they left the coffee shop, walking towards the park where they often met. Max searched for a bench that was far from anyone else, and they sat side by side, still holding hands.

"I have always been so lonely, Teresa. There was never anyone I could talk to about my feelings, except Nathan, but I couldn't talk to him about lots of things because he's younger, and I didn't want to upset him," Max explained. "Until we began to talk in class, and then to meet after school, I didn't have any idea how I would get through the rest of my life."

"I'm so sorry Max. I have friends," Teresa stated, quickly adding, "But no one I could talk with about intellectual subjects, and no one who wanted to share the personal things you and I have ended up talking about." She paused and then asked him with a huge sigh, "How will we survive without each other?"

He shook his head from side to side, unable to answer. His arm snaked around her, and he drew her close, a very brave move for the young man. She was still crying, her tears dribbling down onto her collar and inside her blouse.

"You have brought joy into my life, Teresa," he said. "But I feel like I have to honor my parents, even if I think they're wrong. They really are very decent people."

'Mine are too," she agreed. "My brothers and I are the second generation to live here in America, but my parents are still afraid. I don't think they've ever felt as if they belonged, especially as children."

"Afraid of what?" he asked, though he thought he knew: afraid of being outsiders, ostracized forever. According to his father that was a familiar experience even in the old country if you left your little village. It certainly would have been his parents' experience if they had left their shtetl in the Ukraine to move to Lviv.

Finally Teresa replied, "I think they're afraid that they will never be true Americans."

"I think my parents are afraid of that too. They hate speaking in public because they sound different. I can't tell them they're wrong, because I don't know if they are," Max admitted.

"There is freedom here, but there is also a great deal of prejudice," she agreed. They sat side by side, neither moving, neither knowing what else to say.

"I would rather keep seeing you in the hallway at school, then chance your parents sending you to St. Patrick's, " he said.

"Yes. If we stop seeing each other after school, we would still be able to talk in class, or between classes sometimes. Yes, I agree" Teresa nodded.

They sat together until dusk began to fall, and then walked out of the park together. At the corner they parted as they usually did, Teresa turning the corner and Max crossing the street to head home. Teresa did not look back; Max stood on the sidewalk, watching the place where she had been long after she had disappeared. Then he, too, turned to walk home. He knew he would have to hide his feelings, and did so as soon as he opened the kitchen door. He had had a lot of practice hiding his feelings for someone so young. Even Nate did not realize he was grieving, or that he and Teresa had spoken to one another.

Although they had two classes together, he and Teresa rarely talked outside of class anymore. They didn't decide upon this path, but neither of them could handle the distance they experienced merely having intellectual discussions, so they ceased having any at all. In the spring Max agonized about what girl to take to the prom, since going with Teresa was no longer an option. Finally at Nate's suggestion, he decided to ask Doris, a friend of Helen Welt's who had no plans for the evening and had no expectations of being invited to the prom. She was a studious girl, smart but not terribly personable, perhaps because she was as shy as Max. Doris could not keep the surprise from her face, or the pleasure.

Max quipped, "I didn't want to stay home either. This way neither of us has to."

"Do you know how to dance?" she asked. "I'm not very graceful."

"Nate's been teaching me, so all you should have to do is follow me," he assured her, though he was still quite worried about his abilities in that regard. He and his brother would practice every night in Noah's workshop. His parents realized they should not ask either boy what they were doing out there, and neither did.

The only awkward moment came when Teresa glided by in the arms of the boy who had invited her to the prom. He was a well-built, swarthy Italian boy, and to make matters worse, a very good dancer. Teresa tried to look straight ahead, but couldn't keep herself from glancing his way. The two stared at each other for only a few seconds, but that was enough. Doris sighed, "Ah." When she realized that Max was startled by her simple utterance, and clearly troubled, she added, "Don't worry. No one else noticed. You two have been very circumspect."

Doris had only moved to Elizabeth from New York a few years earlier, when she and Max were in their first year of high school, but they had never talked about her life in the big city. She began to regale him with stories about the Bronx, where she and her family had lived, making him laugh as she described a friend's illness, when she had been carried out of their building on a stretcher and some other neighbor, who had bought a bouquet of flowers for the ailing child, and had thrown them on the prostrate girl because she had had no idea what else to do with them.

"Did you laugh," Max asked her, bemused by the scene she was describing.

"After the attendant had closed the door of the ambulance, I started to laugh. My mother pinched me so I would stop, but she realized no one from Ruth's family remained, so she started to laugh too. I suggested that our laughing would not affect the outcome of my friend's burst appendix, and ii didn't, but my mother wouldn't talk to me until the following morning. She didn't have much of a sense of humor." Years later, when Max got to know Doris' mother because he and his wife and Doris and her husband became good friends, he remembered those words, and couldn't help but agree with them.

Because they were uncomfortable with their lack of grace, Max and Doris left the prom earlier than most of their classmates, including Teresa, who seemed to be having a good time with her good-looking dance partner. Doris had suggested Max take her home since neither was very adept on the dance floor, thanking him for inviting her, since otherwise she would have felt miserable the entire evening because of missing her senior prom. As he draped her shawl around her shoulders, Max could hear Teresa laugh from the gymnasium, a sound he would hear in his dreams for years to come. Of course Doris had no idea why he seemed to hurry her from the building once she was wearing her wrap, because all the noises from the dance floor blended together in her ears. She didn't know anyone well enough to separate one voice from another in the general cacophony of sound. After Doris' front door had closed behind her, Max walked back to the park where he and Teresa used to meet, despite the late hour. He sat there for hours, but not a soul walked by. Eventually he made his way home. He never forgot that evening, even when he was an old man. The memory would bring tears to his eyes for years, even after he was married.

Over the summer before he was to enter Rutgers on a scholarship, Max asked the pharmacist at the drug store where he stocked shelves if he could work longer hours. Since he was particularly competent and even able to fill prescriptions under the tutelage of the older man, his boss readily agreed. When Max was at work he had to concentrate on the tasks at hand, and couldn't spend time daydreaming about Teresa, and the intimate conversations they had shared. He also didn't have the energy to worry about who she was dating by the time he dragged himself home from the drugstore to his mother's pedestrian meals. Beck was married, Min was now in school, and Nell was working and no longer had time to prepare the family meals. Yetta's chicken was usually dry and tough, her beef so overcooked that the grey mass shredded under his knife, and her fish beyond description. Max would force himself to eat, because he knew he needed food to shore up his exhausted body, but he certainly didn't enjoy his mother's repasts. When he complained to Nell about them, she tried to prepare at least one or two of the family dinners, but the rest of the time Min, Noah, Max and Nathan were forced to suffer their mother's sorry attempts at the culinary arts.

One evening when Jules and Lil came to dinner, a meal that Nell had rushed home to prepare to honor the older brother she clearly adored, Jules couldn't help but notice that Max, not ever very talkative, was even quieter than usual. After the meal when he asked his younger brother if anything was the matter, Max shrugged and said he was just tired because of his long hours. Jules went in search of Nate, who was reading in the bedroom he shared with Max. Though it was obvious that Nate knew what was wrong with his brother, he would not say, no matter what tactic Jules tried to dislodge the truth.

Finally Nate muttered, "Why don't you ask him?"

"I just did, and that's why I'm asking you," Jules explained, adding, "I understand. You can't betray a confidence. Just tell him that if he needs a non-judgmental ear, he knows where to go."

Before he left the room, Nate assured him, "It will just take time, Jules, and then he'll be fine," although he was not sure. He had never seen the brother he had always depended upon so despondent.

A few weeks later Max developed a cough that he couldn't seem to shake. One night about ten days after the initial outbreak, Yetta heard him smothering a coughing fit in his bedroom, and poked her husband who was lying in their bed reading The Jewish Daily Forward beside her. This was something he did every night, no matter how tired he was, to keep abreast of world news as well as topics significant to Jewish immigrants.

Without putting down the newspaper, or pausing in the article he was reading, Noah asked, "What is it Yetta? I'm in the middle of an important article on Jewish businesses on the lower East Side." Then he glanced at his wife, and realized from her expression that she was really troubled. "I'm sorry," he apologized as he put the paper across his legs and turned his attention to her. "Something is obviously bothering you. Why don't you tell me what it is?"

"Wait a minute," she said. Then she pointed at the wall separating their bedroom from the bedroom shared by their two youngest sons. "There. Can you hear Max?" she asked him.

Noah frowned, because of course he could, and what he heard did not sound good at all. "How long has he been like this? I'm sorry that I have not been paying attention," he added.

"I don't think any of us has," Yetta murmured, "But I don't think we can ignore his condition any longer."

"No. I will take him to Doctor Glaubman's office on my way to the shop tomorrow morning, so that he will still be able to get to school on time if the doctor thinks he can attend his classes," Noah suggested. Yetta nodded with approval. She knew her husband had a gentler nature than her own, and would be more of a comfort to Max should there be a problem.

The following morning when Noah tiptoed into the boys' bedroom, Nate opened his eyes. No matter what words Noah whispered to him, the younger boy was determined to go to the doctor's office with his father and Max, and quickly dressed and stood by their door so he could not be left behind.

The doctor was sipping his morning coffee behind his receptionist's desk when Noah knocked on the door to his office. When he heard Max, who could not keep back his cough, he motioned them inside to his examination room. The wrenching cough sounded no better to him than it had to the young man's worried parents.

"Come on through," the doctor urged, ushering all of them into the back room, motioning Max to the examination table. Both Noah and Nathan stood to the side, so they would not be in the way.
"Do you want me to put my feet in the stirrups," Max joked, which brought on another round of hacking. No one laughed.

Doctor Glaubman put the stethoscope to his chest. No one said a word, but all of them could tell by the expression that what he was hearing was disturbing him.

"I am starting medical school in a month," Max explained. "There must be something you can give me so that my plans will not be interrupted," he added with obvious concern.

"I'm sorry, son," Doctor Glaubman began, inauspicious words to Max's ears. "There are two sanatoriums within an hour of Elizabeth. My secretary can make some calls to see which one has a bed, and what the cost would be for either one," he continued.

Max became distraught. "But I can't postpone my course of study or stop working. The family needs my support." He was not thinking about how this medical care would be paid for; instead he was worrying about the loss of income for his parents.

Noah laid a hand on his shoulder. "We will deal with that issue later, son. For now we have to take care of your illness."

All of them looked at one another. None wanted to utter the word 'tuberculosis' since that was beyond comprehension, a tragedy for any family in the ghetto of Elizabethport.

Max continued, "When I had the flu I was able to return to school in a few months. I suppose I could contact Rutgers and tell them."

Doctor Glaubman's demeanor was not a happy one. "You might be in the tuberculosis sanatorium for half a year," he explained, though he did not want to dash the hopes of this family he had known for years.

"Only the physician at the clinic will know what your stay there might entail." Finally, the dreaded word had been spoken aloud.

Noah asked him, "How long will it take to decide upon treatment once Max is at the clinic?"

Dr. Glaubman was already standing at the door to the examination room with his hand on the doorknob. "I'm not sure. Let me get Joanie started on those phone calls. You can wait here."

When Glaubman returned he told them that the receptionist was already talking to a nurse at the clinic in the Catskills, which was a bit closer than the other one he had mentioned. Apparently the cost at both clinics was comparable, but this clinic had a bed, so arrangements were being made. When the receptionist had passed along the information to all of them and left the room, Max groaned, "But that will take everything we have saved, and it has taken years for Beck, Nell, Min, and I to set aside those funds."

"Our community is often helpful in situations like these," the doctor reminded them.

"Never for anything this costly," Noah shook his head.

"If the community comes up with a portion of the cost, Rutgers might offer you a larger scholarship once they understand the situation," the Dr. Glaubman said, addressing the family's concerns, which seemed to be focused on the young man's plans, rather than the serious nature of the disease.

Nate finally managed to ask, "Could my brother... how serious....could he....?" without being able to complete the sentence.

"I think we have caught this early enough that it shouldn't be life-threatening," Dr. Glaubman said, sounding quite reassuring. "But you will have to get him to the clinic immediately. If you need a car, you can use mine."

"Thank you," Nate replied immediately. Noah and Max seemed too shocked to say anything.

Glaubman continued, "Arrangements have been made. If you could withdraw your money from the bank, or get them to issue you a check made out to the Saranac Lake Sanatorium, that would be best. It shouldn't take you more than an hour to get there." He then turned to Max. "While your father goes to the bank, you can return home and pack your things. I'm sure Yetta and Nathan will help you. Your family will not be allowed to visit for at least a month, lest they became infected, but then you will be allowed brief visits."

Max had never been away from home, and had always had counted on the comfort of his close-knit family. What the doctor was suggesting shocked him.

"We will find a way, all of us, to continue to set aside money each month, Max," Noah assured him. "For now we had better get started so that we can get you there tonight."

"None of you must hug him or kiss him good-bye, as hard as that will be. It would not help the situation if one of you were to become ill as well. As a matter of fact, I want you, Yetta, and the girls to come in tomorrow morning, so that I can listen to your lungs."

"None of the rest of us is coughing," Nate explained.

"That is a very good sign, but we must still be sure," the doctor said.

Max took charge. Although the news must have been the most distressing to him, he could tell that neither his brother nor his father was capable of making a move. They followed him out of the office. Once they had left, the doctor said to his nurse, "He will heal. But this is nevertheless a tragedy for the Unger's. Nathan was right. Our community could not begin to raise that kind of money. "

"Max will never become a doctor," the nurse agreed, shaking her head sadly. "And he has worked so hard to reach that goal."

"Yes. This is indeed a tragedy."

When Max explained the situation to his mother, she immediately went into his room to fold his clothes, telling him to get the suitcase from beneath the stairs in the basement. They packed in silence. Yetta didn't touch her son, or offer him comfort because she feared she would lose her composure and burst into tears. Both of her sons understood. Besides, their mother had never been a very demonstrative woman.

CHAPTER SEVENTEEN

Ruth raced into the apartment because she knew she was late. It was her night to prepare dinner, and her mother hated to come home and not find the scent of food wafting into the hallway from the kitchen. She believed it was the least her daughters could do for her, since she had the burden of their care, cleaning the apartment, doing the shopping, and all the other chores that comprised their daily life because of her husband's death. If he hadn't been committing adultery, he would still be alive and available to them all, which still infuriated her. Neither daughter had any idea why she was so angry most of the time. As soon as Ruth hung her jacket up in the closet, she heard her mother's voice raised in an all too familiar fury.

"How dare you disobey me, Holly! I said you are going with us to Europe, and you are," she screamed at the top of her voice.

'That can't be good for her 'instrument', her younger daughter thought to herself as she stood in the hallway paralyzed. She knew her sister loathed her mother's horrifying temper. They both did, and had talked about it frequently since it was a subject upon which they could agree.

"I need to be here to deal with my Hunter application!" Holly shouted back.

"You do not!" screeched their mother.

"The secretary in the financial aid office told me I do," Holly's voice wavered. She was clearly close to tears.

"Sniffling will do you no good," her mother declared in a cold, unbending tone. She could really be cruel, with no conception that her daughters might have goals as significant as her own. After all, both girls were almost grown.

"I am not going. I do not care how much you bully me, or what you threaten. If I have to, I will move in with Dorothy next door. I know she would be glad to have my company," Holly said, her tone almost as composed as her mother's. Ruth could well imagine what was going through her mind: she would not demean herself in front of their mother. Ruth would have felt the same way, and often had.

"You will not impose upon my friend!" Adelaide shouted, her voice trembling with distress.
"Fine," came Holly's swift response. "Then I will stay with Becca. Her mother has already told me I am welcome to live with them for the summer. Both of us need to work things out with the financial office."

"You'll never get a scholarship. Your grades aren't good enough," Adelaide replied with infuriating calm.

"Then I'll get a job so that I will be able to go to college later!" Holly shouted back. Ruth could tell she was desperately trying to retain her control.

Adelaide stood in the kitchen, utterly dumbfounded. She couldn't imagine how Becca's mother could have offered this reprise to her daughter. She had thought they were friends, and at the very least, the other woman would have talked to her about the issue before making such an offer to her daughter. Adelaide knew Becca's mother would have sympathized with her concerns had they just talked about them. Holly was a flirt, and could easily get into serious trouble if she were not supervised with great care. Adelaide would not want to take on that kind of burden with Becca, and was certain the other woman would change her mind if she gave it any thought. Perhaps Holly was not being truthful and she hadn't spoken to the woman at all.

"I don't believe you. I am going to call Cynthia right now," Adelaide stormed into the hallway and picked up the phone.

Although Holly had spoken to her friend's mother, she had no idea how the woman would respond to her mother's distress. She might change her mind because she felt she had to be supportive of another mother. She stood in the kitchen doorway, desperate to hear her mother's side of the conversation. Even if she couldn't tell what Becca's mother was saying, she hoped her mother's words would give her the general idea about the direction their conversation was taking.

"Hello Cynthia," Adelaide began. "Yes, I am very busy and feel a bit overwhelmed with all the tasks I have to complete before the Schola departs for our tour."

Then there was a pause. Obviously the other woman was speaking.

"You don't have to take this on, Cynthia. Holly and Ruth have always gone on tour with us every summer," she continued.

Another pause.
"Are you sure it wouldn't be a burden?"

Ruth, who had snuck into the kitchen the back way, had tiptoed inside and taken hold of her sister's hand, giving it a squeeze. Her gesture released Holly's tears. Ruth handed her sister a napkin, which she was able to grab from the holder on the little kitchen table. "It sounds like it's going to be alright," she whispered.

"Do you think? Mama can be so mercurial," Holly whispered back.

Since that was true, Ruth refrained from comment. The two stood in the doorway, silent, clutching each other. Though Ruth dreaded going abroad with their mother alone, she knew Holly should be allowed to stay behind. After all, she was a senior, with adult life just around the corner. When the girls heard their mother make a luncheon date with their friend's mother, they could barely keep themselves from jumping up and down with excitement. They had nary a complaint when their mother entered the kitchen moments later with a request that the two make dinner again the following evening, though they complained a little bit so their mother wouldn't be suspicious. They glanced at one another as soon as she again left the room. In another time and place, the girls would have high-fived.

The following day when their mother explained that she would have to be away from home for the lunch hour, necessitating their doing some of the chopping and paring for the family dinner when they got home from school as well as their usual chores, neither girl complained. If their mother suspected that they knew where she was going, neither could tell. Holly could barely keep from smiling at her mother as she said her good-byes because she knew she would not be forced to go to

Europe with the family. Becca had assured her that she had discussed the matter with her mother before going to bed the previous evening; in turn, her mother had assured Becca that she would persuade Adelaide to allow Holly to stay with them for the summer.

Much to the shock of the sisters, when their mother returned from the luncheon she told Holly that Cynthia, who had worked part time at Saks Fifth Avenue for years, had managed to secure a summer position for her at the perfume counter. Not only would the young woman be staying in the Bronx rather than going to Europe with her family, she would be earning money as well. This pleased Adelaide almost as much as it did her daughter. When Adelaide told Holly what she would be earning an hour, Holly actually jumped up and down with excitement.

"Mama! Oh Mama. That will pay for my whole first semester!" she squealed, thrilled beyond measure.

"Yes," Adelaide agreed, unable to berate her daughter for her unladylike behavior. Had she been able to do the same, she would have jumped up and down with excitement too. The money Holly would be earning would be a huge help to her. She also understood that her daughter had been truthful. Adelaide thought she should admit this to both Holly and Ruth. After all, when it came time for Ruth to attend Hunter, she might follow Holly's example more easily.

"The money you will earn will be a big help to me. And by the time you enter your second semester, your father's insurance policy will have come through, which should ease our financial burdens," she said.

"What if I like working and earning my own money?" Holly asked her mother.

"I assume you would be able to stay on, working after your classes or on the weekends," Adelaide replied.

The obvious benefits of her older daughter having a job were apparent to both mother and daughter. Adelaide was not unaware of the choices she, herself, had made in the early years of her marriage and was continuing to make about her singing life. Those choices were considered 'outside the pale' by many in the circle of friends she and Simon had acquired during their marriage. It was obvious many of the women thought her singing kept her away from home far too frequently. It even made some of them wonder if she were fulfilling her role as a wife and mother, though none of them ever said anything directly to either Simon or Adelaide about the matter. If the men had spoken to Simon about the Schola Cantorum, she had no idea. She had never asked, afraid to raise the subject despite her husband's obvious pride in her talent. Had he given the matter more thought he might have asked her to give up the singing group. Her husband valued his role as a parent and had always had a difficult time understanding her lack of 'normal' feminine feeling, as he saw it. Adelaide would have been happier without children, something she had never admitted to herself, let alone her husband. How could she begrudge her daughter a little bit of the freedom she herself valued so much?

Nevertheless, it was only after speaking at length with Cynthia about the proposed arrangements for the summer that Adelaide was able to relent. Cynthia was actually much more strict with her daughter because she was home more of the time and held a tight rein on what she allowed and what she did not. Holly would be well cared for, and her interest in boys, which Adelaide thought both out of proportion and even dangerous, would be held in check by her own friend's mother. Of course Holly had no idea this realization had anything to do with her mother's change of mind, but she was so happy to be allowed to stay behind, and so excited about entering the adult world with a job at Saks Fifth Avenue, she didn't give the subject much thought.

When Holly apologized to Ruth for leaving her in the lurch, forcing her to spend the entire summer alone with their mother, Ruth surprised her by admitting she was not upset. With her mother involved in her rehearsals as well as her own life, she would have the time and freedom to explore all the parts of Vienna she had not been allowed to see in their earlier trips with the Schola, including the Bohemian neighborhood with its numerous cafes where literary types drank coffee while discussing their oeuvres over coffee and tea cakes. She, Holly and her father had often marveled at the depth of those discussions while quietly imbibing Viennese concoctions themselves, and eavesdropping with delight. Holly felt a pang of jealousy, plus a soupcon of shame, but then she pictured herself alone in Manhattan, and the feelings passed. Each girl was quite excited about the coming summer, a period that had been looming in each of their minds as a time they each would have to endure. Neither could believe their good fortune.

Ruth was unable to fall asleep for hours that night. She could speak German easily, because her mother and father had always communicated in their native language when they wanted to have a quiet moment, at least until they had realized both of their daughters were able to understand them. Both girls had become bilingual at a very early age. Ruth was translating one of her most recent articles into German in her head, which kept her awake as well. Suddenly she sat bolt upright. What if she were able to translate several of her articles that addressed world issues, and managed to gather the courage to ask one of the literary raconteurs to take a peek, explaining that she was the editor of a school journal at home in New York City. She needn't mention that it was a lowly high school paper; she was sure a college girl would be more interesting to the men and women conversing in those cafes. She could even ask her Aunt Sophia for suggestions about the patrons of the different cafes, even sharing her plan with her aunt, who had often been fairly daring in her own life pursuits. When her sister awakened her in the morning, she realized she must have fallen asleep, but she believed she had been awake most of the night thinking about the vistas opening before her.

She and Greg met each other every morning, usually walking into Evander Childs together discussing the school paper, and the jobs they had yet to complete before they could mimeograph the next issue. When Greg asked her how she was, as he did every morning, she was surprised to realize she was not ready to tell him about the summer trip, or her ideas about how to utilize it. Though he knew she and her family went abroad every summer because her mother's singing group performed there, they hadn't yet talked about the dates because the trip was months away. This hesitance came as a complete surprise, since she was used to sharing everything with him. After all, he was her best friend, even if he was a male, and even if they were now necking whenever they had the chance and were sure no one would catch them at it. The few times she and her sister had talked about kissing and petting, though Ruth and Greg had certainly not progressed that far with their newfound explorations, Holly had gushed that every time she even looked at Al she felt weak in the legs. Greg certainly didn't make Ruth feel that way, which she assumed had to do with the fact that they had been friends for years before either of them had thought about exploring anything else. Or at least that was what she believed. Now she wondered.

It was certainly fun to kiss, even when Greg gently eased apart her lips with his tongue, and her heart probably beat a bit faster when he did, but he didn't make her tummy lurch like Holly's, and she rarely thought about Greg when he wasn't around. Holly seemed to think about Al, and what they were doing with one another, all the time. Or at least that's how it seemed to Ruth, from the few tidbits her sister had shared with her. Then a new thought struck, and she no longer heard a word Greg was saying to her about the article he had written the night before. What if she met a younger man at one of the Vienna cafes, a younger man who did make her gasp, and whom she thought about all the time? What if they, too, kissed, or she let him touch her breasts through her blouse? Her mother would be nowhere near, so she could do whatever she pleased. This had never been a possibility before. She and Greg had never touched other than a clap on the back or shoulder before this year, her father had usually gone to the cafes with both of the girls, either separately or together, and neither had been brave enough to speak to any of the cute boys they had seen anyway. Holly was already stepping out with Al, and Ruth hadn't been interested. For the first time since she had gotten to know Greg, Ruth didn't blurt out her news.
"Did you hear a word I said," Greg asked her with a chuckle.

"Oops," Ruth smiled at him. She was certain her smile must have looked like some kind of weird mask because she felt so uncomfortable, but Greg didn't seem to notice.

"Really, Ruth. Your article doesn't need much work. I'm sure you'll be able to edit it during your study hall, and the paper will go to press today, or the latest, tomorrow," he assured her with a pat to her shoulder. She kept silent because she had no idea how to talk to him about her trip, and certainly not about some of the reasons for her excitement about it. When they parted in the hallway – Greg had world history first period and Ruth had her English class- she felt relief.

It was unusual for her to be distracted in her English class, which was her favorite, and besides she knew the teacher thought well of her, but she could not concentrate and never even raised her hand to join the class discussion about Silas Marner.

Holly was equally distracted. Holly was determined to lose her virginity while her mother and sister were away, and now she was sure she would be able to do just that. She had told no one of her intentions, not Becca, not Al, and certainly not Ruth, who had just begun to neck. Ruth, who was thought to be the more adventuresome of the sisters, would have been horrified, or so Holly believed. She had told her sister on more than one occasion how excited she felt when she and Al were necking, and that when he first brushed her breast through the sweater she had been wearing she had thought she would swoon. That he had actually seen her breasts, as well as touched them several times, she had told no one. She was ashamed of her own recklessness, but the feelings inspired by his hands were too marvelous to give up. Even her shame had not stopped her. When his hand had ventured between her legs, he had been the gentleman, not daring to slide it inside her panties, though that was what she most wanted him to do. At least she hadn't said so, she kept telling herself, as if that made what she had allowed him to do all right.

Holly had been so consumed by her own plans that she had not told Al that she would not be going to Europe with her family, although she had told him weeks before that she didn't want to go. It therefore came as quite a shock when he said, "Holly my sweet. I've agreed to accompany my parents to Europe this summer, so you and I may be able to meet in Vienna, though we'll be traveling through France and Germany as well as Austria." He could not keep the excitement from his voice, but stopped in his tracks when he saw the frown crease her brows. "Whatever is that matter?" he asked. "Don't you want to see me over the summer?" His eyes were serious, though his tone was light. Then he added, "Are you breaking up with me?" with a laugh, because he was a confident young man and knew she was not.

"Oh Al," Holly groaned. "Mama has finally agreed to let me stay in New York!"

"Oh damn!" he exclaimed, unable to keep the curse from escaping. Holly didn't even notice.

"What are we going to do?" she asked, hanging on to his arm for dear life.

Al sighed. "I guess we're going to have to endure a summer apart."

"But I don't want to do that!" she blurted. If he only knew....

"Neither to I. You could tell your mother you've changed your mind," he suggested without much hope. When he realized she had quietly begun to cry, he turned and held out his arms. They stood that way for some time, people detouring around them, some smiling, some irritated. They took one another's hands and continued to walk home.

Holly was so distraught she could not hide her distress from Ruth, whispering that she had been just learned that Al and his parents were going to Europe over the summer and was devastated. Ruth gave her a hug as she murmured, "What an irony." Holly wasn't sure whether her sister meant the news about Al or the hug she had instinctively offered her.

The next morning Al raced up to her in front of the school and exclaimed, "We're going for a medical conference and it only lasts three weeks. So we'll be back, and you and I won't be parted for two whole months!" He was clearly ecstatic, which warmed Holly's heart. By the middle of June he would truly understand why she had been so upset, but for now, she would keep that information to herself. She knew his father had given him some condoms a few months earlier, and was certain they could unearth them together when the time was right. Holly found herself grinning throughout the day. Wouldn't he be surprised!

When Ruth immediately said, "I'm so happy for you," at the news, Holly was almost as surprised as she thought Al would be in June. Ruth was equally surprised because the words were true.
Her feelings about the summer were still a-broil. She would miss her friend Greg, but her boyfriend Greg? She was anxious to see what answers her summer abroad might provide. If a young man appeared

at one of her Aunt's soirees, and made her heart pound in her chest the way Holly had declared hers did every time she saw Al in the hallways of their high school, well, she'd have to decide what to do about her feelings then. She knew she would have no counsel to help her; even her aunt would be horrified that Ruth was considering such a betrayal. No milk had been spilled yet, so why worry about stepping in it? Nevertheless, Ruth was a moral person, and knew she at least had to remind Greg that she would again be away for two months of the summer. She hated talking about it, but talk she did the next day as they walked home from school. He dropped her hand and raced up the hill where they often sat to talk in Crotona Park. He was still having trouble hiding his tears by the time she sat down next to him. Dorothy must be right: Greg's feelings for her were stronger than she had believed them to be. "It's alright, Ruth, my reaction came as a surprise to me as much as it did to you. I'll be fine in a minute or so," he assured her, and he did already seem calmer. Ruth decided to take him at his word because that was way more comfortable. Her doubts about what she was really thinking were pushed away, and she prayed they would stay there. That afternoon was the first time Ruth had pushed away feelings, at least grownup feelings as she thought of them, the first of many times throughout her life. It was not a healthy pattern, but she knew no one who could tell her that.

* * *

Ruth could see her mother's sister, Sophia, standing on her tiptoes as the gangplank was lowered to the dock below, and joyfully blew her a kiss. Sophia, who was a Vienna matron with children of her own, had been quite rebellious in her youth, and recognized a kindred spirit in her youngest niece. Adelaide did not hold her daughter back as she raced down the aisle, merely calling out after her, "Ruthie. You need to come back for your bag. I can't carry the lighter things by myself." A porter on the vessel had already collected their trunks. The teenager spun on her heels, grabbed the small suitcase resting by her mother's feet, spun again, and raced down the gangplank into the arms of her Aunt Sophie. Sophie enfolded the young girl in her arms, stroking her back, saying how pleased she was to see her.

"Me too," Ruth sighed. She really adored her aunt and had often wished her mother's temperament was more like Sophia's. Sophia was older, but seemed to remember being young, unlike Adelaide. Sophia had shared some of her secrets with the young girl the preceding year, when Ruth had talked with her about Greg, about her parents' marriage, about how to proceed in a world that welcomed neither her spirit nor her intelligence.

Sophia had given in to her own parents' wishes about which young man they wanted her to marry, but that was a different era. She believed that Ruth was smart enough to sidestep her mother's desires in that regard in order to fight over more important issues, like pursuing a career, fighting for women's rights, the poor, and most important, her own life choices. Given her sister's own life, the summer tours that Simon never complained about, the late afternoon rehearsals, and the household chores that Adelaide had expected her daughters to take up – Sophia could not understand why she was so rigid about Ruth's gifts and possible choices. She might have given up trying to question her sister about it the preceding summer, but at that time she had also determined to support Ruth in every way she could in her struggles to become the woman she was fully capable of becoming.

The very next afternoon Sophia walked over to her mother's apartment where the Liebman's were staying, and suggested that she and Ruth go for tea at her favorite café. Sophia's mother, who never spent time at the cafes, which she considered an improper environment for a woman, frowned, but said nothing. She loathed fighting with her daughters, and knew any such behavior on her part would infuriate her husband, who was struggling with health issues. She believed, as he did, that Sophia was a very responsible person and mother, so perhaps she was just being old-fashioned. She also knew her granddaughter would love the tumult of the cafes, which she herself had often witnessed when she had been perusing the wares at her favorite shops in the same area. Her excitable and curious granddaughter would enjoy herself, and Sophia would never suggest something that could be remotely dangerous, even if she, herself, found such places overwhelming.

As soon as they were seated, Sophia pointed out the board behind the server's table, the day's special pastries listed in no apparent order. Ruth's rapt expression as she took in everything around her amused her aunt, from the cacophony of conversation, to the clothing the women wore, to the number of women sharing a pastry with a friend although no man was in site, and finally to the scents that wafted from the bakery within the tiny outdoor café. She could hear the men at the next table discussing the new ideas of an Austrian doctor named Freud, ears perking up to listen.

"I haven't heard much about this at home," she told her aunt, asking, "Are his ideas about behavior really so radical?"

"The editors of the Wiener Zeitung seem to think so, and so does my husband, "Sophia replied. "But most of my friends don't talk about it much."

"Why?" her curious niece asked her.

"I suppose because our husbands discourage such conversation. Most men don't seem terribly interested in why human beings behave the way they do," she replied after a moment's thought.

"Are you?" Ruth asked her. She, herself, hoped Sophia did, because then she could talk even more freely about her feelings for Greg, and about a possible career at New York Magazine.

"I'm curious about everything we do," Sophia said with a laugh, and then asked her niece what she wanted to eat of drink. Ruth grinned at her with delight, glancing at the steaming coffee drink a waiter was setting down in front of the man sitting to her right.

"Does your mama let you have coffee in the afternoon," Sophia asked her with a smile.

"Not often," Ruth admitted.

"Then we won't tell her. Why don't we share a sacher torte as well," she suggested, "Everyone in Europe comes here to indulge in them."

"Mama makes sachertorte sometimes – she really is a marvelous baker – but I would love to try one here, in the city where she was born!" Ruth declared, eyes sparkling with excitement.

As soon as the waiter departed with their order, Sophia exclaimed, "How perfect. I was hoping they would drop by for afternoon tea!"

Ruth turned to see three young women entering the café. They looked unbelievably sophisticated to her, which made her want to hide her own attire, a suit she and her mother had picked out in New York City before they had departed. At the time both Ruth and Holly had been thrilled; neither had owned a suit before, and the ones they had each chosen had seemed so smart. Now Ruth wished she could duck under the table.

Sophia, always attuned to the feelings of her niece, whispered, "You look lovely Ruth. And if you want to find a European style suit that suits you – 'how clever, don't you think,' she chuckled – we can shop for another one while we're here. " Then she called out, "Lydia, come over here. This is the niece I was telling you about!"

Ruth felt herself flushing, but before she could even try to control it, Lydia and her friends reached their table. "I'm so glad to meet you, Ruth. I have a friend who works at a local journal. He was intrigued when he read a few of your pieces and asked to meet you." Ruth was too shocked to utter a syllable. "Let's pull over some chairs," Lydia suggested, and she and her friends, Suzanna and Carole, did just that. They talked about the latest fashions, the precarious state of both Austria and Germany because of the Great War, London, where Carole had studied painting the preceding semester, and the cafes of Vienna as compared to those in New York. When Sophia suggested they meet again in two days because she had other plans for Ruth the following one, Lydia immediately agreed, saying she would try to set up an appointment for Ruth with her editor friend either at 1, before they were to meet, or afterwards, should he be otherwise occupied at the earlier hour. Sophia, sensing her niece's terror, replied that one would be fine for them both. Lydia stooped to give Sophia a hug, and then impulsively reached down to enfold Ruth as well. Ruth, who was affectionate by nature, immediately hugged her in return, until all of them were exchanging embraces.

As she and Sophia left the cafe with a box of pastries to share with the rest of the family in the morning, Sophia sighed in contentment. "That couldn't have worked out better if I had planned the afternoon in advance." She grasped Ruth's hand, and swinging their arms side by side, the two strolled through the district as they made their way back to the apartment for the sherry that was usually served before dinner in the Lowe household.

After the evening meal, when the men remained seated around the dining room table for conversation, coffee, and cigars, the women retired to the sitting room. Adelaide sat down at the piano and began to noodle around with some chords and Ruth picked up a magazine, which she set down because she was not yet fluent in written German. Without thinking about the effect of what she was about to say, Ruth blurted out, "I translated the article on women wearing slacks into English for practice, mama, if you want me to go get it...," Their mother stopped in the middle of a musical phrase, and even Sophia's mouth opened in surprise.

"When did you do that, Ruth," Adelaide asked her.

Embarrassed, Ruth stammered, "I had trouble falling asleep last night, so I tip-toed back out here, grabbed the magazine and some paper, and began to translate for fun. I knew that was an article that Holly would want to read, and even you, Mama. To prepare for your concert tour," she explained.

Sophia smiled as she said, "How amazing!"

"Not really. I'm taking German in school, and I'm in my third year. Holly is taking Latin," Ruth replied.

Adelaide turned to her younger daughter. "You see! I told you it was more practical to learn a language you would be able to use, especially since the family travels to the continent very year."

Sensing her niece's discomfort, Sophia asked, "Addie. Wouldn't you sing a lieder or two for us?"

Adelaide needed little encouragement to sing, especially since she was a bit nervous about performing in the Vienna music hall where the Schola had been booked for two consecutive evening concerts.

A few days later Sophia and Ruth walked down to a new café Ruth had visited before, and ordered their coffee drinks as well as a few pastries Sophia suggested they share, when they heard, "Ruth! Ruth! Over here!" Carole was already seated at a table with a young woman Ruth had not yet met. As she carried a plate of pastries to the table, Sophia following behind with the coffees, Carole immediately introduced the girls to her older sister. Introductions were made, the pastries placed in the middle of the table with extra forks so they all could share, and the newcomers took their places. Much to Ruth's relief, she was able to follow the discussion and even to enjoy it, joining in right away with animation. A new play was being discussed, so the topic was right up her alley, or Holly's, from whom she had learned a great deal despite herself over the last few years. Within moments Carole had exclaimed, "I'll get tickets for us all, and call Lydia, so she can come too!" which delighted everyone.

Then Carole turned to Ruth, several papers clutched in her hand. "Look what I turned into our school paper! It's going to be published next week, but it isn't nearly as good as yours!"

"View of an American Girl," Ruth read aloud, glancing up with surprise. "Why, this is about meeting me at the Café Central the other day!"

"Yes," Carole continued. "About the clothes you were wearing and that suits like the one you were wearing have not yet become popular in Vienna. I even mention some of your articles, and what you said you were learning at school."

"How does our curriculum compare with yours at the University?" Ruth asked with obvious interest. And they were off and running. Conversation never lagged, all of them again startled when Sophia suggested the time had come to return to their apartment to prepare for the evening meal. On the way home Ruth mused that it was good their mother had already left for Munich with the Schola Cantorum. Startled, Sophia asked her why.

"Because she would not approve of anyone writing about my pursuits," she replied without hesitation.

"Why ever not?" Sophia's voice rose in distress. She truly did admire everything her niece was doing.

"She thinks it isn't a feminine thing to be doing," Ruth muttered, head down, looking at her cup of coffee.

"But she's been giving concerts for years, since she was a teenager," Sophia replied with even more surprise.

"I guess it's OK to sing, but not to write and publish," Ruth said.

"I will speak to your mother," Sophia insisted.

"Please don't," Ruth immediately asked her.

"Ruth, let me try. If anyone can get through to my sister, it's me," she urged. "At least that used to be the case when we were growing up."

Finally Ruth sighed, and nodded her head in agreement. "I've lived with my mother for fourteen years, and I don't think it will do any good," she added. But it did.

* * *

When the family convened for the evening meal at the Unger household, Max was surprised to see that Jules and his wife were joining them. Although Nathan attempted to joke about his brother and wife joining them because they knew it was Beck's night to prepare the evening repast, it was a somber group that actually sat down at the table. After Noah led them in the HaMotzi blessing, Max suggested they talk about the two Sanatorium choices his mother had found, and decide as a group the one that might be better for him.

"I think that should be up to you, Max'l, since you will be the one who will be there," Jules said, his arm around the young man's shoulders.

They were sitting side by side, with Nate next to Max on the other side, and Lil on the other side of her husband.

Max spread the brochures in front of them all. After several minutes Yetta said, "The place in the Catskills is more expensive, but it is also much closer."

"I want my son to be close enough that we can visit him," Noah agreed.

Min asked how much more expensive it was, and Nathan replied, "Forty dollars," in a hushed tone. This was not an insignificant sum for the Unger family.

Yetta spoke up immediately, "I will take in more sewing work, even if it means working on the Sabbath," which silenced everyone.

Close to tears, Max told her, "Mama, I can't let you do that," but was constrained from continuing by the glare leveled at him by his mother.

Jules gave his shoulder another squeeze. "I've looked at both brochures, and I, too, think it's worth the extra money to have Max closer to us all. There is now a sign in my office listing out new hours; we will be open on Saturdays after the midday meal when we have returned from our prayers."

"I can ask for extra work at the factory," Nell agreed, adding, "There is no reason you, Mama and Papa should have the full responsibility for Max's care."

Even Beck's young husband agreed. "I, too, will be able to contribute at least $10 a month," although they already had one young son, with another on the way. Yetta's eyes filled, but no one declined his offer.

Max cleared his throat. "I have saved over a hundred dollars working for Mr. Shulman. None of you have to pay anything because that will more than cover my expenses for the first year."

"No!" Yetta exclaimed with such ferocity that all of them stared at her. "You must save that money for medical school, so that you can still attend once you are in good health, after you are released."

"I agree," said Noah. "There is always more furniture to repair than I can handle during a work day. I will just expand my hours. We all want you to have the life we have long envisioned."

"What if I spend fifty dollars, and save fifty?" Max asked. "That would certainly pay for pharmacy school."

"But you would be giving up your dream," moaned Nathan.

Max reached across the table, and grasped his younger brother by the wrist. "I enjoy working for Mr. Shulman. I know he would keep me on while I am in school. When I graduate I would become a full time worker, which would ease his load."

"You still would not be able to become a doctor," Yetta growled. "That is not what we agreed upon."

With the wisdom of someone much older Max replied, "Mama, circumstances have changed. We can't ignore that." Though clearly unhappy, Max was determined. "If you all want to contribute to my stay at the Sanatorium, I would be honored. That way I can begin my studies as soon as I am released and should be working full time within a year." When no one else responded, in a whisper he added, "Medical school would take too long, and you all know that."

Again silence descended upon the table. If everyone contributed, there would still be enough funds to send Nell to nursing school. Even Yetta realized that Max would never allow his illness to alter the expectations of his younger siblings. Nell's dreams were as important as his. She was certainly not responsible for his illness.
Jules looked miserable. Even though he was now a professional–dentistry was considered a very honorable career, and one he had struggled to attain–Jules did not have the funds to send his brother to the better and more expensive institution. He could contribute, but now that he and Lil were expecting their second child that was all he could do.

Yetta, who had always been the most sensible about financial matters, finally sighed. "If Max uses half of what he has saved, and each of us adds to that amount, we should be able to cover two years of care. When he can come home, he will be able to continue his education and still become a professional, even if his career will not be the one we had envisioned."

Her words brooked no more discussion. Max would go to the Sanatorium and then he would attend pharmacy school, which would be all he would be able to afford. Everyone knew that he would never become a physician. No one had eaten, and although the food was no longer warm, Beck handed the bowl of boiled potatoes to her father, who helped himself to a potato and then passed the bowl to his wife. The meal was a somber one, although Min tried to engage her sisters in conversation to lighten the mood. Each subject she brought up fell flat, not even Beck willing to engage.

Since none of the men in the Unger household were responsible for after dinner chores, Max slipped out the side door without anyone noticing once the women were doing the dishes in the kitchen. As he had expected, Teresa was already sitting on the bench in the park where they usually met, looking around anxiously because he was quite late. As he sat down beside her, he took her hand in his.

"It isn't good news, is it?" she asked him. All he was able to do was shake his head 'no'. He was afraid that if he spoke aloud, he would begin to cry, and that would have been even more shameful that having TB.

"The doctor said that the test shows that I have tuberculosis," he admitted. Both of them knew that this could be a death sentence if nothing was done. When a tear landed on his hand, Max realized Teresa was crying, and became distraught. "I won't be there more than a year, two at the outside, and then I will come back to Elizabeth. The Sanatorium is in Hunterdon County; my family will even be able to visit." Of course such a trip would have been impossible for Teresa who contributed half of her salary to her family's weekly expenses. They sat side by side, crying as quietly as they could, both of them ashamed of their weakness. They were sitting in a public park. Of course there was no place else they could have gone, but still, they each felt ashamed.

Finally Max was able to contain himself. "You will have to be tested. I will explain to Doctor Glaubman before I leave tomorrow. He is really a very decent man, and will understand. You can stop by after work, and he will perform the test. It's a simple one, and won't hurt," he added.

"I'm not afraid of the pain, or of the results," she told him. "But I don't know how I'll survive without you."

"Me neither. But we'll both have to find a way," Max agreed. "Will you please let Nathan know the results of your test. He will tell me."

"Of course. But I'm not coughing at all, and don't have any trouble breathing, so I'm sure I am fine."

Still, they sat on the bench side by side, holding hands.

"I don't want to leave, but my family may realize I am not at home, and will begin to worry. I have to pack a suitcase," Max said.

"I know. Will you be allowed to write?" she timidly asked, clearly afraid of the answer.

"I don't know. But I think waiting for your letters would be stressful…." He began.

"And that wouldn't help you. Stress might even extend the time it would take you to heal," she completed his thought.

Again silence fell.

"If you find it more stressful to not hear from me, just let Nathan know and I will begin to write," Teresa suggested.

Max actually looked relieved. "That's a very good idea."

Neither of them was willing to release the other's hand.

Teresa chuckled, though not with much enthusiasm. "I don't think Nathan ever thought he'd become a conduit. I am sure he had higher expectations for his calling."

Max leaned over and kissed her cheek. "I will miss you more than you know." He pulled Teresa to her feet, released her hand, and gave her a hug. "I don't care if anyone sees us," he said to still her objections. Then they parted, neither looking back even once to watch the other disappear on their respective park path as it meandered out to the street.

Max didn't think he would ever see Teresa again. Her parents would pressure her to date Catholic boys. Two years was a long time, and twenty was considered way down the path to spinsterhood. He was sure she would marry before he returned to Elizabeth. The following morning his mother, father and Nathan took him to the bus station, where they waited until the last minute for him to board the bus to Glen Gardner. The three of them stood watching the road long after the bus disappeared. Noah put his arm around his wife's shoulders, and with heavy hearts, they all returned to their small home. Nathan did not go to school, but instead helped his parents in the shop that day. None of them wanted to be parted.

* * *

Rosa worked side by side with Ruth setting the fonts for the school paper, writing headlines, and composing short stories to fill the blank pages. In this way the friendship between the two girls developed, until they both realized they felt closer to each other than to anyone else in their large high school. Although neither girl was shy, neither had been well known before they began to publish the journal. They discovered that each had always done what was expected of them, both in school and at home, neither wanting to rock the boat. Ruth had been more adventuresome, at least athletically. Rosa had been afraid of sliding, so she had neither roller-skated nor ice-skated, but both loved to sled in Crotona Park when it snowed. Both were voracious readers, and were able to share their favorite books with one another.

One day Ruth took a big risk, or that was how it felt to her, and told the other girl that her mother disapproved of the work she did on the paper. Rosa's mother, who worked in the family delicatessen, did as well.

"Does she expect you to work there after school?" Ruth asked her.

"Well, I always have. But I told her I would make up the hours I can't work during the week on the weekend," Rosa replied.
"My mother thinks I could take an extra course each semester and finish school sooner if I gave up this 'useless' paper," Ruth sighed.

"I don't think my mother has ever approved of me," Rosa admitted. They spent the rest of the afternoon talking about their home life in greater detail than they ever had before, deepening the friendship that was growing between them. For the first time Ruth had a girlfriend who understood the depth of the grief she still experienced over her father's death. Like Ruth, Rosa's father was the only one in the family who did not see her as unfeminine, and who encouraged both her intellectual and artistic pursuits.

Rosa seemed to have more courage than her new friend, or perhaps her need was greater. "I've noticed that you and Greg spend a lot of time together," she stated, not sure how to continue.

"We've been friends for several years. He doesn't make my heart go pitter pat, but he is a good kisser," Ruth agreed, venturing further into intimacy.

"Oh, I'd love to kiss Rolfe," Rosa sighed, and then flushed scarlet. Nevertheless she continued. Who else would she ever be able to talk to about kissing, about which she knew absolutely nothing? Rolfe was a very popular boy who sometimes wrote articles for the paper. "If I ever got up the courage to talk with him, how would I know if he kissed well," she asked with some concern.

"If it feels good, that's an indication, don't you think?" Ruth replied with a smile.

"Did it feel good right away?" Rosa asked her.

"It was exciting right away, even the idea of it, but it took us awhile to get the hang of it," Ruth admitted. "Now tell me about Rolfe. Do you mean the Rolfe who's in our history class?"

CHAPTER EIGHTEEN

The food at the New Jersey Sanatorium helped Max feel less homesick. It was much better than Yetta's, although he thought that his sister Beck could teach the chef a thing or two about baked goods. Obeying the rules, which were many and tedious, consumed much of his time, and left him very much alone. Although he shared a sleeping porch with four other men, they were not encouraged to spend time with one another lest they become re-infected, or their bodies had more difficulty healing. Contact, patient to patient, was strictly forbidden, although the rule made little sense to Max since all of them had already contracted the disease: what harm could come from the patients spending time with one another? One day when he had been leaving his room for an appointment with the facility nurse, one of his porch mates invited him to take a walk in the garden upon his return, laughing out loud when Max stuttered aloud about the 'no contact' rule.

"Everyone here is screwing their way to health," Jack said when he could stop laughing. "No one pays any attention because it doesn't make any difference anyway." Max had been so absorbed in learning his new routine and obeying the rules, he hadn't noticed anyone socializing beyond the scheduled time on the 'healing porches' and meals in the community's dining hall.

"I'd love to!" he declared with obvious enthusiasm. He was utterly sick of his own company, and thrilled that he might possibly find another human being with whom he could converse and share ideas. The books he had brought with them were no longer offering the relief they had at first, and besides, he had almost finished the entire pile.

He did have two concerns. He and Teresa had done some light petting, but that was as far as they had ventured by the time they entered college. Max was so heart-broken at the loss of her in his life he hadn't had the heart to look at the girls who were attending the same classes he was in New Brunswick. It seemed obvious to him that his new friend had a lot more experience with women, and believed he could not possibly still be a virgin. He didn't discover how wrong he was until their fourth get-together weeks later, when both young men began sharing about their day-to-day lives in more than a bare bones way.

"I think now is the time to change our status," Jack declared, adding, "If we have to live in this place for years, we have to find something positive in that reality."

"Do you think our parents would prefer we do the deed with a Jewess or a Gentile?" Max asked with a chuckle.

"My parents never even talked about kissing, so I have no idea," Jack quipped. "Are you sure your parents knew there was anything else to be done in that department?"

"I have two brothers and three sisters," Max replied with his typical dry wit.

Both boys were silent as they trudged around the grounds, a task they now completed every day, convinced the exercise would shorten their stay at the Sanatorium. Finally Jack muttered, "I don't think my parents would care which religion I defiled, if I chose to not wait until my wedding night."

Max felt a lurch in his stomach. He knew Noah and Yetta would both be appalled by this conversation, although he suspected his brother, Jules, would not. He found himself wondering if Jules and Lil had gone all the way before they were actually married. They had certainly been openly affectionate for months before the big day, but both had also been very respectful of their parents' wishes. Now that Teresa was someone from his past, and there was no one he wanted to date let alone marry, the prospect of waiting for years to discover the joys of love making seemed a very long time indeed.

"Have I lost you as a friend, Max? You're not horrified, are you," Jack asked, with a quiver in his voice.

"Of course not," Max assured him, touching his friend's shoulder briefly to reassure him. "I was just thinking about my parents." Then he sighed.

"Mine would be horrified too," Jack admitted.

"But they come from a different time," Max suggested after a few seconds. "I would love to talk to my older brother, Jules, about sex, but I don't think I have the courage."

"I'm amazed you would even consider talking to him," his friend said. "The only one in my family I could talk to - no, scratch that. There isn't anyone I would dare approach about that particular subject." "They might sit shiva for you," Max laughed.

"Absolutely," the other young man agreed. Neither was sure they were kidding. Their parents would be very upset that they were even talking about sex, let alone contemplating engaging in it.

"Does that mean we should just stop talking about this," Jack asked Max.

Max sighed, but nevertheless replied, "I don't think so."

"Good. I don't either."

They both hesitated when they reached the patio door. "I think we should each choose a gentile girl," Jack suggested, and they both burst out laughing. Olivia, their favorite nurse, was opening the door to walk across the lawn to the pharmacy.

"Share the joke, boys. I could use a good laugh!"

When she noticed the appalled glance that passed between the two young men, she laughed and added, "I know. Not for a woman's ears," and went on her way.

This time both of them sighed, only this time it was with relief. "We'll have to be more circumspect with our conversations," Max suggested as he ushered his friend through with a flourish.

"No kidding," was all Jack could manage. His heart was racing so fast he thought he might faint.

The next day when Max was checking out the new Sinclair Lewis novel from the Sanatorium's library, a young woman who lived a floor below him noticed and remarked, "I think I prefer Fitzgerald, but my roommate loves Sinclair Lewis."

Falling into step with one another turned out to be as natural as breathing. They agreed that reading not only helped pass the time, but gave them joy as well as relief. The only other young woman Max had ever known who loved reading as much as he did was Teresa. Perhaps, as Jules had suggested on his last visit, there would be other 'fish in the sea' once he stopped mourning her loss. That first day the two discussed Howard's End, which both had read, agreeing to read another of Forster's novels at the same time so they could discuss it. Much to his surprise Max discovered that Suzanna, his new friend, had already finished 'Sons and Lovers', considered a very risqué choice, especially for a girl. Max was as excited by the prospect of being able to share the ideas within the books he was reading, as he was about meeting a very interesting young woman. When the two scholars made their way to the dining hall and their evening meal, Jack could not believe his eyes.

"She's the best looking girl in this place," he declared once they had separated and Max had filled his tray and sat down beside him.

Max felt his face begin to flush, and turned to glance her way. She was indeed very pretty, with long blond hair curling at the collar of her starched blue blouse, and blue eyes made even more noticeable by her attire. She smiled at him, which increased the flush in his cheeks before he was able to turn away.

"Holy cow! And I thought you were shy like me," Jack blurted.

"I am," Max tried to defend himself. "We were both checking out books at the library and started to talk about them. That's all," he added, the words sounding lame even in his own ears.

"Maybe I should take up reading. I never had time outside, what with school, and working at my Dad's butcher shop," Jack mumbled.

"I think my mother is convinced that one of the reasons I got sick was that I was always reading under my covers at night after I had finished everything else I had to do," Max grinned. "But here you are, proving her wrong."

Jack grinned back at him. "Who knew there were other things to be gained from reading those books you're always buried in."

Max laughed. 'I sure never thought it would send Susanna my way."

"Oh. Now we're on a first name basis," Jack groaned.

"I don't know her last name. Do you?" Max asked him.

"No. I wonder if she's gentile or Jewish."

"You're thinking I should…with her? No, I don't think so." Max was obviously horrified.

"Why not? Because she's smart, or maybe Jewish?" Jack asked him in a teasing manner, although he actually was curious about his friend's answer.

The question certainly gave the thoughtful young man pause. "I wonder if that makes me a bigot. I guess I should give some thought to that," Max replied, clearly troubled. Then, mouth full, he added, "Maybe I'll stay a virgin a little while longer." The two friends smiled at each other, pals again. After the noon meal both boys repaired to their cottage to lie down in their rooms, along with the rest of the patients. Even after two months, Max still felt tired a great deal of the time, which disturbed him greatly. Knowing that his new friend suffered from the same malaise didn't make him feel any better about it. He wanted to go home to begin the rest of his life. After all, he was a high school graduate; even if medical school was now out of the question because of the unexpected expense of his stay in the Sanatorium, his idea to attend pharmacy school had become a plan. That plan was helping to assuage the pain of giving up a lifelong dream, and making him anxious to begin. He would have to save the money to attend, and obviously couldn't pursue this new path until he returned home. He only hoped the actual work would be close enough to the field of medicine to hold his interest, as well as enable him to eventually support a wife and family.

He and Teresa were writing letters to each other every week despite their intentions to the contrary, which Max waited for by the time Friday rolled around. He hadn't heard from her the preceding week, which did concern him. Although he knew he didn't have the courage to marry her against the wishes of his parents and cause them more pain than his illness already had, his heart had not caught up with his head. When he didn't hear from her by Monday, his depression increased. Her parents had been pushing her to date a boy who had gone to the local Catholic high school because they had long been social acquaintances with the young man's parents. She hadn't written about that issue for a few weeks; Max assumed she had gone on a date to please them, and worried that perhaps a second date had transpired as well. The boy had been in his biology class, and was good looking and intelligent, though not particularly intellectual. Nevertheless, the young man was taking night classes at Rutgers and still lived in Elizabeth with his parents, around the corner from Teresa and her family. Max couldn't bear the thought that by the time he was able to leave this facility, she would be beyond his reach completely, even as a friend. If she became engaged, he doubted they would be able to spend any time together, let alone the hours they had been used to sharing with one another. That loss was unimaginable.

At home in Elizabeth Yetta and Noah were very troubled that no one in the family had been to visit Max. He and his wife still worked very long hours and even Nathan was now working every afternoon after school at the law office of a family friend in downtown Elizabeth. Nevertheless, one night at dinner they all came to agreement about who should visit. Noah suggested he speak to the attorney at the law office, but Nathan was adamant that he should take on that task. After all, he was almost a grown man, and felt it his responsibility to ask for time off to take the bus to visit his brother in Glen Gardner. The ride would take hours each way, but it wouldn't necessitate an overnight stay, so he would only miss one afternoon of work, and one full day of school. The morning he was to leave, Yetta was both grim-mouthed and silent at the breakfast table. She knew that the family decision about Nathan being the one to travel to the Sanatorium was the correct one, but she was still furious that she was not the one who would be visiting her child.

When his brother came into the waiting area, Nathan was shocked by his appearance although it hadn't changed particularly in the few months he had been away. Nathan supposed he had forgotten that Max had become so drawn looking and thin, with a continuous flush on his cheeks, which if anything, had intensified. Nathan noticed quite quickly that all of the other patients they passed in the halls or out on the spacious grounds also had odd blotches of pink on their cheeks. Rather than making them look healthy, as if they had been in the sun, they looked odd, and unwell.

"You are looking good," he told Max anyway, because he had no idea what else to say. By the time the nurse came to tell the brothers that it was time for the afternoon rest period, Nathan was surprised at how quickly the hours had passed. Max had wanted to hear every tidbit of information about their family, from Beck's pregnancy, to Min's involvement with Morris, a young man he had known, though only slightly, from Battin High School. Nathan shared some stories about his romance with Helen, which was proceeding much too quickly in Yetta's opinion, but Max was not surprised. He liked Helen, who was quirky, with a wonderful giggle and a lively mind. He was relieved that his brother was talking about attending Rutgers with a scholarship, which he had already been offered, and afterwards doing a two-year course in the law. He loved the discussions he was having with his boss, one of the best attorneys in Elizabeth at the time, and one who was clearly urging Nathan to pursue this path. Marriage would have to wait.

When Nathan hurried off to catch the last bus back to Elizabeth in the late afternoon, Max experienced an emptiness he had never known before, even when he had first arrived at the Sanatorium. He and his little brother had been the best of friends since Nathan had learned to walk. They not only shared a history, but an understanding of one another, their place in the Unger family, and the values that had been imbued in both of them by their parents. To be able to talk with someone with no need of much explanation was a gift Max had never fully appreciated before. He had taken his relationship with Nathan for granted, not because he didn't value him, but because he had assumed it would be life-long, wherever their individual lives would take them. That both would stay in Elizabeth was a given. That their friendship would deepen throughout their lives as they shared their experiences and continued to enjoy one another's company was as well. Max sat on the verandah of his cottage because he felt too tired to walk in the garden. Telling Nate about his life in this place, and hearing about Nate's plans for his future had exhausted, as well as inflamed him. When Jack sat down next to him, he could tell Max was spent, and didn't try to begin a conversation. He merely squeezed his friend's knee, and again, Max felt grateful. Because he too, was ill, and had also had a visit with his only sister, he understood.

The following morning he and Jack sat side by side in the sun, wrapped in their warm woolen blankets, and talked about their families. Jack, who was Jewish with parents much less religious than Max's, expressed great compassion about his friend's love of Teresa and the impossibility of their joining their lives together.

"Even my Pop would be distressed if I wanted to marry a Catholic girl. Letting the Pope into our business? Heaven forbid," he exclaimed in mock horror, at which Max had to laugh.

"My father never said that, but I'm sure that's how my mother feels. No one but her can make the decisions for any of us," he sputtered.

Both young men fell silent. Finally Jack asked him, "Do you really think it's impossible for you to pursue Susanna…in…for…" he stuttered, with no idea how to continue.

His friend actually shivered at the thought. "It would be more likely that I would date her and then even marry her if her family lived anywhere near ours in Elizabeth. But she is from Pennsylvania, so that isn't a possibility."

"You sure enjoy being with her!" Jack exclaimed.

"That I do. She has almost read as many books as I have, and loves to talk about the ideas in the novels we're both reading, and that is a real joy," Max agreed.

"You know what I think?" his friend asked.

"I know you're going to tell me," Max quipped. His sense of humor had increased since his admission to the Sanatorium, although he still considered himself a serious person. He knew Teresa would be pleased by this addition to his personality. There it was again, that name: Teresa. How could he feel like this, and still be experiencing nightly dreams where he was in Susanna's arms, and they were both in a state of almost complete dishabille? He had not told either his brother or his new friend about his nightly emissions because he was utterly ashamed of them. He would never have even mentioned them to Jules, so there was no one to tell him that such things were normal for young men. Even if he had wished he could find a book that would have explained what was happening to him, he would never have asked the librarian for it. How would he explain what he wanted, and why? Never.

The next day, walking with Susanna, he discovered that she loved Mozart. He had only heard one of the concertos she mentioned on their brief stroll in the garden, but looked forward to asking his oldest brother to bring him a recording of it when he came to visit. Of course he would also need a whole new set of books, since he had already finished two of the novels Nathan had brought him from the library. Fortunately, their favorite librarian in Elizabeth had heard that Max had been sent to a Sanatorium and received permission from her boss to lend Nathan several books for him, waiving the rule that the books be returned in three weeks time. Both women realized that the Unger family would never have been able to afford to buy books for Max, but nevertheless wanted him to have pleasure as he healed from the frightening disease that had felled him. She had even suggested a new author, a woman named Virginia Woolf, whom she had greatly enjoyed, though she was not sure if a young male reader would feel the same about this exciting young author. Of course that was the first book he had read and passed on to his female friend, who was thrilled. She had heard of Woolf, and was quite excited to be able to read a woman other than George Elliot.
"When did you realize 'he' was a 'she'? Max asked her. Had he not looked at the back flap, he might not have known himself.

"My English teacher told me about her," Susanna chuckled. "We were both always looking for female authors."

"They don't think the same way as men," Max agreed.

"What do you mean?" she asked, staring at him with a quizzical gaze.

She gave him the time to ponder his answer, walking quietly beside him around the pathways in the garden. "You come at ideas from several directions at once, and we – men – approach thoughts head on. Do you understand what I mean?" he asked.

"Oh yes," she replied, with a broad smile. "I certainly do."

"I think your gender may have the right idea, but it's too late for me to change my spots," he admitted thoughtfully.

"See! That's another difference. I don't think it's ever too late for anything," she exclaimed. By then both of them were tired, and agreed to return to the chairs in the main building's solarium, content to sit side by side reading. Whether any other patients were indulging in more advanced romantic behavior, Max had no idea. He also lacked the courage to ask anyone. Putting an arm around her shoulder from time to time as they walked was as far as he had been able to progress.

That evening a Chaplin film was being shown in the auditorium. Max invited Jack to walk over to the main building with him and Susanna, who joined them from the women's cottage as they made their way there. The three sat together, Jack as impressed with this young woman as Max. He found her friendly, inquisitive – though hardly intrusive – funny and smart. She seemed genuinely interested in his life, where he came from, his family, and his plans once he was released from the Sanatorium. Though Jack preferred the evenings when they played games like bingo and dominoes, he enjoyed the film as well as the discussion that Max and Susanna engaged in as they made their slow trek back to their respective cottages. All three were tired, but nonetheless none of them wanted to walk with any haste. When Susanna asked Jack what his thoughts were about Chaplin, and his supposed political beliefs, he was startled, but didn't hesitate to reply. The young woman had a way of making him comfortable with his beliefs, even if they differed from hers. He had never talked to a woman about anything serious before. Truth be known, he had rarely talked to anyone of the opposite sex at all, even when the occasion permitted discussion, because he was too shy. In this way, he and Max were a lot alike, which probably had a great deal to do with their becoming friends in the first place.

"I love the concerts," Max explained, "because my father always listens to the radio in the evening after a long day of work. He especially loves Mozart and Bach."

"Mine too," Susanna agreed.

Jack felt left out. His family didn't even own a radio because they had given their old model to his older brother when he had moved out of the house to begin work at a factory in the next town. His mother believed his brother needed the comfort of familiar programs more than they did; Jack and his other brother agreed, as did his dad. Neither Susanna nor Max noticed his silence.

Later in the week when one of the patients was asked to entertain them with a violin solo, Susanna turned to Max with a smile. They had been talking about this particular Mozart sonata that very afternoon, having discovered it was a favorite for them both. That evening, when the three were returning to their respective cottages, Susanna asked each of the young men about their schooling, as well as their plans for their futures in that regard. She had not known that Max had planned to pursue a career in medicine, and neither had Jack. Neither of them commented on this disclosure, since all three knew it would now be impossible. Susanna quickly shared that she had plans to become an elementary school art teacher, but wasn't sure she would have the time or energy to work full time while she saved the money to pursue that goal anymore. Both of the boys urged her to find a way; both assured her that she would make a marvelous teacher, and that her small Pennsylvania town would be lose out if she didn't. Max even suggested her town hold a fundraiser to pay for her expenses, both boys sure she would receive a scholarship for her studies at the Institute of Fine Arts in Philadelphia. They have seen her drawings, and been especially impressed by the collages she has shown them because of her use of leaves and twigs as well as paints and crayons. For the first time in their acquaintance, Susanna was speechless. She could not even look at either young man because she felt so embarrassed by such praise. Her parents thought her 'scribblings' a waste of time, although she had never told Max or Jack about that, and would never have volunteered to show them her work had Max not come upon her sketching on a bench outside one afternoon.

"How did you end up here?" Jack asked her.

Susanna answered without any hesitation. "I was a teacher's aid in the very elementary school I attended. My mentor noticed my cough, which I thought was normal, at least for people who grew up in my neighborhood."

Max was appalled. "Did she tell the Principal?" he asked.

"Oh no. But she was concerned, and said she thought I needed to see a doctor, which I knew I couldn't afford. She understood and told me about a clinic in downtown Philadelphia, where she said I probably wouldn't have to pay anything at all."

"I don't know if that's a good thing or not," Max exclaimed with some distress.

"It was the right thing for her to do, Max," she told him. "Otherwise I could have infected everyone in my family, and that would have been a disaster!"

For a while none of them said another word. They all knew she was right, sad as that was. When they reached the door of her cottage, Max asked, "Has anyone else in your family contracted TB?"

"No," she replied with obvious relief. "Everyone is fine. When they told me they were all putting aside money every week so that I could still go to college, I told them to stop. If they don't eat properly, one of them could very well become ill."

Once he and Jack were alone, Max admitted that he was having trouble sleeping, which was worrying him. What if he was getting worse again?

"That happened to me, too, when I had been here for a few months, but Nurse Flynn assured me that was to be expected," Jack assured him. "It took months for me to develop a pattern that helped me sleep through the night," he added.

Max sighed. "I hope that is true for me as well. I sometimes lie awake for hours in the middle of the night, or it certainly feels that way."

"You know, since they offer enjoyable activities here like seeing Charlie Chaplin movies, maybe it wouldn't be bad if we both relapsed," Jack tried to joke. Max glanced at him, but couldn't even smile.

"Not funny, huh?" he agreed, and the two opened their cottage door. Neither had much else to say as they made their nightly ablutions, and both lay awake consumed with their own worries before drifting off to sleep.

* * *

It took me a while to get this was in Europe hmm

One afternoon Al dropped by the Berkowitz apartment to tell Adelaide and Ruth that he and his family were leaving for the country to stay with some cousins the following afternoon. Since Adelaide had gone to the market with her sister to shop for vegetables, Al gave the message to Ruth. Her heart raced when he sat down next to her on the couch, which she tried to disguise as best she could. Shame that she should be so excited by this rare opportunity to have a conversation with her sister's beau, rendered her tongue-tied. He would know that she was a black-hearted vixen if she revealed even a smidgen of what she was really feeling, so she struggled to think of something to say that would be innocuous enough to send Al on his way.

"Hey, why don't we walk over to the Café Central and have a cup of espresso," he suggested with some excitement. "This time of day there are usually poets and writers there, which I know would interest you."

Ruth had no idea how he knew that, since she had rarely said anything to him at all, let alone engage in a literary discussion. "I probably would enjoy that," she mumbled, head down.

"Come on, Ruth. Holly won't mind. She's the one who told me about your success with the school newspaper in the first place," he urged.

This was totally shocking. That Holly would have talked about her at all was surprising enough, but the notion that her sister would have touted her abilities to anyone, let alone her boyfriend, was beyond belief. She found herself standing still so that Al could wrap her shawl around her shoulders, and followed him out the front door of her Aunt and Uncle's house. His touch sent a shiver up her spine, which she was not able to suppress.

Al, misunderstanding completely, suggested they return to the house for a warmer wrap, but finally believed her assurances that she was fine since she had only shivered once and did seem to be alright. They slowly walked to the café side by side, his shoulder and upper arm occasionally brushing hers, but Ruth somehow managed to contain herself although inside she was a-boil. Grateful to have arrived at the coffee house, which she had only been to a couple of times because her mother thought she was too young to frequent such a place, she was relieved to finally step inside, away from Al's strong shoulder. The cacophony of noise that greeted them when Al opened the door for her was almost deafening. People were grouped in two's, three's, and even occasionally five's or six's, seated at tables where all of these groups were engaged in heated discussions. Ruth had no idea where to go, though she would have liked to eavesdrop on every single table. Al waved to three young people sitting in a booth at the edge of the room, and put his hand in the small of her back to guide her to their table. That gesture almost became her undoing. Her legs became wobbly, but she stepped forward in the hopes that walking would steady them, and, fortunately, that was the case.

One of the young women and the fellow who was obviously her companion, were arguing about the Grand War and Austria's ostensible reasons for joining the fray. Like Ruth, the young woman thought the war a dreadful mistake. The young woman had marched with groups opposed to conflicts between nations, instead wanting representatives from the various countries to attend a conference as a way to find solutions for their differences. Since the end of the debacle, as the women described it, the renewed anti-Semitism in Austria was a concern to all of the young people seated at the table. Despite herself, Ruth immediately joined the discussion, asking question after question about the situation, finally voicing a concern that the state of affairs they were describing were certainly concerning as well as personal. Was there a chance that the anti-Jewish feelings could become the basis for another European war? She was passionate in her belief that war was evil, and was clearly disturbed. She asked for a piece of paper from the notebook one of the girls was holding, saying she wanted to write an article about the situation for her school newspaper. When she noticed the smile teasing the corners of Al's utterly appealing lips, she was startled, but then was quickly pulled back into the conversation by one of the young men at the table. Soon the three men were talking about their chances of being called upon to fight if war did break out, Jonas saying he was the most likely candidate, since he was almost finished with his college course, and already twenty years old. Ruth took notes the enter time, intent upon getting down every word. Jonas had talked to his parents about leaving Austria should tensions between Jews and gentiles became more extreme, but his parents were Austrians through and through and would not consider it.

"Do you think you are in danger now?" Ruth asked with trepidation. She had overheard her aunt and uncle talking about some hate-filled slogan that had been painted on a wall near their home in Vienna, but couldn't believe it was as serious a problem as they supposed. After all, she hadn't read anything about the dangers of anti-Semitism in the New York papers.

He shrugged. Nina, a friend of her cousin's Ruth had met on her family's last trip to Europe, disagreed. "I don't know. The schism in my history class is growing wider, and we seem to be dividing along religious lines," she said, brow furrowed.

"But what could they do, the people who dislike the Jews?" Al asked, finally as engaged in the discussion as his companion. He, too, was twenty. No one at the table had an answer, though all of the young people did seem worried.

"You will be safe if war is declared here," Jonas assured Al. "I don't think it likely that your President would allow his young men to cross the ocean only to die on foreign soil a second time."

"I'm not so sure. If an entire race was at risk, I think he would be morally compelled to help them," he murmured, suddenly genuinely worried.

Alarmed, Ruth turned to him and blurted, "You wouldn't enlist, would you, Al?"

Al grasped her hand in reassurance, explaining that he didn't believe in war as an answer to problems between races, religions or nations either, but that if his country entered the fray, he would probably feel compelled to join them. Especially if his cousins and their friends were in danger.

Nina, the young woman with whom Ruth had been conversing, turned to the table at large with a mock frown. "I don't know what is the matter with the male gender. Even as boys they seem to see no way out of joining a fight when it's in progress!" she teased, trying to lighten the tone.

"You're one of the smartest boys in your class. You need to stay in college," Ruth ordered, turning towards Al. She could have kicked herself for sounding so serious, but the entire discussion had upset her a great deal. Another war? Problems for Jews in Europe? What would that even mean?

Al was quite delighted by Ruth's concern. He grinned, grabbing her hand again, much to her delight, which of course she tried to hide. Ruth found herself wondering if Holly had felt her tummy lose it's moorings when Al held her hand, and almost lost the direction of the conversation, so tumultuous were her feelings about the young man whose hand was grasping hers. The exciting sensations had squelched any of the dismay about the situation in Austria that she had been experiencing just moments before. "I never thought you felt that way, little sister!" Al exclaimed, the 'little sister' all but ruining the moment for Ruth.

"She's awfully courageous for a 'little sister'" Jonas quipped. "If this is your first time in Vienna, Ruth, I'd be more than happy to be your tour guide," he added, much to Al's obvious displeasure.

Ruth was about to explain that she had been to Vienna several times with her family when her mother's chorus had come to sing at the Rathaus, but Al squeezed her hand even tighter. "Oh, Ruth is well cared for here in Vienna. My family makes the voyage from the States to the Continent every summer, so I'm more than able to show her the sights she has yet to see here," he explained firmly but with a light tone of voice.

"It seems you've already been noticed, Ruth," Jonas declared with a broad grin. "If your knight in shining armor doesn't suit your needs, feel free to call upon me. I'm usually here at the Central every afternoon."

Ruth's heart was thumping madly in her chest. She was not the 'pretty' sister, and had never received this kind of attention. That Al, whom she had longed for from afar the entire year, had proffered one of the offers reigning down upon her in the bustling café was more than she had imagined even in her dreams. She managed to blurt a 'thank you' and she and Al left the café shortly afterwards with a promise they would return in a day or two. As they turned the corner on their way back to her Aunt Sophia's apartment, Al took her arm, swinging it back and forth as they marched up the block. He began to laugh, the sound contagious.

"You're a very clever girl, Ruth," he managed in-between guffaws. She shrugged as she skipped along beside him.
"I'm used to reading for my articles, that's all," she said, which sent him into gales of laughter yet again.

Finally he managed to contain himself. "You have to stop doing that," he told her.

"Doing what?" she asked in all innocence.

"Making excuses for your ideas," he replied, adding, "You are very clever."

By the time they reached Sophia's brownstone, Ruth felt as if she were flying. She could not understand what he saw in Holly. Though bright, she hid her intelligence, determined to make her way in the world with her pretty face. Ruth had no such thing to fall back upon, and therefore had never considered that option. She had always known it was her brain and gifts as a writer that would sustain her out in the world and was already honing those skills.

Holly had moped around the house after Al had left Vienna with his family, which Ruth completely understood now. Had Al been her boyfriend, she would have felt bereft at his absence. When Sophia invited Ruth to go on a shopping expedition with her, one she knew her older sister would have enjoyed, Ruth was ashamed yet again to feel such delight; she would relish her time alone with Sophia, the day hers to savor for herself.

Their first stop was the hair salon, where Ruth was now a regular. She needed no prodding from her aunt anymore, and readily slipped into the seat in front of her favorite hair stylist to have her bob trimmed. As the young man clipped, stepping back every few seconds to view the fruits of his labor, he and Sophia chatted about the dangers of the political situation in the same breath as their views on the latest fashions. He suggested the best place to find slippers that would be sure to complement the dress Sophia wanted to find for Ruth to take home with her when she and her family returned to New York. Too excited to remain silent, Ruth told both of them about a pair of ballet-like dress shoes she had seen on Graben in Stephansplatz, in rapid and completely comprehensible German, even impressing her Aunt with her fluency.

"You speak our language like an Austrian not an American, liebchen," the hair stylist said with some surprise.

Ruth explained, "I have been speaking both languages since I was a child. At first it was easier than talking to my Mama in English, but as she improved, I used my native tongue more often."

"You certainly haven't lost your abilities in German," Sophia agreed, ruffling the top of her head despite the stylist brushing away her fingers, which he said were 'destroying the artistry' of his hair cut.

When her Aunt chose the very dress Ruth had been eying for days in their favorite dress shop near the plaza, Ruth could not keep back her gasp of pleasure.

Sophia smiled with real affection as she handed the garment to her niece. "I think the lavender will look marvelous with your skin tone, and the cut of the neck is perfect for your Austrian hair style," she said as she ushered her niece into the dressing room. When Ruth emerged from the little stall, Sophia sighed with delight.

"We must buy you that pair of pumps to complement this dress. You look utterly lovely," she said to her niece, smiling broadly.

"But when would I ever wear something like this after we leave Vienna?" Ruth protested.

"Don't your school have a big dance at the end of this year?" Sophia asked.

Ruth visibly brightened. "Yes, we have a senior prom!" she declared.

"You see!" said her Aunt.

The only thought coursing through Ruth's whirling brain was that the only escort she wanted was Al, but he couldn't take her because they would be back in New York by then and he would again be dating her older sister. He probably wouldn't even notice her once they returned home, she thought, trying to accept that grim reality. She supposed Greg would have to do, and then felt horrible because she knew how much he longed for her to feel about him the way she felt about Al.

Instead of turning towards the tram that would take then home, Sophia headed in the opposite direction, smiling at her niece's confusion. As soon as she noticed the 'Hotel Sacher' sign, Ruth realized what Sophia had in mind. The evening they had arrived in Vienna, Sophia's maid had brought one of the famed sachertortes to the table for desert. The confection was chocolate, with apricot jam between the layers, and an absolutely amazing frosting of hard, dark chocolate, a swirl of white chocolate on the top. Perched upon the swirl was a circle of dark chocolate with the words 'Hotel Sacher' in the middle. This too was edible. Their first evening in Vienna Ruth and Simon had eaten every mouthful, though Adelaide politely left the circle of chocolate on her plate as she had been taught.

What was most revealing to Ruth was learning where her mother had learned her skills as a parent. A more forbidding woman than her tightly coiffed grandmamma, with her high colored black dresses and tightly pinned bun, Ruth had never met. How Sophia retained her buoyant spirit, Ruth had no idea and was too polite to ask, although she certainly wanted to know. She was determined to pluck up her courage before their departure since she believed the answer to her salvation with her own mother might lie in her Aunt's answer.

After her first few bites, the image of Al indulging in such a sinful pleasure popped into her head, making her smile. Fortunately Sophia assumed she was smiling because of the pleasure of the pastry itself.

"I'm afraid neither of us is going to eat a very good supper this evening," Sophia said, speaking around the little piece of torte still resting on her tongue. Then she swallowed, and continued. "I know I should have waited until I swallowed, but I often behave in ways that surprise certain members of my family."

"Have you ever felt ashamed?" Ruth asked.

Sophia shrugged her shoulders, clad in white-ruffed silk. "In the beginning. But after awhile it made me feel as if I wasn't trapped in the world in which I was raised."

"It sounds very liberating," the teenager replied, her mouth also half full of melting chocolate. The two began to laugh, delighted conspirators. At that moment Ruth knew there was nothing she couldn't share with her Aunt, a belief that never altered during their lifetimes.

The next morning Ruth came down to the breakfast room earlier than she usually did. Her mother could not keep the surprise from her face, although she attempted to camouflage it with a bite of toast.

'The things we do with food in our mouths,' her daughter thought as she sat down across from Adelaide, delighted by the surprise on her mother's face.

"To what do we owe this appearance?" she asked with a smile.

"I was hoping I could go to your rehearsal, Mama, so that I might see what it is you do all those afternoons when you are away from home in New York," Ruth breathlessly announced. Silence reigned, her mother too startled to speak.

Finally Adelaide took a deep breath and said, "Why Ruth, I would be happy to have you attend my rehearsal."

Before Ruth could faint from the shock of her mama's positive response, Adelaide continued. "You do realize that the rehearsal could continue for over four hours, and that you would have to be silent as a lamb the entire time?"

"If I bring my journal so I can take notes, would that insult anyone in the chorus, or your choir master?" Ruth asked her mother.

Even Adelaide had to smile. "No. I doubt he would even notice, though I'm sure Jenny will want to know what you are writing about."

"And what will you tell her?" Sophia asked her sister.

"I will say that my talented daughter is taking notes for an article she plans to write in the newspaper she edits for her high school in America," declared Adelaide, head and shoulders held high.

At first Ruth was too stunned to respond, although she could feel the eyes of both her Aunt and mother upon her. "Would you really want me to do that?" she asked.

Her mother nodded once, her Aunt smiling broadly with obvious delight.

Had Simon been alive, he might have kissed his youngest daughter on the cheek as 'his two women' walked out the front door of Sophia's house after breakfast. Neither realized they were both thinking about him, and his reaction to their breakfast conversation.

Al had told Ruth that he and his family would be returning from Salzburg two days before Adelaide's concert, which his family planned to attend as guests of the Liebman's, but she didn't see him that entire day. By the time the butler announced his arrival the following morning while the family was still ensconced around the breakfast table, Ruth hoped she did not seem nonplused.

"I am sorry to be interrupting your breakfast," Al began as soon as he entered the dining room. "I had told Ruth we would be returning to Vienna yesterday, and I didn't want any of you to be worried that anything untoward had happened to us."

Adelaide said nothing, too startled to speak at first. "That was good of you, but I don't think any of us was concerned," she sputtered.

"Oh no," Ruth agreed, although she had been devastated. The relief she was experiencing because of this information – he had wanted to see her! – brought a flush of shame to her cheeks, which she managed to cover by bringing her serviette to them.

"Have a seat, Al," Sophia suggested, motioning to the empty chair that Holly would have been occupying had she been willing to come to Europe with the family. This realization brought even more shame to Ruth's heart. What was wrong with her? Perhaps she truly was a feral beast.

After an appropriate amount of time spent sharing stories of Salzburg, where the Schola would be singing later in the month, life in New York, and in particular the schooling Al and Ruth were receiving at Evander Childs High School, he and Ruth excused themselves and left the room. He again suggested a visit to the café, which sent her head spinning. Of course she couldn't go with him, which made her miserable. Why had she told her mother she wanted to attend her rehearsal?

When Ruth told Al that she would be attending the rehearsal all morning and well into the afternoon he immediately suggested he meet

519

her at the rehearsal hall after four, so they could sneak over to the Central Café for a quick snack before they both had to return to their respective apartments. He was clearly delighted to learn that he and his family would be sharing a box with the Liebman clan at the Vienna concert. When she returned to the dining room, her mother looked at her with some interest.

"He gave me something he bought in Salzburg for Holly, and I said I'd give it to her when we go home, since we are returning to New York before they are," she blurted although he had done no such thing. She had no idea why she had said so, or what she, herself, could buy for her sister that she could say came from her beau. She hoped no one remembered her remark, because purchasing something as if it came from him would magnify the lie. Besides, Holly would thank him for the gift, whatever it was, and Al would have no idea what she was talking about. Ruth couldn't explain it to him, because she wouldn't know how to justify her need to lie in the first place. Her crush on Al was becoming more of a problem than she wanted to admit to herself.

Despite her best efforts to limit her contact with him, the very idea of him still made her heart beat with abandon. If he tried to kiss her, an action she longed for him to take, she had no idea what she would do. Of course she knew allowing such a thing would be wrong. She was Holly's sister, after all, and knew how devastated she could have been had Holly been seeing Greg in New York while she was away. And she didn't love Greg, at least not in the way Holly seemed to love Al, or, for that matter, she herself. How had she gotten herself into this untenable situation?

Nevertheless, the evening of the concert she asked her mother if she could use a touch of her rouge, as well as a little dab or two of her perfume behind her ears before Adelaide left to 'prepare her voice' with the rest of the members of the chorus for that evening's concert. Instead of becoming irritated, her mother seemed amused by the request, and actually lightly dabbed her lips with color as well before she raced out the front door to join the group members waiting for her on the pathway.

"You look lovely, Ruthie," her Aunt told her when she realized she was gazing at herself in the downstairs hall mirror. "The frock we picked out is the perfect color, and shows off your frame to great advantage," she added, lightly brushing her shoulders. Indeed, as she looked at herself in the mirror, she couldn't help but agree. For once she didn't look awkward, ungainly, or somehow not quite right. She loved the frock, and the white, ballet-like slippers she had chosen to wear with it were perfect. As she, Sophia and her husband left the apartment Ruth found herself wondering what Al would think about her costume, and then, of course, felt deeply ashamed. Sophia's husband thought she was blushing because their next door neighbor's son was clearly looking at her with admiration, and suggested she get used to such glances. "You're a striking looking young woman," he told her.

She would have preferred he had said she was a very pretty one. The look on Al's face almost brought tears to her eyes as he helped her off with her wrap at the concert hall. Although she and her family sat in the front of the box that had been reserved for them, with Al and his parents in the seats behind them, she was certain she could feel his breath on her neck. She didn't know if she was anxious because her mother was about to sing a solo in front of such a huge audience, or because her sister's beau was seated behind her with his family. When his mother gasped as Adelaide stepped forward and began to sing her solo, Ruth turned around with a big smile, proud, for once, of the mother she had been given.

Although the applause at the end of the concert was thunderous, Adelaide did not step forward to be honored separately until a man in the audience chanted her name, along with a 'bravo', which was taken up by most of the audience, at least in the orchestra. Adelaide seemed so tiny on the large stage, even in comparison with her fellow group members. It was strange for Ruth, who thought of her mother as quite powerful since her opinions usually ruled their home. Her Aunt grasped her hand and held on, whispering, "Isn't it marvelous?" Ruth shook her head in amazement. Even in New York her mother had never received such overwhelming adulation.

"If it was me, I think I would have fainted," she whispered to Sophia, who turned and grinned at her.

"No way, my dear Ruth. You are one of the bravest people I know," she replied, which shook the young woman's very foundation. Her

Aunt thought this of her? Those words would remain with her for years and never lose their glow. Even had her mother uttered them, they would not have had the same affect since Sophia was the person Ruth, herself, most admired. During the intermission, she floated out to the lobby, accepted a fizzy water and cookie without even noticing, and didn't realize until they returned to their seats that she had consumed both. Even talking to Al during the intermission paled in comparison to such praise.

Adelaide seemed somewhat shocked by her reception as well, barely able to compose sensible sentences in response to the Austrians who crowded into the dressing room afterwards. Sophia understood immediately, and easily fielded most of the questions directed at her sister until she was able to answer them herself. Ruth wasn't sure if she was pleased or jealous. Then she relented, gave her mother a very big hug, and told her how proud she was. Adelaide just beamed. She didn't even notice that Al's hand was resting on her daughter's shoulder, although her sister's husband certainly did.

'Uh oh,' he thought. He was delighted for his younger, and less attractive niece, but he also understood there might be hell to pay when both families returned to New York. Her Uncle was sure that Ruth had no idea he, too, thought she was less than pretty, although he also believed that his niece already had a sense of style, a trait that would more than compensate for her lack of beauty. She might, in time, become quite stunning, especially given her intelligence and vivacious personality.

When Molly, Sophia's oldest daughter, suggested the younger set all repair to a local cafe catering to their age group in the evenings, Ruth didn't even hear the remonstrance's of the adults. She would be spending even more time with Al! Her Uncle reminded them to return home by 11, which was later than Ruth had ever been allowed to stay out in America. She was in a fog, which her Uncle also noticed, urging her in a gentle whisper to 'wake up', which she tried to do without much success.

When Al's arm brushed hers as they left the small dressing room, she felt as if she had been struck by lightening. Afraid to glance at him, she could feel the tremors in his arm, which seemed to indicate that he was as affected by this accident as she. Thrilled, she had no idea what either of them would do about Holly, or if he was even thinking about her sister. Would he consider their conversations, and the electricity shooting from one to the other, a brief moment in time, one that carried no weight in the grand scheme of things? She could never ask, but she was also unable to keep her thoughts from straying to her sister, and the betrayal she was engaged in. Even if he never touched her with purpose, she longed for him to do just that: which made her what? Certainly not the good girl her father had always assured her she was.

When all of the young people were seated at a round table in the back room of the café, Al again rested his hand on her shoulder, and leaned down to ask her what she wanted from the bar. Since she knew she had no hope of sleeping during the night, she asked for an espresso, a drink she had already learned to love during the brief time they had been in Vienna on this visit, the only visit where she had been allowed to try such a thing. He squeezed gently, and then, eyes twinkling, said he would find a treat to go with the strong coffee concoction. He and the boy who had been talking to Molly walked towards the counter together, already deep in conversation, both laughing at something that had been said. Ruth could not believe he could carry on a normal conversation, or that he could laugh with such a light heart. When he returned to the table with two glasses of scotch whiskey as well as her espresso, setting two of the drinks in front of her, she gawked at him, totally shocked. She had not ever had a taste of liquor before, and knew her mother would have been horrified that this young man had bought her the scotch. It had been her father's favorite drink.

"I won't tell if you don't," he teased, amused by the expression on her face. "If you don't like it, don't worry. One of us will drink it, since wasting is not acceptable."

All she could manage was a shake of her head. Al took his seat next to her, picked up his glass, and waited for her to do so as well. The scotch burned her throat, but she was surprised to discover she like the taste. "I see why my father had a glass every night before dinner, which sure irritated my mother," she said, and then started to giggle.

"You can't be tipsy already," he teased her again.

"No. I was picturing the look on her face if she could see what I am drinking," she replied. "I hope my father is smiling in his grave," she added, the sadness she still felt at his loss visible for a second or two.

Then a waitress brought a tray of pastries to the table and set them in the center, with utensils for them all. "Eat heartily," Al suggested, "And save a bit for last. Your mother will never know, and the pastry will mask the scent. And I promise to get you back to Adelaide's intact!"

At this last remark, Ruth looked even more shocked. Al could not hold back his laughter, which erupted with loud, hilarious hiccups. Ruth, though scarlet, couldn't help laughing as well.

Molly quipped, "What you boys will need to do is help us get back to the house on our own two feet!" This caused general hilarity all around the table.

"I'm not a total innocent," Ruth declared to the table at large. "My sister and I have been allowed a glass of wine at the dinner table for several years." Of course she immediately regretted the remark, since the last person she wished to bring to the table was that sister.

"Ah yes," her cousin smiled. "That is the 'cultured' thing to do." "Stop," begged one of Molly's friends, tears streaming down her cheeks. "My parents have done that for years too. They'd die if they knew what my sister and I do when we go out with all of you."

Ruth finally understood the slang phrase 'eyes wide as saucers'. Her daring friends in New York would never have dreamed of going to any club, since none catered to the young, let alone having an actual drink in one. Her cousin leaned over and whispered, "Relax. You'll be just fine, I promise. Just sip slowly and don't have more than one. I never do either."

CHAPTER NINETEEN

Ruth realized she had begun to breathe again after Molly had told her to relax, and tried to concentrate on the conversation. Molly and her friends seemed much more worldly than she, and more knowledgeable about the world. For the first time in many years she felt too timid to join in the conversation about the need for the nations of Europe to join together to deal with world issues, and hoped, as did the others, that the League of Nations would serve such a purpose. Ruth thought the United States would still join the group, but she had no reason for her belief, so she didn't speak up. At first she just listened intently, and then began to ask questions because of her natural curiosity. Finally she became so involved in the argument she began to voice her opinion before she realized she had joined in.

"It would certainly be a stronger union if our country joined the group," she mused aloud.

"I agree," one of Molly's friends jumped right in.

"And maybe African countries should be included," another suggested.

The group argued about how such a union of nations might be organized, and whether or not there should be a central office or meeting place for such a group, and then started to argue about an Austrian issue that Ruth had never even heard about. Again she realized how far away America was, and how little interest there seemed to be about European issues there. Perhaps because these young people lived in a small country surrounded by other small countries, each with separate issues and concerns, they felt a need to be knowledgeable about the European issues. They could be directly affected by the decisions and actions of the countries surrounding Austria, while in her own country there was just Canada and Mexico. Canada had never been a concern, and there had been no real issues with Mexico in over fifty years.

By the time they all rose to return to their respective homes, Ruth had completely forgotten that Al had been sitting beside her. Nevertheless, when he held out her coat, his hand brushing hers as she put her arms into the coat sleeves, the jolt that shot through her body reminded her quickly enough. When he moved over to Molly to help her cousin slip into her wrap, she stood still as a statue, hoping no one noticed her apparent inability to even take a step towards the door of the café.

"Hey, that's my job," another young man jokingly suggested, stepping in front of Al to help Molly with her wrap. Al returned to Ruth's side with dispatch, his hand immediately encircling her elbow as he steered her away from the table behind the others. Once they were outside, he slid his hand down to hers, enfolding it with his larger one, as if such an action were the most natural thing in the world. To object would have drawn attention to his action, so she did not. He smiled at her, and swung her arm in a wide arc as they followed the others to the corner. After they had crossed the street, he did not let go of her hand, and kept it in his even after they entered the park that would take them back to Molly's house. Suddenly Ruth realized that Molly and her young man were not behind them. She and Al were utterly alone at the entrance to the huge park. Mutely she followed him down a side path, although she was well aware this was not the most direct route back to her Aunt's house. When he pulled her onto the grass, she didn't object either.

By the time he tilted her head up to his, she was in a total daze, though not so completely out of touch that she didn't feel his lips upon hers, the marvelous softness of them, and the tickle of his tongue against her own. She had no idea what to do. Pulling away would have been the proper and correct action, but she had longed for this moment for so many months she didn't have the strength. Neither did she object when he kissed her again, and then again, and then she was responding with a passion equal to his, engulfed in the sensations brought on by their actions. Kissing had never felt like this with Greg. Ruth had assumed it was something only novelists wrote about, making up the feelings of their characters as they made up every other part of their narrative. Even the female writers she enjoyed, like Jane Austen, must have experienced this she thought as they kissed again and again, before she found the presence of mind to pull away.

"Whatever's the matter, little Ruthie," he asked her, stroking her hair, her cheek, her shoulders.

"Holly's…my … sister," she stammered, continuing, "This is wrong. You know it is."

The look he gave her was filled with sadness.

"We can't do this," she added. "We must stop now."
"I know you are right, my sweet. I was wrong to start, but I've never shared my feelings with anyone else before," he tried to explain.

"Surely you've kissed Holly," she said, desperately wanting him to deny it even though she knew it to be true.

"Yes, I have," he admitted. "But it never felt like this. I don't understand what is happening either, but I know it's real," he added.

"She's so much prettier than I am," Ruth muttered, head bowed.

Al replied, "It has nothing to do with looks," though those were not the words she wanted to hear. "You excite every inch of me, even my mind. I think this is what a man is supposed to feel when he loves a woman."

Ruth began to cry, despite her best efforts to hold back her tears.

"My dear, dear Ruth. The last thing I want to do is upset you," he stammered, continuing to stroke her hair.

"I wish it were different, but it isn't," was all she could manage.

"But it could be…." He disagreed.

Ruth shook her head adamantly. "We can go on being friends, arguing about the world…"

"We never argue," he interrupted, smiling at her. "That's what's so amazing to me. We take each other's side with other people, always."

Ruth again nodded, but this time in agreement.

Al continued. "We agree on everything as far as I can tell."

"Except kissing," she demurred.

"I doubt you disliked the kissing, my sweet. What we disagree about is who should be kissing whom," he suggested.

"Yes. Because Holly is your girlfriend," Ruth reminded him. Al merely sighed.

"I could never be a communist," Ruth added, almost in a whisper.

Again Al sighed. "Actually, Ruth, I'm not sure I could be one either."

"But you've gone to meetings," she objected.

"That's true. To see what I thought of the communist party in New York," he admitted.

"And? What did you?" she asked him.

"They're a bit too dogmatic for my taste," he replied, again with a smile. "Haven't you ever gone to a meeting of some club or another to see what you thought of the people in it as well as their aims?"

"At Evander. When I was figuring out which clubs to join, and what kind of time they would take. But that's different," she argued.

"Yes. It is. But I didn't join, Ruth. I just attended two meetings."

"Why did it take two meetings?" she asked, genuinely curious.

"Because some of their ideas mirror my own. It's their behavior and rules that don't," he explained.

During their entire conversation, Ruth found herself backing up, until she was standing in front of a park bench. "You don't have to be afraid of me," he chided.

"I don't want you to kiss me again," she told him.

"Yes you do, but you think it's wrong," he replied.

"Don't you?" she demanded.

He hesitated and then quietly answered, "Yes."

"We can be friends," Ruth said yet again.

"Even though that isn't what either of us wants," he agreed.

"I couldn't do this to Holly, Al. And I hope you couldn't either," Ruth explained.

"I don't think I should be her boyfriend anymore," he muttered.

"That's for you to figure out," she said very quietly. "But even if you break up with her, we can't be together."

"Ever?" he asked her, distressed.

This time it was Ruth who sighed. "I haven't thought very far ahead. So I don't know about 'ever'."

He smiled again. "That's a relief."

"Do you really think this is funny?" she asked in disbelief.

"Not at all," he replied. "Sometimes I joke when I have no idea what to say. Actually I feel very sad, Ruthie."

Then he took her hand and kissed it. She found herself unable to object. He could tell she was again very close to tears, so he let go of her hand.

"I won't do that again either, Ruth. "

"That's good," she murmured.

"But we can be friends, and work on the school paper together when you come to Hunter?" he asked.

She agreed they could do that, although she had no idea how she would be able to work side by side with him, writing articles and setting type. She knew she would want to reach over and brush his hair as it fell across his brow, feel the heat of his body next to hers, their shoulders rubbing. But her first loyalty had to be to her blood relation, and as much as she resented her sister – her beauty, her easy manner, her popularity – she would be loyal.

They both stood, having sat down on the bench somewhere during the course of their conversation in the park. Ruth realized they had been sitting at the foot of a hill very like the one she used to skate down as a little girl. "I broke my leg on a hill like this one in Crotona Park," she blurted, and described the spin, the pain, and the man who had helped her home. She still met him when she had time, sharing thoughts and feelings over a cup of coffee. Al was ashamed that he was jealous, but didn't tell her that. Instead he asked if he could help her cross the busy street. She nodded in agreement. When they reached the other side, he let go of her arm. Ruth assumed this would be the last time they would touch. They said goodbye, and turned to go in separate directions. They both looked unbearably sad.

Two days later Al and his family left Vienna. Sophia had noticed the difference in their behavior with one another, hadn't said anything to her niece about it. She knew instinctively what had happened. Al was Holly's beau, even though she realized it was Ruth he had come to love. It was also clear that her niece felt the same way about Al, but Sophia understood that neither of them would ever betray Holly. At least her niece wouldn't.

Although Adelaide's concert was over, and they would be leaving in a few days as well, Sophia intended to buy her niece at least one more frock. To forestall objections, she would look for one by herself that did not necessitate another pair of shoes. Simon would have been her ally, but Simon wasn't with them anymore. Nevertheless Sophia knew that Adelaide had always given in to her older sister, and this situation would be no different. The dresses would complement the spirit of her youngest, even if no one would think she was a beauty when she wore them. How could Addie object?

For Ruth the days after Al's departure passed in a blur. Sophia kept her busy during the day, and took her to several soirees in the evening, which were exciting despite Al's absence. She walked over to the Central Café by herself several afternoons, engaging in conversations that were quite stimulating. Her German was improving, so she could even express fairly complicated opinions, which was indeed a great deal of fun. On her way home each afternoon she couldn't help but include Al in those conversations, knowing without even thinking about it what he would have said. This would have to be enough, she told herself. She longed to be done with Vienna and to return home to Greg. If she continued to go out with him, she hoped that watching her sister with Al would be less painful. Of course it wouldn't be. But Greg was safe, and safe seemed the wise choice.

* * *

Max and Susanna often took long walks in the garden in the late afternoons, at first only talking about the books they were reading, although their conversations eventually wandered into the personal realm. It was Jack who informed them that the Sanatorium was aflutter with speculation about the nature of their relationship. Max was horrified. Despite the many conversations he and Jack had engaged in about losing their virginity, he certainly didn't want anyone to believe Susanna was 'that kind of girl'.

"Of course I still want to gain some experience here," he sputtered, to which Jack replied, "What kind of experience?" Max was so appalled, he couldn't even laugh.

"Really! Susanna isn't like that," he repeated, feeling an overwhelming need to convince his friend at least.

"You know," Jack said after a few minutes. "All of the girls here are 'nice'." Which was, of course, true.

"Maybe we'll have to wait until we return home," Max managed.

"God," Jack moaned. "I hope not!" He had been 'walking out' with another patient named Deborah, who was both a smart and a looker. "That hasn't kept me from imagining," he added mournfully.

Even Max had to laugh. "Dreaming is a lot different from doing," he added.

"Well I, for one, still want to do!" Jack declared.

"I'm not so sure. What happens afterwards? We just leave?" he asked Jack.

"I guess first we better get some condoms," Jack quipped, his usual comedic self.

"Do you know how to use those things?" Max stammered.

"Nope. Maybe we could practice together with a banana."

"Good Lord. I think I'm going to wait," came Max's ready response. "I can't even imagine."

However, his nightly dreams belied these protests. He frequently awakened bathed in sweat, which even the nurse believed was related to the tuberculosis. The first time he was jolted awake with a sudden excretion from his penis he was shocked, and then mortified. Jules had told him about such things when he and Teresa had first begun to step out, but Max had never before suffered from that indignity. Because he had denied that he was thinking about Susanna in a sexual way, he didn't even tell Jack about ejaculating. He assumed that's what it was, and cleaned all offending signs from his sheets. That a nurse would see such a thing was not to be imagined. Max would have been equally shocked to learn that the nurses in the men's wing of the sanatorium had become quite accustomed to wet dreams, and hardly thought about them at all. Though none of the nurses had been taught about this male aberration in nursing school, they had learned from one another that it occurred with such frequency that they had all concluded it must be normal.

If anything Max became even more careful in his encounters with Susannah. He certainly didn't want her to realize that he was dreaming about her in a sexual way, if not thinking such thoughts on a conscious level. As long as she had no reason to think he was being disrespectful, he felt exonerated. There was nothing he could do about what other patients thought.

One afternoon he rose from his chair on the sun porch next to Jack to join Susanna in their usual meeting place. Jack, who had drifted into a pleasant afternoon slumber in the sun, murmured, "Is it already that time?" because he had planned to meet Deborah on the long unpaved driveway that led into the Sanatorium at the same time. Max pulled the blanket from around his friend's legs, and said, "Rise and shine!"

"You louse!", Jack complained. "I was totally content until you so rudely interrupted my dreams." By then he, too, was standing. Both young men folded their blankets and set them down at the foot of their Adirondack chairs. "Clearly we've been well trained by our mothers," Jack joked. Most of the other young men frequently left their blankets in a tangled mess. The two left the porch side by side and arm in arm, until Max headed for the grounds behind the main building, and Jack, briskly walked towards the front drive. He turned and called over his shoulder, "I couldn't walk this quickly even a month ago!" The two grinned at each other. Their health was improving.

As Max reached the rose bushes that were just beginning to bud behind the patient's apartments, he wondered how long both he and Susanna would be in residence at the Sanatorium, and then felt immense shame. He knew he was wondering because he wanted to have the time to pursue the adventures that until then he had only been imagining. He had never even kissed his fellow patient in the two months he had been in residence, so he understood that the likelihood of consummating their relationship was slim. Nevertheless his nocturnal dreams, with their unintended consequences, had become more frequent, and were a source of anxiety for the young man. When he saw Susanna walking among the blooms, some already in full flower, his breath quickened. He slowed his steps so that he could control himself before he reached the young woman.

"Well, hello! I thought you had forgotten me," she declared with a smile upon his approach. Her cheeks were quite flushed, not a good sign in a tuberculosis sanatorium.

"Never," Max declared quite seriously.

"Good," she nodded as she reached for his hand, and pulled him towards the grove of trees that bordered the grounds behind their dormitory. Max felt perplexed since they rarely walked in this direction, but he followed her anyway. He was finding it difficult to breathe, and hoped she wouldn't think this worrisome. He knew his labored breathing had nothing to do with his illness. Could this well-brought-up young woman possibly be having the same thoughts he was having?

When he ducked beneath a branch of one of the maple trees on the edge of the small copse of trees, he almost bumped into Susanna, who had stopped and turned to face him. Before he could say a word, she had placed her hands beneath his chin, tilting it down, and then stood on her tiptoes so that she could reach his lips. He was totally nonplussed, then he thought, 'Her lips feel very different from Teresa's', and then he was kissing her with total abandon.

When he finally leaned back, Susanna sighed, "Thank goodness. I didn't think you'd ever do that. More please."

Max laughed aloud, although Susanna quickly placed her hand across his mouth, whispering, "Someone might hear us and wonder why we are behind this bush," which sent them both into gales of laughter that they desperately tried to stifle.

Max managed to sputter, "I know one way to stop us both," which didn't work at all. Both were convulsed, holding their aching bellies.

Max finally clamped his mouth over hers. Not only did this silence them both, it also felt utterly marvelous. Locked in his embrace, Susanna nevertheless seemed to be unbuttoning her shirtwaist, which was shocking but also unbelievably thrilling. When he slid his hand inside her blouse and cupped it over one of her breasts, they both swayed and then she, and finally he, managed to control their knees.

She wore no slip, which was very unusual in the early 20's. Max suddenly realized that his new friend had planned this day, and the events that were to occur over the course of the afternoon well in advance.

"You're not wearing a slip," he gasped when they again came up for air.

Her smile was huge. "Wasn't that thoughtful of me?" she giggled, and then sighed, "Oh my."

"I wonder if it feels this way to my parents?" Max mused aloud as he stroked her left breast through the fabric of her bra. Her nipple responded to his touch, rising to greet his active fingers. Because their hips were touching, she could feel his response as well, much as he tried to hide it. He felt angry at his lack of self-control until she, too, gasped.

"I have wanted to know for so long how that would feel." Then she asked him, "Does it always get so.... large?"

When he instinctively tried to pull away in embarrassment she drew him even closer. "Don't do that. It's marvelous."

He thought he would collapse when she reached down and began to stroke him through his pants. He groaned aloud, but didn't try to stop her. He knew he was showing a lack of respect, but what she was doing felt so very pleasurable. Even Teresa had never dared to do such a thing.

"If I'm going to die I want to experience all of life," she told him.

"You're not going to die," Max almost shouted, so distressed was he by this pronouncement. He didn't know if that was true. Her cheeks really were very pink, not suffused in a normal way, but white with bright pink circles on each one.

Looking directly into his eyes, she murmured, "I really am very sick, Max." He tried to kiss her fears away, but again stopped when her fingers began to struggle with the buttons of his pants.

"Oh Susanna!" he gasped. "You shouldn't."

"I know that," she said but didn't stop what she was doing. They both looked down as she released him, and his penis popped out of the opening.

"My oh my, " she sighed. "Would you be horrified if I touched it?"

He shook his head, unable to verbalize his permission. She could feel his body tense. After only a few seconds, he called out 'Eh' shivering, while he tensed, trying to suppress it.

"Let it out, my dear," she urged, and then he did. Immediately he was filled with shame.

"I'm so…." he began but she again covered his mouth with her free hand.

"Shhh." And then, "What should we do with it?"

They both fell silent, though she still held his penis, somehow unwilling to let go of it.

"Now's when I need that slip," she chuckled.

Max pulled his shirt out of his pants, and then did the same with his undershirt, holding it out to her. "We can use this," he suggested, which they did. He told her he thought he could rinse it out in his bathroom without any of his roommates being any the wiser. He would then hang it outside his window.

As they slowly walked back to the dormitory hand in hand, Susanna mused, "I wonder what everyone else does with the…I don't really know what to call it."

"We could look it up in the library," Max suggested, which brought a smile to both of their lips.

"I think I'm really going to do that," she admitted with a nod, adding, "And I'm also going to bring a blanket out here and hide it behind a tree. That will be much more comfortable than the ground, and I don't want to wait until winter."

"It would be pretty cold," Max agreed, heart pounding. This was not how he had envisioned this momentous event when he and Jack had been discussing it. He also realized he would not share this experience, or the one he was about to embark upon, with his friend. This was private and belonged only to him and Susanna.

Before they parted at the patio doors she said, "If we wait until the first snowfall, than we'll have no place to go," and was gone. He followed shortly thereafter.

The following morning Max had his bi-monthly physical exam. Because the doctor had an emergency that morning with another patient, Max was kept waiting for almost half an hour. By the time he was ushered into the examination room, he was very anxious. Not about the exam, which was fairly perfunctory, but about being too late to take care of the tasks he needed to complete in order to meet Susanna for their walk in the afternoon. Of course he knew they would not be walking, which was why he was so nervous. First he and the doctor exchanged pleasantries. They had been meeting every other week for over two months, and had talked about many aspects of medicine. The doctor knew Max had been preparing for a career in that field before his illness had felled him, and had discussed the possibilities that might still be open to him. Finally, the doctor began his exam. He listened to the young man's chest, tapping each time he moved his stethoscope, and then he sent him for an x-ray. When Max asked if that could be postponed until the following visit, the doctor said no. He hadn't had a chest x-ray during his last exam, and it was necessary to keep track of his recovery, which, the doctor assured him, was proceeding nicely. Max was told to take off his shirt and his undershirt, fortunately laundered the evening before and dried on the tree limb outside his window, and proceeded to the x-ray room. There he was left to languish for another fifteen minutes, until finally the procedure was completed and he was free to leave. By then he realized he only had time to grab a bite of lunch, and then rest for an hour on the sun porch, but not enough time to prepare for his hour with Susanna. He was distraught in the dining room, which she could see from across the room. She, too, became upset, managing to leave the facility at the same time as Max.

"Was your exam a problem?" she asked with some urgency.

"Oh no" he assured her. "But I haven't had a chance to collect the things we will need for our stroll this afternoon."

Susanna's smile was very reassuring. "We can walk tomorrow," she suggested, emphasizing the verb, which left no doubt that she understood his meaning.

"Yes," Max admitted with some relief, although he certainly did not want to wait.

They parted so they could each lie down on their respective lounges, which were not side-by-side. As Max walked down the hall towards the porch, he realized he was momentarily alone. As he passed the linen closet, he opened the door, reached inside, and grabbed a blanket from the bottom shelf. It was only a short detour to the field where he and Susanna usually walked, and took mere seconds for him to stash the blanket behind a tree beneath a pile of leaves to protect it in case there was rain overnight. It certainly wouldn't have improved their plans if the blanket became soaking wet. He was only minutes late to the porch and his place upon it. Only Jack noticed his tardy arrival, but when he raised his eyebrows, Max merely shrugged. "Nature called," he whispered as he slipped into his chair beside him, and then closed his eyes. He didn't want to engage in further conversation because he knew his friend's intuitive sense would pick up on his tension and suspect something momentous might be afoot. That evening he had a very difficult time falling asleep. He hadn't thought about condoms, and would have had no way to purchase any, but he thought he should talk to Susanna about it before it was too late. Neither of them needed a pregnancy that was for sure. The last thing he noticed before he fell asleep were the stars twinkling in the sky outside, which he could clearly see through the window beside his bed. He smiled, and drifted off slowly.

The following morning Susanna had her physical exam, which took a long time, increasing Max's anxiety. He had awakened with the thought that some of the more adventuresome patients might already have purchased condoms, or would know how he could find some. Although he had rarely spoken to any of the more popular and socially active patients at the Sanatorium, he took a deep, metaphorical breath and approached a handsome and popular young man named William after their breakfast meal.

"Clearly you are more than meets the eye, Unger," he crowed, grinning broadly. Then he ordered Max to 'come with me', which he did. When the young man handed him several condoms, he couldn't keep the smile from his face. "Please don't tell anyone," Max asked, adding, "Neither of us wants to succumb to this damned disease without experiencing what love is all about."

William looked him up and down with a great sadness: his cheeks carried a reddish hue even brighter than Susanna's. "Do you want to know how we get them?" he asked Max.

"Yes. I would very much like to know that," Max replied. He realized the other young man, though tempted, would probably not tell anyone about Max and Susanna's plans. He, too, was very ill, and understood the peril threatening the young couple. William explained that one of the nurses, though he wouldn't say who, took pity on their condition and bought the things, which William and his friends paid for and then parsed out to those in need. Max realized what an innocent he had been. Where all this hanky-panky had been going on, he had no idea, and decided not to ask. If he and Susanna had found a spot, given their natures, he was certain the others who were exploring their lives as sexual beings had used their imagination to take care of that problem as well.

When Susanna appeared in the dining room, Max grinned for all he was worth, relieved to see that she smiled right back at him, shaking her head to indicate she understood. Because the morning had already passed, and a session on the sun porch was required, they both understood they would have to wait until after their naps. Neither had any idea how they would sleep, but they both did, warmed into slumber by the warmth of the sun's rays, and the disease that was ravaging their young bodies. When he awakened, Max felt marvelous. He had been concerned that he would be too full to perform, whatever that meant, but the hour of rest had helped him digest his lunch, which had been replete with protein and vegetables. He couldn't believe how hungry he had felt at the noon repast, stuffing his mouth with both the brisket and potatoes and then taking a second portion of both, as well as eating the entire pudding that was placed in front of him for desert. He rarely felt as hungry, but had no idea if that was due to his improving health or his excitement about what was to transpire that very afternoon if all went according to plan.

He had been reading all that he could find in the library about the sex act, huddled in a little cubicle on the second floor, but the information was merely technical, and certainly didn't offer advise on how long to partake in each of the activities described as part of the process. He only hoped he wouldn't become so terrified that his penis would deflate, making penetration impossible. He also could not tell from the few pictures he could find of both the male and female sexual organs, how he could possible gain entry to the portal he so wished to penetrate. The contortions he believed necessary didn't even appear to make such an act possible, although he knew it must be because his own parents had managed to produce six progeny. For the life of him he couldn't picture either of them engaging in such shenanigans. His father was more adventurous, at least in his efforts to start and maintain his business; nevertheless, Max wondered how had he figured it all out. In those days he doubted there were any available books that would have described at least some of what was necessary and certainly no pictures. Picturing his mother lying beneath Noah gave him heart palpitations, so he decided to forgo that line of thought. If his parents had been able to figure it out, and had kept indulging, it must not be as difficult as the books made it seem. Still, he wished he had been able to ask Nathan to bring him 'Lady Chatterley's Lover', a new novel that had caused quite a stir, and was bound to be more informative about the feeling part of the experience.

When Nathan arrived for his next visit, he was obviously bursting with news, so Max decided to wait to ask him for the notorious novel. Max had heard some of the boys whispering before falling asleep at night, and the word, foreplay, was a word that was repeated quite often.

"You know I've talked a little bit about Helen Horowitz," Nate blurted as soon as he sat down on the sun porch next to his brother.

Max grinned as he replied, "Endlessly."

"Do you remember her", Nathan asked him.

"Of course I do. She's very pretty, and has an adorable giggle," Max replied.

"When did you hear her giggle?" Nathan asked, quite startled, sighing before his brother could even reply. "It is adorable...."

"She usually walks home with Doris Davies, and I've been behind them a couple of times. You're blushing, Nathan. I guess this is serious," Max added, waiting for a response. Since Nathan was only a junior in high school, this really was news.

"I know we're both very young, but I think I'm falling in love with her," muttered his younger brother.

"How does she feel about you?" Max asked the obvious question.

More blushing. "The same way, I'm pretty sure."

"Is she smart enough for you, Nate?" Max asked. "You don't want to get bored in a year or two."

Nathan replied with great earnestness. "We talk about so many subjects. Her father gets The Atlantic Monthly and one other magazine, and she reads both from cover to cover. I've never known a girl who did that."

"Gee," blurted a startled Max. "I haven't either."
"We've talked about getting a copy of Scientific America on Broad Street, though I admit I'm more interested in that than she is," mused Nathan.

"Has she taken any science classes at Battin?" Max asked, quite surprised.

"No. That's why she asked about it. She's curious about lots of stuff I didn't expect," Nate replied.

"Does anyone at school know you and Helen are walking out?" Max asked. He and Teresa had been so secretive. But of course Teresa was not Jewish.

"I don't think so. Sometimes we walk home together, but she's usually with Doris. We meet later in the afternoon, before she has to help her mother prepare dinner," his brother replied.

Both young men were silent, and then Nathan spoke, head lowered, even embarrassed in front of his brother, the person he was closest to in the world.

"We hold hands in the park. I can't believe what that feels like," he murmured.

"When I was meeting Teresa and would take her hand, my whole arm felt hot," Max agreed.

Nathan's expelled his breath in a rush and then looked around the porch, sure anyone within five feet could hear him. No one appeared to be paying attention to the Unger brothers at all. He then continued in a whisper, "She let me kiss her yesterday." It was perfectly obvious that Nathan was quite amazed by the experience.

"Isn't kissing grand?" his older brother asked him, a huge grin plastered across his face. No matter how much he wanted to be equally forthcoming, Max found himself unable to tell his brother about Susanna, perhaps because he couldn't bear to admit to anyone, even his younger brother, what they were planning. A good girl didn't contemplate such things, and Susanna was nothing if not good. Had they not been so ill, neither of them would have been thinking about finding a secret place where they could explore one another's bodies to their hearts content. To do so would have seemed disrespectful to the usually dutiful Max.

Nevertheless, he smiled broadly at his younger brother because he didn't believe there was anything wrong with kissing. His father had urged 'waiting for marriage', although Max thought Noah had been discussing the entire process, not just the kissing that might lead to all the rest.

"I feel like a jerk," Nathan blurted. "I haven't asked you a thing about how you're feeling."

"What's going on with you and Helen seems more important. Certainly more fun," Max replied.

"Do you feel any better?" Nate asked, though both boys were still smiling at each other.

"Yes, actually I think I do. How do my cheeks look?" Max asked him.

"Not nearly as flushed," Nate replied. "I noticed as soon as I walked into the room, but didn't even think to say anything." He paused for a second and then muttered, "I really am a jerk."

"No you're not. You're infatuated, if not in love," Max answered.

"What's the difference?" Nathan asked him.

"I'm not sure, but I believe falling in love is more significant. We can be infatuated with a girl we don't belong with."

"Like Teresa?" Nate couldn't help but ask.

"I was in love with her, and she was in love with me. That's not why we couldn't be together." Max said with obvious sadness.

"Don't you think it would be hard to marry someone who wasn't Jewish?" Nate asked him.

"I'm not sure. If you're both bright, and you think through the whole thing and really want to make it work, maybe it can," Max said.

"I'm really sorry. Now that I feel the way I do, I really understand."

Max sighed. "I was trying to picture her face when I was falling asleep a few days ago, but I just couldn't. How could that be?" Max asked him.

"I have no idea," Nathan responded with dismay. "I'd like to think I'd never forget Helen's face, but I don't know if that's true. If I didn't see her for months and months, who knows what would happen."

"Maybe it means we didn't love each other as much as I thought we did," Max mused aloud.

"I don't think that's it. I heard what you shared about her night after night, and I saw you together a few times. What you both felt was obvious to me, even when I was just a sophomore," Nathan replied.

"I think so too. But why can't I remember every detail of her face?" Max asked him.

"I don't know that, but I do know how much you loved her," his brother answered. The duty nurse approached them with some hesitation because the intensity of their conversation was apparent to her. "I'm sorry, Max. But it's time for your brother to leave. I've let you two visit ten minutes longer than I should have. I can't have you tiring yourself out, can I?" she asked, though not expecting a reply. The question was obviously rhetorical.

Although he realized he should sleep, or certainly rest, Max was unable to calm his nerves after Nathan's departure. He lay awake on the chaise next to Jack, unsuccessful despite closing his eyes and taking several deep breaths in an effort to relax. Nothing helped. He knew Jack was looking at him, but did not open his eyes. He knew what he was about to do was probably wrong, but both he and Susanna were determined. Sharing this secret with Jack still seemed dishonorable, so Max remained rigid. He could feel Jack's body go slack and soon heard his friend's deep and regular breaths. Despite all efforts to the contrary, Max could not erase the image of Susanna's breast from his brain. He actually feared it might fill the entire room and everyone else would see it, although his rational mind assured him this was absurd. There wasn't an hour in his life, even years later, that took as long to tick away, but finally, the bell sounded, and the men around him began to awaken and stretch. Since several of the patients at the Sanatorium often strolled around the grounds after nap time, no one took note of his leave-taking, which he tried to navigate with as much nonchalance as possible.

By the time he reached the fountain in the center of the yard where he and Susanna had agreed to meet, his knees felt so rubbery he thought he might fall over. But when he saw her standing there, pride kept him vertical. He thought about Nathan and Helen and their innocent kisses, shamed by his deception. He and Susanna were going to do much more than kiss, but they might both be dying, or that was what he told himself. His brother and his love would probably live long lives, and probably live them side-by-side. They would have plenty of time to explore that aspect of love. Susanna had not noticed his approach because she was facing the bushes on the far side of the clearing. Despite the fact that she was not facing in his direction, the angle of her body told the tale well enough. She was terribly sad, which he couldn't understand.

"Are you alright?" he asked as soon as he reached her side.

Startled, she turned and gasped. "Oh. I thought you had changed your mind," she whispered although no one but Max could have heard her.

"Of course not," he replied. "I just didn't want to rush, or have Jack or anyone else notice when I left."

He took her hand and led her to the tree where he had buried the blanket under the pile of fall leaves. As he bent down to retrieve it Susanna took hold of his arm.

"I thought maybe you didn't find me attractive enough," she said.

Max stood and put his arms around her. "How could you think that?" he asked. "You are the most attractive woman here." This sentiment restored her sense of humor.

"Not in the entire state of New Jersey?" she asked him.

"New Jersey, New York and Pennsylvania combined," he replied without a moment's hesitation, making them both laugh.

They stood chest-to-chest, Max's arm draped awkwardly across her shoulders. Then he realized that Susanna was flushing a fairly bright shade of pink bearing no relation to the illness they both suffered from.

"If you're not ready...," he began.

All Susanna could manage was a shake of her head, indicating this was not so. Max leaned over and kissed her, in awe of his own daring. Her lips felt soft, like silk, no, like the velvet his mother often used in the garments she made for the women in their neighborhood. He tried to vanquish his mother from his mind, kissing Susanna with even more abandon. Although she had no idea why his passion seemed to be increasing, Susanna responded in kind. Max was still clutching the blanket, still folded in the wrapping it had been in when he had stolen it from the laundry closet. Finally, Susanna pulled away.

"I think you better unfold that thing so that I can help you spread it on the ground, " she boldly suggested. "We wouldn't want to get all wet from last night's rain."

"You're right," he agreed with a chuckle. "If I don't, all our secrecy will be in vain."

Together they spread the blanket, both shaking slightly, both noticing, and then both sinking to their knees. When he again took her in his arms, she said with a smile, "It might be more comfortable if we lie down," which lightened the mood.

"I've been reading everything I could find on this subject so I would have some idea what I'm supposed to do," Max admitted to her, lying nose to nose.

"And what did it say?" she asked him with genuine interest.

At first Max hesitated, and then he smiled at her. "Why don't I show you?"

CHAPTER TWENTY

By the time Ruth returned from Europe with her mother, Holly was in a social whirl. Several different young men rotated through their front door, each one introduced to their mother, and then disappearing, a new, but always attractive and educated one taking his place. They came and went with a speed that made Ruth's head spin. She often wondered how her mother felt about the parade, but was afraid to ask her. When she heard Adelaide conversing with Mrs. O'Reilly in whispers late at night, she assumed the topic was Holly and her young men, although she could have been mistaken. Of course her sister rarely talked to her either, although she did make several comments about men of little worth, which, according to her, encompassed most men she had ever known. Al was not to be seen. Ruth assumed he had broken up with her sister, given her experiences and conversations with him in Vienna, but had no way of finding out for sure.

Then one afternoon she was walking in Crotona Park, an activity she enjoyed on a daily basis because the exercise wiped away any anxiety she might have been feeling, a common occurrence for her. When she squatted on the pathway to retie her shoelace, which had come undone, she heard a familiar male voice say, "Ruth. Dear Ruth. And how are you finding the Bronx, now that you've seen more of the world?"

She looked upwards, right into the face of the young man who had not called her since their return from Vienna, despite not dating her sister anymore. "Fine," she said with confidence. She was damned if she was going to let him know how disappointed she was that he had not reached out to her.

"When do you start your classes at Hunter?" he asked, as if her attendance was a foregone conclusion.

"Next fall, I suppose. I haven't even graduated from Evander yet you know," she replied, rising to her feet. Kneeling below him felt quite uncomfortable.

With a broad grin Al held out his hand to help her up. "But you're always ahead of the pack. I assumed you'd applied, and thought you might even have heard back."

"I haven't heard from them, and I haven't heard from you," she replied, feeling quite brazen. Truthfully, she wanted to know why he had never called. Of course her chest pounded as she waited for his response.

"Holly and I broke up," he said finally, even adding, "I figured I was persona non grata in the Liebman houschold."

Ruth was delighted to be able to say, "No one in the Liebman household has talked about you at all."

At that, Al raised his eyebrows.

"Do you really think you are the center of Holly's universe?" she asked him with obvious disdain, quite startled that she was sticking up for her older sibling.

Al sighed. "No, I don't. But she sure is making a wide swath at Hunter," he replied.

"What amazes me is that they're all so good-looking," Ruth found herself blurting.

"That doesn't surprise me at all," Al laughed. "You, on the other hand, would gravitate towards the smart men, although I'm sure an attractive countenance wouldn't detract."

Ruth had no idea how to respond. She hadn't gravitated towards anyone at all, attractive or otherwise, and of course, no one at Evander had ever glanced her way. She still believed she frightened every male student at the high school except Ben. Unfortunately Ben did not cause chest flutters or weakness of knee.

"Perhaps there'll be a bigger pool at Hunter," she suggested and then turned to continue her stroll through the park.

Al didn't try to stop her, but looked sad as she glanced back at him. Then she rounded the bend, and he was no longer visible. He hadn't moved an inch after she had walked away.

A few nights later Holly was in a complete fury as the two of them were completing their toilette before repairing to their shared bedroom. "Did one of your gentlemen friends break up with you this time instead of the other way around?" Ruth asked her in a teasing tone. Actually she wanted to lighten her sister's mood, which was very dark indeed.

"No," Holly sighed. "It's that damned Al. I thought I was shed of him, and didn't care anymore, and then he asked me out and I went," she began.

Her sister merely tilted her head with the invitation to go on. She was too shocked to utter a word.

"He has always appreciated my body, but this time around it was apparently not enough," she quipped, her wry tone belying the hurt behind it.

Ruth felt like stone. She could not believe that Al had renewed his relationship with her sister after his time with her in Vienna, especially the physical part. "Holly, you…didn't…" she stammered, unable to complete the sentence. How could she ask her sister if she had been sleeping with someone, especially that someone?

"We slept together before you left for Europe. Kissing seemed rather beside the point now," she replied with a sigh. "Don't worry. I didn't take any risk. If either of us became pregnant it might send our mother around the bend, don't you think?"

"You don't have to worry about me in that regard," Ruth said, still reeling from her sister's revelations. When she turned the light out seconds later, she lay awake for some time, wondering about the perfidy of men.

Out of the dark Holly whispered, "Don't trust any of them. They have no idea what feelings are about, and just want to get us to take down our bloomers."

At that, Ruth sighed, which made Holly begin to laugh. "Don't worry, sis. By the time you get to Hunter, you'll be beating them off with your wit and obvious smarts."

Ruth would have preferred to be beating them off with her ravishing beauty, but was practical enough to know that would not be the case. Holly didn't suggest that possibility and neither had her father during the many conversations she had had with him over the years until the day he had died. "At least I'll have something to recommend me," she quipped.

"Quite a lot," her sister agreed, much to Ruth's surprise. Wonders never ceased. Her sister seemed to think she might have something to offer men as well as the world at large. If only she felt the same way about herself.

A few days later, Adelaide asked her younger daughter to return to the dining room table after the dishes had been washed, dried and placed in the hutch, an antique from the old country that had always been in their New York apartment. Ruth had no idea how her mother had managed to pack it and send it to the states. Adelaide rarely asked to speak with her if Holly was not in attendance, so she was rather nonplussed. But she acceded to the request without demur, sensing that something serious was afoot.

Her mother was opening several ledgers and spreading other papers in front of her on the mahogany table and didn't even glance up as Ruth entered the room. She sat down quietly across from her mother, until Adelaide indicated that her daughter should take the seat next to her.

"When I began to sing in Europe every summer with the Schola, I asked you father to take over our financial records," she explained, continuing, "Apparently, although he ran his own business, he did not have a head for numbers, at least household ones."

Ruth still had no idea how this related to her, or why Holly wasn't being included in the conversation.

Adelaide continued. "Your father appears to have made some very poor investments, and neither of us was ever very good at saving, something our accountant often chided us about."

Ruth remained silent, not sure what she could even contribute to such a conversation. She wished Holly had been asked to join them, a thought that came as quite a surprise. Her sister never even wanted to be involved in household tasks, let alone matters that related to the running of their little domain in the Bronx.

"You look worried, but you don't need to be. There is enough that we won't have to move from our apartment or sell some of our furniture to make ends meet," Adelaide explained, trying to sound reassuring. Since Ruth had never imagined either eventuality, she did not find her mother's words comforting.

"I'm not sure where all of this information is leading us," she murmured, at a loss of how else to respond.

At that, her mother looked up, and mother and daughter found themselves staring into each other's eyes. This was such an unusual occurrence that it rendered them both speechless, at least for the moment.

Finally Ruth managed to continue. "You don't have to hurry. I was just saying that I don't understand yet."

"Ruthie, I am sorry to tell you that there won't be enough to pay for both you and Holly to attend Hunter for the three-year program," her mother blurted. The breath seemed to leave Ruth's body. She had always assumed she would attend college since she was the 'smart' daughter. Holly was only biding her time until she found the boy she would marry.

"But Mama. You and Papa always said..." she began, her mother interrupting her.

"I know what we said, Ruth. But now only one of your parents has income to contribute to our household, and it just won't be enough," Adelaide replied quietly. "I truly am sorry, but I don't know what I can do about this."

The expression on her face made it clear to her daughter that her mother really did feel remorse.

"Last year Simon told me we couldn't move to Hillsdale as we had hoped," Adelaide continued. "I should have given more thought to why that was so, but I did not. I had my own concerns…" she paused, and then lowered her eyes. "There is really no excuse."

Ruth spoke before she had fully taken in her mother's words. "Hillsdale was always father's dream and not yours." She felt her eyes fill, and lowered her head. She had been dreaming about Hunter College, and what she would learn there ever since she had entered Evander Childs High School as a freshman. She had no idea what kind of life she could have without a college diploma. She was a woman, and that was a big enough deterrent.

"That is true," agreed her mother. "But I should have given more thought to why he wasn't taking steps to fulfill it." Then they both fell silent.

"I had my rehearsal schedule," Adelaide began, Ruth interrupting this time.

"Yes. Moving would have made getting to your rehearsals in Manhattan even more difficult."

"Thank you, Ruth. That is also true."

Again silence fell. Ruth suddenly pictured her application to Hunter, waiting to be filled out on her little desk in the bedroom she shared with Holly. Beneath it she could also see the two teacher recommendations, glowing with praise. After reading them she had been certain of her admittance to the revered public institution. She felt humiliated, although the situation was not of her making. There was no one she could even talk to about it, except, perhaps, Ben. Then Al's face popped into view, but she extinguished his image immediately, believing he would think less of her if she could not attend college. He was already in his third year there, and would of course finish his studies, even if he planned to enter his father's clothing business in Manhattan.

Her mother cleared her throat. "I will not be touring this summer with the Schola, but will be working here in their office instead, helping with tour arrangements, hotels and such," she said. Startled, Ruth realized her mother was silently crying.

"Mama, it is not your fault," she assured Adelaide, although she was not sure. Perhaps her mother should have questioned her father more carefully.

Adelaide's sigh was so deep that Ruth was sure her sister could hear it beyond the closed dining room door. "That is very generous, even if it is probably not true. Not my fault alone, but my fault nevertheless."

"But you have been touring since I was a child," Ruth blurted.

"Not for pay, my dear. The organization did support us by paying our fare to the Continent, and most of our hotel stays. We were fortunate to have family we could stay with there, at least when we were in Austria. I will be paid if I work in the office," Adelaide explained, unable to continue because she was crying more fully by this point.

Despite the lack of warmth between mother and daughter, Ruth realized that her mother's situation was at least as bad as her own, if not worse. She had always known that her mother lived for her singing. Her life without the Schola Cantorum was even more difficult to imagine than her own without college. She turned and reached out for her mother and the two sat there, clinging to one another for a few minutes. Neither would have been comfortable with more. Adelaide was the first to pull away.

"We will both work and save, Ruth, putting what we earn into a savings account that will accrue interest. You will only have to postpone your college career," she suggested, though both already knew the probability of that was unlikely. "Besides, Holly has only a year and a half more, and then she, too, will get a job and contribute to our little fund."

With a lack of generosity not typical of her nature, Ruth thought her sister's willingness to contribute unlikely as well, but she knew enough not to voice her opinion on the matter. Even if her sister had not found a husband by then, she had long been selfish about her own needs, or so Ruth had always believed. What her parents had thought about that unpleasant character trait had never been discussed. That their mother had had no control over her older daughter, at least in the last few years, had been obvious to both her daughters. Two years hence would be no different, Ruth thought to herself.

After the three of them had finished their supper, Adelaide said a few sentences about the impasse before she left the kitchen. Holly turned to her sister with dismay.

"But Papa always intended for you to attend Hunter!" she gasped.

"Papa isn't here," Ruth replied, surprised by how much she sounded like their mother.

"Ruth. Even for you, that is…unfair," Holly murmured. "I do realize you must be very upset. I'm not nearly as smart as you are, and I know I would have been devastated if I couldn't have gone to Hunter."

Because she did not want Holly to see how upset she was she attempted to hold back her tears, only realizing how unsuccessful she had been when Holly handed her an unused dish towel from the drawer.

"I could call the woman who was my supervisor at Sacks last summer. She was quite nice, and I'm sure would try to find a place for you," Holly suggested, adding, "We can all put away money for you, and I can join Mama and you once I am out in the work force."

Ruth was so startled that her sister had come up with this notion and so quickly, that her sobs intensified. "I have to stop or Mama will hear me," she managed, surprised and relieved when Holly held out her arms. The last time they had hugged one another had been at Simon's funeral. They must have hugged each other when they were little girls, Ruth thought, but she could not remember. At least she could remember being held by her mother, although those occasions had been rare.

Holly quickly discovered that her former supervisor no longer worked at Sacks, which she didn't tell her younger sister. Instead she called her old high school friend Dinah, whose mother had begun working there a few years earlier to supplement the family's income. Holly had always suspected the woman had actually taken the job because she was bored with her life as a hausfrau and cook. She understood that was how she would have felt taking care of a home, children, and a husband as well as having to prepare and cook meals night after night with no respite. Better to have several beaus than to settle on one and be burdened with a ball and chain for the rest of her life. She never intended to marry, something she had decided at the age of 10, and didn't see her resolve in that regard ever weakening.

Dinah was very pleased to see her. They gossiped about their old friends at Evander, sharing information about how each one was faring, and then Dinah suggested they go to the kitchen, since her mother was already chopping vegetables for the family's evening meal.

Holly's mouth formed into a moue of sympathy. "I have to help my mother with chopping almost every night. If it's taught me anything it's that I'm never going to have a family!" she declared.

Dinah laughed aloud. "I actually don't mind cooking, but I'm sure going to have a maid do the cleaning. So I guess I won't be able to marry someone who's just starting out or doesn't have a hefty inheritance."

At that Holly also began to laugh. "I'll have to give your idea some thought," she giggled. "I do like kissing so your idea might actually work for me."

"What about more than kissing?" her friend asked, causing Holly to flush to the roots of her very full, auburn hair.

With lowered head Holly murmured, "That too," which caused more laughter from Dinah. After some initial embarrassment Holly joined in with that as well.

"Come on. We can talk about kissing later on. Believe me, I won't forget," said a grinning Dinah. "But right now, let's go see my mother."

As soon as Mrs. Moscowitz had slid her casserole into the oven, she washed and dried her hands on a damp towel hanging over the back of a chair, wiped her forehead, which was beaded with sweat, and sat down at the kitchen table across from Holly and her daughter.

"So my sweet. What is it you wanted to talk to me about?" she asked without indulging in any chitchat. Salad fixings were still laid out on the counter, drying on a linen cloth, potatoes waiting to be peeled, cut up, and boiled as well.

"Oh Mrs. Moscowitz," Holly stammered. "I don't mean to take you away from your dinner preparations."

The woman smiled warmly, admitting, "I'm more than happy to be taking a break, Holly. Thank you for giving me a decent excuse."

Holly smiled back at her, took a deep breath, and began.

"My younger sister, Ruth, needs to find a job but has no real training. Since my father's death..." she paused.

"You needn't say another word, my dear. I don't know what this household would do without two incomes. I'm very sorry this is the case for Ruth, but I understand perfectly," Mrs. Moscowitz explained.

"I'm not sure what kind of job she could even find," Holly continued, the older woman again interrupting.

"I've heard a great deal about your little sister already," she said. "She began publishing a school journal herself, with a few friends, of course, but she was the leader of the group. I gather she is extremely bright, with a caustic wit as well."

"That's true, although I prefer listening to it when it's directed at someone else," Holly replied. Mrs. Moscowitz laughed at the comment.

"Can your sister type and take shorthand?" she asked as soon as she was able.

Holly hesitated. "I know she can type because of the journal, but I'm not certain if she's able to write or understand shorthand," she admitted, not wanting to have to answer the question at all.

Mrs. Moscowitz patted her hand in reassurance. "That's no problem at all. If she doesn't, I would be more than happy to teach her. Can you find out by tomorrow?" she asked.

"I'm sure I can. But I know she wouldn't want to inconvenience you and neither would I," Holly replied.

"Don't you worry your pretty little head about that," the older woman said, lighting a cigarette, something Holly had never before seen a woman do. She hoped she wasn't gaping.

"I asked because there's going to be an opening for a secretary in the executive offices. With your sister's abilities, and some copies of the journal, I'm sure I could secure her the position if she can fulfill those two requirements by then," she concluded.

Holly was thrilled, which in turn, pleased Dinah's mother who rose from the table to stub out her cigarette in the sink, and toss it in the garbage can below. "And now I need to return to making sure this family has enough to eat this evening," she said.

"Thank you so much. I'll go right home and ask Ruth, if she's there. I'm sure she will be since she helps my mother every night with our family's supper preparations," she explained.

Mrs. Moscowitz turned, obviously startled by this revelation. "Every night? Even with her duties at the journal?"

"Yes," Holly replied, startled at the pride she felt as she answered, adding, "I should help more."

"Yes you should," Mrs. Moscowitz agreed, squeezing Holly's shoulder as she passed her chair. "And now I'm sure you will."

Which Holly did that very evening, much to the surprise of both Ruth and their mother. As the three worked together, squeezed in side by side at the kitchen counter, she told them about her conversation with Mrs. Moscowitz. Adelaide expressed her delight immediately, surprising both girls, and Ruth asked if she thought it would be too late to call Dinah's mother on the tenants' phone in the hallway outside their apartment. Holly was sure it was not, so Ruth grabbed a sweater and charged down the hall to make the call. When she returned, she was beaming.

"Mrs. Moscowitz wants me to come to her house after my editorial meeting tomorrow afternoon so that she can begin my shorthand lessons," she exclaimed, face flushed with pleasure. "She said she will tell her boss what she is doing, and set up a meeting for me with him."

"That's quite exciting, Ruth," her mother agreed, for once not chastising her youngest daughter for her unladylike enthusiasm. Then she added, "Did Mrs. Moscowitz indicate what she thought your chances were at securing such a job, even though you don't yet know shorthand?" The question came as a bit of a damper to Ruth's ebullient mood.

"She said she will tell him I will be a quick learner because I am very bright," Ruth nevertheless murmured with some amazement. "Can you imagine? I hope I can live up to her expectations."

When Holly exclaimed that she was certain her sister would not have a problem, Ruth had no idea what to say. She had run out of words. Neither her mother nor her sister had ever seemed to admire her skills or abilities before. By the time she was brushing her teeth, she felt almost numb with shock. But she knew feeling would return, and would be quite wonderful when it did.

The day of her interview at Saks Fifth Avenue Ruth donned one of the dresses she had bought in Vienna with her Aunt Sophia, and was turning this way and that examining herself in the small mirror in her mother's bedroom behind the closed door, when she heard a knock. Her mother had already left for her rehearsal so Ruth almost jumped out of her skin, as well as the new dress. Holly opened the door holding one of her purses in her right hand.

"I think this will look better than the big satchel you always take to school," she said. Ruth knew it was one of her favorites, and was again nonplussed. "Relax," her sister continued. "You can't do any damage to a leather purse except forget to bring it home, and you can't do that because you wouldn't be able to get on the subway without it."

"Hahaha, very funny," Ruth replied, and then hit her head in emphasis. "My transit pass will be inside it, so how could I leave it behind!"

"Exactly!" The two sisters grinned at each other. Of course Ruth was well aware that Holly had never offered such a thing before.

"You don't have to feel guilty..." she told her sister.

"Of course I do. You should be the one going to Hunter. But Mama wouldn't let me quit, even if I wanted to," she said. "Take the purse and shut up."
At that Ruth had to laugh. "This is all so new," she said.

"Having the interview, needing a job to help support the family, my helping you – what?" Holly asked her.

"All of the above, I think," Ruth nodded. "Oh my. I have no idea what you do at a job interview!"

Holly replied, "You act interested and curious about everything 'Saks'. That's your personality anyway."

"Don't you have a class at 11? We could walk to the subway together," Ruth suggested. When the sisters parted at the token booth, each headed for a different track, Ruth impulsively reached out and gave her sister a quick hug, and then, hearing the approach of her train downstairs, raced off before Holly could respond. Left behind beside the tollbooth Holly was surprised by the pounding of her heart: she was anxious about the interview, almost as anxious as Ruth. She really wanted her sister to get this job because she knew Ruth had a sense of style that would be apparent to the person who would become her supervisor at Saks. Even without college, her sister would be able to make a good and exciting life for herself.

Sitting in the half empty subway car on the way into Manhattan from the Bronx, Ruth felt depressed. She, too, thought she should have been the one attending Hunter, though her sister's words and actions had really helped allay such thoughts. They both understood that they each had a path to follow, one that had not been chosen by either one of them. As each station whirled by on the local track, Ruth realized she was also a little bit excited. She, too, believed that if she were offered this job, she would not remain a secretary for very long. It would have come as a complete surprise had she realized Holly had been having the same thought, in a day that seemed to be packed with surprises. Her plan was to observe every position Saks had to offer once she was hired at the famous department store, and set her sights on the one that best suited her abilities.

The last thing she expected before she was ushered into the office for her interview was to find a woman sitting behind the large, imposing mahogany desk in the middle of the room. Several clothes racks were arrayed behind her, the most stunning suits Ruth had ever seen hanging on one, and delicious, billowy party dresses on another. She hadn't for a moment imagined that someone of her own gender might occupy the position of department head. For once in her life she was relieved that she wasn't particularly pretty. She assumed a pretty apprentice would be more of a threat to a female boss than a plain one. A man, of course, would have preferred her sister, and a man had been what she had expected.

The woman wasted no time. "Why is such a bright girl applying for a job as a glorified secretary?" she asked.

Startled, Ruth replied truthfully, "My older sister is already attending Hunter College. My father died last year, and my mother doesn't have the funds to send us both there." Holly's suggestion that she be herself seemed the right choice. She was quite comfortable with her response and the questions that were sure to follow.

"I'm sorry. Libby Moscowitz didn't tell me," the woman behind the desk explained. "If you are able to rise in the hierarchy of this department, will I have to worry that you will quit when you have sufficient funds to attend Hunter?"

"I don't know. I hadn't thought about it," Ruth replied, following the path of truthfulness she had decided upon.

"Well, an honest applicant. That's refreshing. My name, by the way, is Mrs. Gelb. Antonia Gelb."

"How do you do, Mrs. Gelb. It's good to meet you," Ruth said, actually meaning it. She could tell they were both enjoying the interview, which increased the young woman's confidence.

"Do you think you will be a secretary your whole life?" Gelb asked, which elicited a huge smile on the face of the young woman sitting across from her. This made the supervisor smile as well. "I didn't think so."

"I discovered I have a sense of style when my family was in Vienna last summer because I spent time with my Aunt Sophia while my mother was rehearsing," Ruth elaborated. She assumed this information about her life outside of the working world would be interesting to this woman, and she was not mistaken.

Antonia Gelb raised her eyebrows. "And what was your mother rehearsing?"

"My mother has been singing with the Schola Cantorum for many years," Ruth explained, adding, "She is one of their foremost soloists."

"I'm impressed. Not only are you smart, but you have obviously led an adventuresome and cultured life," the woman said. "Let me tell you what concerns me. If nothing more interesting opens up in this department, will you stay until it does?"

Ruth had to think for several seconds before she replied. "That would depend on how long it takes. I think five years would be a long time for me to work as a secretary and still be content," she replied with candor.

"I agree. That's a very good answer. And I don't think that will be a problem anyway," the woman said, smiling at her. "I understand you are learning shorthand."

"Yes. Mrs. Moscowitz has been teaching me. I think I will be proficient at it within the next couple of weeks. If I wasn't compiling my final issue of the journal at Evander, I'm sure it wouldn't take as long," she clarified.

"I'm sure not," said her potential boss, eyes twinkling. "I would be more than willing to recommend you to one of my colleagues in another department if your skills are not adequately utilized here."

"Thank you very much," Ruth exclaimed, very much hoping her jaw was not wide open.

"Is it fair to say you could start in a month?" Mrs. Gelb inquired.

"Oh yes. We graduate in three weeks. If I can start then, would you like me to call you?"

The two women, one young, one middle-aged, smiled across the table at one another. "I would like that indeed", the older one replied. "I think we are going to work well together."

"So do I," came Ruth's ready response.

"I'm glad you agree," her future boss said with some asperity. She stood, extending her hand to her new secretary. She was also obviously pleased that the hand that met hers was firm and not slack, another sign of the young woman's confidence. After Ruth turned and left her office, Antonia sighed with relief, She had despaired of finding anyone who could meet her expectations, having interviewed at least five young women before Ruth. She needn't have worried. Ruth Liebman more than met them.

Ruth ran, skipped and raced to the subway station, euphoric. She knew neither her mother nor sister would believe she had gotten this job while still in high school, and that her friend's mother would be keeping an eye on her. She was also excited for herself. If she could not go to Hunter with her sister, this job seemed better to her than any she could have imagined. Yes, she would be a secretary, but she also believed there would be room for advancement when she was ready, and that her new boss, who had also risen through the ranks of the men in the top jobs at Sacks, would be a champion of her career path as well.

"You got the job!" Holly all but shouted as Ruth walked into the kitchen where she and her mother were busy at the counter, as usual chopping up vegetables for supper.

"I did! And she knows I can't start until after graduation, isn't that something?" Ruth beamed at them both.

Adelaide moved over to the cabinet across from the counter, where she kept the family bottle of sherry, and put it on the kitchen table. "Ruth, why don't you get three sherry glasses from the dining room," she suggested.

"But Mama, those glasses are our best stemware," she protested.

"And when [what] better time to use them. You have been hired by Saks Fifth Avenue, and that is a reason to celebrate!" her mother replied.

When Ruth returned to the kitchen with two of the glasses, her mother filled them with the Bristol Cream, ready for Ruth to reappear so she could pour the third. The three women stood side by side and sipped the thick, creamy liquid, all grinning like silly little airheads, as Adelaide called women who stayed at home and did nothing adventuresome with their lives. Again she felt grateful to Simon, who had allowed her to pursue her dreams, and had even encouraged such a thing. On the ship that had brought her to Ellis Island, she never would have thought a singing career possible. She had spent much of the journey crying in her cabin when her roommate had left it for her daily strolls on the deck, not savvy enough to enjoy one moment of the trip. Imagining

563

that she would be making such a voyage not only once again, but many times, to sing al over the Continent in the famous New York City choir would have been beyond her wildest fantasies.

* * *

As he touched her breasts in absolute wonder, marveling at the rosy nipples with their darker pink areolas, he couldn't help wondering what awaited him below. He and Teresa had never advanced any further than her breasts, although she had become daring enough to stroke his penis through his pants the last time they had been together. When Susanna reached for his fly, he thought she would stroke him in the same way, and almost gasped aloud when she unzipped him and then released his penis, stroking his naked member tentatively at first. It didn't take long, however, for her hand to become bolder in its exploration. As her fingers meandered over his testicles, he groaned with disbelief.

"Someone might catch us," he gasped, silenced when she whispered 'shhh'.

Then she raised her hips and lifted her skirt so she could reach beneath it, sliding her panties down her thighs and over her ankles, tossing them into the bush behind them.

"Susanna, you don't have to," Max began but she put her fingers to his lips, shaking her head as well.

A smile suffused her face, giving it a luminous quality, which silenced him. Max began to unbutton his own shirt, suddenly not embarrassed at all by his penis, which was still standing up stiffly, almost like a soldier in a military unit, he thought to himself as button after button came undone. It was Susanna who reached up for his belt buckle with one hand, continuing to massage him as she did so.

The smile she bestowed upon him was filled with sweetness. "I thought I would be embarrassed by this, but I'm not at all!" She added with a sigh of utter contentment, "What a marvelous looking organ."

Then she took his free hand and guided it beneath her skirt. The moisture he found there made it quite easy to rub his hand around the entire area, which startled him. At first he wasn't sure if it was his groans he was hearing, or Susanna's, and then realized he was hearing them both. It all felt so marvelous that he couldn't get himself to stop, although he thought that might be the more gentlemanly choice. They had time to consummate the act, weeks in fact, to get there. Suddenly Susanna reared up beneath his fingers and let out the most amazing cacophony of sounds he had ever heard. He leaned over and began to kiss her, and then he, too, uttered groans unlike any that had ever escaped his lips before. When the liquid he feared would spurt forth began to erupt, although he was desperately trying to hold it back, she laughed aloud.

"How absolutely amazing!"

"I'm afraid it's going to be sticky," he apologized, to which she just laughed again.

"You have a hanky, don't you?" she asked him. "I think we're going to have to ask Jack where he gets those condoms sooner than we thought?" she mused with a very wide smile.

'I will bring some tomorrow," Max agreed. He was't sure he would be able to rise and walk back to his dormitory but hadn't the will to voice such a concern.

Susanna sighed and said, "I'm not sure my legs will be able to get me out from behind this bush and across the lawn," at which Max had to laugh. "I was thinking the exact same thing," he admitted. "Maybe you're not meant to," she said, looking down at him. His penis was again standing at attention. Again she reached out and grasped it in her hand. "Oh my," she moaned, and then he was holding himself above her. "Please, oh please yes," she moaned, eyes bravely staring into his. "I never knew I was a hussy or that it was a wonderful thing to be!"

Max needn't have worried about how to do what he needed and wanted to: his member had a life and brain of its own, and quickly slid inside her.

"Go slowly," she sighed. "I am still a virgin."

He was able to refrain from moving his hips faster and faster, although how, he had no idea. "I don't think that's strictly true," he suggested, which sent them both into a paroxysm of laughter. "We have to stop laughing or I'll slip out," he gasped, and then said, "Maybe I better do that anyway, since I don't have the condoms today." They lay side by side, staring into each other's eyes, smiling, excited, and finally, content.

"Thank you so much," she exhaled, her breath catching.

"I think that's what I should be saying" said Max. "I never imagined...."

"Neither did I."

Max had no idea why she would thank him for deflowering her, or what his responsibilities might be now that he had. He liked this woman enormously, and was utterly grateful for the liberties she had allowed him, but wasn't sure that he loved her. The descriptions he had read in novels he had taken from the library about love did not match his feelings at all. Perhaps, he thought, he was just lacking in proper emotional range. Of course he couldn't share any of this with Susanna, because he understood that she would find his musings hurtful.

"I so wanted to have this experience before I died," she sighed. "Don't," she said, her fingers again gently brushing his mouth. "I could see the truth in the nurses eyes when the doctor was examining me. My cheeks are much more flushed than yours."

Not knowing what to say in response, Max took her hands in his, and brought them to his lips. Then he whispered, "We never really know." Her eyes filled with tears. No matter how quickly he wiped them away, more came rushing down her cheeks until he finally stopped.

"Will you promise never to forget me?" she asked him in a whisper.

His eyes filled, and he could not hold back his tears either. "Of course," he finally replied, adding, "How could I?"

"I would love to be able to go back to teaching when I leave here, even if I don't have much time left. But I don't think my parents will allow it," she sighed.

"We could both talk to them if you think that would help," he suggested.

Her eyes glowed for a second, and then were still. Again she sighed. "I suppose we could try, but I doubt it would work."

"Would your school allow you to return?" he asked.

"I hadn't even thought about that. Probably not, because they do think we are contagious, even if the disease is no longer spreading," she mused. "That makes me so sad."

"What do you think you will do?" he asked, because he knew she would go mad if she had nothing to occupy her agile and curious mind.

"I've been thinking about that. Some of the parents might let the children come to my parents' home if I wear a mask," she said.

"Sounds like a very good idea to me. Have you spoken to your mother or father about it, so they could inform some of the parents before you are released?"

"Do you think I should?" she asked him, sounding hopeful for the first time in months.

He replied, "Absolutely," although in truth he had no idea if she would ever be released. Her illness might have progressed too far already for that to be safe, for her, her parents, or anyone else who might come into contact with her.

"Then I will," she agreed, smiling with her entire body. He felt some concern that she would be deeply disappointed when that plan was laid to rest, but she interrupted his thoughts with a question. "What do you hope to do when you go back home?"

"I'm going to apply to Rutgers Medical College," he replied without a moment's hesitation. "Of course I'll have to save enough money first."

Although he didn't share his doubts with Susanna, Max was riddled with them. 'Who knew if he'd ever recover, or be released from the Sanatorium?' 'What if he wasn't accepted in medical school?' 'What if he couldn't save enough money because he also had to contribute to the Unger household?' And on and on. He also believed there was no harm in dreaming, if not for himself, then certainly for his friend.

"I would have so liked to marry, but I know that will never happen for me," she murmured, as if saying it any louder would make her death come to pass even more quickly. Max didn't argue with her. Even if she were able to go home, she would never be strong because her illness had done too much damage to her lungs. Most men wanted children eventually, so there wasn't much likelihood of Susanna finding someone who wouldn't be afraid of the state of her health or bothered by her inability to bear children. Since they came from different states and weren't members of the same faith, they had always known there would be no future for them as a married couple. Neither chose to pretend this wasn't so; neither had ever mentioned the possibility of marrying after they were both released. Susanna was Quaker, and came from a small town in Pennsylvania. Max could picture her congregation saying the bans, and shuddered within. What his family would say would not be very different from what Nathan had said about his potential union with Teresa. Being a Quaker was not as bad as being Catholic, but it still was not being a Jew, even a reform Jew. A reform Jew would be difficult enough for his parents to accept, and Max understood this with every fiber of his being.

The two lovers lay side by side, content with what they had, neither troubled by the fact that the relationship would go no further. Max was more concerned that what they were doing with one another was wrong, but his concern wasn't stopping him from planning for the following day. He didn't think that Jack would laugh when he asked to borrow a few condoms, since he was hoping to eventually use them himself, with a new patient, perhaps.

After Max walked Susanna back to her dormitory, he made his way to the porch, and lay down on a chaise, covering himself with a blanket because he suddenly felt chilled. He didn't understand why Susanna believed she was going to die. He knew the doctors told her exactly what they always told him: that he was improving. He lay there wondering if that meant they were lying to him. He only coughed after he had eaten something now; Susanna coughed often, even sometimes when he leaned over to kiss her. If he asked his doctor, would the man tell him the truth? He decided to ask his nurse first; she was more likely to be truthful because she believed none of them would heal completely if they carried unrealistic dreams within their hearts. As he drifted into sleep, he told himself he would not even tell Susanna who and what he had asked, let alone what the answer had been. 'If I'm told she is improving, I think I will tell her, even though she may be irritated that I asked,' was the last thought he had before he slept.

CHAPTER TWENTY-ONE

Ruth dreamed of asking Al to her Senior Prom, and woke up bathed in sweat. In her dream he had turned her down, shocked that she would even consider such a thing, which would surely hurt her sister. That afternoon when she and Greg were working head to head on the layout of the last journal offering, she asked him if he had any interest in going to the prom. Since he rarely spoke to any girl besides Ruth, he eagerly accepted her invitation even though he had known for some time that the girl he pined for only thought of him as a friend. Still, he knew he would never forget that he had gotten to take her to their Senior Prom, and for years it was the highlight of his life. Although they eventually lost touch with one another, he never did forget the first girl he had loved, or their night together at the prom.

At supper after she had gotten home from school that day, Ruth told both her mother and sister that she would be going to the prom with Greg. Her mother said that was wonderful, but her face betrayed her. Ruth had no idea why her mother would begrudge her this senior ritual, one that her sister had talked about for weeks after the event the year before until it had even become boring to Ruth. When she and Adelaide were standing side by side at the kitchen counter cleaning up Adelaide finally cleared up the mystery. At first Ruth was relieved that her mother didn't have anything against her attending the prom.

"Ruth," her mother had begun in a very quiet voice. "I don't think I have the money to purchase a new dress for you for the prom. "

"Oh!" Ruth muttered and then stopped, having no idea how to continue. She knew she couldn't attend the prom in one of her school frocks. Even if no one laughed, she would have known what her classmates were thinking, or worse, whispering, and that would have been unendurable. Did this mean she couldn't go to the prom after all?

"Do you remember the dress Holly wore to my concert in Vienna two years ago?" Adelaide asked her, voice quivering. Her mother's voice never trembled. Ruth realized that she was very upset about the situation too. She tried to remember the garment and then suddenly the image popped up in her mind's eye.

"It was blue, wasn't it? With lots of chiffon?" she asked her mother.

"Yes. I hung it in mothballs in my closet. I think we should take it out and see if it fits you," she continued.

"Holly's always been bustier than I am," Ruth hesitated.

Much to her surprise, her mother smiled at her and grasped her hand. "Isn't it a good thing that you're not the busty one, my dear?"

Ruth had to laugh. "You mean you can always take it in so it looks like it's my dress," she agreed.

And so it did. Holly told her she looked lovely in the frock, and even Ruth had to agree. The blue of the bodice suited her as it had Holly, since both had blue eyes, Ruth's rounder and filled with curiosity about almost everything. The night of the prom Adelaide not only allowed her to wear make-up, she outlined her younger daughter's eyes with kohl and applied a pink lipstick she had bought for the occasion. Adelaide usually wore a dark red color because Simon had liked it. Even after his passing that was the color she bought when a tube ran out. Pink would have felt silly to her, but she believed it would suit her daughter, and it did.

By the time Greg arrived at their apartment door with his little wrist corsage, Ruth felt as if she were floating on air. If that was true, she thought, she would be taller than Greg, and she giggled.

"Ruth, " her mother commanded. "Don't do that. It ruins the entire impression!"

Ruth had stopped giggling by the time her sister opened the front door and Greg stepped inside, but she had done so only with enormous effort. When Greg's jaw dropped, it was extremely gratifying, even if they were just friends.

"You…look…fantastic!" he said, mouth still agape. The two smiled broadly at one another, Adelaide and Holly standing arm in arm in the foyer. As the door closed behind them, Ruth heard her sister say, "She looks as good as she can," her mother shushing her and adding, "She looks good, period," which was even more gratifying.

Unbeknownst to anyone, Ruth had taught herself the Charleston, which she adored, and she taught Greg, right on the dance floor. Much to her shock, a circle formed around them, and suddenly they were the only two dancing, everyone else clapping in rhythm and cheering them on. It was a thrill: she felt pretty for the first time in her life, and believed she was a good dancer. That belief remained life-long, and was a gift she passed on to her younger daughter years later. She and Greg enjoyed every dance, even though both admitted afterwards that they had each thought they might drop from exhaustion. Neither did, and both had the night of their lives.

Several weeks later when the last issue of the journal came out, at least the last issue that she would oversee, Ruth could not believe her eyes. Greg and the other editors had totally redesigned the front page without her knowledge. Her picture was centered there with a long article beneath it about the journal's beginnings, touting the editor and her efforts to create a news outlet for creative students at their high school. Without her hard work, the article suggested, Evander Childs would have had to wait years longer for a school magazine. At the party for the final issue of the year – the journal would continue with a new, sophomore editor who had been elected by all of the reporters that had worked on the journal over the preceding two years – Ruth was buoyant and all smiles. No one knew that she had had to fight back tears, not even Greg. She understood this was the last school event she would ever attend, she who had loved every minute she had spent within the walls of Evander Childs, even the 'hated' physics class she had endured in her junior year. That night when she crawled into bed after two in the morning, she noticed that Holly's bed was empty. She knew her sister had been sneaking out at night to meet her latest beau, but had never told their mother. For once, she didn't care if it was Al. She had finally left him behind.

Ruth's first week at work at Saks Fifth Avenue was a nightmare. She had felt confident about her shorthand, but as it happened, her boss spoke rat-tat-tat when he dictated a letter, unless he was still thinking about what he wanted to say. He rarely called Ruth into his private office until he was ready; sometimes the new secretary had to piece together what her boss had actually said once she was transposing her little squiggles into actual words and typing them on a piece of paper. She often had to correct her initial copy by hand, and then retype it, which made the project take longer than she felt it should. Fortunately Mrs. Gelb had convinced her new boss, Michael Bronfman, that his new recruit might need some breathing room so that she would grow into the job, and he followed her advise. He did expect that when his new secretary handed him the letter to sign, it would be perfect. She often had to type several of his missives after she had gotten him coffee and Danish from the cart that appeared on their floor well before 9 AM, but rarely touched her own coffee before it had turned cold. She developed an abiding dislike of cold coffee and never again drank any, even when she was well into her fifties. Bronfman never seemed to notice. He did seem pleased when she asked him on her second day at Saks whether he would prefer the same Danish every day, or would prefer she choose something different each morning and surprise him.

"Let's try it that way," he said with a shrug. "No one's ever made that suggestion to me before. Probably didn't have the courage to fuel my displeasure."

Of course Ruth worried about the same thing, but figured there weren't that many pastry choices, so how many bad selections could she make? He never complained about his morning repast the entire year she worked for him before he suggested that she be promoted. Bronfman was in charge of marketing for the prestigious store, and as such, had to read the Times, The Herald, The Tribune, and The Daily News to see what the other significant department stores were advertising about their products. Ruth began to read them too, often finishing two of the newspapers before arriving at work in the morning. After a few months she felt confident enough to tell him what the men's department was offering at Gimbels, or what Macy's was selling on its first floor. Although at first Bronfman merely grunted, she could tell he found her observations interesting. Although these extra tasks barely gave her a moment to breathe, Ruth believed that her initiative would help her become more in life than a secretary if she could not attend Hunter and become a journalist.

Despite the fact that he rarely complimented her, especially in those first months, Ruth enjoyed learning about the job he did, which was, of course, much more interesting than her own. She tried to learn as much as she could about his marketing choices, afraid to ask what his reasoning was directly, but quick and bright enough to figure out patterns when there were any. Saks and Macy's only advertised in the New York Times, while Gimbels seemed to prefer the Herald, From this she deduced that Gimbels favored a working class clientele. People who couldn't afford to shop in small New York City shops might be able to buy children's clothes at Gimbels, pants for the mister, and some everyday dresses for mom without totally straining the family budget.

Although her boss was often short-tempered, and rarely complimented her, Ruth could tell from his facial expressions that he actually found her suggestions useful. When he asked her opinion about an advertisement he was planning to pay for in the Herald, Ruth suggested he focus on women's everyday wear instead of dress frocks, since even middle class girls dressed on a budget. Although Saks catered to the wealthy, she suggested it might be useful to expand their clientele as a way to compete with the other department stores springing up around the city. She told him she often browsed the aisles at Macy's, and of late had noticed that some of the women sharing those aisles with her were very well dressed. Women loved a bargain, she told him, and she saw no reason to assume wealthy women weren't like the women she knew personally in that regard. Although he didn't tell her she was the cause for the change, a few months later Saks opened a bargain aisle on the floor catering to women's clothing. That way when seasonal items were discarded they could often be found in this new area at a discount, which cut down on loss and actually began to make money for the company. She might have liked it if he had shared his decision with her, even if he hadn't told her that her remarks had influenced him, but he was not that kind of man. She understood his character and had smiled all the way home on the subway the day he had proudly showed her his new 'brain child'. 'His?' she wanted to scream, but knew better. If she kept paying attention she was sure Bronfman would have more 'new ideas'. If he couldn't credit her with any of them, perhaps he would give her a recommendation so she could move up in the hierarchy at Saks to become an assistant buyer, or to a position in the executive branch of the store that was more significant than that of a mere secretary. She could bide her time.

From its inception Saks catered to the upper crust of New York City. Initially when she began working there, Ruth felt uncomfortable since her mother rarely shopped at Saks, even when the upper class department store had first opened, despite the fact that she and Simon lived a comfortable life. Simon, in particular, expected his wife and his daughters to be well dressed, which meant wearing clothes that people living alongside Central Park wore. That may have been the reason he supported his wife's musical endeavors. Although they were artistic in nature, the singers were each given a small stipend to help them pay for their own needs when they travelled on the Continent. This income was a big help to the family, expanding their coffers so that his 'girls' could wear clothes that suited their class. When he died, of course the family fortunes changed. Because of the financial advise Addie was given at the time of her husband's death, she became much more cautious about what she was willing to spend on her daughters' attire as well as her own. By that time both Holly and Ruth knew the difference between well-made clothing and dresses that could be found in the street bins on the lower east side. Holly had been repairing tears in her frocks since she had entered Hunter College, and had begged her mother to allow her to take a part-time job so she could keep abreast of current fashions. In high school that was not even a consideration for Ruth. Adelaide did without, as did her youngest daughter, so the college girl would feel on equal footing with her peers.

When Ruth received her first paycheck from Saks, she immediately went to Gimbels to find a few frocks that were not only au courante but well made as well. She combed the racks, and managed to find two dresses, leaving her with enough money to contribute to her mother's food budget. She had already bought a monthly subway pass, so she knew she could get to work and back without worrying about that. She would have also stayed up late into the night creating a pattern for a dress she could make herself, as she and Holly had sometimes done in high school, but Adelaide did not want Ruth developing TB, or other illnesses that were rampant among the poor from lack of sleep. They were not poor, and would never appear to be so, at least if Adelaide could help it. She made two dresses for her younger daughter after Ruth had come home with her purchase from Gimbels. She not only felt guilty that her smart and opinionated daughter could not attend college, she felt sympathy for the young woman's desire to look stylish. After all, Holly was not only prettier, but still wearing clothes that enhanced her natural beauty because Holly's clothing was in the college budget outlined by all three of them. Adelaide believed it was her duty to help her younger child enhance her minimal physical attributes, and so she sewed. She never told Ruth why she was making her the dresses, but Ruth knew anyway. She had once overheard her parents having a fight about her looks, and knew her mother believed that finding her a husband would be a difficult task. Now that she was making a financial contribution to the household, Ruth assumed that her mother was helping her so that the men she met at work might find her if not beautiful, at least not displeasing.

Because she knew her mother was doing her best to help her, Ruth went out of her way to help her mother on the weekends. She often took charge of mopping the kitchen floor, polishing the silver, which her mother had always loathed doing, and taking over in the kitchen, seasoning the roast, paring the potatoes and cutting the vegetables for dinner. Holly contributed with baked goods, little Danish pastries and yeast cakes, which they kept in the breadbox all week long. She and Holly both took the little yeast cakes into the city with them several days a week. Ruth made sandwiches for both of them every evening because they were often in a hurry in the morning, grabbing some Danish for breakfast they could eat on the train as they raced out the door. Because she was so busy both at home and in the office, Ruth rarely accepted an invitation to join the other secretaries for lunch at one of the tiny delis on the side street bordering Saks Fifth Avenue. She would eat her sandwich at her desk, usually with a cup of strong coffee, although that didn't keep her from resting her head on her arms and drifting off to sleep until she heard the voices of the other women returning from lunch. She would then race to the ladies room to splash cold water on her face, dashing back to her typewriter, her fingers busily clacking away by the time Bronfman returned moments later from his frequently liquid lunch.

After several months at Saks, Ruth noticed that one of the other secretaries usually ate lunch at her desk as well, and approached her to suggest they eat together. Mina had never even entertained the notion of attending college because her family couldn't have afforded such a thing, given that she had three brothers who would have been given the opportunity had the family been able to send anyone. Her brothers, bright, every one, according to Mina, all worked on construction crews. There were many in the growing city now that both builders and architects were recovering from the depression. She and Ruth quickly discovered that they shared a wry sense of humor as well as a voracious appetite for the written word. It took them longer to share personal stories. When they trusted each other enough, they quickly realized they both had judgmental mothers, even though Mina's had never dreamed of having a career. Only Ruth walked the uneasy path behind a successful mother and college-educated sister. Both young women had felt inferior for one reason or another, and both were able to offer support to the other because their mutual compassion was instantaneous.

Since her return from her summer in Europe with her mother, where she had attended not only Addie's concerts but gone to the symphony with her coffee house friends, she hadn't had the time, or funds, to do the same in New York. One afternoon Mina invited her to attend an evening with her favorite quartet in Greenwich Village. At first Ruth hesitated but then picked up the phone on her desk and placed a call to her mother, hoping to catch Adelaide before she left for her own rehearsal in Manhattan. At first Adelaide reminded Ruth of all the chores she had yet to complete at home, but could not deny her own frequent defection from completing the very same ones herself.

"I want you to be very careful," her mother finally relented. "Don't talk to the young men who will be in the audience with you."

Totally startled, Ruth asked her, 'Why not?"

"You may not know this," Adelaide replied, "But artist types are often irresponsible. More significant where you are concerned, many have very loose morals and might try to persuade you to partake of…" there she hesitated before continuing, "activities that would not be good for you. Men only marry certain kinds of women, you know," she declared, thus completing her thoughts on the matter.

Ruth found herself wondering if her mother had any idea that her older daughter had already had two such boyfriends, and had been deflowered at least a year earlier. Ruth herself would have gladly made the same choice, but hadn't yet found a boy who interested her enough.

When she walked into the art gallery with Mina, the first thing she noticed was the wood sculptures that had been placed on pedestals all around the room, some large and imposing, others smaller, with intricate detail. Her eyes darted from one to another, amazed that one person could create such widely divergent pieces. She assumed the works had been created by one person, and was correct. Mina strode over to an interesting looking man with a thatch of black hair and an unintended beard that was already darkening his skin. As she followed her friend Ruth wondered if he had shaved right before coming to the gallery, or if he had only done so in the morning. Either way the growth was significant, and must have been a burden. At least it would have been for her. Of course he probably didn't need to race out of his apartment every morning to make sure he arrived at a job on time; she hoped he sold enough to be able to forego that life chore. As she stood behind Mina she noticed the paintings that were hung at infrequent intervals along the wall, and walked over to read about the artist who had painted them. Much to her amazement, one artist had created all of the sculpted pieces as well as the paintings, and had been doing both for over ten years. He didn't look more than thirty to her, but perhaps pursuing his muse kept him young in spirit.

"Ruthie. I want you to meet my friend, Richard Levine," Mina gushed. When Ruth turned around, she was momentarily flustered to find herself face to face with the swarthy young artist. 'Not so young,' she reminded herself. "Hello. I have to tell you that I find the depth of your work impressive. Do you always sculpt in wood?" she asked, the first of many questions she longed to ask him.

"I've been working with wood for over two years now, and I prefer it to clay," Richard replied, answering her question with a smile. He talked with her for a few minutes about his work, and then was dragged off by another woman who said she had to introduce him to a new gallery owner. At first Ruth was sorry to see him go; talking with an artist about his work, and what it took to create his pieces, had been fascinating. She realized that she had never asked her own mother, an artist of a different kind, how she chose her the pieces she sang, or even how to sing them, and for once, felt chagrin over her lack of interest in the artist in her own family.

Then she and another woman, whose name she discovered was Lisbeth, began to discuss one of the busts that Richard had carved as soon as Ruth realized that the other young woman had been the model for the piece. It turned out that Lisbeth had grown up in the same building as the artist in Brooklyn, had graduated from Brooklyn College, and was now working as a secretary at a small publishing house in Manhattan. She had various suggestions for Ruth on how she might manage to attend college given her exemplary high school record, even writing down some catalogues she could explore at her leisure in the library. She had several friends who had worked full or part time, and still taken college courses, most graduating in time.

"How many years did it take them?" Ruth asked, afraid to hear the answer.

"Some managed it in five years, but most took six or seven," Lisbeth replied, not surprised by Ruth's deep sigh. "It is a long time, and could take longer since you'd have to reapply every year for financial aid."

"Not likely," Ruth shrugged. "I really have to earn a decent living to help my family. My father died a few years ago...."

"I'm so sorry," Lisbeth interrupted, inspiring another shrug. Then the sculptor joined them, turning to Ruth immediately.

"Could I talk to you for a few minutes?" he asked. Lisbeth quickly tore a sheet of paper from the pad she had been carrying to write down her suggestions to Ruth, adding her own phone number before she handed it to her.

"I'd like to get together again too," Ruth smiled at the other woman. "I have really enjoyed talking to you."

Then Richard led her to a quiet corner of the gallery. Without preamble he said, "I'd like to use you as a model," which actually made her laugh aloud.

"I'm sure my mother would love that!" she sputtered.

His laughter joined hers, baritone and alto mixing well.

"You can be fully clothed, at least until I reach the neck, and then you might need to lower your blouse," he said. "Actually I only want to sculpt your face."

"But I'm not pretty," Ruth blurted, instantly ashamed. 'I sound idiotic,' she thought, but had no idea what to add to what she had already announced.

"I think you're striking," the sculptor told her. "And that's what I'm looking for."

This time Ruth interrupted. "I'm not seeking a compliment, I really mean it. I'm totally shocked, I guess, by your request.

He grinned at her. "I'd love to do a full body piece, but that isn't really what I intended. I think your face is marvelous."

"Thank you. I haven't ever thought…I must sound very silly," she babbled on.

He reached up and brushed the planes of her cheeks as well as her nose, which she knew was overly large because her mother had been telling her that as long as she could remember.

"Marvelous, truly," he said, dropping his hand. "Really."

"I work fulltime," she explained, as if that would make the venture impossible.

"Evenings work for me," he said.

"You're not going to drop this, are you?" she asked him with some measure of irony.

"No," he agreed. "If you don't agree here in the gallery, I'll get your number from Lisbeth, or from Mina. We've all known each other since we skinned knees side by side in Williamsburg."
This intrigued the daredevil in Ruth, who asked, "Did you do that often?"

"According to all of our mothers, who are also friends," he replied. "So. Can I talk you into sitting for me this coming weekend?"

"You are pushy," she murmured, but she was obviously intrigued. "I could come on Tuesday. My mother has a rehearsal that evening, so I wouldn't have to explain my absence to her," she added, despite herself

""One evening won't be enough," he prodded.

"Are you like this all the time?" she asked him.

"Only when I really want something," he answered.

"I bet that's fairly often," she muttered.

"You see. We already understand one another," he grinned again.

"Well, I understand you," she quipped.

"A second evening, or over the weekend?" he again asked.

"You are relentless. My mother sings every Sunday morning at the Ethical Society – I'll tell you what that is another time. So I could come then as well, if I find the experience bearable," she agreed, though with less enthusiasm than she had originally.

"I really do think I'll be able to create a very interesting piece with you. I frequently pay my models a small stipend," he explained, eyes twinkling.

"Now it sounds like you're trying to bribe me," she complained.

"Partly. But it's also true. And if you do work fulltime, I know that filling up your evenings and Sundays must not be very appealing," he explained.

"That's certainly true," she said with a shake of her head.

He persevered. "So, though I'm trying to persuade you, I also think you're the kind of model I should, and usually do, pay," he explained. "I should have said that from the beginning."

"Yes, you probably should, though I don't think it would have made much difference. I just never thought anyone would ever want to paint or sculpt me, because I'm not..." she trailed off before he interrupted with a gentle smile, "Pretty."

Not wanting to cry, because of course that was what she had been about to say, she bowed her head, and mumbled, "Low blow."

"Maybe I should tell you that conventionally pretty women don't interest me all that much, either personally or professionally. They're usually dull, which you are not," he said.

"But I am striking," she reminded him with her usual wit.

"You are. And you shouldn't disparage that trait. You are also witty, intelligent, and great fun to talk to," he said seriously but lightly. Noticing her expression, he added, "And I have a girlfriend. We're engaged, and plan to marry over the summer."

Ruth grinned broadly, and said, "Too bad!" They both laughed aloud. "So how much are you going to pay me for this honor?" she asked him.

"How about a dollar twenty-five an hour?" he asked her.

Her smile was broad and swift. "For that I can set aside Madame Bovary. It's more than I make at Saks!"

Richard was clearly impressed with the former. "In French or in English."

"Unfortunately English. I love reading fiction. It's a great pleasure, so what do you think?"

"Bring it along. I don't have a copy. When we take breaks in-between the sketch and starting to carve, you may want to read," he suggested. With that they parted. Mina was into a very animated conversation, so Ruth waved at her and left the gallery. Mina lived in Brooklyn, so she and Ruth had agreed they didn't have to stay at the gallery to support one another. If one of them was ready to leave, she should leave. Ruth felt as if she was flying all the way to the 8th Street Subway station. She was 'striking'! That phrase had seemed a curse when her mother uttered it, but maybe it wasn't. She made a commitment to herself to dress accordingly, and find clothes, even if she could afford fewer things, that enhanced her look. She might even ask Richard what kinds of dresses, skirts and sweaters he would suggest, or even what colors would best suit her, if they became friends as he chipped away at the wood block that would eventually look like her face.

* * *

Years later, when Max had been married for some time, he finally stopped feeling guilty about his relationship with Susanna. They hadn't slept together frequently because they had both been very concerned about pregnancy, even though Max had bought several packages of condoms through Jack and they had used them religiously. Neither trusted the things, and Max certainly wondered about the morality of what he and she were doing. He also doubted his ability as a lover. He had read everything he could find on the subject, although there wasn't much, but hadn't felt comfortable talking about how to please her with anyone, even Nathan. He knew his younger brother and Helen were exploring each other's bodies as well, but the brothers had never talked in detail about what this exploration entailed. At one point Susanna had taken his hand and placed it between her legs, and then laid her own hand atop his, using her fingers to guide his until he was stroking her wetness and she let go. He believed that the little bump he could feel was the clitoris, about which he had managed to find an article in a rather risqué magazine, because she lay back with a moan. When he finally pulled his hand back, she had moaned, "Oh, not now!" so he had continued until her entire body had writhed beneath him, and she had emitted tiny squeals that at first frightened him. When she again lay back on the blanket with a sigh, her smile one of obvious contentment, he realized that he had just experienced his first female orgasm, or maybe his second. 'So that's what the sounds she made were about,' he thought. And though he never came to believe he was a 'lover' he did learn how to please a woman because of his initial sexual exploration with the young woman he had met in a sanatorium that treated people suffering from a disease that could easily have killed them all.

Unfortunately, a year after he had been released, he received a letter from a staff person there who had known of his friendship with Susanna, informing him that she had passed away. The nurse wrote that she had hesitated to write to him, but knew they had been friends and thought he would want to know. He had been thinking of writing to a nurse on his floor anyway, because he hadn't heard from Susanna in a couple of months. She didn't write often as her condition worsened, and Max had been worried. Consumed as he was with his classes in pharmacy school he hadn't penned a letter in a awhile either, another guilt he would carry for years afterwards. She had a reason for not writing: her deteriorating health; he did not, no matter how busy he might have been. He, of all people, should have known how difficult it would have been to still be a resident at the Sanitorium and have no one to whom you could confide your fears. Susanna had had some friends besides him, but no one she was close to. He also knew that after he had been released, she had begun to spend even more time alone, to grieve his loss, and to attempt to cope with her worsening physical condition.

Because Max had never confided to anyone about what had taken place between the two - that he had left Elizabeth a virgin to find healing for a pernicious disease and returned cured, but no longer a sexual novice. Who would he have told? Certainly not his parents. Not even Nathan, who hadn't shared his exploits with Max either. The two brothers never lost their reticence about discussing sexual matters. For Max if a woman succumbed to his charms and he talked about it, he would have been tarnishing her reputation. After all, while he was in pharmacy school he never had intercourse, or even attempted more than light petting with a woman whose reputation and character were less than stellar. The only person he told about his entire experience at the Sanatorium was the woman he eventually married, and that was years after he had been a patient, and lover, there.

That he again started seeing Teresa in secret was another reason for him to tell no one about the young woman who had filled his days, as well as his dreams at night, while he was a patient. The only person who knew about this new and secret liaison was Nathan, who had told his older brother that he was very concerned about this development. "What will you do?" he had asked him. What, indeed? Both brothers knew he could never marry the girl. Their father would be distressed, their mother destroyed. It was the Irish Catholic boys who beat up Jewish kids in the Elizabeth ghetto. To marry a Catholic would be inexcusable in their eyes, even if Teresa's brothers had never engaged in such behavior. Her family would be no different. Though the Jews in Elizabeth rarely perpetrated violence on anyone, there wasn't one resident there who was unaware of the violence that was enacted, often monthly, against their tribe. Nathan had reason to be concerned, which Max well knew.

He and Teresa met, and talked, and kissed, and touched, but Max never pressured her to take off her clothes in his presence, or to engage in the full range of sexual activities. Not only did he feel this would show a lack of respect, but he feared he would have to explain how he had learned all that he had learned since their time together in high school. One afternoon when they were lying on her bed at her parents' house before either had returned from their workday, Teresa began to cry. She took his hand and brought it to her waist, making it clear she wanted him to take it the rest of the way.

"I can't, Teresa," he moaned.

"But I want you to," she whispered.

"It isn't because I don't want to. But we can't marry and that could ruin your life. I care about you too much to do that to you," he whispered in turn, though why he whispered he wasn't sure, since no one was in the house but them.

"I'm glad you care about me," Teresa said with a sarcasm that was rare for her.

"I love you. You know that," he sighed.

"I…guess I needed to hear you say it," she said. "Will we forget about each other once we're married to other people," she wondered moments later, trying not to cry.

In a fierce whisper, Max hissed, "I will never forget you. And I don't think I will ever love another woman the way I love you, even if I marry!"

They left it at that, neither willing to stop seeing one another, but neither having the courage to let go. It would take months for them to take that step, months neither would ever forget.

Made in the USA
San Bernardino, CA
23 September 2016